Countering Terrorism

The BCSIA Studies in International Security book series is edited at the Belfer Center for Science and International Affairs at Harvard University's John F. Kennedy School of Government and published by The MIT Press. The series publishes books on contemporary issues in international security policy, as well as their conceptual and historical foundations. Topics of particular interest to the series include the spread of weapons of mass destruction, internal conflict, the international effects of democracy and democratization, and U.S. defense policy.

A complete list of BCSIA Studies appears at the back of this volume.

Countering Terrorism

Dimensions of Preparedness

Arnold M. Howitt and Robyn L. Pangi, editors

BCSIA Studies in International Security

in cooperation with the Executive Session on Domestic Preparedness

The MIT Press
Cambridge, Massachusetts
London, England

This book was typeset in Palatino by Wellington Graphics and was printed and bound in the United States of America.

Library of Congress Control Number: 2003109413

ISBN : 0-262-08324-8 (hc)
0-262-58239-2 (pb)

On the cover: Construction workers place concrete barriers near the base of the Washington Monument on August 22, 1998, in an attempt to bolster security around the structure. The security measures come in the wake of the U.S. attacks on suspected terrorist targets in Sudan and Afghanistan and threats of retaliation by Islamic extremists. AP Photo/William Philpott.

Printed in the United States of America

10   9   8   7   6   5   4   3   2   1

Contents

*In fond and grateful memory of John "Jack" Fanning,
Chief of Hazardous Materials Operations,
New York City Fire Department,
and member of the Executive Session on Domestic Preparedness.
He gave his life in New York City
at the World Trade Center towers on September 11, 2001,
selflessly seeking to save those endangered by the terrorism
that he had energetically sought to avert.*

Acknowledgments

Producing any book—let alone a collection of essays by many authors—creates a host of debts that can never be fully credited. In this case, the number of people who deserve thanks is legion.

Our greatest debt is to the essay authors. They have provided their best thinking and hard efforts—and have tolerated our incessant questions and requests for updating as the steps of the publication process and the pace of recent U.S. history have seemed to conspire against effective reporting of their insights. To them, we offer sincere thanks for making this book possible.

Nearly all of these essays were written for or by the Executive Session on Domestic Preparedness (ESDP), an ongoing project at the John F. Kennedy School of Government at Harvard University. Established in 1999, ESDP is a research program that taps the expertise of a standing task force of leading practitioners and academic specialists concerned with terrorism and emergency response. Sponsored by the U.S. Department of Justice, ESDP brings together senior officials from federal, state, and local governments with Harvard faculty and researchers. As a group, ESDP members have grappled with the complex problems of preparing the country for an emergent security threat, challenged and learned from each other, and then sought to promote their collective and individual insights to the professional communities in which they operate.

The "practitioner" members of ESDP are a remarkable group of public servants, whose efforts on behalf of the citizens of the United States deserve the humble thanks of us all. We—and all of the Harvard faculty and researchers who have interacted with them—have learned much about the difficulties and possibilities of preparing the homeland for terrorism. Greatly admiring their skill and dedication and valuing them as friends, we could write at length about each; but limits of space prevent more than naming them: Thomas Antush, Joseph Barbera, Bruce Baughman, Peter Beering, Thomas Burnette, Hank Christen, Rebecca Denlinger,

Frances Edwards-Winslow, John Fenimore, Ellen Gordon, Margaret Hamburg, Clarence Harmon, Thomas Kinnally, Robert Knouss, Peter LaPorte, Bruce Lawlor, Marcelle Layton, Scott Lillibridge, John Magaw, Paul Maniscalco, Gary McConnell, Stanley McKinney, Andrew Mitchell, Paul Monroe, Phillip Oates, Charles Ramsey, Leslee Stein-Spencer, Darrel Stephens, Steven Storment, Patrick Sullivan, Ralph Timperi, and Alan Vickery.

The Harvard members of ESDP—Graham Allison, Alan Altshuler, Ashton Carter, Richard Falkenrath, Frank Hartmann, Philip Heymann, Juliette Kayyem, Matthew Meselson, Steve Miller, Terry Scott, and Jessica Stern—are also dedicated and accomplished individuals whom we thank for their commitment to the project, many thoughtful ideas, and generosity and friendship. The Kennedy School's Dean Joseph Nye has been an ESDP participant, supporter, and unflagging enthusiast for the project's efforts.

Both editors owe special thanks to Richard Falkenrath, who provided much of the initial stimulus and "thought-provocation" that got them involved in preparedness studies. His book, *America's Achilles Heel* (MIT Press, 1998), was a timely call to confront U.S. vulnerabilities to terrorism. To act on these concerns, Falkenrath co-founded ESDP with Arnold Howitt, and among many other actions, he played a part in the genesis of a number of the essays in this volume. His departure from the Kennedy School in early 2001—first for service at the National Security Council and then at the Office of Homeland Security—was a serious loss for ESDP and the School but a major gain for the country.

Our colleagues on the ESDP staff have been wonderful compatriots—thought-provoking, generous friends who know how to laugh as well as work hard. Juliette Kayyem and Rebecca Storo are at the hub of these relationships and contributed to this project in many ways, large and small. Frank Hartmann has been a superbly skillful conference facilitator and an irreplaceable source of wisdom about the executive session "art form," which he is significantly responsible for developing at the Kennedy School. Kerry Fosher, Kendall Hoyt, Rebecca Horne, and Greg Koblentz have all provided important support and help.

No simple tribute is enough for Patricia Chang, ESDP's able research assistant, who has labored long and hard on every aspect of the book, contributing significantly to the intellectual substance and rolling up her sleeves cheerfully to do the less glamorous tasks of cajoling authors and preparing a manuscript.

The Kennedy School of Government is a wonderful place at which to think about and seek to influence public policy and management, and this is particularly the case at the two research centers that cosponsor

ESDP—the Belfer Center for Science and International Affairs and the Taubman Center for State and Local Government. As directors of these two Kennedy School research centers, Graham Allison and Alan Altshuler have both participated in ESDP and generously provided full administrative support and personal backing. We gratefully thank them and our many colleagues at these Centers who have contributed ideas, provided encouragement, or simply been good friends.

In particular, the Belfer Center's Sean Lynn-Jones and Karen Motley have our hearty thanks for providing guidance and support in preparing this manuscript for publication. We also thank the skillful freelance editors who have worked on individual essays in this volume. Miriam Avins, Pat Deutch, John Gravois, Teresa Lawson, and Diane McCree have effectively pushed all of the authors and editors to make our ideas more forceful and transparent.

At the Office for Domestic Preparedness in the Office of Justice Programs, U.S. Department of Justice, which has provided the financial support for ESDP's work, Andy Mitchell has been a stalwart supporter and a source of insight and good sense. Susan Obuchowski has also been an invaluable friend and skillful administrative intercessor.

Finally, we offer bountiful thanks to our spouses, Maryalice Sloan-Howitt and Corey Sassaman. We salute them not alone for their loving support and tolerance when our work hours and grim professional preoccupations invaded our personal lives (though they amply deserve that thanks) but also for the times when they *weren't* so tolerant or actively diverted us (which, in truth, is part of why we married them). Arnold Howitt also thanks his children—Mark, Alexa, Molly, and Matt—who bring him so much joy and inspire a large measure of his motivation to make the future better.

Arnold M. Howitt
Robyn L. Pangi

Cambridge, Massachusetts
February 2003

Introduction

Arnold M. Howitt and Robyn L. Pangi

The terrorist attacks that occurred in the fall of 2001 have changed Americans' perception of domestic and international terrorism. They have forced the nation to reevaluate its state of readiness to detect, prevent, and respond to attacks. Both attacks clearly demonstrated the shortcomings of existing institutions and showed the need for a sharper focus on preventing or mitigating the impact of terrorism and also on developing improved capabilities of emergency response.

On September 11, 2001, 19 hijackers commandeered four commercial aircraft as weapons against U.S. targets. Two of the fuel-laden aircraft slammed into New York City's World Trade Center towers: American Airlines Flight 11 hit the north tower at 8:45 A.M., and United Airlines Flight 175 hit the south tower at 9:03 A.M. A third plane—American Airlines Flight 77—destroyed part of the Pentagon when it crashed into the building at 9:43 A.M.. The fourth kamikaze mission was thwarted when passengers refused to give hijackers full control of the aircraft. United Airlines Flight 91 crashed in a field in Somerset County, Pennsylvania, at 10:10 A.M. Altogether, nearly 3,000 people lost their lives, hundreds more were injured, and millions were affected.

Shortly after the hijackings, a series of anthrax attacks was carried out using the U.S. Postal Service as a delivery system. Between September 22 and November 21, unknown numbers of people were exposed to anthrax spores, resulting in 22 confirmed or suspected cases, and of those cases, five deaths. Approximately 32,000 people took antibiotics as a precaution against possible infection.

The attacks originated on September 18 when envelopes mailed from Trenton, New Jersey, containing *Bacillus anthracis* were sent to the various destinations. On September 22, an editorial page assistant at the *New York Post* noticed a blister on her finger. She later tested positive for the skin form of anthrax. On September 26, a postal worker in Trenton visited a physician to have a lesion on his arm treated. One day later, a letter carrier at the West Trenton post office developed a lesion on her arm. Over the next few days, people associated with the ABC and NBC television networks discovered signs of cutaneous anthrax, including the seven-month-old son of an ABC producer in Manhattan, who spent time at the network offices and later developed a cutaneous anthrax rash.

More than a thousand miles away on September 30, 2001, Robert Stevens, photo editor at the *Sun*, a weekly supermarket tabloid in Boca Raton, Florida, fell ill. Two days later, Ernesto Blanco, mailroom employee at American Media Inc., publisher of the *Sun*, was admitted to the hospital with heart problems. Within a few days, authorities confirmed that Stevens had inhalation anthrax, the most deadly form of the disease. On October 5, Stevens died. His death was the first U.S. death from inhaled anthrax since 1976 and only one of 18 documented cases in the previous 100 years. On October 18, Ernesto Blanco was diagnosed with inhalation anthrax; he was released from the hospital 23 days later.

Also in October, letters sent to the government offices of Senators Tom Daschle and Patrick Leahy tested positive for anthrax. Two Washington postal workers died from inhalation anthrax; five others were sickened. Authorities in Washington, D.C., responded more dramatically than those in other affected locations: Congressional office buildings were closed for long periods during the investigation and decontamination, and more than 30,000 people thought to be at risk in the region took antibiotics as a precautionary measure.

Yet, the threat was uncontained. Two less readily explained deaths occurred in late October and late November. Kathy T. Nguyen, an employee of Manhattan Eye, Ear, and Throat Hospital, with no direct connection to the media, Congress, or the postal service, died of inhalation anthrax on October 31. Perhaps even more perplexing, on November 21, Ottilie Lundgren, a 94-year-old woman from Oxford, Connecticut, died from inhalation anthrax. Like Kathy Nguyen, Lundgren had no known connection to media outlets or government offices.

Taken together, suicide jetliner attacks on the World Trade Center towers and the Pentagon, soon followed by anthrax-laced letters dispatched to journalists and U.S. senators, gave Americans stark notice of their vulnerability to terrorists. The events of September 11 catapulted terrorism to a high priority on the nation's policy agenda. Yet in the rush to develop visible remedial programs to correct some of the revealed shortcomings, such as bolstering air and border security and creating an

Office and Department of Homeland Security, there is a risk that critical components of readiness will be overlooked. In the quest to improve domestic preparedness, policymakers and practitioners need a systematic way to evaluate the threat situation, policy and programmatic needs, and alternative solutions.

This volume contributes to that purpose. It opens with four articles that review the strategic and organizational issues of domestic preparedness. It then analyzes four emerging threats: biological attacks and nuclear attacks on humans, biological attacks on crops and livestock, and "cyber" attacks that target information infrastructure. The third section of the book addresses the capacity that must be built to deal with these and other emerging threats. The existing U.S. legal framework, medical capacity, and communications infrastructure all provide examples of preparedness gaps that may be overlooked if the United States continues to prepare for familiar instead of unexpected threats. Finally, the book looks to the international arena in order to learn from other countries such as Israel, Japan, and the United Kingdom, which have all experienced terrorism.

Strategies and Institutions

The essays in this section provide critical overviews of the complexities of preventing and responding to terrorism. All four analyze the impediments to and opportunities for improving homeland security. The authors agree that change is difficult: policy cycles cause public and governmental attention to ebb and flow dramatically; embedded bureaucratic missions and routines yield slowly to even incremental change; the structure of federal operations encompasses competing power centers that inhibit coordinated action across agencies; and institutional interests reinforce reluctance to relinquish any responsibilities and related budget allocations.

In "The Architecture of Government in the Face of Terrorism," Ashton Carter begins by looking at why the United States was surprised by the events of September 11 and concludes that post–Cold War complacency, lack of counterterrorism infrastructure and strategy at the federal level, and the complexities of managing such a vast and institutionally diverse effort all contributed to lack of preparedness. In order to improve homeland security, Carter calls on the U.S. government to think carefully through a national strategy and method of implementation for homeland security.

Prior to the September 11 attacks, the post–Cold War "A-list" security issues that the Bush administration focused on were the collapse of Moscow's power and the growth of Beijing's military and economic might. After September 11, the administration was forced to focus on the proliferation of weapons of mass destruction (WMD) and the potential for catastrophic terrorism—terrorism causes mass casualties or serious damage to the economy or vital infrastructure. Yet Carter asserts that increased awareness is insufficient to improve homeland security because the "security institutions of the U.S. government are particularly ill-suited to deliver homeland security." His paper offers practical recommendations for improving domestic preparedness. These include adopting the military mechanism of "red team/blue team" (devising means of attack and countermeasures to thwart it) research and development, devising a budget strategy, enhancing forensic capabilities, shifting intelligence strategies from surveying individuals to surveying means, and updating legal preparedness for emergency situations. His suggestions for international policy include developing a transnational intelligence- sharing protocol and engaging the international community in verifiable arms control agreements.

In "Intergovernmental Challenges of Combating Terrorism," Arnold Howitt and Robyn Pangi assess the difficulties and opportunities of working through the decentralized and institutionally fragmented federal system in the United States. They show how various networks of organizations for both prevention and emergency response cut across state and local levels of government and interact with private institutions. During the 1990s, recognizing the emerging terrorist threat, Congress and the executive branch established a number of new federal programs to provide grants and technical assistance to state and local governments. These initiatives, however, were only loosely coordinated and did not provide for the new comprehensive capacity needed to prepare for potential terrorist attacks. Since September 11, the federal government has intensified efforts to prepare state and local institutions. Nonetheless, this aid remains fragmented and does not fully address the diverse needs of large cities and small communities, metropolitan-scale regional organizations, and states of varying size.

An improved national system of prevention and emergency preparedness for terrorism in the United States will inevitably rely on these subnational institutions for detailed policy development and operational capabilities. More emphasis on regional collaboration of local governments, with strong reinforcement by the states, will make this effort more effective and cost-efficient. The immense diversity of governmental structure, geography, and economic and social institutions in the United States, however, dictates that no cookie-cutter approach to building improved capabilities will work effectively. On the one hand, a strong federal role is essential in setting the agenda for state and local government action, providing fiscal incentives and technical assistance to facilitate change and supplying critical specialized capabilities and backup. But, Howitt and Pangi argue, federal policy must also "recognize the need for *customized replication* of operational capabilities" in many separate places, with substantial variation. "Strategies explicitly or implicitly striving for standardization are likely to confront political and organizational resistance and are likely to contain design flaws that would impede or subvert implementation under at least some conditions prevailing in specific states or localities."

In "Dealing with Terrorism," Philip Heymann explores how the world has changed since September 11 and offers possible alternatives to reestablish the perception of security that Americans enjoyed prior to September 11. Heymann questions why "the United States seemed so much better protected against terrorism within its boundaries than other countries, such as United Kingdom, Germany, France, and Spain (each of which suffered sustained terrorist campaigns)." The paper considers, but rejects as unsupported, five hypotheses: superior intelligence capabilities, the reputation of the United States as a difficult and risky target, fear on behalf of countries friendly toward the terrorist organization of alienating the United States, reluctance on behalf of terrorist organizations to inflict mass casualties, and finally, a unique combination of specific vulnerabilities that were exploited by the September 11 attackers. Heymann concludes that each of these explanations is flawed. He suggests that in order genuinely to protect the American people and reduce fear, government must take relatively "massive steps," such as increased efforts at prevention, intelligence-sharing, and military action that will "reinforce the reluctance of any nation to tolerate groups planning attacks on the United States."

In the final paper in the first section, "Lessons of the 'War' on Drugs for the 'War' on Terrorism," Jonathan Caulkins, Mark Kleiman, and Peter Reuter probe another large-scale national initiative in search of strategies to assist in the fight against terrorism. Counterdrug operations, they argue, are similar to the current war on terrorism in certain respects: the rhetorical use of war imagery; the relative importance of prevention over punishment; cycles of political attention and inattention; difficulties in engaging and coordinating many agencies at several levels of government into a single mission; the need for international cooperation; and the problem of tacit or overt state support of illicit operations. The two campaigns, however, are dissimilar in many other ways: there is a higher tolerance for failure in the drug war than in the war on terror; counterdrug operatives can interrupt their targets at supply and demand points that do not exist in comparable form in terrorist operations; and there is a greater ability to harden targets against terrorism than against drug dealers.

The authors conclude that critical differences in the two "wars" mean that enforcement tactics relevant to the war on drugs cannot be simply transferred to counterterrorism. Both deterrence and incapacitation of terrorists hold considerably more promise for counterterrorism than for counterdrug efforts. Border control, on the other hand, while necessary, is not likely to be a major way of preventing terrorism. The experience of the White House drug czar, moreover, is cautionary against hopes that the Office of Homeland Security or the new Department of Homeland Security will be effective in coordinating federal terrorism prevention and preparedness efforts.

Emerging Threats

At first glance, biological terrorism, nuclear terrorism, agricultural terrorism, and cyberterrorism seem to have little in common. Yet the chapters in this section reveal several common themes. Each of these threats is a relatively new security concern. None is widely understood or appreciated by the public. Indeed, sometimes they have not been a primary concern for some key players responsible for preventing or responding to an attack. Yet, of necessity, the response to each requires the cooperation of myriad federal, state, and local agencies, the private and public sectors, and international partners—including many that do *not* traditionally play a role in national security affairs.

"During the fall of 2001, biological terrorism was transformed from a possibility to a reality." In "Biological Terrorism: Understanding the Threat and America's Response," Gregory Koblentz introduces the reader to biological weapons: their lethality, methods of delivery, and targeting. In addition to providing an overview of biological agents, the paper highlights their potential effects, including their psychological impact. It also details current preparedness initiatives by various government and private health agencies to create the capacity to respond to bioterrorism. With billions of dollars of new money allocated to countering bioterrorism over the next several years, limited resources are no longer as severe a hindrance to enhancing U.S. preparedness. What remains a problem, Koblentz notes, is the lack of a "national strategy that integrates the preparedness efforts and response plans of the public health, medical, national security, and law enforcement communities" to counter bioterrorism.

In "Nuclear Terrorism: Risks, Consequences, and Response," Jim

Walsh looks at the potential of nuclear terrorism—whether the use of a nuclear weapon, an attack on nuclear facilities, or the use of a radiological weapon or "dirty bomb"—from the perspective of state and local officials who may have to respond. These threats should not be conflated in the national debate about terrorism, since they have widely varying levels of risk and possible consequences. Walsh carefully assesses these risks, explores the challenges that each type of event would pose for the responding institutions, and recommends how states and localities should prepare, with a particular emphasis on public information and communication capabilities.

The overwhelming concern for policymakers today is the threat of terrorism against humans. But another serious concern is the use of a weapon of mass destruction against animals or plants, an issue introduced by Jason Pate and Gavin Cameron in "Covert Biological Weapons Attacks against Agricultural Targets: Assessing the Impact against U.S. Agriculture." While an attack against U.S. agriculture remains a low probability threat, "the economic impact of such attacks is, potentially, enormous." As "mad cow disease," which was first diagnosed in the 1980s, and the outbreak of hoof-and-mouth disease in the United Kingdom in 2001 showed, the United States must prepare regardless of whether an outbreak of disease affecting livestock or agriculture occurs naturally or intentionally. "Differentiating between naturally occurring outbreaks of disease and those caused purposefully by subnational entities is extremely difficult and may be impossible, if no group or individual comes forward to claim responsibility for the outbreak." Fortunately, the preparations are similar, although not identical. An intentional attack would require a strong role for law enforcement, but the basic epidemiological surveillance, removal of contaminated product, public information campaign, and economic damage control would be the same. Also required are improved federal, state, and local response capabilities, upgraded research facilities, and the development of a cohesive national strategy. Farming practices, such as diversity of agriculture, can also help reduce vulnerability of livestock and crops to disease. In addition, although all forms of terrorism can have an international component, the reliance of agriculture on international markets is a key cause of financial losses associated with disease outbreaks or agroterrorism.

Attacks on humans, animals, and plants are only one end of the spectrum of potential terrorist attacks. As Michael Vatis highlights in "Cyber Attacks: Protecting America's Security against the Digital Threat": "In addition to such physical attacks . . . the United States remains highly vulnerable to another form of attack: a 'cyber attack' against the computer networks that are critical to our national security and economic prosperity." Not all cyber crimes are political, but they can severely damage the U.S. politically and economically. Vatis details the types of perpetrators likely to carry out a cyber attack, defined as "computer-to-computer attacks to steal, erase, or alter information or to destroy or impede the functionality of the target computer system." He notes that there are several different types of attacks, the motives for which range from pranks to attempts to bring down entire infrastructures, including power grids. He also notes that a direct relationship persists between cyber attacks and physical attacks. Following the collision between a U.S. surveillance plane and a Chinese fighter aircraft, for example, cyber attacks against both involved parties spiked.

Like the targets of biological or agroterrorism, "the private sector owns and operates most of the nation's essential networks . . . and employs many of the field's leading technical experts. . . . " The Bush administration, like the Clinton administration, is reluctant to impose regulations requiring private companies to take security measures. Yet internationally and domestically, there is a need for improving private sector security, securing information, empowering institutions, creating a comprehensive legal framework, and improving local capabilities.

Capacity Building

Preparing for terrorism requires the development of organizational capacity to carry out tasks that are not part of the normal portfolio of agency actions or that involve extraordinary degrees of effort under emergency conditions. In the wake of the World Trade Center, Pentagon, and anthrax letter attacks, public agencies and key private organizations have been carefully evaluating the areas requiring improved response capabilities.

The essays in this section highlight three important elements of readiness for terrorism: legal authority, health care capacity, and communications interoperability. Like counterterrorism and domestic preparedness in general, none of the issues discussed is a completely new concern for policymakers or first responders. In current form, however, existing capabilities in most locales in the United States would be severely taxed by a WMD terrorist attack—or by a natural disaster, such as a hurricane or earthquake, or from a technological disaster, such as a serious industrial explosion. Indeed, the attacks on September 11 and the subsequent anthrax letters revealed gaps in all three capability areas. A serious, sustained crisis caused by a biological weapons attack, for example, would certainly create enormous stress on health care facilities of all types, and many areas currently lack appropriate legal authority to cope with the demands of such an attack.

Juliette Kayyem's essay, "U.S. Preparations for Biological Terrorism: Legal Limitations and the Need for Planning," deals with legal preparedness. Many states have public health laws drafted early in the twentieth century. They currently lack appropriate legal authority to deal with the demands of a serious bioterrorism attack, including the possibility of quarantine, mandatory evacuation, involuntary medication, and other actions that clearly test the boundaries between individual rights and public safety. As Kayyem argues, therefore, "cautious and realistic legal planning, in advance of an attack, that appreciates both the difficulties that the United States could face in the event of a terrorist attack and the need to be respectful of the rule of law is crucial." She notes, in particular, that, "a biological terrorism event . . . will challenge the explicit balance this country has tried to maintain between security and liberty."

Kayyem points out that the current approach of passing piecemeal legislation at the federal and state levels after a crisis is suboptimal; it allows gaps to remain and redundancy to dominate. Moreover, in the aftermath of an attack, laws more restrictive of individual liberties may be enacted in the name of fighting terrorism that would not pass in less strenuous times. She concludes that, "with appropriate statutory revisions, a thorough search of authorities, and a clear triggering event providing for broader powers during a biological terrorist attack, legal preparation can be improved."

In the next chapter, "Ambulances to Nowhere: America's Critical Shortfall in Medical Preparedness for Catastrophic Terrorism," Joseph Barbera, Anthony Macintyre, and Craig DeAtley address the problem of medical surge capacity. After more than a decade of health care cost containment efforts (e.g., hospital mergers and closures, federal Medicare and Medicaid funding changes, and the managed care revolution in private medical insurance), hospitals and other acute care facilities have little reserve capacity to handle the unusual increases in demand that would accompany a major terrorist attack or a severe disaster of another kind. This deficiency has recently been starkly revealed even under "normal" conditions by well-publicized incidents of emergency rooms going on "bypass" and refusing to accept patients. The health care system in most cities would therefore be severely overtaxed by a mass casualty terrorist attack. "As concerns for WMD terrorism rise," the authors note, "incorrect assumptions are being made about existing medical capabilities to treat mass casualties. In reality, hospital surge capacity and specialized medical capability across the United States has never been more restricted." Historically, expectations for casualty loads have been for "numbers in the teens, not thousands, and planning has been performed accordingly." The authors suggest several models that may lead to better medical preparedness, ranging from tax incentives to cost sharing to mandatory certification.

Viktor Mayer-Schönberger, in "Emergency Communications: The Quest for Interoperability in the United States and Europe," addresses another problem that confronts emergency response agencies: communication equipment that is incompatible with that of other response agencies. Interoperability is "the ability of public safety personnel to communicate by radio with staff from other agencies, on demand and in real time." Many people assume that fire, police, and Emergency Medical Service (EMS) personnel from different counties and states can talk not just to colleagues *within* their profession but to colleagues *in all* of these professions. Yet, this capability is currently lacking in most jurisdictions in the United States. As the attack on Columbine High School in 1999 dramatically revealed, response personnel from different disciplines or different communities could not communicate with one another. In a catastrophic terrorist attacks, or any large-scale disaster, this could have tragic consequences, ranging from casualties from "friendly fire" to overlooked victims.

The interoperability problem has been dealt with more effectively in Europe, Mayer-Schönberger demonstrates. "In the United States, interoperability has suffered from strategic misalignment and haphazard implementation. European interoperability policies have fared better, not because of a general advantage in the strategies chosen, but because of a better fit between means and ends." Mayer-Schönberger suggests that three steps are required to achieve interoperability: "inventing the appropriate technology, setting common standards and frequencies, and providing adequate funding." Europe was able to surpass the United States in all three, thanks to a mixture of ingenuity and good fortune, and "today is well on its way toward an integrated continent-wide public safety radio communications network providing comprehensive interoperability on all levels." In the United States, turf battles, budgetary restrictions, and hesitation by the federal regulatory agency have stymied the development of a universal communication system.

Lessons Learned from International Cases

The final section of the book describes important lessons from experiences with terrorism abroad. The cases of Israel, Japan, and the United Kingdom provide valuable insights for preventing terrorism and responding to attacks from weapons of mass destruction.

Until the 1990s, the United States was largely insulated from terrorism, especially on home soil—a fact that distinguished the United States from many other democracies. These essays explore the experiences of three nations forced to confront large-scale or chronic terrorism. Israel and the United Kingdom have faced sustained political violence. They have shaped important aspects of their legal and public safety systems and political and social networks around the threat of terrorism. Japan, on the other hand, is noteworthy for facing the first WMD terrorist attack in recent history. Its experience with sarin attacks by the cult Aum Shinrikyo was the impetus for the United States to begin seriously preparing to manage the consequences of WMD terrorism. The Japanese experience is similar in important respects to the U.S. experience, since to date both have faced only isolated incidents of terrorism, yet have encountered terrorism with weapons of mass destruction. These international cases offer instructive perspectives for the United States as this country works to craft a nationwide strategy for combating terrorism that is consistent with the values and traditions of a liberal democracy.

Ariel Merari, in "Israel's Preparedness for High Consequence Terrorism," looks at the response to terrorism in Israel prior to the escalating violence experienced in the winter and spring of 2002. Merari explains that, "in many respects the Israeli public and government have regarded terrorism as a war, rather than as a problem of law and order that merely requires suitable police measures." Israel has enacted emergency powers, but has chosen to complement them with a more aggressive military posture in defending its homeland. Legal measures allocate certain offenses to the jurisdiction of military courts, allow harsher punishment for terrorism-related offenses, and give the government the power to censor mail, the press, and books. These measures also include the power to restrict movement, confiscate houses deemed used for terrorism or related activities, confiscate property, and impose curfews. Finally, measures include the proscription of "unlawful associations" that advocate, incite, or encourage bringing down government by violence.

Yet, "Israel's greatest investment in combating terrorism has been, by far, in the development of defensive measures in all three categories of terrorist operations [domestic terrorism, the border area, and international terrorism]." Defensive measures, such as hardening targets; involving the public in homeland security, such as by establishing civilian guard units in every urban locale; striking preemptively, like the bombings of Palestinian headquarters; searching cars at roadblocks; and tightening aviation security are all hallmarks of Israeli counterterrorism. Other aspects of preparedness have also evolved in response to the threat. For example, Israel has developed a hospital rotation list, maintained by the health ministry, for an event involving mass casualties. In the event of an attack, the hospital next on the list receives notification. In part, this may also reflect the possibility of WMD terrorism, which has been very real in Israel for at least a decade. If the use of a chemical agent is suspected, that information is conveyed even before it is confirmed. A trained team performs decontamination on site. First responders are also schooled in recognizing symptoms of illness caused by biological weapons. There are stockpile and distribution systems for medications and personal protection, i.e. gas mask, kits are everyday gear for many Israelis. In fact, "given its unique experience managing significant terrorist events and its nationwide readiness for state-sponsored chemical and biological attacks, Israel is probably better prepared than any other country for an unconventional terrorist attack."

Robyn Pangi, in "Consequence Management in the 1995 Sarin Attacks on the Japanese Subway System," uses the attack by Aum Shinrikyo to analyze elements critical to any consequence management program. Japan's political response to terrorism is less geared toward prevention than those of either Israel or the United Kingdom and is more oriented toward the management of terrorism. There are many possible explanations for this focus. First, the Aum Shinrikyo attack was an isolated incident, and many Japanese considered Aum an oddity, rather than a terrorist organization capable or interested in a sustained campaign of violence. Second, Japan tends to be more interested in alleviating the root causes of violence and simultaneously shuns military force or anything that can be viewed as an infringement of civil rights. Third, the attacks revealed several gaps in preparedness that were relatively easy to address and did not require a full-scale overhaul of the system.

Perhaps the greatest lesson that Japan taught the world was the need to be prepared to manage the consequences of WMD terrorism. At the time of the attack, Japan did not have fully developed response plans; intergovernmental and interjurisdictional relationships; a public affairs strategy; or decontamination, health care, and emergency communication capacities. Moreover, even the basic legal framework for prosecuting the perpetrators of a chemical attack was missing. In response to the attack, Japan began a concerted effort to fill these gaps. Decontamination kits were disseminated to hospitals; legal loopholes regarding the prosecution of Aum Shinrikyo were closed; communications systems and strategies were strengthened; and an overflow medical facility was completed. Perhaps the most important point that the United States can take home from Japan's experience, however, is that the need for coordination is paramount: "even when each agency does its job, the lack of cross-agency communication and cooperation hinders effective response and recovery operations."

The United Kingdom provides an example of a nation that has responded to terrorism with, among other tools, a strong law enforcement regime. Laura Donohue chronicles the development of the current system in her article, "Civil Liberties, Terrorism, and Liberal Democracy: Lessons from the United Kingdom." Sweeping legal provisions were first enacted as a temporary measure in 1922, when "Northern Ireland sought to quell rising violence through the temporary use of emergency powers." Far from being temporary, however, the emergency measures were extended repeatedly over the course of 80 years and remain in effect today.

Were they effective? In many respects, yes: after imposition of emergency measures in Northern Ireland, "a high of 80 murders and 58 attempted murders in April 1922 plummeted to one murder and 11 attempted murders by September of that year. These figures continued to fall throughout the balance of 1922 and into 1923." Similar results followed the introduction of other emergency measures. Yet in the Northern Ireland conflict, emergency measures did not stand alone: improved intelligence, the cutoff of U.S. funding to the Irish Republican Army (IRA), and international attention all played significant roles. At the same time, the emergency measures imposed significant costs to civil liberties. Once instituted, moreover, these emergency measures have had unexpected durability, proving difficult to repeal. The apparent success of the measures, coupled with the fact that it was politically unfeasible to repeal a measure labeled counterterrorist without seeming to support terrorism, "transferred the burden of responsibility from those seeking to extend anti- terrorist law to those seeking to repeal it." As a result, these "emergency measures," which were intended to be temporary, instead have extended over the course of nearly a century.

Preparing for Terrorism

The essays in this volume provide a detailed look at many complexities of dealing with the terrorist threat against the United States. The authors have explored how effective our institutions and strategies are, how different forms of terrorist attack pose varying types of problems, what kinds of capacity should be developed to better prepare our institutions for an actual attack, and what lessons the experiences of other developed nations subjected to terrorism can provide. Together these essays provide a valuable resource for the public discussion and debate that should take place as the United States confronts its vulnerability to attack.

Part I
Strategies and Institutions

The Architecture of Government in the Face of Terrorism

Ashton B. Carter

On September 11, 2001, the post–Cold War security bubble finally burst. In the preceding 10 years, the United States and its major allies failed to identify and invest in the prevention of "A-list" security problems that could affect their way of life, position in the world, and very survival. Instead they behaved as if lulled into a belief that the key security problems of the post–Cold War era were ethnic and other internal conflicts in Bosnia, Somalia, Rwanda, Haiti, East Timor, and Kosovo. Peacekeeping and peacemaking in these places, although engaging important humanitarian interests, never addressed the vital security interests of the United States, and none of these conflicts could begin to threaten its survival. As if to confirm this point, the official military strategy of the United States centered not on peacekeeping but on the challenge of fighting two Desert Storm reruns, one in Korea and one in the Persian Gulf, at the same time. The two-major-theater-war doctrine at least had the virtue of addressing threats to vital U.S. allies and interests. But as the decade wore on, it was increasingly apparent that although important interests were at stake in both major theaters, in neither was U.S. survival in question. The A-list seemed empty, so policy and strategy focused on B- and C-level problems instead.[1]

The author is grateful for the support of the Carnegie Corporation of New York, the John D. and Catherine T. MacArthur Foundation, the Packard Foundation, the Simons Foundation, and the Herbert S. Winokur, Jr., Fund for support of this work. The author has benefited from discussions with William J. Perry, John P. White, and Herbert S. Winokur, Jr., and from the editorial and research assistance of Gretchen M. Bartlett in the preparation of this essay.

1. This argument and the corresponding A-, B-, and C-lists are derived from Ashton

A-list threats, such as the threat posed by the Soviet Union for the preceding half-century, were indeed absent but only if threat is understood as the imminent possibility of attack defined in traditional military terms. If taken instead to denote looming problems that could develop into Cold War–scale dangers, the A-list contained at least four major underattended items in the 1990s: the collapse of Moscow's power; the growth of Beijing's military and economic might; proliferation of weapons of mass destruction; and the prospect of catastrophic terrorism. Upon taking office, George W. Bush and his administration claimed to be formulating their strategy around the first two of these items, in a self-proclaimed return to big power realism. But in the wake of the World Trade Center and Pentagon attacks of September 11, the Bush administration is instead finding its agenda dominated by catastrophic terrorism, for which it appears no more or less prepared than its predecessor Bush and Clinton administrations.

The challenge of catastrophic terrorism is destined to be a centerpiece of the field of international security studies. Today the focus is on a particular nest of Islamic extremists who operated freely from the failed state of Afghanistan. But in April 1995, the last time that a building in the United States—the Alfred P. Murrah Federal Building in Oklahoma City—was destroyed in a terrorist attack, the perpetrator was homegrown, an embittered American nihilist operating in the vast anonymity of modern society. One month earlier, an obscure cult in Japan released sarin nerve gas in a Tokyo subway and attempted an airborne anthrax attack. Indeed, the varieties of extremism that can spawn catastrophic terrorism seem limitless, and social scientists have not studied them as thoroughly as they have the dynamics of great power rivalry. What is clear is that war-scale destructive power is becoming increasingly available as technology advances. The same advances heighten the complexity and interconnectedness of civilization, making society more vulnerable at the same time as technology delivers to small groups destructive powers that were formerly the monopoly of states. Thus, if security is understood to be the avoidance and control of mass threat, catastrophic terrorism must occupy a central place in security studies, a status that "ordinary" non-mass terrorism never achieved.[2]

B. Carter and William J. Perry, *Preventive Defense: A New Security Strategy for America* (Washington, D.C.: Brookings, 1999).

2.   Studies dealing with catastrophic terrorism include: Richard A. Falkenrath, Robert D. Newman, and Bradley A. Thayer, *America's Achilles' Heel: Nuclear, Biological, and Chemical Terrorism and Covert Attack* (Cambridge, Mass.: MIT Press, 1998); "A False Alarm (This Time): Preventive Defense against Catastrophic Terrorism," in Carter and

The resulting agenda of analysis and policy development is broad. First, the motivations and root causes of catastrophic terrorism—inscrutable as they may now seem—must eventually yield, at least in part, to careful study.[3] Second, the potential of catastrophic terrorism to transform traditional international relations should also be studied, and its policy consequences propounded, as the great powers—the United States, Europe, Japan, Russia, and China—set aside some of the lesser issues that divide them and acknowledge a greater common interest in protecting their homelands.[4] This essay concerns a third dimension of policy: the need to reengineer the architecture of governance—security

---

Perry, *Preventive Defense*, pp. 143–174; Ashton B. Carter, John M. Deutch, and Philip D. Zelikow, "Catastrophic Terrorism: Tackling the New Danger," *Foreign Affairs*, Vol. 77, No. 6 (November/December 1998), pp. 80–94; Robert T. Marsh, John R. Powers, Merritt E. Adams, Richard P. Case, Mary J. Culnan, Peter H. Daly, John C. Davis, Thomas J. Falvey, Brenton C. Green, William J. Harris, David A. Jones, William B. Joyce, David V. Keyes, Stevan D. Mitchell, Joseph J. Moorcones, Irwin M. Pikus, William Paul Rodgers, Jr., Susan V. Simens, Frederick M. Struble, and Nancy J. Wong, *Critical Foundations: Protecting America's Infrastructures: The Report of the President's Commission on Critical Infrastructure Protection* (Washington, D.C., October 1997); The Gilmore Commission, James S. Gilmore III, James Clapper, Jr., L. Paul Bremer, Raymond Downey, George Foresman, William Garrison, Ellen M. Gordon, James Greenleaf, William Jenaway, William Dallas Jones, Paul M. Maniscalco, Ronald S. Neubauer, Kathleen O'Brien, M. Patricia Quinlisk, Patrick Ralston, William Reno, Kenneth Shine, and Ellen Embrey, *First Annual Report to the President and the Congress of the Advisory Panel to Assess Domestic Response Capabilities to Terrorism Involving Weapons of Mass Destruction I: Assessing the Threat* (Washington, D.C., December 15, 1999), <http://www.rand.org/nsrd/terrpanel/terror.pdf>; The Gilmore Commission, James S. Gilmore III, James Clapper, Jr., L. Paul Bremer, Raymond Downey, Richard A. Falkenrath, George Foresman, William Garrison, Ellen M. Gordon, James Greenleaf, William Jenaway, William Dallas Jones, Paul M. Maniscalco, John O. Marsh, Jr., Kathleen O'Brien, M. Patricia Quinlisk, Patrick Ralston, William Reno, Joseph Samuels, Jr., Kenneth Shine, Hubert Williams, and Ellen Embrey, *Second Annual Report to the President and the Congress of the Advisory Panel to Assess Domestic Response Capabilities to Terrorism Involving Weapons of Mass Destruction II: Toward a National Security for Combating Terrorism* (Washington, D.C., December 15, 2000), <http://www.rand.org/nsrd/terrpanel/terror2.pdf>; and The National Commission on Terrorism, Ambassador L. Paul Bremer III, Maurice Sonnenberg, Richard K. Betts, Wayne A. Downing, Jane Harman, Fred C. Iklé, Juliette N. Kayyem, John F. Lewis, Jr., Gardner Peckham, and R. James Woolsey, *Countering the Changing Threat of International Terrorism*, report of the National Commission on Terrorism (Washington, D.C., June 5, 2000), <http://www.fas.org/irp/threat/commission.html>.

3. Jessica Stern, *The Ultimate Terrorists* (Cambridge, Mass.: Harvard University Press, 1999); Philip B. Heymann, *Terrorism and America: A Commonsense Strategy for a Democratic Society* (Cambridge, Mass.: MIT Press, 1998).

4. See Stephen M. Walt, "Beyond bin Laden: Reshaping U.S. Foreign Policy," *International Security* 26, No. 3, (Winter 2001/02), pp. 56–78.

institutions and their modes of operation—to acknowledge that war-scale damage results from terrorism.[5]

The Governance Issue

Post–Cold War complacency was only one reason that the United States found itself so surprised by, and so unprepared for, the onset of catastrophic terrorism and the mission of homeland security. Greater awareness of the threat since September 11 alone will not rectify this problem. A deeper reason is that the security institutions of the U.S. government are particularly ill-suited to deliver homeland security. There is a fundamental managerial inadequacy, as basic as that of a corporation with no line manager to oversee the making of its leading product.

Pundits debate whether the campaign to prevent catastrophic terrorism is a "war" or not. If one sets aside semantics and asks the practical managerial question: can U.S. preparations for war be easily adapted to preparation for catastrophic terrorism? The answer is "no." Preparations for war in the military, diplomatic, and intelligence senses are the province of institutions—the Departments of Defense and State and the intelligence community—whose focus and missions have been "over there," in the fields of Flanders, the beaches of Normandy, the jungles of Vietnam, and the desert of Kuwait. Their opponents have been foreign governments, and even against them, these U.S. institutions have not been asked to defend the U.S. homeland in recent history, except through the abstraction of nuclear deterrence.

If catastrophic terrorism cannot really be treated as a war, then perhaps it should be conceived of as a crime. But the U.S. law enforcement paradigm is also ill-suited to deal with catastrophic terrorism. This paradigm centers on the *post facto* attribution of crimes to their perpetrators and to prosecution under the law. So deeply entrenched is this model that four weeks after the September 11 attacks, the attorney general had to prod the Federal Bureau of Investigation (FBI) publicly to shift its efforts

---

5. "Countering Asymmetric Threats," Ashton B. Carter and William J. Perry with David Aidekman, in Carter and John P. White, eds., *Keeping the Edge: Managing Defense for the Future* (Cambridge, Mass.: MIT Press, 2001), pp. 119–126; The Hart-Rudman Commission, Gary Hart, Warren B. Rudman, Anne Armstrong, Norman R. Augustine, John Dany, John R. Galvin, Leslie H. Gelb, Newt Gingrich, Lee H. Hamilton, Lionel H. Olmer, Donald B. Rice, James Schlesinger, Harry D. Train, and Andrew Young, *Road Map for National Security: Imperative for Change: The Phase III Report of the U.S. Commission on National Security/21st Century* (Washington, D.C., February 15, 2001).

from "solving the case" to preventing another disaster.[6] Additionally, if the focus of the war model is on foreign perpetrators, the focus of the law enforcement model is on the American citizen. Neither model encompasses the transnational drifter that is characteristic of the al Qaeda operative.

Early in the Bush administration, the new director of the Federal Emergency Management Agency (FEMA) asserted that catastrophic terrorism was neither a war nor a crime but a disaster and thus, the province of his agency, even obtaining a presidential directive to that effect.[7] In so doing, he reversed the position taken by previous FEMA management, which regarded catastrophic terrorism as a new mission with no funding and thus to be avoided. But even armed with a presidential directive, FEMA seemed unable to convince anyone that acts of God and acts of terror were similar enough that a managerial solution was to be found in combining them.

Thus, the federal government lacked a managerial category for catastrophic terrorism, which is neither war, crime, nor disaster, as conventionally understood. Preparations for confronting mass terrorism therefore proceeded haltingly in the 1990s. Some progress was made when preparedness was tied to specific events, such as the 1996 Atlanta Olympics.[8] But elsewhere, the preparations were more the result of the efforts of a few well-placed individuals in the Departments of Defense, Justice, and Health and Human Services who had become concerned about the problem, than of any overall managerial scheme. As the decade wore on, money began to flow to such programs as training state and local governments in confronting weapons of mass destruction.[9] But these efforts

---

6.   Philip Shenon and David Johnston, "F.B.I. Shifts Focus to Try to Avert Any More Attacks," *New York Times*, October 9, 2001.

7.   Vernon Loeb, "Cheney to Lead Anti-Terrorism Plan Team: New FEMA Office Will Coordinate Response Efforts of More Than 40 Agencies, Officials Say," *Washington Post*, May 9, 2001, p. A29.

8.   John Buntin, Kennedy School of Government case study, Parts A–C: "Security Preparations for the 1996 Centennial Olympic Games (Part A)," Case No. C16–00–1582.0; "Security Preparations for the 1996 Centennial Olympic Games: Seeking a Structural Fix (Part B)," Case No. C-16–00–1589.0; "Security Preparations for the 1996 Centennial Olympic Games: The Games Begin (Part C)," Case No. C16–00–1590.0.

9.   Defense against Weapons of Mass Destruction Act 1996 (Nunn-Lugar-Domenici), Public Law 104–201 (H.R. 3230), September 23, 1996, National Defense Authorization Act for Fiscal Year 1997, 104th Cong., 2d sess., <http://www.fas.org/spp/starwars/congress/1996/pl104–201-xiv.htm>.

were largely the result of congressional initiative and inevitably reflected constituent interests. They did not lead to the development of a program to build a national capability for combating catastrophic terrorism.

Outside the federal bureaucracy, even less was done. State and local governments, key to both prevention and response to this new threat, generally lacked the resources and specialized knowledge to combat catastrophic terrorism. The role of the private sector—for example, in protecting critical infrastructures, such as communications and power networks, from disruption or in funding protection through insurance—remained undefined.

Before September 11, 2001, therefore, the U.S. government did not have a managerial approach (i.e., a framework for bringing responsibility, accountability, and resources together in sharp focus) to deliver a key public good—security in the homeland against catastrophic terrorism. This managerial deficiency was not unique to catastrophic terrorism. The post–Cold War world spawned a host of novel security missions for government: peacekeeping and post-peacekeeping civil reconstruction, counterproliferation, threat reduction, information warfare, and conflict prevention (or "preventive defense"). Although it is widely agreed that the United States needs to be able to accomplish these missions (even if debate continues over exactly when and where it should perform them), no fundamental changes have been made in the security architecture to create better institutions and capabilities for them.

Indeed, at least on paper the federal structure has changed little since the first burst of innovation in the aftermath of World War II and the onset of the Cold War. No comparable burst occurred in the 1990s. It is as though corporate America was managing the modern economy with the structures of the Ford Motor Company, the Bell System, and United Fruit. Company managements spend a great deal of thought and energy on organizing their functions to align executive authority with key products. The federal government disperses executive authority so thoroughly that few individuals believe they are accountable for any of the government's key security outputs. People rise to the top of the Washington heap because of their policy expertise, not their managerial expertise. Those senior executives who are managerially inclined find their tenures so short and precarious that there seems to be little reward in making changes in "the system" that will make it possible for their successor's successor to be more effective.[10]

---

10. Ashton B. Carter, "Keeping the Edge: Managing Defense for the Future," in Carter and White, *Keeping the Edge*, pp. 1–26.

Above all, the federal government in the past few decades has eschewed creating new institutions for new missions, such as preparedness for catastrophic terrorism. The political climate in the United States has been hostile to "big government," and existing cabinet departments staunchly defend their heritages and authorities, many of which are enshrined in 200 years of statute. The sense of departmental entrenchment is mirrored on Capitol Hill, where separate authorization and oversight committees protect each "stovepipe"—national security, law enforcement, disaster relief, public health, and so on—as jealously as the executive agencies do themselves.

It is not surprising, therefore, that the specter of catastrophic terrorism occasions deep reflections on the nature and structure of governance in the United States. What needs to be done next cannot be understood without reference to these problems and past attempts to overcome them.

Four Failed Approaches

In broad outline, four approaches to managing the mission of homeland security have been proposed: the command and control approach of the Clinton administration; the lead agency approach; the Department of Homeland Security approach; and the appointment of a White House coordinator or "czar."

The Clinton administration defined its approach in command and control terms: which federal agency should be in charge of dealing with catastrophic terrorism? Initially, the administration determined that the Department of Justice would "have the lead" in domestic terrorist incidents, while the Department of State would do so in incidents abroad. This approach both reinforced the false distinction between domestic and foreign terrorism and focused on actions in progress, rather than on advance detection, prevention, and protection. Later, the Clinton administration promulgated two Presidential Decision Directives—PDD-62 and PDD-63—which further apportioned the matter of "who's in charge" among the existing agencies according to their traditional functions.[11] Thus, for example, PDD-63 assigned protection of the financial system to

---

11. Address by President Bill Clinton at the U.S. Naval Academy, May 22, 1998; White House fact sheet, Combating Terrorism, PDD/NSC-62, Protection against Unconventional Threats to the Homeland and Americans Overseas, May 22, 1998, <http://www.fas.org/irp/offdocs/pdd-62.htm>; White House fact sheet, PDD/NSC-63, Critical Infrastructure Protection, May 22, 1998, <http://www.fas.org/irp/offdocs/pdd/pdd-63.htm>.

the Treasury Department. The fact that this department had no funds, no technology, and little authority to regulate in the field of cybersecurity did not deter the authors of PDD-63. In fact, by focusing on the question of who is in charge, the command and control approach presumed that the government possessed the capabilities to combat catastrophic terrorism; all that was required was to marshal them effectively under a clear command system. The result was the creation of a host of unfunded mandates—responsibilities assigned with no plan for providing the means to fulfill them. The administration made no provision to build new capability, which was—and remains—the crux of the matter.

A second approach considered a single lead agency as having the homeland defense mission. In this approach, the proposed lead was usually the Department of Defense (DOD). DOD was presumed already to have much relevant technology, an ample budget, and a reputation for carrying out its mission more effectively than most other government agencies.[12] But this approach failed because too much of the relevant capability—for example, for surveillance of potential terrorists on U.S. territory—fell beyond DOD's traditional purview. The Pentagon shared the disinclination to arrogate such sweeping new authorities to itself and proclaimed itself willing to take a strong, but follower, role if another agency would lead the effort.

A third approach resulted in the creation of a Department of Homeland Security, which was signed into law in late November 2002. This approach seeks to escape the problem of interagency coordination by concentrating the catastrophic terrorism mission in a single agency. It recognizes that none of the existing cabinet departments was a natural lead agency, and that their ingrained cultures would not easily incline them to adopt the new mission. The fallacy in this approach is that interagency coordination could be thus avoided. Suppose, for example, that the Department of Homeland Security sought to develop a more rapid means of determining whether someone was exposed to anthrax. It would soon discover that this effort was redundant with DOD's efforts to develop the same detector technology for battlefield exposure, in accordance with its traditional mission. The problem of interagency coordination would not be eliminated but only complicated by the introduction of this new agency. Aggregating functions such as customs, immigration, border patrol, and coast guard into the new agency might be efficient, but it can hardly be said that this entity should have the lead in homeland de-

---

12. See Joseph S. Nye, Jr., Philip D. Zelikow, and David S. King, eds., *Why People Don't Trust Government* (Cambridge, Mass.: Harvard University Press, 1996), p. 9 and references therein.

fense, or that its creation eliminates the inherently interagency nature of responding to catastrophic terrorism.

A fourth approach to organizing the federal government to combat catastrophic terrorism is to appoint a White House coordinator or "czar." President Bush named Pennsylvania governor Tom Ridge to such a post within one month of September 11 (though he subsequently moved Ridge to the newly created Department of Homeland Security). This approach is the least problematic, because it recognizes that the essence of the solution is the coordination of a wide range of government functions behind a new priority mission. White House czars, however, have usually been ineffective. With no resources or agencies of their own, such czars must usually cajole cabinet departments into doing what the czar prescribes. The czar's instructions inevitably compete with other needs and tasks of the department, and the final outcome of the competition is determined by the cabinet secretary (invoking legal authorities, usually of long standing) and the relevant committees of Congress, not the czar. After the czar is overridden a few times, lower-level bureaucrats conclude that they can ignore the czar's directives. As the Washington, D.C., saying about czars goes, "The barons ignore them, and eventually the peasants kill them."

The Crux of the Managerial Challenge

A solution to the managerial challenge of catastrophic terrorism should have two features that the approaches outlined above lack. First, it should acknowledge the inherent and ineluctable interagency nature of the problem and abandon any idea of creating a single lead agency that does the entire homeland security job.[13] Second, the approach should begin the long process of providing the United States with a stock of essential capabilities—tactics, technology, and institutions—that the federal departments, state and local governments, and private sector currently lack. Interagency coordination implies a White House focus. But this focus should not be a "czar" who tries to assume or direct the daily functions of all the agencies involved but an "architect" who designs the capabilities that these agencies need to address the problem. In short, the important function of the White House architect is *program* coordination, not policy coordination or command and control.

---

13. This does not rule out the desirability of creating an agency to combine the functions of such border-related agencies as the Coast Guard, Border Patrol, Immigration and Naturalization Service, and Customs. Accomplishing this bureaucratic feat, however useful, would require the full-time attention of a senior manager with presidential and congressional support.

Perhaps the most apt analogy for the job required of the White House is provided not by any war that the United States has fought, but rather by the Cold War. In 1949, Josef Stalin's Soviet Union exploded an atomic bomb over the steppes of Kazakhstan. Although no U.S. citizens died in that distant blast, Americans were suddenly gripped by the prospect of warlike damage being visited upon their homeland by a shadowy enemy with global tentacles. George Kennan, the U.S. diplomat, warned of a long twilight struggle that would test U.S. patience and resolve. The nation mobilized over time a response that was multifaceted, multiagency, and inventive. The United States built nuclear bombers, missiles, and submarines for deterrence and retaliation; it launched spy satellites for warning. It deployed air defenses around the nation's periphery and attempted missile defenses, to raise the price of attack. Civil defense programs sought to minimize casualties if the worst happened. Special relocation sites and procedures were instituted to ensure continuity of constitutional government if Washington, D.C., were destroyed. The North Atlantic Treaty Organization (NATO) and other alliances were formed to get more friends on the U.S. side, and the Marshall Plan sought to ensure that economic desperation did not become Stalin's ally. U.S. leaders further recognized that this new reality was so dangerous that they needed a capacity to analyze, reflect, and learn, not merely react. They founded such think tanks as the RAND Corporation to devise innovative methods for coping with the era's new danger. In time, ideas such as the theory of deterrence and the theory of arms control were elaborated, which were not obvious in 1949, but which helped the world navigate through 50 years of Cold War. With difficulty and many mistakes, the nation also learned to deal with fear of a threat at home, without hunting "reds" in the State Department and Hollywood. The Cold War effort was massive, extended throughout most of the federal government, and was coordinated by the White House.

Designing a similar long-range program to counter catastrophic terrorism is the task of the Bush White House in the aftermath of September 11, 2001. The National Security Council (NSC) cannot do the job for two reasons. First, it does not normally convene the full range of departments, such as Justice and Health and Human Services, required for this effort. The NSC has focused largely on foreign problems. More fundamentally, since Dwight Eisenhower's day, the NSC has slowly lost the capacity for program coordination and become a policy coordination body only.[14]

---

14. John Deutch, Arnold Kanter, and Brent Scowcroft with Chris Hornbarger, "Strengthening the National Security Interagency Process," in Carter and White, *Keeping the Edge*, pp. 265–284.

That is, it brings the national security agencies together to decide upon a common policy but does not oversee or influence their internal capabilities or budgets. Indeed, the NSC's staff is renowned for its diplomatic and policy expertise, but few have experience managing programs or agencies.

President Bush was therefore correct not to give the homeland security job to the NSC, but instead to establish the Office of Homeland Security (OHS) and later, the Department of Homeland Security, both headed by Governor Ridge. As Director of the Office of Homeland Security, it was up to Governor Ridge to avoid the fate of White House czars who try to "run things" from the White House. Instead of taking a command and control approach, Ridge needed to adopt the architect's programmatic approach—designing a multiyear, multiagency plan that will materially increase the capabilities of the existing departments and agencies, so that they can play their part in the campaign against catastrophic terrorism. To a limited extent, he did so. Such an approach would have had the additional salutary effect of overriding the tendency, prevalent as the fiscal year 2002 budget was finalized in the aftermath of September 11, for individual agencies and their oversight committees to craft their own responses to the counterterrorism challenge. In many cases, these responses amounted to little more than long-standing budgetary requests to which the label "counterterrorism" was conveniently applied. Elsewhere, multiple agencies vied to make investments that were duplicative, and each too small to do the job, where a single large investment by only one of them is needed.

The Role of the Office of Homeland Security

The original charter for the Office of Homeland Security uses the word "coordinate" 29 times to describe what its authors imagined was the essence of this managerial task. A large fallacy lies in the idea that "coordination" describes what the nation in fact needs. The nation's capabilities for homeland security, even optimally coordinated, are simply not adequate to cope with twenty-first century terrorism. All the managerial models advanced and tried over the past decade for counterterrorism—coordinator, czar, lead agency—have made this mistake. The result is a "come as you are party," to which each agency shows up with whatever capabilities its previous history happens to have bequeathed to it. What is needed is far less a coordinator of what exists, than an architect of the capabilities we need to build.

The homeland security program might be organized functionally, according to a time line extending from before a hypothetical incident of catastrophic terrorism to its aftermath. In the first phase, the United States needs better capabilities for *detection* of catastrophic terrorism. This involves surveillance of persons and motives—a delicate matter—but also surveillance of potential means of destruction, such as crop dusters, germ cultures, and pilot instruction. Surveillance of means raises far fewer civil liberties issues than does surveillance of persons, and it might be much more effective. A group that evades surveillance becomes subject to *prevention* by efforts to keep destructive means out of its hands. The Nunn-Lugar program to safeguard Russian nuclear weapons and fissile materials is an example of a prevention program. The next stage is *protection*—making borders, buildings, airplanes, and critical infrastructures more difficult to breach, disrupt, or destroy, through technical design and procedures. Protection might also mean making people more resistant to disease through vaccination and other public health measures. *Interdiction,* or "crisis management," seeks to disrupt and destroy potential perpetrators of catastrophic terrorism and their base of support before they can mount an attack, as in the U.S. campaign in Afghanistan. *Containment,* or "consequence management," means limiting the level of damage and the number of casualties by organizing emergency response, public health measures, and restoration of critical functions in the aftermath of a terrorist attack. *Attribution* refers to the capability to find the perpetrators of an act (e.g., by typing an anthrax culture or performing radiochemical analysis of nuclear bomb debris) and to choose retaliation, prosecution, or other response. Finally, as with the RAND Corporation in the Cold War, the nation will need a capacity for *analysis and invention*—studying terrorist tactics and devising countermeasures, understanding motivations and modes of deterrence, drawing lessons from past attacks, creating new technologies, and developing a systematic strategy plan.

As architect, the director of OHS would first identify needed capabilities and then assign resources to the various agencies to build those capabilities. This approach would give the architect budgetary authority (the key to his influence) to apply that influence where it is needed most: capacity building. Where no agency naturally forms the right base to build on, the architect should recommend new agencies. The result, schematically, would be a multiagency, multiyear investment and management plan that can be arrayed on a spreadsheet as in Figure One. In each box would appear the agency's responsibility, if any, for possessing capability in that function, with a plan to develop that capability over a period of years. The president would approve such a matrix for each fiscal year, extending five years into the future, and would send it to the Congress with his annual budget submission. Although Congress would of course

Figure 1. Dimensions of a Homeland Security Program: The Architect's Plan.

	Detection	Prevention	Protection	Interdiction	Containment	Attribution	Analysis and Invention
Justice/FBI							
Defense							
Intelligence							
Health and Human Services							
Border (Coast Guard, Border Patrol, Customs, Immigration, etc.)							
FEMA							
Other (Energy, Transportation, Agriculture, State, etc.)							
New Federal Agencies or Nonprofit Institutions							
State and Local Government (supported by federal grants)							
Private Sector (via regulation, subsidy, and indemnification)							

have the last word on the budget, experience shows that Congress makes only marginal adjustments where there is a strong and clear presidential program on a subject of great national importance.

The Role of the Department of Homeland Security

The Department of Homeland Security (DHS) is an appropriate ingredient or output of the architect's plan, but not a substitute for the architect. While DHS contains much, it also omits much—the Central Intelligence Agency (CIA), Department of Defense, and Federal Bureau of Investigation, in particular. An architect is needed for *all* of the agencies involved. Therefore, the founding of DHS must not be viewed as supplanting OHS.

In order for DHS to be successful, the administration must first successfully complete the reorganization of the border, transportation, and emergency management agencies that have been transferred to DHS, improving their management and focusing them on their new priority. Most reorganizations in the federal government are only partially completed. Agency heads, after first fighting the merger, will next aim to send their weakest performers to the new agency and keep their very best. Temporary inconveniences associated with the reorganization—moving people into new office buildings, for instance—will be argued as detracting from day-to-day pursuit of the urgent mission of homeland defense. Government unions, strong in some of the agencies included in the new DHS, will scrutinize personnel policies. Congress will need to disband influential committees with established relationships and constituencies. All this is necessary but difficult. A reorganization done halfway could make things worse.

Finally, DHS still needs to do truly new things and not merely gather together old functions under one roof. The department's most important contributions could be in intelligence analysis and science and technology. Indeed, two of the five undersecretary positions in DHS are assigned these functions; the other three undersecretary positions are in charge of aggregating existing border/transportation and emergency management functions and administration.

The nation will continue to struggle with the organization and management of the "homeless mission" of homeland security. Since October 8, 2001, we have had an Office of Homeland Security in the White House, and since November 25, 2002, a Department of Homeland Security, which swore in Tom Ridge as a cabinet-level secretary on January 24, 2003. Both are needed to make a home for this mission, but each has a distinctive role to play. Creation of DHS in no way supplants the paramount need for a strong White House OHS. The DHS should not just bring order and focus to existing functions but should accomplish new functions, as part of an aggressive reorganization developed by the OHS. Such new functions include the development and practice of new types of intelligence and new security technology and techniques.

Key Ingredients of the Homeland Security Program

The homeland security program will have many key components. Below are a few illustrative examples.

RED TEAM, BLUE TEAM

Most Americans were probably not shocked to learn on September 12, 2001, that the U.S. government did not have advance information about the dozen or so individuals residing in the country who plotted and took part in the airline suicide attacks of September 11. They probably were deeply disturbed to learn, however, that the government was as heedless of the tactic used as it was of the perpetrators. The airline security system inspected for guns and bombs, not knives; aircrews were trained to deal with hijackers who sought hostages or conveyance to Cuba, not kamikaze attack. In retrospect, a huge gap existed within the U.S. air safety system. Terrorists detected the gap before the security system did—and exploited it.

To avoid tactical surprise of this kind, the homeland security effort needs to adopt a standard mechanism of military organizations: competing red and blue teams. The red team tries to devise attack tactics, and the blue team tries to design countermeasures. When the United States developed the first stealth aircraft, for example, the air force created a red team to try to detect and shoot it down. When the red team identified a weakness in the stealth design, the blue team was charged to fix it, systematically balancing risk of detection against the cost and inconvenience of countermeasures.

A comparable red/blue team mechanism should be the central feature of the program for homeland security. To work, the mechanism must be systematic and institutionalized, not *ad hoc*. It must be independent of the interests—airlines, for example—that stand to be inconvenienced by its findings. It must have the money to conduct experiments, tests, and inspections, not just paper studies. It must be knowledgeable about the technologies of terrorism and protection. Above all, it must be inventive. These criteria all argue for founding a new institution outside of, but close to, government. Models include the National Academy of Sciences, the RAND Corporation, the Mitre and Mitretek Systems Corporations, the Institute for Defense Analyses, and other nonprofit research organizations established during the Cold War.

SCIENCE AND TECHNOLOGY

American society has many weaknesses in the battle against catastrophic terrorism. It is large and open. Its infrastructures are complex and interconnected. It values free movement, free speech, and privacy. Its commanding international position is a lightning rod for many international grievances. The United States must therefore draw on its key strengths in ensuring homeland security, among which inventiveness, derived from its huge science and technology base, is probably most important. The U.S. military has long sought to use superior technology to offset its opponents' favorable geography, superior numbers, and willingness to suffer casualties.[15] The homeland security effort requires a program of contract research and technology development that should be conducted outside of government, in universities and private companies. The contracting methods should permit small and entrepreneurial commercial companies that are the drivers of new technology, and not just large government contractors, to participate in the effort. Biotechnology companies, which unlike the aerospace and information technology industries have never had strong ties to national security, should be induced to participate.[16] Finally, "centers of excellence" in counterterrorism should be established. These centers should set out to develop the same depth of expertise represented by the Los Alamos, Lawrence Livermore, and Sandia National Laboratories in the field of nuclear weapons design during the Cold War.

TRANSNATIONAL INTELLIGENCE

A number of studies have called attention to the problem of combining information derived from foreign intelligence collection with information derived from domestic law enforcement.[17] The rules governing collection in the two categories differ for the important reason that U.S. citizens en-

---

15. William J. Perry, "Desert Storm and Deterrence," *Foreign Affairs,* Vol. 70, No. 4. (Fall 1991), pp. 64–82; Ashton B. Carter with Marcel Lettre and Shane Smith, "Keeping the Technological Edge," in Carter and White, *Keeping the Edge,* pp. 129–163.

16. Joshua Lederberg, ed., *Biological Weapons: Limiting the Threat* (Cambridge, Mass.: MIT Press, 1999), chap. 1.

17. Gilmore Commission, *First and Second Annual Reports to the President and the Congress;* Carter, Deutch, and Zelikow, "Catastrophic Terrorism"; Hart-Rudman Commission, *Road Map for National Security;* Heymann, *Terrorism and America.*

joy protections from surveillance that do not apply to the overseas activities of the intelligence community. There is no reason, however, why information of both types, collected by the U.S. government in accordance with the respective rules for each, cannot be combined and correlated. The barriers to doing so are largely bureaucratic. These barriers need to be surmounted in an era when individuals move easily across borders, and when groups fomenting terrorism are likely to be transnational in their membership.[18]

INTELLIGENCE OF MEANS

Surveillance of the *means* that terrorists employ is potentially more important than surveillance of *persons*, and raises far fewer civil liberties issues. Placing all Middle Eastern male noncitizens resident in the United States under surveillance, for example, is both objectionable and impractical. But inquiring after all those who take flying lessons but are not interested in learning to take off or land, who rent crop dusters, or who seek information on the antibiotic resistance of anthrax strains or the layout of a nuclear power plant, is feasible and may be extremely useful.

Likewise, it is undesirable to restrict access by citizens to the Capitol building and congressional office buildings, but there is no fundamental technical barrier to seeding these buildings with sensors that would promptly, and with a low rate of false alarms, detect the presence of anthrax on surfaces and in ventilation systems. Nuclear weapons are much harder to detect, but the streets in the vicinity of the White House could be laced with sensitive detectors that would stand a good chance of detecting a nuclear or radiological weapon. Although these detectors would individually have a high rate of false alarms, when networked so that their outputs are correlated in space and time, they could constitute an effective warning system. Such a system is preferable to registering truck drivers or other methods of surveilling persons in the White House vicinity.

CONTROL OF WEAPONS AND MATERIALS

10 years into the Nunn-Lugar program to safeguard nuclear, chemical, and biological weapons and materials in the former Soviet Union, the job remains unfinished.[19] In addition to continuing to support and greatly

---

18. A specific proposal for combining CIA and FBI intelligence on transnational terrorism is contained in "A False Alarm (This Time)," pp. 143–174; Carter, Deutch, and Zelikow, "Catastrophic Terrorism."

19. See Matthew Bunn, *The Next Wave: Urgently Needed New Steps to Control Warheads and Fissile Material* (Washington, D.C.: Carnegie Endowment for International Peace

expand this program, the effort must be extended to Pakistan, where an arsenal of substantial size may fall prey to growing extremism.

THE COSTS OF PROTECTION

Protective measures for homeland security cover a wide spectrum of possibilities: vaccines, air defenses around the White House and nuclear power plants, electronic firewalls around information networks, to name just a few examples. The investments required could be enormous. Who will pay? Private investment could be mandated by regulation. Government could bear or subsidize the costs. Or apportionment of risk and blame could be left to the insurance marketplace and tort courtrooms. The answer will vary from case to case, but the federal government needs to devise a strategy. Crafting the right regulations and legislation, as well as putting the right subsidies into the federal budget, will be a key responsibility of the homeland security architect.

INTERDICTION

Soon after September 11, President Bush enunciated a principle of U.S. policy against catastrophic terrorism that, if pursued to its logical conclusion, would establish interdiction as an ongoing effort, rather than an episodic response to actual attacks. In his first major public pronouncement following the September attacks, the president said, "Either you are with us, or you are with the terrorists."[20] This would seem to imply the need for a continuing program to preempt attack from groups that profess an intention to carry out mass terrorism and to apply pressure, including attack, against those who actively support or harbor them. Taken literally, such a program of interdiction would have profound consequences for U.S. foreign policy, for alliances such as NATO, and for international organizations such as the United Nations.

PUBLIC HEALTH SURVEILLANCE AND RESPONSE

Containment of the damage from an incident of mass terrorism requires that the public health and agricultural systems establish capabilities that go well beyond their accustomed mission of protecting against naturally occurring dangers. The powers of the public health authorities to man-

---

and Harvard Project on Managing the Atom, April 2000); Howard Baker and Lloyd Cutler, cochairs, *A Report Card on the Department of Energy's Nonproliferation Programs with Russia* (Washington, D.C.: U.S. Department of Energy, Secretary of Energy Advisory Board, January 10, 2001).

20. President George W. Bush, Address to a Joint Session of Congress and the American People, U.S. Capitol, September 20, 2001.

date disease surveillance and impose such remedies as quarantine are broad, a holdover from the nineteenth century. These authorities need to be updated to encompass man-made pandemics. The private health care system overall, which under the doctrine of managed care is designed to have the least possible excess capacity during normal times, will need to provide such surge capability as extra hospital beds and stockpiled medications carefully chosen and sized for possible bioterrorism.

STATE AND LOCAL FIRST RESPONSE

Since 1996, the Nunn-Lugar-Domenici legislation, has provided state and local first responders with the equipment and training to enhance their vital role in consequence management.[21] Defining the ongoing federal role in supporting state and local government is a major task of the counterterrorism program.

FORENSICS FOR ATTRIBUTION

Ever since U.S. Air Force aircraft sampled the first residue from the Soviet Union's nuclear weapons testing in the 1950s and deduced their detailed design, radiochemical analysis of bomb materials and debris has developed into a sophisticated science. A corresponding effort to type bioterror agents and their chemical preparations is required to attribute attacks to their perpetrators. At this time the FBI, the DOD, and the Centers for Disease Control and Prevention all have forensic programs, but none is adequate for counterterrorism purposes. The counterterrorism program architect will need to decide which of these programs will be funded to provide the greatly expanded capability that the nation needs.

MOBILIZATION AND SUNSET

Until the mid-twentieth century, successful prosecution of war depended on the ability to mobilize nations and armies. A similar concept is useful in the war on terrorism. In the face of reasonably credible and specific information about actual or imminent mass terrorism, extraordinary measures might be advisable that are undesirable when there are no such warnings. In an emergency, the government will assume special authorities, restrict movement and other freedoms, and impose economic dis-

21. Falkenrath, Newman, and Thayer, *America's Achilles' Heel;* and Richard A. Falkenrath, "The Problems of Preparedness: Challenges Facing the U.S. Domestic Preparedness Program," BCSIA Discussion Paper 2000–28, ESDP Discussion Paper 2000–05 (Cambridge, Mass.: Belfer Center for Science and International Affairs and Executive Session on Domestic Preparedness, John F. Kennedy School of Government, Harvard University, December 2000).

ruptions as the nation hunkers down. It is important to the quality of civil society in the long run that this mobilized state be clearly distinguished in statute and procedures from "normal" times, when catastrophic terrorism is an ever present, but not a specifically anticipated, contingency. Experience in the United Kingdom during its century-long struggle against Irish terrorism suggests that, even in liberal democracies, powers granted to the government in the name of imminent terrorism are seldom rescinded when the threat recedes.[22] It is therefore important to write into any statute or regulation conferring extraordinary powers on the government, a sunset clause describing the time and method of demobilization that places the burden for extending the mobilization squarely on the government's ability to produce credible and specific information of imminent threat.

Conclusion

Merely coordinating the existing capabilities of the United States to counter catastrophic terrorism is not adequate to protect the nation or the international order from this major new challenge, because the existing capabilities fall far short of what is needed. Nor is it practical to imagine having someone in the federal government who is truly in charge of a mission that inherently cuts across all agencies of the federal government, state and local government, and the private sector. What is required instead is a multiyear, multiagency program of invention and investment devised in the White House, embedded in the president's budget submissions and defended by him to Congress, and supported by appropriate law and regulation. This program should cover all phases in the war against catastrophic terrorism—detection, prevention, protection, interdiction, containment, attribution, analysis, and invention. If President Bush's secretary of homeland security assumes the role of architect of such an effort, he will provide future presidents with the tools that they will need to cope with this enduring problem.

---

22. Laura K. Donohue, "Civil Liberties, Terrorism, and Liberal Democracy: Lessons from the United Kingdom," BCSIA Discussion Paper 2000–05, ESDP Discussion Paper 2000–01 (Cambridge, Mass.: Belfer Center for Science and International Affairs and Executive Session on Domestic Preparedness, John F. Kennedy School of Government, Harvard University, August 2000).

Intergovernmental Challenges of Combating Terrorism

Arnold M. Howitt and Robyn L. Pangi

In the wake of the attacks on the Pentagon and World Trade Center and the anthrax letter mailings, elected officials at all levels of government pledged firmly to take all steps necessary to protect the American people. The challenges are great, particularly as the nation contemplates other emerging threats, such as radiological ("dirty bomb") weapons attacks and infectious bioterrorist agents, including smallpox. Large uncertainties abound. The variety and geographic scope of possible threats is immense, and the future level of terrorist activity in the United States is unknown.

The government's response is most familiar and visible at the federal level, where numerous agencies play important roles in combating terrorism. The task is by no means exclusively federal, though, but cuts across the broad intergovernmental system, encompassing federal, state, and local agencies. States and localities possess many of the operational resources and much of the critical authority needed to detect, prevent, and, when necessary, respond to terrorism. The complexities of this system must be taken into account as a national strategy emerges and core capacities of government are enhanced.

This essay reviews why preparing for terrorism in the context of U.S. federalism poses significant institutional challenges, surveys federal policies—both before and after September 11—to build up state and local capabilities, and examines how states and localities have responded to the new realities that suicide jetliner attacks and anthrax letters on U.S. territory signify.

Institutional Challenges of Preparedness

The United States has two loosely coordinated systems of institutions relevant to, but not primarily focused on, combating terrorism. The first set of institutions, concerned with *prevention and mitigation* of domestic and international threats to civil society, is almost entirely governmental. It includes agencies responsible for law enforcement, border management, intelligence, and military functions. The second set of institutions, concerned with *emergency or disaster response*, cuts across governmental and private sector boundaries, with key roles played by nongovernmental organizations. This system includes emergency services (e.g., fire suppression and hazardous materials containment), health care, and incident management and coordination. Post–September 11, these institutions are being transformed to increase system integration and to enhance the focus and priority given to the terrorist threat. Substantial efforts are necessary, however, to establish stronger interconnections and relationships between and within these two institutional systems.

Historically, there are weak interconnections between the prevention/mitigation functions and emergency/disaster response functions. The first mission is primarily oriented toward external invasions of U.S. territory and major domestic disruptions of civic order—events that have occurred very infrequently historically. Emergency response institutions effectively specialize in natural disasters (such as hurricanes, tornados, floods, earthquakes, winter storms, forest or wildland fires, or widespread disease) or technological emergencies (such as hazardous materials spills, plane or train crashes, urban fires, or industrial explosions). They do not generally work closely with the institutions concerned with prevention (e.g., law enforcement and the National Guard), except in extraordinary circumstances, such as the urban riots of the 1960s or the Los Angeles riot of 1992, or when maintaining order during natural or technological disasters. As a consequence, neither the prevention nor emergency response systems have previously seen the need for tight institutional coordination or operational integration.

Even *within* the mostly separate prevention and emergency response systems, the public agencies and private organizations that contribute to these missions are not highly integrated.

Achieving greater integration requires meeting significant organizational challenges. First, these agencies and organizations, in the main, operate independently; in the course of their regular work, they interact with each other only episodically rather than systematically. Police departments, for example, carry on their daily functions of order maintenance and law enforcement with relatively little contact with other elements of the prevention system, except for criminal prosecutors and the courts. They have less well developed cooperative ties with the rapidly expanding private security industry, which provides contract guard service and other forms of protective services, primarily to private business firms. Police agencies do periodically work on specific cases with the specialized federal agencies dealing with drug or firearms enforcement, border security, or immigration violations, but these interactions are far less structured and frequent than relationships with the courts. Even less frequent and less structured are relationships among police agencies, national intelligence agencies, and the military. The results are weak formal coordination mechanisms, unclear authority relationships, and few interpersonal ties among officials of different organizations. This independence of operation is not exceptional; it is characteristic of interorganizational relationships in both the prevention and emergency response sectors.

Another barrier to integrated action is the decentralized and diverse institutional structure of U.S. federalism. Federalism is a fundamental and deeply rooted feature of the U.S. constitutional tradition, under which each state determines its own substate institutional structure.[1] The sheer number of institutions below the state level is enormous: the United States has more than 87,000 independent units of county, municipal, school, and special district government—not counting separate agencies of each governmental unit (i.e., the police, fire, and emergency management departments of a particular city).[2] Adding to the complexity, the locus of specific governmental responsibilities and the formal authority structure of substate institutions vary substantially from state to state. State finance systems vary widely as well—both in the nature and relative importance of specific revenue sources and in the division of revenue raising authority between the state and local governments.

This cross-state and within-state variation makes it difficult for the federal government—whether Congress or executive agencies—to devise national policies and design grant and technical assistance programs that are well suited to the needs of all locales. Individual state and local governments are typically given considerable latitude to customize solutions within the general scope of federal policies—a result also connected to state sensitivity to prescription by the federal government. The fragmen-

---

1. See, for example, Thomas J. Anton, *American Federalism and Public Policy: How the System Works* (Philadelphia, Penn.: Temple University Press, 1989).

2. U.S. Department of Commerce, Economics and Statistics Administration, Bureau of the Census, *1997 Census of Governments, Vol. 1, Government Organization*, GC97 (1)–1 (Washington, D.C.: U.S. Government Printing Office, 1999), pp. 1, 3.

tation of subnational government also makes it difficult to organize prevention and emergency response functions across jurisdictional boundaries in a given metropolitan area or state.

In most specific functional areas, moreover, planning, operating, and financing responsibilities are shared among several levels of government, but the division of responsibility varies widely from one function to another. Key emergency management functions are located throughout the intergovernmental system—at the federal, state, county, and municipal level.[3] Domestic law enforcement, though, is primarily a local government function, with more specialized roles played by state and federal law enforcement agencies. Urban fire protection capacity is even more concentrated at the local level. By contrast, military capacity is overwhelmingly federal, with the exception of the National Guard, which, under normal circumstances, operates under state authority. Public health responsibilities, as another example, are more evenly distributed across levels of the federal system.

In some functional areas, particularly health care, private sector organizations, rather than public agencies, are key institutional actors. In many states, emergency medical services are provided mainly by private sources—for example, hospitals, ambulance companies, physicians, and technicians. Especially for emergency services, moreover, volunteers may play a critical role in some settings—working through established organizations, such as the American Red Cross, or as individuals who offer their time and skills in a particular situation.

Yet another layer of complexity in U.S. federalism arises because the distribution of *operational* responsibility for a particular government function does not necessarily correspond to the distribution of *financing* responsibility. State and local revenue raising and spending systems are highly complex. In most states, local governments raise most of their revenues from local sources as authorized by state law. But states raise revenue directly not only for their own operations but also for redistribution to substate institutions—both for general and specific purposes. The federal government also plays a part in state and local finance by providing a wide range of grants-in-aid and subsidies. Federal funds sometimes go directly to states (which then may or may not funnel all or part of a particular source to localities) and sometimes directly to localities. Although in most functional areas federal assistance to states and localities repre-

---

3. U.S. Department of Commerce, Economics and Statistics Administration, Bureau of the Census, Government Finances, 1998–99 (Washington, D.C.: U.S. Government Printing Office, 2001), p. 1.

sents a relatively small portion of total funding for those levels, federal aid may be an important source of funds for innovation.

The federal system is thus extraordinarily complex—in terms of the number of independent units and the great variation in institutional structure, financing, sharing of functions across levels of government, the involvement of private organizations and volunteers, constituencies and accountability relationships, and operating capacity. The diversity of institutional forms below the federal level produces complicated stakeholder relationships and dynamic structures of accountability to voters and taxpayers. The elected officials of each jurisdiction must be responsive to their own constituents—voters and interest groups—who may have quite different conceptions of policy and differing priorities from those in other jurisdictions or at other levels of government.

Domestic Preparedness Policies Prior to September 11

Within this complex framework, policymakers have sought, over the past decade, to establish a series of programs designed to prepare the nation to manage the consequences of a large-scale terrorist attack. Much of the early effort was spurred on by a series of terrorist incidents at home and abroad in the mid-1990s, which resulted in several initiatives undertaken by the federal government—collectively referred to as the domestic preparedness program.

On February 26, 1993, the World Trade Center was damaged when a bomb was detonated in an underground parking garage. The attack, carried out by Mahmud Abouhalima and Ramzi Yousef, killed six people and injured thousands more. On April 19, 1995, Timothy McVeigh bombed the Alfred P. Murrah Federal Building in Oklahoma City, killing 169 people. Shortly before, on March 20, 1995, members of the Aum Shinrikyo cult in Japan released the nerve agent sarin into the Tokyo subway system. This attack, the first large-scale terrorist attack with a weapon of mass destruction in modern history, resulted in 12 deaths and nearly 1,000 injuries. Bombings of U.S. embassies in Nairobi, Kenya, and Dar es Salaam, Tanzania, on August 7, 1998, killed 301 people and wounded more than 5,000.

These events convinced many that a new era had dawned.[4] Terrorist attacks were being directed at U.S. interests; it was no longer a problem

---

4. See the Advisory Panel to Assess Domestic Response Capabilities for Terrorism Involving Weapons of Mass Destruction ("The Gilmore Commission"), "Countering the Changing Threat of International Terrorism," June 7, 2000; and the General Ac-

mainly for other countries. In addition, terrorism could strike on U.S. soil, and anti-American terrorism could originate at home or abroad. Weapons of mass destruction, moreover, could be obtained or developed by sophisticated terrorists and terrorist organizations. Despite agreement that a new threat was emerging, the domestic preparedness measures initiated in the 1990s did not originate as a comprehensive strategy or action plan. Rather, they emerged from several venues in different forms: congressional earmarks, executive orders and administrative measures, agency reorganization, and—less frequently—state and local government initiatives.

Momentum for creating a counterterrorism program built slowly. In September 1994, more than a year after the first World Trade Center attack, Congress made it a crime to provide material support or resources to terrorists. The executive branch took action in January 1995, when President Clinton issued Executive Order 12947, naming 12 foreign terrorist organizations and freezing their assets.[5]

After the Tokyo subway attack and the Oklahoma City blast, however, Congress and the Clinton administration took stronger steps. In June 1995, President Clinton released Presidential Decision Directive (PDD)-39, "U.S. Policy for Combating Terrorism," which called for heightened counterterrorism activities, clarified federal agency roles and responsibilities for terrorism, and designated the Federal Bureau of Investigation (FBI) as the lead federal agency for crisis management and Federal Emergency Management Agency (FEMA) for consequence management with regard to domestic terrorism. PDD-39 did not, however, provide budgets for these newly assigned roles.

In April 1996, Congress passed the Anti-Terrorism and Effective Death Penalty Act. The legislation gave the Department of Justice (DOJ) a series of discrete congressional earmarks for specific counterterrorism projects. Later that same year, the Defense Against Weapons of Mass Destruction Act—otherwise known as the Nunn-Lugar-Domenici Amendment—was passed by Congress and directed the Department of Defense

---

counting Office, "Combating Terrorism: Selected Challenges and Related Recommendations," GAO-01–822 (September 2001).

5. Executive Order 12947: Prohibiting Transactions with Terrorists Who Threaten to Disrupt the Middle East Peace Process (January 23, 1995), named Abu Nidal Organization (ANO), Democratic Front for the Liberation of Palestine (DFLP), Hizballah, Islamic Gama'at (IG), Islamic Resistance Movement (HAMAS), Jihad, Kach, Kahane Chai, Palestinian Islamic Jihad-Shiqaqi faction (PIJ), Palestine Liberation Front-Abu Abbas faction (PLF-Abu Abbas), Popular Front for the Liberation of Palestine (PFLP), and Popular Front for the Liberation of Palestine-General Command (PFLP-GC), as foreign terrorist organizations.

DOD) to train and equip federal, state, and local agencies. In Fiscal Year (FY) 1998, Congress earmarked $17 million for a "Special Equipment and Training Grant Program" housed in the Department of Justice. A new Office for State and Local Domestic Preparedness Support (subsequently renamed the Office for Domestic Preparedness) was established to implement this program. This office also was given responsibility for the Nunn-Lugar-Domenici program, which was transferred from DOD to DOJ.

Congress and the administration also created specialized programs in several federal departments. After the sarin attacks in Tokyo, the Office of Emergency Preparedness, a small office in the Department of Health and Human Services (HHS) responsible for the National Disaster Medical System, began the Metropolitan Medical Response System program, which supported city and regional efforts to prepare emergency medical providers for the consequences of a chemical weapons incident. The Centers for Disease Control and Prevention in HHS also instituted the creation of a pharmaceutical stockpile in May 1998. In the Department of Defense, the U.S. Marine Corps created the Chemical and Biological Incident Response Force—a deployable unit containing the majority of the Corps' existing chemical and biological defense capabilities. In March 1998, Secretary of Defense William Cohen announced the creation of special National Guard teams to support areas attacked with weapons of mass destruction.

The proliferation of federal programs aimed at states and localities, as well as the increased federal counterterrorism agency activities, led to demands for better integration of these efforts. In May 1998, President Clinton issued PDD-62, "Protection Against Unconventional Threats to the Homeland and Americans Overseas," which established the Office of National Coordinator for Security Infrastructure Protection and Counterterrorism in the National Security Council to coordinate federal efforts. Paralleling these efforts to make the federal program more coherent, however, was further expansion. On the same day that he issued PDD-62, President Clinton also announced PDD-63, "The Critical Infrastructure Protection Directive." In June 1998, the White House requested almost $300 million additional dollars for domestic preparedness programs. In October 1998, the Attorney General announced the creation of a new National Domestic Preparedness Office in the FBI, intended as a national clearinghouse of information for state and local response agencies.

Even before the attacks in September and October 2001, however, it was clear to many that much more needed to be done to coordinate the nation's capacity to combat terrorism. The intergovernmental dimensions of this problem were highlighted in May 2000 by a congressionally mandated exercise for top officials, called TOPOFF. TOPOFF simulated simultaneous attacks in three U.S. cities: a biological release in Denver, Colorado; a chemical release in Portsmouth, New Hampshire; and a radiological release in Washington, D.C. The exercise revealed significant shortcomings in the state of domestic preparedness. Primarily, there was an obvious lack of established authority roles, too little familiarity with incident management systems, and cultural and institutional barriers to timely information sharing. In addition, limited public health resources, lack of medical capacity, and logistical hurdles, evident in the simulation, would have crippled the response effort in an actual emergency.[6]

Like many emerging policy areas in the past, the domestic preparedness program has grown in a disjointed manner. Some initiatives were congressional earmarks provided without a request from the administration or unfunded congressional mandates; these directed federal agencies to do something they had not been doing before or were now being asked to do differently. Moreover, some of these initiatives had little stability. As noted, the Nunn-Lugar-Domenici Act training program for first responders was transferred from DOD to DOJ after only three years. (In 2002, President Bush twice proposed another transfer—first to FEMA and then to the Department of Homeland Security.)

No mechanism for coordinating the domestic preparedness program existed at the outset, nor was any one agency "in charge" of central coordination. Attempts to designate lead federal agencies (as in PDD-39), even for specific aspects of preparedness, were largely unsuccessful. It was difficult, if not impossible, for one cabinet agency to coordinate another's activities; the National Security Council (NSC) staff lacked sufficient resources and authority to carry out its coordination assignment, and NSC lacked the contacts and experience to lead state and local agencies effectively.

At the state and local level, domestic preparedness efforts, with few exceptions, were reactive. States and localities were less likely than federal authorities to consider terrorism their responsibility. An attack in the domain of any particular subnational government was much less likely than the risk to the nation as a whole. Even after Timothy McVeigh's attack in Oklahoma City, terrorism seemed part of the realm of national security, foreign affairs, and defense policy—not local law enforcement. At the state and local levels, moreover, few stakeholders were actively advocating increased preparedness expenditures, except as federal subsidy reduced local costs. A few jurisdictions, notably New York City, which had

---

6. Donald A. Henderson, Thomas V. Inglesby, Jr., and Tara O'Toole, "A Plague on Your City: Observations from TOPOFF," *Clinical Infectious Diseases*, No. 32, (October 5, 2000) pp. 436–445.

experienced the first attack on the World Trade Center, were aggressively building up their emergency response capabilities and establishing closer relations with the FBI and other federal agencies concerned with prevention; but most jurisdictions mainly participated in federal programs like first responder training and planning for the Metropolitan Medical Response System.

Post–September 11 Federal Policies

The terrorist attacks on the United States in the fall of 2001 vaulted preparing for terrorism from an issue with occasional attention but low visibility overall to an issue of national prominence and high priority. Since September 11, there has been almost universal acceptance, among policymakers, practitioners, and civilians, that the suicide jetliner attacks and the subsequent anthrax attacks were not isolated incidents, but rather represent a potential trend of more destructive attacks on Americans, whether serving abroad or going about their daily business at home. In response to this threat and in an effort to mitigate the physical, emotional, and economic impacts that terrorism has on Americans, government at all levels is sharpening its focus on homeland security. Many aspects of the new homeland security campaign are familiar, because they were integral pieces of the domestic preparedness program. Others are new but represent old concerns.

Perhaps the most visible change is the budget. Shortly after the attacks, Congress and the Bush administration agreed to $20 billion to promote homeland security, including funds to upgrade intelligence and security, provide recovery assistance to disaster sites, help victims' families, increase numbers of law enforcement personnel, provide health care for displaced Americans, and purchase irradiation equipment to sanitize the mail. According to the Government Accounting Office (GAO), in FY 2002, $19.5 billion in federal funding was allocated for homeland security. In addition, Congress passed an emergency supplemental appropriation of $40 billion, of which $9.8 billion was dedicated to strengthening defenses at home. The total represents a 50 percent overall increase in federal funding from FY 2001 to $29.3 billion. The proposed budget for FY 2003 contains another significant increase to $37.7 billion. However, the President's FY 2004 budget proposals, reflecting a major change in the federal fiscal situation, did not appreciably increase this amount.

NEW EMPHASIS ON PREVENTION
Immediately after the terrorist attacks on September 11, Congress initiated action to create a Transportation Security Administration (TSA) in

the U.S. Department of Transportation (DOT).[7] Responsible ultimately for protecting all modes of transportation, TSA's initial and quite formidable task was taking over responsibility for screening passengers and luggage in airports. (TSA was subsequently transferred from DOT into the new Department of Homeland Security.)

Prevention also became a key focus of law enforcement and intelligence activities. The FBI and the Justice Department began shifting their focus to the prevention and detection of terrorist attacks.[8] Attorney General John Ashcroft ordered a "wartime reorganization" of the Justice Department. This restructuring involves shifting $2.5 billion from Justice Department programs that do not focus on counterterrorism to those that do. The restructuring will also move 10 percent of funds and investigative and legal jobs from Washington, D.C., to field offices around the nation; it will also add FBI agents, immigration screeners, and prosecutors. What this entails is rethinking the allocation of responsibility for law enforcement in the federal system. "Traditional" crimes like bank robberies and narcotics investigations may now be handled mainly by local law enforcement. Thus, issues that were previously considered highly important within the Justice Department have been relegated to much lower priority.

The FBI restructured its headquarters' functions in two phases. Phase One addressed management shortcomings, while phase two was intended to refocus the FBI's mission by increasing the emphasis on counterterrorism, cyber attacks, and relations with state and local enforcement. In early steps, the FBI implemented a new aggressive and controversial approach—one that aims to prevent terrorist acts by rounding up suspects early on; it follows Attorney General Ashcroft's policy of preemptive arrests and detentions, instead of waiting to identify all members of the terrorist cell or waiting for terrorists to reach the final stage of action.

To push this process even further, in February 2003, the Administration announced that the counterterrorism staffs of both the FBI and the Central Intelligence Agency (CIA) would be co-located in a single office complex and coordinated by the director of the CIA to promote far closer

---

7. *Aviation and Transportation Security Act*, Public Law 107–71 (November 19, 2001). Available at <http://www.tsa.dot.gov/interweb/assetlibrary/Aviation_and_Transportation_Security_Act_ATSA_Public_Law_107_1771.pdf >.

8. As Attorney General Ashcroft proclaimed, "defending our nation and its citizens against terrorist attacks is our first and overriding priority." Terry Fieden, "Ashcroft vows changes to focus on terrorism prevention," (November 8, 2001) at <www.cnn.com/2001/LAW/11/08/inv.justic.revamp>.

collaboration between domestic and foreign intelligence collection and analysis.[9]

NEW EMPHASIS ON BIOTERRORISM

At its inception, the domestic preparedness program treated all weapons of mass destruction as if they would require a traditional "lights and sirens" approach, similar to a fire or hazardous materials spill. Over the last decade, however, it has become apparent that an attack with a biological weapon will require different avenues of detection, methods of treatment, and levels of investigation. This point was driven home after the anthrax attacks—a very limited terrorist campaign that had far-reaching effects.

After the anthrax attacks, the Bush administration sought $11 billion over two years to protect the nation against bioterrorism. The budget included $5.9 billion to finance improvements in the nation's public health system, in addition to the $1.4 billion that Congress approved in the previous fiscal year and a $3.7 billion request subsequently approved for countering bioterrorism. The budget provided $650 million to stockpile vaccines and antibiotics in the event of a disease outbreak, as well as appropriations for increased high security laboratory capacity and expanded research.[10]

NEW EMPHASIS ON STRATEGY AND COORDINATION

Previously, domestic preparedness involved the active participation of about 40 federal agencies, in addition to the countless stakeholders at the state and local level. The new focus on homeland security is even broader and more intensive, including a greater emphasis on infrastructure protection, border control, aviation security, and greater military involvement in domestic affairs. Such a broad based effort, with the involvement of so many stakeholders across levels of government and the public and private sectors, requires a coherent strategy and some form of organizational coordination.

As an immediate response to the September 11 attacks, President Bush created a White House Office of Homeland Security to develop and coordinate a comprehensive national strategy to strengthen protections against terrorist threats or attacks in the United States. This new compo-

---

9. Eric Lichtblau, "Threats and Responses: Intelligence; F.B.I. and C.I.A. to Move Their Counterterror Units to a Single New Location," *The New York Times* (February 15, 2003), p. A1.

10. Samuel Goldreich, "Agencies, Committees Vie for Bioterrorism Funding," *CQ Daily Monitor*, Vol. 38, No. 15A (February 7, 2002) p. 13.

nent of the Executive Office of the President, headed by former Pennsylvania Governor Tom Ridge (later appointed the first Secretary of the Department of Homeland Security), was charged with coordinating federal, state, and local counterterrorism efforts. Each state has initiated a similar team. Every state and a number of cities have appointed a homeland defense coordinator since September 11. Antiterrorism task forces were created by U.S. Attorney General John Ashcroft, who directed every U.S. Attorney district to establish an antiterrorism task force, which coordinates the "dissemination of information and the development of investigative and prosecutorial strategies for dealing with terrorism."[11] The task forces have three purposes: to act as a "conduit for information" about suspected terrorists between federal and local agencies; to serve as "a coordinating body" for operational plans that prevent terrorism; and to provide a "standing organizational structure" for a coordinated response to a terrorist incident in that district. Ninety-three anti-terrorism task forces (in many cases, co-existing with joint terrorism task forces previously established by the FBI to coordinate with state and local police and sheriffs) were created to "integrate the communications and activities of local, state, and federal law enforcement."[12]

As 2002 progressed, however, it became clear that those actions did not suffice. Picking up on a proposal made by the U.S. Commission on National Security/21st Century in January 2001,[13] a number of congressional voices pressed the Bush Administration to reorganize components of the federal bureaucracy into a new cabinet-level agency to protect the United States from terrorism. In June 2002, President Bush made this idea his own, proposing a sweeping reorganization of agencies to create a new Department of Homeland Security.[14] Congress enacted a bill after 2002 elections that incorporated most of the president's proposals. It moved the Coast Guard and Secret Service into the new department and established four major functional "directorates" that absorbed many other ele-

---

11. Letter to mayors from Attorney General John Ashcroft, September 19, 2001, at <www.usmayors.org/executivedirector/attygeneral_091901.pdf>.

12. Attorney General John Ashcroft, testimony before the Senate Committee on the Judiciary (December 6, 2001) at <judiciary.senate.gov/te120621f-ashcroft.htm>.

13. This report, *Roadmap for National Security: Imperative for Change*, issued by a commission headed by two former senators widely respected on national security issues, Gary Hart and Warren Rudman, had received relatively little public attention when issued on January 31, 2001, but its ideas became far more influential in the aftermath of September 11. Available at <www.nssg.gov/phaseIII.pdf>

14. "Remarks by the President in Address to the Nation." Available at <www.whitehouse.gov/news/releases/2002/06/20020606–8.html>

ments of existing agencies and departments. These were Border and Transportation security (including the Transportation Security Administration, Customs Service, security functions of the Immigration and Nationalization Service, the Office for Domestic Preparedness, and Animal and Plant Health Inspection Service); Emergency Preparedness and Response (including the Federal Emergency Management Agency and Office of Emergency Preparedness); Science and Technology, and Information Analysis and Infrastructure Protection.

SWEEPING CHANGES IN LEGISLATION

There has also been a proliferation of new legislation—so much, that in the four months after September 11, 98 percent of all legislation proposed by the House of Representatives related to terrorism. More than 323 bills and resolutions were introduced in the Congress, and 21 laws and resolutions were adopted. One of the more important, the Antiterrorism Bill of 2001 (The USA PATRIOT Act) passed both the House and the Senate quickly, with very little opposition. Among other provisions, the bill, signed into law in late October 2001, expands law enforcement powers, permits roving wiretaps, reduces the barriers to surveillance and information sharing, and makes it easier to search property as well as to detain individuals.

NEW FOCUS ON VULNERABILITIES AND THREAT ASSESSMENT

One of the greatest challenges at all levels of government is assessing the threat. This involves understanding the motivations of terrorists, the vulnerabilities of potential targets, and a locale's readiness to respond in case of attack. At the local level, many cities have been reassessing what is at risk, and local emergency agencies are reevaluating what is needed to effectively respond in the event of another terrorist attack. After September 11, numerous threat advisories were communicated to the public, with few or no details and even fewer specific preventive recommendations. The frustration of state and local leaders and the public as a whole stimulated the creation of a revised threat assessment system. The proposed Homeland Security Advisory System was unveiled in March 2002, with the intent of identifying threat levels in a relative scale. The five levels of alert were expressed in a color scheme: low (green), guarded (blue), elevated (yellow), high (orange), and severe (red). The threat level was initially set at yellow, temporarily increased to orange for several weeks in 2002 around the anniversary of the September 11 attacks, and then raised to orange again in February 2003. This system provided a greater measure of clarity about the meaning of federal warnings and let federal, state, and local agencies establish predetermined plans and actions to implement at times of heightened alert. It did little, however, to improve the underlying problem of judging the nature and extent of threats to specific localities at particular times.[15]

The View from the States and Cities

Federal policy advocates robust state and local capacity for terrorism prevention and response. President Bush's FY 2003 budget proposed expanded programs to assist state and local governments, notably for public safety equipment and training and disease monitoring and surveillance systems to detect bioterrorism. But the possibility of large-scale federal aid was highly constrained as a result of a near recession, federal tax cuts, the war in Afghanistan, and increased overall defense spending. Although some in Congress strongly advocated more intergovernmental aid, the administration was wary of committing large amounts of money to support core state and local operations—such as law enforcement, fire protection, and emergency medical services—which it viewed as a state and local, not federal, responsibility. Until the new Republican majorities in both houses took office, partisan divisions in Congress during the 2002 election year blocked the passage of most appropriations bills until early 2003, delaying provision of most aid to states and localities even further. The president's proposals for FY 2004 showed only a modest 7.4 percent increase over FY 2003, and it did not contain major increases or new initiatives for state and local government functions.[16]

In this context, state and local governments have begun to probe what "homeland security" means in practical terms. These questions became even more acute as many states and localities encountered severe budget shortfalls in late 2002 and 2003, which some called the worst since the end of World War II.[17] Is each state, county, city, and town across the United States equally vulnerable to terrorism? What should prudent leaders, responsible for particular cities or states, be doing to prepare? How much can they depend on higher levels of government for preven-

---

15. See, for example, Philip Shenon, "Threats and Responses: Domestic Security; Balancing Act for Washington in Terror Alerts," *The New York Times* (February 16, 2003), p. 1.

16. Department of Homeland Security, *Budget in Brief*. Available at <http://www.dhs.gov/interweb/assetlibrary/FY_2004_BUDGET_IN_BRIEF.pdf>

17. Michael Janofsky, "The President's Budget Proposal: Deficits; States' Budget Gaps Widen Nearly 50% in Two Months," *The New York Times* (February 5, 2003), p. A16.

tion and emergency response? How can states and localities pay for increased preparedness when a nationwide economic slowdown has cut their revenues, and myriad demands for tax reduction and other public services are competing for available funds?

Perspectives on these issues vary considerably depending on particular institutional vantage points. In the immediate aftermath of September 11, major cities and large special districts (e.g., airport and port authorities or regional transportation agencies) saw themselves potentially at risk like New York City or Washington, D.C. Many made substantial expenditures on security. Personnel costs spiked upward, largely because of overtime payments to police officers, firefighters, and emergency medical technicians responding to anthrax scares or assigned to precautionary protective duties. Many jurisdictions invested in new equipment, such as protective gear for first responders and communication upgrades, and scheduled broad based training for personnel who might have to recognize or respond to a biological or chemical weapons attack. Hospitals and public health agencies, whether municipal or regional, faced similar pressures.

These were not onetime investments. The need for enhanced vigilance by law enforcement agencies has no obvious termination point. Equipment purchases have life cycle implications for maintenance and eventual replacement. Training commitments imply "refresher" needs for those initially trained and systematic training of new personnel.

Given this need for constant reinvestment, the leaders of major cities and institutions are increasingly worried about how they will sustain the costs of security post–September 11. Although citizens remain concerned, most leaders see no organized constituencies backing significant local security expenditures, impelling local officials to ask whether it is feasible to sustain public support for these measures.

By contrast, smaller communities generally face a different situation. Despite diffuse public anxiety, many see little realistic threat of terrorist attack. Some, however, fear that specific facilities, e.g., industrial plants or bridges, may be targets. Even in the immediate aftermath of September 11, however, because most small communities had limited fiscal means and insufficient operational flexibility to take significant new security steps, they had little choice but to depend on state and federal protection.

For their part, most governors and legislatures took steps post–September 11 to augment preparedness, mainly by naming state-level homeland security directors to seek stronger coordination of local and state efforts and by selectively providing new resources to bolster existing state functions. Although state governments control limited first responder assets in emergencies, they command important backup resources, including the National Guard and state emergency management agencies. States also maintain specialized services and facilities, such as state public health laboratories, on which even large cities like New York rely. In most states, these laboratories were heavily taxed after September 11 with thousands of suspected anthrax letter hoaxes that needed to be analyzed. In addition, because of regulatory responsibilities for many types of infrastructure, such as water supply and power systems, and industries like agriculture, states went on alert to protect these potential terrorist targets. State governments, moreover, could be called upon to play more direct terrorism response roles in the future, effectively superseding local response, as they do in natural disasters, if emergency needs outstrip the capabilities of small communities or counties.

Like big cities, therefore, states are pondering their realistic vulnerability to attack and their capacity to pay for enhanced security among many competing demands, particularly in the severely constrained fiscal environment of 2003. Facing an uncertain terrorist threat, how reliant must each jurisdiction be on its own preparedness for emergencies? In the highly decentralized system of U.S. federalism, does homeland security require costly and duplicative capacity building? Or can the federal government and individual state and local jurisdictions effectively mesh their efforts, as the United States seeks to enhance and institutionalize its preparedness for terrorism?

The Potential of Regional Cooperation

Large gains can be achieved from regional partnerships to prepare for terrorism and other emergencies. Improving preparedness for terrorism is an expensive, time-consuming, and exacting task. Even large cities may lack sufficient resources to prepare for a huge surge of demand for emergency services. For many smaller localities and organizations, which start from a lower base of emergency management capability and often lack adequate fiscal and management resources, effective preparedness is infeasible. It would be wasteful, moreover, to replicate capabilities in every community, especially highly specialized equipment and training, since many are likely never to use them.

Effective collaboration across jurisdictional boundaries is essential to encourage compatibility in equipment and operational planning, minimize redundant investments in specialized equipment, reduce geographic gaps in preparedness by smaller communities, spur joint training and exercises, and broker stronger mutual assistance agreements. Cooperation is necessary not only within metropolitan areas but also among states closely linked economically or through infrastructure systems, such as transportation, water supply, and power grids.

Regional arrangements—metropolitan and interstate—have great promise but also require much work to overcome problems of institutional complexity, cost sharing, liability, and turf protection. Successful efforts to foster cooperation should not only achieve common goals but also create specific benefits for individual "partners," such as equipment or training grants, to motivate potential partners in return for their commitment to cooperative relationships. Timely, focused information-sharing from pooled and coordinated state and local sources, for example, can be a major incentive for cooperation. Furthermore, opportunities to lower the costs of providing security or emergency response capability are attractive incentives for collaboration. Equipment sharing and mutual aid arrangements among jurisdictions, for example, reduce the need for each partner to procure specialized gear or to provide for peak needs. Providing even modest financial subsidies for cooperation in the form of grants from federal or state governments can make it easier to achieve collaboration.

Reducing the costs and risks of cooperation increases the willingness of potential partners to collaborate. For example, transaction costs—the hassle of repeatedly making agreements among jurisdictions—can impede cooperation. Developing standard mutual aid agreements and communication systems that make it easier to work together and reach decisions can reduce transaction costs. Jurisdictions may also be reluctant to cooperate because of perceived risks from collaboration, such as damage to equipment, injuries to personnel, or liability for actions taken while aiding a partner. These can be reduced by state legislation to provide insurance against loss or to protect jurisdictions from liability claims.

Developing regional collaboration structures requires thoughtfully addressing governance issues, but this may require prior development of trust among the potential partners. *Ad hoc* accomplishments may be necessary first steps to more extensive cooperation. As initial interactions produce results, the development of trust among collaborating jurisdictions can allay mutual suspicions that partnership is a means of exploitation. To make cooperation feasible, large communities or counties must be prepared to make some accommodations to small communities. Large jurisdictions may have to accept governance arrangements that give reassurance to jurisdictions concerned that their independence is at stake. Small jurisdictions, moreover, may lack sufficient means to contribute their share of financial resources. The benefits of effective collaboration among the larger jurisdictions may make these accommodations to smaller entities acceptable.

Conclusion: Intergovernmental Roles in Perspective

Although individual states and localities are often policy innovators, their successful initiatives diffuse to other jurisdictions unevenly and relatively slowly. A strong federal role is therefore crucial. Only federal leadership and financial incentives can generate broad state and local action in a short time frame. Federal policy guidance and technical assistance about "best practices" are also needed to structure program activities unfamiliar to many jurisdictions, particularly when compatibility from state to state is desirable.

Federal *financial* incentives are important, moreover, not only to jump start action but also to sustain state and local commitment. Prevention, mitigation, and response capabilities for terrorism are difficult to maintain, because they are likely to be used infrequently, if at all. Federal funding that encourages an "all-hazards" approach to domestic preparedness, which emphasizes strategies and equipment that can be used in more routine emergency situations, as well as in response to terrorist attacks, can anchor state and local commitment, even if there are few influential local stakeholders to advocate sustained funding when headlines and public attention shift to other issues.

Despite a crucial federal role, however, big cities and major independent metropolitan institutions, such as airports, port authorities, transit agencies, and hospital systems, must be the bedrock of terrorism preparedness below the national level. They have analytic and planning capabilities to assess and prioritize vulnerabilities and frame appropriate policies for the future. In addition, they command core operational capabilities—such as police, fire, hazardous materials, public health, and emergency medical services—necessary for rapid, effective response. Big city governments and metropolitan agencies can provide these capabilities on a sufficiently large scale and with detailed jurisdictional knowledge that surpasses what federal or state governments can provide. Big cities and metropolitan agencies would also inevitably play a critical role if terrorists struck in smaller communities or rural areas.

State governments also have critical functions, including their significant specialized resources and backup capabilities. At least as importantly, states are well positioned to take the lead in promoting metropolitan and regional cooperation. Cooperation is essential not only within metropolitan areas, but also, in many areas, between states closely linked economically or by infrastructure systems, such as transportation, water supply, and power grids. Effective collaboration across jurisdictional boundaries is necessary to encourage standardization or compatibility in equipment acquisition and operational planning, minimize duplicative investments in specialized equipment, reduce the geographical gaps in preparedness by smaller communities, and coordinate joint training and exercises.

The implications for federal policy are clear. National policies to enhance domestic preparedness for terrorism—whether prescribing regulations, initiating programs, providing financing, or proposing coordination methods—must recognize the need for *customized replication* of operational capabilities. Preparedness structures must be built in many separate places, with substantial variation. Strategies explicitly or implicitly striving for standardization are likely to confront political and organizational resistance and are likely to contain design flaws that would impede or subvert implementation under at least some conditions prevailing in specific states or localities.

As the United States confronts the uncertain but enduring threat of terrorism, it must strengthen its capacity to prevent and respond to attacks at all levels of government. The great challenge facing the nation in further developing its domestic preparedness program is not only to achieve coordination of effort and function within levels of government, but also to make the intergovernmental relationships work effectively.

Dealing with Terrorism after September 11, 2001: An Overview

Philip B. Heymann

For the United States, the world has changed dramatically since September 11, 2001. We no longer feel secure, although we cannot measure the extent of the danger. Being less secure means, irresistibly, that we have to take steps, costly in any of a variety of ways, to help reestablish safety.[1] What are the possibilities for stopping groups, organized largely abroad, from undertaking sustained campaigns in the United States of lethal terrorism? That—and not the more traditional problem of occasional, low-level terrorism—is the subject of this essay.[2]

---

1. We have other goals besides increasing safety and reducing fear, but some of these are less important and, others will follow naturally from the first two. The additional goals that I have in mind are these: we have to maintain our foreign alliances, formal and informal. That requires not only mutual benefit but also maintaining a persuasive moral and legal justification behind our military, diplomatic, and economic actions abroad. We have to maintain trust in—and avoid fear of—our government for all significant sections of the population. That requires effectiveness and fairness in our response. We want to punish wrongdoers simply because that's right, and we would like to build as broad as possible a military, legal, and moral commitment to oppose all forms of terrorism—even those that do not threaten us. None of these is comparable in importance to creating safety and ending fear.

2. Developing as complete a list as possible of what we can do to recreate safety and reduce fear is of course only part of the problem. What will work and won't work depends upon understanding how the possibilities relate to the military, political, and cultural situation in which the options may be used. Even if an option would be effective in a specific context, whether to adopt it depends upon its costs not only in dollars and American lives, but also in terms of our values—the immensely important degree to which American citizens, our allies, and those suspicious of us can accept what we are doing as right or necessary. An important implication of this is that, when we put together a portfolio of actions, it is necessary to describe them in terms of a unifying

The list of options depends on how much in the way of human, financial, moral, and political resources the United States is prepared to invest in its capacities for prevention, consequence management, deterrence, and retaliation. This, in turn, depends on whether the United States should anticipate a sustained terrorist campaign—either by Osama bin Laden or by others inspired by his success—and to what extent any such campaign would involve other immense attacks. Even discounting the threat of bin Laden himself, the case for a major investment in counterterrorism and homeland defense seems strong.

One way to approach how much danger Americans have to fear is to ask, as many have before, why the United States seemed so much more protected against terrorism within its boundaries than other countries such as the United Kingdom, Germany, France, and Spain (each of which has suffered sustained terrorist campaigns.) If we knew what "prevented" such attacks in the United States before, and if we judge what September 11 has changed, either in our understanding of that mystery or in terrorist capacities and attitudes, we might be better able to estimate the future.

Here are the possibilities: perhaps the United States was better able than its allies to detect any plans of attack within its boundaries. Certainly the Federal Bureau of Investigation (FBI) has aborted several major intranational attacks. On the other hand, the bombing of the World Trade Center on two different occasions, the U.S. embassies in Kenya and Tanzania, and military bases in Saudi Arabia do not support this theory. Either U.S. targets were never better protected than those of our allies that had been attacked in the past, or terrorist organizations, such as al Qaeda, have developed new and unanticipated capabilities (such as a cadre of trained terrorists, some of whom are willing to die to attack more effectively.)

A second possibility looks at reputation, not reality. Perhaps terrorist groups believed, whether correctly or mistakenly, that it was not possible, or it was too risky to engage in terrorism in the United States—at least by means of any massive attack. If so, what the attacks on September 11 would have shown is that we had surprising vulnerabilities (particularly to suicide terrorists). Whatever psychological barrier of fear there was seems to have fallen with the World Trade Center towers.

A third explanation of the rarity of attacks within U.S. borders by foreign-based terrorists is that they may have recognized that a condition

---

theme. Very different actions—and very different reactions of others—will depend on whether, for example, our unifying theme is to protect ourselves or to defeat terrorism, whomever it may attack.

of their organizational existence in a sheltering country, such as Syria, Iraq, or Iran, was not to bring down the wrath of the United States on their hosts. If so, the vigor of the U.S. response to the Taliban regime in Afghanistan is critical, both because of how it affects what it does to that particular haven for terrorism and what it conveys to other potential havens.

As for massive attacks, terrorists have long been believed to be reluctant to engage in so lethal an operation, preferring the obvious benefits of a sympathetic audience to the anger generated by mass casualties. This fourth possibility, as well as the technical difficulty of the enterprise, may have explained the relatively small size of terrorist attacks in the past and may have prevented biological and nuclear terrorism. If so, the events of September 11 and the terrorist use of anthrax thereafter suggest that moral restraints no longer provide much security against massive attacks.

Each of these explanations of changes in the conditions of our prior domestic tranquility would suggest the need for a very substantial investment in reestablishing domestic security, even if the United States were not confronted with a threatening opponent who commands extensive public support in Muslim countries.

Only a fifth possible explanation of the events of September 11 is slightly more optimistic, emphasizing the uniqueness of U.S. vulnerability on that day. Possibly, the only innovation to disturb the security Americans felt before that date was that the terrorists discovered the remarkable capacity of combining suicide terrorists with a sky full of commercial jetliners and a haven, Afghanistan, that would permit the planning and financing of an attack, unacceptable to other terrorist havens, by a group that saw no advantage to restraint in selecting its targets. But the anthrax attacks in the fall of 2001 ended that basis for limited optimism. And even to prevent commercial flights being used as missiles, radical changes in U.S. protections against hijacking (as well as in protection of targets from other forms of attack from the air) and powerful steps to reinforce the reluctance of any nation to tolerate groups planning attacks on the United States would still be needed to reduce the risk greatly.

In the final analysis, the case for massive steps seems convincing. But what could they be?

Possible Responses to a Terrorist Threat

Responses to terrorism can be categorized in any of several ways. They can be either backward- or forward-looking. Thus, as punishment, they can be considered inseparably joined—by a demand for justice—to an event that has already occurred; as prevention, they can be intended to affect the probability or nature of a future danger. A response can be both at once. Punishment of those involved in one terrorist attack may be a preventive step with regard to a future terrorist attack, as well as a morale-sustaining form of retribution for the first. And there is more than prevention and punishment. The purposes may be not only to prevent future attacks and to remedy in some sense what has already happened, but also to reduce greatly the cost to the United States of future attacks that we cannot prevent by organizing to deal intelligently with their consequences.

Because of the overriding importance of the goals of creating safety and a sense of security, I focus here on forward-looking ways of preventing a campaign of massive terrorism. Still, within this category, there are critical distinctions. Most important by far, actions can be at home and thus, within U.S. control, or they can be taken abroad, requiring cooperation and alliances but also offering significant opportunities missing at home. Terrorists from abroad will presumably appear in the United States—their target country—in fewer numbers and for shorter periods than abroad in their home base. Moreover, to the considerable extent that terrorists in a haven abroad are likely political challengers of a nondemocratic regime, they are potentially subject to control by a dictator's internal security apparatus, using techniques that the United States would not tolerate at home.

So a central issue becomes: can the United States motivate the often politically risky use of that foreign apparatus against terrorists who enjoy local public support but who threaten U.S. territory? Tolerance or support of the terrorists may be motivated by sincere beliefs of the government or by fear of a restive population supportive of the terrorist cause. To offset either of these, the United States has at its disposal the threat of military strikes, diplomatic and economic sanctions, and the promise of a range of rewards. The United States also has some, albeit limited, capacity to reduce the anger or the danger of the groups that the haven government fears.

Perhaps the last of these is the most important action that the United States can take to make its leverage effective: reducing the threat of potentially violent or mass opposition to any government pursuing terrorists on U.S. behalf. That requires the United States to take more seriously its importance to the hopes and self-esteem of those large parts of foreign populations that are now hostile to any governments that support the United States. Foreign assistance and a determined effort to persuade hostile populations that we do not want to be an enemy are thus critical steps, not because they are likely to reduce the number of potential terrorists to a safe number, but because they are likely to make it possible for a friendly state to do that. For the harder job of preventing terrorists from reaching their targets while they remain temporarily in the U.S. territory, the United States must rely on its intelligence and law enforcement organizations.

To capture all of these options, one must begin with a description of what a terrorist group based abroad needs for a sustained campaign of large-scale attacks on U.S. targets. To accomplish such a campaign, a terrorist organization must have sufficient financing, a flow of recruits, and the capacity to retain their commitment and loyalty. It must train them in the variety of skills (organizational, technical, tactical, et al.) that executing a terrorist campaign requires. It must be able to provide them with the necessary resources, including information, to create and use the weapons needed to attack a target. It must furnish a means of getting access to the target for those carrying out the operation. All of this requires creating and maintaining an enduring organization and managing it. Last, and implicit in the others, it must be able to carry out all these steps in secrecy (or some of them with the tolerance of those who might otherwise prevent them).

Many of these measures can be taken abroad. As for each of these requirements one must ask: what makes it easier and what could make it more difficult for a terrorist group to accomplish the essential steps and what is the available capacity to affect either? The answers provide not only our options, but also permit a rough estimate of the limits of the effectiveness of each separately and all together.[3]

RECRUITMENT

First, consider reducing the availability of recruits or making it more difficult to maintain the commitment of members. That could be accomplished by, for example: reducing grievances; preventing "schooling" in anger and hatred; denying the solidarity values of charismatic leadership, colleagueship in a shared battle, and heroism, including martyrdom; providing disincentives, such as capture and punishment; denying incentives in terms of the results the terrorists seek; or even providing support for groups or causes the terrorists oppose.

---

3. The advantage of approaching options in this way is that it breaks the difficult task of imagining a full range of possibilities into two more manageable parts. I have listed a half dozen goals that a terrorist group would have to accomplish to mount a sustained campaign of massive attacks on the United States from abroad. There may be more or other ways of dividing up what terrorists must do, but the number is manageably small. Then, imagining what the United States or supportive nations can do to interfere with each of those steps again presents a relatively manageable problem.

Some of these options are inconsistent with others. Reducing grievances to discourage support of terrorism *after* a terrorist event has taken place or has been threatened may appear like a victory to potential recruits, thus rewarding those leaders who threaten terrorism. Other steps that the United States can take or urge others to take may also be just as likely to increase recruitment as to reduce it. Assassinations may create martyrs and thus stimulate imitation, with a greater effect on total commitment than the deterrence resulting from the assassination. Any step that threatens in a way that suggests unfairness can have the same effect. Recruitment to the Irish Republican Army (IRA), for example, increased sharply during some periods of overly vigorous British action against suspects.

Many of the steps necessary for recruiting terrorists may be readily discoverable by internal security agents of a somewhat despotic host government if it wants to stop the terror. To recruit for any sizeable organization requires at least minimal forms of advertising, and this exposes the organization to informants. Training in anger and hatred requires schools or other meeting places that can be discovered. Charismatic leadership requires exposure. What is likely beyond U.S. reach—recruitment abroad—can be greatly affected by the activities of the host country.

Why is effective action against recruitment largely beyond the reach of U.S. agents? Some steps are hardly feasible. Denying the capacities needed to teach anger and hatred is one. Others seem likely to be ineffective. It is doubtful whether the limited U.S. ability to successfully capture and try individual terrorists will provide much disincentive to recruitment, particularly in the case of suicidal terrorists. Even for a non-suicidal terrorist, the United States can hardly increase the already severe sanctions if a terrorist is caught. Increasing the disincentive to terrorism requires increasing the risk of apprehension and detention—a form of risk that may be hardly noticed by the most motivated fringe of any passionate movement.

This pessimistic picture of the prospects of independent U.S. efforts to reduce terrorist recruitment could be qualified to some extent by adopting a scheme of deterrence that systematically punishes terrorism, not by punishing the individual terrorists, but by harming their cause by providing advantages to people and causes that the terrorists fear and detest. One can imagine this sanction being a very good reason for even the most dedicated and zealous to forgo terrorism, if the terrorist campaign was rational, either at the level of recruitment or at the level of management. The problem, as Prime Minister Ariel Sharon may be learning in Israel, is that this sanction necessarily provides "new evidence" of hostility—the effect of which in reinforcing hatred may overwhelm any deterrent effect.

Reducing the total number of recruits to a number too small to mount a sustained campaign of terrorism requires steps that reach all the way to the most angry and hostile fringe of the population that feels aggrieved and in need of heroes. In the case of Muslim fundamentalists, this seems unlikely, whether we are discussing deterrence or reducing grievances or changing the atmosphere in which youth are brought up to be terrorists.

Access to Targets and to the Resources and Skills Necessary for Attacking Them

To carry out the September 11 attacks in New York, the terrorists had to find a way to bring two huge explosives into the World Trade Center buildings. Access to the buildings from the air was uncontrolled. To get the huge explosives—the needed resources—they had only to get control of planes leaving Boston with enough fuel to take them to California. To direct the planes, they had to have at least minimal flight skills and information about navigating. To take over the controls of the plane, they needed numbers (four or five persons) and at least primitive weapons.[4]

The possibilities for preventing the repetition of such an event come directly out of this, admittedly partial, list of what the terrorists had to have or do. Many of these steps had to take place within the United States. The government has since taken steps to strengthen controls on access to planes (the needed explosive resources), to the controls of planes (the cockpit), and even to the buildings that might be targets from the air. (President George W. Bush has authorized firing on planes that may be targeted on buildings.)

It is easy enough to make the case for forbidding weapons on planes, preventing passengers from entering the pilot compartment, and prohibiting planes flying in airspace near attractive targets. But denying an individual access enjoyed by others to a plane or, before that, to pilot training or to other skills that might prove critical to a terrorist attack depends on being able to match a record of who may intend violent harm with who is obtaining dangerous resources or access to targets. Access controls can be no better than the three conditions that they require: a record of who may be dangerous; a reliable identification of an individual seeking access; and the ability to match these quickly.

---

4. We could make a similar list for use of the mail to deliver anthrax.

The United States may obtain access to a membership list of those who belong to dangerous organizations from informants, spies, or foreign intelligence agencies, If not, it can sometimes develop evidence of who is dangerous by combining pieces of information about an individual and his activities. Although taking one or two steps along the six- or eight-step path to bringing a weapon into dangerous contact with a tempting target may not warrant suspicion, taking three or four steps along that path may be very suspicious. With computer technology, the United States can combine information obtained from monitoring who is seeking access to potentially dangerous resources and potentially tempting targets and identify those unlikely to be engaged in an innocent activity. By combining that information and then assessing the package, the United States can develop a picture that may justify either denying access or further investigation of the person seeking access and of any others or any organization with whom he is closely associated.

The role of foreign governments at this stage is likely to be mainly in helping to produce a thorough list of suspects. The target, by my assumption, is in the United States, so access must be obtained inside U.S. borders by the terrorists. Generally, it is far riskier to try to import the necessary resources for attacking the target than to acquire the resources within the United States.

The limits of U.S. ability to weaken or defeat a campaign of terrorism by controlling access to targets and to needed information and resources are important and perhaps not obvious. The resources (even explosives) and the needed information (often available on the Internet) are now freely available in the United States. Take explosives as an example. Congress could pass something comparable to the Brady Law to monitor purchases. Alternatively, it could require markers to be placed in explosives to let authorities know the source of the explosives used in an attack. But dangerous possibilities for evasion would remain and even a rudimentary effort to limit information about how to make or use explosives or other weapons may be constrained by the First Amendment to the Constitution or defeated by Internet access.

There are two extremely troublesome problems that govern any efforts to deny access to targets and resources. First, there is the problem of "fresh faces," about whom no one—not we nor our allies—have information suggesting terrorist leanings. The number of such fresh faces may be very large. Second, those providing for national security often do not know which targets to protect and which resources to deny. The United States can and does tightly control access to a relatively small percentage of the attractive targets, but there are far too many to rigorously limit access to every target whose loss may have a major effect on feelings of security in the United States. Similarly, there are a large number of resources that might be useful in a terrorist attack, many more than one could sensibly monitor.

The result is that the United States can be prepared for attacks on certain targets (e.g., the White House) or types of targets (e.g., reservoirs), and it can attempt to control access to certain types of dangerous resources (commercial airliners filled with fuel). But it cannot even monitor access to all targets and all destructive resources, let alone deny access or limit access to those persons who are demonstrably "safe." So those charged with our security must guess. They have to choose the targets that they want most to protect and also choose the targets that may be most attractive to terrorists, then design access controls for these two sets of targets. They also have to guess which are the most dangerous resources, or the ones most easily used by terrorists and try to control access to these.

The inability to identify the dangerous resources to which terrorists want access is somewhat less of a problem with regard to the most dangerous forms of terrorism: the use of biological or nuclear weapons. Only a relatively few places in the world, perhaps 17 states, have the skills necessary to develop a biological weapon or the radioactive material necessary to develop a nuclear weapon. The United States should and does monitor the latter. It must also monitor and regulate any access to the information, skills, and resources necessary to make a biological weapon. Our failure in this regard helps explain the difficulty we have had finding those responsible for mailing anthrax.

The danger is great enough for the United States to treat any state that refuses the monitoring as itself a suspect. But that requires the United States to accept monitoring on its territory, as it has not yet done with regard to biological and chemical weapons. By international treaty, the nations of the world can and should also make any private or state cooperation in furnishing skills or resources to someone known to be making a nuclear, chemical, or biological weapon a universal crime (i.e. an act punishable in every nation in the world, regardless of where it occurred).

The United States does not currently have a domestic organization with the skills, training, or inclination to address these questions of prevention. Even if it did, it would still have to recognize that the price of access controls will be substantial inconvenience, such as waiting in longer lines at airports; that asking guards or businesses to find a needle of suspicion in a haystack of legitimate access to targets and resources is complicated by the inherent boredom of the task; and that simplifying the problem involves a dangerous trade-off of the many risks of ethnic profiling for more convenience to most Americans.

The problem of denying access to resources for a terrorist attack changes radically if the needed resources are being provided by another nation—for example, one of the 17 or so with biological weapons programs. State support for a campaign of terrorism against the United States by providing skills, resources, technical information, and even help in entering the country and getting to the target poses special risks but also offers special opportunities.

The capacity of the terrorist organization is likely to be vastly increased by this support. At the same time, the likelihood that the United States can learn of the support and therefore deter the state supporter and the terrorist group that relies on that support is also increased. The United States has massive military forces, conventional and unconventional. Every nation has the right, under Article 51 of the United Nations Charter, to act in self-defense, unless and until the Security Council acts. Deterring a state that provides resources to those planning terrorist attacks against another nation is well within the scope of Article 51 and the precedents that the United States created in military responses to attacks secretly supported by Libya, Iraq, and now Afghanistan.

Organizational Capability and Secrecy

To mount a sustained terrorist campaign against the United States, more than four or five or even 20 individuals are necessary. There has to be a relatively sizeable ongoing organization to raise money, recruit, train, establish contacts for help with resources and skills, choose targets for maximum impact, and so on. The small operational cells for such an organization, al Qaeda, were able to work in the United States for some years prior to September 11, 2001. It is in fact very difficult for a law enforcement or internal security agency to detect the activities of small numbers of people, even if they are illegally within the United States.

But the mass of the organization, al Qaeda, was detectable and its general location—Afghanistan—was easily discovered. The final requirement for terrorists to mount a sustained campaign from abroad against the United States is that they be able to build and maintain for sustained periods a significant organization abroad, despite the efforts of law enforcement and internal security agencies in the states where the organization is located.

That capacity may depend upon the host state's tolerance of the organization's activities, as in the case of Afghanistan. The U.S. response to open tolerance of those preparing to attack its territory should be severe military, diplomatic, or economic sanctions against the haven.

But to prevent the terrorist organization from operating, the host state would have to do far more than deny or hide open support. It would have to use its domestic intelligence and law enforcement capacities to find and punish the terrorists. The more undemocratic—the more despotic—the state, the more likely these capacities will be adequate for the job, because intelligence agents will already have been trained to protect the undemocratic government against its challengers. Fortunately, it is in such despotic states that al Qaeda finds most of its supporters and its havens. Unfortunately, such states generate substantial and threatening dissident movements and are understandably reluctant to inflame them by curtailing their hostility to the West.

The internal security tasks are not ones that the United States could carry out itself. The critical question thus is: what limits does the United States face in compelling this extremely valuable support? It could demand access for investigators or even military forces to help conduct law enforcement operations in Iran, Iraq, Syria, Libya, Sudan, or Afghanistan. But these states are highly unlikely to agree to that sacrifice of sovereignty. Even Saudi Arabia would not allow the FBI to freely investigate the 1996 bombing of the Khobar Towers. Even if all agreed, moreover, the capacity of U.S. agents to find terrorists in an unfriendly setting, without taking over the country and mounting a costly and repressive occupation, is likely to be very low indeed.

If the United States located and captured terrorist leaders, it would remain difficult to try them and prove personal guilt beyond a reasonable doubt. For this reason the United States declined efforts to try the Palestine Liberation Front leader, Abul Abbas, for the seizure of the *Achille Lauro* and murder, and, in 1996, Osama bin Laden for his terrorist efforts. Assassination of a leader may create in the terrorist group a vacuum of leadership or demoralization or a harmful conflict over new leadership. But it also carries the threat of retaliatory efforts (such as Israel experienced with the assassination of its minister of transportation), the recruitment benefits of martyrdom, and the profound embarrassment of mistaken identity.

So the United States will have to rely on the efforts of law enforcement and internal security forces of states where the terrorist organization is operating. Careful analysis suggests that threats alone will be inadequate to create reliable cooperation. Some states will lack the competence really to help, and other states that do not believe in the cause will make efforts too halfhearted to be effective but real enough to be indistinguishable from sanctionable incompetence. And there is little that the United States will be able to do when a state, where terrorists may be planning attacks, plausibly claims it cannot find them. Greece's leading terrorist group, "November 17" operated in Greece against the United States for decades without "detection" by the Greek government.

In sum, all that the United States can accomplish by threat of military force or other sanctions is to end state support or tolerance of terrorism where it is now available and open, or where it is likely to be discovered. That will not prevent secret support or tolerance, which may continue but in a carefully concealed form, as many believe happened after the United States bombed Libya in 1985 in retaliation for its terrorism against American soldiers at a disco in Berlin. Similarly, U.S. intelligence agencies suspected that East European communist states were supporting various terrorist groups in the West, but they could not prove it until after those regimes had collapsed. That concealed support can continue at least as long as the host state can pretend to be unable to locate, let alone control, the terrorist organization. In the absence of proof of bad faith, any U.S. military response will threaten the continued support of coalition partners and cause widespread suspicion of injustice within the United States and abroad.

With feigned good faith a disabling effective reply to military threats, the best bet—one that the government is currently pursuing—is a combination of military threat, economic or political inducements, and a moral campaign against terrorism. To win the sincere cooperation of states where terrorist organizations are located, the United States will have to form mutually beneficial alliances as well as make a persuasive ideological case against terrorism wherever it takes place and whomever it targets, not just terrorism targeted on the United States. The former will require rewards as well as threats. The latter will require abandoning support for groups that are attacking civilians in any country whose enthusiastic support the United States wants in tracking down terrorist organizations. The case made will have to be that no one's terrorists are "freedom fighters."

Even if the United States can coax or coerce the full support of a state where an organization such as al Qaeda is located, that may not end the threat. Terrorist organizations whose support has been withdrawn by one state may find alternative support in another state that is unrelentingly hostile to the United States and prepared to bear the consequences. Iraq and Sudan come quickly to mind as possible hosts. And, not to be forgotten, the terrorist organization may be able to operate despite good faith efforts to eliminate it by the state where it is located. After all, even the British could not disable the IRA during its most dangerous years, and

U.S. authorities took years to apprehend abortion clinic bomber Eric Rudolph, who was also charged with bombing the Atlanta, Georgia, Olympic Centennial Park in 1996. Like organized crime, a terrorist group may be able to survive the most steely of state opposition.

Penetrating Terrorist Secrecy in the United States

The task of defeating secrecy must take place in the United States, where the terrorist event occurs, as well as abroad, where the terrorist organization is housed. As discussed above, penetrating its secrecy abroad requires the coaxed or coerced cooperation of the host country and its vigorous use of intelligence capacities going far beyond what many democratic states would tolerate from their governments. Effectively keeping tabs on the small part of the organization that is operating in the United States may be far more difficult.

The core difficulty lies in the initial detection of a dangerous group worth following. Once such a group is detected, most nations, including the United States, have a range of devices for learning about the activities of the group. That includes not only informants and undercover government agents but also electronic surveillance, highly sophisticated physical surveillance, and more. Government surveillance powers are somewhat greater, and available resources are far greater in combating international terrorism than in pursuing crime. The great difficulty is in detection of a dangerous group in the first place, without massive and constant spying on all citizens.

Within the United States, the presence of a dangerous group or individual may be revealed by information about its activities from a foreign intelligence or law enforcement agency. The United States learned of the presence within its borders of Mohamed Atta, the apparent leader of the September 11 attacks, months earlier. A state can also match a master list of suspected terrorists against information as to who is entering the country, who is in particularly dangerous locations, or who is purchasing particularly dangerous materials. The first is made far more difficult by the ease of illegal entry from Canada or Mexico, combined with the ease of entry—legally or illegally—into those countries.

But what about "new faces" without terrorist records? What can the United States learn about the presence of dangerous groups by detecting activities that only members of a dangerous group are likely to undertake? Certain fermenting equipment would be an unlikely purchase by anyone other than either the operator of a brewery or someone considering biological terrorism with anthrax. Simple checks could place purchasers in one category or the other. Although the use of different people or false identity papers to make different purchases is an obvious way for terrorists to avoid detection while purchasing ingredients that may be monitored, looking for linkages among the locations of purchases or the mode of payment may help.

The United States can offer either of two types of reward for information leading to the identification of new suspects. Large and well-advertised financial rewards, sometimes accompanied by the protection of being admitted to the United States, have led to revelations about terrorists. Ramzi Yousef, the mastermind of the first World Trade Center bombing in 1993 and the author of a plan to simultaneously attack a number of U.S. airliners crossing the Pacific Ocean, was caught by using offers of rewards on matchbooks. Alternatively, people arrested know that they can reduce their sentence or even obtain immunity by revealing information about far more serious past crimes or future dangers. Terrorism plainly qualifies. Both of these systems of rewards need better advertising.

Conclusion

I have argued that, with a predominant goal of reestablishing citizen safety and a feeling of security, the dangers of the present situation warrant considering even quite costly alternatives. Then, I have tried to show how one can generate, and crudely assess, a list of alternatives to be considered by the United States in dealing with the serious danger of an organized campaign of terrorism based abroad.

The result of this exercise is a moderately optimistic conclusion. It is likely that, at low cost to citizens of the United States, it can threaten damage and offer incentives that more than offset the benefits to almost any state of harboring terrorists. And the states that harbor terrorists have the capacity, in the form of internal security forces, to prevent sustained terrorist campaigns against the United States. Beyond that, some effective steps can be taken at home, even in the short time span and with the small cell structure that the terrorists will require in the target country.

Deciding precisely what to do requires more than recognizing trade-offs and competition among the items on a list of what could be done to discourage terrorism. Not every harboring state and not every terrorist group will behave in a uniform way. The alternatives have to be considered in the far more detailed context of a particular terrorist threat: its leadership, capacities, beliefs, culture, alliances with states and other organizations, and so on.

Deciding on a portfolio of actions and a theme to unify and reassure Americans and recruit allies, the final step, depends on also addressing intangible as well as tangible costs. The choices made in dealing with the dangers of terrorism, will, in very significant ways, reveal and alter our national values.

Lessons of the "War" on Drugs for the "War" on Terrorism

Jonathan P. Caulkins, Mark A. R. Kleiman, and Peter Reuter

Efforts to prevent repetitions of the September 11 incidents have been called "the war on terror." This suggests analogies to the "war on drugs," and there have been attempts to use these comparisons to draw conclusions about the appropriate shape and likely success of the counter-terrorism campaigns.[1] Making new problems seem familiar by seeking out analogies is both a natural psychological response and a rational analytical strategy.

In this essay, we argue that the similarities between the problem of illicit drug distribution and the problem of foreign-based terrorist activity go deeper than the "war" metaphor. In each case, the problem is both important and somewhat inchoate. In each case, the problem has both domestic and transnational aspects. In each case, law enforcement is indispensable but not itself a complete solution. In each case, there is great reluctance to accept an ongoing high level of damage but great difficulty in formulating a strategy to bring that damage down to a level that seems acceptable. In each case, the tendency to think that "tougher is better" may not be justified by results. In each case, coordinating efforts across governments, across levels of government, across agencies, among disciplines, and across the public, private, and civic sectors is both highly important and very difficult.

But terrorism is also unlike drug distribution in vital ways: the scale of the activity to be suppressed; the structure of the organizations whose

---

1. Michael Massing, "Home-Court Advantage: What the War on Drugs Teaches Us about the War on Terrorism," *American Prospect*, Vol. 12, No. 21 (December 3, 2001).

schemes we must try to foil; the motivations of their participants; the scale, structure, and direction of the related financial transactions; and the tolerance for failure. Even if, as some argue, "the war on drugs has been a failure," that would not imply the inevitable failure of the attempt to suppress terrorist actions. Nor can we simply adopt wholesale for counterterrorism successful strategies and tactics from the anti-drug effort.

For each major drug control program and for each policy choice, therefore, we ask if there are relevant parallels and lessons to be drawn for fighting terrorism. We organize our comparisons within six topics: crime control and investigation within the United States; the use of prison to incapacitate offenders; control efforts outside the United States and at the border; financial investigation and control; overall coordination of enforcement efforts; and rhetoric, media, and communications issues.

A note is in order concerning the scope of this analysis. Domestic production does exist for both drugs and terrorism (it now seems likely that the anthrax attack of fall 2001 originated from domestic rather than foreign activity). Both domestic drug dealing and terrorism may involve U.S. citizens using commodities that are legal to possess and use in routine circumstances (sniffing gasoline or glue; using legally owned firearms to conduct violent mass attacks). There are also forms of domestic production of drugs, or of terror, that involve contraband, such as synthesizing methamphetamine or building bombs on U.S. soil. Drugs can be sold, and terrorist actions committed by lone individuals or tiny groups with no connections to larger organizations. However, like others who draw analogies between counterdrug and counterterror operations, we focus on the more international and more organized ends of this spectrum of activity.

There are qualitative differences between domestic and international operations, including what we can reasonably expect of efforts to control them. It is hard to imagine how enforcement could completely eradicate homegrown marijuana or the manufacture of bombs from easily available commodities; however, just as "merely" shrinking consumption of foreign-produced cocaine by 50 percent would constitute an enormous victory, so would "merely" eliminating organized international terrorist activities against the United States. (The death toll from the World Trade Center attack exceeded manyfold the toll from all other terrorist actions on U.S. soil in the past generation.) What changed on September 11 was the level of concern about international terrorism directed at U.S. targets, so that is our focus.

Crime Control and Investigation

Although both drug traffickers and terrorists commit crimes, the two problems display as many differences as similarities when viewed as crime control targets. A basic difference is that while terrorism may have sponsors, it has no true "consumers" the way black market crimes such as drug distribution have. There is therefore no clear analogy in counterterror efforts to "demand reduction" efforts in drug control policy. Modifying U.S. foreign policy to appease terrorists may (or may not) reduce terrorists' motivations to attack, but it would be more akin to addressing so-called "root causes" of drug abuse, such as poverty and family instability, than to drug prevention or treatment.

Counterterrorism policy can attempt to harden targets. The parallel is found in aspirations of "crime prevention through environmental design."[2] For example, just as drug markets may be closed down by redesigning streets or traffic patterns, some terrorist threats could be foiled by reinforcing cockpit doors and keeping vehicles away from buildings. However, both terrorist organizations and drug dealers are capable of adapting to control efforts in ways that diminish the effectiveness of those efforts.[3] Drug smugglers modify routes to evade interdiction pressures; terrorists can adapt to target-hardening by choosing different targets.

Even at the investigative level, apparent similarities are soon revealed as basic differences. Drug enforcement attacks ongoing activity: most targets of investigation have sold drugs many times before and hope to continue doing so on a weekly or monthly, if not daily, basis; the next drug transaction typically looks a lot like the last one. By contrast, counterterrorism efforts seek to halt the targeted activity before it occurs: ideally, would-be terrorists are arrested before their first attack, or at least, perpetrators of past attacks are prevented from committing another attack (which would, in all likelihood, be very different in location, method, and target) rather than merely being apprehended after completing their crimes.

---

2. Clarence Ray Jeffrey, *Crime Prevention through Environmental Design* (Beverly Hills, Calif.: Sage Publications, 1971).

3. Jonathan Caulkins, Gordon Crawford, and Peter Reuter, "Simulation of Adaptive Response: A Model of Drug Interdiction," *Computer and Mathematical Modelling*, Vol. 17, No. 2 (1993), pp. 37–52. See also Ian O. Lesser, Bruce Hoffman, John Arquilla, David Ronfeldt, and Michele Zanini, *Countering the New Terrorism*, MR-989-AF (Santa Monica, Calif.: RAND, 1999).

Undercover operations in which law enforcement personnel imper-
sonate offenders are common in drug investigations. Undercover drug
investigations routinely allow organizations under surveillance to deliver
drugs to customers; indeed, enforcement agencies have from time to time
assisted drug traffickers by operating transportation and money laundering facilities, in order to obtain leads against "higher-ups."

Undercover activity against terrorist organizations, by contrast, is
complicated by the need to stop any known future action that may risk
injury or harm to others. Nevertheless, undercover investigation can play
a valuable role in counterterrorism efforts. A parallel is found in one of
the essential contributions of undercover drug investigations: making
drug market participants suspicious of strangers who show an interest in
drug transactions. Thus, the existence of undercover operations hampers
all drug operations, not just those directly targeted. Similarly, even if enforcement agencies find it difficult or impossible to penetrate terrorist
cells, their efforts to do so may still hamper cooperation among cells by
making them more suspicious of strangers. Moreover, efforts by terrorist
cells to confirm the trustworthiness of others may create vulnerabilities,
for example, when they seek to contact a higher-level leader, by travel in
person or by electronic means, to gain such confirmation.

Efforts to prevent and punish any kind of crime should take into account the basic organizational structures of the activities they target. Here
too there are important differences between drug dealing and terrorism.
Drug distribution is highly atomistic. Between production in Colombia
and sale on the street, cocaine passes through a half dozen or so arm's-
length transactions between people who may know very little about each
other.[4] At all market levels below the very top, few organizations cover
large geographic areas, any given city will have multiple operations, and
most participants have redundant potential transaction partners (i.e.,
could buy from, and sell to, more people or organizations than they currently do business with). Hence, drug distribution networks are resilient
precisely because they are networks, not monoliths or hierarchies. Individual nodes are expendable, because there are multiple paths through
the network from source to customer, and new branches are created con-
stantly.

However, an open organizational pattern also creates opportunities
for law enforcement. For example, drug dealing organizations are sometimes in violent competition for markets and customers, and dismantling
one such organization benefits others. Enforcement can take advantage of

---

4. Jack K. Riley, *Snow Job: The War against International Drug Trafficking* (Westport,
Conn.: Greenwood Press, 1996).

this, either by getting one group to inform against another or by making intergroup or intragroup violence the target of investigative efforts. There is, in general, no comparable incentive for different terrorist organizations or cells to interfere with each other; within the same general movement, they may even cooperate.

Terrorist organizations are more vertically and horizontally integrated than drug distribution networks.[5] Given this integration (although the "new" terrorist organizations may have more of a network structure and may thus be more resilient than the terrorist organizations of the 1970s and 1980s), enforcement activities may take as a useful model traditional organized crime enforcement, rather than drug enforcement. A prime example is that of the families of La Cosa Nostra (LCN); their capacity to extort and to corrupt was unique and could not be duplicated by others, even if specific pieces of illicit business, say, loan-sharking, were taken over by other enterprises. Although law enforcement prosecuted people for labor racketeering, gambling, prostitution, drug dealing, and the like, it was not aimed at those illicit industries, but rather at a small list of organizations, each with a finite, though changing, list of members. The anti-drug effort has led to no better than a standoff. By contrast, the organized crime enforcement effort has been an overwhelming success. There is no place in the United States today where La Cosa Nostra is a significant aspect of social, economic, or political life; no other group has filled the niche that LCN once occupied. The country is clearly better off without its loan-sharking, drug dealing, and prostitution linked to a cluster of organizations with important connections to politics, organized labor, and licit commerce, wielding significant corrupt influence over local enforcement agencies.

While a variety of other changes, notably legalized gambling and trucking deregulation, contributed to the process, enforcement and prosecution efforts started by Attorney General Robert F. Kennedy in the past quarter-century deserve a substantial amount of credit. The successful effort to crush LCN provides lessons, both encouraging and cautionary, for counterterrorism efforts. It shows both the feasibility of eradicating a set of organizations designed to be enforcement-resistant and some of the hard to achieve agency characteristics that such a success requires.

When Kennedy decided to make La Cosa Nostra his target, he created a career service organized crime prosecution effort, reporting administratively to the criminal division in Washington, D.C., rather than to the semi-independent U.S. attorneys' offices, each headed by a presiden-

---

5. John Arquilla and David Ronfeldt, *Networks and Netwars: The Future of Terror, Crime and Militancy*, MR-1382-OSD (Santa Monica, Calif.: RAND, 2001).

tial appointee (usually one with political connections and often one with political ambitions). The prosecutors in the Organized Crime and Racketeering section's city-based "strike forces" had both the patience to make long cases and, after a while, the trust of the investigators who worked with them. Cases began to be planned from the beginning, with investigative effort targeted on the elements that would have to be proven at trial. The goals were to put the leadership of each organized crime "family" behind bars and to challenge LCN's control of key institutions.

Success was slow at first. New statutes, such as the Racketeer Influence and Corrupt Organizations (RICO) law, and new administrative mechanisms, such as the Witness Protection Program (designed to overcome LCN's well-earned reputation for taking revenge on informants), took time to develop and implement. But no one in the organized crime effort needed to run for anything; they could afford to wait. As more and more high-ranking mobsters went to prison for long terms and informing was no longer perceived as a death sentence, organized crime figures began to form informant relationships with investigators as potential lifelines, spreading distrust even among "made" family members. Eventually, family by family, the mob cracked under the pressure.

The organized crime enforcement story is not a uniformly cheerful one. Both the U.S. Constitution and the ethics of investigation were from time to time stretched to the breaking point and beyond. In at least one case, the exclusive focus on LCN led to the formation of an unsavory relationship between the organized crime investigators in one Federal Bureau of Investigation (FBI) office and a non-Italian crime "family" that was much more powerful, both criminally and politically, than the rather insignificant LCN group it was informing against. But the bottom line is that LCN, a major institution in the United States from the 1920s through the 1960s, has become more or less a fossil.[6]

One major difference between the organized crime enforcement effort and any campaign that might plausibly be mounted against terrorism is that La Cosa Nostra was almost entirely domestic; this made its activities and leadership vulnerable to domestic law enforcement. In contrast, al Qaeda's operations are largely international and, therefore, less vulnerable to purely domestic enforcement. However, the dismantling of the Medellin cartel also offers a basis for optimism with respect to the elimination of international terrorist organizations. After the Medellin group assassinated Colombia's leading presidential candidate in 1989,

6. Peter Reuter, "The Decline of the American Mafia," *Public Interest*, No. 120 (Summer 1995), pp. 89–99.

the central government, with U.S. assistance, was able, over a three-year period, to capture or kill all its leaders. While cocaine and heroin production continue in Colombia, the capacity of drug organizations to contend for political power in Colombia has not been reproduced. This suggests that eliminating al Qaeda, for example, might have lasting value.

Incapacitation and Replacement

The criminal justice system is customarily thought of as affecting crime rates in three ways: through deterrence—making crime so unprofitable that criminals pursue other activities; rehabilitation—reforming convicted offenders; and incapacitation—physically separating offenders from potential victims, typically through incarceration. However, experts and the public alike have largely lost faith in the effectiveness of deterrence and rehabilitation against crime, so the focus is increasingly on efforts to incapacitate.[7] However, the supply of drugs is little affected by incapacitation, because incarcerated offenders are easily replaced.[8] Although incapacitation may be somewhat effective with "predatory" crimes, such as burglary, the incapacitation effect of imprisoning a drug dealer is close to zero. Even high-level drug dealers and entire drug distribution organizations have proven to be replaceable, with at most, a brief interruption of supply.[9] As long as there are drug buyers, the financial rewards of supplying their drugs will attract new organizations to replace the old. The new organizations may not be as efficient as the ones destroyed, but the differences, in terms of drug prices and availabilities, are small.

There may be much more promise in the removal of a relatively small number of terrorists, especially when it comes to suicide operations. Despite its ample funding, over the past decade al Qaeda has mounted no more than one successful operation every year or so.[10] Nor is there a "de-

---

7. Peter W. Greenwood, C. Peter Rydell, Allan F. Abrahamse, Jonathan P. Caulkins, James Chiesa, Karyn E. Model, and Stephen P. Klein, *Three Strikes and You're Out: Estimated Benefits and Costs of California's New Mandatory Sentencing Law*, MR-509-RC (Santa Monica, Calif.: RAND, 1994).

8. Mark A.R. Kleiman, "The Problem of Replacement and the Logic of Drug Law Enforcement," *Drug Policy Analysis Bulletin*, No. 3 (September 1997).

9. Peter Reuter, R. MacCoun, and P. Murphy, *Money From Crime: A Study of the Economics of Drug Dealing in Washington, D.C.* (Santa Monica, Calif.: RAND, 1990).

10. Yoram Schweitzer "The Bin Laden Principle," The International Policy Institute for Counter-terrorism, on-line article series, (2001) <www.ict.org.il>.

mand" for terrorist acts in the sense that there is a demand for heroin, so there is no mechanism that automatically replaces terrorists, in the same way that the market replaces drug retailers.

The focus on specific individuals and organizations that has proven futile in reducing the supply of drugs may well be more effective in controlling the level of terrorist activity. "Brand names" and organizational identity may be more important to terrorism than they are to drug dealing. Both voluntary fund-raising and extortion for the benefit of terrorist organizations rely on donors' perception that the organization is one that they support or that they fear; in contrast, cocaine consumers and lower-level dealers are largely indifferent to the provenance of the goods that they purchase.

In efforts to constrain drug dealing, the limiting factor is the capacity to incarcerate the numbers involved, not the ability to arrest.[11] More than one million Americans sell cocaine in any given year; imprisoning all of them would be extraordinarily expensive.[12] By contrast, locking up all of the individuals in the United States who are working to commit lethal terrorist attacks would put no strain on the prison system. The problem is catching them.

If enforcement aims to make carrying out an activity impossible, rather than merely punishing one group of perpetrators, it must somehow destroy a resource that cannot easily be replaced. No resource in the drug arena seems scarce enough; organizational capacity, drugs, and the willingness to take risks to produce, smuggle, and sell them have all proven to be replaceable. Terrorism may be different in this respect. The requisites for a successful terrorist operation seem to be: knowledge of how to create damage or ingenuity in developing new methods of doing so; access to the requisite material means; a supply of operatives willing to kill and perhaps to die; the ability to raise money and move it around internationally; an organization capable of putting these requisites together to carry out operations across borders; and motivation, either intrinsic or extrinsic.[13] The combination of these factors may prove hard to

11.   Jonathan P. Caulkins and Philip B. Heymann, "How Should Low-Level Drug Dealers Be Punished?" in Philip B. Heymann and William N. Brownsberger, eds., *Drug Addiction and Drug Policy: The Struggle to Control Dependence*, (Cambridge, Mass.: Harvard University Press, 2001), pp. 206–238.

12.   Jonathan P. Caulkins, "The Cost-Effectiveness of Civil Remedies: The Case of Drug Control Intervention," in Jorraine Green Mazerolle and Janice Roehl, eds., *Crime Prevention Studies*, Vol. 9 (1998), pp. 219–237.

13.   Bruce Hoffman, *Re-thinking Terrorism in Light of a War on Terrorism*, CT-182, (Santa Monica, Calif.: RAND, 2001).

reproduce; if so, a terrorist group dismantled by enforcement may not be replaced. Thus incapacitation efforts could prove more successful against terrorism than against crimes such as drug dealing.

Control of Sources Outside U.S. Borders and Interdiction at the Borders

Offshore production locations are an important resource for cocaine and heroin production. This has generated hopes of eradicating the drug problem at its source, but production locations are hard to shut down and easy to replace.[14] The number of viable source countries for terrorism may be smaller than those for drugs.[15] That concentration allows for better targeting of enforcement; there is less scope for the "production" of terrorism to move from one country to another to avoid enforcement pressure.

Neither drug production nor recruiting and training terrorists requires much acreage or a special climate; they can be done almost anywhere. What is required is some degree of support or at least tolerance by the local government such as:

- actual state sponsorship of specific acts, such as Libya and the Lockerbie bombing;
- state aid and support for organizations that operate elsewhere, such as Iran and Hamas;
- allowing fund-raising, as with al Qaeda in Saudi Arabia;
- allowing operations or bases within national borders, whether by policy, as with Afghanistan and al Qaeda, or due to weakness, as in Somalia.

State sponsorship of terrorism takes all of these forms. For illegal drugs, the most common scenario is the last, in which a country passively allows trafficking within its borders, because the local government is too weak, too corrupt, or too besieged by other priorities to take effective ac-

---

14. Paul B. Stares, *Global Habit: The Drug Problem in a Borderless World* (Washington, D.C.: Brookings Institution, 1996).

15. The United States currently designates seven countries as state sponsors of terrorism: Cuba, Iran, Iraq, Libya, North Korea, Sudan, and Syria. See Meghan L. O'Sullivan, "Dealing with State Sponsors of Terrorism," in *America's Response to Terrorism*, Analysis Paper No. 6 Brookings Institution (October 25, 2001), at <www. brook.edu/views/articles/osullivan/2001statesponsors.htm>. However, this does not mean that those designated are the only source countries for terrorism.

tion to prevent it. Even growers of drug crops require only that the source country's government be weak, not that it provide direct support for drug cultivation. Corruption may be necessary, but this is hardly a scarce resource: so many nations offer systemic corruption that the drug industry is moderately mobile internationally. Opium production and heroin manufacturing in Colombia, for example, grew very rapidly in the 1990s; distribution channels moved quickly from Thailand to Burma in the 1980s in the face of growing Thai enforcement pressure.

Recruiting and training terrorists often benefit from the acquiescence or even complicity of host governments, not just their weakness. However, after the U.S.-led coalition's invasion of Afghanistan, fewer countries may be willing to offer such protection.[16]

The military assault on Afghanistan's Taliban underscores another difference between international counterdrug and counterterror operations. U.S. drug law enforcement must respect the sovereignty of other countries (the invasion of Panama in 1989 to remove General Noriega notwithstanding—this seems to have been more an effort to remove a particularly repressive dictator that was rationalized by drug charges, than it was a drug control operation). In contrast, however, the foreign-supported killing of civilians on U.S. soil is perceived as justifying an entirely different level of response.

Comparisons to counterdrug policy are more useful with regard to border interdiction, which has been a central component of the drug control effort. Interdiction has driven smuggling out of the hands of amateurs and into the hands of professionals; it also maintains a differential between the price of drugs overseas and those sold in the United States that is enormous compared to conventional transportation costs (the price for a kilogram of cocaine as it travels from Bogotá to Miami increases by $15,000, while Federal Express might charge $100 to ship a package of that weight between those two cities).[17] However, border interdiction has not succeeded in shrinking the availability of cocaine and heroin in the United States. Similarly, while border control is likely to play a supporting role, it will not play a key role in helping reduce terrorism risks for the United States.

Terrorism, like drug dealing, often involves a flow of criminals and

16. Daniel L. Byman, Peter Chalk, Bruce Hoffman, William Rosenau, and David Brannan, *Trends in Outside Support for Insurgent Movements*, MR-1405-OTI (Santa Monica, Calif.: RAND, 2001).

17. Jonathan P. Caulkins and Peter Reuter, "What Price Data Tell Us About Drug Markets." *Journal of Drug Issues*, Vol. 28, No. 3 (1998), pp. 593–612.

materials across international borders—locations at which the government has unique legal powers of investigation and apprehension. However, the sheer numbers of people and vehicles crossing those borders makes the interdiction problem one of finding a few needles in many haystacks. The difficulty of that problem varies depending on the source country; the greater the legitimate flow, the harder it is to detect the criminals or the contraband that they conceal. The United States has more residents from Colombia than from any other South American nation and a substantial licit import trade from Colombia; thus, a Colombian drug trafficker does not stand out from the background of Colombian-born legal visitors, permanent residents, and naturalized citizens, and a shipment of Colombian cocaine marked "coffee beans" from the background of actual coffee imports. Traffickers or drug shipments from, say, Bolivia would be much easier to detect, because they would be a larger fraction of the total traffic from that country.

A similar problem arises with "dual-use" materials, whether it is the type of fertilizer used to make the Oklahoma City bomb or box cutters and airliners turned to lethal uses on September 11: the threat does not stand out from the background. On the order of 300–400 metric tons of cocaine and some multiple of that amount of marijuana enter the United States each year. Those quantities are a tiny, tiny fraction of the corresponding numbers for legitimate commerce, and that is what makes interdiction so difficult. About 25–40 percent of cocaine shipments are seized; heroin is more compact and therefore easier to hide, thus its seizure rate is closer to 10 percent.[18] The constant development of new technologies for detecting drugs has been countered by improved smuggling technology. It is hard to estimate what fraction of drug couriers are caught. It may be quite large, but only because each individual makes so many trips; the probability of getting caught on any one entry into the United States is very small.

The problem is clearly even greater for terrorism control at borders. It is harder to find a kilogram of heroin than a ton of marijuana and harder still to detect lethal quantities of toxins and infectious agents. Thus searches based on specific intelligence, not just random searches, become correspondingly more valuable. At the same time, the stakes are much higher: "leakage" rates that may be acceptable for drugs are far too high for terrorism. Stopping 90 percent of the drugs entering the United States would be a spectacular success, but letting through even

---

18. Peter Reuter, "The Limits of Drug Control," *Foreign Service Journal*, Vol. 79, No. 1 (January 2002), pp. 18–23.

10 percent of terrorists or materials for major terrorist acts could be a disaster.

This pessimistic assessment does not imply that border interdiction has no useful role. Besides forcing the use of more difficult and expensive smuggling techniques and thus shutting out amateurs, interdiction creates two different vulnerabilities for criminals. One is that the material itself may be seized. For drugs, this rarely matters much, since the material is cheap and replaceable. Even with seizure rates of 25–40 percent, cocaine keeps flowing in at prices that, while high compared to legal drugs such as tobacco and alcohol and to refined agricultural products that are legal such as sugar, are still low enough to retain a mass market. Many potential terrorist materials are likely to be similarly replaceable, although others, such as fissile material, may not be; individuals who are trained and committed to terrorism are surely harder to replace than drug couriers.

The other vulnerability that smuggling creates for terrorists and drug dealers is that shipments may be traced to their senders or recipients, which puts the personnel of the operation at risk of arrest. This tends to be the more important risk of the two from the perspective of drug dealers and may prove so for terrorists as well. But tracing a shipment to its recipient often involves letting the delivery be consummated; the fault-intolerant climate of counterterrorism efforts makes such "controlled deliveries" much more troublesome where terrorist materials are involved than it is for drug shipments.

Financial Investigation and Control

International terrorism and drug dealing both involve moving money around, but the sums are of entirely different orders of magnitude. The September 11 actions are estimated to have cost only about half a million dollars, which is roughly nine minutes' revenue in the U.S. cocaine market. The direction of flow is also different. Money in the drug business all moves up: first from the customers to low-level dealers and then up the domestic supply chain; eventually, some of it goes to overseas suppliers. Money sources and flows in the terrorism business are more complicated, and the foot soldiers are more likely to receive money from above than to send it up the chain.[19] These transactions will require new approaches in criminal financial investigation.

---

19. Stefan Leader, "Cash for Carnage: Funding the Modern Terrorist," *Jane's Intelligence Review*, Vol. 10, No. 5 (1998), p. 36.

For drug traffickers, paying fees to money launderers or even losing an occasional bank account is just a cost of doing business. But moving money also creates vulnerability to investigation.[20] Money laundering investigations are even more useful for their potential in catching major figures (as described above with regard to organized crime) than for the actual financial penalty represented by the cash and property seized.

It is not clear whether the same is true for counterterrorism operations. The half-million dollars estimated for the September 11 operation is less than one-quarter of one percent of al Qaeda's estimated financial resources. On the other hand, not every would-be terrorist leader inherits as much money as Osama bin Laden. Terrorism *per se* expends rather than makes money, so at least for individuals or cells isolated from such central bank accounts, money could become a resource constraint.

The other half of the financial crimes aspect of the counterterrorism effort is preventing fund-raising for terrorist operations, both in the United States and abroad. Again, this has no direct parallel in drug investigations.

What is clear is that if drug traffickers had the incentive to fund terrorists, they have the financial wherewithal to do so. Most drug traffickers are apolitical, being more interested in making money than advancing a political agenda. But some terrorist organizations clearly can and do resort to drug trafficking to fund their politically motivated operations.[21] Concerns about "narco-terrorism" have been discussed by analysts and policymakers for at least 15 years.[22] While drug revenues may be important for terrorists, terrorists are unimportant for drug trafficking, simply because there are relatively few of them. Moreover, they are, certainly from the U.S. point of view, not located in dangerous places: neither Colombia nor Mexico, which account for the vast majority of U.S. drug imports, have much involvement in international terrorism. Keeping drug revenues in the hands of old-fashioned greedy criminals rather than criminals with an anti-U.S. political agenda would be desirable, but to what extent drug enforcement could be crafted to this end is a question yet to be explored.

---

20. Mark A.R. Kleiman, *Against Excess: Drug Policy for Results* (New York: Basic Books, 1992).

21. Michael A. Sheehan, statement prepared for the U.S. House Judiciary Committee, Subcommittee on Crime (December 13, 2000) See <usinfo.state.gov/topical/global/drugs/00121303.htm>.

22. Michael Satchell, "Narcotics: Terror's New Ally," *Newsweek* (May 4, 1987), p. 30.

COORDINATION AND ORGANIZATION

Counterdrug and counterterrorism efforts alike transcend jurisdictional and organizational boundaries, which make coordination and organization of efforts important to their overall success. The coordination challenges have proved substantial for drug control and are likely to be even greater for terrorism control, because terrorist organizations cross jurisdictional boundaries even more than individual drug organizations do. No one international drug organization operates in more than a handful of countries, and no domestic drug organization operates in more than a handful of cities. The geographic reach of the al Qaeda organization is far greater than that of any drug organization. During investigations of drug operations that span local jurisdictional boundaries, joint federal-local task forces have been created to pool information; something parallel but more ambitious may be needed to pool counterterrorism information effectively.

U.S. anti-drug efforts involve more than a score of federal agencies, as well as uncounted state and local agencies. At the federal level alone, there are significant efforts by the Bureau of Prisons, the Drug Enforcement Administration (DEA), the Federal Bureau of Investigation (FBI), the Customs Service, the Coast Guard, the Defense Department, the Education Department, the Department of Veterans Affairs, and the Substance Abuse and Mental Health Services Administration; each of these nine agencies spends more than a half billion dollars a year on anti-drug efforts.

The problem is larger than just coordinating the 18,000 law enforcement agencies within the United States.[23] Effective drug control requires international collaboration. There have been some successes in international cooperation on drug enforcement, such as the dismantlement of the Italian Mafia heroin operations during the 1980s and 1990s.[24] However, those collaborations have involved stable and strong governments, which is not typical of those that serve as hosts for terrorist organizations.

The problem extends beyond coordinating investigative agencies. Terrorism, like drugs, is a crime problem, but it is also much more. Whereas the United States views drugs largely as a crime problem, other countries view it more as a public health problem.[25] It is both and also in-

23. Kathleen Maguire and Ann L. Pastore, *Sourcebook of Criminal Justice Statistics 2000* (Washington, D.C.: U.S. Department of Justice, Bureau of Justice Statistics, Government Printing Office, 2001).

24. Letizia Paoli, *Mafia Brotherhoods: Organized Crime, Italian Style* (New York, New York: Oxford University Press, forthcoming).

25. Ministerial Council on Drug Strategy, *National Action Plan on Illicit Drugs: 2001 to*

volves educational agencies (e.g., for drug prevention), diplomats, the military, housing authorities, and many other agencies.

Coordinating either drug control or terrorism control is further complicated in the United States because it spans so many levels as well as functions of government.[26] Sellers of drugs that evade federal interdiction efforts are arrested by the city, prosecuted by the county, and imprisoned by the state. Children in local housing authority projects may do poorly in city schools if their addicted parents fail at the federally funded, county contracted treatment programs that are run by nonprofit agencies. The range of jurisdictions and agencies involved is similar for terrorism: the failure of more than a dozen federal intelligence agencies to detect a plot to circumvent Federal Aviation Administration security procedures implemented by private contractors at municipally operated airports resulted in the seizure of commercial airliners that crashed into commercial and government buildings that were national icons. The first responders to the resulting disasters included city, county, state, federal, and nonprofit emergency response teams.

The Office of National Drug Control Policy (ONDCP) was created in 1989 with an announced mission of giving coherence to U.S. anti-drug efforts. The office has a number of resources: a director with cabinet status, the central role in promulgating an official National Drug Control Strategy, statutory authority to "certify" agency budgets as adequate to the needs of that strategy as well as to propose midyear reallocations of resources within and across agencies, and management of a performance indicator system.

The ONDCP's budgetary authority is, however, much weaker than it appears. The power apparently offered by the budget reallocation authority is virtually unusable: not only would using it start a war with the agency involved, in which the Office of Management and Budget Director and the president would have to back the ONDCP director, but, in most cases, it would require the approval of the chairs and ranking members of the relevant appropriations subcommittees.

The National Drug Control Strategy is, as a practical matter, developed by a process of interagency negotiation that essentially gives the agencies a veto over anything that they find objectionable. Little as it is able to influence federal spending, the ONDCP has even less control over

2002–03 (Canberra, Australia: Commonwealth Department of Health and Aged Care, 2001).

26.   Patrick J. Murphy, Lynn E. Davis, Timothy Liston, David E. Thaler, and Kathi Webb, *Improving Anti-Drug Budgeting*, MR 12–62-ONDCP/NSF (Santa Monica, Calif: RAND, 2000).

the actions of state and local governments, even when federal dollars are being spent. Thus, the ONDCP director must rely primarily on the "bully pulpit" offered by the office, but this approach is only intermittently successful.

These cautions are all likely to apply to any "homeland defense"office in the White House. The budget process and the difficulty of influencing the actual behavior of any agency from outside will drastically limit the actual power of any homeland defense entity. Former Governor Tom Ridge, while Director of the Office of Homeland Security (OHS), was not a czar any more than the drug czar; "czardom" is not consistent with the way the federal government operates, either in the executive branch or the legislative branch. Thus, ONDCP does not offer a practical model for the coordination of the U.S. counterterrorism effort.

In creating the new Department of Homeland Security (DHS), also headed by Governor Ridge, President Bush and Congress have created a unit that combines coordination with substantial operational capacity of its own, mostly by absorbing existing agencies (or pieces of existing agencies) into a new structure. This approach poses different challenges but not necessarily less daunting ones. Importing existing operational units means importing as well their existing personnel, organizational cultures and loyalties, and networks of relationships with clients, other agencies, and the legislature; how responsive the old units will be to the new superstructure is always an open question. Once combined into a new agency, existing units can be reorganized, but that poses problems of its own. The Drug Enforcement Administration, created in 1974 by combining elements of the Customs Service with the Bureau of Narcotics and Dangerous Drugs, remained divided for years between veterans of the two different units.

Moreover, the very sweep of the homeland protection mission guarantees that a new department will include only some of the relevant operational capacity. (For example, the Federal Bureau of Investigation remains outside the Department of Homeland Security.) That will complicate the efforts of Secretary of Homeland Security Ridge, who has operational authority to coordinate the efforts of units outside his immediate control; the functions of referee and team captain do not easily co-exist. The Director of Central Intelligence, for example, is in principle both the chief of an operating agency, the Central Intelligence Agency (CIA), and the coordinator of the entire intelligence community, including units of the Defense and State Departments. But the fact that the holder of that position is virtually always referred to as the "CIA Director" testifies to the extent to which he is identified with the agency he actually runs.[27]

An alternative model would have the Congress appropriate large sums to the Department of Homeland Security, with the expectation that most of those sums would be transferred to operating agencies under interagency agreements executed at the discretion of its director. If Secretary Ridge truly had the ability to choose whether, say, $100 million in counterterrorism law enforcement funding went to the FBI for investigations or instead to the Customs Service to strengthen border inspections, the agency could wield enormous power. But such authority would be virtually unprecedented, and there are strong reasons, arising from competition among Congressional committees and among agencies to doubt that it would be granted or that, if granted, it could be effectively wielded and retained over time.

Another approach to U.S. anti-drug efforts that may offer useful lessons for counterterrorism was the establishment of a distinct enforcement agency whose sole mission is counterdrug operations: the Drug Enforcement Administration. There is no analogous enforcement or intelligence organization dedicated to counterterror operations. The DEA is not small: its budget is $1.7 billion for fiscal year 2003; it has a staff of 9,200, half of whom are special agents (i.e., criminal investigators with arrest powers), and it has experienced recent growth. Nevertheless, it represents only 18 percent of all federal domestic counterdrug enforcement efforts.[28] Predictably there have been coordination problems between the DEA and other agencies, including the FBI. The single purpose character of the DEA means, among other things, that drug enforcement will not be entirely neglected when some other problem dominates public attention. The constancy of DEA's attention to the drug problem contrasts with the rapid cutback in the Customs Service's counterdrug efforts as it shifted efforts to the counterterrorism mission after September 11.

Rhetoric, Media, and Communication Issues

Part of managing a public policy problem is managing public perceptions of the problem and associated control efforts. The rhetorical and political

---

27. For a devastating analysis of the design problems in national security management, see Amy B. Zegart, *Flawed by Design* (Stanford, Calif.: Stanford University Press, 2001.

28. ONDCP, National Drug Control Strategy: FY2003 Budget Summary (Washington, D.C.: 2002), pp. 6–8.

dynamics of the "war against drugs" have been problematic and offer some sobering cautions for the counterterrorism effort.

Counterdrug and counterterrorism measures have costs other than overt monetary expenditure, especially their impacts on civil liberties. Testing junior high school athletes for drug use may or may not reduce drug use; it certainly leads to more intrusions by the state in the lives of families and individuals. Counterterrorism efforts are already affecting the ease of movement of noncitizens. The "war" metaphor encourages decision-makers and the public to ignore those costs, because "there is no substitute for victory." If the "war on terrorism" were indeed a time-limited campaign against existential threats from specific entities whose defeat could be clearly defined, that would be appropriate. Hence, declaring war on the Taliban, for example, makes more sense than declaring war on terrorism.

There is a price to be paid if the U.S. government is not careful and precise in its rhetoric. For example, it cannot expect the media to be friendly forever. Journalists often prefer writing stories about how incompetent or corrupt the government is rather than writing about how difficult the problem is that the government is facing. The media's tendency to look for morality plays and formulaic coverage can hamper the government's ability to take the right steps against terrorism, and this problem is only exacerbated by imprecise language. For example, the press has already given a considerable mauling to ONDCP's rhetorical efforts in television and print advertisements linking that war against terror with the war against drugs by assertions that buyers of drugs are supporting terrorism.[29]

Rhetorical contexts that reward "get-tough" soundbites at the expense of nuanced reasoning can lead to direct harms. For example, minor and peripheral players, such as drug couriers ("mules") and providers of false documents, may be easier to capture than the kingpins (this is clearly so with drug dealing, in part simply because there are many more workers than kingpins). The danger lies in the temptation to ratchet up sanctions, inflicting disproportionate punishment on these minor figures. There are, likewise, peripheral players in terrorism, such as producers of counterfeit identification documents or bureaucrats who are bribed to issue licenses to transport hazardous waste. Increasing the punishment risk that they face can have benefits if it deters them sufficiently to make their services hard for terrorists to acquire, or if it coerces them into offering useful information to law enforcement authorities. However, these

---

29. A. Trafford, "Second Opinion: Drug Users as Traitors," *Washington Post*, February 12, 2002, p. HE01.

benefits must be weighed against valid considerations of justice and cost, with recognition that, as a practical matter, these harms fall disproportionately on racial and ethnic groups who are minorities in the United States.

Conclusions

Here are the six lessons that we draw from this analysis:

First, the enforcement problems are very different for the two campaigns, and therefore, methods and ways of thinking drawn from the counterdrug effort cannot simply be applied to the counterterrorism effort. Drug dealers have customers; terrorists have supporters and victims. Drug organizations are mostly anonymous and interchangeable, thus making the removal of any one or few number of limited usefulness. In contrast, terrorist organizations appear to be highly individual and may take a long time to replace, so that the removal of even one, such as al Qaeda, may make a large difference to the threat faced in the United States. The largely successful campaign against La Cosa Nostra, which dismantled a specific group of organizations, may provide many more useful lessons than the drug enforcement effort.

Second, in the absence of the virtually automatic replacement mechanism that frustrates drug law enforcement, both deterrence and incapacitation hold out substantial promise in controlling terrorism.

Third, border control, although it may be necessary and useful, is unlikely to play a major role in preventing terrorism. The counterdrug experience with interdiction is sobering: making U.S. borders impermeable to cocaine and heroin has proven impossible. In a free society with substantial international trade and tourism, "sealing" the borders is not practical. Permitting the continued smooth flow of commerce and traffic has taken priority throughout the "war on drugs." Border interdiction is likely to be even less successful against relatively small numbers of terrorists and material that, in the wrong hands, can be dangerous even in tiny quantities, such as biological agents or radioactive material. Random, as opposed to intelligence-driven, searches may deter some amateurs but are likely to pick up little contraband.

Fourth, drug dealers need to launder the money that flows up from retail dealing to higher-level sources. Terrorists need to raise money and to distribute it down to operatives on the ground. Thus, while criminal financial investigation has a role in counterterrorism operations, that activity will not much resemble the financial aspects of counterdrug efforts. Preventing terrorists from dipping into the rivers of drug money that flow around the globe (not nearly as great as rumored but more than

Table 1. "War" on Drugs vs. "War" on Terrorism.

Program/Function	Role in Counterdrug Efforts	Role in Counterterrorism Efforts
Demand side interventions	Relevant	Not applicable
Domestic investigation	Important, expensive, and frustrating	Stronger parallel with organized crime enforcement than drug enforcement
Incapacitation	Usefulness is constrained by numbers and replaceability	No reason not to pursue with long sentences
Source country operations	Qualitatively different, so no conclusions drawn	Qualitatively different, so no conclusions drawn
Interdiction at borders	Useful but not decisive	Useful but not decisive
Financial investigation and control	Useful but not decisive	Useful but not decisive
Coordination	Extremely vexing problem	Problems even more severe
Rhetoric	War metaphor and "tough-on-drugs" litmus test problematic	Choose rhetoric thoughtfully

large enough to satisfy the relatively modest needs of terrorism) seems important, but the task of figuring out how to shape drug enforcement to disadvantage terrorist-linked groups remains before us.

Fifth, coordination problems are immense, and merely naming a "czar" is not a solution, as the experience of the "drug czar" illustrates. Neither controlling drugs nor controlling terrorism is primarily a criminal justice problem, and the agencies that must work together—criminal justice, military, public health, and others—are very different in mission and culture. The Secretary of DHS will need to be supplemented by new coordinating mechanisms, because the structure of the federal executive and legislative branches, and in particular the budget process, makes it virtually impossible for the head of any one agency to exert effective control over the activities of other agencies. The problems are only multiplied in attempts to influence the actions of state and local agencies (as well as private and voluntary sector entities), even when those agencies and entities receive federal funds.

Sixth, the rhetoric that gets the most applause from domestic publics today may not create the best long-term prospects for maintaining support for the counterterrorism effort. Table 1 summarizes the analogies between the "war on drugs" and the "war on terrorism," and their implications.

The problem of large-scale terrorism aimed at targets within the United States is new. It is much too early to judge how permanent that problem is: whether the September 11 attacks will eventually be seen as causing a significant increase in the domestic risk from such acts or will instead stand out like the Chicago fire of 1871 or the 1900 Galveston flood—not as a precedent but as a unique event. To some extent, that may be determined by the adequacy of the policy response. But there is no set of lessons from the "war on drugs" that can be used straightforwardly to shape policy against the new threat.

Part II
Emerging Threats

Biological Terrorism: Understanding the Threat and America's Response

Gregory D. Koblentz

During the fall of 2001, biological terrorism was transformed from a possibility to reality. Prior to September 11, 2001, biological terrorism was viewed as a "low probability, high consequence" event. Experts debated whether or not terrorist groups had the motivation and capability to develop and use biological weapons. The suicide hijackings on September 11, 2001, which destroyed the World Trade Center, damaged the Pentagon, and killed an estimated 3,000 people demonstrated that some terrorist groups have the motivation and capability to cause mass casualties. In the aftermath of September 11, 2001, biological terrorism became a central focus of concerns about future terrorist attacks. On October 5, 2001, Robert Stevens, a 63-year-old photo editor with American Media Inc. in Boca Raton, Florida, died of inhalation anthrax and became the first fatality due to biological terrorism in U.S. history.[1] Over the next two months, spores of *Bacillus anthracis* (the organism that causes anthrax) contained in letters mailed to media outlets in New York and Florida and to elected officials in Washington, D.C., infected 22 individuals, of whom five were killed.[2] Although only a small number of people were directly affected,

---

1. The contamination of salad bars with *Salmonella typhi* by the Rajneesh cult in The Dalles, Oregon, in 1984, sickened hundreds but did not cause any fatalities. Thomas J. Torok, et al., "A Large Community Outbreak of Salmonellosis Caused by Intentional Contamination of Restaurant Salad Bars," *Journal of the American Medical Association*, Vol. 278, No. 5 (August 6, 1997), pp. 389–395.

2. The letters containing *Bacillus anthracis* caused 11 cases of inhalation anthrax and 13 cases of cutaneous anthrax (eight confirmed and four suspected). The twenty-third case occurred in March 2002 when a laboratory worker became infected with cutaneous anthrax after improperly handling vials containing *B. anthracis*. Centers for Dis-

these letters forced the closure and decontamination of several buildings and disrupted the operations of the U.S. Congress and U.S. Postal Service. Besides the estimated 32,000 individuals who took antibiotics due to possible exposure to the anthrax-containing letters, countless more treated themselves with ciprofloxacin hydrocloride (Cipro®) or hoarded medicine. The anthrax letter attacks also spawned a host of subsequent hoaxes and false alarms that further heightened the public's sense of insecurity and anxiety. The financial cost has also been significant: hundreds of millions of dollars have been spent responding to and mitigating the consequences of these attacks.

Just as the methods and sophistication of the terrorist attacks on September 11, 2001, were unexpected, so too were the use of letters to deliver *B. anthracis* spores and the quality of the spores in the letters. The anthrax letter attacks have led to a new understanding of *B. anthracis*, the organism, and anthrax, the disease, which will contribute to future efforts to combat this threat. The ability of doctors to save more than half of the people infected with inhalation anthrax, the most severe form of the disease, was a significant achievement. However, it was also clear that despite the attention and funding devoted to bioterrorism preparedness over the past several years, the government was ill-equipped to handle even a small-scale incident. The shortcomings in the government's response to the attacks and the inability of law enforcement agencies to apprehend the perpetrator(s) have further reduced the public's confidence in the nation's preparedness for terrorism, especially mass casualty attacks.

As a result of the September 11, 2001, attacks and the anthrax letter incidents, federal spending on biological terrorism preparedness has increased dramatically. During 2002 and 2003, the Bush administration plans on spending $11 billion to defend against this threat. The Department of Health and Human Services (HHS) alone received $2.8 billion to combat bioterrorism in 2002, 10 times as much as it received in 2001. Since 1996, the federal government has been engaged in a large-scale effort to prepare for a potential terrorist attack in the United States with a weapon of mass destruction (WMD).[3] The threat of terrorists employing

---

ease Control and Prevention, "Update: Cutaneous Anthrax in a Laboratory Worker—Texas, 2002," *Morbidity and Mortality Weekly Report,* Vol. 51, No. 22 (June 7, 2002), p. 482.

3. For details about these efforts, see Gregory Koblentz, "Overview of Federal Programs to Enhance State and Local Capability to Respond to WMD Terrorism," ESDP Discussion Paper ESDP-2001–03, John F. Kennedy School of Government, Harvard University, April 2001.

biological weapons has been a source of great concern to officials involved in domestic preparedness activities for several years. A 1996 survey by the National Governors Association found that states were not prepared to deal with the threat of biological weapons.[4] A July 1999 National Guard Bureau report to Congress concluded that, "there is insufficient capability to determine that a biological attack has occurred, make timely identification of biological agents, provide treatment to mass casualties, and contain the event. In sum, the United States is ill-prepared to respond to attacks involving biological agents."[5] According to the Department of Justice's *Five-Year Interagency Counterterrorism and Technology Crime Plan*, "By far, our greatest deficiency in regard to WMD lies in our limited capability to detect, prevent, and respond to the use of biological agents."[6] U.S. vulnerability to biological terrorism has also been demonstrated in numerous exercises and simulations.[7]

Concern about the use of biological weapons by terrorists was driven in part by reports that Aum Shinrikyo, the Japanese cult responsible for the nerve gas attack in the Tokyo subway system in 1995, had also developed biological weapons. The group was reported to have disseminated, without success, *B. anthracis* and botulinum toxin (a highly lethal toxin produced by the bacteria *Clostridium botulinum*) and to have experimented with *Coxiella burnetti* (the causative organism for Q fever) and the hemorrhagic fever virus Ebola.[8] Aum Shinrikyo, it was feared, had

---

4. National Governors Association, "Terrorism: Is America Prepared?" issue brief, February 2, 1997.<www.nga.org/Pubs/IssueBriefs/1997/970202terrorism.asp>.

5. National Guard Bureau, *Report to Congress: Enhancing the National Guard's Readiness to Support Emergency Responders in Domestic Chemical and Biological Terrorism Defense* (Washington, D.C.: Government Printing Office, 1999), pp. 17–18; <www.ngb.dtic.mil/wmd/report/reportcover.htm>.

6. Department of Justice, *Five-Year Interagency Counterterrorism and Technology Crime Plan*, unclassified edition (Washington, D.C.: Government Printing Office, 1999), p. 36.

7. Judith Miller, "Exercise Finds US Unable to Handle Germ War Threat," *New York Times*, April 26, 1998, p. A1; Thomas V. Inglesby, Rita Grossman, and Tara O'Toole, "A Plague on Your City: Observations from TOPOFF," *Clinical Infectious Diseases*, Vol. 32 (2001), pp. 436–445; Richard E. Hoffman and Jane E. Norton, "Lessons Learned from a Full-Scale Bioterrorism Exercise," *Emerging Infectious Diseases*, Vol. 6, No. 6 (November–December 2000); Thomas V. Inglesby and Tara O'Toole, "Shining Light on Dark Winter: Lessons Learned," *Biodefense Quarterly*, Vol. 3, No. 2 (Autumn 2001).

8. For an early assessment of Aum's biological weapons program, see John Sopko and Alan Edelman, "Global Proliferation of Weapons of Mass Destruction: Study on the Aum Shinrikyo," staff statement in Senate Committee on Governmental Reform, Permanent Subcommittee on Investigations, *Global Proliferation of Weapons of Mass Destruction, Part I* (Washington, D.C.: Government Printing Office, 1996), pp. 63–64. Subsequent reports indicate that Aum was less successful than initially believed in

broken a long-standing taboo among terrorist groups and was the harbinger of other nonstate actors interested in causing mass casualties and capable of acquiring nuclear, biological, and chemical weapons. The rise of these groups, coupled with major domestic terrorist attacks in the United States, raised the specter of a WMD attack occurring on U.S. soil.[9]

The proliferation of biological weapons and the ties that many of the states with biological weapons programs have with international terrorist groups has also contributed to the perceived increase in the threat posed by biological terrorism. In the 1990s, the problem of biological weapons proliferation was highlighted by revelations about the Iraqi and former Soviet offensive biological weapons programs and intelligence that indicated that at least 10 other nations were pursuing offensive biological warfare programs.[10] The vigor with which Iraq and the former Soviet Union pursued biological weapons belied the conventional wisdom that

---

cultivating pathogenic organisms. Aum apparently failed to produce a lethal strain of botulinum toxin and had access to only a harmless vaccine strain of anthrax. There is no evidence Aum obtained strains of either Q fever or Ebola. See Milton Leitenberg, "Aum Shinrikyo's Effort to Produce Biological Weapons: A Case Study of the Serial Propagation of Misinformation," *Terrorism and Political Violence,* Vol. 11, No. 4, pp. 149–158; Advisory Panel to Assess Domestic Response Capabilities for Terrorism Involving Weapons of Mass Destruction, *First Annual Report to the President and the Congress: Assessing the Threat* (Washington, D.C.: Government Printing Office, 1999), pp. 48–51.

9. The emerging trend in terrorist interest in causing mass casualties and employing WMDs is described in Richard Falkenrath, Robert Newman, and Bradley Thayer, *America's Achilles' Heel: Nuclear, Biological and Chemical Terrorism and Covert Attack* (Cambridge, Mass.: MIT Press, 1998); Jessica Stern, *The Ultimate Terrorists* (Cambridge, Mass.: Harvard University Press, 1999); and *Terrorism with Chemical and Biological Weapons: Calibrating Risks and Responses,* ed. Brad Roberts (Alexandria, Va.: Chemical and Biological Arms Control Institute, 1997).

10. For details about the Soviet Union's biological warfare program, see Ken Alibek with Stephen Handelman, *Biohazard: The Chilling True Story of the Largest Covert Biological Weapons Program in the World* (New York: Random House, 1999). The best summary of what is known about the Iraqi biological weapons program is United Nations Security Council Document S/1999/94, Annex C: Status of Verification of Iraq's Biological Warfare Programme, January 25, 1999, <www.un.org/Depts/unscom/s99–94.htm>.

For an assessment of the extent of the proliferation of biological weapons, see unclassified statement for the record by Special Assistant to the DCI for Nonproliferation John A. Lauder on the Worldwide WMD Threat to the Commission to Assess the Organization of the Federal Government to Combat the Proliferation of Weapons of Mass Destruction, April 29, 1999, <www.cia.gov/cia/public_affairs/speeches/archives/1999/lauder_speech_042999.html>.

had prevailed since the early 1970s: these weapons were of limited military utility. The economic chaos in Russia since the breakup of the Soviet Union has also intensified fears that scientists from the now defunct Soviet biological weapons program would work for other nations or terrorist groups attempting to develop these weapons.[11] All seven nations on the State Department's list of state sponsors of terrorism are believed to have or to be developing biological weapons.[12] The United States' clear superiority in conventional weapons, demonstrated repeatedly in the 1990s, has led to an expectation that a future enemy may seek to avoid a direct confrontation on the battlefield and instead rely on the covert use of a nuclear, biological, or chemical weapon against U.S. forces or civilian targets in the United States.[13] Biological weapons, cheaper and easier to produce than nuclear weapons and more lethal than chemical weapons, are now perceived as the weapon of choice for both state and nonstate actors seeking to inflict maximum damage while minimizing the risk of detection and retaliation.[14]

This chapter examines U.S. preparedness for an act of biological terrorism and the current status of efforts by the federal government to improve national, state, and local capabilities to recognize and respond to such an attack.[15] The first section provides an overview of bioterrorism

---

11. Jonathan B. Tucker and Kathleen M. Vogel, "Preventing the Proliferation of Chemical and Biological Weapons Materials and Know-How," *The Nonproliferation Review* (Spring 2000).

12. The seven nations are Cuba, Iran, Iraq, Libya, North Korea, Sudan, and Syria. Department of State, *Patterns of Global Terrorism 2001* (Washington, D.C.: Government Printing Office, 2002).

For information on the biological weapons programs of these countries, see Department of Defense, *Proliferation: Threat and Response* (Washington, D.C.: Government Printing Office, 2001); John R. Bolton, Under Secretary for Arms Control and International Security, "Beyond the Axis of Evil: Additional Threats from Weapons of Mass Destruction," Remarks to the Heritage Foundation, Washington, D.C., May 6, 2002; Central Intelligence Agency, *Unclassified Report to Congress on the Acquisition of Technology Relating to Weapons of Mass Destruction and Advanced Conventional Munitions, 1 January Through 30 June 2001*, January 30, 2002, <www.cia.gov/cia/publications/bian/bian_jan_2002.htm>.

13. Department of Defense, *Proliferation: Threat and Response* (Washington, D.C.: Government Printing Office, 1997), p. iii.

14. United States Commission on National Security in the 21st Century, *New World Coming: American Security in the 21st Century: Supporting Research and Analysis*, September 15, 1999, p. 50.

15. Additional studies on this topic include Amy Smithson and Leslie-Ann Levy, *Ataxia: Chemical and Biological Terrorism and the U.S. Response* (Washington, D.C.: Henry

and the ways in which preparing for and responding to bioterrorism differs from that for other forms of terrorism.[16] The second section describes current programs underway in the United States to prepare for and respond to biological terrorism. In an address to the National Academy of Sciences, D. A. Henderson, then head of the Center for Civilian Biodefense Studies at Johns Hopkins University, stated that it is "near impossible to summarize succinctly the status of what is best characterized as a miscellaneous array of fragmented, poorly coordinated initiatives."[17] Nonetheless, that is exactly what this section attempts to do. The final section concludes with some observations on areas of preparedness that require additional attention.

Overview of Biological Terrorism

Biological terrorism can take many forms. The spectrum of potential scenarios ranges from localized food contamination with a common bacteria to the dissemination of anthrax or bubonic plague in a subway station to the infection of an airplane full of people with smallpox. Scientists at the Centers for Disease Control and Prevention (CDC) have estimated that a bioterrorism attack that exposed 100,000 people to *Francisella tularensis* (the causative agent of tularemia) could cause 6,000 fatalities and have an economic impact of almost $4 billion. If anthrax were used instead, fatalities and costs would increase fivefold.[18] Appendix A presents additional

---

L. Stimson Center, October 2000); *Bioterrorism in the United States: Threat, Preparedness, and Response* (Washington, D.C.: Chemical and Biological Arms Control Institute, November 2000); *Third Annual Report to the President and the Congress of the Advisory Panel to Assess Domestic Response Capabilities for Terrorism Involving Weapons of Mass Destruction* (Washington, D.C.: RAND Corporation, December 2001).

16. Although biological agents can also be used to attack crops and livestock, this essay focuses solely on biological terrorism aimed at humans. For in-depth treatments of the former subjects, see Jason Pate and Gavin Cameron, *Covert Biological Weapons Attacks Against Agricultural Targets: Assessing the Impact Against U.S. Agriculture,* ESDP Discussion Paper ESDP-2001–05, John F. Kennedy School of Government, Harvard University, August 2001 and Anne Kohnen, *Responding to the Threat of Agroterrorism: Specific Recommendations for the United States Department of Agriculture,* ESDP Discussion Paper ESDP-2000–04, John F. Kennedy School of Government, Harvard University, October 2000.

17. Donald A. Henderson, "US Response to Possible Bioterrorism," address to National Academy of Sciences, May 2, 2000, <www.hopkins-biodefense.org/pages/events/speeches.html>. In November 2001, Dr. Henderson was appointed to lead the bioterrorism preparedness efforts of the Department of Health and Human Services.

18. Arnold Kaufmann, Martin Meltzer, and George Schmid, "The Economic Impact

estimates of the effects of a bioterrorist attack, on a crowd in a large indoor arena and a city the size of Boston. This first section provides an overview of biological terrorism. The first part describes likely agents, production and delivery methods, targets, and bioterrorism scenarios. The second part examines how a covert attack may unfold and the challenges that it would present to local, state, and federal responders. The section concludes with a summary of the implications for preparing for and responding to an act of biological terrorism.

Agents, Delivery Methods, Targets, Scenarios

BIOLOGICAL AGENTS

Roughly a dozen microorganisms—mainly bacteria and viruses—and toxins are viewed as likely candidates for use in biological warfare or biological terrorism (see Appendix B). Once bacteria and viruses have infected a host, they begin to multiply rapidly, thus enabling a relatively small dose to result in the death or debilitation of the host within days, weeks, or months. Biological toxins, in contrast, do not replicate in the body, so the exposure dose itself is what causes the illness. However, toxins are extraordinarily lethal, the most potent being 100,000 times more toxic than sarin. Toxins can be thought of as chemicals that are produced by living things: by animals (venom from snakes), plants (ricin from castor beans), or microorganisms (botulinum toxin is produced by the bacteria *Clostridium botulinum*). The agents listed in Appendix C are those designated by the CDC as "critical agents" because of the ease with which they can be disseminated or transmitted from person to person, their lethality, their potential to cause public panic, and the degree of special preparations that must be made by the public health and medical communities to diagnose the agent and treat infected individuals.[19] In general, these agents can cause moderate (30 percent) to very high (90–100 percent) fatality rates if treatment is not provided in a timely fashion, or if there is no treatment available once a person begins to show symptoms. Thus, these agents require early diagnosis for medical intervention to be

---

of a Bioterrorist Attack: Are Prevention and Postattack Intervention Programs Justifiable?," *Emerging Infectious Diseases*, Vol. 3, (April–June 1997).

19. The criteria employed by CDC to select and prioritize potential bioterrorism threat agents is described in Lisa D. Rotz, Ali S. Khan, Scott R. Lillibridge, Stephen M. Ostroff, and James M. Hughes, "Public Health Assessment of Potential Biological Terrorism Agents," *Emerging Infectious Diseases*, Vol. 8, No. 2 (February 2002), <www.cdc.gov/ncidod/eid/vol8no2/01–0164.htm#1>.

successful. It should be noted, however, that this list does not encompass the full range of naturally occurring pathogens and toxins that have been weaponized by state-sponsored biological weapons programs or employed by terrorists in the past. Prior to 2001, the only confirmed act of biological terrorism in the United States utilized the organism *Salmonella enterica* serotype typhimurium, a common cause of food poisoning.[20] In addition, it is possible to create new strains of existing agents to enhance their virulence or resistance to antibiotics.[21]

PRODUCTION

The barriers to acquiring biological weapons are relatively low.[22] Information on agents, as well as production and dissemination techniques, is available from public sources. Seed stocks of agents can be obtained from the environment, from commercial sources, or by theft from a government, university, or private laboratory. In addition, production equipment is widely available, and the skills necessary for such production are not highly specialized. Production activities can be conducted safely with minimal precautions and are not likely to create a unique signature that can be identified by law enforcement agencies before a terrorist attack. In addition, the amount of biological agent required to cause mass casualties can be measured in tens to thousands of grams, reducing the size of the requisite production facilities and dissemination devices. (By comparison, the amount of chemical agents required for a large-scale attack would be measured in tens to hundreds of kilograms, and an improvised nuclear device would probably weigh more than 1,000 kilograms).

Biological agents can be produced in two versions: as a liquid slurry or as a dry powder. The slurry is easier to produce but is more difficult to disseminate than the dry version. In addition to their ease of dissemination, dry agents are typically more concentrated, and therefore, more potent than liquid agents. The processing of the dry agent, however, presents additional safety problems to the would-be terrorist.[23]

---

20. Tojork, op cit.; W. Seth Carus, "The Rajneeshes (1984)," in *Toxic Terror: Assessing the Use of Chemical and Biological Weapons*, ed. Jonathan Tucker (Cambridge, Mass.: MIT Press, 2000), pp. 116–137.

21. Raymond A. Zilinskas, "Possible Terrorist Use of Modern Biotechnology Techniques," Paper Presented at Conference on Biosecurity and Bioterrorism, Instituto Diplomatico "Mario Toscano," Rome, Italy, September 18–19, 2000.

22. This section is derived from Falkenrath, Newman, and Thayer, *America's Achilles' Heel*, pp. 113–126.

23. William C. Patrick III, "Biological Warfare: An Overview," in *Director's Series on Proliferation*, ed. Kathleen Bailey, No. 4 (May 1994), p. 4.

To assess the threat posed by terrorist acquisition of biological weapons, the Defense Threat Reduction Agency (DTRA) commissioned a team in 1999 to build a small-scale biological agent production facility using $1.6 million and commercially available equipment.[24] The project demonstrated that such a facility could be built and operated without generating suspicion. However, both the Central Intelligence Agency and General Accounting Office (GAO) have noted that producing biological weapons is significantly harder than commonly portrayed in the media.[25]

DISSEMINATION

The weaponization and dissemination of a biological agent is the most significant challenge to a potential bioterrorist. The Aum Shinrikyo cult in Japan, even with hundreds of millions of dollars and well-educated scientists, failed on seven separate occasions to successfully aerosolize virulent strains of anthrax and botulinum toxin.[26] According to the GAO, "terrorists working outside a state-run laboratory infrastructure would have to overcome extraordinary challenges to effectively and successfully weaponize and deliver a biological agent and cause mass casualties."[27] Unlike chemical agents such as mustard and VX, biological agents cannot be absorbed through the skin; they must enter the body through inhalation, ingestion, or cuts in the skin. The most effective means of infecting a large number of people is to create an aerosol of respirable particles in the one to five micron range.[28] Aerosols would be the preferred delivery

---

24. Judith Miller, Stephen Engelberg, and William Broad, *Germs: Biological Weapons and America's Secret War* (New York: Simon & Schuster, 2001), pp. 297–298.

25. General Accounting Office, *Combating Terrorism: Need for Comprehensive Threat and Risk Assessments of Chemical and Biological Attacks*, NSIAD-99–163, September 1999, p. 13; statement by Special Assistant to the DCI for Nonproliferation John A. Lauder on the Worldwide Biological Warfare Threat to the House Permanent Select Committee on Intelligence, March 3, 1999, <www.cia.gov/cia/public_affairs/speeches/archives/1999/lauder_speech_030399.html>.

26. David E. Kaplan, "Aum Shinrikyo (1995)," in *Toxic Terror: Assessing the Use of Chemical and Biological Weapons*, ed. Jonathan Tucker (Cambridge, Mass.: MIT Press, 2000), p. 221; W. Seth Carus, *Bioterrorism and Biocrimes: The Illicit Use of Biological Agents in the 20th Century* (Working Paper National Defense University, Washington, D.C., July 1999), p. 56.

27. General Accounting Office, *Combating Terrorism: Need for Comprehensive Threat and Risk Assessments of Chemical and Biological Attacks*, NSIAD-99–163, (Washington, D.C.: Government Printing Office, 1999), p. 13.

28. A micron is one-thousandth of a millimeter. A human hair has a diameter of about 50 microns. Particles smaller than one micron will be exhaled instead of being trapped in the lungs. Particles larger than five microns will not be able to penetrate past the upper respiratory tract.

method for biological agents since the infectious dose of most agents is generally lower if inhaled than if ingested, and the lethality of some agents is significantly higher if the agent has been inhaled and deposited in the lungs. In addition, small-particle aerosols are able to stay airborne longer, thus increasing the potential area of infection.[29] Creating a respirable aerosol is difficult but can be accomplished with modifications to off-the-shelf equipment.[30]

A critical variable affecting the dissemination of biological agents is meteorology. Most microorganisms are fragile and thus are susceptible to environmental conditions, such as ultraviolet radiation and humidity. Aerosols are also delicate creations and can be disrupted or rendered ineffective by very low or very high wind speeds, unstable atmospheric conditions, and urban terrain.[31] Moderate snow and rain will not affect a biological aerosol.[32] In general, the best times to disseminate biological aerosols to minimize the impact of meteorological degradation are at sunset, at night, or shortly before daybreak.[33] Thus, an open-air biological weapons attack would require extensive planning and access to accurate meteorological information for the target area. Releasing a biological agent in a confined space, such as a building or subway station, eliminates these obstacles.

There are three main ways that terrorists could disseminate a biological agent as an aerosol. The simplest method is to place the agent in a porous or breakable device and rely on external pressures to expel the agent. However, this method requires a high quality agent to be successful. This method was employed by the perpetrator(s) of the anthrax letter attacks.[34] Devices using explosive energy are simple but also an in-

---

29. Leroy Fothergill, "The Biological Warfare Threat," in American Chemical Society, *Nonmilitary Defense: Chemical and Biological Defenses in Perspective,* Advances in Chemistry Series No. 26: American Chemical Society (July 1960), p. 26.

30. Department of Health and Human Services, *Proceedings of the Seminar on Responding to the Consequences of Chemical and Biological Terrorism,* (Washington, D.C.: Government Printing Office, 1995), pp. 1–63.

31. Frederick Sidell, William Patrick, and Thomas Dashiell, *Jane's Chem-Bio Handbook* (Alexandria, Va.: Jane's Information Group, 2000), pp. 237–239.

32. Patrick, "Biological Warfare," p. 5.

33. Fothergill, "The Biological Warfare Threat," p. 26; Patrick, "Biological Warfare," p. 5.

34. The U.S. Army experimented with this method in the 1960s by filling light bulbs with simulant agent and dropping them onto subway tracks. See William Patrick III, "Biological Warfare Scenarios," in Scott P. Layne, Tony J. Beugelsdijk, and C. Kumar N.

efficient means to create an aerosol of properly sized particles. An explosive device also provides an obvious indication of an attack, although the contents of the device may not be determined immediately. Devices employing gaseous energy are more efficient than explosive devices, are widely used in industrial and agricultural applications, and could even be built from scratch.[35]

Contamination of food would be easier to accomplish, since sophisticated aerosolization devices would not be required, and could also infect a large number of people. In 1984, the Rajneesh cult in Oregon successfully infected at least 750 people by contaminating restaurant salad bars.[36] In contrast to popular beliefs, contamination of water supplies is not believed to be an effective method for infecting a large population.[37] Wells, service reservoirs, and water mains serving smaller populations could however be vulnerable.[38] It is also possible to use vectors, such as mosquitoes, fleas, and ticks, to spread disease.[39]

Biological weapons are uniquely suited for covert delivery. Given the small amount of a biological agent needed to infect a large population, the dissemination device for such an agent can be relatively compact. In addition, aerosols of biological weapons are tasteless, odorless, and invisible. Finally, the delayed time of onset for the diseases caused by these biological agents would enable terrorists who employed them in an attack to leave the affected region or even the country before the first victim even became symptomatic. The prospect that a terrorist could conduct a biological weapons attack covertly and escape retaliation reduces the utility of deterrence for preventing such attacks.

Patel, eds., *Firepower in the Lab: Automation in the Fight Against Infectious Diseases and Bioterrorism* (Washington, D.C.: Joseph Henry Press, 2001), p. 223.

35.   William C. Patrick III, "Biological Terrorism and Aerosol Dissemination," *Politics and the Life Sciences* (September 1998), pp. 208–210; Falkenrath, Newman, and Thayer, *America's Achilles' Heel*, pp. 119–123.

36.   Tojork, et al., "A Large Community Outbreak of Salmonellosis," p. 167.

37.   Carus, *Bioterrorism and Biocrimes*, p. 20; Falkenrath, Newman, and Thayer, *America's Achilles' Heel*, p. 120; Sidell, Patrick, and Dashiell, *Jane's Chem-Bio Handbook*, p. 242.

38.   Al Venter, "Poisoned Chalice Poses Problems: The Terrorist Threat to the World's Water," *Jane's Intelligence Review*, (January 1999); W. Dickinson Burrows and Sara E. Renner, "Biological Warfare Agents as Threats to Potable Water," *Environmental Health Perspectives*, Vol. 107, No. 12 (December 1999), pp. 975–984; J.C. Cotterill, *Major Conclusions from a Study of the Feasibility of Clandestine Chemical Attack on Water Supplies in War* (London: Home Office, 1982).

39.   Sidell, Patrick, and Dashiell, *Jane's Chem-Bio Handbook*, p. 242.

TARGETS

Buildings and other confined spaces present an inviting target to a bioterrorist, since releasing an agent indoors reduces the unpredictable effects of the environment on an aerosolized agent, dissemination of an aerosol may be enhanced by a building's air circulation system, and even low concentrations of an agent in a confined space will infect a large number of people, if they are exposed long enough.[40] Releasing an agent indoors would also bypass protective features, such as positive pressure systems and filters on air vents designed to prevent contamination from the outside. Preventing a terrorist from smuggling a small amount of a biological agent and a dispersal device into a building would be extraordinarily difficult.[41]

A terrorist seeking to maximize the number of casualties caused by a biological weapon could conduct an attack so that the victims would be geographically dispersed by the time that they become symptomatic and require hospitalization. This tactic could significantly delay recognition of the attack by physicians or public health personnel by reducing the number of victims presenting at any one medical treatment facility and hinder an effective response by increasing the barriers to communication between medical treatment facilities and public health departments located in different cities, states, or even countries. Based on these criteria, the most likely targets for a bioterrorist seeking to inflict mass casualties would be those that are indoors, have a high volume of traffic, and are frequented by people from outside the city or state in which the target is located. Thus, major transportation hubs, sports arenas, convention centers, special events, and tourist attractions would be the most likely targets for this type of bioterrorist attack. Terrorists more interested in causing mass disruption than mass casualties may select targets for their symbolic importance or adopt tactics that increase the likelihood of an attack being detected early in order to generate higher levels of fear and panic.

Based on the available evidence, it appears that the perpetrator(s) of the fall 2001 anthrax attacks did not intend to cause many, if any, casual-

---

40. Department of Health and Human Services, *Proceedings of the Seminar on Responding to the Consequences of Chemical and Biological Terrorism*, Bethesda, Md. (July 14–15, 1995), pp. 1–59.

41. Biological weapons expert William C. Patrick III reports that he has never been stopped and questioned by security guards at federal buildings or airports regarding the vials of biological simulants and munitions props he carries with him for lectures. William Broad and Judith Miller, "Bill Patrick: Once He Devised Germ Weapons, Now He Defends against Them," *New York Times* (November 3, 1998), p. D1.

ties. Instead the purpose was apparently to generate media attention and political action. Unlike the massively destructive suicide hijackings on September 11, 2001, the anthrax letter attacks seemed to adhere to the axiom that "terrorists want a lot of people watching, not a lot of people dead." This interpretation is supported by the choice of targets—media outlets and U.S. senators—and the enclosure in the letters of notes warning of anthrax or advising the recipient to take penicillin. These features of the attacks ensured intense media coverage and high-level attention by policymakers while minimizing the risk to those opening the letters. Indeed, the fatal cases of anthrax were contracted primarily by postal workers and others who were unknowingly exposed to *B. anthracis* spores.

PLANNING SCENARIOS

Planners must consider three generic scenarios for a biological terrorist event. The first scenario encompasses threats, hoaxes, or suspicious packages involving biological agents. Between 1997 and September 11, 2001, the Federal Bureau of Investigation (FBI) recorded 503 threats to release biological agents, of which the threat most cited was anthrax.[42] In the two months following September 11, 2001, the FBI responded to over 7,000 suspicious anthrax letters, received an estimated 29,000 telephone calls from the public about suspicious packages, and initiated 305 new anthrax related investigations.[43] As the anthrax letter incidents in 2001 demonstrated, these threats and suspicious packages must be taken seriously. If handled improperly, these events will consume valuable resources, cause temporary disruptions for entire buildings or city blocks, and create public panic.[44] A comprehensive strategy for addressing biological terrorism must take these types of incidents into account.[45]

---

42. Prepared Statement of James F. Jarboe, Section Chief, Counterterrorism Division, Federal Bureau of Investigation before the House Judiciary Committee, *Penalties for Terrorism Hoaxes*, November 7, 2001; Prepared Statement of Robert Burnham, Chief, Domestic Terrorism Section, Federal Bureau of Investigation before the House Commerce Committee, Subcommittee on Oversight and Investigation, *Threat of Bioterrorism in America: Assessing the Adequacy of Federal Law Relating to Dangerous Biological Agents,* May 20, 1999.

43. Prepared Statement of James F. Jarboe, Section Chief, Counterterrorism Division, Federal Bureau of Investigation before the House Judiciary Committee, *Penalties for Terrorism Hoaxes,* November 7, 2001.

44. See John Buntin, *Anthrax Threats in Southern California,* Case No. 1577, Case Program, John F. Kennedy School of Government, Harvard University, Cambridge, Mass., May 2000.

45. Leonard A. Cole, "Bioterrorism Threats: Learning From Inappropriate Responses," in Lloyd Novick and John Marr, eds., *Public Health Issues in Disaster Preparedness* (Gaithersburg, Md.: Aspen Publishers, 2001), pp. 64–74.

The second scenario, the no-notice release of a pathogen, is the most challenging bioterrorism scenario. Historically, fewer than five percent of actual or attempted conventional terrorist bombings have been preceded by a threat.[46] Terrorism analyst Bruce Hoffman has noted the emergence of a trend in the 1990s in which responsibility for the most lethal terrorist attacks goes unclaimed.[47] In addition, by providing notice, a terrorist would negate one of the primary advantages of biological weapons: the difficulty in diagnosing and recognizing an attack in time to provide effective treatment. Warning the authorities of an impending attack would also prevent the terrorists from taking full advantage of the disease's incubation period to cover their tracks and avoid capture. Although the anthrax letter attacks demonstrated that terrorists may be willing to forgo the element of surprise in order maximize disruption rather than casualties, a no-notice release presents the most difficult challenge and therefore, should be the primary basis for emergency response planning.

The third scenario is a credible threat of a biological terrorist attack. There have been no publicly reported cases of this occurring. In 1997, however, FBI Director Louis Freeh stated that most threats to use chemical or biological weapons, "have made little mention of the type of device or delivery system to be employed, and for this reason have been deemed technically not feasible. Some threats have been validated."[48] The FBI, with the assistance of other agencies, conducts threat assessments based on behavioral, technical, and operational criteria.[49] Once a threat has been validated and is deemed credible, the FBI will notify the Department of Homeland Security and other relevant federal agencies.[50] The extent to which federal, state, and local agencies have examined and addressed this type of scenario has not been analyzed in any systematic fashion.

---

46. Department of Justice, *State and Local Domestic Preparedness Stakeholders Forum*, Washington, D.C., August 27–28, 1998, p. 28.

47. Bruce Hoffman, "Why Terrorists Don't Claim Credit," *Terrorism and Political Violence*, Vol. 9, No. 1 (Spring 1997), pp. 1–6.

48. Statement of Louis Freeh, Director, Federal Bureau of Investigation, before the Senate Appropriations Committee Hearing on Counterterrorism, May 13, 1997.

49. Senate Committee on the Judiciary, Subcommittee on Technology, Terrorism and Government Information, *Biological Weapons: The Threat Posed by Terrorists* (Washington, D.C.: Government Printing Office, 1998), pp. 146–147.

50. Office of Homeland Security, *National Strategy for Homeland Security* (Washington, D.C.: White House, July 2002), pp. 16–17.

CHARACTERISTICS OF A BIOTERRORISM INCIDENT

The characteristics of any biological terrorist attack will be highly dependent on the agent employed, the delivery system chosen, and the venue targeted. It is possible, however, to make some generalizations based on the biological agents of greatest concern. First, a biological attack via aerosol is unlikely to be detected until patients present with symptoms, unless biological aerosol detection equipment is present where the attack is conducted. Contamination of food and water can also be done covertly. Second, the first indicators of the attack may be individuals seeking medical attention, either from their own doctors or hospital emergency departments. Thus, in the event of a biological terrorist attack, doctors, nurses, and epidemiologists will be the first responders, not police officers and firefighters. Third, the initial symptoms of many biological agents are either nonspecific or are similar to those of naturally occurring diseases.[51] The initial symptoms of agents such as anthrax, tularemia, staphylococcal enterotoxin B (SEB), and Q fever mirror those of influenza. A few diseases such as plague, smallpox, and the viral hemorrhagic fevers cause lesions, rashes, and other cutaneous manifestations that could alert a doctor to the presence of an agent of biological terrorism.[52] Unless physicians have a heightened index of suspicion based on clinical observations or epidemiological features of an outbreak, however, early victims of a bioterrorist attack are likely to be misdiagnosed with more common and less severe illnesses, such as influenza.[53] The proper treatment of several victims of inhalation anthrax in fall 2001 was delayed due to misdiagnosis.[54]

---

51. *Medical Management of Biological Casualties Handbook, Fourth Edition* (Frederick, Md.: United States Army Research Institute of Infectious Diseases, February 2001), pp. 10–11.

52. By the time these cutaneous manifestations typically present, however, the disease is no longer responsive to medical treatment. In addition, since these diseases are all contagious, those with whom the patient has had close contact, as well as the patient's health care providers, may already have been infected by the time the disease is diagnosed. Thomas McGovern, George Christopher, and Edward Eitzen, "Cutaneous Manifestations of Biological Warfare and Related Threat Agents," *Archives of Dermatology* 135 (March 1999), pp. 311–322.

53. In examining patients with a fever and a cough, sore throat, hoarseness, or a head cold, doctors correctly ruled out bacteria as a cause of infection 60 percent of the time and correctly identified bacteria as the cause 50 percent of the time. David Lieberman, Pesach Shvartzman, Igor Koronosky, and Devora Lieberman, "Aetiology of Respiratory Tract Infections: Clinical Assessment versus Serological Tests," *British Journal of General Practice*, Vol. 51, No. 473 (2001), pp. 998–1000.

54. John A. Jernigan, "Bioterrrorism-Related Inhalation Anthrax: The First 10 Cases

Fourth, to be effective, treatment of many diseases caused by biological weapons must begin before the onset of symptoms or shortly after onset.[55] Therefore, an incorrect diagnosis could mean that the patient does not receive the proper, and possibly lifesaving, medical treatment for the agent to which he or she has been exposed. Standard laboratory analysis of clinical specimens requires growing samples of organisms in culture, which could take 24 to 48 hours.[56] Of the agents of greatest concern, anthrax, tularemia, and some of the viral hemorrhagic fevers respond to medical treatments initiated more than 24 hours after the patient becomes symptomatic. The cases of inhalation anthrax in 2001 demonstrated a survival rate of 55 percent, a significant improvement over earlier rates of 10–20 percent.[57] However, this success was dependent on the early initiation of appropriate antibiotic treatment.[58]

Fifth, unlike other forms of terrorism, the effects of bioterrorism are delayed. The incubation period of a biological agent varies depending on such factors such as the virulence of the pathogen, the dose received, and the strength of the individual's immune system. As a result, the onset of symptoms among the infected population could be distributed over a period of days to weeks, roughly in the shape of a bell curve. This characteristic of bioterrorism provides the public health system with a window of opportunity to recognize that an outbreak is underway and to begin investigating its scope, source, and severity.[59] Thus, the initial epidemiolog-

---

Reported in the United States," *Emerging Infectious Diseases*, Vol. 7, No. 6 (November–December 2001), pp. 933–944.

55. *Medical Management of Biological Casualties Handbook*, p. 11.

56. Institute of Medicine and National Research Council, *Chemical and Biological Terrorism: Research and Development to Improve Civilian Medical Response* (Washington, D.C.: National Academy Press, 1999), p. 79.

57. John A. Jernigan, et al., "Bioterrorism-related Inhalational Anthrax: The First 10 Cases Reported in the United States," *Emerging Infectious Diseases*, Vol. 7, No. 6 (November–December 2001), pp. 933–944; Thom A. Mayer, et al., "Clinical Presentation of Inhalational Anthrax Following Bioterrorism Exposure: Report of 2 Surviving Patients," *Journal of the American Medical Association*, Vol. 286, No. 20 (November 28, 2001), pp. 2549–2553; Luciano Borio, et al, "Death Due to Bioterrorism-Related Inhalational Anthrax: Report of 2 Patients," *Journal of the American Medical Association*, Vol. 286, No. 20 (November 28, 2001), pp. 2554–2559.

58. Of the six patients who received antibiotics with activity against *B. anthracis* on the same day that they were admitted to the hospital, all six survived. Four patients were already exhibiting fulminant signs of illness when they first received antibiotics with activity against *B. anthracis,* and all four died. Jernigan, p. 940.

59. An act of bioterrorism is likely to expose more members of a population to a pathogen simultaneously, resulting in a more compressed epidemic curve than a natu-

ical investigations in a bioterrorism attack may be triggered by reports of a large or unusual outbreak of influenza given the time of year or an outbreak of an unknown or unusual disease.[60]

Sixth, there is a significant potential for person-to-person transmission of some diseases. Plague, smallpox, and some of the viral hemorrhagic fevers are contagious and can be spread from person to person with varying degrees of ease. Smallpox is the most communicable of the critical agents. In 1970, a single case of smallpox in Germany resulted in 19 other cases, the quarantine of an entire hospital, including staff and patients for four weeks, and the vaccination of 100,000 people.[61] On average, each case of smallpox can be expected to infect 10 other individuals.[62] In Madagascar in 1997, one patient with pneumonic plague transmitted the disease to 18 other people.[63] Therefore, early diagnosis of a contagious disease is crucial for enabling medical treatment facilities to protect their staff and other patients from infection, as well as to begin treating people who have had contact with infected individuals.[64]

Finally, there is an important, but poorly understood, psychological component to biological terrorism.[65] Although all forms of terrorism aim

---

ral outbreak. Outbreaks of foodborne illnesses can also present a compressed epidemic curve, however, so this is not a definitive indicator of bioterrorism. Julie Pavlin, "Epidemiology of Bioterrorism," *Emerging Infectious Diseases*, Vol. 5, No. 4 (July–August 1999).

60.   Outbreaks of rare diseases or diseases not endemic to the area are not necessarily indicators of bioterrorism, however, as the West Nile Virus outbreak in New York City in late 1999 demonstrated.

61.   D. A. Henderson, "Bioterrorism as a Public Health Threat," *Emerging Infectious Diseases*, Vol. 4 (July–September 1998).

62.   D. A. Henderson's testimony before Senate Appropriations Committee and Senate Veterans Affairs Committee, *Bioterrorism: Domestic Weapons of Mass Destruction* (Washington, D.C.: Government Printing Office, 2000), p. 56.

63.   M. Ratsitorahina et al., "Epidemiological and Diagnostic Aspects of the Outbreak of Pneumonic Plague in Madagascar," *Lancet* (January 8, 2000), pp. 111–113, cited in Thomas Inglesby et al., "Plague as a Biological Weapon: Medical and Public Health Management," *Journal of the American Medical Association*, Vol. 283, No. 7 (May 3, 2000), p. 2283.

64.   Joseph Barbera, et al., "Large-Scale Quarantine Following Biological Terrorism in the United States," *Journal of the American Medical Association*, Vol. 268, No. 21, December 5, 2001, pp. 2711–2717.

65.   For studies on the potential psychological effects of a biological terrorism attack, see Cleto DiGiovanni, "Domestic Terrorism with Chemical or Biological Agents: Psychiatric Aspects," *American Journal of Psychiatry* (October 1999), pp. 1500–1505; David Siegrist, "Behavioral Aspects of a Biological Terrorism Incident," presentation to the Association for Politics and the Life Sciences Convention, Atlanta, Georgia, September

to intimidate and influence governments or particular segments of the population, the use of disease-causing organisms, particularly contagious ones, would add a new and more horrifying dimension to an attack. As Harvard University political scientist Jessica Stern has noted, although one cannot predict ahead of time the scope of a biological terrorism attack, "what we can predict is that the radius of psychological damage would exceed that of injury and death."[66] Biological weapons are insidious, mysterious, frightening, and unknown. The association of disease and pestilence in biblical texts as forms of divine wrath adds to their mystique. As the anthrax letter attacks demonstrated, a biological terrorism attack could have a direct effect psychological impact not only on the victims, their families, and individuals involved in responding to the attack but on the nation as a whole.[67] Public anxiety regarding biological terrorism manifested itself by runs on gas masks, hoarding of antibiotics, and measures to reduce the possibility of contracting anthrax from contaminated mail.[68]

IMPLICATIONS

Responding to an attack with a biological weapon is fundamentally different from responding to other terrorist attacks, even those involving nuclear or chemical weapons. Health care providers and public health officials will be the first responders to such an attack. As the anthrax letter attacks demonstrated, the current level of preparedness for responding to even a small-scale biological terrorist attack is low. This low level of readiness is driven by the nature of the modern health care system, exacerbated by the traditional lack of communication between the medical and public health communities, and reinforced by the long-term neglect of both communities by public safety and national security agencies.

The first opportunity for a disease outbreak to be recognized as an act

---

2, 1999; Anne Norwood, "Psychiatric Aspects of Chem/Bioterrorism," presentation to the American Medical Association Annual Meeting, Chicago, Illinois, June 19, 1999, <www.ama-assn.org/meetings/public/annual99/edu/norwood.ppt>.

66. Jessica Stern, *The Ultimate Terrorists* (Cambridge, Mass.: Harvard University Press, 1999), p. 30.

67. Robert Blendon, et al., "The Impact of the Anthrax Attacks on the American Public," *Medscape General Medicine* Vol. 4, No. 2, 2002.

68. Don Oldenburg, "Stocking Up in Hopes Of Breathing Easier," *Washington Post,* October 10, 2001, p. C01; Melody Petersen and Robert Pear, "Anthrax Fears Send Demand for a Drug Far Beyond Output," *New York Times,* October 16, 2001, p. A1; Ceci Connolly and Ellen Nakashima, "CDC Sets 'Tips' on Handling Mail; Precautions Aimed at Cutting Risk From Anthrax Traces," *Washington Post,* December 6, 2001, p. A26.

of biological terrorism would present itself to physicians in emergency departments, intensive care units, and primary care settings. In medical school, students are trained with the maxim, "when you hear hoofbeats, think horses, not zebras." Anecdotal evidence suggests that the index of suspicion for biological agents of concern is still fairly low. As recently as 1999, only one of 17 doctors in the Pittsburgh area was able to recognize the distinctive rash caused by smallpox.[69] A similar test was conducted at Johns Hopkins University Hospital, and none of the doctors quizzed recognized the symptoms of inhalation anthrax.[70] Two-thirds of the respondents to a more scientific survey of emergency medicine physicians conducted in 1998 considered their ability to recognize and clinically manage victims of biological terrorism to be less than adequate.[71] More recent surveys of hospital preparedness for WMD incidents also indicate that significant shortfalls exist in training, planning, and equipment.[72] Thus, the first wave of victims of a biological terrorist attack is unlikely to receive proper treatment or trigger an alarm, unless physicians have a heightened index of suspicion.[73]

In addition, the capacity of the medical community to manage a large-scale outbreak of infectious disease is low. During planning for a biological terrorism tabletop exercise held in Boston, hospital representatives indicated that as few as 80 patients requiring critical care would saturate their patient care capabilities.[74] In recent years, hospitals have been cutting beds and staff to minimize excess capacity, and cities have been

---

69. "Pittsburgh Doctors Fail Pop Quiz Testing Reaction to Mock Outbreak," *Associated Press*, February 14, 2000.

70. John G. Bartlett prepared statement before the Senate Committee on Health, Education, Labor and Pensions Subcommittee on Public Health in *Bioterrorism: Our Frontline Response; Evaluating U.S. Public Health and Medical Readiness* (Washington, D.C.: Government Printing Office, 1999), p. 46.

71. N. Pesik, M. Keim, and T.R. Sampson, "Do US Emergency Medicine Residency Programs Provide Adequate Training for Bioterrorism?" *Annals of Emergency Medicine*, Vol. 34, No. 2 (August 1999), p. 175.

72. Donald C. Wetter, William E. Daniell, and Charles D. Treser, "Hospital Preparedness for Victims of Chemical or Biological Terrorism," *American Journal of Public Health*, Vol. 91, No. 5 (May 2001), pp. 710–716; Kimberly N. Treat, et al., "Hospital Preparedness for Weapons of Mass Destruction Incidents: An Initial Assessment," *Annals of Emergency Medicine*, Vol. 38, No. 5 (November 2001), pp. 562–565.

73. Christopher Richards, Johnathan Burstein, Joseph Waeckerle, and H. Range Hutson, "Emergency Physicians and Biological Terrorism," *Annals of Emergency Medicine*, Vol. 34, No. 2 (August 1999), pp. 183–190.

74. Gregory Koblentz, *Enhancing Massachusetts' Preparedness for Biological Terrorism*, Master's Thesis, John F. Kennedy School of Government, April 6, 1999, p. 21.

losing emergency departments as a result of cost-cutting measures. Based on experience with the 1999–2000 flu season, serious shortages of health care providers and beds are expected to develop during a large outbreak.[75] Financial pressures also severely limit the ability of hospitals and doctors to enhance their preparedness.[76] Unlike fire departments, emergency medical services, and law enforcement agencies, there is typically no established mutual aid system for health care facilities. In the event of a bioterrorism incident that affects a wide geographic area or has the potential to do so, hospitals that are hard pressed to maintain the standard of care for their regular flow of patients may be unable or unwilling to provide assistance to other facilities. There is also the risk that even a small outbreak, magnified by media reports, could overwhelm local medical facilities with the "worried well."

The public health surveillance system currently in place at state and local levels is incapable of detecting a bioterrorism incident in a timely fashion. Currently, the public health system relies on physicians and laboratories to submit to their public health department, usually by facsimile or mail, reports of notifiable diseases or unusual outbreaks.[77] Such passive surveillance systems, however, are "notorious for their poor sensitivity, lack of timeliness, and minimal coverage [and] the quality of information is greatly limited."[78] In addition, "the reliability of passive surveillance systems is often quite low."[79] Thus, the public health system may not be able to detect an outbreak and identify its parameters in time to initiate an effective response.[80] Less than 10 percent of county public

---

75. Monica Schoch-Spana, "Hospitals Buckle during Normal Flu Season: Implications for Bioterrorism Response," *Biodefense Quarterly*, Vol. 1, No. 4 (March 2000), p. 1.

76. Joseph A. Barbera, Anthony G. Macintyre, and Craig A. DeAtley, *Ambulances to Nowhere: America's Critical Shortfall in Medical Preparedness for Catastrophic Terrorism*, Executive Session on Domestic Preparedness Discussion Paper ESDP-2001–07, John F. Kennedy School of Government, Harvard University, Cambridge, Mass., October 2001.

77. The list of notifiable diseases is compiled by state and federal epidemiologists, but the CDC has no authority to force states to adopt the CDC's preferred list. Therefore, the list of notifiable diseases varies slightly from state to state. The CDC-developed list includes anthrax, botulism, plague, and tularemia, but not smallpox or the viral hemorrhagic fevers. CDC, *Nationally Notifiable Infectious Diseases, United States*, 2000, <www.cdc.gov/epo/dphsi/infdis.htm>.

78. Institute of Medicine and National Research Council, *Chemical and Biological Terrorism*, p. 66.

79. Ibid., p. 67.

80. Michael T. Osterholm, Guthrie S. Birkhead, and Rebecca A. Meriwether, "Impediments to Public Health Surveillance in the 1990s: The Lack of Resources and the Need

health departments report that they are fully prepared for biological terrorism.[81] Deficiencies affecting state and local public health departments include the lack of comprehensive response plans, sufficient numbers of properly trained personnel, robust communication capabilities, and advanced laboratory detection systems.[82]

Another important implication of a no-notice release is that unless federal response assets are pre-positioned at the site of a release because of a special event, local and state governments will have to rely on their own resources until federal assistance can be mobilized and deployed. In addition, specialized military WMD terrorism response units at the state and national level, such as the National Guard's Weapons of Mass Destruction Civil Support Teams (WMD-CSTs, formerly known as RAID teams) and the Marine Corps' Chemical Biological Incident Response Force (CBIRF), have few of the capabilities required to assist state and local authorities in detecting a covert bioterrorist attack or treating bioterrorism casualties. As a result, the foundation of U.S. biological terrorism preparedness must be enhancing state and local capabilities for detecting and responding to outbreaks of infectious diseases. Programs to achieve this goal are described in the next section.

Origin and Evolution of Biological Terrorism Preparedness Programs

BACKGROUND

Concerted efforts to prepare for an act of biological terrorism in the United States did not emerge until 1998. The focus of the early domestic preparedness efforts, initiated in 1996, centered on chemical terrorism, motivated by Aum Shinrikyo's development and use of the nerve gas sarin. The primary recipients of federal domestic preparedness assistance were the traditional first responders: law enforcement agencies, fire departments, hazardous materials teams, bomb squads, and emergency medical services.[83] During the initial phase of this domestic preparedness

for Priorities," *Journal of Public Health Management Practice,* Vol. 2, No. 4 (1996) pp. 11–15.

81.   National Association of Counties, *America Secure: A Survey of County Public Health Needs and Preparedness,* January 2002, <www.naco.org/pubs/surveys/pubhealth/ pubhlth.pdf>.

82.   National Association of County and City Health Officials, "Assessment of Local Bioterrorism and Emergency Preparedness," *Research Briefs,* October 2001; Association of Public Health Laboratories, "State Public Health Laboratory Bioterrorism Capacity," *Public Health Laboratories Issues in Brief,* October 2002.

83.   For a summary of federal domestic preparedness efforts, see Gregory Koblentz,

initiative, biological weapons were lumped into the "chem-bio threat," and the unique challenges posed by biological weapons were not fully recognized. By 1998, however, several programs were underway to address the threat posed by biological terrorism.

White House interest in biological terrorism was piqued by a federal interagency tabletop exercise held in March 1998 that revealed significant gaps in the nation's preparedness for biological terrorism.[84] In April of that year, President Clinton and senior federal officials met with a group of outside experts to discuss the role of biotechnology in responding to the threat of biological weapons.[85] This group submitted a plan to the president in early May, recommending improvements in both research and development and public health surveillance and the creation of a national stockpile of drugs and vaccines to counter a biological terrorist attack. The cost of these efforts over five years was estimated at $420 million.[86] Later that month, President Clinton announced a major new initiative to enhance preparedness for biological terrorism, including the creation of a civilian stockpile of pharmaceuticals and stepped-up research on new drugs and diagnostic tools.[87] In June, the White House requested that an additional $294 million be added to the administration's request for domestic preparedness programs, including funding for the pharmaceutical stockpile, increased research and development, and enhancing public health surveillance.[88]

Preparing for biological terrorism involves a range of activities undertaken by multiple agencies at the local, state, and federal levels of government, as well as private entities, such as hospitals and health care

---

Overview of Federal Programs to Enhance State and Local Capability to Respond to WMD Terrorism, ESDP Discussion Paper ESDP-2001–03, John F. Kennedy School of Government, Harvard University, April 2001.

84. Judith Miller and William Broad, "Exercise Finds U.S. Unable to Handle Germ War Threat," *New York Times,* April 26, 1998, p. A1.

85. White House, "Roundtable on Genetic Engineering and Biological Weapons," press release April 10, 1998.

86. William Broad and Judith Miller, "Germ Defense Plan in Peril as Its Flaws Are Revealed," *New York Times,* August 7, 1998.

87. White House, press release, "Remarks by the President at the United States Naval Academy Commencement" (May 22, 1998).

88. White House, press release, "President Requests Additional Funding for Protection against Biological and Chemical Terrorism," press release, June 9, 1998. According to Frank Young, former director of the Office of Emergency Preparedness (OEP) and moderator for the April 1998 meeting, of about 75 percent of the group's recommendations were included in this funding request. Lois Ember, "Bioterrorism: Combating the Threat," *Chemical and Engineering News,* July 5, 1999, p. 15.

providers.[89] The General Accounting Office has identified 20 federal agencies that have a role in preparing for or responding to biological terrorism.[90] Key agencies that play important roles in preparing for and responding to biological terrorism are the Department of Health and Human Services (HHS), Department of Homeland Security (DHS), Department of Defense (DOD), Department of Energy (DOE), Department of Justice (DOJ), and Department of Veteran Affairs (VA).[91]

The primary beneficiary of this increased focus on the threat of biological terrorism was the Department of Health and Human Services (HHS). Under a May 22, 1998, Presidential Decision Directive (PDD) 62, "Protection Against Unconventional Threats to the Homeland and Americans Overseas," HHS was designated "the lead agency to plan and to prepare for a national response to medical emergencies arising from the terrorist use of weapons of mass destruction."[92] HHS also received a majority of the new funding for countering bioterrorism during this period. As a result of the White House initiative in mid-1998, the HHS budget for domestic preparedness increased from $16 million in 1998 to $255 million in 2000.[93] HHS received $290 million for domestic preparedness activities in 2001 and, in early 2001, requested $348 million for 2002.[94] As a result of the department's increased involvement in counterterrorism and homeland security planning, HHS Secretary Donna Shalala observed, "This is the first time in American history in which the public health system has been integrated directly into the national security system."[95] Prior to the

---

89. For a comprehensive discussion of the role of interagency and intergovernmental coordination in domestic preparedness, see Arnold Howitt and Gregory Koblentz, "Organizational Capacity and Coordination: Obstacles and Opportunities for Preparing for Domestic Terrorism," discussion paper, Executive Session on Domestic Preparedness, Cambridge, Mass., forthcoming.

90. General Accounting Office, *Bioterrorism: Review of Public Health Preparedness Programs*, GAO-02–149T, October 10, 2001, p. 8.

91. For a summary of the research and preparedness activities of these agencies, see General Accounting Office, *Bioterrorism: Federal Research and Preparedness Activities*, GAO-01–915, September 2001.

92. Presentation by Matthew Payne, HHS Liaison to the National Domestic Preparedness Office, at Defense Week Conference, "Weapons of Mass Destruction and Domestic Preparedness III: Interoperability & the Medical Management of a Bio-Terrorist Incident," Washington, D.C., November 3, 1999.

93. Office of Management and Budget, *Annual Report to Congress on Combating Terrorism*, July 2001, p. 8.

94. Ibid.

95. Office of the White House Press Secretary, "Press Briefing by Attorney General

creation of the Department of Homeland Security, three organizations within HHS were responsible for preparations to detect and respond to a biological terrorism incident and to enhance local bioterrorism preparedness: the Office of Emergency Preparedness (OEP), the Centers for Disease Control and Prevention (CDC), and Health Resources and Services Administration (HRSA).[96]

OEP, located within the U.S. Public Health Service, originally had the responsibility within HHS for managing and coordinating federal health, medical, and health-related social services for major emergencies and federally declared disasters, including acts of terrorism. OEP was the first federal agency to begin preparing local first responders for a terrorist attack involving a WMD, with the establishment of the first Metropolitan Medical Strike Team (MMST) in 1995, in the Washington, D.C., metropolitan area. This system became the prototype for the Metropolitan Medical Response Systems (MMRS) that OEP established in 97 cities between 1997 and 2002.[97] OEP is also a participant in the National Disaster Medical System (NDMS), a joint effort between federal agencies and private hospitals throughout the nation to provide medical treatment to casual-

---

Janet Reno, Secretary of HHS Donna Shalala, and Richard Clarke, President's National Coordinator for Security, Infrastructure and Counterterrorism," January 22, 1999.

96. Research and development of new technologies to detect, treat, or counter biological weapons is vital to long-term bioterrorism preparedness but is outside of the scope of this chapter. Bioterrorism research within HHS is conducted primarily by the National Institute of Allergy and Infectious Diseases (NIAID) of the National Institutes of Health (NIH). See National Institute of Allergy and Infectious Diseases, *NIAID Biodefense Research Agenda for CDC Category A Agents*, February 2002 and National Institute of Allergy and Infectious Diseases, *NIAID Strategic Plan for Biodefense Research*, February 2002.

For information on bioterrorism-related research conducted by the Department of Defense, see Department of Defense, *Chemical and Biological Defense Program, Volume 1: Annual Report to Congress*, April 2000; *Report of the Defense Science Board 2000 Summer Study on Defense Against Biological Weapons: Leveraging Advances in Biotechnology and Medical Informatics to Improve Homeland Biodefense Capabilities* (Washington, D.C.: Office of the Undersecretary of Defense for Acquisition, Technology and Logistics, October 2001); *Report of the Defense Science Board/Threat Reduction Advisory Committee Task Force on Biological Defense* (Washington, D.C.: Office of the Undersecretary of Defense for Acquisition, Technology and Logistics, June 2001).

For information on bioterrorism-related research conducted by the Department of Energy, see Department of Energy, *Chemical and Biological Nonproliferation Program Strategic Plan* (Washington, D.C.: Department of Energy, 1999) and National Nuclear Security Administration, *Chemical and Biological National Security Program FY00 Annual Report* (Washington, D.C.: Department of Energy, March 2001).

97. Prepared Statement of D.A. Henderson, Director, Office of Public Health Preparedness, Department of Health and Human Service before the House Science Committee, *Science of Bioterrorism: Is the Federal Government Prepared?*, December 5, 2001.

ties of a war or major disaster. OEP has trained and equipped four volunteer medical teams, called National Medical Response Teams (NMRT)s, which are part of NDMS, to be able to provide medical treatment to the victims of a chemical or biological weapon attack.[98]

The mission of the CDC is "to promote health and quality of life by preventing and controlling disease, injury, and disability."[99] In late 1998, CDC established its Bioterrorism Preparedness and Response Program (BPRP) to lead an agency-wide effort to prepare for and respond to acts of terrorism that involve the actual, threatened, or suspected use of biological or chemical agents. In addition to upgrading CDC's epidemiological, surveillance, and laboratory capabilities, BPRP also initiated a grant program in 1999 to improve the capacities of municipal and state health departments to detect and respond to a terrorist attack involving a biological or chemical agent. Between 1999 and 2001, CDC awarded more than $130 million in grants to support these programs at the state and local levels.[100] Besides providing grants specifically designed to enhance public health laboratories, CDC established the Laboratory Response Network (LRN) to link public health departments at all levels to advanced diagnostic capabilities. The network is designed to increase the number of laboratories capable of detecting critical biological agents, reduce the time needed to confirm the presence of a critical agent in a clinical or environmental sample, and improve the communication of testing results within the public health community.[101] CDC also established the Health Alert Network (HAN) to provide state and local public health agencies with more sophisticated communications capabilities to facilitate public health surveillance, information sharing, and distance training. Finally, CDC established a National Pharmaceutical Stockpile (now known as the Strategic National Stockpile) to ensure that sufficient quantities of antibiotics, vaccines, and medical supplies can be rapidly supplied to jurisdictions targeted by a biological weapons attack.

The mission of the Health Resources and Services Administration is to improve the nation's health by extending health care services to underserved populations, particularly women, children, and rural

---

98. Robert Knouss, "NDMS," *Public Health Reports,* Vol. 116, Supplement 2 (2001) pp. 49–52.

99. CDC website, <www.cdc.gov/aboutcdc.htm>.

100. Prepared Statement of D.A. Henderson, Director, Office of Public Health Preparedness, Department of Health and Human Service before the House Science Committee, *Science of Bioterrorism: Is the Federal Government Prepared?*, December 5, 2001.

101. CDC, "Biological and Chemical Terrorism," p. 10.

areas.[102] HRSA became involved in bioterrorism preparedness after the anthrax letter incidents highlighted the importance of hospitals and health care providers in detecting and responding to biological terrorism. In 2002, HRSA established a Bioterrorism Hospital Preparedness Program for the states and three largest cities (Chicago, Los Angeles, and New York) to upgrade the readiness of health care facilities to handle a bioterrorism incident. This grant program will support efforts by hospitals to develop comprehensive response plans, conduct needs assessments, upgrade laboratory and decontamination infrastructure, acquire personal protection equipment, and conduct training and exercises for health care providers.[103]

Following the terrorist attacks on September 11, 2001 and the subsequent anthrax letter attacks, the Bush administration launched a major initiative to enhance U.S. preparedness for terrorism. The centerpiece of the Bush administration's efforts to enhance the nation's preparedness for terrorism is the creation of a Department of Homeland Security, which was signed into law in late November 2002 and officially established in late January 2003. In addition, funding for homeland security was dramatically increased. Both of these actions will have a dramatic impact on U.S. preparedness for biological terrorism.

BIOTERRORISM PREPAREDNESS AND THE DEPARTMENT OF HOMELAND SECURITY

On June 6, 2002, President Bush proposed merging 22 federal agencies with responsibilities for different aspects of homeland security into the cabinet-level Department of Homeland Security (DHS). The creation of this department, with more than 170,000 employees, resulted in the largest federal government reorganization since the end of World War II. The new department is responsible for guarding the nation's borders, protecting transportation systems and other critical infrastructure, enhancing the preparedness of state and local first responders, coordinating research and development relevant to homeland security, managing federal emergency response activities, analyzing terrorism-related intelligence, and coordinating bioterrorism preparedness programs.

With regard to biological terrorism preparedness, the Department of

---

102. Health Resources and Services Administration, "Role and Function in Relation to Emergency Preparedness and Reaction," undated, <www.hrsa.gov/bioterrorism.htm>.

103. Health Resources and Services Administration, *Bioterrorism Hospital Preparedness Program Cooperative Agreement Guidance*, February 15, 2002, <www.hrsa.gov/bioterrorism.htm>.

Homeland Security has absorbed the office of the Assistant Secretary for Public Health Emergency Preparedness, including the Office of Emergency Preparedness, the National Disaster Medical System, and the Metropolitan Medical Response System, from HHS and the Strategic National Stockpile from CDC.[104] The transfer of OEP and its related programs will strengthen the ability of DHS to serve as the single source of federal assistance for state and local first responders. The expansion of the CDC's pharmaceutical stockpile into a strategic reserve of crucial supplies for use in responding to nuclear, biological, chemical, radiological, or conventional terrorist attacks warranted its transfer to DHS. In addition, DHS is to sponsor efforts to develop a national biological terrorism detection system based on public health surveillance and the monitoring of private databases as well as networks of sensors to detect the release of pathogens in densely populated areas.[105] With regards to research and development relevant to biological terrorism, DHS will take over several programs run by the Departments of Energy and Defense. HHS will continue to set priorities, objectives, goals, and policies for its research on bioterrorism countermeasures while developing a coordinated research strategy with DHS.[106]

The reorganization of homeland security responsibilities raised some concerns about its adverse impact on biological terrorism preparedness. Public health-related programs have a dual purpose: to enhance preparedness for biological terrorism and naturally occurring infectious disease outbreaks. The infrastructure, planning, and expertise developed using grants from these programs is designed to upgrade the day-to-day capabilities of public health agencies, as well as their ability to respond to a mass casualty attack or public health emergency. Granting DHS control over these programs, including the responsibility for setting program priorities, could have impeded efforts to integrate bioterrorism-related assistance into the broader mission of preventing, detecting, and responding

---

104. The position of the Assistant Secretary for Public Health Emergency Preparedness, with responsibility for OEP, NDMS and MMRS, was created on June 12, 2002, under The Public Health Security and Bioterrorism Preparedness and Response Act of 2002 (Public Law 107–188).

105. Judith Miller, "U.S. Is Deploying A Monitor System for Germ Attacks," *New York Times*, January 22, 2003, p. A1; William Broad and Judith Miller, "Health Data Monitored for Bioterror Warning," *New York Times*, January 27, 2003, p. A1.

106. Details on the reorganization of homeland security responsibilities and the establishment of the Department of Homeland Security can be found in: President George W. Bush, *The Department of Homeland Security*, June 2002; Homeland Security Act of 2002; Office of Homeland Security, *Department of Homeland Security Reorganization Plan*, November 25, 2002. All available at <www.whitehouse.gov/homeland/>.

to outbreaks of infectious disease and other public health emergencies.[107] As a result of these concerns, HHS retains responsibility for setting the priorities and goals of programs to enhance state and local preparedness for bioterrorism to DHS. The legislation establishing DHS tasks HHS with coordinating its bioterrorism strategy with DHS and collaborating with the department to measure the progress of its bioterrorism preparedness efforts.[108]

FUNDING FOR BIOTERRORISM PREPAREDNESS

The homeland security reorganization effort has been accompanied by a massive increase in spending on homeland security and bioterrorism preparedness. The Bush administration has dramatically expanded and accelerated existing bioterrorism preparedness programs and established new programs to enhance the readiness of hospitals and health care providers. On January 10, 2002, President George W. Bush signed an appropriations bill containing $2.9 billion for the bioterrorism preparedness programs of HHS, 10 times as much as spent in 2001.[109] In 2002, the Strategic National Stockpile program received $645 million to increase the number of ready-to-deploy caches of pharmaceutical and medical supplies from eight to 12 and to expand the holdings of anti-anthrax antibiotics sixfold. In addition, $512 million was used to purchase 204 million doses of smallpox vaccine. CDC received $116 million to enhance its laboratory and epidemiological capacity. During 2002, HHS disbursed over $1.1 billion to state and local public health agencies, municipalities, and hospitals. CDC provided $918 million in grants to state public health agencies, while OEP provided $51 million to communities for emergency preparedness and $20 million to expand MMRS to 25 additional cities (bringing the total to 122 cities representing 80 percent of the nation's population). A new program established by HRSA to provide bioterrorism-related training, equipment, and exercises to hospitals disbursed $125 million in 2002. Finally, the National Institutes of Health (NIH) received $248 million for research on defenses against biological weapons.[110]

---

107. General Accounting Office, *Homeland Security: New Department Could Improve Coordination but May Complicate Public Health Priority Setting*, GAO-02–883T, June 25, 2002; Marilyn Werber Serafini, "Public Health Officials Nervous About Plan to Move HHS Agencies," *Government Executive Magazine*, September 24, 2002.

108. See Section 305 of The Homeland Security Act of 2002 (H.R. 5005).

109. "Bioterror Funding Provides Blueprint to Build a Strong New Public Health Infrastructure," *HHS News*, January 25, 2002.

110. Ibid.

Perhaps the most innovative aspect of this new initiative is the requirement that states develop bioterrorism preparedness and response plans to be eligible for the bulk of HHS bioterrorism funding. States are expected to develop plans for responding to biological terrorism or natural disease outbreaks, assess their capabilities to implement their plans, and indicate how they will use grant assistance to build the capabilities necessary to realize their plans. In 2002, HHS distributed over $1.1 billion to upgrade state and local public health infrastructure and enhance hospital preparedness: 20 percent was distributed in January with the other 80 percent following in June, after HHS reviewed the bioterrorism preparedness plans submitted by the states.[111] This requirement provides a strong incentive for states to improve the coordination of their bioterrorism preparedness efforts, incorporate private health care institutions into preparedness planning, and develop comprehensive plans for detecting and responding to infectious disease outbreaks.

In February 2002, President Bush requested $37.7 billion for homeland security in 2003, up from $19.5 billion in 2002. Of this amount, $5.9 billion would be for bioterrorism, up from $5.1 billion in 2002. Under this proposal, HHS is slated to receive $4.3 billion for bioterrorism activities in 2003. While grants to public health agencies will remain relatively steady at about $900 million, assistance to hospitals and health care providers will grow to $618 million. Funding for the national stockpile will actually decrease from one billion to $400 million, due to the large one-time purchases of extra antibiotics and smallpox vaccine in 2002. Bioterrorism research by NIH will rise sharply from $248 million in 2002 to $1.7 billion in 2003.[112]

Appendix D contains a breakdown of funding to combat biological terrorism between 1998 and 2003. Table One provides information on HHS spending to defend against biological terrorism. As Figure One in Appendix E illustrates, HHS devoted roughly two-thirds of its resources to programs to prepare for and respond to terrorism, while research and development efforts received the other one-third. Among the programs to enhance preparedness and response capabilities, most of the funds were earmarked for public health surveillance and stockpiling pharmaceuticals (Figure Two, Appendix E). As Figure Three illustrates, HHS allocates a significant portion of its bioterrorism funds to enhancing state

---

111. "HHS Announces $1.1 Billion in Funding to States For Bioterrorism Preparedness," *HHS News,* January 31, 2002; "HHS Approves State Bioterrorism Plans So Building Can Begin," *HHS News,* June 6, 2002.

112. President George W. Bush, *Securing the Homeland, Strengthening the Nation,* February 2002, p. 30.

and local readiness. While the bulk of research and development funds were initially earmarked for the development of new vaccines, the post-September 11 infusion of funds into NIH is split among basic research on the microorganisms of greatest concern, the development of new vaccines and therapeutics, and construction of new research facilities. (Figure Four, Appendix E).

This section provided background on the origins and evolution of U.S. bioterrorism preparedness programs. The following section describes the federal programs currently in place to improve the nation's capacity to detect and respond to a biological terrorist attack and the coordination of the nation's efforts toward those goals. When evaluating the current and proposed measures to combat biological terrorism, one should keep in mind the following admonition: "It has to be acknowledged that it will be impossible to prevent ALL mortality, no matter how good a technology can be developed, and no matter how much money we are willing to spend to enhance our response."[113] The goal should not be invulnerability but the development of capabilities at the federal, state, and local levels that will allow the United States to mitigate so successfully the effects of a biological attack that terrorists will find this method ineffective and unappealing.

Programs to Improve Detection and Recognition of Biological Terrorism

The key to mounting an effective response to a bioterrorism attack is early warning. The earlier an attack is detected, the earlier treatment of those affected by the attack can be started and precautions taken to prevent further transmission of the disease, if it is contagious. A study by scientists at the CDC found that the single most important means of reducing casualties caused by bioterrorism is rapid recognition of the attack and identification of the agent. According to the study, "arithmetic increases in response time buy disproportionate increases in benefit (preventing losses)."[114] Unfortunately, the task of increasing detection and response time is much more complicated for a biological attack than for a nuclear, chemical, conventional, or radiological attack: unlike biological

---

113. Institute of Medicine and National Research Council, *Chemical and Biological Terrorism*, p. viii.

114. Arnold Kaufmann, Martin Meltzer, and George Schmid, "The Economic Impact of a Bioterrorist Attack: Are Prevention and Postattack Intervention Programs Justifiable?," *Emerging Infectious Diseases*, Vol. 3, April–June 1997.

agents, each of these weapons has an immediate and readily detectable signature.

There are two general methods of detecting a covert attack with a biological weapon. The first is the public health model, which relies on the collection, analysis, and investigation by public health departments of data generated by physicians and clinical laboratories. This model is effective only after an attack has taken place and victims become ill and seek medical attention. The public health system is capable of detecting a disease outbreak, however, regardless of its cause or route of infection. Thus, investments in the public health system for the purpose of preparing for bioterrorism can also contribute to efforts to fight naturally occurring diseases. The second method of detecting a covert biological attack utilizes sensors to detect and identify aerosol clouds of biological agents. This method could detect a biological attack with an aerosolized agent while it was underway and, theoretically, provide enough warning to allow prophylaxis of exposed individuals before they became ill.

This section examines the role of the public health system in detecting an outbreak caused by the intentional release of a pathogen, programs underway to enhance the effectiveness of this system to provide prompt and accurate information on infectious disease outbreaks, and the status of biological aerosol detectors that have been deployed or are under development to provide near real-time warning of a bioterrorism attack.

Public Health

The public health system is designed to detect outbreaks of illnesses, discover their source, and intervene to save lives, as well as to conduct research to prevent, or at least detect more quickly, future outbreaks. The public health model has four components: diagnosis, surveillance, epidemiology, and laboratory analysis. Physicians can play a crucial role in detecting a bioterrorism event. An alert physician may recognize an individual's symptoms as being caused by an unusual or rare disease or note an unusual epidemiological pattern in a large number of patients with similar symptoms.[115] In the more likely event that a disease outbreak caused by bioterrorism goes undetected by physicians because of the

---

115. In New Mexico in 1993, an astute physician, on the basis of only two unusual cases, alerted public health authorities to what turned out to be an outbreak of hantavirus pulmonary syndrome. Prepared statement of James Hughes, Director, National Center for Infectious Disease, CDC, before Senate Committee on Appropriations, Subcommittee on Department of Labor, Health and Human Services, and Education and Related Agencies, *Preparedness for Epidemics and Bioterrorism,* June 2, 1998.

nonspecific symptoms of the victims, and the "noise" of other medical problems masks the "signal" of a bioterrorism incident, the next line of detection is the public health surveillance system. Physicians and clinical laboratories provide the crucial inputs for this system. Laboratories also play a vital role by providing definitive confirmation of a disease outbreak and determining the strain of a particular organism involved in the outbreak. Even after an outbreak is detected, its cause and scope may not be readily apparent. Thus, epidemiologists must begin investigations to determine the scope and severity of the outbreak, its cause, and the population at risk. In the event of an intentional release of a pathogen, law enforcement agencies will also launch criminal investigations to identify and apprehend the suspected perpetrators. Efforts currently underway to enhance the capabilities of these components of the public health system to detect and recognize a bioterrorism event are described below.

Diagnosis

The federal government currently follows a three-prong strategy for improving the ability of health care professionals at the local level to accurately diagnose an outbreak of a biological agent.[116] First, OEP has contracted with professional medical organizations to develop a standard curriculum for training medical personnel on how to recognize and manage victims of a WMD attack. Second, DOD, OEP, and CDC offer training and educational materials. Third, OEP, CDC, and HRSA provide funding to state and local governments that can be used to conduct training of health care providers. These programs have now been consolidated under the leadership of DHS and HHS.

CURRICULUM DEVELOPMENT

In 1998, OEP commissioned the American College of Emergency Physicians (ACEP) to establish a task force of professional medical organizations that would develop a curriculum and standards for educating health care providers in recognizing and treating victims of nuclear, biological, and chemical weapons. The task force issued its final report in April 2001.[117] OEP has also funded the development of clinical guidelines

116. Of course, individual doctors, state and local governments, and institutions, such as hospitals and medical organizations, have taken the initiative and utilized their own funds to provide invaluable training and education to a number of health care providers. This section, however, focuses on federal efforts, since these are the most visible and form the foundation for efforts by other entities.

117. Office of Emergency Preparedness and American College of Emergency Physicians, *Developing Objectives, Content, and Competencies for the Training of Emergency Med-*

for use by civilian health care providers in treating victims of chemical and biological agents. This curriculum and these standards and guidelines are prerequisites for any large-scale training and education effort.

TRAINING AND EDUCATION

A 1995 HHS review of training available to health care providers on the medical response to a WMD terrorist incident found such training "almost totally lacking."[118] Since that time, federal agencies have established multiple training programs on diagnosing and treating victims of biological agents for physicians and other health care providers.

The Domestic Preparedness Program, established within the DOD in 1996 to train the largest 120 cities on how to prepare for and respond to a WMD terrorism incident, included a "Hospital Provider" course for emergency department physicians and nurses. As of May 1, 2000, more than 22,000 individuals in 82 cities, including 5,400 hospital providers, had received this training.[119] The goal of the course was to train physicians and nurses on how properly to decontaminate, triage, diagnose, and treat victims of a WMD attack and protect themselves and other patients while doing so.[120] The length of the course (eight hours) has reportedly made it difficult, however, for physicians and nurses to attend.[121] The entire city training program was transferred to DOJ in October 2000.[122] DOJ's first responder training program is now administered by DHS.

Another training mechanism is the Noble Training Center at Fort McClellan, Alabama, operated by OEP. The facility, a converted former Army hospital with 100 beds, is the only mock hospital in the United

---

ical Technicians, Emergency Physicians, and Emergency Nurses to Care for Casualties Resulting From Nuclear, Biological, or Chemical (NBC) Incidents: Final Report, April 23, 2001, <www.acep.org/1,2676,0.html?ext=.pdf>.

118. Cited in Department of Justice, Five-Year Interagency Counterterrorism and Technology Crime Plan, p. 52.

119. Email communication with an official with the Domestic Preparedness Program, Soldier Biological and Chemical Command, Department of Defense, May 18, 2000.

120. Solider Biological and Chemical Command Fact Sheet, "Training Program: Hospital Provider," August 2, 1999, <dp.sbccom.army.mil/fs/dp_hospital_provider.html>.

121. E. M. Eitzen, "Education Is the Key to Defense against Bioterrorism," Annals of Emergency Medicine, Vol. 34, No. 2 (August 1999), p. 222.

122. President William Clinton, "Designation of the Attorney General as the Lead Official for the Emergency Response Assistance Program under Sections 1412 and 1415 of the National Defense Authorization Act for Fiscal Year 1997 (Public Law 104–201)," memorandum, April 6, 2000.

States devoted to medical training for diagnosing and treating victims of conventional or WMD terrorist incidents.[123] The training, based on the curriculum developed by the ACEP-led task force, will be offered free of charge to hospital administrators, emergency department physicians and nurses, and paramedics.[124] This facility will have the capacity to train 2,500 students each year.[125]

A third mechanism is distance-learning courses sponsored by the CDC. In September 1999, the CDC and United States Army Medical Research Institute on Infectious Diseases (USAMRIID) cosponsored a video broadcast on bioterrorism and public health that reached more than 17,000 health care and public health professionals.[126] In the fall of 2001, CDC reached more than one million health professionals using satellite and web broadcasts.[127] In addition, HAN was used to deliver updates on the public health and medical aspects of terrorism and the anthrax attacks, reaching an estimated 7 million health professionals.[128] CDC plans on using HAN to conduct training for the public health community on a regular basis.[129]

Finally, the network of more than 1,500 nonfederal hospitals enrolled in the National Disaster Medical System (NDMS) provides another mechanism for training health care providers. NDMS is a joint program of

---

123. U.S. Public Health Service, "The U.S. Public Health Service Noble Training Center," fact sheet, undated.

124. Telephone interview with official of the U.S. Public Health Service Noble Training Center, April 27, 2000; Rose Livingston, "New Center Trains for Chemical Attacks," *The Birmingham News,* January 28, 2000.

125. Office of Management and Budget, *Annual Report to Congress on Combating Terrorism,* July 2001, p. 23.

126. CDC, *National Bioterrorism Preparedness and Response Initiative Briefing Packet,* April 17, 2000.

127. Prepared statement of Edward Baker, Director, Public Health Practice Program Office, Centers for Disease Control and Prevention before the House Committee on Government Reform Subcommittee on Technology and Procurement Policy, *Bioterrorism Preparedness: CDC Efforts to Improve Public Health Information at Federal, State, and Local Levels,* December 14, 2001. The CDC also provides a streaming-video version of these broadcasts over the Internet, <www.bt.cdc.gov>.

128. Prepared statement of Edward Baker, Director, Public Health Practice Program Office, Centers for Disease Cotnrol and Prevention before the House Committee on Government Reform Subcommittee on Technology and Procurement Policy, *Bioterrorism Preparedness: CDC Efforts to Improve Public Health Information at Federal, State, and Local Levels,* December 14, 2001.

129. CDC, "Facts about the Health Alert Network," undated, <www.phppo.cdc.gov/han/>.

DOD, DHS, and VA and the private sector to provide staffed, acute care beds for treating large numbers of people. NDMS operates during peacetime after a major disaster or as a backup to the military medical system during a conflict. PDD-62 mandated that the Public Health Service and Department of Veterans Affairs provide WMD training to the hospitals participating in the NDMS. The Public Health Service received one million dollars to carry out this mission in 2000 and provided the VA with another $832,000 in September 2001. An assessment of hospital training needs and the development of a pilot training module was scheduled to take place during 2002.[130] The training curriculum under PDD-62 will be based on the recommendations of the ACEP task force. Another potential training mechanism for physicians that has gone unutilized to date is the VA's own hospital system.[131] The VA has been granted neither the mandate nor the funding to conduct WMD preparedness training at its own facilities, even though each year more than half of all medical students and a third of postgraduate physicians in training (residents) receive some of their training at VA hospitals.[132] The Public Health Security and Bioterrorism Preparedness and Response Act of 2002 (Public Law 107–188) authorized $133 million for the VA to enhance the readiness of its facilities and employees to respond to a WMD terrorism incident.[133]

GRANT ASSISTANCE

HHS and DHS also provide grants to state and local governments that can be used to train health care providers and acquire pharmaceuticals necessary in cases of biological weapons attack. OEP's Metropolitan Medical Response System (MMRS) program, now part of DHS, provides

---

130. Prepared statement of Frances M. Murphy, Deputy Under Secretary for Health, Department of Veterans Affairs, before House Veterans Affairs Committee, Subcommittee on Oversight and Investigations, *VA's Role in Educating Health Care Professionals to Diagnose and Treat Casualties of Weapons of Mass Destruction*, November 14, 2001.

131. Kenneth Kizer, Thomas Cushing, and Robyn Nishimi, "The Department of Veterans Affairs' Role in Federal Emergency Management," *Annals of Emergency Medicine*, Vol. 36, No. 3, September 2000, pp. 255–261.

132. Senate Appropriations Committee and Senate Veterans Affairs Committee, *Bioterrorism: Domestic Weapons of Mass Destruction* (Washington, D.C.: Government Printing Office, 2000), pp. 32–33; Statement of Cynthia A. Bascetta, Director, Health Care-Veterans Health and Benefits Issues, General Accounting Office, before the House Committee on Veterans Affairs, *Homeland Security: Need to Consider VA's Role in Strengthening Federal Preparedness*, October 15, 2001.

133. "Rockefeller Secures $133 Million for VA Hospitals to Prepare For Possible Bioterrorism Attacks," *U.S. Senate Committee on Veteran Affairs Press Release*, May 24, 2002.

grants of up to $550,000 to cities to establish integrated plans to provide hospital, pre-hospital, and public health response to WMD terrorism. These funds can be used to conduct training or exercises and purchase medical supplies such as antibiotics. Although the MMRS program initially focused on enhancing preparedness for an act of chemical terrorism, in 1999 OEP required MMRS cities to develop response plans for a bioterrorism incident, including plans for conducting mass prophylaxis and mass patient care, managing mass fatalities, and carrying out environmental remediation. Through 2002, OEP contracted with 122 cities to develop MMRS programs, which will provide coverage of 80 percent of the nation's population.[134] An additional $60 million has been requested for MMRS for 2003.[135]

The Bush administration has also requested $100 million in 2003 for HHS to provide bioterrorism education to health care professionals, poison control centers, and emergency medical services.[136] The $40 million earmarked for the poison control centers and emergency medical services will be administered by the Health Resources and Services Administration (HRSA).[137] At this time, it is unclear how the $60 million designated for health care professionals will be utilized or disbursed.

Surveillance and Epidemiology

In the absence of a definitive diagnosis by a physician of symptoms related to a biological weapons attack, the passive surveillance system operated by local and state health departments provides the next opportunity for recognizing an act of bioterrorism. Public health surveillance provides crucial data to decision-makers by identifying public health problems and evaluating the effectiveness of interventions to halt or mitigate these problems. Surveillance also serves to trigger epidemiological investigations that can provide more detailed information about these attacks than passive surveillance systems. If an intentional release of a pathogen were suspected, law enforcement agencies would be called in

---

134. "Bioterror Funding Provides Blueprint to Build a Strong New Public Health Infrastructure," *HHS News*, January 25, 2002.

135. Bush, *Securing the Homeland, Strengthening the Nation*, p. 32.

136. "HHS Bioterrorism Preparedness Funding Proposal Includes $518 Million For Hospitals, Up 284 percent," *HHS News*, February 5, 2002.

137. Health Resources and Services Administration, "Role and Function in Relation to Emergency Preparedness and Reaction," undated, <www.hrsa.gov/bioterrorism.htm>.

to conduct a criminal investigation.[138] This type of investigation could also provide public health officials with a better understanding of the scope, nature, and cause of a particular outbreak. Given the similarity of the symptoms of some critical biological agents with those of common diseases, the potential for naturally occurring emerging diseases to strike in unexpected places, and modern medicine's incomplete understanding of many diseases, clearly differentiating between a natural outbreak of an unusual disease and a man-made epidemic may not be an easy task. As Margaret Hamburg, former Assistant Secretary of Health for Planning and Evaluation, has observed, "Clearly there is a gray area between how you would recognize a low-grade bioterrorist incident versus a naturally occurring outbreak of disease."[139] To maximize the benefit from bioterrorism preparedness, programs instituted at the state and local levels should build capacity or capabilities that will be needed for events other than bioterrorism, either on a routine basis or in an emergency.

The integration of medical and public health surveillance and epidemiology is crucial for early recognition of unusual disease outbreaks, as the case of New York City's 1999 West Nile Virus outbreak clearly demonstrated. The outbreak originally came to the attention of the city's public health department through a call from an infectious disease specialist who had two patients with similar symptoms. A follow-up by city epidemiologists revealed two more cases and eventually led to the recognition that an emerging disease had struck New York City.[140] This lesson is also apparent from the experience in the southwestern United States with hantavirus. In 1993, after a physician reported that two young healthy adults had succumbed to an unknown respiratory infection, an epidemiological investigation identified 17 additional cases and led to the first identification of hantavirus in the United States.[141]

The current national disease surveillance system is incapable of detecting a biological terrorist act in a timely manner. For example, CDC maintains a national surveillance system to track the weekly total num-

---

138. Jay C. Butler, et al., "Collaboration Between Public Health and Law Enforcement: New Paradigms and Partnerships for Bioterrorism Planning and Response," *Emerging Infectious Diseases*, Vol. 8, No. 10 (October 2002), pp. 1152–1156.

139. Margaret Hamburg, Assistant Secretary of Health, quoted in "Bioterrorism: Policy, Technology, Nature of the Threat," *The Officer* (March 2000).

140. Monica Schoch-Spana, "A West Nile Virus Post-Mortem," *Biodefense Quarterly*, Vol. 1, No. 3 (December 1999), p. 1.

141. CDC, *Preventing Emerging Infectious Disease: A Strategy for the 21st Century*, October 1998. <www.cdc.gov/ncidod/emergplan/9obj11.htm>.

ber of deaths and deaths from pneumonia and influenza in 122 cities across the country.[142] Although the early symptoms of several critical agents resemble those of pneumonia and influenza, CDC does not receive the information until two to three weeks after date of death.[143] By that time, an outbreak of anthrax or plague would have already taken its toll. CDC's national infectious disease surveillance system is currently being modernized under a program called the National Electronic Disease Surveillance System (NEDSS), but this is a long-term effort.[144] In the interim, CDC has several programs in place to enhance the surveillance and epidemiological capabilities required to rapidly and accurately detect and identify an infectious disease outbreak.

IMPROVING THE SYSTEM

In recognition of the limited utility of the passive surveillance systems currently in place, CDC launched a program in 1999 to provide grants to state and municipal health departments to modernize their information technology systems and develop new surveillance systems and methods that could provide earlier recognition of a disease outbreak, whether natural or intentional.[145] Between 1999 and 2001, CDC awarded more than $130 million in grants to support these programs at the state and local levels.[146] A major focus of CDC efforts to enhance public health surveillance has been on upgrading the information and communications capabilities of local public health agencies. A February 1999 survey of public health agencies found that 20 percent lacked email, 50 percent lacked high-speed Internet access, and 45 percent did not have broadcast fax capability for use in emergency notification.[147] HAN will enable state and local health agencies to improve their connectivity with each other, the medical community, and the CDC. HAN will be used for routine reporting of surveillance and epidemiological information, rapid two-way com-

---

142. This system covers one-third of the deaths in the United States.

143. CDC, "121 Cities Mortality Reporting System: History," January 21, 2000, <www.cdc.gov/epo/dphsi/121hist.htm>.

144. Telephone interview with an official with the Epidemiology Program Office, CDC, May 3, 2000.

145. The laboratory component of the CDC program is described in the following section.

146. Prepared statement of D.A. Henderson, Director, Office of Public Health Preparedness, Department of Health and Human Services before the House Science Committee, *Science of Bioterrorism: Is the Federal Government Prepared?*, December 5, 2001.

147. Centers for Disease Control and Prevention, *Public Health's Infrastructure: A Status Report*, March 2001, p. 8, <www.phppo.cdc.gov/documents/phireport2_16.pdf>.

munication regarding public health emergencies, and training for public health personnel through distance-learning technologies. Improved communication capabilities and enhanced surveillance technologies could also be used on a daily basis by public health departments to fulfill their core mission.[148] The goal of HAN is to provide coverage to 90 percent of the nation's population.[149] Between 1999 and 2001, roughly $68 million was distributed to state and local public health departments under the HAN program.[150] An additional $78 million was appropriated for 2002, and another $202 million was requested for 2003.[151]

The CDC also provided $28 million in funding in 1999 and 2000 to state and local public health departments to enhance their surveillance and epidemiological capabilities.[152] These funds can be used to hire additional personnel, develop new means for gathering and analyzing data, create response plans, train staff, and conduct exercises. In 2002, CDC initiated a program to place a specially trained epidemiologist in every metropolitan area with a population greater than 500,000.[153] Instead of relying on physicians and laboratory reports of specific diseases, health departments are encouraged to conduct surveillance based on syndromic indicators, such as upper respiratory symptoms, influenza-like illnesses, or gastrointestinal illnesses. Gathering this type of data requires public health departments to seek new sources of information and establish ties with new partners. Other sources of information that could be used to conduct surveillance for unusual disease outbreaks include poison control centers, 911 call centers, health care organizations, veterinarian labs and clinics, animal health agencies, commercial pharmacies, coroners,

---

148. A program similar but unrelated to HAN is Electronic Laboratory Reporting (ELR). Under this program, Hawaii developed an electronic reporting system for the state's three largest commercial clinical labs. The results were significant. The state health department recorded a 2.3-fold increase in notifiable disease reports, reports were received five days earlier, and they were more likely to be complete and have patient contact information to facilitate epidemiological follow-up. Paul Effler et al., "Statewide System of Electronic Notifiable Disease Reporting from Clinical Laboratories," *Journal of the American Medical Association*, (November 17, 1999), p. 1845.

149. "Federal Funds For Public Health Infrastructure Begins to Flow to States," *HHS News*, January 25, 2002.

150. CDC, "The National Bioterrorism Preparedness and Response Initiative," March 13, 2000.

151. Bush, *Securing the Homeland, Strengthening the Nation*, p. 32.

152. Centers for Disease Control and Prevention, "The National Bioterrorism Preparedness and Response Initiative," March 13, 2000.

153. "Bioterror Funding Provides Blueprint to Build a Strong New Public Health Infrastructure," *HHS News*, January 25, 2002.

and medical examiners. Spikes in the volume of calls to any of these agencies, or unusual patterns or numbers of symptoms or deaths reported to them, could be useful indicators that a major public health emergency is underway. Aberrations in one or more of these surveillance systems could serve as a trigger for epidemiological investigations, active surveillance, or heightened vigilance with respect to reports from standard public health surveillance systems. The West Nile Virus outbreak in 1999 illustrated the need for improved coordination between public health agencies and animal and wildlife health communities.[154]

New York City was the first city to develop a system that collected these types of information.[155] The Mayor's Office for Emergency Management created a citywide list of daily health indicators, including emergency medical services' runs, deaths, emergency hospital admissions, and sales of over-the-counter antidiarrheal medicines, which are reported to the office on a daily basis.[156] The CDC grant assistance enables state and local public health agencies to adopt the New York City model. The Boston Public Health Commission, for example, is working with local hospitals to obtain the daily figures for the number of visits to emergency departments, urgent care centers, and admissions to medical intensive care units. These figures are combined with 911 call data submitted by the city's emergency medical service and mortality data (which is already collected by the city) and compared to baseline data from 1999 to provide early warning of a disease outbreak or other public health emergency.[157] Similar systems are also being developed by health care organizations and universities around the nation.[158] Despite the proliferation of these

---

154. General Accounting Office, *West Nile Virus: Preliminary Information on Lessons Learned*, HEHS-00–142R, (Washington, D.C.: Government Printing Office, 2000), p. 4.

155. Interview with Jerome Hauer, Director, Mayor's Office of Emergency Management, City of New York, March 1, 2000.

156. Prepared statement of Jerome Hauer, Director, Mayor's Office of Emergency Management, City of New York, before Senate Health, Education, Labor and Pensions Committee, *Bioterrorism: Evaluating U.S. Public Health and Medical Readiness*, March 25, 1999; interview with Jerome Hauer, March 1, 2000.

157. Kathy Brinsfield, et al., "Using Volume-Based Surveillance For An Outbreak Early Warning System," *Academic Emergency Medicine*, Vol. 8, No. 5 (May 2001), p. 492.

158. Liz Kowalcyk, "Program May Spot Bioterror Early On: Harvard Vanguard Surveillance Could Be Model for Rest of US," *Boston Globe*, November 20, 2001; Cindy Hall, "Stanford Tests Bioterror Early Warning System: ER Computers Track Trends in Symptoms," *San Francisco Chronicle*, November 19, 2001; Christopher Snowbeck, "Pitt Computer Network Forms a DEW Line Against Epidemics," *Pittsburgh Post-Gazette*, February 6, 2002; Ross Lazarus, et al., "Use of Automated Ambulatory-Care Encounter

syndromic surveillance systems, CDC has yet to conduct systematic testing of these systems to determine which are the most sensitive, specific, and cost effective.[159]

PILOT PROJECTS

The Departments of Defense and Energy have initiated pilot projects that could become the foundation for civilian syndromic surveillance systems being developed by the Department of Homeland Security.[160] As part of a program to conduct global epidemiological surveillance of the health of its military and civilian employees, the DOD has developed a prototype syndromic surveillance system to detect disease outbreaks for military facilities in the Washington, D.C., area called Electronic Surveillance System for the Early Notification of Community-based Epidemics (ESSENCE). Since 1999, this system has been used to detect disease outbreaks, including bioterrorism.[161] After September 11, 2001, the geographic coverage of the system was greatly expanded, and work began on upgrading the system to incorporate civilian sources of data and additional health indicators.[162]

The DOE has a project underway in New Mexico to enhance hospital-level surveillance by equipping the emergency and urgent care departments of a University of New Mexico hospital with touch screen computers tied directly to the state's office of epidemiology.[163] The Rapid Syndrome Validation Project (RSVP) system will allow physicians to input age, sex, certain respiratory and gastrointestinal symptoms, and zip

---

Records for Detection of Acute Illness Clusters, Including Potential Bioterrorism Events," *Emerging Infectious Diseases*, Vol. 8, No. 8 (August 2002), pp. 753–760.

159. However, CDC has taken the first step by creating an analytic framework that can be used to compare the effectiveness of different syndromic surveillance systems. See Daniel Sosin, "Draft Framework for Evaluating Syndromic Surveillance Systems for Bioterrorism Preparedness," undated, <www.cdc.gov/epo/dphsi/phs/syndromic.htm>.

160. William Broad and Judith Miller, "Health Data Monitored for Bioterror Warning," *New York Times*, January 27, 2003, p. A1.

161. Kendall Brown, et al., "Identification and Investigation of Disease Outbreaks by ESSENCE," Presentation to National Syndromic Surveillance Conference, New York City, September, 23–24, 2002.

162. Gerry J. Gilmore, "DoD Database Provides Global Tripwire for Bio-Terror," *American Forces Press Service*, December 17, 2002.

163. Ian Hoffman, "Tracking Diseases Via Computer," *Albuquerque Journal*, March 27, 2000; Jonathan Knight, "Epidemiology Gains an Ally in Bioweapons Surveillance Project," *Nature*, May 17, 2001, p. 228.

codes for home and work. The system will then display a color-coded map of clusters of patients with similar symptoms.[164]

ENHANCED SURVEILLANCE FOR SPECIAL EVENTS
The CDC has also developed a specialized system to provide enhanced surveillance during special events. The system was first used in Seattle for the World Trade Organization (WTO) meeting in November–December 1999. It was also used in 2000 during the Republican and Democratic national conventions and the Super Bowl. The WTO Enhanced Surveillance Project established an active surveillance system in the emergency departments of eight hospitals in Seattle and King County, which monitored more than 10,000 clinical visits.[165] The system was used to monitor key syndromes, such as sudden death and botulism-like illness, and send the data directly to the epidemiology office in the county public health department. Although the system operated successfully and was praised by participating hospitals, it was suitable for use only for a short period because of the heavy demand it placed on the public health agency and emergency departments.[166] In addition to providing near real-time surveillance of the city's emergency departments, the project also raised the doctors' awareness about public health surveillance and bioterrorism and improved communications between the hospitals and the public health department.[167]

Laboratory Identification of Biological Agents

Since most of the critical biological agents that the CDC has identified as posing the greatest threat to the public are not endemic to the United States, there has traditionally been little capacity or expertise at the state or local level to identify these agents. To remedy this problem, the CDC established the Laboratory Response Network (LRN) to build capacity at the state and local level and establish links between public health departments at all levels to advanced diagnostic capabilities. The network has

---

164. Alan P. Zelicoff, et al., *The Rapid Syndrome Validation Project (RSVP)*, SAND No. 2001–2754J, August 2001, <www.cmc.sandia.gov/bio/rsvp/SAND%20No.pdf>.

165. Seattle and King County Department of Public Health, "WTO Enhanced Surveillance Project: Local and National Collaboration Leads to Success," *Epi-Log*, Vol. 39, No. 12 (December 1999), pp. 1–2.

166. Telephone interview with Jeffrey S. Duchin, Chief, Communicable Disease Control and Epidemiology, Seattle and King County Department of Public Health, April 20, 2000.

167. Ibid.

both reduced the time required to confirm the presence of a critical agent in a clinical or environmental sample and increased the capacity of laboratories to process such samples.

LABORATORY RESPONSE NETWORK

The laboratories participating in the LRN are divided into four levels depending on their capability to safely handle and identify critical biological agents.[168] Level A labs are public health and clinical labs with low-level biosafety features and will employ only standard microbiological techniques, which can take up to 48 hours to identify an organism.[169] If a specimen is suspected of involving a critical agent, it will be forwarded to the nearest Level B or C lab.[170] Likewise, environmental specimens believed to contain a critical agent (such as those obtained from a suspicious package) will be transported directly to a Level B or C lab. Level B labs are state and local public health labs capable of testing for specific agents and will be used to screen samples to prevent the overloading of Level C labs. Level C labs are located at state health agencies, universities, or federal facilities and will be able to conduct advanced diagnostic tests, such as nucleic acid amplification and molecular fingerprinting. Level D labs are specialized federal labs operated by CDC and USAMRIID at Fort Detrick, Maryland, that have experience identifying rare, unknown, or genetically altered pathogens at the highest level of biosafety. CDC's Rapid Response Advanced Technology (RRAT) laboratory serves as the key entry point for all unknown or suspicious biological specimens sent to the CDC. The RRAT is on duty 24 hours a day, seven days a week and screens specimens before sending them to one of the agent-specific specialty labs at CDC.[171]

Members of LRN tested over 125,000 clinical specimens and over one million environmental samples in response to the anthrax letter attacks and the subsequent hoaxes and false alarms.[172] The volume of laboratory testing required by the B. anthracis-contaminated letters far surpassed the

---

168.   This description of the LRN is drawn from CDC, "Biological and Chemical Terrorism," p. 10.

169.   Institute of Medicine and National Research Council, Chemical and Biological Terrorism, p. 79.

170.   In the event that a specimen is suspected to contain smallpox or a viral hemorrhagic fever, such as Ebola, the specimen will be transported by the FBI directly to the CDC. Telephone interview with an official with the BPRP, CDC, April 27, 2000.

171.   Telephone interview with an official with the BPRP, CDC, April 27, 2000.

172.   "CDC's Terrorism Preparedness: One Year Later," CDC Telebriefing Transcript, August 27, 2002, <www.cdc.gov/od/oc/media/transcripts/t020827.htm>.

expectations of public health officials and would have been impossible for CDC to handle without the cooperation of public health laboratories in the LRN.[173] By August 2002, LRN included 200 public health laboratories, with at least one in every state.[174] The LRN will be enhanced by an NIH initiative to construct six new high-containment laboratories to conduct biodefense-related research. These labs will also be available for use in processing clinical and environmental samples in the event of a bioterrorism attack.[175]

GRANT ASSISTANCE

As part of the LRN program, CDC provides state health departments and a small number of municipal health departments with funds to develop enhanced capabilities to rapidly and accurately detect critical biological agents.[176] CDC is also posting agent-specific laboratory protocols on the Internet, as well as establishing an online order service for the necessary test reagents.[177]

TRANSPORTABLE LABORATORIES

Besides the central laboratories that are part of the LRN, several federal agencies maintain or are developing mobile or transportable laboratories to detect biological agents.[178] The Naval Medical Research Institute (NMRI) currently has a deployable field laboratory that can provide confirmatory diagnoses.[179] The Marine Corps' CBIRF, the FBI's Hazard-

---

173. Bradley Perkins, Tanja Popovic, and Kevin Yeskey, "Public Health in the Time of Bioterrorism," *Emerging Infectious Disease,* Vol. 8, No. 10 (October 2002), p. 1016.

174. "CDC's Terrorism Preparedness: One Year Later," CDC Telebriefing Transcript, August 27, 2002, <www.cdc.gov/od/oc/media/transcripts/t020827.htm>.

175. Martin Enserink, "One Year After: Hunt for NIH Funds Fosters Collaboration," *Science,* September 6, 2002, pp. 1630–1631.

176. CDC, "The National Bioterrorism Preparedness and Response Initiative," March 13, 2000.

177. CDC, *National Bioterrorism Preparedness and Response Initiative Briefing Packet.*

178. The commercially available handheld detectors, called "tickets," have proven to be of limited utility because of their lack of sensitivity and specificity. Institute of Medicine and National Research Council, *Chemical and Biological Terrorism: Research and Development to Improve Civilian Medical Response,* p. 87; "Use of Onsite Technologies for Rapidly Assessing Environmental Bacillus anthracis Contamination on Surfaces in Buildings," *Morbidity and Mortality Weekly Report,* Vol. 50, No. 48 (December 7, 2001), p. 1087.

179. Institute of Medicine and National Research Council, *Chemical and Biological Terrorism,* p. 87.

ous Materials Unit (HMRU), and the National Guard's WMD-CSTs all plan to field mobile labs.[180] The CDC also plans to equip its bioterrorism response team with suitcase-sized systems based on polymerase chain reaction technology.[181] These systems could be useful for forensic purposes, guiding environmental remediation, or bolstering the diagnostic capabilities available at the local level during crisis or consequence management.

Aerosol Detection

The second method for detecting a covert biological attack using aerosols of pathogens is through the use of special sensors. Aerosols are invisible and odorless clouds of microscopic particles and therefore, cannot be detected by the human senses. Although special equipment for the detection and identification of aerosols has been developed by the federal government, this technology is neither available to all jurisdictions nor is it capable of detecting all types of critical agents. A 1999 DOJ counterterrorism needs assessment found that "biological agent detection technology has not yet provided a complete, affordable capability."[182] Furthermore, a 1999 National Research Council and Institute of Medicine study found that continuous, real-time monitoring for aerosols of biological weapons is feasible only for special events, or when intelligence indicates a potential threat in a specific locale.[183] While DOD fielded the original devices capable of conducting this type of detection, DOE installed such a system around Salt Lake City, Utah, for the 2002 Olympic games.

The DOD deployed a biological aerosol detection system, called Por-

---

180.   Lois Ember, "Marines Offer Rapid Response to Chemical/Biological Terrorism," *Chemical and Engineering News,* July 1, 1996, pp. 22–23; Steve Vogel, "High-Profile Marine Unit Moving Here," *Washington Post,* January 8, 2000, p. B1; Federal Bureau of Investigation, *FBI Laboratory Annual Report 1998,* p. 3; Federal Bureau of Investigation, *FBI Laboratory Annual Report 1999,* (Washington, D.C.: Government Printing Office, 1999), p. 4; prepared statement of Charles Craigin, Acting Assistant Secretary for Reserve Affairs, Department of Defense, before the House Committee on Government Reform, National Security, Veterans Affairs, and International Relations Subcommittee, *Combating Terrorism: The National Guard Rapid Assessment and Initial Detection (RAID) Teams,* June 23, 1999.

181.   Telephone interview with an official with the BPRP, CDC, April 27, 2000.

182.   Department of Justice, *Responding to Incidents of Domestic Terrorism: Assessing the Needs of the State and Local Jurisdictions, Phase I Report,* (Washington, D.C.: Government Printing Office, 1999), p. 22.

183.   Institute of Medicine and National Research Council, *Chemical and Biological Terrorism.,* p. 95.

tal Shield, at such events as the 1997 Group of Eight international economic summit in Denver, Colorado, and North Atlantic Treaty Organization (NATO)'s 50th anniversary summit in Washington, D.C., in 1999.[184] The Pentagon maintains the capability to deploy this system to special events anywhere in the United States.[185] Portal Shield began as an advanced technology demonstration in 1996 to detect, identify, and warn of a biological warfare attack against overseas ports and airbases. It is currently installed at facilities in South Korea and the Arabian Peninsula.[186] The system comprises a network of automated sensors that can detect eight agents (plague, tularemia, anthrax, cholera, SEB, ricin, botulinum, and brucellosis) in less than 25 minutes.[187] If two or more sensors detect a biological agent, an alarm rings at a computer station. A false positive rate of less than 0.5 percent using the system has been reported.[188] A limitation of this system is that it is designed to provide coverage of an area several square kilometers in size, not an entire city.[189] The only other operational biological aerosol detection system is the Army's Biological Integrated Detection System (BIDS). Although the BIDS has the advantage of mobility, since it is mounted on a truck, it is not fully automated and thus takes longer to identify biological agents. The most recent version of this system is able to detect eight different biological warfare agents and requires up to 30 minutes to identify the organisms in the cloud.[190] In 2002, the Department of Defense launched a new program to develop a prototype early warning system for urban areas in the United States. The goal is to produce a system integrating aerosol detectors, syn-

---

184.   Department of Defense, *Nuclear Biological Chemical Defense Annual Report to Congress 2000*, (Washington, D.C.: Government Printing Office, 2000), p. A-3.

185.   Telephone interview with an official with the Joint Program Office-Biological Defense, Department of Defense, May 1, 2000.

186.   Department of Defense, *Nuclear Biological Chemical Defense Annual Report to Congress 2000*, p. A-3; "Bases in Korea and Mideast to get Bio-Warning Networks," *Defense Week*, January 26, 1998.

187.   Department of Defense, *Nuclear Biological Chemical Defense Annual Report to Congress 2000*, p. A-3. The list of agents is from Institute of Medicine and National Research Council, *Chemical and Biological Terrorism*, p. 87.

188.   Telephone interview with an official with the Joint Program Office-Biological Defense, DOD, May 1, 2000.

189.   Ibid.

190.   *Chemical and Biological Defense Program Report to Congress, Volume I* (Washington, D.C.: Department of Defense, April 2002), pp. A-2, A-3.

dromic surveillance, and information from private databases by 2004.[191] The program has reportedly been transferred to DHS.[192]

The Department of Energy, as part of its Chemical and Biological Nonproliferation Program, developed the Biological Aerosol Sentry and Information System (BASIS) to provide continuous monitoring of a large area for airborne biological agents during the 2002 Winter Olympics. BASIS consisted of a network of 50 sensors, urban hazard assessment models, a command and communication system, and decision support tools for emergency management planners in Salt Lake City. Aerosol samples were collected from sensors and analyzed at a central laboratory, with the results being fed directly to the special event's operations center. Since the system is still under development, operational parameters, such as sensitivity, specificity, speed, accuracy, and types of agents detected are not currently available.[193] This project has been transferred to DHS.

While DOD, DOE, and DHS continue to develop new generations of sensors, their utility in providing early warning of a biological terrorist attack will remain limited. According to the Defense Science Board, "Biological sensors will remain imperfectly reliable, environmentally sensitive, slow, range-limited, and difficult to operate for the foreseeable future."[194] Rigorous and systematic testing of newly developed sensors deployed in operational settings will be required to give public health and safety officials sufficient confidence in the systems to integrate them into their bioterrorism preparedness and response plans.

Programs to Enhance Response to Biological Terrorism

Once a biological terrorist attack has been detected or recognized, federal, state, and local agencies, as well as organizations in the private sector,

---

191. "DOD Announces Biological Defense Homeland Security Initiative," *Department of Defense News Release*, August 27, 2002; Gerry Gilmore, "DOD to Develop Biological Agent Early Warning System," *Armed Forces Press Service*, August 27, 2002; "DOD Biodefense Officials Cite Need for Standoff Detection, Analysis," *Inside the Pentagon*, August 29, 2002, p. 1; Shane Harris, "Defense Launches Plan to Fight Bioterrorism Attacks," *Government Executive Magazine*, August 28, 2002.

192. William Broad and Judith Miller, "Health Data Monitored for Bioterror Warning."

193. DOE, *Chemical and Biological Nonproliferation Program Annual Report 1999*, pp. 39, 49, 173–175; DOE, *National Security R&D Portfolio: FY99–2001*, (Washington, D.C.: Government Printing Office, 2000), p. 147.

194. *Report of the Defense Science Board/Threat Reduction Advisory Committee Task Force on Biological Defense*, Office of the Undersecretary of Defense for Acquisition, Technology and Logistics, June 2001.

will have to mobilize rapidly and deploy a wide range of resources to contain and mitigate the consequences of the attack. A large-scale biological terrorist incident could generate from hundreds to hundreds of thousands of casualties and worried well. Even a small-scale incident, infecting dozens or hundreds of people, could overwhelm the medical resources of a large city. Although early warning is essential, agencies at all levels of government must also have the appropriate response capabilities in place and plans to utilize these capabilities in concert with other agencies. This section divides the current efforts to enhance local, state, and federal response capabilities into four categories: planning, medical response, decontamination, and mass immunization and prophylaxis.

PLANNING

FEDERAL. DHS is responsible for the federal response to a WMD terrorist incident. DHS, acting through FEMA, will use the Federal Response Plan (FRP) to coordinate its activities with the other federal agencies that participate in consequence management. Within the FRP, HHS is the lead agency for health and medical services under Emergency Support Function #8. PDD-62 has reinforced the lead role played by HHS in preparing for and responding to medical emergencies.[195] Since 1996, HHS has had a plan in place to address the specific requirements of combating biological terrorism.[196] The plan describes the assignment of responsibilities for the separate bureaus and offices within the department, as well as the mechanisms for coordinating with other agencies. As of this writing, this plan has apparently not yet been updated, however, to take into account significant recent developments in domestic preparedness programs. In April 2000, CDC published a strategic plan for preparing for and responding to biological terrorism that provided a comprehensive description of the CDC's ongoing preparedness programs, but devoted only one paragraph to how the CDC or other federal agencies would respond to a biological terrorism incident.[197] As Dr. D. A. Henderson has noted, "There is, as yet, no agreed upon national strategy or plan to deal with bioterrorism."[198] As the anthrax letter incidents demonstrated, this

---

195. Hamburg testimony before Senate Appropriations Committee and Senate Veterans Affairs Committee in *Bioterrorism: Domestic Weapons of Mass Destruction* (Washington, D.C.: Government Printing Office, 2000), p. 14.

196. HHS, *Health and Medical Services Support Plan for the Federal Response to Acts of Chemical/Biological (C/B) Terrorism*, (Washington, D.C.: June 21, 1996).

197. CDC, "Biological and Chemical Terrorism," p. 9.

198. D. A. Henderson, "US Response to Possible Bioterrorism."

problem continues to hinder U.S. efforts to respond to biological terrorism.

STATE AND LOCAL. Planning for a bioterrorism incident is also lacking at the state and local level. Two-thirds of local health departments have not yet developed an emergency response plan that addresses bioterrorism.[199] Plans for rapid epidemiological investigation, laboratory identification of unknown agents, and conducting mass prophylaxis campaigns would also be useful for dealing with pandemic influenza and outbreaks of emerging infectious diseases. Hospitals could also benefit from planning for dealing with mass casualty incidents and small-scale disease epidemics.

Numerous federal agencies have efforts underway to assist state and local governments in developing plans for preparing for and responding to a bioterrorism event. Between 1999 and 2001, the CDC distributed roughly $12 million to state and municipal health agencies to develop model bioterrorism preparedness and response plans.[200] In order to encourage planning at the state level, HHS withheld 80 percent of the one billion earmarked for strengthening state and local public health infrastructure in 2002 until states developed comprehensive plans for how they will utilize the funding.[201] In 2002, HHS also initiated a program administered by the Health Resources and Services Administration (HRSA) to disburse grants to hospitals to conduct planning for bioterrorism and other mass casualty incidents.[202] At the municipal level, OEP requires each of the cities participating in the MMRS program (122, as of 2002) to develop response plans for a bioterrorism incident, including plans for improving early recognition of a bioterrorism incident, providing mass prophylaxis and mass patient care, managing mass fatalities, and ensuring environmental surety after an event.[203] HHS and DOD have also pub-

---

199. National Association of County and City Health Officials, "One Year Later: Improvements in Local Public Health Preparedness Since September 11, 2001," *Issue Brief*, November 2002.

200. CDC, *National Bioterrorism Preparedness and Response Initiative Briefing Packet.*

201. "Federal Funds for Public Health Infrastructure Begin to Flow to States," *HHS News*, January 25, 2002.

202. Health Resources and Services Administration, "Role and Function in Relation to Emergency Preparedness and Reaction," undated, <www.hrsa.gov/bioterrorism.htm>.

203. OEP, *MMRS Statement of Work Bio Add-On*, draft, January 31, 2000, <207.91.118.34/Public/NewsStand/Documents/MMRS_SOW_BIO.pdf>.

lished guidelines for state and local agencies regarding how to plan for a bioterrorism incident.[204]

Although all U.S. hospitals are required to have disaster plans, few are believed to have plans that address the unique demands of a bioterrorism incident, such as large-scale victim isolation, laboratory work with dangerous organisms, critical care availability, access to appropriate antibiotics and vaccines, and the handling of large numbers of corpses.[205] Even a small-scale infectious disease outbreak, especially one amplified by the media, could create conditions that would overwhelm a hospital that lacked cooperative relationships with other hospitals, as well as public health and safety agencies. In response to this lack of planning, a team from the CDC and the Association for Professionals in Infection Control and Epidemiology devised a model bioterrorism readiness plan for health care facilities in 1999 and posted it on the Internet.[206] In addition, the American Hospital Association, with the support of OEP, published a report in August 2000 highlighting the key issues facing hospitals in preparing for mass casualty incidents.[207] Internal, facility-specific planning is essential, but there is also a need for hospitals to shift their planning perspective from that of an autonomous and self-sufficient actor to that of an interdependent actor integrated into an interagency, multi-jurisdiction system. A significant step forward in this regard was the promulgation of new guidelines by the Joint Commission on Accreditation of Healthcare Organizations (JCAHO), the nation's primary standard-setting and accrediting body for hospitals, that requires hospitals to prepare all-hazard emergency management plans.[208]

A crucial element for effective planning is conducting realistic exer-

204. Soldier Biological Chemical Command, *Improving Local and State Agency Response to Terrorist Incidents Involving Biological Weapons*, August 1, 2000, <dp.sbccom.army.mil/fr/bwirp_interim_planning_guide.pdf>. Centers for Disease Control, *The Public Health Response to Chemical and Biological Terrorism: Interim Planning Guidance for State Public Health Officials*, July 2001, http://www.bt.cdc.gov/Documents/Planning/PlanningGuidance.pdf>.

205. Richards, et al., "Emergency Physicians and Biological Terrorism," p. 187.

206. *Bioterrorism Readiness Plan: A Template for Healthcare Facilities*, APIC Bioterrorism Task Force and CDC Hospital Infections Program Bioterrorism Working Group, April 1999, <www.cdc.gov/ncidod/hip/Bio/13apr99APIC-CDCBioterrorism.pdf>.

207. American Hospital Association, *Hospital Preparedness for Mass Casualties*, August 2000, <www.ahapolicyforum.org/policyresources/MOdisaster.asp>.

208. Prepared statement of Dennis O'Leary, President of the Joint Commission on Accreditation of Healthcare Organizations, before the House Committee on Energy and Commerce Subcommittee on Oversight and Investigations, *Review of Federal Bioterrorism Preparedness Programs from a Public Health Perspective*, October 10, 2001.

cises. Cities participating in the Domestic Preparedness Program (formerly run by DOD and DOJ and now administered by DHS) have conducted a bioterrorism tabletop exercise as part of the training. Field exercises for biological terrorism are more difficult to conduct, however, because of the potential disruption to daily operations in participating hospitals and public health agencies. A biological terrorism field exercise was scheduled to be held in New York City in September 1999 but was postponed indefinitely due to the West Nile encephalitis outbreak which began that August. The first full-scale biological terrorism field exercise took place in May 2000 in Denver, as part of the "Top Officials" (TOPOFF) exercise cosponsored by DOJ and FEMA. The exercise highlighted the complexity of decision-making during a fast-moving infectious disease outbreak, the lack of well-rehearsed mechanisms for distributing antibiotics on a large scale, the inability of hospitals to handle mass casualties, the need for the public health community to develop new partnerships with the public safety community, and the lack of planning on containing an epidemic.[209] In response, the Bush administration has requested funding for hospitals to participate in state-sponsored bioterrorism exercises.[210]

MEDICAL RESPONSE

A bioterrorist incident would most likely create a grave medical emergency. As a government-commissioned task force of health care providers noted in a recent report on medical preparedness for a WMD incident, "Unless such an attack is announced, the local health care system, especially emergency departments, will be the first and most critical line of defense for detection, notification, rapid diagnosis, and treatment."[211] The current level of readiness in the medical community to handle such an incident, however, is low. According to a DOJ study, "Most of the as-

---

209. Thomas V. Inglesby, Rita Grossman, and Tara O'Toole, "A Plague on Your City: Observations from TOPOFF," *Clinical Infectious Diseases*, Vol. 32 (2001), pp. 436–445; Richard E. Hoffman and Jane E. Norton, "Lessons Learned from a Full-Scale Bioterrorism Exercise," *Emerging Infectious Diseases*, Vol. 6, No. 6 (November–December 2000).

210. More specifically, the Bush administration has requested $73 million for hospitals to participate in state-sponsored bioterrorism exercises. Bush, *Securing the Homeland*, p. 32.

211. Task Force of Health Care and Emergency Services Professionals on Preparedness for Nuclear, Biological and Chemical Incidents, *Executive Summary: Developing Objectives, Content and Competencies for the Training of Emergency Medical Technicians, Emergency Physicians, and Emergency Nurses to Care for Casualties Resulting from Nuclear, Biological or Chemical (NBC) Incidents*, contract no. 282–98–0037 (July 2000), p. 3.

sessments agree that medical and hospital personnel are not prepared to provide the necessary support to address a WMD incident. Most medical personnel lack the skills to treat WMD victims, and hospitals may lack the equipment and capacity to handle casualties."[212] Dr. D. A. Henderson has noted that even "hospital executives [have] concluded that no U.S. hospital is prepared to deal with community-wide disasters, for a host of financial, legal, and staffing reasons."[213] This finding has been validated by surveys of hospital preparedness for WMD incidents.[214] The American Hospital Association has estimated that the nation's acute care hospitals would require over $11 billion to be adequately prepared to handle mass casualty incidents involving a weapon of mass destruction.[215]

As the medical community continues the trend of reducing costs by cutting staff and bed capacity and closing emergency departments, its preparedness to address mass casualty incidents, such as bioterrorism, erodes. As a result, the health care system today is extremely inelastic and incapable of responding to large-scale public health emergencies. To illustrate the lack of capacity to handle a large number of critically ill patients, consider that in Boston, as few as 80 patients requiring critical care would saturate the local hospitals' patient care capabilities.[216] In the view of Michael Osterholm, former state epidemiologist for Minnesota, the capacity to provide intensive care to 2,600 patients is "not available anywhere in the country."[217] Financial pressures generated by the managed care environment limit the ability of hospitals and doctors to enhance their readiness.[218] In addition, unlike fire departments, emergency medi-

212. Department of Justice, *Responding to Incidents of Domestic Terrorism*, p. 24.

213. D. A. Henderson, "Nation Is Perilously Unprepared for a Bioterror Event," *The Star Tribune*, August 9, 2000.

214. Wetter et al., "Hospital Preparedness for Victims of Chemical or Biological Terrorism," pp. 710–716; Treat, et al., "Hospital Preparedness for Weapons of Mass Destruction Incidents: An Initial Assessment," pp. 562–565.

215. American Hospital Association, *Hospital Resources for Disaster Readiness*, November 1, 2001, <www.aha.org/Emergency/Readiness/ReadyAssessmentB1101.asp>.

216. Gregory Koblentz, "Enhancing Massachusetts' Preparedness for Biological Terrorism," Master's thesis, John F. Kennedy School of Government, Harvard University, April 6, 1999, p. 21.

217. "Doc: U.S. Not Set for Bio Attack," *Associated Press*, June 2, 2000.

218. Joseph A. Barbera, Anthony G. Macintyre, and Craig A. DeAtley, *Ambulances to Nowhere: America's Critical Shortfall in Medical Preparedness for Catastrophic Terrorism*, Executive Session on Domestic Preparedness Discussion Paper ESDP-2001–07, John F. Kennedy School of Government, Harvard University, Cambridge, Mass., October 2001.

cine, and law enforcement agencies, there is no established mutual aid system for health care facilities. In the event of a bioterrorism incident that affects a wide geographic area, or has the potential to do so, local hospitals that are hard pressed to maintain the standard of care for their regular flow of patients—not to mention the added burden of bioterrorism casualties or worried well—may be unable or unwilling to provide assistance. Based on the consequences of the 1999–2000 flu season, serious shortages of health care providers and beds can be expected in the event of a bioterrorism incident.[219] Thus, federal assistance will be required to boost local medical care capabilities and sustain that level throughout the aftermath of a bioterrorist attack.[220] Federal assets, however, should not be expected in less than 24 hours after notification. Thus, the initial burden of a medical response will fall on local and state resources.

MASS CARE. The primary source of federal medical assistance in a bioterrorism attack will be the National Disaster Medical System (NMDS), a joint effort of DOD, DHS, and VA. Through NDMS, the federal government can provide both civilian and military medical teams to supplement local health care providers, as well as evacuate patients from the affected area to receive care at a hospital participating in the NDMS.

The principal medical support assets provided by NDMS are the 30-member Disaster Medical Assistance Teams (DMATs). The 27 Level one teams can be mobilized within hours and are able to sustain their operations for up to 72 hours.[221] An additional 30 teams, some capable of providing specialized services, such as pediatrics, burn treatment, and mental health care, are capable of deploying in one to three days.[222] OEP has also upgraded four DMATs, called National Medical Response Teams (NMRTs), with additional equipment and specialized training to provide

219. Monica Schoch-Spana, "Hospitals Buckle during Normal Flu Season: Implications for Bioterrorism Response," *Biodefense Quarterly*, Vol. 1, No. 4 (March 2000), p. 1.

220. Unlike a conventional terrorist attack that produces a surge of patients at hospitals for a few hours, an act of biological terrorism could produce waves of victims seeking medical care over the course of several days. Henry Siegelson, "Aftermath: Hospitals Are on the Front Lines after Acts of Terrorism," *Health Facilities Management*, (January 1990).

221. Prepared statement of Gary Moore, Acting Deputy Director, Office of Emergency Preparedness, HHS before the House Committee on Government Reform, Subcommittee on National Security, Veterans Affairs, and International Relations, *Domestic Preparedness Against Terrorism: How Ready Are We?* March 27, 2000.

222. Institute of Medicine and National Research Council, *Chemical and Biological Terrorism*, p. 25.

medical treatment to the victims of a chemical or biological weapon attack.[223] Each team has access to a cache of specialized pharmaceuticals to treat up to 5,000 people exposed to a chemical weapon and hundreds of people exposed to a biological agent.[224] The DMATs and NMRTs rely on volunteer medical personnel who are federalized for deployment to the scene of a disaster or terrorist incident. In the past, these units have also been pre-positioned in anticipation of major storms and for special events.

Contrary to conventional wisdom, the military cannot provide significant specialized medical assets on short notice in the event of a bioterrorism incident. The Pentagon's dedicated WMD terrorism response teams—the Marine Corps' Chemical and Biological Incident Response Force (CBIRF and the National Guard's Weapon of Mass Destruction-Civil Support Teams (WMD-CSTs)—have limited medical care capabilities.[225] The military's premier infectious disease laboratory— USAMRIID—plans to deploy only one physician with experience in treating casualties of a biological warfare agent to the scene of an attack, and then only in an advisory role.[226] Although DOD has a large pool of medical personnel, the bulk of them are located in the reserve force rather than on active duty.[227] These units are not designed to deploy at short notice to domestic events.

---

223. The NMRTs are based in Denver, Colorado; Winston-Salem, North Carolina; Los Angeles, California; and Washington, D.C. The D.C. team does not deploy outside of the metro area. Prepared statement of Robert Knouss, Director, Office of Emergency Preparedness, Department of Health and Human Services, before the Senate Judiciary Committee, Youth Violence Subcommittee Hearing, on *Training First Responders into the 21st Century*, June 11, 1999.

224. Senate Appropriations Committee and Senate Veterans Affairs Committee, *Bioterrorism: Domestic Weapons of Mass Destruction*, p. 9.

225. CBIRF has a 27-member medical unit. The unit does not however, include antibiotics in its stockpile. GAO, *Combating Terrorism: Chemical and Biological Medical Supplies Are Poorly Managed*, HEHS/AIMD-00-36, (Washington, D.C.: Government Printing Office, 1999), p. 4. Each WMD-CST has a four-member medical team. Jay Steinmetz, "Military Support for Response to Attacks Using Weapons of Mass Destruction," presentation to Worldwide Chemical Conference, Fort McClellan, Alabama, June 23–25, 1998.

226. *Joint Chiefs of Staff (JCS) J-3 Weapons of Mass Destruction (WMD) Handbook*, (Washington, D.C.: Government Printing Office, 2000), p. 72, <www.anser.org/homeland/featured.cfm>.

227. The Army Reserve holds 59 percent of the Army's medical assets. Jack Siemieniec, "Army Reserve Gears Up for Civil Support Mission," *ArmyLink News*, March 22, 2000.

PATIENT TRANSPORT. The National Disaster Medical System is also capable of evacuating patients from stricken areas and placing them in hospitals outside of the affected area. The Department of Defense is charged under the FRP with providing the transportation assets necessary for this mission. More than 1,500 nonfederal hospitals participate in NDMS and would be able to accept patients in the event of an incident. As noted above, the critical care capabilities of many cities are quite limited and could be easily overwhelmed by a large outbreak of bioterrorism-related illness. The patient relocation function of the NDMS is rarely utilized, however, and has never been exercised with a mass casualty scenario.[228] In addition, relatively few hospitals or local jurisdictions have experience interfacing with this system. Even if the NDMS patient relocation system functioned smoothly following a biological terrorism incident, it is expected that only noninfected patients would be transported out of the area to free beds for the bioterrorism victims.[229] This approach is necessary to contain the scope of the outbreak and minimize the disruption of the operations of other hospitals. In addition, in the event that the biological agent employed by the terrorists was lethal and contagious, there are an extremely limited number of assets to safely transport patients with such diseases and of health care facilities capable of providing intensive care to such patients in a high biosafety environment.[230] Thus, based on current federal plans and capabilities, local hospitals and health care providers, supplemented by state and federal assets, will bear the brunt of providing treatment to the casualties of a biological terrorist attack.

Decontamination

Terrorists who employ biological weapons in an aerosol form may also contaminate items and surfaces along the path of the aerosol. This risk is reduced by the fragility of most biological agents of concern and the

---

228.   Telephone interview with an official in the Emergency Management Strategic Healthcare Group, Veterans Health Administration, Department of Veterans Affairs, August 23, 2000.

229.   This is the concept of operations in Soldier and Biological Chemical Command, *Improving Local and State Agency Response.*

230.   USAMRIID maintains two aeromedical isolation teams (AITs) that can each transport one patient at a time under high-biosafety conditions. USAMRIID is also the only facility in the United States that can provide patient care under high-biosafety conditions. Its capacity is limited, however, to a 16-bed biosafety level three ward and a four-bed biosafety level four ward. George Christopher and Edward Eitzen, "Air Evacuation Under High-Level Biosafety Containment: The Aeromedical Isolation Team," *Emerging Infectious Diseases,* Vol. 5, No. 2 (March–April 1999).

difficulty in re-aerosolizing particles in the one to five micron range that pose an inhalation hazard.[231] Regardless of the objective assessment of the risk posed by contamination, however, the public will likely demand that areas affected by a biological weapon be decontaminated to remove even residual amounts of pathogens from the environment.

The anthrax letter attacks highlighted the importance of decontamination as part of a comprehensive response to an act of bioterrorism. Although most biological agents of concern are fragile organisms that will die upon exposure to sunlight, *B. anthracis* has the ability to encapsulate itself in a protective shield, called a spore, and lie dormant for long periods of time. The high degree of purity of the *B. anthracis* in the letters sent to media outlets and elected officials contributed to the contamination problem.[232] In addition, the novel form of delivery employed by the terrorist(s) led to a long-standing underestimation of the degree of contamination caused by the letters.[233] As a result, dozens of locations were contaminated, ranging from mail boxes to rooms to entire buildings. On January 22, 2002, the Hart Senate Office Building, where the anthrax letter addressed to Senator Daschle was opened, was declared clear of contamination and ready for occupancy.[234] As of early 2003, the two other major sites of *B. anthracis* contamination, the American Media Inc. building in Boca Raton, Florida, and the Brentwood post office in Washington, D.C., remained closed due to contamination.[235]

---

231.   Amnon Birenzvige, *Inhalation Hazard From Reaerosolized Biological Agents: A Review*, CRDEC-TR-413, Chemical Research, Development and Engineering Center, U.S. Army Armament Munitions Chemical Command, Aberdeen Proving Ground, Maryland, September 1992; J.A. Garland, J. Watterson, P.N. Jayasekera, and D.W. Jones, *The Hazard from Reaerosolised Biological Warfare Agents, Final Technical Report*, DERA, CBD Porton Down, Prepared for European Research Office of the U.S. Army, London, England, August 1999.

232.   John Lancaster and Dan Eggen, "Anthrax on Senate Letter Called Potent," *Washington Post,* October 17, 2001, p. A1; Joby Warrick, "Powder Used in Anthrax Attacks 'Was Not Routine,'" *Washington Post,* April 9, 2002, p. A9.

233.   This continued failure to appreciate the ability of letters containing dry powder of small particles to cause extensive contamination was particularly striking in light of research that demonstrated this potential problem. B. Kournikakis, et al., *Risk Assessment of Anthrax Threat Letters* (Defense Research Establishment Suffield, England, September 2001).

234.   Environmental Protection Agency, "Anthrax," August 8, 2002, <www.epa.gov/epahome/hi-anthrax.htm>.

235.   Scott Shane, "Cleanup of Anthrax Will Cost Hundreds of Millions of Dollars," *Baltimore Sun,* December 19, 2002, p. A1.

Mass Prophylaxis and Immunization

Providing antibiotics, vaccines, and other medical supplies to exposed and at-risk populations will be crucial for saving lives after an act of bioterrorism. Epidemiological and criminal investigations will provide critical inputs to a mass treatment campaign by specifying the nature of these populations and the scope of the outbreak. During the course of a mass prophylaxis and immunization campaign, public health officials must remain mindful of the adverse effects associated with selected pharmaceuticals and the development of antibiotic resistance that results from excessive or inappropriate usage.[236] A successful mass immunization and/or prophylaxis campaign will have three main components: planning, personnel, and pharmaceuticals.

PLANNING

Providing drugs to large numbers of people poses severe logistical challenges. Planning is essential to ensure that the maximum number of people receive the appropriate medicine in a timely fashion. New York City's Office of Emergency Management has conducted planning for this type of public health activity. The city's point of distribution plan has been adopted in part by the U.S. Army Soldier and Biological Chemical Command (SBCCOM) as a model response plan and is under review by several other cities as well.[237] The TOPOFF exercise in May 2000 included a biological field exercise in Denver that utilized this model for distributing antibiotics, but an analysis of this segment of the exercise is not currently available.[238] In August 2000, SBCCOM published a guide for state and local agencies on how to plan for a bioterrorism incident that included a section on mass prophylaxis.[239] In November 2001, CDC issued an interim plan for responding to an outbreak of smallpox and began training public health officials on how to respond to such an outbreak. In September 2002, an updated plan was pub-

---

236. E. Navas, "Problems Associated with Potential Massive Use of Antimicrobial Agents as Prophylaxis or Therapy of a Bioterrorism Attack," *Clinical Microbiology and Infections*, Vol. 8 (2002), pp. 534–539.

237. Telephone interview with Jerome Hauer, former Director, Mayor's Office of Emergency Management, City of New York, April 26, 2000.

238. CDC deployed only personnel, not pharmaceuticals, to Denver as part of the TOPOFF exercise. Telephone interview and email communication with CDC official, July 18, 2000.

239. SBCCOM, *Improving Local and State Agency Response*.

lished.[240] Hopefully, the requirement by HHS in 2002 that states develop comprehensive bioterrorism response plans before they receive the bulk of their money will result in a higher level of preparedness at the state and local levels, as well as tighter integration with federal response plans. However, the extent and quality of planning will only be assessable by the use of exercises or simulations.

PERSONNEL

Mass prophylaxis and immunization is labor intensive. For example, even a scaled-down version of New York City's point of distribution model applied to a community of 100,000 people would require 654 personnel to provide ciprofloxacin or doxycycline pills (the antibiotics of choice for treating inhalation anthrax) to the entire community.[241] Local hospital personnel would likely be unable to participate in such an effort because of the already limited number of staff available at most institutions and the necessity of treating the regular flow of patients, as well as bioterrorism casualties and the worried well. Although the New York City plan envisions utilizing minimally trained personnel to administer pills, this may not be possible if the required prophylaxis needs to be administered intravenously or by injection. Michael Osterholm, former chief epidemiologist for Minnesota, has estimated that no public health department could provide prophylaxis or immunizations to more than 10,000 people per day.[242] Thus, federal assets such as DMATs, NMRTs, and military medical personnel will probably be required to participate in any mass prophylaxis or immunization campaign.

PHARMACEUTICALS

Pharmaceuticals are obviously critical to mass prophylaxis and immunization campaigns. At the local level, the demands of managed care have forced hospitals to minimize their supplies of pharmaceuticals to a just-in-time inventory. Thus, sufficient quantities of the appropriate antibiotics may not be readily available in a bioterrorism incident to begin chemotherapy. Given the need for antibiotic therapy to extend from one to six weeks for most diseases of concern, even a modest bioterrorism incident could consume very large quantities of antibiotics. As part of the

---

240. The plan is available at <www.bt.cdc.gov/agent/smallpox>.

241. Prepared statement of Jerome Hauer, March 25, 1999.

242. Michael T. Osterholm, "How to Vaccinate Thirty Thousand People in Three Days: Realities of Outbreak Management," *Public Health Reports*, Vol. 116 (2001) Supplement 2, p. 16.

MMRS program sponsored by OEP, cities can use a portion of their grant assistance to maintain small stocks of crucial drugs.[243] OEP urges cities to plan conservatively and have sufficient pharmaceuticals on hand for their entire population for 24 hours.[244] Prior to special events, cities and local hospitals have taken steps to increase their holdings of key pharmaceuticals, but it is unlikely that this practice could be sustained indefinitely in the absence of an immediate threat.[245]

The two pharmaceutical stockpiles established by HHS for rapid delivery to the scene of an infectious disease outbreak are scheduled to be transferred to DHS.[246] Each of the four NMRTs established by OEP possesses a small cache of pharmaceuticals for treating 80 people for four weeks for several different types of bacterial infections.[247] The three teams and their associated stockpiles can be deployed within four hours of notification.[248] These teams and their caches can also be pre-positioned at special events.

In 1998, CDC established a national pharmaceutical stockpile for the treatment of millions of victims of bioterrorism. The national stockpile consists of two elements: 12-hour push packages and vendor-managed inventory. The push packages are palletized sets of medical supplies, such as bandages and dressings, pharmaceuticals (mainly antibiotics), and medical equipment, such as intravenous supplies and ventilators.

---

243. The extent to which this is being done, however, has not been assessed in any reliable or systematic way.

244. OEP, *MMRS Statement of Work*, draft, January 31, 2000, <207.91.118.34/Public/NewsStand/Documents/MMRS_SOW.pdf>.

245. "Hospitals Stockpiling Antidotes against Biological Weapons for WTO Meeting," *Associated Press*, November 9, 1999; Troy Anderson, "L.A. Hospitals Readied for Terror Attacks," *Los Angeles Times*, July 23, 2000; Marie McCullough, "Bioterror Scenarios Drawn Up," *The Philadelphia Inquirer*, July 23, 2000.

246. Contrary to its name, CBIRF does not maintain a cache of pharmaceuticals for treating victims of biological terrorism. Prepared statement of Carlos Hollifield, Commander, CBIRF, United States Marine Corps, Department of Defense, before House Committee on Government Reform, Subcommittee on National Security, Veterans Affairs and International Relations, *Combating Terrorism: Management of Medical Stockpiles*, March 8, 2000.

247. Senate Appropriations Committee and Senate Veterans Affairs Committee, *Bioterrorism: Domestic Weapons of Mass Destruction* (Washington, D.C.: Government Printing Office, 2000), p. 9.

248. The NMRT based in Washington, D.C., does not deploy. Prepared statement of Dr. Knouss, Director, Office of Emergency Preparedness, Department of Health and Human Services, before House Committee on Government Reform, Subcommittee on National Security, Veterans Affairs, and International Relations, *Combating Terrorism: Management of Medical Stockpiles*, March 8, 2000.

The first push package became operational in December 1999, and by 2001 there were eight push packages in place.[249] The antibiotics stockpiled are for the treatment of anthrax, plague, and tularemia—the three bacterial agents identified by the CDC as posing the most critical threat. These packages will comprise roughly 20 percent of the entire inventory. The other 80 percent will come from inventories maintained by manufacturers and prime vendors. The vendor's inventory can be shipped to arrive 24 and 36 hours after notification. Following the September 11, 2001, terrorist attacks, a push package was deployed to New York City within seven hours of receiving notification.[250]

The content and mission of the stockpile were expanded after September 11, 2001, and, as a result the name, of the program was changed to Strategic National Stockpile. In 2002, CDC received $645 million to expand the stockpile from eight push packages to 12. As part of this effort, the CDC will increase the holdings of anti-anthrax antibiotics, such as ciprofloxacin and doxycycline, to enable the post-exposure prophylaxis of 12 million persons.[251] In addition, the stockpile will include potassium iodide pills to counteract the effects of radiation exposure.[252] The stockpile is scheduled to be transferred to DHS in 2003. The decision to deploy the national stockpile will be made by the Under Secretary of Homeland Security for Emergency Preparedness and Response.[253]

Future expansion of the stockpile may include treatments for botulinum toxin and the viruses that cause hemorrhagic fever. These high-priority agents on the CDC's critical agent list currently have limited therapeutic remedies, so pharmaceuticals for these agents have not been included in the national stockpile. There are no licensed antiviral drugs or vaccines for use against the most worrisome of the viral hemorrhagic

249.   House Committee on Government Reform, Subcommittee on National Security, Veterans Affairs, and International Relations, *Combating Terrorism: Management of Medical Stockpiles,* March 8, 2000; Telephone interview and email communication with CDC official, July 18, 2000.

250.   Prepared statement of D.A. Henderson, Director, Office of Public Health Preparedness, Department of Health and Human Services before the House Science Committee, *Science of Bioterrorism: Is the Federal Government Prepared?*, December 5, 2001.

251.   As of late 2001, the stockpile contained enough antibiotics to provide post-exposure prophylaxis to two million persons. Department of Health and Human Services, "Bioterror Funding Provides Blueprint to Build a Strong New Public Health Infrastructure," *HHS News,* January 25, 2002.

252.   "Health Officials Mull Bioterror Steps," *Associated Press,* January 13, 2002.

253.   Homeland Security Act of 2002 (H.R. 5005).

fevers.[254] Although experimental trials with antiviral drugs and antibody therapy have been found to be effective against viral hemorrhagic fevers caused by arenaviruses, such as Lassa fever, the Argentine hemorrhagic fever, and Bolivian hemorrhagic fever, none have been effective against filoviruses, such as Ebola and Marburg.[255] Given the relatively short time of onset for symptoms of botulinum toxin (generally between 24 and 36 hours) and the need to administer the antitoxin before the onset of symptoms, the prospects of supplying the antitoxin in time to help exposed individuals who have not yet developed symptoms are dim.[256] However, CDC has begun to study the utility of including the antitoxin in the stockpile, perhaps for pre-positioning at special events.[257]

ANTHRAX AND SMALLPOX VACCINES

Biological weapons are unique among the weapons available to terrorists in that soldiers or civilians can be protected against them long before an attack through the use of vaccines.[258] By stimulating the production of antibodies, vaccines prime the body's immune system to recognize and attack intruding pathogens. While vaccines are generally viewed as the most effective defense for military forces against a biological warfare attack, it is also recognized that this form of defense has severe limitations, particularly for defending civilian populations.[259] For vaccines to be

254. Luciana Borio, et al., "Hemorrhagic Fever Viruses as Biological Weapons: Medical and Public Health Management," *Journal of the American Medical Association*, Vol. 287, No. 18 (May 8, 2002), pp. 2391–2405.

255. David R. Franz, et al, "Clinical Recognition and Management of Patients Exposed to Biological Warfare Agents," in Joshua Lederberg, ed., *Biological Weapons: Limiting the Threat*, pp. 69–70.

256. Franz, "Clinical Recognition and Management of Patients Exposed to Biological Warfare Agents," p. 73; Stephen S. Arnon, et al., "Botulinum Toxin as a Biological Weapon: Medical and Public Health Management," *Journal of the American Medical Association*, Vol. 285, No. 8 (February 28, 2001), pp. 1059–1070.

257. Mike Toner, "US Stockpiling Drugs," *Atlanta Journal and Constitution*, January 29, 2002, p. A1.

258. Richard O. Spertzel, Robert W. Wannemacher, and Carol D. Linden, *Global Proliferation: Dynamics, Acquisition Strategies, and Responses. Volume IV: Biological Weapons Proliferation* (Washington, D.C.: DNA, September 1994). p. 71.

259. David Franz, "Physical and Medical Countermeasures to Biological Weapons," in Kathleen Bailey, ed., *Director's Series on Proliferation*, No. 4, 1994, pp. 59–60; Don T. Parker, Dale O. Galloway, J. Clifton Spendlove, *Defense Against Biological Attack: A General Assessment* (Dugway, Utah: U.S. Army Dugway Proving Ground, May 1975), p. xiii.

effective, planners must be able to meet the following conditions: identification of the specific target population, knowledge of the specific threat agent, availability of the appropriate vaccine, and time for the vaccine to be administered to the target population before an attack.[260] These conditions are difficult to meet when the threat is posed by secretive terrorists armed with unidentified agents who will strike against an unspecified target without warning. It would be neither feasible nor desirable to vaccinate civilians against every possible bioterrorist agent for which a vaccine is available (and there are several for which no vaccine exists). As a result of these considerations, a 1999 National Research Council-Institute of Medicine study concluded, "vaccination has limited value as a primary defense for civilian populations."[261] Although vaccines were not originally included in the CDC's pharmaceutical stockpile program, after September 11, 2001, and the subsequent anthrax letter attacks, a decision was made to include vaccines for anthrax and smallpox in the stockpile. Both of these vaccines are unusual, since in addition to their protective properties, they also have therapeutic value, and thus are uniquely well-suited for use in both pre-exposure and post-exposure scenarios.

The decision by CDC to include the anthrax vaccine in its stockpile was apparently predicated on the ability of anthrax spores to remain dormant in hosts for 60 days or longer.[262] Due to this possibility, in December 2001, CDC made the vaccine available to postal workers and U.S. Senate staffers possibly exposed to anthrax spores who had completed their 60-day course of antibiotics, if they wished an additional precaution.[263] The vaccine would continue to provide protection against anthrax to recipients after they ceased their antibiotic regimen. Although only 152 of the estimated 5,000 people believed to have been exposed to anthrax spores chose to receive the vaccination, public health officials continue to view the vaccine as an important tool in the event of another anthrax attack.[264] In June 2002, DOD and HHS announced that the growing an-

---

260. Franz, "Physical and Medical Countermeasures to Biological Weapons," p. 60.

261. Institute of Medicine and National Research Council, *Chemical and Biological Terrorism*, p. 131. See also Philip Russel, "Vaccines in Civilian Defense against Bioterrorism," *Emerging Infectious Diseases*, Vol. 5, No. 4, (July–August 1999), pp. 531–533.

262. Thomas Inglesby, et al., "Anthrax as a Biological Weapon, 2002: Updated Recommendations for Management," *Journal of the American Medical Association*, Vol. 287, No. 17 (May 1, 2002), pp. 2236–2252.

263. Statement by the Department of Health and Human Services Regarding Additional Options for Preventive Treatment For Those Exposed to Inhalational Anthrax, December 18, 2001.

264. Ceci Connolly, "Workers Exposed to Anthrax Shun Vaccine," *Washington Post*,

thrax vaccine stockpile, produced by the troubled firm BioPort, would be split roughly evenly between the two agencies.[265] HHS had received an initial shipment of 220,000 doses of the vaccine in December 2001 but is believed to be seeking to stockpile enough vaccine to immunize one million people.[266] In October 2002, HHS signed contracts worth $22 million to procure 25 million doses of a second-generation anthrax vaccine for the national stockpile. The new vaccine is expected to be ready by the end of 2003 and offer substantial improvements over the existing vaccine, such as requiring fewer doses to provide immunity and causing fewer adverse reactions.[267]

The World Health Organization (WHO) declared smallpox eradicated in 1980, and the remaining stocks of the virus were believed to be confined to laboratories in Atlanta and Moscow. However, in the 1990s, evidence emerged that during the Cold War, the Soviet Union engaged in a massive program to weaponize smallpox and improve the weapon through the use of genetic engineering.[268] In addition, concerns arose that other nations with biological weapons programs retained secret stocks of the virus.[269] Since routine immunizations of Americans ended in 1972 and the vaccine requires a booster shot every 10 years to remain effective, most Americans in 2001 were now highly susceptible to this dreaded disease. In addition, only 15 million doses of vaccine were available, and several ancillary supplies and drugs, including the diluent needed to reconstitute the freeze-dried vaccine, sterile bifurcated needles to administer the vaccine, and vaccinia immune globulin (VIG) for the treatment

---

January 8, 2002, p. A6; Thomas Inglesby, et al., "Anthrax as a Biological Weapon, 2002: Updated Recommendations for Management," *Journal of the American Medical Association*, Vol. 287, No. 17 (May 1, 2002), pp. 2236–2252.

265. "Special Briefing on Anthrax Vaccine Program," *Department of Defense News Transcript*, June 28, 2002, <www.defenselink.mil/news/Jun2002/ t06292002_t0628ww. html>.

266. Nicholas Wade, "U.S. Seeks Anthrax Vaccine for Almost a Million People," *New York Times*, October 31, 2001, p. B9; Ceci Connolly, "CDC Gets Pentagon's Anthrax Vaccine," *Washington Post*, December 13, 2001, p. A10.

267. "Two Companies to Develop New Anthrax Vaccine," *Washington Post*, October 4, 2002, p. A15; "New Anthrax Vaccine Gets Green Light," *Science*, Vol. 296 (April 26, 2002), p. 639.

268. Ken Alibek with Stephen Handelman, *Biohazard: The Chilling True Story of the Largest Covert Biological Weapons Program in the World–Told From the Inside by the Man Who Ran It* (New York: Random House, 1999); Jonathan B. Tucker, *Scourge: The Once and Future Threat of Smallpox* (New York: Atlantic Monthly Press, 2001).

269. William Broad and Judith Miller, "Government Report Says 3 Nations Hide Stocks of Smallpox," *New York Times*, June 13, 1999, p. A1.

of adverse reactions to the smallpox vaccine, were also in short supply.[270] Given the high degree of transmissibility of smallpox, even a small initial outbreak can explode into a major epidemic.[271] The Dark Winter bioterrorism simulation in 2001 demonstrated the potential consequences of a failure to identify and respond rapidly to a covert attack with smallpox.[272] The smallpox vaccine can be used not only to protect individuals not yet exposed to the virus, but if administered within four days of infection, it can prevent or substantially mitigate the development of the disease. There is no licensed antiviral drug available for smallpox, although animal models indicate that cidofovir may have some utility. Thus, having adequate stockpiles of vaccine is crucial to responding to an outbreak of smallpox to prevent the disease from spreading beyond the initial group of infected individuals.[273]

In the wake of the suicide hijackings and the anthrax letter attacks in 2001, HHS accelerated its plans to expand the nation's smallpox vaccine stockpile and develop guidelines for using the vaccine and responding to an outbreak of smallpox. Prior to September 11, 2001, CDC had planned on acquiring 40 million doses of smallpox vaccine from the biotech company Acambis, with the first deliveries set for mid-2004.[274] Subsequently, Secretary of Health and Human Services Tommy Thompson announced that the government would acquire enough smallpox vaccine for every man, woman, and child in the United States—300 million doses—by the end of 2002.[275] Overall, the Bush administration plans on spending over $1 billion on smallpox-related preparedness activities in 2002 and 2003.[276]

There is also the question of how to use vaccine stockpiles dur-

---

270. James W. LeDuc and John Becher, "Current Status of Smallpox Vaccine," *Emerging Infectious Diseases*, Vol. 5, No. 4, (July–August 1999), pp. 593–594.

271. Smallpox has the potential to multiply tenfold every two weeks. Donald A. Henderson, et al., "Smallpox as a Biological Weapon: Medical and Public Health Management," *Journal of the American Medical Association*, Vol. 281, No. 22 (June 9, 1999), p. 2132.

272. Tara O'Toole, Michael Mair, and Thomas V. Inglseby, "Shining Light on Dark Winter," *Clinical Infectious Diseases*, Vol. 34 (2002), pp. 972–983; Peter J. Roman, "The Dark Winter of Biological Terrorism," *Orbis* (Summer 2002), pp. 469–482.

273. Henderson, "Smallpox as a Biological Weapon," pp. 2131–2132.

274. James W. LeDuc and Peter B. Jahrling, "Strengthening National Preparedness for Smallpox: An Update," *Emerging Infectious Diseases*, Vol. 7, No. 1 (January/February 2001), p. 155.

275. Judith Miller and Sheryl Gay Stolberg, "Sept. 11 Attacks Led to Push For More Smallpox Vaccine," *New York Times*, October 22, 2001, p. A1.

276. Bush, *Securing the Homeland*, p. 32.

ing peacetime and in the event of an outbreak. In June 2001, the Advisory Committee on Immunization Practices (ACIP)—a group of 15 outside experts who advise HHS and CDC on vaccination policies—recommended that the smallpox vaccine be offered on a voluntary basis to public health and hospital workers who are part of pre-designated smallpox response teams. The estimated number of personnel who would be vaccinated under this program would be 15,000. Given the low level of risk from smallpox and the adverse effects associated with the vaccine, ACIP recommended against vaccination of the general public.[277] During the fall of 2002, HHS presented smallpox vaccination options to President Bush. Under one option, the vaccine would be offered to 500,000 public health and medical personnel who would most likely be the first responders to a smallpox outbreak. Another option would be to expand this vaccination effort to all 10 million medical, public health, emergency response, and public safety personnel in the nation. A third option would be to offer the vaccine to the general public, once it is licensed in 2004.[278] On December 13, 2002, President Bush announced a three-phase vaccination policy starting with the immunization of up to 500,000 public health and medical workers beginning in January 2003, followed by 10 million emergency responders, and offering the vaccine to the public in 2004.[279] Due to the lack of an imminent threat and the adverse reactions associated with the vaccine, the vaccine is being offered on a voluntary basis. Despite the resistance of some healthcare facilities and providers to the vaccination policy and organizational difficulties at the state and local level, immunization of health and medical workers began in late January 2003.[280]

In addition to the debate over the proper pre-attack vaccination pol-

277. Lawrence Altman, "Panel Rules Out Smallpox Shots for All," *New York Times*, June 21, 2002, p. A16; *Draft Supplemental Recommendations of the ACIP: Use of Smallpox (Vaccinia) Vaccine*, June 2002, <www.bt.cdc.gov/agent/smallpox/vaccination/acip-guidelines.asp>.

278. Lawrence Altman and Sheryl Gay Stolberg, "Smallpox Vaccine Backed for Public," New York Times, October 5, 2002, p. A12; Laura Meckler, "Smallpox Vaccine May Appear Slowly," *Associated Press*, October 4, 2002.

279. Richard Stevenson and Sheryl Gay Stolberg, "Bush Lays Out Plan on Smallpox Shots," *New York Times*, December 14, 2002, p. A1; Jon Cohen and Martin Enserink, "Rough-and-Tumble Behind Bush's Smallpox Policy," Science, Vol. 298, December 20, 2002, pp. 2312–2316.

280. Vicki Kemper, "States Lag at Start of Smallpox Program," Los Angeles Times, January 17, 2003; Donald McNeil, Jr., "Health Care Leaders Voice Doubts on Smallpox Inoculations," New York Times, January 30, 2003, p. A13; Donald McNeil, Jr., "Smallpox Inoculations Begin With 4 Connecticut Doctors," New York Times, January 25, 2003, p. A10.

icy, there is also controversy over the most effective means of responding to a smallpox outbreak. The global smallpox eradication campaign found the "ring vaccination" method to be highly effective in containing and halting smallpox outbreaks. This strategy seeks to locate and isolate smallpox victims and identify and immunize their close contacts with the goal of containing the spread of the virus.[281] In contrast, the mass vaccination strategy seeks to reduce the pool of susceptible people before an attack (build herd immunity) and prevent a covert attack with smallpox from growing into an epidemic. [282] In September 2002, the CDC issued guidelines to state health departments on the development of plans to conduct mass vaccinations in the event of a smallpox outbreak.[283] This plan does not supplant the "ring strategy" that was the focus of earlier versions of the CDC plan, but a mass vaccination program is now more feasible given the large stockpile of vaccine, and such a program may also appear more desirable in light of studies that question the effectiveness of ring vaccination to control an outbreak in a large metropolitan area.[284] Policies governing the utilization of the smallpox vaccine promise to remain hotly debated for the foreseeable future.[285]

Conclusion

The terrorist attacks on September 11, 2001, and subsequent anthrax letter incidents have transformed biological terrorism from a *low-probability risk* to a *high-priority threat*. With $11 billion being allocated to countering biological terrorism in 2002–2003 and the prospect for more funding in the future, the level of resources is no longer a limiting factor in enhancing

---

281. F. Fenner, D.A. Henderson, I. Arita, Z. Jezek, and I.D. Ladnyi, *Smallpox and Its Eradication* (Geneva: World Health Organization, 1988); Centers for Disease Control and Prevention, *CDC Interim Smallpox Response Plan and Guidelines,* Draft Version 2.0.

282. William J. Bicknell, "The Case for Voluntary Smallpox Vaccination," *New England Journal of Medicine,* Vol. 346, No. 17 (April 25, 2002), pp. 1323–1325.

283. Centers for Disease Control and Prevention, *Interim Smallpox Response Plan and Guidelines, Version 3.0* (Atlanta, Ga.: CDC, September 23, 2002).

284. Edward H. Kaplan, David L. Craft, and Lawrence M. Wein, "Emergency Response to a Smallpox Attack: The Case for Mass Vaccination," *Proceedings of the National Academy of Sciences,* Vol. 99, No. 16 (August 6, 2002), pp. 10935–10940. The results of this study are in dispute, however. See M. Elizabeth Halloran, Iraq M. Longini, Jr., Azhar Nizam,and Yang Yang, "Containing Bioterrorism Smallpox," *Science,* Vol. 298, November 15, 2002, pp. 1428–1432 and Jim Koopman, "Controlling Smallpox," *Science,* Vol. 298, November 15, 2002, pp. 1342–1344.

285. Anthony Fauci, "Smallpox Vaccination Policy: The Need for Dialogue," *New England Journal of Medicine,* Vol. 346, No. 17 (April 25, 2002), pp. 1319–1320.

U.S. preparedness. The most urgent need is for a national strategy that integrates the preparedness efforts and response plans of the public health, medical, national security, and law enforcement communities in the United States. The impact that infectious disease outbreaks, both natural and man-made, can have on the health and security of the United States has risen to the top of policymakers' agendas and fostered new relationships among these communities.[286] However, the coordination and communications problems that bedeviled federal agencies responding to the anthrax letter incidents demonstrate that these relationships have not yet blossomed into full partnerships. The creation of the Department of Homeland Security will not lead to the centralization of bioterrorism preparedness under one agency. Thus, interagency and intergovernmental coordination will remain a crucial element of preparedness. As the anthrax letter attacks highlighted, even small acts of biological terrorism can have a disproportionate impact on public perceptions and behavior, particularly if government agencies and health care organizations are caught unprepared. A national strategy to counter biological terrorism must not treat this threat as just another emerging infectious disease. Biological terrorism is not only a public health problem and a medical emergency but also a heinous crime and a threat to national security. U.S. research and preparedness efforts have to be guided by this broader conception of the threat and not be limited to a narrow definition of the problem.

---

286.   See Christopher Chyba, *Biological Terrorism, Emerging Disease and National Security* (New York: Rockefeller Brothers Fund, 1998) and *Contagion and Conflict: Health as a Global Security Challenge* (Washington, D.C.: Chemical and Biological Arms Control Institute and Center for Strategic and International Studies, January 2000).

Appendix A. Potential Casualties from Biological Terrorism.

AGENT	AMOUNT	AREA AFFECTED	POPULATION EXPOSED	ESTIMATED FATALITIES
		Indoor Attack (Arena)[1]		
Anthrax	1–100 liters of liquid slurry	inside building	10,000–50,000	8,000–40,000
Brucellosis	1–100 liters of liquid slurry	inside building	10,000–50,000	160–800 (8,000–40,000 sick)
		Open Air Attack (Boston)[2]		
Point Source				
Anthrax[3]	30 kg dry powder	10 km^2	50,000	25,000
Line Source				
Anthrax[3]	100 kg dry powder	140 km^2	560,000	280,000
Brucellosis[4]	50 kg dry powder	20 km^2	100,000	200 (36,000 sick)
Q fever[4]	50 kg dry powder	>40 km^2	200,000	85 (100,000 sick)
Plague[5]	50 kg dry powder	20 km^2	100,000	8,500 (25,500 sick)
Tularemia[5]	50 kg dry powder	40 km^2	200,000	25,000 (75,000 sick)
Anthrax[6]	50 kg dry powder	40 km^2	200,000	80,000 (20,000 sick)

SOURCES: Richard Falkenrath, Robert Newman, and Bradley Taylor, *America's Achilles Heel: Nuclear, Biological and Chemical Terrorism and Covert Attack* (Cambridge, Mass.: MIT Press, 1998); World Health Organization, *Health Aspects of Chemical and Biological Weapons* (Geneva: WHO, 1970); Office of Technology Assessment, *Proliferation of Weapons of Mass Destruction: Assessing the Risks* (Washington, D.C.: Government Printing Office, 1993).

1 Falkenrath, Newman, and Taylor, *America's Achilles Heel*, pp. 152–153. These estimates are based on a concentrated liquid agent slurry, low-efficiency aerosol dispersal, high inhaled dose, and the assumption that early medical treatment is not provided to the victims.

2 These estimates are for attacks using high-quality dried agents disseminated with a high-efficiency device. Whereas states with advanced biological weapons programs would be capable of conducting such an attack, nonstate actors would face significant challenges in mastering the relevant skills and technologies. "Line source" refers to the dissemination of a biological agent from a moving vehicle (ship, aircraft, or other). This is a more efficient means of spreading an agent over a large area than a single, or "point," release.

3 OTA, *Proliferation of Weapons of Mass Destruction*, pp. 53–54. Estimates are for an attack against a city with a population density equivalent to Boston's (5,000 people per square kilometer) under moderate weather conditions and assume that no medical treatment is provided to the victims.

4 WHO, *Health Aspects of Chemical and Biological Weapons*, pp. 96–99. Estimates are for an attack against a city of 500,000 people with a population density equivalent to Boston's (5,000 people per square kilometer) under ideal weather conditions and assume that no medical treatment is provided to the victims.

5 Ibid., p. 99. Assumes that victims do not receive medical treatment.

6 Ibid., p. 99. Assumes that victims do not receive medical treatment.

Appendix B. Characteristics of Select Biological Agents.

Disease	Transmit Man to Man	Infective Dose (Aerosol)	Incubation Period	Duration of Illness	Lethality (approx. case fatality rates)	Persistence of Organism	Vaccine Efficacy (aerosol exposure)
Inhalation anthrax	No	8,000–50,000 spores	1–6 days*	3–5 days (usually fatal if untreated)	High	Very stable—spores remain viable for 40 years in soil	2 dose efficacy against up to 1,000 LD_{50} in monkeys
Brucellosis	No	10–100 organisms	5–60 days	Weeks to months	< 5% untreated	Very stable	No vaccine
Cholera	Rare	10–500 organisms	4 hours–5 days	> 1 week	Low with treatment, high without	Unstable in aerosols & fresh water; stable in salt water	No data on aerosol
Glanders	Low	Assumed low	10–14 days via aerosol	Death in 7–10 days in septicemic form	> 50%	Very stable	No vaccine
Pneumonic Plague	High	100–500 organisms	2–3 days	1–6 days (usually fatal)	High unless treated within 12–24 hours	For up to 1 year in soil; 270 days in live tissue	3 doses not protective against 118 LD_{50} in monkeys
Tularemia	No	10–50 organisms	2–10 days (average 3–5)	> 2 weeks	Moderate if untreated	For months in moist soil or other media	80% protection against 1–10 LD_{50}
Q Fever	Rare	1–10 organisms	10–40 days	2–14 days	Very low	For months on wood and sand	94% protection against 3,500 LD_{50} in guinea pigs
Smallpox	High	Assumed low (10–100 organisms)	7–17 days (average 12)	4 weeks	High to moderate	Very stable	Vaccine protects against large doses in primates

Appendix B. *Continued.*

Disease	Transmit Man to Man	Infective Dose (Aerosol)	Incubation Period	Duration of Illness	Lethality (approx. case fatality rates)	Persistence of Organism	Vaccine Efficacy (aerosol exposure)
Venezuelan Equine Encephalitis	Low	10–100 organisms	2–6 days	Days to weeks	Low	Relatively unstable	TC 83 vaccine protects against 30–500 LD_{50} in hamsters
Viral Hemorrhagic Fevers	Moderate	1–10 organisms	4–21 days	Death between 7–16 days	High for Zaire strain, moderate with Sudan	Relatively unstable—depends on agent	No vaccine
Botulism	No	0.001 g/kg is LD_{50} for type A	1–5 days	Death in 24–72 hours; lasts months if not lethal	High without respiratory support	For weeks in nonmoving water and food	3 dose efficacy 100% against 25–250 LD_{50} in primates
Staph Enterotoxin B	No	0.03 g/person incapacitation	3–12 hours after inhalation	Hours	< 1%	Resistant to freezing	No vaccine
Ricin toxin	No	3–5 g/kg is LD_{50} in mice	18–24 hours	Days—death within 10–12 days if ingested	High	Stable	No vaccine

SOURCE: *Medical Management of Biological Casualties Handbook, Fourth Edition* (Frederick, Md: United States Army Research Institute of Infectious Diseases, February 2001), pp. 10–11. Note: The infectious dose represents the number of organisms needed to infect 50% of the exposed population. Individual susceptibility may vary.

LD_{50} = Lethal dose for 50% of exposed population

*During a 1979 outbreak of inhalation anthrax in Sverdlovsk in the Soviet Union, the incubation period ranged from two to 43 days with two-thirds of the patients falling sick and dying within two weeks. Jeanne Guillemin, *Anthrax: The Investigation of a Deadly Outbreak* (Berkeley, Calif.: University of California Press, 1999), pp. 235–237.

Appendix C. Critical Biological Agents.

Category A (highest priority) agents include organisms that:

- can be easily disseminated or transmitted person-to-person;
- cause high mortality, with potential for major public health impact;
- may cause public panic and social disruption;
- require special action for public health preparedness.

Category A agents include:

- *Variola major* (smallpox)
- *Bacillus anthracis* (anthrax)
- *Yersinia pestis* (plague)
- *Clostridium botulinum toxin* (botulism)
- *Francisella tularensis* (tularemia)
- *Filoviruses*
  (Ebola hemorrhagic fever)
  (Marburg hemorrhagic fever)
- *Arenaviruses*
  Lassa (Lassa fever)
  Junin (Argentine hemorrhagic fever)
- *Related viruses.*

Category B (second highest priority) agents include those that:

- are moderately easy to disseminate;
- cause moderate morbidity and low mortality;
- require specific enhancements of CDC's diagnostic capacity and enhanced disease surveillance.

Category B agents include

- *Coxiella burnetti* (Q Fever)
- *Brucella species* (brucellosis)
- *Burkholderia mallei* (glanders)
- *Burkholderia pseudomallei* (melioidosis)
- *Rickettsia prowazekii* (typhus)
- *Chlamydia psittaci* (psittacosis)
- *Alphaviruses*:
  Venezuelan, Eastern, and Western equine encephalomyelitis
- Ricin toxin from *Ricinus communis* (castor beans)
- Epsilon toxin of *Clostridium perfringens*
- *Staphylococcus* enterotoxin B.

A subset of List B agents includes pathogens that are food- or waterborne. These pathogens include but are not limited to:

- *Salmonella species*
- *Shigella dysenteriae*
- *Escherichia coli* O157:H7
- *Vibrio cholerae*
- *Cryptosporidium parvum*

Category C (third highest priority) agents include emerging pathogens that could be engineered for mass dissemination in the future because of:

- availability;
- ease of production and dissemination;
- potential for high morbidity and mortality and major health impact.

Category C agents include:

- *Nipah virus*
- *Hantaviruses*
- *Tick-borne hemorrhagic fever viruses*
- *Tick-borne encephalitis viruses*
- *Yellow fever virus*
- *Multidrug-resistant tuberculosis*

Appendix D. HHS and CDC Spending on Biological Terrorism Preparedness.

Table 1. Department Of Health And Human Services Funding For Domestic Preparedness, FY 1998–2003 (Millions)

Function	FY98 Actual	FY99 Actual	FY00 Actual	FY01 Enacted	FY02 Enacted	FY03 Requested
Preparing For And Responding To Terrorism	**0**	**138.5**	**145.6**	**174.5**	**2485**	**2378**
Medical Responder Training and Exercises	0	3	1	2	140	651
Other Planning and Assistance to State/Locals	0	14.5	16.5	17.4	20	60
Other	0	4	3.1	5.6	83	123
Public Health Infrastructure and Surveillance	0	62	68	91.4	1034	1101
Special Response Units	0	4	5	6.1	51	43
Stockpile of Vaccine and Therapeutics	0	51	52	52	1157	400
Research And Development	**15.9**	**34.8**	**109.7**	**116.1**	**398**	**1833**
Basic Research incl. Gene Sequencing	13	17.2	29.7	35.4	178	440.6

Appendix D. *Continued.*

Table 1. *Continued*

Function	FY98 Actual	FY99 Actual	FY00 Actual	FY01 Enacted	FY02 Enacted	FY03 Requested
Detection/Diagnostics	0	5.7	5.9	6.1	?	?
Modeling, Simulations, System Analysis	0	0	0	0	?	?
Other	0	1.85	0	0	154	521
Personal/Collective Protection	0	0	0	1.2	?	?
Therapeutics, Treatments, and Vaccines	2.9	10.1	74.1	73.4	66	786.2
Total	**15.9**	**173.4**	**255.3**	**290.6**	**2883**	**4211**

NOTE: The totals for FY2002 and FY2003 do not include $97 million and $99 million, respectively, for the Food and Drug Administration's food safety program.

SOURCE: Office of Management of Budget, *Annual Report to Congress on Combating Terrorism*, July, 2001, pp. 19–36; "Bioterror Funding Provides Blueprint to Build a Strong New Public Health Infrastructure," *HHS News*, January 25, 2002; President George W. Bush, *Securing the Homeland, Strengthening the Nation*, February 2002; Tara Palmore et al., "The NIAID Research Agenda on Biodefense," *ASM News*, Vol. 68, No. 8 (2002), p. 379.

Appendix E.

Figure 1. Department of Health and Human Services Spending on Domestic Preparedness.

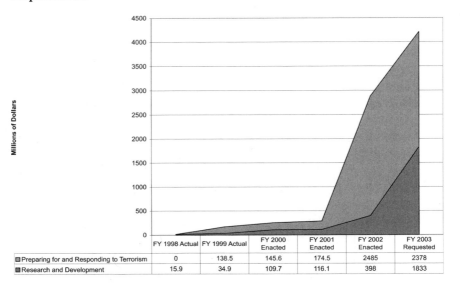

	FY 1998 Actual	FY 1999 Actual	FY 2000 Enacted	FY 2001 Enacted	FY 2002 Enacted	FY 2003 Requested
Preparing for and Responding to Terrorism	0	138.5	145.6	174.5	2485	2378
Research and Development	15.9	34.9	109.7	116.1	398	1833

Figure 2. Department of Health and Human Services Spending on Preparing for and Responding to Terrorism.

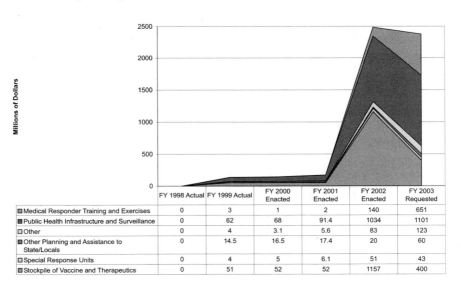

	FY 1998 Actual	FY 1999 Actual	FY 2000 Enacted	FY 2001 Enacted	FY 2002 Enacted	FY 2003 Requested
Medical Responder Training and Exercises	0	3	1	2	140	651
Public Health Infrastructure and Surveillance	0	62	68	91.4	1034	1101
Other	0	4	3.1	5.6	83	123
Other Planning and Assistance to State/Locals	0	14.5	16.5	17.4	20	60
Special Response Units	0	4	5	6.1	51	43
Stockpile of Vaccine and Therapeutics	0	51	52	52	1157	400

Figure 3. Department of Health and Human Services Assistance to State and Local Authorities.

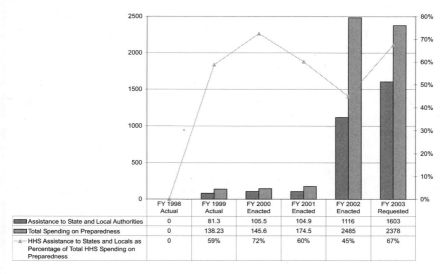

	FY 1998 Actual	FY 1999 Actual	FY 2000 Enacted	FY 2001 Enacted	FY 2002 Enacted	FY 2003 Requested
Assistance to State and Local Authorities	0	81.3	105.5	104.9	1116	1603
Total Spending on Preparedness	0	138.23	145.6	174.5	2485	2378
HHS Assistance to States and Locals as Percentage of Total HHS Spending on Preparedness	0	59%	72%	60%	45%	67%

Figure 4. Department of Health and Human Services Spending on Research and Development.

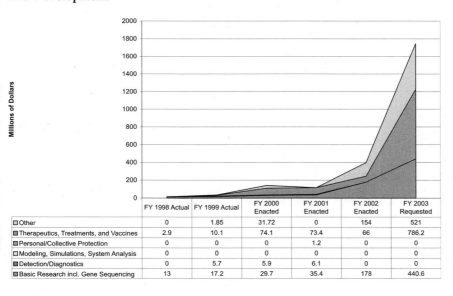

	FY 1998 Actual	FY 1999 Actual	FY 2000 Enacted	FY 2001 Enacted	FY 2002 Enacted	FY 2003 Requested
Other	0	1.85	31.72	0	154	521
Therapeutics, Treatments, and Vaccines	2.9	10.1	74.1	73.4	66	786.2
Personal/Collective Protection	0	0	0	1.2	0	0
Modeling, Simulations, System Analysis	0	0	0	0	0	0
Detection/Diagnostics	0	5.7	5.9	6.1	0	0
Basic Research incl. Gene Sequencing	13	17.2	29.7	35.4	178	440.6

Nuclear Terrorism: Risks, Consequences, and Response

Jim Walsh

Americans have lived with the fear of nuclear attack for over a half century. The decaying system of fallout shelters bears testament to a time when schoolchildren learned to "duck and cover," and there was a deep anxiety about the age of the atom. Today, threats of nuclear war and nuclear proliferation persist, but many worry that a new danger threatens the United States—a terrorist attack involving nuclear bombs, materials, or facilities.

This essay looks at the problem of nuclear terrorism and, in particular, at the role of state and local officials who may have to respond to such an event.[1] The first task is to define what is meant by the phrase "nuclear

Several people provided intellectual and editorial support for this essay, including the members of the Harvard International Working Group on Radiological Weapons, the members of the Executive Session on Domestic Preparedness, Annaliis Abrego, Leah Litman, Joe Pace, and Malini Daniel.

1. On nuclear terrorism in general, see Committee on Science and Technology for Countering Terrorism, National Research Council, "Nuclear and Radiological Threats" in *Making the Nation Safer: The Role of Science and Technology in Countering Terrorism* (Washington D.C.: National Academy Press, 2002); Jessica Stern, *The Ultimate Terrorists* (Cambridge, Mass.: Harvard University Press, 1999); Graham Allison. "Could Worse Be Yet to Come?" *The Economist* (November 1, 2001); Matthew Bunn, "Preventing Nuclear Terrorism." Testimony before the Subcommittee on National Security, Committee on Government Reform, United States House of Representatives. (September 24, 2002); Jim Walsh, "Nuclear Regimes and Nuclear Terrorism," Testimony before the Subcommittee on International Security, Proliferation and Federal Services of the Senate Committee on Governmental Affairs, *Multilateral Non-proliferation Regimes,*

terrorism." Three versions of nuclear terrorism are discussed: 1) use of a nuclear weapon, 2) operations against nuclear facilities that may result in the release of radioactivity, and 3) the use of radiological materials for purposes of contamination (e.g., with a radiological dispersal device or "dirty bomb"). Following a discussion of the consequences and risks associated with each scenario, the focus turns to state and local response. The characteristics of radiation-related incidents are reviewed, and special attention is given to the problem of public communications. The essay concludes with a brief look at how state and local authorities can prepare for and even prevent these kinds of attacks.

Threats and Risks

The phrase "nuclear terrorism" is used to describe a variety of incidents with wildly different characteristics. It covers both low probability–high consequence events like a terrorist employing a nuclear weapon as well as higher probability–low consequence events like those involving a crude radiological bomb. For the sake of completeness, this essay considers a broad range of scenarios, but the analytical emphasis is on the kinds of events that state and local officials are most likely to confront.

Terrorist Use of a Nuclear Weapon

A terrorist use of a nuclear weapon, even a crude fission device, would represent an unparalleled event in U.S. history. Depending on the size of the device, its location, and other variables, tens or hundreds of thousands of people could be killed in just the first few hours. A three mile area around the explosion would be devastated—a scene characterized by collapsed buildings, radiation, and, perhaps most deadly of all, firestorms. In addition, there would be the secondary, but not trivial, problem of radioactive fallout.[2]

How would a terrorist group get its hands on a nuclear weapon? Three scenarios are widely discussed: 1) a terrorist group builds its own

---

Weapons of Mass Destruction Technologies and the War on Terrorism, February 12, 2002, pp. 1–12; and Richard A. Falkenrath, Robert D. Newman, and Bradley A. Thayer, *America's Achilles' Heel: Nuclear, Biological, and Chemical Terrorism and Covert Attack*, (Cambridge, Mass.: The MIT Press, 1998).

2. On weapons effects, see Samuel Glastone and Philip J. Dolan, editors, *The Effects of Nuclear Weapons*, third edition (Washington, D.C.: Government Printing Office, 1977); Richard L. Garwin, "Nuclear and Biological Megaterrorism," 27th Session of the International Seminars on Planetary Emergencies, August 21, 2002, see http://www.fas.org/rlg/020821-terrorism.htm.

nuclear weapon, 2) a nuclear weapons state willingly transfers a nuclear weapon to a terrorist group, and 3) a terrorist group steals a nuclear weapon from a nuclear weapons state. Each is considered in turn.

Terrorists Build Their Own Nuclear Weapon

Of the three scenarios, a homemade nuclear weapon is the least likely. Despite stories that any bright college student can master the basics of bomb design, the historical record suggests that building a nuclear weapon from scratch is no small technical achievement. Even decades after the first nuclear bomb was built and used, national governments have had difficulty crossing the nuclear threshold. Iraq, for example, devoted billions of dollars and thousands of personnel to its bomb program in the 1970s and 1980s but, despite that effort, was unable to produce a working nuclear weapon.[3] Most countries that did develop nuclear weapons had to marshal a relatively large fraction of their country's financial and scientific resources to accomplish that objective. Terrorist groups, by contrast, command a tiny, tiny fraction of the resources available to governments.[4]

Moreover, the history of modern terrorism, a record that extends across literally thousands of incidents this past decade alone, indicates that most terrorists lack the technical sophistication to successfully pursue nuclear weapons. Indeed, virtually all terrorists have been content to follow the path of least resistance and instead employ conventional means of attack—truck bombs, plastic explosives, grenades, and the like.[5]

---

3. On Iraq's nuclear program, see, for example, Joint Intelligence Committee, *Iraq's Weapons of Mass Destruction*, (London: The Stationary Office, 2002); U.N. Security Council Document S/1997/779 [Fourth Consolidated Report of the Director General of the IAEA, under paragraph 16 of the Security Council Resolution 1051], October 8, 1997; Marvin M. Miller, "The Iraqi Nuclear Program: Past, Present and Future?," paper presented for the Conference on Non-Proliferation, IGC, University of California, held at Limassol, Cyprus, August, 18, 1995; Robert E. Kelley, "Two Substantially Different Approaches to Proliferation: The Cases of South Africa and Iraq," paper presented for the Conference on Non-Proliferation, IGC, University of California, held at Limassol, Cyprus, August, 18, 1995.

4. Al Qaeda and the Aum Shinrikyo cult in Japan, for example, enjoyed substantially greater financial resources than any other terrorist group. The Aum is reported to have had assets worth one billion, while al Qaeda's resources have been reported to be as high as $300 million. Neither figure comes close, however, to the resources available to midsized industrialized country, let alone the United States.

5. On terrorism, in general, see Bruce Hoffman, *Inside Terrorism*, (New York: Columbia University Press, 1998); Rohan Gunaratna, *Inside Al Qaeda Global Network of Terror*, (New York: Columbia University Press, 1998); Martha Crenshaw and John Pimlott, ed-

This low-tech approach fits well with the organizational "cell" structure used by most terrorist groups. In a cell structure, members in the organization know only a few others and work on a compartmentalized piece of an operation. Large, complex scientific projects—like building a nuclear weapon—require a completely different kind of organization, one in which groups of scientists and engineers know each other and exchange ideas in order to solve the technical obstacles that inevitably arise.[6] Nuclear weapons also require large stationary facilities, which are often vulnerable to detection. Such facilities run against the terrorists' interest in decentralized networks, secrecy, mobility, and the capacity to reconstitute themselves following successful police actions.

Still, some officials worry that a small group of highly trained individuals may be able to build a bomb of their own.[7] What makes this scenario at all plausible is the availability of large volumes of unprotected plutonium and highly enriched uranium (HEU) scattered across the former Soviet Union and other countries. Plutonium and HEU are the key ingredients for a nuclear weapon; no terrorist or country can make a nuclear weapon without possessing one of these materials. The production of fissile material is the most technically challenging part of a bomb program but, with 600 metric tons of these materials in storage in Russia alone (not to mention other nuclear weapons states such as Pakistan or some non-nuclear weapons states such as Japan), acquiring the special materials for bomb construction may not be as difficult as it once was.[8]

itors, *Encyclopedia of World Terrorism* (Armonk, N.Y.: M.E. Sharpe, 1997); Jim Walsh, ed., *Terrorism Documents of International and Local Control,* (Dobbs Ferry, N.Y.: Oceanna Publications, 2002).

6.   This tension between a desire for secrecy and compartmentalization on the one hand and the need for scientific collaboration and exchange on the other was evident in the Manhattan Project and other bomb programs. See, for example, Richard Rhodes, *The Making of the Atomic Bomb,* (New York: Simon & Schuster, 1986).

7.   J. Carson Mark et al., "Can Terrorists Build Nuclear Weapons?" in Paul Leventhal, and Yonah Alexander, *Preventing Nuclear Terrorism* (Lexington, Mass.: Lexington Books, 1987). Exercises conducted at the nation's nuclear weapons laboratories reportedly suggest that a small team with modest scientific training and the requisite materials could successfully construct a nuclear device. In general, however, estimates of this kind tend to underestimate the real world difficulties that proliferators encounter.

8.   Matthew Bunn, John P. Holdren, and Anthony Wier, *Securing Nuclear Weapons and Materials: Seven Steps for Immediate Action* (Cambridge, Mass.: Harvard University Managing the Atom Project and Nuclear Threat Initiative, May 2002), see http:// www.nti.org / e_research/securing_nuclear_weapons_and_materials_May2002.pdf; Matthew Bunn and George Bunn, "Strengthening Nuclear Security Against Post-September 11 Threats of Theft and Sabotage," *Journal of Nuclear Materials Management,* Spring 2002.

As it stands, however, no terrorist group is known to have come close to developing a nuclear weapon. Al Qaeda, probably the most sophisticated and well-financed international terrorist group in existence, has repeatedly expressed interest in nuclear weapons but has exhibited no capacity to execute such a project.[9]

The problem, however, is that the future may not be like the past. One can imagine a terrorist group of the future assembling a team of competent scientists and engineers and stealing enough fissile material for a crude device. The plain fact is that such a possibility, though not suggested by past experience, cannot be ruled out.

Transfer of a Nuclear Weapon by a Nuclear Weapons State

According to this scenario, a terrorist group acquires a nuclear weapon from a so-called "rogue state." Like the first scenario, this series of events is possible but, thus far, contradicted by empirical experience.

At no time in modern history has a government transferred any weapon of mass destruction—chemical, biological, radiological, or nuclear—to a terrorist group. If anything, national governments seem particularly careful about who controls such weapons. From a country's perspective, a terrorist group would appear to be a particularly unreliable partner. Terrorists often turn on their patrons, and, for their part, countries frequently stab their terrorist allies in the back once their foreign policy objective is accomplished. In short, it would seem foolish for a government to share its most precious weapons with violent, unreliable *non*state actors.

Recent events, however, illustrate at least two circumstances in which such a scenario appears at least plausible. One is suggested by the relationship between Afghanistan's Taliban and al Qaeda. Imagine, for example, that it is September 2001, but that the Taliban and al Qaeda control Pakistan, Afghanistan's eastern neighbor. Given those circumstances, it is certainly conceivable that the Taliban would have shared its (i.e., the Pakistani) nuclear stockpile with al Qaeda, particularly once U.S. forces began their post–September 11 military action. Similarly, recent events in Iraq have prompted speculation that a bloody tyrant on the verge of defeat might be tempted to provide a terrorist group with weapons of mass destruction as a last act of contrariness or revenge.

The Iraq–al Qaeda scenario seems unlikely, in part, because Saddam

---

9. David Albright, Kathryn Buehler, and Holly Higgins, "Bin Laden and the Bomb," *Bulletin of Atomic Scientists,* Jan.–Feb. 2002; Mike Boetcher and Ingrid Arnesen, "Al Qaeda Documents Outline Serious Weapons Program," *CNN,* January 25, 2002.

Hussein and Osama bin Laden are enemies, and in part, because an Iraq *in extremis* would more likely rely on its own operatives, not fanatical foreigners. Still, the picture is suggestive. A different set of players, at a different time, operating under the same conditions could conceivably lead to the transfer of the world's deadliest weapon.

Terrorists Steal a Nuclear Weapon

This last possibility, that a terrorist group is able to steal a useable nuclear weapon, represents a more realistic and uncomfortable possibility. A terrorist group that steals a nuclear weapon needs neither the technical sophistication traditionally required to build a weapon nor the permission of a suspicious dictator. It only requires that a government be sufficiently corrupt, inept, or challenged by crisis to lose control over a single weapon. This scenario also assumes that the weapon in question lacks a device that would prevent unauthorized use (e.g., a permissive action link, commonly found in U.S. and Russian nuclear weapons) or that the group can somehow overcome these protections.

What makes this scenario more likely than the "build-your-own" or the "gift" scenarios is that there is an abundance of evidence that governments can lose control of their nuclear stockpile. To begin with, countries sometimes lose their nuclear weapons outright. In the movie, the *Sum of All Fears*, terrorists acquire a nuclear weapon that Israel lost during the 1973 War. Pure Hollywood? Not really. The United States did, in fact, lose a nuclear weapon in the 1960s. A U.S. bomber flying near Polmares, Spain, crashed following a mid-flight accident. It took three months before the last of its nuclear bombs was recovered.[10]

Less innocent chains of events are also possible. Recent reports that Pakistani nuclear scientists sympathetic to al Qaeda met with bin Laden are again illustrative. No one has suggested that these Pakistani scientists were planning to give al Qaeda a nuclear weapon. Instead, it is thought that the scientists were simply briefing al Qaeda leaders on the basics of nuclear weapons. Still, given that sort of cooperation, it is not unreasonable to posit a situation in the future in which an official from a nuclear

---

10.   John German, "Palomares 'Bomb Number Four'—It Crashed, It Fell, It Sank, But (Whew!) It Never Blew Up, *Lab News*, January 19, 1995, see http://www.sandia.gov/LabNews/LN01–19–96/palo.html; Robert W. Simmons, "Nuclear Weapons Accident: Learning from the Palomares, Spain, 1966 Incident," *Ordnance* (February 1993), pp. 5–9; Air Force Surgeon General's Office, *Palomares Nuclear Weapons Accident, Revised Dose Evaluation Report*, April, 2001; Scott Sagan, *Limits of Safety*, (Princeton, N.J.: Princeton University Press, 1993), p. 178.

weapons state is persuaded by money, ideology, or grievance to help a group steal a nuclear weapon.

Finally, it is worth pointing out the obvious—no country lasts forever. Over human history, countries have come and gone. Yugoslavia and the Soviet Union are just two of the more recent examples. When countries collapse, their protection over nuclear weapons may become suspect. When the Soviet Union fell, 600 metric tons of nuclear material were left unprotected. Some day, Pakistan, China, North Korea, or any of the nuclear weapons states may break up or implode. What will happen to their nuclear weapons and nuclear materials?

One factor that helps reduce the risk of lost or stolen weapons is that, compared to the tons of fissile material, a modest number of warheads is fairly easy to count and track. Moreover, governments have a strong interest in maintaining control of these weapons. On average, one should expect that most countries, most of the time, take good care of their nuclear inventories. Unfortunately, when it comes to nuclear weapons, a system that is "mostly" secure may not be sufficient.

Attacks on Nuclear Facilities

A terrorist attack using a nuclear weapon represents a classic high consequence–low probability event. A second category of nuclear terrorism, an assault on a nuclear facility (e.g., a nuclear power plant or spent fuel storage facility) is a scenario that may be equally frightening in the popular mind but, in fact, poses fewer dangers to residents near the target facility. Even a worst-case attack or act of sabotage at a nuclear facility would result in far fewer deaths and injuries than the use of a nuclear weapon.[11]

Indeed, the United States and other countries have already experienced a number of high profile mishaps related to the operation of nuclear installations. Some names are familiar (Three Mile Island, Chernobyl), others are less so (Windscale, Tokaimura). These nuclear accidents resulted in unhealthy exposures to radioactivity, but the death toll

---

11. On nuclear facilities and terrorism in general see, Bruce Hoffman, *Terrorism in the United States and the Potential Threat to Nuclear Facilities*, (Santa Monica, Calif.: RAND, 1986); Paul Leventhal and Yonah Alexander, *Preventing Nuclear Terrorism* (Lexington, Mass.: Lexington Books, 1987); Mason Willrich and Theodore B. Taylor, *Nuclear Theft: Risk and Safeguards*, (New York: Ford Foundation, 1974); *Threat of Sabotage and Terrorism to Commercial Nuclear Powerplants*, Hearing before the Subcommittee on General Oversight and Investigations of the Committee on Interior and Insular Affairs, House of Representatives, 100th Congress, second session, March 9, 1988, (Washington, D.C.: Government Printing Office, 1988).

was not catastrophic. In most cases, the life of the nation—if not the local community—carried on as before.

In the United States, a terrorist could target any of the 103 civilian nuclear power plants located at 65 sites across the country. The sites also contain much of the nation's 42,000 tons of spent fuel, most of which is stored in temporary cooling ponds awaiting transfer to a permanent storage facility. The power plants and related on-site storage ponds are likely to be the most tempting targets for terrorists given their size and proximity to population centers, but terrorists could conceivably target military nuclear facilities or one of several dozen small research reactors.

Analysts who worry about attacks on the nation's nuclear power plants cite two concerns. One is that the terrorists may be able to rupture the core or otherwise damage the reactor in such a way that it results in a Chernobyl-style release of radioactivity and contaminated material. A second possibility is an attack on the adjacent spent fuel storage facilities could induce a radioactive fire that would send a plume of highly radioactive waste into the sky, which could be carried by the wind to communities both near and far.

By law, civilian nuclear power plants are required to establish a "design basis threat" (DBT) and take steps to protect the plant from the threat. The DBT is intended to characterize the threat that a particular facility is most likely to face. For most U.S. installations, this threat has been traditionally conceived of as an assault by a small group of commandos attempting to gain access to the plant.

Following the attacks of September 11, 2001, officials began to reassess and consider whether other threats are equally likely. In particular, there has been new attention given to the threat posed by a hijacked airliner being flown into a power reactor or spent fuel pond. 21 of the nation's nuclear power plants are located within five miles of an airport, and few have been designed in a way that takes into consideration this particular threat.

Are nuclear power plants at risk of a terrorist strike? It is difficult to say, in part, because there is both good news and bad news about the vulnerability of U.S. nuclear facilities. One piece of good news is that terrorists generally prefer "soft targets." Soft targets, such as buses and nightclubs, do not have specific security measures intended to prevent terrorism and are thus easier to attack with greater likelihood of success. Nuclear power plants, by contrast, have fences, guard posts, and security personnel who are in place to defend against a terrorist operation. They are hard targets.

The bad news is that despite a general preference for soft targets, there are a variety of indicators that some terrorist groups, notably al

Qaeda, may have an interest in targeting civilian nuclear reactors. Documents allegedly found in al Qaeda safe houses in Afghanistan and information collected from captured al Qaeda operatives appear to corroborate this interest. Indeed, strikes against power plants are consistent with bin Laden's often-articulated strategy of hitting targets that would hurt the U.S. economy.

The other piece of bad news is that while the Nuclear Regulatory Commission (NRC) requires plant operators to provide for security against the DBT, the reality is that NRC efforts in this area leave much to be desired. The commission has never given security a high priority, and, in past years, it has supported moves to shift the burden of security from the agency to industry. Even after September 11, it took months for the agency to require that the nation's nuclear plants step up their security measures. The NRC does require that power plants undergo periodic testing with mock commando raids, but the results of that testing have not been very encouraging. Most of the plants perform poorly on these tests, even under the most unrealistically favorable conditions (e.g., being given the date and time of the mock attack in advance).

A potential saving grace here—and the last piece of good news—is that some recent calculations suggest that it may be quite difficult from an engineering standpoint to induce a catastrophic event at a power plant. New post–September 11 analyses of the plane-into-the-reactor scenario, for example, maintain that a reactor would be able to withstand such an impact and maintain the integrity of the reactor core. Not surprisingly, others fault the studies for their methodology and contest these claims.[12]

In sum, terrorists will be drawn to nuclear facilities for some reasons and discouraged from attack for other reasons. Nuclear power plants have made preparations for terrorist attacks, which is more than can be said for much of U.S. energy infrastructure, but these preparations are likely insufficient. Terrorists may strike, and may successfully execute an attack, but despite their efforts and the deficiencies of plant security, the assault may not generate the spectacular result they seek, in large measure because of technical and engineering obstacles. At the end of the day, it is difficult to come to hard conclusions about the probability and

12. Douglas Chapin et al., Nuclear Power Plants and Their Fuel as Terrorist Targets," *Science*, Vol. 297 (September 20, 2002), pp. 1997–1999; Edwin S. Lyman, Statement on the *Science* article "Nuclear Power Plants and Their Fuel as Terrorist Targets," (Washington, D.C.: Nuclear Control Institute, 2002); Elizabeth Shogren, "A Year Later; Nuclear Facilities," *Los Angeles Times,* September 11, 2002, p. 14; Stephen Koff, "NRC Chief Reports No Specific Threat to Nuclear Plants," *Cleveland Plain Dealer,* September 11, 2002, p. A8.

likely consequences of an attack on domestic nuclear facilities. What is
not in doubt is that there are a number of measures that could be implemented to reduce vulnerabilities. Chief among these is the placement of
spent fuel in dry casks, a step that power plants will be required to take
in any case, if their waste is to be shipped to a permanent storage facility
such as the one planned for Yucca Mountain in Nevada.

Radiological Attacks

Like assaults on civilian nuclear facilities, a terrorist's use of radiological
material would be far less devastating than a use of a nuclear weapon.[13]
On the other hand, it represents the most likely scenario for nuclear terrorism.

A radiological weapon—also known as a dirty bomb, a trash bomb,
or a garbage bomb—is not a nuclear weapon. It is simply a conventional
weapon such as a truck bomb or a satchel filled with dynamite that also
contains radiological material. When the bomb goes off, it does not alter
the structure of an atom as a nuclear weapon would. Instead, it disperses
radioactive contamination. Despite its name, a radiological weapon does
not kill primarily by radiation. The vast majority of people killed in a
dirty bomb attack will be killed by the conventional blast, not the radiation effects. An elevated level of radiation will likely add marginally to
the cancer death rate for a given area, but the main and immediate effects
of such a weapon would likely be fear and economic disruption.[14]

The chances that a U.S. city will be the target of a radiological
weapon attack are difficult to assess. On the one hand, radiological weapons are not the weapons of choice among terrorists. As noted earlier, the
overwhelming majority of terrorist incidents have involved conventional
explosives, not weapons of mass destruction or mass disruption.[15] In

---

13. On radiological weapons and attacks in general, see Nuclear Regulatory
Commission, "Fact Sheet on Dirty Bombs," (Washington, D.C.: National Research
Council, July 2002), see http://www.nrc.gov/reading-rm/doc-collections/
fact-sheets/ dirty-bombs.html; Michael A. Levi and Henry C. Kelly, "Weapons of Mass
Disruption," *Scientific American*, November, 2002; Virginia Department of Emergency
Management, "Nuclear and Radiological Weapons: Description," (Richmond, Va.:
VDEM, 2002), see http://www.vdem.state.va.us/prepare/terrorismtoolkit/
terrguide/ weapons/nuclear.htm.

14. National Council on Radiation Protection and Measurements, *Management of Terrorist Events Involving Radioactive Material*, NCRP Report No. 138, (Bethesda, Md.:
NCRP, October 2001).

15. Though many countries looked at and, in some cases developed, radiological
weapons as part of a more general nuclear weapons program, no country has actually

fact, no person has ever been killed by the terrorist use of radiological material, and no more than a handful of incidents are known to have occurred.[16]

Analysts who worry about the radiological threat point out, however, that dirty bombs pose the fewest technical barriers of any weapon of mass destruction and fit well with most terrorist groups' training, experience, and organizational structure. The radiological materials that might be used in a radiological weapon are widespread, and the task of constructing a dirty bomb is easier than either building a nuclear weapon or inducing a reactor meltdown. Moreover, there are some indications that groups like al Qaeda have an interest in nuclear materials.[17]

Rating the Risk

How much danger do these three versions of nuclear terrorism pose? How worried should we be, and should the public be more worried about some scenarios more than others? There is no one answer, but a reasonable approach might compare the risks and consequences of nuclear terrorism with the risks and consequences of other known threats. In this case, one can compare nuclear terrorism with the dangers posed by conventional terrorism and by chemical and biological terrorism.

Based on historical evidence, conventional attacks—even mass casualty conventional attacks—are more likely to occur than any form of

---

used a radiological weapon. In the 1940s, the United States developed a plan for using radiological weapons against Soviet forces in the event that they overtook Saudi oil fields. The idea was to contaminate them until such time as U.S. forces were ready to retake them. More recently, there have been claims that Iraq tested a radiological weapon. On U.S. plans for radiological weapons, see Steve Everly, "1950 Memo Shows U.S. Mulled Radiological Attack," *Kansas City Star*, February 19, 2002, p. A1. On Iraq's efforts see, William J. Broad, "Document Reveals 1987 Bomb Test by Iraq," *The New York Times*, April 29, 2001, p. A8; Khihir Hamza, *Saddams' Bombmaker*, (New York: Scribner, 2000), p. 175.

16. Gavin Cameron, "Potential Sources of Radionuclides from Terrorist Activities: New challenges in Radioecology," paper presented at International the Conference on Radioactivity in the Environment, Monaco, September 2–5, 2002, (Østerås, Norway: International Union of Radioecology, 2002).

17. Kimberly McCloud and Matthew Osborne, WMD Terrorism and Usama Bin Laden, CNS Reports,(Monterey, Calif.: Center for Nonproliferation Studies, Monterey Institute for International Affairs, 2001), see http://cns.miis.edu/pubs/reports/binladen.htm; Bob Woodward, Robert G. Kaiser and David B. Ottaway, "Concern Over 'Dirty Bomb' Affects Security," *Washington Post*, December 4, 2001; David E. Kaplan and Douglas Pasternak, "Terror's Dirty Secret", *U.S. News & World Report*, December 3, 2001.

WMD terrorism. Since 1990, there have been over 4,000 international terrorist attacks, and only a handful of chemical, biological, or nuclear incidents.[18]

One can also compare nuclear terrorism with chemical and biological terrorism. Each of these forms of terrorism is rare. There have been a handful of chemical episodes, and it was only in the 1990s that the world witnessed the first fatality due to a terrorist chemical attack. Biological incidents have also been rare, the first U.S. fatality occurring during the fall 2001 anthrax attacks. In terms of consequences, only an extremely sophisticated biological weapon could approach the devastation caused by a nuclear weapon. Chemical and radiological attacks, most biological weapons attacks, and assaults on nuclear power plants would likely generate roughly similar results, for example, between one and one thousand deaths per attack, with the average number of deaths being on the lower end of the scale.

Within the domain of nuclear terrorism, attacks with radiological weapons or assaults on nuclear facilities are more likely than the use of a nuclear weapon. It is difficult to say, however, whether radiological or facility-based terrorism is more likely. Over time there have been a greater number of attacks on nuclear facilities than attacks with radiological weapons, and there is some evidence that al Qaeda has actively considered an operation against a nuclear power plant. On the other hand, nuclear facilities are hard targets and thus less attractive from a terrorist standpoint. Given those added burdens and the widespread availability of radioactive material, a radiological attack may be the preferred option.

Obviously, this comparison does not take account of important consequences such as economic dislocation, psychological effects, clean-up, and remediation. One might expect, for example, that clean-up costs would be substantially larger for a radiological or nuclear facility attack than for a conventional, chemical, or biological attack. Still, the comparisons provide a rough ordering.

The most likely events (e.g., standard conventional attacks; low to moderately successful chemical, biological, radiological, and facility-related incidents) will have smaller consequences. More deadly attacks (conventional mega-terrorism, highly successful radiological, chemical, and facility-related incidents) may very well take place, but with less frequency. Catastrophic attacks (nuclear weapons, high-success biological weapons) are the least likely but cannot be ruled out.

---

18. Department of State, "Patterns of Global Terrorism 2001," Appendix I Statistical Review, (Washington, D.C.: Government Printing Office, May, 2002).

Response: The Role of State and Local Officials

As with most emergencies, state and local officials will be the ones who will first grapple with the realities of a terrorist attack. Any terrorist strike brings special challenges for government officials, but this is especially true in the case of nuclear terrorism. This section examines a few of the unique burdens associated with this kind of attack. It focuses, in particular, on the less catastrophic types of nuclear terrorism (i.e., attacks involving radiological material and nuclear facilities) and not the use of a nuclear weapon.[19]

Three topics are examined. The first is the "information paradox" that defines nuclear terrorism. The second is a brief survey of some of the issues government responders will confront across the life cycle of a nuclear terrorist event. The third is a more detailed look at one of those issues: public communications.

NUCLEAR TERRORISM AND THE INFORMATION PARADOX

For state and local officials, terrorist events involving radiation or radioactive materials are marked by a fundamental characteristic: there is a great deal of information about radiation but no information or experience with radiological attacks.

Radiation is one of the most studied topics of the twentieth century. Governments, universities, corporations, interest groups, and others have sponsored an enormous amount of research on the health effects of radiation. Nuclear issues—nuclear weapons, nuclear energy, nuclear medicine, and nuclear waste—have been a familiar feature of the public and policy landscape for decades. By contrast, there is virtually nothing written about the problem of radiological or nuclear terrorism. No one has ever died from a terrorist attack employing nuclear materials, and in fact, no terrorist has ever detonated an explosive radiological dispersal device.

This is a mixed and peculiar blessing that makes it both easier and more difficult for government responders. On the positive side, for example, there is a tremendous amount of good science on the effects of radiation. The United States knows much more about radiation than it does about anthrax, for example. On the other hand, radiation's prominence as an issue means that most everyone has an opinion about it. It is a subject

---

19. Such attacks are far more likely and of roughly comparable magnitude. A terrorist use of a nuclear weapon, by contrast, represents a fundamentally different category of effects and consequences. It is also an event that would likely a) overwhelm the capacity of local officials and b) bring the immediate intervention of federal authorities.

that has generated decades of debate, controversy, and in some cases, governmental scandal.

For state and local authorities, the abundance of information can also be both a help and a hindrance. Many state and local governments, particularly those with nuclear facilities, have had to develop mechanisms for dealing with nuclear-related issues, including regulation, transportation, environmental oversight, and emergency response. Every state with a nuclear power plant, for example, has an emergency response plan and at least some personnel familiar with health physics. On the other hand, these procedures and resources will be insufficient, or in some cases, inappropriate for the challenges posed by a terrorist attack. Indeed, the presence of an existing bureaucratic structure for dealing with radiation accidents or non-hostile events may *inhibit* the ability of governments to respond to a new threat.

GOVERNMENT RESPONSE OVER THE LIFE CYCLE OF A NUCLEAR EVENT
Given the half-lives and latent health effects of some radioactive elements, a successful terrorist attack using radiological materials or against a nuclear facility will likely pose immediate, intermediate, and long-term policy challenges for area officials. These challenges will require governments to balance a number of competing and important interests.

In the days and weeks immediately following an attack, policymakers will have to contend with crisis management and consequence management. Unlike most natural disasters or even most terrorist attacks, responding to a radiological-related event requires addressing both real and perceived dangers. Health systems will need to respond to the medical needs of the victims, but they will also have to deal with the "worried well" who fear they may have been exposed to radiation.

One of the key challenges will be resolving jurisdictional issues. Terrorist attacks, particularly those involving nuclear facilities, will require the cooperation and coordination of a variety of governmental authorities. At the local level, that would include law enforcement, public health, environmental, and occupational safety agencies, among others. Moreover, state and local authorities will have to integrate their work with a number of federal agencies—e.g., Federal Emergency Management Agency (FEMA), Nuclear Regulatory Commission (NRC), Environmental Protection Agency (EPA), Department of Energy (DOE)—who may have competing interests. If radioactive material is dispersed in such a way that it crosses state lines, then there will be the additional need for interstate coordination. It would not be reassuring to the public, for example, to hear officials from different states offer widely differing assessments or advice.

In the intermediate term, the most difficult issues will likely involve the economic consequences of an attack and the need for cleanup and remediation. Depending on the particulars of the incident (the chemical composition of the radioactive material, the area of dispersion, the concentration of dispersion, and other related factors), a terrorist event could contaminate commercial buildings, transportation nodes, and other areas that could affect the local economy. A key issue will be the cleanup standard: how clean is clean? How much radiation, above natural background radiation, will be acceptable? This is a question that is likely to generate different answers. The NRC and the EPA, for instance, have very different views on the acceptable risks posed by radiation. Views among the public will also likely vary depending on their circumstances, e.g., whether they are homeowners, out-of-area customers, or parents with kids in the local schools.

In the long term, many of these issues will likely decline in intensity. The invisibility of radiation makes it particularly frightening, but it also makes it easier to ignore over time. Fifteen years after Chernobyl, many of the Scandinavian cities that found themselves showered with radioactive fallout have returned to equilibrium. Indeed, a return to normalcy is most likely in those places where options are limited. If businesses cannot move their operations, if residents cannot sell their homes, and if workers cannot move elsewhere for employment, then the pre-attack status quo may return rather quickly. This is all the more likely because any post-attack health effects will be difficult to distinguish and diffused over time. Nevertheless, some public health and environmental issues will persist, and locales whose economic resources are highly mobile or whose economic welfare depends on the perception of outsiders (e.g., tourists) may face continuing issues relating to economic revitalization.

Psychological Consequences and Public Communications

The research literature on radiological weapons and terrorism against nuclear facilities is exceedingly small, and it tends to follow a common pattern. Most treatments of the topic state up front that, as a general rule, the number of radiation-induced deaths and injuries from these kinds of terrorist attacks would be small, at least in relation to the casualties caused by the blast effects from the conventional component of a dirty bomb. These articles point out that the psychological and social consequences, on the other hand, may be severe. Unfortunately, most articles offer this conclusion but then gloss over the topic of psychological and social consequences and instead focus on physical health risks and first responder issues.

This essay also fails to treat the likely psychological and social consequences of a nuclear terrorist event in sufficient detail, but it does briefly examine one piece of the psychological dimension. Indeed, it is one aspect of the problem over which state and local officials have some control: public communications.

Any government faced with a terrorist attack will have to adopt a communications strategy. Such a strategy will have several goals, including obtaining the public's compliance with certain emergency directives (e.g., evacuation versus shelter in place) and minimizing fear and other potential psychological effects of the attack. Presuming a local authority knows what it wants the public to do immediately following such an attack, the odds are good that the public will follow the government's advice. Indeed, the history to date suggests that eliciting emergency compliance is easier than allaying public fear.[20]

It is fear, however, that is the core problem. Terrorist attacks, especially those involving radiation, are first and foremost about creating fear. A government's communications strategy thus plays a radically different role than it may play during a natural disaster. Disasters also cause fear, but that is neither their "goal" nor their most pronounced effect. Moreover, the fear resulting from a natural disaster does not affect the likelihood of future natural disasters. Such is not the case with terrorism. If a terrorist attack is successful in causing fear, it increases the odds that such an attack will be replicated. An effective communications strategy is, in essence, a counterterrorism tool. This is a frame of reference that differs greatly from traditional conceptions of emergency public communications.

The post–September 11 anthrax attacks vividly illustrate some of the difficulties that efforts at public communication may encounter. Governmental communications during the height of the anthrax attacks were plagued by problems, including changing assessments about the causes of contamination; varying statements about the nature of the contamination; statements concerning the health risks that were retracted (especially in the case of the postal workers, who were first told that they were not in danger); the virtual absence of any information from the Centers for Disease Control and Prevention (the agency considered the most knowledgeable about anthrax); the inelegant and hardly reassuring communications transition from local to federal officials; and statements by government agencies that encouraged widespread fear (e.g., the Postmas-

---

20. Ronald W. Perry, "Disaster Warnings as Risk Communications: Stimulating Immediate Citizen Action," June 2002.

ter General's announcement suggesting that all Americans were at risk of receiving an anthrax-laced letter).

In addition to these pitfalls, a radiation-specific communications strategy will encounter special challenges. Many of these are rooted in the information paradox described earlier. Two of these challenges are described below.

No Monopoly over Information

As was suggested above, there is no lack of information and opinion about the dangers of radiation. Contrast that with the anthrax incidents, where few people outside of government possessed information about weaponized anthrax, and fewer still had the ability to independently collect such information. This is not true with radiation. Any individual or any television station can order a Geiger counter from the Internet and collect readings on their own. Media outlets will also have a wide range of experts that they can interview. In this context, the media's desire to appear evenhanded and, thus, present opposing views, could mean that the airwaves will carry a variety of competing claims that the public will have to assess.

Others, besides worried citizens and the media, may also join the fray. A variety of interest groups, such as environmentalists and the nuclear energy industry, to name just two, will likely have strong feelings about the issue of radiation and may feel compelled to provide their own views and findings.

In an environment of high interest, low barriers to entry, and competing claims, government authorities will have to provide information that is timely. Any vacuum left by the absence of official information will be filled by other sources eager to offer their opinions. It will also require that officials be prepared to answer competing claims and explain why their information is more reliable. They will have to make this case to a public that is nervous about terrorism and suspicious about anything involving the issue of radiation.

Questions of Legitimacy

The sheer number of players that may seek to join a public discussion of radiation health risks is one issue that state and local communications strategies will have to address. Another is the issue of legitimacy. Even if officials respond promptly with quality information, it will be for naught if that information is not perceived as credible. Unfortunately for officials dealing with a radiation-related terrorist incident, there is a long and un-happy government track record in this area, including radiation experiments on human subjects, the exposure of soldiers and workers, and scandals involving various DOE facilities. This history may encourage skepticism of legitimate government claims.

The good news is that lessons derived from this long history of radiation and public communications can be used to help inform the actions of officials dealing with today's nuclear threats. The record suggests both actions to avoid and ideas to pursue when trying to reassure the public—openness, the involvement of stakeholders, and good science being key features of a successful strategy.[21]

Another piece of a successful strategy is preparation. What can local officials do to prepare for a radiological-related terrorist incident? The next section highlights some initial steps and discusses ways to prevent nuclear terrorism from happening.

Preparation And Prevention

The fight against nuclear terrorism has many components—securing vulnerable nuclear materials abroad, reducing the amount of nuclear material in use, reducing the number of countries with nuclear weapons, and reducing the size of nuclear stockpiles, to name a few. Many of these steps require action by federal authorities or international agencies. State and local governments also have a critical role to play. Their most important contributions are in the areas of preparation and prevention.

PREPARATION

Preparation will enable state and local authorities to minimize the consequences of a nuclear terrorist attack. It will help save lives and moderate the economic cost. In doing so, it will reduce the chances that nuclear terrorism will be perceived as an effective tactic.

State and local officials wanting to prepare for nuclear terrorism have an obvious starting point: current state and local radiological emergency plans. Existing plans typically focus on a nuclear power plant accident, but they provide a good first step. A radiological emergency plan will identify some of the resources available for governmental response and may provide a statutory or administrative platform for radiological ter-

---

21. Still, the lessons from past radiation-related controversies have their limits. DOE has wrestled with issues of public reassurance, but with the luxury of not having to worry about other parts of the equation, e.g., the economic consequences of losing 10 blocks of a city center.

rorism planning. Programmatically, that means that local officials have to initiate a process for rewriting the radiological emergency plan.

After starting with the radiological emergency plan, officials will have to go beyond it to incorporate the resources and agencies needed to respond to the particular demands of a terrorist attack. With the appropriate intragovernmental team in place, officials should begin to address the information paradox—that much is known about radiation and little about radiation-related terrorism. Officials can get a better handle on the threat posed by these forms of terrorism by staging tabletop and field simulations and using case studies of roughly analogous events, e.g., Chernobyl or the Aum Shinrikyo subway attack. Officials should also game out the communications piece and simulate an environment in which both a government's facts and legitimacy are contested.

PREVENTION

Imagine that you are a senior public official in a U.S. city. One morning you wake up to receive notification that the radiological materials used in an attack was traced back to a facility in your jurisdiction. Preventing radiological attacks or September 11–style attacks against nuclear power plants depends, in part, on actions by state and local authorities. Perhaps the best example of prevention is the control of radiological material. A domestic terrorist employing a radiological weapon would, in all likelihood, construct a device using a domestic source of radiological material. International terrorists could acquire the material outside of the United States, but they also could send operatives into the United States to procure domestic radiological material.

Today there are roughly two million radioactive sources licensed in the United States by the NRC. The commission also reports that since 1996, almost 1,500 radioactive sources were reported missing, more than half of which are presumed lost or stolen. Local authorities have strong self-interests—legal, public health, and environmental interests—in making sure that radiological materials in their jurisdictions are secure. This security depends on being able to inventory and monitor radiological sources. It also requires the safe storage and disposal of that material.

Conclusion: The Challenge of Nuclear Terrorism

There has never been a terrorist nuclear attack on U.S. soil, and so not surprisingly, most of us are not prepared to respond to such an event. Though the chances of such an attack are lower than the chances of a conventional terrorist attack, the risk is still high enough to warrant a strong response by local decision-makers, especially those in the nation's major cities.

An effective response to the threat of nuclear terrorism will require a commitment to planning, preparation, and prevention. State and local authorities can have a direct and sizeable impact on the likelihood and consequences of a terrorist strike, but doing so will require effort and change. In particular, it will require a different response model. Nuclear terrorism is not the same as a hazardous waste spill or an accident at the local power plant. Terrorism raises the stakes and introduces new complicating factors. To meet the challenge of nuclear terrorism, local officials will have to change their established plans and organizational procedures—a process that is difficult given the realities of bureaucratic politics. The new emergency plan will have to include law enforcement, competing federal agencies, and the capacity to coordinate with other states. Most important of all, it will have to develop a communications strategy that can function in hostile environments.

Meeting these objectives will not be easy, but the odds of success will increase substantially if the state authority assigns a single person to be responsible for coordinating efforts relating to nuclear terrorism. There are communities of people in every state—in health physics, in universities, in the public health community, in law enforcement—who are knowledgeable, concerned, and ready to address the problem. The task for local officials is to provide them with a structure and a political mandate that will enable them to move forward.

These steps—appointing a lead person to coordinate the state's prevention and response efforts; building the appropriate intragovernmental team; using simulations and case studies to test communications and other response capabilities—are relatively small steps that carry modest financial commitments. In today's world, a world in which there is no shortage of nuclear materials or people willing to use them, these small steps can save lives and preserve the long-term economic health of a community. One can hope that it will never come to that, but wisdom dictates that we prepare and do so sooner rather than later.

Covert Biological Weapons Attacks against Agricultural Targets: Assessing the Impact against U.S. Agriculture

Jason Pate and Gavin Cameron

Since 1995, analysts, policymakers, and the news media in the United States have focused unprecedented attention on the threat of terrorism involving weapons of mass destruction (WMD), particularly chemical and biological weapons (CBW). More recently, the threat of a biological attack against an agricultural target, often labeled "agricultural terrorism" (or "agroterrorism" for short), has become a concern for policymakers and practitioners. The purpose of this essay is to analyze, by investigating previous acts of agroterrorism and by looking at natural disease outbreaks, what economic and social impact an agroterrorist attack would have in the United States.

The essay begins with a discussion of the definition of agricultural terrorism. It then examines the historical record of agricultural terrorism cases and attempts to categorize such incidents by motive. Next, the essay reviews a number of naturally occurring outbreaks to provide a basis for determining the impact disease in the agricultural sector may have. To assess the vulnerability of the vast U.S. agricultural economy to terrorist attacks using biological weapons (BW), it then analyzes the diversity of U.S. agriculture and comments on the feasibility of attacking regionally focused crops. The essay then attempts to qualify and quantify the costs associated with an agroterrorist attack and the government-led effort to safeguard against or prepare to mitigate the effects of an attack, should one occur. Finally, the essay draws some conclusions from the data.

Definitions

Before looking to intentional and natural disease outbreaks and contamination in an effort to understand what economic impact a subnational

BW attack against an agricultural target would have, it is necessary to define the term "agricultural terrorism." One key issue in arriving at such a definition is how to categorize covert BW attacks. Are all such attacks terrorism? In some cases, where there is a terrorist group or individual using BW against agriculture, the term "agricultural terrorism" would obviously apply. In others, the motivations for the attack are criminal in nature with no link to furtherance of an ideological goal. Even in such cases, however, the attack is likely to have a psychological impact that goes beyond the immediate effects of the attack, a subsequent terrorizing effect. For this reason, these cases are covered in the analysis presented here, even though they cannot, by any reasonable definition, be included as terrorism *per se*. This essay defines agroterrorist attacks as subnational attacks against agriculture; to provide as comprehensive analysis as the data allow, we use the term subnational BW attacks against agriculture to include all of these cases. Though cumbersome, this term allows for more accurate analysis. Although attacks using chemical or even conventional weapons against agricultural targets could be considered examples of subnational agricultural attacks, for the purposes of this study, subnational agricultural attacks refers to the use of *disease* against agricultural targets, including crops and livestock, in an effort to cause widespread damage to or destruction of the target. This is a separate issue from the use of agents to contaminate specific products; in those cases, the target is actually people, and the incidents look more like consumer product tampering. However, because of the paucity of incidents of actual agricultural terrorism, this essay provides an overview of product contamination cases for context. Because chemical destruction is by nature self-limiting, we have chosen to look specifically in this essay at disease—at attacks using a biological agent.

It would be extremely difficult for a terrorist group to perpetrate a significant biological attack against the agricultural economy in the United States for several reasons. First, although obtaining and effectively delivering a biological agent is theoretically possible, given perpetrators who were motivated to do so, this vulnerability does not necessarily translate into a threat. Some agricultural agents can be obtained relatively easily and crudely delivered, but to cause a truly catastrophic incident may require a more sophisticated approach. Second, because crops and livestock in the United States generally appear in multiple locations across the country; eliminating a segment of the agricultural economy would require a multi-pronged attack and a sophisticated understanding of the economy. Although not impossible, this type of attack presents significant obstacles. Third, the U.S. agricultural economy has in

place networks and plans to respond to an attack once detected, and surveillance of crop and animal disease in the United States is extraordinarily sophisticated. Even if a terrorist group managed to deliver a biological agent effectively against a target, the effects of the attack would
likely be severely limited by the U.S. response. Fourth, although a determined group could conceivably carry out a devastating attack, there is no
evidence of terrorist groups with the motivation to carry out a catastrophic attack against U.S. agriculture. It is clear, however, that more research is required before an accurate assessment can be made of the
threat terrorism poses to the U.S. agricultural economy.

Although often cited cases of subnational BW agricultural attacks
have involved threats of contamination of specific products, causing
significant economic losses through diminished consumer confidence,
they did not threaten the loss of an entire segment of the agricultural sector. Although the diffusion, both geographically and typologically, of agricultural production across the United States makes a catastrophic attack
on or the total elimination of a significant portion of the national agricultural economy highly unlikely, regional economies could be significantly
affected. Moreover, certain segments of the agricultural economy in the
United States may be sufficiently concentrated or sufficiently unique that
an attack against them could have major regional consequences.

Incidents Involving Subnational BW Agricultural Attacks

Historically, agroterrorist attacks have been relatively rare occurrences.
As of August 2, 2000, the database of WMD Terrorism Incidents at the
Center for Nonproliferation Studies, Monterey Institute (the database),
held 21 incidents that may be classified as subnational BW agricultural
attacks—only a small fraction (2.5 percent) of the total number (853) of incidents contained in the database.[1] Moreover, although high profile con-

---

1. The Monterey Institute WMD Terrorism Database, created in 1997, is a unique
open-source database of worldwide incidents involving sub-national actors and chemical, biological, radiological, or nuclear materials from 1900 to the present. CNS staff
members designed an extensive information collection system to gather data from the
Internet and news media sources, using a lengthy search string based on specific
WMD agents and materials. Each year, staff members review approximately 200,000
documents and identify relevant incidents based on specific criteria. Accidents, individual poisonings/murders (except for political assassinations), and purely criminal
incidents with no intent to cause indiscriminate casualties are excluded from the database. Anomalous or bizarre cases are assessed on an *ad hoc* basis by the staff as consistently as possible. Selected incidents are then researched and entered into the database

cern over the potential threat is a relatively new phenomenon and has centered in the United States, the historical record indicates that acts of agricultural terrorism have been perpetrated worldwide for decades. Of the 21 incidents of subnational CBW agricultural attacks in the database, five occurred in the United States, four occurred in Israel, and others took place in Canada, China, Sri Lanka, the Philippines, Australia, Uganda, and Kenya, and throughout Europe. Clearly, then, the threat of agricultural terrorism, which has been limited thus far, is not specific to the United States.

MOTIVATION: EXTORTION, INTIMIDATION, AND ECONOMIC PUNISHMENT

Agricultural attacks have predominantly been used as a means of extortion, intimidation, or economic punishment, rather than to injure or kill humans. The earliest incident in the database occurred in Kenya in 1952, when members of the Mau-Mau, an anticolonialist group, inserted the latex of the African milk bush plant into cuts made in the skin of 33 steers, eight of which died.[2] Within the United States, members of the Ku Klux Klan supposedly poisoned the water supply of cattle owned by a group of Black Muslims in Ashville, Alabama, in March 1970. A local veterinarian identified the poison as cyanide, and it killed 30 cattle and sickened nine others.[3] The incident may have been part of a sustained campaign of intimidation by the Klan against the owners of the farm.

A number of cases worldwide and the majority of cases in the United States reflect the targeting of exports or products rather than agriculture *per se*. In the 1980s, Huk terrorists poisoned Dole pineapples in the Philippines that were meant for export. However, the contaminated pineapples were discovered and destroyed before any harm was done.[4] In September 1997, an ex-Kurdistan Workers Party member claimed that the group

---

according to standardized coding criteria and typologies. For security reasons, access to the Monterey WMD Terrorism Database is restricted to law enforcement agencies and other qualifying entities, including certain international organizations and government agencies. For more information, contact Jason Pate at CNSDB@miis.edu.

2. Seth Carus, "Bioterroism and Biocrimes: The Illicit Use of Biological Agents in the 20th Century," National Defense University, Washington D.C., Working paper, August 1998 (March 1999 revision), p. 73.

3. "Poison Is Suspected in Death of 30 Cows On a Muslim Farm," *New York Times*, March 16, 1970, p. 30; James Wooton, "Black Muslims Would Sell Farm to Klan," *New York Times*, March 17, 1970, p. 32; "Wallace Seeking More Policemen," *New York Times*, December 12, 1971, p. 50.

4. Ron Purver. "Chemical and Biological Terrorism: The Threat According to the Open Literature," CSIS/SCRS (June 1995), <www.csis-scrs.gc.ca/eng/miscdocs/biblio_e.html>.

planned to target Turkish vegetable exports.[5] In July 1986, threats from the Azanian Peoples Liberation Front, an anti-apartheid group, were published in the Canadian press to the effect that South African fruit would be poisoned with a toxic chemical.[6] Although no poisoned fruit was discovered, two Canadian supermarket chains ceased sales of all South African fruit.[7] The South African fruit sales ceased because of the poisoning threat at the time with no clear indication from the two supermarkets when sales would resume. Within the United States, exports have also been a target: in January 2000, an email message spread to Internet users that warned that Costa Rican bananas were contaminated with necrotizing fasciitis, a disease caused by flesh-eating bacteria.[8] The email message was signed "Manheim Research Institute Center for Disease Control, Atlanta, Georgia," which is a false organization according to the Centers for Disease Control and Prevention (CDC).[9] No basis was discovered for the threat, and it is doubtful whether it is possible, even theoretically, to contract the disease as a consequence of eating food.[10]

MOTIVATION: POLITICAL

Although their impact is primarily financial, agricultural attacks have obvious social consequences as well that may be used as a tactic for political as well as criminal purposes. In fact, of the 21 cases of subnational BW agricultural attacks in the database, only five were classified as criminally motivated. This is partly a consequence of the database's inclusion criteria,[11] but it is nevertheless extremely significant that 16 incidents were

---

5. Shyam Bhatla Naxos and Leonard Dayla, "Poison bomber offers secrets for sanctuary," *The Observer,* September 28, 1997, available at http://www.byegm.gov.tr , accessed on May 21, 1998.

6. Purver, "Chemical and Biological Terrorism: The Threat According to the Open Literature."

7. "Quebec's largest food distributor removes S. African fruit," *Reuters,* July 11, 1986; Michael Babad, "Threats halt sales of S. African fruit at Canadian stores," *United Press International,* July 15, 1986; Michael Babad, "Canadian stores stop selling South African fruit," *United Press International,* July 16, 1986.

8. David Emery, "The Great Banana Scare of 2000," (February 23, 2000), <urbanlegends.agends/library/weekly/aa022300a.htm>.

9. Emery, "The Great Banana Scare of 2000."

10. "Banana Fits," Urban Legends Reference Pages: Toxin du jour (Banana Fits), <www.snopes.com/toxins/bananas.htm>, accessed on July 27, 2000; "False Internet Report about Bananas," National Center for Infectious Diseases, ov/ncidod/banana.htm, accessed on May 31, 2000; "E-mail at UC Riverside Helped Spread Hoax About Bananas," Los Angeles Times, February 16, 2000, p. A18.

11. See footnote one.

classified as politically motivated; agricultural terrorism is a means of political as well as financial extortion.

In fact, when people have been injured or even killed as a result of agricultural terrorism, it has generally been when the incident is politically motivated but closely resembles consumer product tampering. In 1978, the Arab Revolutionary Council used liquid mercury to poison citrus fruit exports from Israel to Europe. Israeli orange exports were reduced by 40 percent, and twelve people were injured when they ate contaminated oranges.[12] In this case, though, despite the injuries, the primary target of the attack was the Israeli economy. A more serious case was uncovered in May 2000, when inspectors from the Israeli Agricultural Development Authority discovered that Palestinians had been using counterfeit stamps on expired and salmonella-ridden eggs that were then sold throughout Israel. Although they had been operating the scheme for 18 months, it is unclear how many contaminated eggs were sold or how many people were sickened as a result. In September 1999, two Israelis died of salmonella as a result of eating contaminated eggs. According to Israeli news sources, there may have been "widespread food poisoning in the Israeli Defense Force and among tourists" as a result of the Palestinians' actions.[13] Clearly, in this case, the intended impact was not only economic, but also disruption of the Israeli military and society, a direct and politically motivated attack on people.

Pro-Palestinian groups, more than other terrorist organizations, appear to have used politically motivated product tampering agricultural terrorism as one in a series of strategies. In each case, the actions of such Palestinian groups are examples of the product-tampering type of agricultural terrorism. In 1974 in Genoa, Italy, the "Revolutionary Command" announced that it had "injected toxic substances into Israeli-

---

12.   Joseph Douglass Jr. and Neil C. Livingstone, *America the Vulnerable: The Threat of Chemical and Biological Warfare* (Lexington, Mass.: Lexington Books, 1987), cited in Ron Purver, "Chemical and Biological Terrorism: The Threat According to the Open Literature," (Canadian Security Intelligence Service, unclassified, June 1995), pp. 87–88; Yonah Alexander, "Will Terrorists Use Chemical Weapons?" *JINSA Security Affairs* (June–July 1990), p. 10 cited in Purver, "Chemical and Biological Terrorism," pp. 87–8.

13.   "Counterfeit stamps put on diseased eggs," *Ha"Aretz*, May 23, 2000, available on http://www3.haaretz.co.it/eng/scripts/print.asp?id=78775, accessed on June 23, 2000; "Warnings of contaminated eggs being sold with official stamp," *Israel Wire*, May 26, 2000, com/new/00526/00052626.html, accessed on June 23, 2000; "Woman dies from salmonella," *Israel Wire*, September 13, 1999, com/New/990913/99091328.html, accessed on June 23, 2000.

produced grapefruit."[14] In 1979, the Arab Revolutionary Council threatened to contaminate a range of Israeli agricultural exports to Europe.[15] In April 1988, again in Italy, the Organization of Metropolitan Proletariat and Oppressed Peoples, acting in support of the Palestinian *intifada*, claimed to have injected poison into Israeli grapefruit. Grapefruit contaminated with a non-harmful agent were discovered in Naples and Rome, and the Italian government then withdrew all Israeli grapefruit from sale.[16] Interestingly, Israeli individuals or groups have targeted Palestinian agriculture too, but such attacks have been directed against crops rather than exports. Therefore, they have had a more direct, although possibly less widespread, impact than that achieved by Palestinian undermining of consumer confidence in Israeli fruit.[17]

Elsewhere in the world, agriculture has been targeted for a range of political objectives. In 1977, Ugandan dissidents threatened to poison the country's coffee and tea crops in an effort to severely affect Ugandan foreign exchange, thus undermining the economy.[18] The LTTE (Tamil Tigers) threatened to use biological weapons to attack Sri Lankan crops in the mid-1980s.[19] In January 1984, Pater Vivian Wardrop threatened to use foot-and-mouth disease (FMD)[20] to attack livestock in Queensland, Australia, unless prison reforms were undertaken.[21] In none of these cases

---

14. The RAND-St. Andrews Terrorism Chronology: Chemical/Biological Incidents, 1968–1995, RAND Corporation, Santa Monica, Calif.

15. Ibid.

16. Ibid.

17. Other examples of agroterrorism on behalf of pro-Palestinian groups include: in October 1997, settlers from Gosh Etzion sprayed a chemical on grapevines in two Palestinian villages south of Bethlehem. The settlers supposedly destroyed hundreds of vines and up to 17,000 metric tons of grapes. In June 2000, settlers from Efrat released sewer water onto Palestinian fields in Khaddar, near Bethlehem. Farmers estimated their losses at around $5,000. Although the settlers were undoubtedly pursuing a campaign to drive Palestinian farmers from the land, it is unclear whether they sought to do so by poisoning crops with sewage or by simply flooding the fields with the water.

18. RAND-St. Andrews Terrorism Chronology.

19. Carus, "Bioterrorism and Biocrimes."

20. FMD is a highly infectious wasting disease that affects ungulates (hoofed animals) and which is characterized by blistering on the foot and around the mouth of the animal.

21. Purver, "Chemical and Biological Terrorism," p. 35; Tony Duboudin, "Murderer in court over virus threat," *The Times*, February 22, 1984, p. 5; *Reuters*, December 5, 1984.

was there any indication that an attack had actually been perpetrated or that an agent for use against agriculture had been successfully acquired.

MOTIVATION: INDIVIDUAL REVENGE

Forms of subnational agricultural attacks have been used as a means of settling personal scores. In the mid-1990s, a farmer in China used rat poison to kill 12 of his neighbors' water buffalo, along with four of his neighbors, supposedly because they were better off than he.[22] In 1997, Brian W. 'Skip" Lea, of Berlin, Wisconsin, used the fungicide folpet and the illegal pesticide chlordane to contaminate products manufactured by National By-Products, a supplier for Purina Mills animal feed that he regarded as a business competitor.[23]

MOTIVATION: SINGLE ISSUE FANATICISM

More interesting was the 1989 case of the Breeders, a previously unknown group that threatened to spread the Mediterranean fruit fly (Medfly) throughout California if aerial spraying of pesticides continued in the state. The Medfly infestation in California at that time was unusually large and had a number of characteristics that led investigators to conclude a deliberate infestation was being propagated. No one was ever caught for promoting the spread of the Medfly, however.[24] The case had a number of noteworthy aspects, particularly in that the motivation for the action was environmentalism. Although causing economic damage seems the most likely political reason to perpetrate an act of agricultural terrorism, the Breeders case shows that some single-issue groups may be similarly interested in such a tactic. Protesters concerned with genetically modified foods, as well as environmentalists, seem plausible candidates to consider an act of agricultural terrorism or agro-sabotage. The Breeders used a biological means, the Medfly, to attack crops in Califor-

---

22. "The Poisoned World—1998," University Sains Malaysia (1998), U.S.m.my/diary/text298.html, accessed March 29, 1999.

23. Gretchen Schuldt, "Man indicted on charges of tainting animal feed; Berlin plant contaminated with toxic pesticide in 1996," *Milwaukee Journal Sentinel,* September 15, 1999, p. 1; Richard P. Jones, "Product Recalled in Four States; Animal Feed Tainted in Act of Sabotage," *Milwaukee Journal Sentinel,* January 4, 1997, p. 1; "MDA Investigates Possible Feed Contamination," *Newswire,* January 6, 1997.

24. John Johnson, "Female Medfly Found in Sun Valley Close to Area Targeted Earlier," *Los Angeles Times* January 4, 1990, p. B3; Ashley Dunn, "Officials Advertise to Contact Mystery Group Claiming Medfly Releases," *Los Angeles Times,* February 10, 1990, p. B3; Stephanie Chavez and Richard Simon, "Mystery Letter Puts a Strange Twist on Latest Medfly Crisis," *Los Angeles Times,* December 3, 1988, p. B1 (Orange County Edition).

nia. By contrast, most attacks have either been hoaxes or relied on chemical agents to attack agriculture. It is biological, not chemical, weapons, however, that can potentially have the most widespread effects on agriculture.

Naturally Occurring Outbreaks of Disease

There have been very few instances that could be deemed "agricultural terrorism" in the United States; the empirical data is therefore quite limited. Although there have been some well-known cases of agricultural product contamination, these cases did not target crops or livestock and were thus not examples of subnational actors seeking to eliminate a specific crop or portion of the agricultural base. Without a set of cases to examine, it is extremely difficult to predict accurately what an incident of agricultural terrorism would involve, how it would present itself, how it would be detected, and what its consequences would be.

By looking at natural outbreaks of disease in segments of the agricultural economy in the United States and other countries, however, it may be possible to identify and quantify the actual impact of an attack against U.S. agriculture. These outbreaks, although they do not carry with them the same level of psychological impact that is normally associated with terrorism, do provide a baseline for economic analysis and estimates of disease impacts on local, regional, and national economies.

Beginning in February 2001, a major outbreak of FMD occurred in the United Kingdom (UK) and spread to France, the Netherlands, and Ireland. Affecting cloven-hoofed animals, such as cattle, pigs, and sheep, the viral infection resulted in widespread import bans on livestock and dairy and meat products from European Union (EU) countries. The disease is extremely infectious and can be spread either by direct or indirect (e.g., by dirty straw or human clothes) contact with an infected animal. The British outbreak originated in a single pig herd in northeastern England, where animals ate swill containing infected meat imported illegally from East Asia. (FMD is endemic in areas of Africa, the Middle East, and Asia.) As the origin of the British outbreak shows, the FMD virus can survive processing, explaining the ban not only of live animals from affected countries but also of many animal products as well.

Between February 20, 2001, and February 1, 2002, 2,030 separate cases of FMD were reported in the UK, and a much smaller number of possible cases had been reported in France, the Netherlands, and Ireland.[25] Al-

---

25. The most recent case occurred on September 30, 2001. UK Department for Envi-

though the disease has a relatively low mortality rate—around five percent of affected animals, mostly those that are young or old—it has a major economic impact. The meat and milk producing capacity of affected animals drastically declines, and there is an increased incidence of miscarriages in animals that have suffered the disease. Within the UK, compensation was available, so it was more economical for a farmer to slaughter the animal than to keep it. More importantly, however, recovered animals may still be viral carriers, presenting a continued threat of infection and increasing the incentive to destroy such animals.[26]

As well as incurring import bans, the outbreak of FMD restricted movement of livestock within the UK. Markets closed, and only a small number of animals from unaffected herds were moved to slaughterhouses, under tightly controlled conditions. Since culled animals from affected herds must be burned, rather than sold for meat, the restricted number of animals being slaughtered for food resulted in a shortage that had to be satisfied by importing meat from outside the United Kingdom at an increased cost to consumers.

The economic costs to farmers and the wider agricultural sector was devastating. Even those farms that were unaffected stood to suffer huge losses, because the disease compelled all livestock markets to be shut

---

ronment, Food and Rural Affairs (DEFRA), "Foot and Mouth Disease," defra.gov.uk/footandmouth, accessed on February 1, 2002.

26. Although vaccines are available to counter the disease, these should ideally be administered before an animal is exposed to FMD. This is complicated further, as there are seven major strains of the disease and several subtypes, limiting the scope of a vaccination to be effective against all varieties of the disease. The "killed" vaccines offer protection for just six to nine months, so animals must be repeated immunized. More important still is the need to sell meat to countries free of FMD. A vaccinated animal can neither be distinguished from one that has had the disease nor does vaccination prevent an animal from acting as a carrier. Vaccination, therefore, is an expensive option, particularly in countries where the disease is not endemic and also has implications for trade. Consequently, the more common response has been to destroy every cloven-hoofed animal on affected farms. "Foot and Mouth Outbreak: Special Report," *BBC News Online*, available at <news.bbc.co.uk/hi/english/in_depth/uk/2001/foot_and_mouth/default.stm>, accessed on May 14, 2001. Britain ultimately slaughtered 4,080,001 animals with foot-and-mouth disease or from infected farms. However, a further 2,573,317 animals were slaughtered under the Animal Welfare Disposal Scheme and the Light Lambs Disposal Scheme for farmers not hit by foot-and-mouth disease but whose stock was suffering from movement restrictions. UK Department for Environment, Food and Rural Affairs figures, cited in Ann Treneman, "The new haves and have-nots" The Times, January 31, 2002, Section 2, pp. 2–5; European countries have also slaughtered thousands of animals that may have come into contact with British livestock. See also "Foot-and-mouth disease: The costs and cures," Business News Special, *The Economist*, March 31, 2001, available at <www.economist.com/printedition/displayStory.cfm?Story_ID=549904>, accessed on April 2, 2001.

down; most farmers had no income, only expenses, for several months. Moreover, the economic prospects for such farmers were grim: they were forced to retain animals past the optimum time to ship them off to slaughter, and when the markets finally opened, the price of meat fell, because every farmer was in the same situation and flooded the market. Moreover, while there was compensation for farms where animals were slaughtered as a direct consequence of FMD (either due to infection or prevention), the compensation for indirectly affected farms was less certain. Even the money for slaughtered animals is unlikely to be sufficient to return farms to pre-disease levels. The government money was based on stock valuation, rather than being compensation for lost income. Once the outbreak was over, the cost of new animals for replacing herds and flocks was high due to the short-term scarcity of breeding stock.

The FMD outbreak had significant political implications: the British government felt obliged to postpone both a national election and local elections. The government's handling of the crisis became a source of political debate, and the government department responsible for agriculture—the Ministry of Agriculture, Fisheries and Food (MAFF)—found itself under pressure, being accused of bungling the prevention and control of the disease. MAFF was ultimately closed and replaced by a new government department with rearranged responsibilities—the Department for Environment, Food and Rural Affairs.

However, it is hard to suggest that the outbreak presents a strategic threat to the UK economy: agriculture and even the associated loss of tourism are not significant enough. Farming currently represents 0.9 percent of UK gross domestic product (GDP) and employs 1.5 percent of the UK workforce. The FMD epidemic is likely to continue to reduce the value of the agricultural sector, as some farmers decide that their compensation does not permit a return to the occupation that offered economically marginal returns, even before the outbreak. However, the economically more significant impact of the disease was on tourism. Although FMD only very rarely affects humans (when it presents itself as flu-like symptoms), tourist bookings for holidays in the UK were severely affected by the disease outbreak.

Differentiating between naturally occurring outbreaks of disease and those caused purposefully by subnational entities is extremely difficult and may be impossible, if no group or individual comes forward to claim responsibility for the outbreak. Epidemiological evidence may suggest intentional spread of disease, for example, the appearance of a strain of disease not endemic to the region or the occurrence of the disease at several nonproximal sites simultaneously. Even this type of information, however, may not be completely reliable. The outbreak of West Nile virus in the northeastern United States that began in September 1999 is such an example, being a naturally occurring outbreak of an exotic, non-indigenous disease never previously seen in the United States.[27] In addition, if it were discovered that a particular outbreak had been intentionally caused, would it be in the public's best interests to make that information widely available? Doing so could create panic and incidentally assist the goals of the perpetrator. Naturally occurring outbreaks continue to have economic impacts, but thus far, subnational attacks against agricultural targets have been limited in scope and sophistication. Technical obstacles to effective acquisition, maintenance, and delivery of microorganisms partially explain the limited scope of such attacks, but a more telling explanation is that there is little evidence that subnational groups are interested in this type of attack.

It is widely acknowledged that usable agricultural pathogens are likely to be more easily acquired than are their human equivalents. Dissemination of these agents may also be extremely straightforward, in some cases, such as that of some rusts or FMD, which supposedly require no more than swabbing an infected animal or crop and transferring the sample to a healthy animal or crop elsewhere. The theory holds that these highly infectious diseases would then spread naturally within their new host population. However, rigorous surveillance, quarantine, and eradication programs are likely to help curtail the spread of such diseases, and crop pathogens are generally vulnerable to environmental factors such as light, heat, and wind. Even with frequent transport of agricultural goods across the country, it is reasonable to hope that outbreaks initiated or spread by such methods may be contained within a region. In such circumstances, the attack need not be catastrophic. To achieve widespread effect in all but the most localized crops (such as almonds), multiple attacks would likely be necessary. Discussion of such an approach is beyond the scope of this paper, but it clearly increases the quantities of agent required and the likelihood of being apprehended.

Diversity of U.S. Agriculture

Part of the reason that the United States has been able to avoid some of the most catastrophic consequences of agricultural pestilence has been the diversity of the national agricultural economy.[28] In 1997, the market

27. Jennifer Steinhauer, "Outbreak of Virus in New York Much Broader Than Suspected," New York Times, September 28, 1999, p. A1.

28. The information in this section was obtained from <www.usda.gov> and email

value of agricultural products sold in the United States was more than $208 billion. Although some states clearly had disproportionate shares of the total, it was widely distributed across the states. California was the leading agricultural state, with products valued at $25.2 billion, or 12.1 percent of the U.S. total; Texas was second with $13.4 billion, followed by Iowa ($12.8 billion), Nebraska ($10 billion), and Illinois ($9 billion). The top five states accounted for 34 percent of the U.S. total. However, 27 states, spread across the country, had agricultural products valued at more than $3 billion; 20 states had more than $4 billion of business, and 9 had $6 billion.

A similarly diverse geographical pattern can be seen among individual agricultural products, particularly major crops and livestock. Of the leading states, measured by cash receipts in 1997, Texas produced about 16 percent of U.S. cattle and calves and about 22.5 percent of U.S. cotton; California about 17.2 percent of U.S. dairy products and 14.7 percent of the country's hay; Iowa about 18.5 percent of U.S. corn, 22.4 percent of the country's hogs, and 17.9 percent of its soybeans; Georgia about 16.1 percent of U.S. broilers; and Kansas about 16.8 percent of U.S. wheat. Clearly, although there are some regional concentrations, such as cattle and corn in the Midwest, the scale of production and geographical distances involved offer some level of protection against catastrophic attacks.

Some other crops are far more concentrated and thus potentially substantially more vulnerable to a major attack. Using 1997 cash receipts figures from within the United States, 92.2 percent of grapes, 47 percent of tomatoes, 33.8 percent of oranges, 77.8 percent of lettuce, 100 percent of almonds, and 75.5 percent of strawberries were grown in California; 41.3 percent of tobacco in North Carolina; 53.5 percent of apples in Washington; 38.9 percent of peanuts in Georgia; 43.3 percent of rice in Arkansas; and 65.7 percent of oranges in Florida.

Even within individual states, crops may be further concentrated, making them more vulnerable to attack. Three adjacent counties in California—Fresno, Madera, and Tulare—produced 55.1 percent of all U.S. grapes in 1997. Another striking example is lettuce. California cultivated 77.8 percent of U.S. lettuce in 1997, and 57 percent of the national acreage for lettuce production was in six bordering counties in that state: Santa Cruz, Monterey, San Benito, Fresno, San Luis Obispo, and Santa Barbara. Strawberry production provides another impressive illustration. A little over 41 percent of Californian strawberry production, which comprises

exchanges with Jim Tippett, State Statistician for the California Department of Agriculture.

over 75 percent of total U.S. production, was in two contiguous counties (Santa Cruz and Monterey), and another 33 percent of Californian production was in two nearby counties (Santa Barbara and Ventura).

In addition to these specific concentrations, it is important to note that a few counties spread over many square miles in the relatively compact San Joaquin Valley produce most of these crops. A disease that could affect several crops would have even greater impact on regional economies and aggregate production, thereby increasing the apparent vulnerability of certain sectors of the U.S. agricultural economy.

This geographical diversity of agriculture in the United States can be slightly misleading: although spread over several states, 70 percent of U.S. beef cattle is raised in an area with a 200 mile radius. Moreover, the concentration of animals on individual farms can also magnify the impact of an attack. Large poultry farms may have hundreds of thousands of birds; dairy herds can have thousands of heads of cattle. Some animals, such as pigs and poultry, are often raised intensively and in close quarters. In such cases, even where a disease does not compel that an entire farm be slaughtered, the spread of the disease in such confined conditions may be rapid and extensive. Intensive farming, using large-scale and automated feeding, also increases the scope for attacks that use animal feed as the means of delivery. By contaminating the feed on such a farm, an attacker could legitimately hope to reach a high proportion of the animals.[29]

A similar phenomenon is observable in arable farming in the United States. It is common practice even for large farms to focus on one or two crops, rather than grow a range of different ones. It is therefore entirely possible to threaten thousands of acres of farmland with a single pathogen because all the fields are planted with the same crop. In such circumstances, even effective surveillance may be a challenge: on large farms, production methods such as spraying and harvesting are highly automated, so it may be weeks before there is an appreciation of the problem. In the meantime, the pathogen may have been widely disseminated by the wind and by insect, bird, or animal vectors.[30] The danger is compounded by the dependence of U.S. agriculture on a few regions for seeds. The Idaho valley provides most of the seed in the country. This greatly increases the opportunities for contaminating seeds and causing a

---

29. Corrie Brown, "Agricultural terrorism: A cause for concern," *The Monitor*, Vol. 5, Nos. 1–2, pp. 6–8.

30. Mackenzie, "Run, Radish, Run," pp. 36–39.

"sleeper" outbreak of disease, capable of blighting crops across the United States.

In summary, the U.S. agricultural sector, as a whole, appears to be sufficiently diverse and vast as to be invulnerable to a catastrophic sub-national BW attack with a significant economic impact. That said, certain portions of the agricultural economy may nevertheless be concentrated or organized in such a way that a sophisticated attack could have significant economic consequences at the regional, state, or local level.

Costs

INTENTIONAL ATTACKS

It is useful to examine the economic impact of the incidents of agricultural terrorism from the Monterey Institute Database. In 12 cases, no costs could be identified beyond the cost of harassment from the threats. In four cases, the perpetrators were able to kill animals, and in two of these four, people were killed as well. In only five cases is it possible to attribute financial costs to the activities. In one case, 17,000 metric tons of grapes were destroyed. In another, 300 pounds of feed were stopped from distribution, but it is unclear whether Purina destroyed the feed or simply tested it for contamination. In a third, Palestinian farmers lost an estimated $5,000. In a fourth case, two supermarket chains in Canada stopped importing South African fruit, but reports gave no estimate of losses in currency. In the most significant case, Israeli orange exports were reduced by 40 percent, but again, reports gave no estimate of costs incurred. In two of the more significant cases, the incident looked more like product tampering than an attack against agriculture. In the other cases, costs were extremely limited and minimal. The historical record therefore suggests that it is difficult to achieve significant damage against agricultural targets, with the possible exception of product tampering.

NATURALLY OCCURRING DISEASE

A report by accountants PricewaterhouseCoopers on the cost of the FMD outbreak suggested that although the cost to UK agriculture would be between £500m and £1.6 billion, the total cost of the crisis for the UK in 2001 could be between £2.5 billion and £8 billion, or between 0.3 percent and 0.8 percent of Gross Domestic Product.[31] Pounds lost in tourist revenue

---

31. "Foot-and-mouth disease: The costs and cures," Business News Special, *The Economist*, March 31, 2001, <www.economist.com/printedition/displayStory.cfm?Story_ID=549904>, accessed on April 2, 2001.

numbered in the billions.[32] The direct cost to the UK taxpayer, by February 2002, was less than had appeared likely six months earlier. The Department for Environment, Food and Rural Affairs estimated that the true figure was £2.06 billion.[33] Clearly, a major disease outbreak, such as FMD, has the potential to be catastrophic on an individual farm level, significant to the agricultural sector, but may not be devastating to the economy as a whole. The same distinction could apply in the United States. In 1999, the sector of the economy directly related to agriculture represented 1.3 percent of U.S. GDP[34] and in 2000, employed 2.6 percent of the U.S. workforce.[35]

In the Netherlands in 1997, five million pigs had to be slaughtered as a result of swine fever. Since the disease, though harmless to humans, is highly lethal to pigs and extremely contagious, entire herds of affected pigs have to be killed to contain its spread. Due to restrictions on the transportation and sale of pigs, which were necessary to control the disease spread, the Dutch government had to impose breeding bans, and 1.5 million piglets had to be slaughtered to relieve the pressure on overcrowded sties. The cost of compensation for the cull and cleanup of affected farms is estimated at $2 billion. Of this sum, the Dutch government contributed $900 million, and the European Union (EU) contributed $1.1 billion from the EU agricultural fund. Moreover, pig breeding usually contributes about $2.25 billion to Dutch exports; the disease knocked a half point off the country's GDP for the year.[36]

A 1999 dioxin (a highly carcinogenic substance) contamination in Belgium cost Belgian food producers and farmers hundreds of millions of dollars. The incident arose from contaminated feed and led to bans of Belgian eggs, poultry, and also beef, pork, and some dairy products

---

32. "After foot and mouth," *The Economist*, May 3, 2001, <www.economist.com/printedition/displayStory.cfm?Story_ID=611386, accessed on May 14, 2001.

33. This figure included £1.05 billion as compensation for animals slaughtered, £255 million for cleaning and disinfecting, £171 million for disposal and transportation of carcasses, £29 million for seized and destroyed items, and £15 million for veterinary costs. UK Department for Environment, Food and Rural Affairs figures, cited in Ann Treneman, "The new haves and have-nots" *The Times*, January 31, 2002, Section 2, pp. 2–5.

34. "Gross Domestic Product by Industry data," U.S. Bureau of Economic Analysis, available at http://www.bea.doc.gov/bea/dn2/gposhr.htm#1993–99, accessed on April 9, 2001.

35. "Comparative Civilian Labor Force Statistics, Ten Countries, 1959–2000," U.S. Bureau of Labor Statistics, available at http://www.bls.gov/flsdata.htm, accessed on April 9, 2001.

36. Roel Janssen, "Swine Fever strikes," *Europe*, No. 371, November 1997, p. 43.

across the European Union. It is believed that the original contamination was at Verkest, a company providing animal fats to animal feed manufacturers. The impact continued to spread: nine Belgian, one Dutch, and one French feed manufacturer were supplied with contaminated products, leading to bans on all EU chicken and pork in the United States, Japan, and Brazil. By September 1999, estimates of the cost of the incident to Belgian farmers varied at between $750 million and $1.5 billion, and the Belgian government estimated that it had cost the country around $900 million in lost tax revenue, chemical testing, and veterinary bills.[37]

When FMD struck Taiwan in 1997, over four million pigs had to be slaughtered. Before the outbreak, the swine industry represented nearly 60 percent of Taiwan's livestock products. After the outbreak, pork prices collapsed, and it was estimated that damage to the Taiwanese economy might include $3 billion of lost sales, the jeopardizing of 50,000 jobs, and a half point slowdown in the country's economic growth.

Within the United States, the economic consequences of naturally occurring outbreaks have been less catastrophic than overseas. In 1999, the Mexican fruit fly threatened agriculture across California when it was discovered in San Diego and Fallbrook Counties. The fly attacks more than 250 species of fruits, nuts, and vegetables, laying eggs in ripening fruit and, thus, spoiling it for sale and consumption. The agricultural economy in San Diego County alone is worth $1.2 billion, but it is difficult to determine the effects of subsequent bans on fruit exports from the county by the Australian, New Zealand, Taiwanese, and Japanese governments. Mediterranean fruit flies were discovered in Riverside County, and guava flies were found in Fresno County. According to the California Department of Food and Agriculture, the state's worldwide fruit exports were valued at about $2 billion in 1997, and 1997 combined fruit, nut, and vegetable production was almost 39 million tons, or more than half of total U.S. production.[38] Within the state, 132,000 jobs and $13 billion depend directly or indirectly on fruit farming. However, thanks to a rigorous program of quarantine and eradication, the damage to Californian agriculture was a mere fraction of these figures.

In 1994, late blight, the fungal disease that caused the Irish potato famine in the 1840s, caused $100 million damage in the United States. The costs of attempting to suppress the late blight within the country equaled the direct losses. The majority of seed potatoes come from a single region,

37. Dick Leonard, "Scandals damage farmers' influence," *Europe,* No. 388, September 1999, p. 44. "Wrap-Up," *Chemical Week,* September 22, 1999, p. 24.

38. "California Agriculture," California Department of Farms and Agriculture.

Europe, so the late blight developed into a worldwide problem, with out-breaks in the Middle East, South America, Asia, and Africa, as well as Europe and North America. In 1997, the International Potato Center in Lima, Peru, estimated losses worldwide from late blight were about $3 billion annually. In 1995, growers in Washington and Oregon alone lost $30 million. In 1994, a single New York grower lost $1 million, despite extensive use of pesticides, as marketable yields fell by 80 percent.

One of the means employed to control the worldwide spread of pathogens is export controls. The World Trade Organization has "phyto-sanitary" rules that permit even a minor disease outbreak to compel the cessation of a crop's export. This can be seen in the example of the fruit flies in California or in the case of karnal bunt in Arizona. In the latter example, a relatively mild but highly infectious pathogen was discovered in Arizona wheat. In one day, 32 countries banned U.S. wheat imports. It cost the United States hundreds of millions of dollars to eradicate the fungal pest and threatened the country's $5 billion of annual wheat exports.[39]

Societal and Political Costs

Although this essay takes note of the direct economic impact of sub-national BW agricultural attacks, a range of costs, in the wider sense, would be associated with such an attack. If crops or livestock are destroyed, then, obviously, that has a financial impact on the grower or breeder. Depending on the scale of the attack, however, it might have an impact on consumers, both in confidence, in the case of product tampering, and in produce prices. Clearly, if a particular crop is in short supply, or if it has to be imported from a more remote region, then the price of that crop will rise. An example of this phenomenon attributable to natural causes occurred in 1999, when frost decimated the California orange crop, so that oranges had to be shipped from Florida to markets, such as the West Coast, usually served by oranges from California, resulting in a rise in orange prices. Such an occurrence also has a ripple effect: the increase in the price of oranges adversely affected the Florida juice industry even though the frost had hit California. The increased costs were passed to the consumers of orange juice and table oranges.

Equally, though, a range of individuals and businesses are likely to suffer as a result of the secondary impact of subnational BW agricultural attacks. For example, if a crop is decimated, agricultural workers are

---

39. Mackenzie, "Run, Radish, Run."

likely to be seriously affected unless they can find alternative employment. In January 1999, for example, unemployment in Tulare County, California, hit 20 percent, largely as a result of the area's spoiled orange crops. A range of industries may depend on certain crops or livestock: a terrorist attack on cattle, like a natural outbreak, would affect not only the farmer, but also the livestock shippers, stockyards, slaughterhouses, distributors, and so on. The economic impact of an incident depends not only on the scale of an attack, but also on the targeted crop or livestock. Where there are substitute goods for those that have been targeted, the economic impact can be reduced. Equally, some livestock or crops have more elastic supply than others, so that output can readily be expanded to fill a gap in the market. For example, because pigs have large litters and reach maturity relatively quickly, the supply of hogs is much more flexible than that of cattle.

Apart from the loss of immediate revenue from a subnational BW agricultural attack, there is also the risk of long-term loss of market share. If distributors, wholesalers, and retailers find acceptable and affordable alternative sources of agricultural produce to replace those affected by the attack, they may not return to their original supplier, even after the crisis has passed. This might be not only a consequence of subnational BW agricultural attacks, but conceivably a motive for them as well. Competitors in a particular market could see these attacks as a means of increasing their market share at the expense of their rivals.

Obviously, a range of other potential costs may also be incurred as a result of a subnational BW agricultural attack. Crops or livestock may need to be replaced. The expense of doing so could be particularly heavy, if breeding stocks have to be replaced to replenish supplies of produce. Depending on the agent used to attack agriculture, the affected area will likely need to be decontaminated. Additional costs may include not only "cleaning up" the agent, but also the collection and destruction of infected crops or livestock. If dealing with a virulent and readily transmissible agent such as FMD or certain wind-borne plant pathogens, the need for collection and destruction may extend from those livestock or crops already affected to those in the vicinity, due to the need to establish a *cordon sanitaire* to control the spread of the disease.

Finally, agricultural terrorism may generate political costs. Some of these costs apply to any act of terrorism: the loss of confidence and credibility stemming from a government's inability to protect the country. Specifically, however, terrorism involving BW attacks on agriculture may also result in a heightened need for interagency cooperation, possibly at local, state, and national levels, and calls for increased action against further attacks.

In summary, subnational BW agricultural attacks, like naturally occurring disease outbreaks, may involve a range of costs, both direct and indirect, overt and hidden. Therefore, when discussing the economic impact of such attacks, it is important to be clear which costs are being incurred and by whom.

Costs Associated with Preventing or Mitigating the Effects of an Agroterrorist Attack:

Programs to ensure preparedness for such an attack remain largely the purview of a limited part of the U.S. Department of Agriculture (USDA), which has begun to improve its capabilities to respond in the event of a disease outbreak in animals or crops.[40] In an effort to address the potential threat of attacks against agricultural targets, USDA has developed a six-point strategy to ensure the security of U.S. agriculture, including terrorism prevention and deterrence, international cooperation, domestic consequence management planning, research on counterterrorism capabilities, protection of critical infrastructure, and protection of food supply.[41] This wide-ranging and somewhat vague list resembles many other agencies' counterterrorism plans. Interagency groups have proliferated, as a characteristic of U.S. CBW counterterrorism planning in recent years. Several other U.S. agencies besides USDA now have some role in preparedness for agricultural terrorism, including the National Security Council and the Department of Justice (DOJ).[42]

Under the new Department of Homeland Security (DHS), the Animal and Plant Health Inspection Service (APHIS) and the Plum Island Animal Disease Center will be the main agencies responsible for preventing and responding to agroterrorism. Both agencies will transfer into DHS from the U.S. Department of Agriculture (USDA), with APHIS situated in the DHS Directorate of Border and Transportation Security, and the Plum Island Animal Disease Center relocating to the DHS Directorate of Science and Technology. Although budgets within the four DHS divisions have not yet been allotted to specific agencies, the Directorate of Border and Transportation Security will receive an estimated $16.9 billion for 2003 and $16.7 billion for 2004, while the Directorate of Science and Technol-

---

40. "The Threat of Biological Terrorism to U.S. Agriculture," U.S. Department of Agriculture, undated.

41. Statement by Floyd P. Horn, Administrator, Agricultural Research Service, U.S. Department of Agriculture, before the U. S. Senate Emerging Threats and Capabilities Subcommittee of the Armed Services Committee, October 27, 1999, p. 5.

42. Ibid.

ogy will receive an estimated \$3.4 billion for 2003 and \$3.3 billion for 2004.[43]

APHIS' responsibilities in DHS include inspection of agricultural imports and exports through U.S. borders, such as inspections of passengers, luggage, and cargo. APHIS will also be involved in protecting U.S. animals and agriculture from disease, possibly brought about by acts of agricultural terrorism, so that the nation's food supply is not endangered.

The Plum Island Animal Disease Center's role in the new Department of Homeland Security is to protect U.S. animals and agriculture by researching and countering agroterrorism. Through experimentation and research, this center hopes to better prepare itself in aiding the efforts to identify acts of agroterrorism quickly.

USDA requested a total of \$41.3 million for counterterrorism in fiscal year (FY) 2001, \$39.8 million of which (or 96 percent) is devoted to defense against WMD.[44] In FY 2000, WMD defense accounted for \$7.3 million of \$12.3 million or 59 percent of the total.[45] Clearly, USDA has focused significant resources on addressing this problem. For comparison, the Department of Health and Human Services (HHS), the agency responsible for public health, including the Centers for Disease Control and Prevention (CDC), requested \$265.4 million for counterterrorism activities for FY 2001, all of which were WMD-related, representing a decrease in funding from \$277.6 in FY 2000.[46] The HHS FY 1999 figure, however, was \$173.1 million, indicating either that HHS was able to capitalize sooner on the attention given the WMD threat or that the threat was perceived as more pressing in HHS's jurisdiction.[47] DOJ requested \$254.7 million in WMD-related funding in FY 2001, an increase of \$37.5 million over the previous year.[48] In the U.S. national security community, funding for WMD-related programs has tripled since 1998, but the figures remain a small portion (less than 10 percent) of the total for counterterrorism generally.[49] Other agencies' funding for WMD defense pro-

---

43. Office of Management and Budget, *Department of Homeland Security;* accessed on February 3, 2003 at http://www.whitehouse.gov/omb/budget/fy2004/print/homeland.html.

44. "Federal Funding to Combat Terrorism, Including Defense against Weapons of Mass Destruction FY 1998–2001," <http://cns.miis.edu/research/cbw/terfund.htm>.

45. Ibid.

46. Ibid.

47. Ibid.

48. Ibid.

49. Ibid.

grams has also increased but, in no case, has the proportion of WMD funding in the total counterterrorism budget been so great as in the case of USDA. That said, USDA's funding levels, seen as a proportion of the U.S. budget, trail those of other agencies dramatically in WMD-related appropriations, because the domestic preparedness program until very recently has focused on preventing and mitigating attacks targeted directly at humans. The heightened focus on terrorism against agriculture represents a new stage, one with the object of protecting U.S. strategic assets, such as agriculture.

In addition, USDA has requested funding to upgrade a research facility at Plum Island, New York, to Biosafety Level 4, capable of and dedicated to the study of animal and plant pathogens, although local public opinion and congressional representatives have mixed views on the issue.[50] Building on these indicators of growing official attention to the threat of attacks against agricultural targets, including congressional hearings on the issue, news articles have begun to reflect concerns that U.S. agriculture is vulnerable to attack using biological weapons, and arguably this vulnerability, as well as the theoretical ease of carrying out such attacks covertly, makes agricultural targets particularly appealing to terrorists.[51] Terrorists may also find these types of targets appealing because they do not target humans directly and may therefore be more easily justified. Indeed, a recent influential U.S. government report asserted that the "U.S. agricultural sector is especially vulnerable to agroterrorism" and that "a successful attack could result in local or regional economic destabilization" and affect international commerce.[52] The U.S. agricultural sector, including all elements directly or indirectly related to agriculture, represents about 13 percent of the U.S. gross national product and is enormous and diverse; few specific threat assessments of vulnerability exist.[53]

---

50. David Ruppe, "Battle Over Plum Island," *ABCNews.com*, accessed January 20, 2000.

51. Steve Goldstein, "'Agroterror' Fears Awake; U.S. Crops Seen as Vulnerable," *The Arizona Republic*, June 26, 2000, p. A12; and "Experts Warn of "Agroterrorism" Threat," *Associated Press*, December 2, 1999).

52. "First Annual Report to the President and the Congress of the Advisory Panel to Assess Domestic Response Capabilities for Terrorism Involving Weapons of Mass Destruction: Assessing the Threat," December 15, 1999, p. 12, <www.rand.org/organization/nsrd/terrpanel/>, accessed on June 23, 2000.

53. Statement by Floyd P. Horn before the Emerging Threats and Capabilities Subcommittee, October 27, 1999, p. 3.

Conclusion

Because of the ease of perpetrating an attack, agriculture throughout the world and the United States is extremely vulnerable. However, achieving widespread impact from such an attack may be significantly more difficult. In reality, there appear to have been relatively few such attacks worldwide that have even sought catastrophic consequences. Rather than seeking to eradicate a crop or type of animal from a country's agricultural economy, most attackers have focused on damaging consumer confidence. This has meant that such attacks have been much closer to examples of product tampering than to the devastating strikes that have been the focus of a growing number of government reports, academic articles, and newspaper columns. The economic impact of such attacks is, potentially, enormous: within the United States, agriculture is an industry worth hundreds of billions of dollars and, directly or indirectly, employing millions of people. The willingness and ability of an attacker to jeopardize more than a fraction of that, however, appears limited. Moreover, the size of the United States and the range of agriculture within the country make it likely that even a major attack would be highly damaging rather than crippling to the country's economy. In addition, although the relative ease of releasing BW agents against agriculture compared to that of BW agents against human targets implies that BW attacks against agriculture could be quite effective, the potential ease of delivery may be offset by these limiting factors. Effective delivery would at the very least require a sophisticated, multi-pronged attack to achieve major effects, one also capable of overcoming the environmental barriers to effective dissemination.

Historically, most attacks against agriculture worldwide have been directed at consumer confidence and could more legitimately be described as credible threats than as genuine attacks. The number of actions directed against agriculture *per se* has been limited, and none appears to have occurred on the scale presently being envisaged. However, relatively little is known or understood about the threat of subnational BW agricultural attacks. Although the potential vulnerability to attack could be enormous and could have economically disastrous impacts on individual farms and, possibly, on specific segments of the agricultural economy, the agricultural economy as a whole, as well as the entire U.S. economy, are unlikely to be significantly affected. However, there is currently a gap between what has actually occurred in previous incidents and this perceived danger. Further research needs to be undertaken to ascertain whether there is a genuine danger and whether the terrorist threat has evolved to the point that terrorists now see agriculture as a worthwhile target. Alternatively, this perceived danger may simply be the latest example of vulnerability-driven, rather than intent-driven, threat assessments. In either case, it is important that more work be undertaken to ascertain the scope of the problem and determine the best means of minimizing the danger.

Cyber Attacks: Protecting America's Security against Digital Threats

Michael A. Vatis

Information technology pervades all aspects of our daily lives. . . . Its presence is felt almost every moment of every day, by every American. It pervades everything from a shipment of goods, to communications, to emergency services, and the delivery of water and electricity to our homes. All of these aspects of our life depend on a complex network of critical infrastructure information systems. Protecting this infrastructure is critically important. Disrupt it, destroy it or shut it down . . . and you shut down America as we know it and as we live it and as we experience it every day. We need to prevent disruptions, and when they occur, we need to make sure they are infrequent, short and manageable. This is an enormously difficult challenge.

—Tom Ridge, Secretary of the Department of Homeland Security[1]

The events of September 11, 2001, underscored the vulnerability to foreign attack of the territory of the United States itself, in a way not seen since Pearl Harbor. Since that day, the federal government, the media, and the American public have been intensely focused on taking measures to protect us from similar attacks—or from even more devastating attacks involving weapons of mass destruction (WMD), such as nuclear, biological, chemical, or radiological weapons.

This essay was prepared with the able assistance of Matthew Funk and Kathleen Cassedy, Research Associates at the Institute for Security Technology Studies at Dartmouth College.

1.   Transcript of Governor Ridge's October 8, 2001, comments, Office of the Press Secretary, U.S. Government, "New Counter-Terrorism and CyberSpace Security Positions Announced," October 9, 2001, <www.whitehouse.gov/news/releases/2001/10/20011009-4.html>.

In addition to such physical attacks, however, the United States remains highly vulnerable to another form of attack: a "cyber attack" against the computer networks that are critical to our national security and economic prosperity. Attackers may use computers to target the networks that operate banking and financial institutions, voice communication systems, electric power grids, emergency rescue networks, health care systems, water resources, oil and gas infrastructures, or crucial governmental functions. The growing complexity and interconnectedness of these and other critical infrastructure networks render them increasingly vulnerable to attack. While a physical attack on an infrastructure is likely to be carried out only by terrorists or hostile foreign nation-states, cyber attacks may be carried out by a wide array of adversaries, from teenage hackers or protest groups to organized crime syndicates, terrorists, or foreign nations. As a result, the problem of cyber attacks is enormously broad and complex. It requires that we have in place both protective and reactive measures to deal with all of these potential scenarios.

The threat is also challenging in another way. As a former Secretary of Commerce put it:

This is the first time in American history that we in the federal government, alone, cannot protect our infrastructure. We can't hire an army or a police force that's large enough to protect all of America's cell phones or pagers or computer networks—not when 95% of these infrastructures are owned and operated by the private sector.[2]

Meeting the challenge of cyber security thus requires an extraordinary level of public-private cooperation. Moreover, the global nature of the Internet means that cyber attacks can originate from anywhere in the world and occur with incredible speed. This requires an unprecedented ability by the government to respond quickly and to work effectively with international counterparts.

This essay explores some of the issues that make dealing with cyber attacks such a novel and difficult issue for the government and private sector alike, examines the history of the U.S. government's efforts to prevent and respond to cyber attacks, and concludes with recommendations for improving efforts to prevent and respond to such attacks.

---

2. Remarks by Secretary of Commerce William M. Daley, "Release of National Plan for Information Systems Protection," January 7, 2000, <cryptome.org/cybersec-wh.htm>.

Types of Cyber Attacks

Cyber attacks are computer-to-computer attacks carried out to steal, erase, or alter information or to destroy or impede the functionality of the target computer system. These attacks typically fall into three general categories: 1) unauthorized intrusions, in which the attacker breaks into the computer system using various hacking or "cracking" techniques, or an insider exceeds his or her authorized access in order to do unauthorized things to or on the network; 2) destructive viruses or worms, which spread from computer to computer through email or other forms of data exchange and can cause the loss of functionality of parts of the network; and 3) denial of service (DoS) attacks, which use any of several techniques to bombard the target computer system with communications and overload it, thereby hampering its functionality.[3] This section describes some of the kinds of attacks that cyber attackers have perpetrated and are likely to continue perpetrating against targets in the United States.

WEB DEFACEMENTS AND SEMANTIC HACKS

Website defacements are one of the most common forms of cyber attacks. Groups frequently deface information on government or company websites in order to ridicule the entity that sponsors the site or to spread the groups' own message.[4] Most of these attacks do not have very serious consequences but are a nuisance. The most potentially serious website defacements could result from "semantic hacking," which changes the content of a web page subtly, so that the alteration is not immediately apparent.[5] As a result, false information is disseminated. For instance, in October 2002, hackers reportedly defaced a Venezuelan government website and made it appear as though Venezuelan President Hugo Chavez had issued an order to shoot members of a political opposition party.[6]

---

3. See Michael Vatis, *International Cyber Security Cooperation: Informal Bilateral Models* (Washington, D.C.: Center for Strategic and International Studies [CSIS], 2002). For a thorough enumeration of types of computer security incidents, see Thomas A. Longstaff et al., "Security of the Internet," CERT Coordination Center, <www.cert.org/encyc_article/tocencyc.html#TypesInc>.

4. The website <www.blackhat.info/live/> currently maintains an extensive rolling list of mirrored website defacements.

5. For information regarding semantic hacks and research currently underway to address this problem, see <www.ists.dartmouth.edu/IRIA/projects/d_semantic.htm>.

6. See El Mundo, "Colocan en el web del Gobierno venezolano una falsa orden de Chavez instando a disparar a matar," October 21, 2002, <www.elmundo.es/navegante/2002/10/21/esociedad/1035188416.html>.

An example of a possible semantic attack with far-reaching consequences would be a hack of the website for the Centers for Disease Control and Prevention during a bioterrorism event, in which the text relating to either symptoms or treatment of the related disease were changed, causing citizens and health professionals to have incorrect information and thereby increasing the number of fatalities or critical illnesses resulting from the biological attack. A different example with potentially significant economic consequences would involve a hacker's subtly changing stock information on a financial website to spread false information and manipulate investors to make bad trades.

DOMAIN NAME SERVER (DNS) ATTACKS

Computers connected to the Internet communicate with one another using numerical Internet Protocol (IP) addresses.[7] Computers consult domain name servers (DNS) to map the name of a website (e.g., cnn.com) to its numerical address (e.g., 64.12.50.153). If the DNS provides an incorrect numerical address for the desired website, then the user will be connected to the incorrect server, often without the user's knowledge. A DNS attack can thus be used to disseminate false information, to divert a potential e-commerce customer to a competing business's site, or simply to block access to the original website. For example, in 1997, the owner of an internet domain name registration service placed software on the Internet that involuntarily diverted potential customers from his chief competitor to his own website. He ultimately was apprehended by the Federal Bureau of Investigation (FBI) and pleaded guilty to violating the federal Computer Fraud and Abuse Act.[8]

DISTRIBUTED DENIAL OF SERVICE ATTACKS

Distributed Denial of Service (DDoS) attacks subject web and email servers to overwhelming numbers of communications from other computers. The high volume of communications can slow the functioning of or effectively shut down the targeted system. Hackers can multiply the force of their DDoS attacks by using malicious codes to take control of other users' machines and using these "zombie" machines to send additional communications to targeted servers.

---

7. An IP address is a number that identifies the sender or receiver of information sent across the Internet. For a more detailed explanation of IP addresses, see <whatis.techtarget.com/definition/0,289893,sid9_gci212381,00.html>.

8. See Jonathan Rusch, "The Rising Tide of Internet Fraud," July 9, 2001, <www.cybercrime.gov/usamay2001_1.htm>; "Computer-related Crime: Website Disruption: Case Study," <www.criminaldefense.com/computer_site_disruption.html>.

In October 2002, for example, a large and sophisticated DDoS attack was launched against the Internet's 13 domain name root servers. Although system administrators at the host sites for the root servers were largely able to repel the attack, many government officials and security experts were concerned that Internet traffic around the globe would shortly have begun to experience significant delays and outages if the attack had been sustained for a longer period. As of this writing, the Federal Bureau of Investigation was investigating the attack to determine the identity of the perpetrators.[9]

The previously best-known instance of a DDoS attack occurred in early 2000, when a number of e-commerce and web portals, including Yahoo.com, reported to the FBI that they were experiencing severe DDoS attacks. Working in close cooperation with the private sector, internet service providers, the Royal Canadian Mounted Police (RCMP), the National Infrastructure Protection Center, and FBI field offices conducted an extensive international investigation. The investigation led to the arrest in April 2002 by the RCMP of a Canadian teenager who went by the nickname "MAFIABOY."[10]

MALICIOUS CODE

Worms, viruses, and Trojan horses are types of malicious code.[11] The vulnerabilities that worms and viruses exploit are usually well-known to

---

9. See David McGuire and Brian Krebs, "Attack On Internet Called Largest Ever," *Washington Post*, October 22, 2002, <www.washingtonpost.com/wp-dyn/articles/A828–2002Oct22.html>. The attack actually appears to have occurred in two stages. The main attack began at approximately 5:00 P.M. on Monday, October 21, 2002, against the 13 root servers for the Internet. That attack ceased abruptly after about an hour. At about 11:00 P.M. on the same day, a second DDoS attack was launched against targeted domain name servers that direct Internet traffic to more specific online locations. This attack was also repelled. See McGuire and Krebs, "More Than One Internet Attack Occurred Monday," *Washington Post*, October 23, 2002, <www.washingtonpost.com/wp-dyn/articles/A6894–2002Oct23.html>.

10. Ultimately, Canadian prosecutors charged MAFIABOY with 65 criminal acts, the vast majority of which were acts of unauthorized access into Internet sites. MAFIABOY pleaded guilty to 56 of the counts against him, and in September 2001, he was sentenced to eight months of "open custody," one year of probation, and restricted Internet use. See <www.nipc.gov/investigations/mafiaboy.htm>.

11. A virus is a program or piece of code that is loaded onto a computer without the authorized user's knowledge and runs against the user's wishes. Viruses can replicate themselves. Even a simple virus is dangerous, because it can use all available memory and bring the system to a halt; even more dangerous are those viruses capable of transmitting themselves across networks and bypassing security systems. A worm is a type of virus that can replicate itself and use memory, but does not attach itself to other programs. A Trojan horse is a destructive program that masquerades as a benign applica-

system administrators and can be remedied, but they often go uncorrected on so many systems that worms and viruses are able to cause major problems in the information infrastructure. If maximum destruction is a hostile adversary's goal, malicious code offers a cost-effective way to significantly disrupt the U.S. information infrastructure.[12]

According to one survey, 43 percent of federal information technology managers deem viruses and other types of malicious code to be the biggest threats to their networks.[13] On average, over 30 new viruses are reportedly disseminated daily. Approximately 50,000 viruses exist overall.[14] Examples of destructive malicious code abound. In 2001, the "Code Red" virus alone caused costs that were estimated to reach billions of dollars worldwide.[15] The "Nimda" worm, released on September 18, 2001, was another high-profile, widespread instance of malicious code and is believed to have caused hundreds of millions of dollars in damage.[16] On January 25, 2003, the "SQL Slammer" or "Sapphire" worm was launched, exploiting a previously identified vulnerability in Microsoft's SQL Server 2000. The worm quickly spread around the globe and adversely affected tens of thousands of computers. It reportedly disrupted some bank automated teller machines (ATMs), the electronic reservations system of a major airline, the websites of several financial services firms, and operations of emergency 911 systems outside Seattle, Washington.[17] The prolifera-

---

tion. Unlike viruses, Trojan horses do not replicate themselves, but they can still be destructive. See <www.mcafee.com/anti-virus/virus_glossary.asp>.

12. See Institute for Security Technology Studies, *Cyber Attacks During the War on Terrorism: A Predictive Analysis*, September 22, 2001, <www.ists.dartmouth.edu/ISTS/counterterrorism/cyber_attacks.htm>, p. 16.

13. Richard W. Walker, "Feds Say Virus Threats Keep Them Awake at Night," *Government Computer News*, August 20, 2001, <www.gcn.com/20_24/security/16834–1.html>.

14. See, e.g., Florence Olson, "The Growing Vulnerability of Campus Networks," *Chronicle of Higher Education*, March 15, 2002, reporting statements by Michael A. McRobbie, vice president for information technology at the Indiana University system.

15. Jay Lyman, "In Search of the World's Costliest Virus," *E-Commerce Times*, February 21, 2002, <www.ecommercetimes.com/perl/story/16407.html>. Estimates of damage caused by viruses and worms are at best rough guesses and often lack any clear foundation. However, it is clear from the number of companies that report damage and the types of harm that they report, that malicious code can cause significant economic harm to companies worldwide.

16. Ibid.

17. See SANS Institute, "A Special Report from the SANS Research Office: MS-SQL Server Worm (also called Sapphire, SQL Slammer, SQL Hell)," <www.sans.org/alerts/mssql.php>; Brian Krebs, "Internet Worm Hits Airline, Banks," *Washington Post*,

tion of high-speed networks means that viruses and worms propagate ever more quickly.[18]

EXPLOITATION OF ROUTING VULNERABILITIES

Routers are the "air traffic controllers" of the Internet, ensuring that information, in the form of packets, travels from source to destination. Routing disruptions from malicious activity have been rare, but the lack of diversity in router operating systems leaves open the possibility of a massive routing attack. The malicious reprogramming of even one router could lead to disruption of communication across the Internet.[19]

COMPOUND ATTACKS

By combining different methods of cyber attacks, hackers could launch an even more destructive attack. Another strategy might be to magnify the destructiveness of a physical attack by launching coordinated cyber attacks. For example, attackers might set off a bomb in a heavily populated area and simultaneously disable the community's "911" emergency telephone system to impede the response of police, fire, and rescue personnel.[20]

The Range of Cyber Attackers

The volume, sophistication, and coordination of cyber attacks are increasing. The *2002 Computer Crime and Security Survey*, conducted by the Computer Security Institute and FBI, reports all-time highs in the percentage

---

January 26, 2003, <www.washingtonpost.com/wp-dyn/articles/A46928–2003Jan26. html>; "Internet Worm Keeps Striking," CBSNEWS.com, January 28, 2003, <http://www.cbsnews.com/stories/2003/01/28/tech/main538200.shtml>.

18.   The likelihood of a company's experiencing a virus or worm and the consequent costs approximately doubled each year from 1995 to 1999 and grew approximately 15 percent per year in 2000 and 2001. See Lawrence M. Bridwell and Peter Tippett, *ICSA 7th Annual Computer Virus Prevalence Survey 2001*, 2002, <www.trendmicro.com/NR/rdonlyres/eib3fwut4wpsmhkleyfb6ywdqilofdt7bz2utjxmspsysehu5vkh5zxpwy2qiihx um25ukavqx3kci/icsavps2001.pdf>, p. 1.

19.   See Curt Wilson, "Protecting Network Infrastructure at the Protocol Level," December 15, 2000, <www.netw3.com/documents/protecting_net_infrastructure.doc>. See also ISTS, *Cyber Attacks During the War on Terrorism*, <www.ists.dartmouth.edu/ISTS/counterterrorism/cyber_attacks.htm>, p. 16.

20.   As former NIPC Director Ronald Dick has stated: "'The event I fear most is a physical attack in conjunction with a successful cyber-attack on the responders' 911 system or on the power grid.'" Barton Gellman, "Cyber-Attacks by Al Qaeda Feared," *Washington Post*, June 27, 2002, <www.washingtonpost.com/ac2/wp-dyn/A50765–2002Jun26>.

of respondents who detected system penetration from the outside, denial of service attacks, employee abuse of Internet access privileges, and computer viruses.[21] More recently, Riptech, Inc.'s July 2002, *Internet Security Threat Report, Vol. II*, stated that for the six-month period starting January 1, 2002, Internet-based attacks had increased 28 percent over the previous six months, contributing to a projected annual growth rate of 64 percent.[22] During a single week in 2001, approximately 1,200 U.S. sites, including those belonging to the White House and other government agencies, were subjected to DDoS attacks or defaced with pro-Chinese images. Chinese hacker attacks launched in 2001 were able to reach such a massive scale because numerous hacker groups used password-protected chat rooms and other technologies to coordinate the launch of a joint campaign against U.S. targets.[23] This section catalogues the spectrum of cyber attackers, ranging from hostile foreign governments and terrorists to disgruntled employees and recreational hackers.

INFORMATION WARFARE

Perhaps the greatest potential threat to our national security is the prospect of "information warfare" by foreign militaries against our critical infrastructures.[24] Several foreign nations are already developing informa-

---

21.   *2002 CSI/FBI Computer Crime and Security Survey* (Spring 2002) <www.gocsi.com/press/20020407.html>.

22.   See <enterprisesecurity.symantec.com/content.cfm?articleid=1539&PID=1280755 0&EID=0>.

23.   See *Security Wire Digest*, May 3, 2001, "Chinese-U.S. Cybervandalism Escalates," <www.infosecuritymag.com/2001/may/digest03.shtml#news2> and *iDEFENSE— Current Intelligence*, "Will Chinese Hackers Attack The US Again?" April 22, 2002, <www.idefense.com/Intell/CI041002.html>. The United States is by no means the only nation suffering a growing volume of politically motivated cyber attacks. For example, the number of Indian website defacements attributed to pro-Pakistan hackers increased from 45 in 1999 to 275 in the first eight months of 2001. See Institute for Security Technology Studies, *Cyber Attacks During the War on Terrorism: A Predictive Analysis*, September 22, 2001, <www.ists.dartmouth.edu/ISTS/counterterrorism/cyber_attacks.htm>, p. 5.

24.   "Information warfare" is susceptible to varying definitions but essentially involves the use of information systems to deny, exploit, corrupt, or destroy an adversary's information, information systems, and computer-based networks while protecting one's own. It thus has both offensive and defensive components. I use the term to refer specifically to state use of computer-to-computer attacks and do not include things like propaganda or "psychological operations" which have been included in past Defense Department definitions of "information operations." See Toshi Yoshihara, "Chinese Information Warfare: A Phantom Menace or Emerging Threat," (Strategic Studies Institute, Carlisle, Penna.: November 2001), pp. 3–5, <http://www.iwar.org.uk/iwar/resources/china/iw/chininfo.pdf>.

tion warfare doctrine, programs, and capabilities for use against each other, the United States, or other nations.[25] Some foreign nations are developing information warfare programs because they fear that they cannot defeat the United States in a head-to-head military encounter. Targeting U.S. information systems is a way to strike at what they perceive to be America's Achilles' heel—its reliance on information technology to control critical government and private sector systems. For example, two Chinese military officers published a book in 1999 that promoted the use of unconventional measures, including the propagation of computer viruses, to counter the military power of the United States.[26]

In addition, the line between state-sponsored information warfare and attacks by foreign civilians who oppose U.S. policy is not always easy to draw and may become increasingly murky. During the conflict in the former Yugoslavia in the 1990s, for example, the North Atlantic Treaty Organization (NATO) servers were hit with "ping flood" attacks (a type of denial of service attack), DDoS attacks, and bombardment with emails, some infected with viruses. Simultaneously, hackers defaced military, government, and commercial websites in the United States.[27]

In early 2001, a loose coalition of Chinese hackers, reportedly led by the China Eagle Union hacker group, launched a massive website defacement campaign, combined with DDoS attacks on the Central Intelligence Agency (CIA) and White House websites. This coordinated attack was in direct response to the incident involving a collision between a U.S. surveillance plane and a Chinese fighter jet.[28] These attacks were not, as far as can be told from publicly available information, specifically tied to a foreign government. But such attacks are at least portents of much more serious attacks that foreign adversaries could attempt in future conflicts, including attacks in which governments covertly organize or inspire attacks by seemingly unrelated private individuals.[29]

---

25. Testimony of Director of Central Intelligence George Tenet, Senate Select Committee on Government Affairs, June 24, 1998, <www.cia.gov/cia/public_affairs/speeches/archives/1998/dci_testimony_062498.html>.

26. See English-language translation of Qiao Liang and Wang Xiangsui, *Unrestricted Warfare*, PLA Literature and Arts Publishing House, Beijing, China, February 1999, <www.terrorism.com/documents/unrestricted.pdf>.

27. See Institute for Security Technology Studies, *Cyber Attacks During the War on Terrorism: A Predictive Analysis*, September 22, 2001, <www.ists.dartmouth.edu/ISTS/counterterrorism/cyber_attacks.htm>, pp. 7–8.

28. See iDEFENSE, Inc. white paper, "Inside the China Eagle Hacker Union," April 29, 2002, <www.idefense.com/papers.html>.

29. See generally John Arquilla and David Ronfeldt, eds., *In Athena's Camp: Preparing for Conflict in the Information Age* (Santa Monica, Calif.: RAND, 1997).

Indeed, the ongoing U.S. campaign against terrorism could prompt cyber attacks either by individuals who oppose that campaign or by countries targeted during that campaign. Cyber attacks on Israeli banking and telecommunications systems during the second Palestinian *intifada* should serve as a warning.[30] The Code Red worm, which targeted the White House web site, serves as a reminder that politically motivated cyber attackers may attempt to disable symbols of the U.S. government.[31]

At the time of this writing, Iraq, in particular, is a potential target of U.S. military action, and that country is thought to be developing information warfare capabilities.[32] Because it is relatively easy to disguise the origin of online attacks, the possibility also exists that one nation (or a non-state actor) could launch a cyber attack against the United States but make it appear as though the attack was coming from another country, thereby causing the United States to take retaliatory steps against the wrong country.[33]

FOREIGN INTELLIGENCE SERVICES

Foreign intelligence services have been using cyber tools as part of their information gathering and espionage tradecraft since at least the 1980s. Between 1986 and 1989, for example, a ring of West German hackers penetrated numerous military, scientific, and industrial computers in the United States, Western Europe, and Japan, stealing passwords, programs, and other information, which they then sold to the Soviet Committee for State Security (KGB).[34] Significantly, this was well over a decade ago—ancient history in Internet years. Although very little unclassified information regarding current cyber espionage practices or trends is available, it

---

30. The "cyber jihad" undertaken by hackers supporting the second Palestinian *intifada* had specific stages during which Israeli financial institutions and Israeli telecommunications firms, respectively, were targeted. ISTS, *Cyber Attacks During the War on Terrorism*, <www.ists.dartmouth.edu/ISTS/counterterrorism/cyber_attacks.htm>, p. 7.

31. ISTS, *Cyber Attacks During the War on Terrorism*, <www.ists.dartmouth.edu/ISTS/counterterrorism/cyber_attacks.htm>, p. 10.

32. Testimony of Special Advisor to the President on Cyberspace Security Richard Clarke, Senate Judiciary Committee, Administrative Oversight and the Courts Subcommittee, hearing titled "Administrative Oversight: Are We Ready For A Cyber Terror Attack?" February 13, 2002, <www.techlawjournal.com/security/20020213.asp>.

33. ISTS, *Cyber Attacks During the War on Terrorism: A Predictive Analysis*, <www.ists.dartmouth.edu/ISTS/counterterrorism/cyber_attacks.htm>, p. 13.

34. Clifford Stoll, *The Cuckoo's Egg* (New York: Pocket Books, 1989); Dorothy E. Denning, *Information Warfare and Security* (Reading, Mass.: Addison-Wesley, 1999), pp. 205–206.

seems abundantly clear that foreign intelligence services increasingly view computer intrusions as a useful tool for acquiring sensitive U.S. government and private sector information.[35]

TERRORISTS

The United States has yet to verify a sophisticated cyber attack by a terrorist group. But there is good reason to expect that terrorists will use cyber attacks to disrupt critical systems in order to harm or coerce governments or civilian populations. We have known for some time that terrorists use both information technology and the Internet to formulate plans, raise funds, spread propaganda, and communicate securely.[36] For example, convicted terrorist Ramzi Yousef, the mastermind of the 1993 World Trade Center bombing, stored detailed plans to destroy U.S.-bound airliners on encrypted files on his laptop computer.[37] In addition, U.S. intelligence sources report that al Qaeda is using the Internet to regroup and reorganize forces scattered by the global antiterror campaign and the downfall of Afghanistan's Taliban regime.[38]

Moreover, some groups have already used relatively unsophisticated cyber attacks to disrupt their enemies' information systems. For example, a group calling itself the Internet Black Tigers conducted a successful DoS attack on servers of Sri Lankan government embassies.[39] And a Canadian government report indicated that the Irish Republican Army has considered the use of information operations against British interests.[40] Although terrorists can be expected to continue to prefer physical attacks that cause large-scale death and destruction, the relative ease, low cost, and low risk of engaging in computer-to-computer attacks—and the possibility of using them to impede the government's response to a physical

---

35. Testimony of National Infrastructure Protection Center Director Ronald Dick, House Committee on Energy and Commerce Subcommittee on Oversight and Investigations, April 5, 2001, <energycommerce.house.gov/107/hearings/04052001 Hearing153/ Dick228print.htm>.

36. Testimony of Federal Bureau of Investigation Director Louis Freeh, Senate Select Committee on Intelligence, May 10, 2001, <www.fbi.gov/congress/congress01/ freeh051001.htm>.

37. Denning, *Information Warfare and Security*, p. 68.

38. Ian Bruce, "Al Qaeda Using Internet in Bid to Regroup," *The Herald* (Glasgow, Scotland), March 7, 2002, <www.theherald.co.uk/news/archive/7–3–19102–0–52–33. html>, p. 10.

39. Denning, *Information Warfare and Security*, p. 69.

40. See Canadian Security Intelligence Service's *Counter-Terrorism: Backgrounder Series*, No. 8, August 9, 2002, <www.csis-scrs.gc.ca/eng/backgrnd/back8_e.html>.

attack or maximize the sense of public chaos attending a physical terrorism incident—make cyber attacks an attractive addition to terrorists' arsenal.

Information about the cyber capabilities and intentions of al Qaeda is spotty, but recent reports suggest that the cyber threat from these groups is real.[41] According to information found in seized al Qaeda computers or revealed by terrorists during interrogations by U.S. or foreign officials, al Qaeda has been considering cyber attacks against U.S. infrastructure targets and researching cyber attack techniques.[42] It has also reportedly been gathering information about potential targets of cyber attacks, including the computer networks that control power, transportation, and communications.[43]

As part of a larger inquiry into global threats in February 2002, the CIA was asked to respond to the following questions by the Senate Select Committee on Intelligence: "Do we have any information that al Qaeda had the interest or ability to conduct cyberterrorist operations against the United States? What terrorist groups are the likeliest to conduct such operations?" The CIA responded:

- We are alert to the possibility of cyber warfare attack by terrorists on critical infrastructure systems that rely on electronic and computer networks. Cyber warfare attacks against our critical infrastructure systems will become an increasingly viable option for terrorists as they become more familiar with these targets, and the technologies required to attack them. Various terrorist groups—including al Qaeda and Hizballah—are becoming more adept at using the Internet and computer technologies, and the FBI is monitoring an increasing number of cyber threats.
- The groups most likely to conduct such operations include al Qaeda and the Sunni extremists that support their goals against the United States. These groups have both the intentions and the desire to develop some of the cyberskills necessary to forge an effective cyber attack *modus operandi.*

---

41. See Office of Critical Infrastructure Protection and Emergency Preparedness, Government of Canada, *Threat Analysis: al Qaida Cyber Capability,* December 20, 2001, <www.ocipep-bpiepc.gc.ca/opsprods/other/TA01–001_E.asp>.

42. See Barton Gellman, "Cyber-Attacks by al Qaeda Feared," *Washington Post,* June 27, 2002, <www.washingtonpost.com/ac2/wp-dyn/A50765–2002Jun26>.

43. Ibid.

- Aleph, formerly known as Aum Shinrikyo, is the terrorist group that places the highest level of importance on developing cyber skills. These could be applied to cyber attacks against the US. This group identifies itself as a cyber cult and derives millions of dollars a year from computer retailing.[44]

"HACKTIVISM"

Over the past five years there has been a rise in what has been dubbed "hacktivism"—politically motivated attacks typically against email servers or publicly accessible web pages.[45] Groups and individuals seek to overload email servers and to hack into web sites in order to send a political message. While these attacks generally have not altered operating systems or networks, they can still disrupt services, and by denying the public access to websites containing valuable information, they can infringe on others' right to communicate. One such group, the "Electronic Disturbance Theater," has promoted civil disobedience online in support of its political agenda regarding the Zapatista movement in Mexico and other issues, leading to attacks on the web pages of Mexican President Ernesto Zedillo and the U.S. White House as well as those of the Pentagon and the Frankfurt Stock Exchange.[46] Supporters of Kevin Mitnick, convicted of numerous computer crimes, hacked into the U.S. Senate webpage and defaced it in May and June 1999.[47] Members of the anti-capitalism and anti-globalization movement launched

---

44. Central Intelligence Agency's "Questions for the Record from the Worldwide Threat Hearing," submitted as part of a hearing before the Senate Select Committee on Intelligence, February 6, 2002, <www.fas.org/irp/congress/2002_hr/020602cia.html>. The CIA filed its written responses on April 8, 2002.

45. The term "hacktivism" has been in fairly common usage since at least 1998. Some groups have been using the term to describe their online political hacking activities for even longer. See Niall McKay, *Wired News,* "The Golden Age of Hacktivism," September 22, 1998, <www.wired.com/news/politics/0,1283,15129,00.html>. One of the earliest organized hacker groups to engage in hacktivism is also one of the oldest hacker groups in North America, the Cult of the Dead Cow ("cDc"), founded in Lubbock, Texas. See <www.cultdeadcow.com>.

46. Denning, *Information Warfare and Security,* p. 73; see also David Ronfeldt, John Arquilla, Graham E. Fuller, and Melissa Fuller, *The Zapatista Social Netwar in Mexico* (Santa Monica, Calif.: RAND, 1998).

47. For more information about pro-Mitnick "cyber protests," see "Feds Warn Hackers Will Be Prosecuted; Pro-Mitnick Protest Planned," CNN.com, June 2, 1999, <www.cnn.com/TECH/computing/9906/02/hunting.hackers/>.

DoS attacks during the 2002 World Economic Forum held in New York City. [48]

CRIMINAL GROUPS

Criminal groups are increasingly using cyber intrusions for purposes of monetary gain. In fact, attacks by criminal groups constitute one of the most significant growth areas in the cyber attack arena. In the summer of 2002, for instance, the U.S. Secret Service conducted an investigation into an individual who manually installed key logging software (which covertly monitors and records computer keystrokes while they are being typed) on computers at colleges and universities across the United States. The "malware" was used to steal credit card numbers and other personal information.[49]

In an earlier case, two Russian hackers engaged in a series of computer intrusions, thefts, and extortion attempts against U.S. banks and e-commerce companies. In 2000, the FBI, in an undercover operation, persuaded the two to come to the United States to demonstrate their hacking skills, ostensibly for possible employment. Both were arrested and indicted. One was convicted of 20 counts of conspiracy, computer crime, and fraud.[50] The other is awaiting trial.[51]

In a similar scheme, two Kazakh hackers attempted to extort $200,000 from Bloomberg, L.P., after hacking into Bloomberg's computer system. The two threatened to go public with the security breach if they were not paid. The hackers were arrested in London after a sting operation launched by the FBI and Scotland Yard (with the close cooperation of then-Chief Executive Officer, and now New York City Mayor, Michael Bloomberg) and were extradited to the United States to stand trial in 2003.[52]

---

48. See Noah Shachtman, "Econ Forum Site Goes Down," *Wired.com,* Jan. 31, 2002, <www.wired.com/news/politics/0,1283,50159,00.html>.

49. See "Computer-Crime Incidents at 2 California Colleges Tied to Investigation Into Russian Mafia," *Chronicle of Higher Education,* June 24, 2002, <chronicle.com/free/2002/06/2002062401t.htm>.

50. See the U.S. Department of Justice's press release announcing the conviction of Vasiliy Gorshkov, one of the accused Russian hackers, October 10, 2001, <www.usdoj.gov/criminal/cybercrime/gorshkovconvict.htm>.

51. See the U.S. Department of Justice's press release announcing the superseding indictment of Alexey Ivanov, May 7, 2001, <www.cybercrime.gov/ivanovIndict.htm>.

52. See the NIPC's "Major Investigations: Bloomberg," <www.nipc.gov/investigations/bloomberg.htm>. The trial of one of the conspirators began in February 2003. See Patricia Hurtado, "Trial Begins in Bloomberg Extortion," *Newsday.*

"RECREATIONAL" HACKERS AND VIRUS PROPAGATORS

Virtually every day there is another report about "recreational hackers," or "crackers," who penetrate networks for the thrill of it or for bragging rights in the hacker community, or about virus propagators who, though lacking any specific malicious intent against a particular target, release a virus or worm that causes widespread damage to computer systems. While remote cracking once required a fair amount of skill and computer knowledge, the recreational hacker can now download attack scripts and protocols from the World Wide Web and launch an attack against victim sites. Similarly, a virus propagator can find the basic code for an existing virus and merely adapt it to his particular specifications, rather than having to write the code for his virus from scratch. Thus, while attack tools have become more sophisticated, they have also become more accessible and easier to use.

"Recreational" hacks are numerous and may appear to be benign, but they can have serious consequences. One example from 1997 involved a juvenile who used his personal computer to hack into the telephone system that served the area of Worcester, Massachusetts. The attack shut down telephone service to 600 customers. The resulting disruption affected emergency 911 services as well as the ability of incoming aircraft to activate the runway lights at the Worcester airport. Telephone service at the airport tower was down for six hours.[53] The investigation of this case also revealed a vulnerability in 22,000 telephone switches nationwide that could allow a hacker to take them down with relatively little effort.[54] Because he was a juvenile, however, the hacker was sentenced to only two years probation and 250 hours of community service and was forced to forfeit his computer equipment and to reimburse the phone company $5,000.[55] This case demonstrated that a single individual working from his personal computer could cause serious consequences. It also showed

---

com, February 6, 2003, <www.newsday.com/news/local/newyork/politics/ny-nybloo063118900feb06,0,2666382.story?coll\\7,61\\ny-nycpolitics-print>.

53. Denning, *Information Warfare and Security*, p. 51. See also Defense Technical Information Center (DTIC), "Information Assurance: Legal, Regulatory, Policy and Organizational Considerations," 4th Edition, August 1999, <www.dtic.mil/jcs/j6/j6k/ia.pdf>, pp. 2-7–2-8.

54. Testimony of Michael Vatis, Senate Judiciary Committee Subcommittee on Technology and Terrorism, October 6, 1999, <www.fbi.gov/congress/congress99/nipc10–6.htm>.

55. See U.S. Department of Justice press release, "Juvenile Computer Hacker Cuts Off FAA Tower at Regional Airport," March 18, 1998, <www.usdoj.gov/criminal/cybercrime/juvenilepld.htm>.

that an attack against one critical infrastructure—here, telecommunications—could have cascading effects on other infrastructures, such as emergency services and transportation.

INSIDERS

Disgruntled insiders—meaning current or former employees or contractors—are the most common perpetrators of computer crimes.[56] Insiders do not need a great deal of knowledge about computer intrusion techniques because their familiarity with and access to the systems that they are attacking allows them to damage the system or to steal information relatively easily.[57] There have been many criminal prosecutions involving disgruntled insiders. For example, a former U.S. Coast Guard employee used her insider knowledge and another employee's password and login identification to delete data from a Coast Guard personnel database system. It required 115 agency employees working over 1,800 hours to recover and re-enter the lost data.[58] In another case, a former employee of the Forbes publishing company hacked into the company's systems using another employee's password and login identification, caused the crash of more than half of the company's computer network servers, and erased all of the data on the crashed servers. The losses to Forbes were reportedly over $100,000.[59]

The International Component of Cyber Attacks

Because the Internet spans the globe, Internet attacks can be launched from one country, cross through numerous systems in many other countries, and hit targeted networks in still another country. A typical cyber

---

56. See Sharon Gaudin, "Case Study of Insider Sabotage: The Tim Lloyd/Omega Case," *Computer Security Journal*, Vol. XVI, No. 3 (2000), <www.gosci.com/pdfs/insider.pdf>, p. 8.

57. "The insider poses the greatest threat because they [sic] know where the most critical information is kept and how to bypass the safeguards on the system." James Savage, Deputy Special Agent in Charge of the Secret Service's Financial Crimes Division, quoted in Sharon Gaudin, "Study Looks to Define 'Insider Threat,'" *Network World*, March 4, 2002, <www.nwfusion.com/news/2002/130577_03–04–2002.html>.

58. See Laura DiDio, "U.S. Coast Guard Beefs Up Security After Hack," *CNN*.com, July 22, 1998 <www.cnn.com/TECH/computing/9807/22/coastguard.idg/>. The former employee was convicted and sentenced to five months in prison, five months home detention, and was ordered to pay $35,000 in restitution.

59. Testimony of Michael Vatis, Senate Judiciary Committee Subcommittee on Technology and Terrorism, October 6, 1999, <www.fbi.gov/congress/congress99/nipc10–6.htm>.

investigation can thus require tracing an evidentiary trail that crosses numerous international boundaries.[60] Even intrusions into U.S. systems by a perpetrator operating within the United States may require international investigative activity if the attack is routed through Internet service providers or computer networks located outside the United States. Cyber attackers often purposely take advantage of the complications associated with cross-border law enforcement in an effort to evade prosecution. When evidence is located within the United States, law enforcement authorities can subpoena records, conduct electronic surveillance, execute search warrants, and seize and examine evidence. But U.S. authorities typically can do none of those things overseas; instead, they must depend on the assistance of local authorities.[61] International cooperation is therefore essential to successful cyber crime investigations.

International cyber investigations pose special problems. First, the transient or perishable nature of digital evidence requires more expeditious response than has traditionally been possible in international law enforcement matters. Internet service providers and system administrators of networks are always seeking to discard unneeded information in order to save storage costs. Thus, if digital evidence, such as historical transaction data or "log" information recording certain network activity, is not specifically located and preserved quickly, it may be permanently lost by the time formal legal assistance procedures are completed. Hackers may even return to a network and erase their digital trail if they suspect that law enforcement is watching them. As a result, the delays typically associated with cross-border law enforcement are especially likely to impede an international cyber investigation.

Second, many foreign criminal justice systems are poorly prepared to

---

60. It has been estimated that 70 percent of attacks on computer systems worldwide originate outside the United States. Ranae Merle, "Computer Attacks on Companies Up Sharply," *Washington Post*, January 28, 2002, <www.washingtonpost.com/ac2/ wp-dyn/A46836–2002Jan27>.

61. One notable exception to this principle involves the case of the Russian hacker (see "Criminal Groups," above), who was convicted based in part on evidence collected by the FBI's remote penetration from the United States of a computer located in Russia and the downloading of pertinent files. U.S. prosecutors obtained a search warrant before opening the seized files in the United States, but the seizure occurred without the consent of the system owner or the knowledge of Russian law enforcement. Although a U.S. court found that this search and seizure did not violate any U.S. laws, the incident caused consternation in the Russian government and reportedly led to the filing of criminal charges (unauthorized access to computer information) by Russia's Federal Security Service (FSB) against one of the FBI agents involved in the case. See Mike Brunker, "FBI agent charged with hacking," *MSNBC News*, August 15, 2002, <msnbc.com/news/563379.asp?cp1>.

respond to cyber crimes. While the situation has improved markedly in recent years, some countries still lack substantive criminal laws that specifically address computer crimes. As a result, these countries may lack the authority, not only to investigate or prosecute computer crimes that occur within their borders, but also to assist the United States when it seeks evidence located in those countries.[62] The quickly evolving technological aspects of these investigations also can exceed the capabilities of local police forces in some countries. The limits on the technical savvy of foreign law enforcement officials can thus seriously inhibit U.S. cyber investigations.

Finally, there are few formal mechanisms for international cooperation in cyber investigations. Formal bilateral arrangements for information sharing, generally embodied in "Mutual Legal Assistance in Criminal Matters Treaties" (MLATs), do not exist between all of the countries that may need to cooperate on a cyber crime investigation. As of February 2003, the United States had MLATs in force with only 48 countries (with another 15 countries signed but not yet ratified).[63] Furthermore, many MLATs do not cover computer crimes (either specifically or through broadly applicable general terms), and their procedures are typically time-consuming and burdensome.

Multilateral conventions (informal as well as formal) have proven difficult for a number of reasons. One significant reason is that the growth of computer crime has affected different countries at different rates, meaning that many countries have not yet (or until recently) had to face the problem in a serious way. Countries that have not adopted a rigorous internal approach to the problem of computer crime are ill prepared to enter multilateral negotiations. A second reason is the difficulty of distinguishing what is mere "cyber crime" from that of "information

---

62. The best example of a country's lacking the requisite substantive criminal law involved the ILOVEYOU virus, or "Love Bug," which in 2000 spread around the world in a matter of hours, causing damage estimated in the billions of dollars. Within 24 hours, the FBI traced the virus back to the Philippines and, with the assistance of the Philippines' National Bureau of Investigation, identified the propagator as Onel de Guzman. But the investigation in the Philippines was somewhat hampered by the lack of a specific computer crime statute, and ultimately charges against de Guzman were dropped because of a determination by the government of the Philippines that its general criminal statutes did not apply to the propagation of a computer virus. In June 2000, though, the Philippines approved the E-Commerce Act, which now specifically criminalizes computer hacking and virus propagation. See <www.nipc.gov/investigations/loveletter.htm>.

63. See U.S. State Department, Mutual Legal Assistance in Criminal Matters Treaties (MLATs) and Other Agreements, at <www.travel.state.gov/mlat.html>.

warfare" or cyber espionage.[64] If a foreign intelligence agency committed an intrusion, then that country's government is unlikely to render effective assistance to U.S. investigators.

The effectiveness of informal multilateral initiatives, such as the G8 Subgroup on High-Tech Crime, and informal bilateral efforts between U.S. and foreign law enforcement agencies partly compensates for the weakness of formal mechanisms.[65] However, in light of the continuing rise in the number and gravity of cyber crimes, the expansion of both formal and informal mechanisms for international cooperation is vital to improving U.S. cybersecurity.[66]

The Federal Response to Cyber Attacks

The federal government has for decades devoted substantial resources to building U.S. information infrastructure. A researcher at a govern-

---

64. The case of the West German hackers who sold U.S. military information to the KGB (discussed in "Foreign Intelligence Services") is a good example of a case that initially looked like a relatively benign case of a hacker breaking into a university network but actually turned out to be a case of cyber espionage. See Stoll, The Cuckoo's Egg. The converse can also be true: what looks like a state attack can turn out to be the work of recreational hackers. In February 1998, for example, there were intrusions into numerous U.S. military networks during a period in which the United States was sending troops and *materiel* to the Persian Gulf in anticipation of air strikes against Iraq because of its continued flouting of United Nations resolutions regarding weapons inspections. Some of the computer intrusions were initially traced to the Persian Gulf region. The timing of the intrusions and the initial linkage to the Persian Gulf led many in the Pentagon to believe initially that the Iraqi government was behind the penetrations. But a multiagency investigation led by the NIPC, dubbed "Solar Sunrise," in conjunction with Israeli and other foreign law enforcement agencies, soon determined that the intrusions were the work of two California teenagers, assisted by an Israeli citizen. See Testimony of Michael Vatis, House Committee on Government Affairs, Subcommittee on Government Management, Information, and Technology, July 26, 2000, <www.fbi.gov/congress/congress00/vatis072600.htm>.

65. See Vatis, International Cyber Security Cooperation.

66. One example of a multilateral mechanism for fostering international cooperation on cyber crime issues is the Council of Europe's Convention on Cybercrime, a treaty signed by the Council of Europe's member nations and some non-member "observer" nations (including the United States) in 2001. "The Convention is the first international treaty on crimes committed via the Internet and other computer networks . . . Its main objective, set out in the preamble, is to pursue a common criminal policy aimed at the protection of society against cybercrime, especially by adopting appropriate legislation and fostering international co-operation." See <conventions.coe.int/Treaty/ EN/projets/ FinalCybercrime.htm>. As of February 2003, however, only Albania and Croatia had ratified the treaty. See <conventions.coe.int/Treaty/EN/searchsig. asp?NT=185&CM= &DF=>.

ment-funded think tank developed the precursor to the Internet's essential packet switching technology around 1960, in a research project aimed at providing the U.S. military with a communications system that could survive nuclear attack.[67] The Internet itself grew out of ARPANET, a Department of Defense (DOD) program that developed a communication network to link scientists working on DOD-funded research projects.[68] Government efforts to protect this infrastructure, however, are much more recent.

EARLY EFFORTS AT INFORMATION INFRASTRUCTURE PROTECTION

The federal government began focusing on cyber attacks in earnest during the mid-1990s.[69] Motivated by the bombing of the Alfred P. Murrah Federal Building in Oklahoma City, Oklahoma, the Clinton administration in late 1995 convened the Critical Infrastructure Working Group (CIWG) to assess the vulnerabilities of the nation's "critical infrastructure[s]" to attack and to make recommendations to the president on how to protect them.[70] The CIWG defined as critical infrastructures the "interdependent networks and systems comprising identifiable industries, institutions, and distribution capabilities that provide a continual flow of goods and services essential to the defense and economic security of the United States, the smooth functioning of governments at all levels, and society as a whole."[71]

Moreover, it warned that critical infrastructures were vulnerable not only to physical attacks like the one seen in Oklahoma City, but also to

---

67.   See Janet Abbate, *Inventing the Internet* (Cambridge, Mass.: MIT Press, 1999), pp. 8, 11. The researcher was Paul Baran of the RAND Corporation.

68.   Abbate, *Inventing the Internet*, pp. 43–44.

69.   The National Security Agency, the National Institute for Standards and Technology (NIST) at the Department of Commerce, and some other agencies have worked on computer security issues for many years. But government-wide policymaking to address the vulnerabilities of and threats to vital computer networks and the critical infrastructures that rely on them did not begin until the 1990s, with the rapid growth of the Internet.

70.   The Critical Infrastructure Working Group (CIWG), led by the author on behalf of Deputy Attorney General Jamie Gorelick, comprised representatives from many federal agencies, including the Departments of Justice and Defense, the FBI, and the CIA, as well as the executive office of the president.

71.   Presidential Decision Directive 63 would subsequently define critical infrastructures as "those physical and cyber-based systems essential to the minimum operations of the economy and government." It listed eight critical infrastructure sectors: telecommunications, electric power, transportation, oil and gas delivery and storage, banking and finance, water, emergency services, and critical government services.

"cyber attacks" against the computer networks that are used to control the delivery of vital services. In its January 1996 report, the CIWG recommended the creation of a full-time commission, comprising representatives from both government and private industry, to develop a national strategy for protecting the critical infrastructures and also an interim task force to coordinate the government's existing operational capabilities for responding to infrastructure attacks.[72]

Based on the CIWG's recommendations, President Bill Clinton signed Executive Order 13010 in July 1996, creating the President's Commission on Critical Infrastructure Protection (PCCIP) to study the problem in depth and to develop proposed solutions.[73] The Executive Order also established the Infrastructure Protection Task Force (IPTF). This interagency body, led by the FBI, was designed to facilitate the coordination of existing infrastructure protection efforts in the interim period, while the PCCIP conducted its analysis and developed long-term recommendations.[74]

PDD-63

The PCCIP's final report became the basis for Presidential Decision Directive (PDD) 63, which outlined the federal government's approach to critical infrastructure protection.[75] Signed by President Clinton on May 22, 1998, PDD-63 created intragovernmental and public-private cooperative structures to address policymaking, preventive measures, and operational matters. PDD-62, a classified document that set forth the government's counterterrorism policy, was signed the same day. It created,

---

72. Office of the Attorney General, Memorandum on Critical Infrastructure Security, March 14, 1996, <www.fas.org/sgp/othergov/munromem.htm>, summarizes the work of the CIWG. Senate Governmental Affairs Permanent Subcommittee on Investigation, "Hearing Report: Security in Cyberspace," June 16, 1996, <www.fas.org/irp/congress/1996_hr/s9606051.htm >, summarizes a Senate hearing on the CIWG's recommendations and related matters.

73. Executive Order No. 13,010, 61 Fed. Reg. 37,345 (July 17, 1996), <www.access.gpo.gov/su_docs/aces/aces140.html>.

74. See testimony of Michael Vatis before the Senate Judiciary Committee, Subcommittee on Terrorism, Technology and Government Information, June 10, 1998, <www.fas.org/irp/congress/1998_hr/98061101_ppo.html>, for a brief history of these recommendations.

75. See Critical Infrastructure Assurance Office, "White Paper: The Clinton Administration's Policy on Critical Infrastructure Protection: Presidential Decision Directive 63," May 1998, <www.ciao.gov/resource/paper598.html>. PDD 62 and PDD 63 are summarized in a White House press release dated May 22, 1998, at <www.info-sec.com/ciao/6263summary.html>.

within the National Security Council staff, the position of National Coordinator for Security, Infrastructure Protection, and Counterterrorism to oversee both the counterterrorism and cyber security activities of the federal government.[76]

PDD-63 introduced several mechanisms for improving public-private cooperation. It designated "lead agencies" to work with private industry in each infrastructure sector to address critical infrastructure problems, develop parts of the national plan to protect the critical infrastructure, and engage in education and vulnerability awareness activities with each industry sector.[77] In addition, PDD-63 encouraged the creation of Information Sharing and Analysis Centers (ISACs) in each sector. These centers, located in the private sector, are intended to gather, analyze, sanitize, and disseminate private sector information within each sector and also serve as a conduit for information sharing between industry and government. At least a segment of each of the eight critical infrastructure sectors identified by the federal government has created or is developing an ISAC.[78] PDD-63 also created the National Infrastructure Advisory Council (NIAC), a panel of industry CEOs and other private sector experts, to

---

76. Richard Clarke, a senior NSC staffer who was already responsible for counterterrorism, was appointed to the new post. He would later be named the Chairman of the President's Critical Infrastructure Protection Board and Special Advisor to the President for Cyberspace Security by President Bush. He retired from these positions in February 2003.

77. PDD-63 designated lead agencies as follows: the Commerce Department for information and communications; the Treasury Department for banking and finance; the Environmental Protection Agency for water supply; the Department of Transportation for aviation, highways, mass transit, pipelines, rail, and waterborne commerce; the Justice Department/FBI for emergency law enforcement services; the Federal Emergency Management Agency for emergency fire service and continuity of government; and the Department of Health and Human Services for public health services. It also specified lead agencies for special functions: the State Department for foreign affairs; the CIA for intelligence; the Defense Department for national defense; and Justice/FBI for law enforcement and internal security.

78. For the current and growing list of ISACs, see <www.nipc.gov/infosharing/infosharing6.htm>. See also National Infrastructure Protection Center (NIPC), *Highlights,* April 2001, <www.nipc.gov/publications/highlights/2001/highlight-01–05.htm>; Willard S. Evans, Jr., "Security: Protecting Critical Infrastructures by Sharing Information," *Energy IT,* January/February 2002, <www.platts.com/infotech/issues/0201/0201eit_security.shtml>; Energy ISAC, <www.energyisac.com/>; Association of Metropolitan Water Agencies, *Information Sharing and Analysis Center: Planning for the Water ISAC Implementation,* <www.amwa.net/isac/waterisac.html>; Telecommunications ISAC Information Portal, <www.ncs.gov/InformationPortal/portal.html>; National Association of State Chief Information Officers' Interstate ISAC, <www.nascio.org>; Financial Services ISAC, <fsisac.com>; and Information Technology ISAC, <www.it-isac.org>.

promote cooperation between businesses and government on computer security issues.

On operational matters, the directive formally recognized the creation of the National Infrastructure Protection Center (NIPC), an interagency center that had been created in February 1998 by the Department of Justice and FBI, in conjunction with the Defense Department, the intelligence community, and other agencies. The NIPC served as the operational focal point for information gathering, threat assessment, warning, and investigation of cyber attacks. (As discussed below, most of the NIPC was transferred to the newly created Department of Homeland Security on March 1, 2003. As of this writing, it is not clear how the move will affect the NIPC's name or mission.)

The NIPC's status as an interagency center housed at the FBI and its strong ties with both the private sector and state and local law enforcement were essential to its ability to carry out its operational functions. The FBI's broad legal authority to conduct both criminal and foreign counterintelligence investigations allowed the NIPC to gather and retain the information necessary to determine the source, nature, and scope of an incident.[79] But the broad scope of cyber threats—including foreign espionage, information warfare, and cyber terrorism—frequently implicates the missions and different expertise of the Defense Department, the intelligence community, infrastructure-focused civilian agencies such as the Department of Energy and the Department of Transportation, and state and local law enforcement. Having those agencies, as well as key foreign allies, represented in the NIPC made it easier for the NIPC to tap into those agencies' data, to share information with them, and to quickly engage their operational components when necessary. In addition, the key role of businesses in operating and maintaining most of the critical infrastructures made the NIPC's outreach efforts to the private sector a crucial tool for planning for and mitigating the consequences of cyber attacks.[80]

---

79.   See statement of Michael A. Vatis before the Senate Committee on Judiciary, May 25, 2000, <judiciary.senate.gov/oldsite/52520mav.htm>.

80.   Among these outreach efforts are the Key Asset Initiative and InfraGard. The Key Asset Initiative is a program aimed at identifying, cataloging, and engaging in contingency planning with "key assets." A key asset is defined as an organization, group of organizations, system or groups of systems, or physical plant, whose loss would have widespread and dire economic or social impact. <www.nipc.gov/infosharing/infosharing2.htm>. InfraGard is a cooperative undertaking between the U.S. government (led by the NIPC and FBI) and businesses, academic institutions, state and local law enforcement agencies, and other participants dedicated to sharing information about cyber threats, vulnerabilities, and incidents, thereby increasing the security of U.S. critical infrastructures. See <www.infragard.net/>. Between 1998 and 2003,

PDD-63 also created the Critical Infrastructure Assurance Office (CIAO), located in the Commerce Department, to support the National Coordinator in outreach and policy planning, including the development of the National Plan for Information Systems Protection ("National Plan"), which was released in January 2000. The National Plan outlined the steps that the federal government would take to protect its own information assets and to develop a public-private partnership dedicated to defending the nation's critical infrastructures. Its three objectives were summed up as "Prepare and Prevent," "Detect and Respond," and "Build Strong Foundations."[81]

BUSH ADMINISTRATION POLICY

President George W. Bush established the President's Critical Infrastructure Protection Board (PCIPB) to coordinate federal infrastructure protection efforts and to develop a national strategy for information systems protection.[82] On February 14, 2003, the Bush administration released its "National Strategy to Secure Cyberspace."[83]

The substantive content of the Bush administration's cyber security policy appears similar to that of the Clinton administration. In particular, it continues to emphasize the crucial importance of public-private partnerships, recognizing that the U.S. government currently lacks the legal authority and the capability to single-handedly defend the nation's critical infrastructures. Like its predecessor, the Bush administration is acutely conscious that the private sector owns and operates most of the nation's essential networks and critical infrastructures, that it employs many of the field's leading technical experts, and is therefore a vital partner in the infrastructure protection effort.[84] The Bush administration is

---

InfraGard grew from a pilot program in Cleveland into a national initiative with thousands of members from both the public and private sectors.

81. "National Plan for Information Systems Protection, Version 1.0," 2000, <www.ciao.gov/publicaffairs/np1final.pdf>.

82. See Executive Order 13231, "Critical Infrastructure Protection in the Information Age," October 16, 2001, <www.ncs.gov/ncs/html/eo-13231.htm>. See also Thomas R. Temin, "Bush Establishes Cybersecurity Board," *Government Computer News,* October 22, 2001, <www.gcn.com/20_31/news/17361–1.html>.

83. See "The National Strategy to Secure Cyberspace," <www.whitehouse.gov/pcipb/>. The final draft of the strategy eliminated or watered down proposals, which, in an earlier draft released for public comment, were designed to improve security of private sector networks. See Brian Krebs, "White House Releases Cybersecurity Plan," *Washington Post,* February 14, 2003, <www.washingtonpost.com/wp-dyn/articles/A7970–2003Feb14.html>.

84. As Paul Kurtz, director of Critical Infrastructure Protection for the White House,

also consolidating in the recently created Department of Homeland Security many of the existing federal agencies that have infrastructure protection responsibilities, including most of the NIPC,[85] the CIAO, the National Communications System, the Federal Computer Intrusion Response Capability (FedCirc), and the National Infrastructure Simulation and Analysis Center (NISAC).[86]

On the whole, both the Clinton and Bush administrations have steered clear of requiring companies to institute security measures to protect their networks or imposing legal liability on software or hardware manufacturers whose products contain vulnerabilities, relying instead on the voluntary efforts of industry to improve security.[87] Two exceptions to

stated: "First and foremost, we must form a partnership with the private sector." Maureen Sirhal, "White House Official Outlines Cybersecurity Initiative," National Journal's Technology Daily, January 25, 2002, <govexec.com/dailyfed/0102/012502td1.htm>. Kurtz also noted that the current White House cyber security team was continuing a Clinton administration initiative to ensure that security is built into the next generation of computer systems. Richard Clarke, who headed cyber security efforts for the White House in both the Clinton and Bush Administrations (until January 31, 2003), repeatedly stated that convincing private companies to invest in computer security was a top administration priority. Bara Vaida, "Clarke Presses Private Sector to Protect Against Cyber Attacks," February 14, 2002, <www.govexec.com/dailyfed/0202/021402td1.htm>.

85. Specifically, the administration is moving the analysis, warning, and outreach functions of the NIPC to the Department of Homeland Security, while leaving the investigations and operations arm at the FBI in the Bureau's new Cybercrime Division. See Department of Homeland Security Reorganization Plan, November 25, 2002, <http://www.whitehouse.gov/news/releases/2002/11/reorganization_plan.pdf>, pp. 1–3. This could enhance the NIPC's outreach and analytical capabilities, but the splitting of the investigative and analytical/warning responsibilities into different agencies could impede the flow of information from investigators (at the FBI) to analysts (at DHS), thereby delaying the issuance of warnings and could concomitantly make it more difficult for the investigators to benefit from the work of the analysts. This new approach can succeed only if mechanisms for improved interagency information sharing are instituted—and enforced.

86. Ibid., pp. 3–4.

87. See Hiawatha Bray, Boston Globe, "Cyber chief speaks on Data network security," October 17, 2002, <www.boston.com/dailyglobe2/290/business/Cyber_chief_speaks_on_Data_network_security+.shtml>. Howard Schmidt, who succeeded Richard Clarke as the Chairman of President Bush's PCIPB and was formerly the chief security officer for Microsoft, said: "It's got to be voluntary because if we don't work in a spirit of cooperation and trust, we are shooting ourselves in the foot at the outset." Molly M. Peterson, "Public-Private Partnerships Called Key to Cybersecurity," March 12, 2002, <www.govexec.com/dailyfed/0302/031202td2.htm>. See also Carolyn Duffy Marsan, "Security Chief Details U.S. Cybersecurity Plans," March 12, 2002, <www.nwfusion.com/news/2002/0312cybersec.html>.

this general approach are the Gramm-Leach-Bliley Act[88] (GLB), which imposes information security requirements on financial service companies, and the Health Insurance Portability and Accountability Act[89] (HIPAA), which imposes similar security requirements on health care providers. These acts were passed out of a concern for protecting the privacy of customer and patient data stored electronically, more than out of a concern for the security of computer networks and critical infrastructures. However, if the number and severity of cyber attacks continue to increase, the GLB and HIPAA models for trying to improve security could be extended to other industries.

Recommendations

This section outlines some recommended steps that the government and the private sector can take to protect critical infrastructure networks against digital threats, ranging from near-term operational steps to longer-term policy measures.

EXERCISE HIGH LEVEL OF CYBER ALERTNESS NATIONALLY DURING PERIODS OF CONFLICT

During periods of military conflict and international tension, U.S. government officials and system administrators in both government and industry should be on high alert for the warning signs of impending hostile cyber activity. Cyber attacks increasingly accompany international conflicts. As discussed earlier, for example, cyber attacks followed NATO intervention in Kosovo during the spring of 2000, the April 2001 midair collision between a U.S. surveillance plane and a Chinese fighter aircraft, and other recent international incidents or conflicts. Similar attacks may ensue as the United States carries out military and law enforcement actions against terrorist groups and their state sponsors and also as the United States and allies build up for—and possibly engage in—military

---

88. Gramm-Leach-Bliley Financial Services Modernization Act, Public Law No. 106–102, 113 Stat. 1338 (1999). Section 6801 of the Act requires that financial institutions protect nonpublic personal information by adopting a privacy obligation policy and sufficient safeguards to ensure the security and confidentiality of customer records and information, including information stored electronically.

89. Health Insurance Portability and Accountability Act of 1996, Public Law No. 104–191, 110 Stat. 1988. The Department of Health and Human Services is scheduled to publish in the Federal Register the final rule implementing the security provisions of HIPAA on February 20, 2003. The final rule can be found at <www.cms.hhs.gov/regulations/hipaa/cms0003–5/0049f-econ-ofr-2–12–03.pdf>.

action against Iraq. To prepare for periods of high alert, security officials and network administrators should implement systematic and routine risk assessments of networks, oversee development of an incident management plan, and ensure that law enforcement contact information is readily available in case of attack.

IDENTIFY AND FOLLOW STANDARD "BEST PRACTICES" FOR COMPUTER SECURITY

Agency heads, CEOs, and other leaders must ensure that their organizations' standard operating procedures incorporate existing best practices for security. For too long, security has been, at best, an afterthought for senior executives. Given the extent of damage that can be caused by cyber attacks—both to the enterprise itself as well as to the economy and national security—government and industry leaders alike must ensure that their organizations at least implement state-of-the-art security technology and practices.

SECURE CRITICAL INFORMATION ASSETS

Any host or network component, the loss of whose services may result in serious communications failure, financial loss, or disruption of a vital organizational function should be considered a critical information asset. While cost considerations make extraordinary protection of all systems impractical, measures for securing the most critical systems should be implemented wherever possible. These measures can include backing up data and storing copies off-site, building redundancies into key communications systems, and decoupling systems so that failures are more easily contained within a part of the network or infrastructure. All of an organization's measures to secure critical infrastructure assets should be clearly explained to its members in an enforceable security policy.

EXPAND EXISTING ORGANIZATIONS THAT PERFORM OPERATIONAL WARNING AND RESPONSE FUNCTIONS

The severity of the digital threat has grown much more rapidly than the budgets of the government agencies charged with managing it. The NIPC, for example, received just $27 million in fiscal year (FY) 2002; meanwhile the number of cyber security incidents and the number of computer security vulnerabilities more than doubled in 2001.[90] By one estimate, the worldwide cost of attacks using malicious code in 2001 was

---

90. CERT-CC, "CERT/CC Statistics 1988–2001," <www.cert.org/stats/ cert_stats. html>.

$13.2 billion.[91] While all such estimates must be taken with a large grain of salt, at the very least, a clear trend of significantly increasing costs can be discerned. Yet, U.S. investments in mechanisms that gather information, assess threats, provide warnings, investigate incidents, and assist recovery have not kept pace. This imbalance must be addressed by enhancing the capacities of operational entities that are moving to the Department of Homeland Security as well as those remaining at the FBI, DOD, the intelligence agencies, and elsewhere.

HELP STATE AND LOCAL GOVERNMENTS DEVELOP MORE SOPHISTICATED CYBER SECURITY CAPABILITIES

State and local government employees will be among the first to respond to any terrorist attack in the United States. After September 11, 2001, this assertion is self-evident in the case of physical attacks. But it is also true in the cyber context, particularly since federal response resources will never be sufficient to deal with all cyber attacks. It is therefore imperative to empower state and local governments to help businesses and citizens respond to computer security incidents. At the same time, state and local governments must improve the security of their own computer and communications networks, both to protect those networks for their own sake as well as to preserve government agencies' ability to respond to physical terrorism. A physical attack would have much more severe consequences if terrorists used a cyber attack to disable a jurisdiction's emergency response system or other critical infrastructures. The federal government, in conjunction with industry and academia, should therefore help state and local counterparts develop the capacity to prevent, prepare for, investigate, and recover from cyber attacks.[92]

DEVELOP LEGAL MECHANISMS AND RELATIONSHIPS TO FACILITATE CROSS-BORDER INVESTIGATION AND ENFORCEMENT

As it works to improve cross-border responses to cyber attacks, the United States should focus on expanding formal and informal bilateral

---

91. *Computer Economics, 2001 Economic Impact of Malicious Code Attacks,* January 2, 2002, press release at <www.computereconomics.com/article.cfm?id=133>.

92. One existing example of such assistance involves an agreement between the NIPC and the National Association of State Chief Information Officers (NASCIO) to "allow participating states to begin receiving sensitive alerts regarding cyber and physical terrorism threats" from the NIPC as "the first step toward a full-featured Interstate Information Sharing and Analysis Center (Interstate ISAC)." <www.nascio.org/pressReleases/02_nipc.cfm>. See also NASCIO's Issue Brief, "The Role of the State CIO and IT in Homeland Security," <www.nascio.org/hotissues/hs/StateCIOsandHomeSec.cfm>.

and multilateral cooperative arrangements. The NIPC established programs that strengthen the "trust networks" essential to informal bilateral cooperation: for example, it sponsored classes for foreign law enforcement, developed information-sharing relationships with foreign watch centers, and invited other countries to send liaison representatives to the NIPC. The new Department of Homeland Security should expand such practices. Inevitably, however, the United States will find that a cyber attack has originated from or passed through a country outside of our trust network. It is therefore important that the United States support formal multilateral agreements that will oblige all parties to help one another respond to cyber attacks and that will speed the pace at which cyber attacks are traced and investigated.

EXPAND CYBER SECURITY RESEARCH AND DEVELOPMENT

The U.S. government must expand its support for the development of technologies that build security into new information technologies "from the ground up." The Internet itself was never designed with security as a primary consideration; as a result, vulnerabilities are embedded in the very foundation of our information infrastructure. Much work is currently underway in the private sector to develop new virus detection software, firewalls,[93] and the like. But commercial research is largely focused on existing threats and near-term profit making developments. What remains sorely needed is research that can address the mid- and long-term threats and develop secure, next-generation networks.

To obtain the maximum benefit from cyber security research and development (R&D), however, the nation needs more than just increased funding. The government must also identify priorities for R&D, so that funding entities and researchers alike can focus their activities on the areas of greatest need and highest potential impact. What is needed is a prioritized national agenda for information assurance research and development.[94] In FY 2001, Congress funded the creation of a new organiza-

---

93. Firewalls are dedicated gateway machines with special security precautions, used to service outside networks, especially the Internet. Free On-Line Dictionary of Computing, at the Imperial College of London's Department of Computing, <foldoc.doc.ic.ac.uk/foldoc/foldoc.cgi?firewall+machine>.

94. See, e.g., Institute for Defense Analysis (IDA), *A National R&D Institute for Information Infrastructure Protection (I3P)* (Washington, D.C.: IDA, 2000); Office of Science and Technology Policy (OSTP), "White Paper on the Institute for Information Infrastructure Protection" (Washington, D.C.: OSTP, July 11, 2000). Also recommending additional funding for information security research and development to keep pace with cyber attackers is the Center for Strategic and International Studies (CSIS), *Defending America—Redefining the Conceptual Borders of Homeland Defense—Critical Infrastructure*

tion—the Institute for Information Infrastructure Protection (I3P)—to develop such an agenda and to fund research to address critical R&D priorities.[95] The first I3P research and development agenda was published in January 2003.[96]

EXPLORE NEW LEGAL AND POLICY MEASURES TO INCREASE SECURITY

As discussed above, the federal government's general approach to increasing cyber security has been to rely on criminal law to punish cyber attackers and to trust the voluntary efforts of private industry to build and run more secure systems. To date, however, the government has not only avoided trying to mandate better security through statute or regulation (with the exception of the HIPAA and the Gramm-Leach-Bliley Act), but has also largely failed to create incentives for better security, such as instituting reporting requirements on security practices by publicly traded companies, making changes in tort law to create legal liability for negligent or reckless creation of security vulnerabilities by manufacturers or network operators whose action or inaction causes harm to others, and establishing tax or insurance incentives for companies that take steps to increase security. These types of innovative approaches need to be thoroughly explored by federal and state governments to ensure that the legal, policy, and economic environments contribute to the improvement of the nation's cyber security posture.[97]

Conclusion

Each day, online news services and trade journals report newly discovered computer security vulnerabilities. Most of the hackers who exploit these vulnerabilities lack the political motivation, resources, technical capabilities, and malicious intent of terrorist groups or hostile nations. For

---

Protection and Information Warfare (Washington, D.C.: CSIS, 2000). See also <www. thei3p. org/abouti3p.jsp>, and <www.csis.org/homeland/#reports>.

95. The Institute for Information Infrastructure Protection ("I3P") is a consortium of (as of this writing) 23 leading cyber security and information infrastructure protection research organizations, with strategic direction and management functions provided by the Institute for Security Technology Studies at Dartmouth College. See <www. thei3p.org>. The I3P concept is based in significant part on IDA, *A National R&D Institute for Information Infrastructure Protection (I3P);* and OSTP, "White Paper on the Institute for Information Infrastructure Protection."

96. The I3P R&D agenda can be found at <www.thei3p.org/documents/2003_ Cyber_Security_RD_Agenda.pdf>.

97. The I3P R&D agenda calls for research into such legal and policy measures to foster improved security. *Ibid.,* pp. 38–42.

this reason, most cyber security incidents to date have not inflicted the maximum possible damage on compromised systems, and they rarely, if ever, have injured or killed people. Because so many hackers are content merely to penetrate or deface the systems that they compromise without causing lasting damage, people may underestimate the havoc true cyber terrorists or hostile nations engaged in "information warfare" could wreak on the United States. In addition, the effects of a compound attack—integrating physical and cyber attacks—could be devastating.

Although cyber terrorists and hostile states may be more malicious and destructive than other hackers, all rely on the same basic methods and vulnerabilities to penetrate computer systems. As a result, the best defense against cyber terrorism is to improve mainstream computer security. The federal government must increase resources for institutions that respond to security breaches, expand both formal and informal mechanisms for international cooperation in the investigation and prosecution of cyber attackers, and invest in research to substantially raise the overall security of the systems that underlie our critical infrastructures. Simply patching existing systems is an essential, but temporary solution; the next generation of information technologies must build improved security into their basic structures. This requires an unprecedented level of cooperation among government, industry, and academia.

Part III
Capacity Building

U.S. Preparations for Biological Terrorism: Legal Limitations and the Need for Planning

Juliette Kayyem

September 11, 2001, and the continuing threat of terrorism have focused the attention of the United States on domestic preparedness. Although the likelihood of a domestic terrorist attack may remain low relative to more common threats, such as earthquakes, fires, and street crime, the country is nonetheless preparing first responders; local, state, and federal officials; and the public for what to do and what to expect should an attack occur. This comprehensive effort, funded largely under the umbrella of the domestic preparedness program, began in the mid-1990s, grew throughout the latter half of the decade, and intensified following the attacks on the World Trade Center and the Pentagon on September 11, 2001. Lawyers, however, have only recently begun to consider the issue of domestic preparedness. Any steps to improve preparedness must, of course, involve an assessment by the proper legal authorities to determine their lawfulness and legitimacy.

This essay addresses two significant legal problems with the U.S. domestic preparedness program. It begins by analyzing the doctrinal difficulties inherent in defining a terrorism incident. It then considers—as a distinct subset of terrorism—the particular problem of biological terrorism. Biological terrorism is singled out because, given its nature and potential impact, it will likely affect our present legal regime in ways that are unique (as compared to other forms of terrorism).

Two conclusions follow from this analysis. First, deciding which laws apply best is difficult because most laws were created to deal with situations other than terrorism. Second, laws nevertheless do exist that can be applied to domestic preparedness. Claims to the contrary bolster policymakers' calls for more legislating, but they do so at great risk by potentially threatening to dissuade first responders from utilizing existing tools to combat a terrorist attack. Gaps in the law, in particular with regard to biological terrorism, exist, but these do not require the creation of an entirely new legal regime. Instead, in many cases, they just need to be deciphered within the vast federal and state legal codes. This essay ultimately argues that the concerns with legal preparedness too often mask the more difficult policy and political considerations that must be evaluated in any counterterrorism policy.

Conventional Terrorism and Existing Law

Vague and contradictory laws, overlapping jurisdictions, and procedural and professional divisions among law enforcement, national security, and public health officials have created a confusing set of laws that do not conform easily to the needs of first responders. In a terrorist attack, this confusion could produce at least two unwanted outcomes. First, it could cause institutional inertia, leading ultimately to more deaths and even greater destruction. Second, it could give rise to overreaction and fear, resulting in unnecessary uses of power.

Currently, our law balances government interests against the interests of the public and individuals to determine the proper scope of government authority. This is a balancing of public rights, or the expectation that the government provide safety and security to its citizens, against private rights. During a time of crisis, the balance necessarily shifts heavily in favor of the government. As has been apparent in debates arising from the present "war on terrorism," from the use of military tribunals to increased surveillance of U.S. citizens, the government can often make a strong case for greater powers with little dissent.

The law may seem confusing, because although the necessary authorities often exist, they are not always readily apparent. There is no "law" that applies only to terrorist attacks. Electronic surveillance, for example, is as appropriate for combating terrorism as it is for combating espionage. Thus, an examination of the doctrines of U.S. law is really only a starting point. The U.S. legal regime seeks to balance the often competing needs of defending national security, providing effective law enforcement, and ensuring the individual's rights and liberties. For the most part, this regime has been a successful part of the U.S. effort to combat conventional forms of terrorism. The balance is often not perfect—as experience and history have shown and debates regarding the comprehensive counterterrorism legislation, the USA PATRIOT Act (which was signed into law in late October 2001), continue. At the very least, however, that balance has been the articulated justification for the present state of our legal code.[1]

Lawyers tend to analyze issues in terms of doctrines of law. The law establishes a set of rules and criteria that govern any incident. Table One shows the three categories of law that currently exist; none is a perfect fit for dealing with a terrorist attack. The first category includes laws and regulations that govern governmental conduct and powers during a national security crisis (hereinafter, rules of war), most commonly viewed (and indeed almost always litigated) as powers that exist during wartime. The second group includes laws and regulations that apply to criminal conduct and government action (hereinafter, rules of personal liberty). These are most commonly understood to include the rights of defendants from government action: for example, the right to due process and a speedy trial. These are also understood to include rights that afford certain actions protection from government intrusion, such as the rights to free speech, expression, and equal protection. The third category comprises laws and regulations that establish procedures for dealing with a cataclysmic event (hereinafter, rules for disasters). The Federal Emergency Management Agency's (FEMA) Federal Response Plan (FRP), for example, outlines how the U.S. government should assist state and local governments if a major disaster or other emergency overwhelms their ability to respond effectively to save lives, protect public health, safety, and property, and restore damaged communities.[2]

A terrorist attack on U.S. soil would not exclusively fall into any one of the three categories just described. Rather, it would fall into all three. A terrorist attack is similar to other types of aggression, but it is not always characterized as the kind of event justifying the use of the military and other expansive governmental powers associated with international crisis, a civil war, or a foreign invasion of troops. An act of terrorism is like any other heinous crime, but its impact may be too overwhelming to be contained by the traditional rules of personal liberty. Terrorism is similar to other crises, such as an earthquake or hurricane, but it has security and criminal implications not typically seen in a natural disaster.

Cautious and realistic legal planning, in advance of an attack, that appreciates both the difficulties that the United States could face in the

---

1. Laura Donohue, "In the Name of National Security: U.S. Counterterrorist Measures, 1960–2000," BCSIA Discussion Paper 2001–6, ESDP Discussion Paper 2001–04, John F. Kennedy School of Government, Harvard University (Cambridge, Mass.: August 2001).

2. The FRP is authorized by the Robert T. Stafford Disaster Relief and Emergency Assistance Act, as amended. 42 U.S.C. Sect. 5121, et seq.

Table 1. Categories of Law and Corresponding Authorities.

Area of Law	Authorities
Rules of War	President as Commander in Chief Congressional authority over troops State authority over the National Guard Suspension of "normal" constitutional protections (e.g., writ of *habeas corpus*)

Rules of Personal Liberty	Bill of Rights (First, Fourth, Fifth
	    Amendments), including application
	    to states through the Fourteenth
	    Amendment and case law supporting
	    privacy rights
	Public health laws

Rules for Disasters	FEMA's Federal Response Plan State health, safety, and police laws

event of a terrorist attack and the need to be respectful of the rule of law is crucial. Where more authority is deemed necessary, the government should seek it. Explicit authorization of governmental conduct—for example, a broadening of the scope of the laws regarding the ability to quarantine—would decrease the likelihood of *ad hoc* and unauthorized action by the government. Americans live in a democratic society where federal powers are limited and individual rights are protected. Although additional powers may be required to combat a terrorism crisis, the wisdom of engaging such powers must first be fully explored. Thus, the time for examination and reflection, with a proper balancing, should occur well before a terrorism event. An honest assessment of the laws will show which are necessary, which are expendable, and which need to be clarified. Only then can the even harder political and policy questions be explored (i.e., whether, even if legal, an action is desirable).

An assessment of the laws—which laws are appropriate, which laws need refining, and which laws are missing—is an essential part of any domestic preparedness program. The cost of ignoring the law would only further a terrorist's goal of wreaking havoc. To avoid this outcome, the United States needs to establish a legitimate, well-coordinated counterterrorism strategy that can provide the public with a sense of security and a feeling that everything is being done to ensure that there is minimal mass hysteria and blame. The publication of such a strategy would also underscore the government's responsibility to protect the lives, property, and well-being of its citizens.

To determine whether new, expanded powers are permissible, two potential legal limitations on the federal government's authority must be addressed. First, under the U.S. Constitution, all powers not delegated to the national government under the Tenth Amendment to the Constitution are retained by the states and the people.[3] The war power and the power over foreign affairs, for example, are vested in the national government to the point that state regulation in the same area is essentially precluded. Congress also has the power to regulate commerce, to tax, and to spend. Through the commerce powers, for example, Congress is able to pass legislation affecting a broad spectrum of policies, including race relations, drug policy, and environmental cleanup, since all affect interstate commerce. That power, however, is not absolute; for example, the Supreme Court has limited Congress's ability, under the Commerce Clause, to prohibit the knowing possession of firearms in a school zone, holding that Congress needs to show a substantial and commercial effect before it can regulate any activity, especially in cases where the states have traditionally had control.[4]

Deciding the proper balance of power between the states and the federal government is still, legally speaking, a work in progress. What is clear is that the states retain broad powers in our federal system and the federal government cannot trump the powers reserved to the states. States, for example, maintain police powers to legislate for the health, morals, and well-being of their citizens. While the states are subject to the same requirement as the federal government that their laws not violate personal liberties and freedoms, the states also have broad powers to regulate the conduct of their citizens. The federal structure, therefore, places some restrictions on the national government's ability to expand its powers in order to combat, for example, biological terrorism; in other words, the federal government may not always have the authority to act, even if it so chooses.

Second, limited government in the United States is achieved not only through the constitutional allocation of powers but also through the recognition of the personal rights and liberties of its citizens as protected in the Constitution and the Bill of Rights. These protections apply to state governments and state actors as well; thus, various fundamental guarantees of the Bill of Rights are, through the Fourteenth Amendment of the

---

3. "The powers not delegated to the United States by the Constitution, nor prohibited by it to the States, are reserved to the States respectively, or to the people." U.S. Constitution, Amendment X [1791]. ·

4. *Lopez v. United States*, 514 U.S. 549 (1995).

Constitution, "incorporated" and made applicable to the states.[5] The continuing vitality of the right to free speech, the right to worship, and the prohibition against unreasonable searches and seizures underscores the notion that governmental authority must be balanced and limited.

Determining the appropriate law within each of the three doctrines outlined earlier is essential, so that debates on policy can be decided before an actual terrorist attack. A legitimate legal question, for example, is: do police officers have sufficient reasonable suspicion to enter an apartment house where it is suspected that one, but not all, of the apartments may contain critical information? As a legal matter, the answer is likely "yes."[6] But several policy questions still remain, including: under which circumstances would such a search be permissible? How should the officers behave? How can they best obtain consent from the apartment owners? These policy matters and others, such as when the government would want to impose a quarantine following a biological attack, should not be ignored because of concerns about legal ambiguity. The law, as most lawyers will say, does not provide all the right answers but merely offers guidance.

The Special Case of Biological Terrorism

A biological terrorism event, specifically, will challenge the explicit balance that this country has tried to maintain between security and liberty. As was apparent in the anthrax attacks in 2001 and the response, biological attacks will require different responses than conventional attacks. The huge number of lives at stake, coupled with the unique nature of biological weapons and their ability to infect large populations, will place extreme pressures on those designated to prevent the attack, punish the perpetrators, or manage the consequences if prevention fails.

As a legal matter, the differences between biological terrorism and conventional terrorism are dramatic. The following list depicts the operational areas where policymakers and first responders would require defined powers in the event of a biological event.[7] It is important to understand what would be requested in order to honestly assess whether

---

5. *Mapp v. Ohio*, 367 U.S. 643 (1961). An "incorporated" Bill of Rights guarantee applies against the states to the same extent and in the same manner that it binds the federal government.

6. See *Marlin v. U.S.*, 620 U.S. 547 (2000).

7. The following list of "necessary" powers during a biological terrorism event was compiled during the December 2, 1999, Executive Session on Domestic Preparedness symposium on "Legal Authorities During a Terrorism Event." Participants of the con-

the law is adequate and relevant. If lawyers do not specifically address the needs of policymakers, then the two will be operating in a vacuum. Moreover, lawyers are rarely experts on first responders' needs. In other words, it is outside the capabilities of legal experts, for example, to determine whether quarantine, as a public health matter, may be necessary following a biological agent release. For the purposes of this analysis, then, it is assumed that the powers requested are necessary; the legality of those powers, however, is addressed below.

1. The exigent circumstances of a potential biological terrorism event will require that the president formalize the situation as an emergency so that the necessary powers, such as the power to impose a curfew or federalize the National Guard, can be invoked.

2. Access to public and private commodities, such as food, water, and vehicles, will be necessary in order to provide essential commodities to federal and state emergency workers as well as to ensure that the civilian population has basic necessities. This also includes price controls so that necessary commodities remain accessible to the population.

3. Access to and from infected areas, airports, ocean ports, and highways may need to be controlled.

4. The general prohibition against the use of the military or the Department of Defense for civilian and law enforcement purposes—the *posse comitatus* rules—will need to be evaluated where state and local officials may not have sufficient manpower to effect necessary controls.

5. The traditional divisions between law enforcement and national security entities as well as those between federal, state, and local intelligence; law enforcement; and medical communities, will need to be bridged to ensure that proper notification is provided to first responders and state officials.

6. A serious public relations effort must be sustained in order to control civilian exodus or possible hysteria. This may include restricting media access to threatened geographic areas.

7. The free movement of large segments of the population will likely be restricted, and those who may have been exposed to a biological agent may be quarantined. The notion of quarantine includes forms of isolation, such as requiring contaminated individuals to remain in specially designated areas.

ference, mostly first responders, described the types of powers that they would want in such an event.

8. Present criminal law is both suspect and incident specific: warrants and searches require that the police have a clear sense of the persons and locations under investigation. Despite the potential for devastation and mass casualties in a biological attack, there are no criminal provisions that provide for expansive investigatory powers. This may also limit police from scoping potential terrorist targets or searching broad geographic areas.

9. Many European countries permit the detention of individuals for periods of time when they are thought to be planning, or have been involved in, a terrorist attack. The U.S. criminal justice system has no such provision; however, under immigration laws, detention rules are much less severe. It was under either immigration violations or material witness provisions that a majority of those detained after the September 11, 2001, attacks were held. While recent comprehensive counterterrorism legislation permits the detention of persons for up to one week, it requires the government to release them or file charges within that time.

10. Many terrorists either identify or are affiliated with organized groups, whether ethnic, religious, or cultural. Present law prohibits group-based investigations when members are simply asserting their First Amendment rights. It may be necessary to initiate group-based surveillance or investigations to determine any culpability.

11. Privacy and familial rights require that the bodies of the deceased be released, and thus, they can rarely be examined or held by the state. In a biological terrorist attack, however, the need to protect the general population from infection may outweigh those rights. The state may desire authority to reserve the right to perform autopsies or cremate in the event of a biological terrorist attack.

12. Interstate assistance from health care officials will be necessary to address the threat against the population. Current confidentiality laws generally do not permit the sharing of information about a patient, whether alive or deceased, with law enforcement personnel. Such prohibitions may need to be loosened to provide for the general public safety.

13. Given the likelihood that necessary items—such as food, vaccines, and protective materials—will be in short supply during a biological terrorist incident, the government may require that the private sector produce specific items.

14. Generally, the public cannot be compelled to take medications. If a biological agent is released, however, compulsion may be necessary, despite personal or religious objections, to ensure that infected persons do not contaminate others. Three additional requirements

will be necessary: first, medicines and medical procedures that have not yet been formally approved may be utilized for purposes of prevention and containment; second, children or pregnant women may be required to take medication that has not been tested on their specific subgroups; and finally, first responders may need to use force to administer vaccines to individuals refusing them. Force may also be needed to compel individuals to obey medical instructions, such as agreeing to be quarantined.

Even those not versed in the law will recognize that the procedures and policies described above would constitute a dramatic reorientation of the present U.S. legal order. Table Two highlights some of the most obvious constitutional and statutory questions that these changes will raise.

Locating the appropriate laws will give practitioners a clear sense of where modifications, or full-scale changes, are warranted. In some instances, those changes may not necessarily be desirable from a policy perspective and making them lawful would not cure the deficiency. In other cases, however, the rules can be analyzed to determine how they can best be used and which, if any, triggering event may be desirable in order to ensure that these rules are fully utilized. Some of these authorities overlap with others, and they have been combined for purposes of clarity and legal discussion.

A Model State Emergency Health Powers Act, prepared for consideration by states as they get their public health authorities in order, raises the issues discussed above.[8] The model legislation, however, is limited to health authorities, does not address criminal law enforcement tools that may be needed during a biological terrorism event, and has barely been debated by most state legislatures.

Declaring a Formal State of Emergency and Utilizing the Military for Purposes of Civil Control

The sorts of authorities that may be needed in a biological terrorism event are in some ways similar to those that a president may exercise during a war or natural disaster. One may conceive of three established areas of constitutional authority with regard to the military. At one end of the spectrum is martial law, which basically suspends the Constitution for a

---

8. "The Model State Emergency Health Powers Act," A Draft for Discussion Prepared by The Center for Law and the Public's Health at Georgetown and Johns Hopkins Universities, draft as of December 21, 2001.

Table 2. Legal Issues Implicated During Terrorist Attack.

Desired Power	Potential Constitutional or Statutory Concerns
Declaring a Formal State of Emergency	Article I, Section 8: Congress shall have power "to provide for calling forth the militia" vs. Article III, Section 2: The president shall be commander in chief
Seizure of Community and Private Assets	Fifth Amendment prohibition on government takings without just compensation
Control of Transportation Terminals	Case law recognizes freedom of movement for U.S. citizens; quarantine laws may be too restrictive
Utilization of Military for Civil Control Purposes	Posse Comitatus Act
Required Notification of Appropriate Authorities in states and localities	Law enforcement and intelligence rules proscribe sharing of certain information
Control of Access to Mass Communication	First Amendment protections
Quarantine: Stay in or Go out	Federal quarantine and state and local public health laws provide for very limited quarantine authority by the government
More Liberal Interpretation of General Criminal Law Constitutional Standards	Fourth Amendment prohibition on unreasonable searches and seizures
Detention of Individuals for Short Periods of Time	Fourth, Fifth, and Sixth Amendment protections against detention without criminal basis

Table 2. *Continued*

Desired Power	Potential Constitutional or Statutory Concerns
Investigating Groups before Required "Reasonable Suspicion" is Met	First Amendment freedoms of association; Fourteenth Amendment equal protection rights
Granting of Broad State Authority Over Body of Deceased Individuals	General privacy rights
Loosening of Confidentiality and Licensing Laws to Permit Broader Access and Interstate Travel Rights to Health Officials	General privacy rights; state administrative licensing schemes
Compelling Production of Necessary Goods	Fifth Amendment prohibition on government takings without just compensation
Compelling Citizens to Take Medicine	General privacy rights

period of time. In the middle are the powers of the executive branch during wartime; simply put, the president can exercise such powers as suspending certain rights and ordering the deployment of the military. Although the contours of when an emergency exists are somewhat imprecise, there is no question that the executive branch possesses broad authority during such times. The duty to enforce the laws includes a general authority to protect and defend the personnel, property, and instrumentalities of the United States from harm.[9] At the other end is the doctrine of *posse comitatus,* which prohibits the use of the military in civilian matters but recognizes exceptions during which the military could be called up—insurrections, civil disturbances, counterdrug operations, and counterterrorism operations. The National Guard has both civilian and military responsibilities and is not bound by *posse comitatus* until it is federalized.[10] The National Guard can also be federalized by the president as an option for homeland defense requirements.

Historically, the United States has not emphasized a governmental role in "homeland defense."[11] The attacks of September 11, 2001, changed this significantly, especially with the creation of the Department of Homeland Security. The need for prompt, informed, and effective action in domestic and foreign affairs has meant that in times of crisis, power has tended to flow to the executive branch. While many of the vague, open-ended executive powers provided in the Constitution are technically shared with Congress, presidential initiatives have generally produced only congressional acquiescence, and the courts have tended to avoid judicial review of executive actions, especially in the area of foreign affairs and national security.[12] It does not appear that any additional statutory authority is needed to give the president the power to deal with such a threat: both the courts and history have provided ample support

---

9. Henry P. Monaghan, "The Protective Power of the Presidency," 93 *Columbia Law Review* 1 (1993).

10. The Department of Defense recently approved the creation of National Guard Rapid Assessment and Initial Detection (RAID) teams to assist local and state authorities in assessing the conditions surrounding a WMD emergency and to expedite the arrival of additional state and federal military assets, if necessary.

11. Prior to September 11, 2001, the widespread assumption was that U.S. territory would remain essentially safe. CSIS Report on Military Preparedness for Homeland Defense (1998).

12. See *The Prize Cases,* 67 U.S. (2 Bl.) 635 (1863). (Upholding President Lincoln's order to blockade certain Southern ports); *In re Debs,* 158 U.S. 564 (1895). (Upholding President Cleveland's power to obtain an injunction against the 1895 Pullman Strike and in the absence of any congressional authority since "the wrongs complained of [were] such . . . as affect the public at large").

for an executive guardian role. What policymakers need to determine is less which authority *exists,* and more to which extent use of that authority is *desirable.*

Achieving this balance has historically roused suspicion regarding the elevation of the military's role and a general embracing of *posse comitatus. Posse comitatus* dictates that, "Whoever, except in cases and under circumstances expressly authorized by the Constitution or Act of Congress, willfully uses any part of the Army or the Air Force as a *posse comitatus* or otherwise to execute the laws shall be fined under this title or imprisoned not more than two years, or both."[13] These firm limitations imposed by the law inhibit military activities in day-to-day civilian society. Whether the limitations are desirable has been subject to much debate. Currently, the United States has prepared only for a limited role on the part of the Department of Defense in the event of a biological terrorist attack. The Robert T. Stafford Disaster and Emergency Assistance Act of 1974 authorizes state and local governments to provide direct and primary disaster relief and emergency assistance. Even in the more recent 1996 annex to FEMA's Federal Response Plan (FRP), the government outlines the appropriate role of the military in any terrorist incident as mere support. The sense, however, that the military may be better utilized in more than a supporting role animates the literature on biological terrorism.[14] Without explicit authority, the Department of Defense (DOD) will be unprepared or unwilling to take on a more active role:

The [Posse Comitatus Act] constraints may have been appropriate in the late 1800s, but in a world where non-state groups have access to weapons of mass destruction . . . [constraints] could prove counterproductive. . . . Outdated and inflexible American legislation has produced a patchwork consisting of constitutional and statutory exceptions so that the realities of domestic operations can be performed. Examples include the [Stafford Act] . . . contingency planning for U.S. Army assistance in incidents involving use of chemical and biological weapons of mass destruction on U.S. soil, and various methods to facilitate cooperation between the FBI and the U.S. Army in anti-terrorism. The potential consequences of this approach include a convoluted chain of command and control structure, increased response time, and continuity of operations problems; it also leaves the federal response vulnerable to exploitation by the adversary.[15]

---

13. 18 U.S.C. 1385, sec. 270b.

14. Lewis Libby, "Legal Authority for a Domestic Military Role in Homeland Defense", CISAC Report (2000).

15. Ibid. at 270.

Neither concern about the public response to such an increased role nor the DOD's historical reluctance, however, stand as a legal bar to the use of the military. The Posse Comitatus Act contains a number of exceptions to the general ban, including provisions for "insurrections and civil disturbances,"[16] "humanitarian assistance,[17] and "counterterrorism" assistance in the event of a WMD attack.[18] Given that the law does not bar military involvement in a biological terrorist attack, the question remains: which kind of activities would be appropriate for the DOD to perform?

When, in 1996, Congress authorized military involvement in cases involving WMD, such as agents used for chemical or biological attacks, regulations were required by statute to further delineate the role of the DOD.[19] No such regulations have ever been issued. Yet the law is no bar to the kinds of exercise of authority that may be deemed appropriate in a biological terrorist attack. Whether such authority is desirable is a question that should be answered after the DOD makes clear its plans and intentions. Indeed, in October 1, 2002, the DOD launched the U.S. Northern Command (USNORTHCOM), a military presence in the United States for the first time in its history. The exact contours of USNORTHCOM's authority are still being debated. Nonetheless, the government and the law already contemplate a vast expansion of the military role in a crisis.

---

16.   10 U.S.C. 331, et seq.

17.   10 U.S.C. 401, et seq. The president, by proclamation, has invoked this category in several desegregation cases in the South during the civil rights movement.

18.   10 U.S.C. 382 and 18 U.S.C. 831, et. seq.

19.   The Secretary of Defense is now permitted to provide materials, expertise, and even antidotes to prepare for or respond to emergencies involving nuclear, chemical, and biological weapons of mass destruction. Upon request of the Attorney General, and agreement by the Secretary of Defense, DOD may also assist law enforcement during "emergency situations" involving the use of weapons of mass destruction. The statute defines an "emergency situation" as one where there is "(1) a circumstance involving biological or chemical weapons of mass destruction; (2) a circumstance that poses a serious threat to the interest of the United States; and (3) civilian expertise and capabilities are not readily available to counter the threat immediately posed, [where] special capabilities of DOD are necessary to counter the threat, and enforcement of the criminal statutes would be seriously impaired without DOD assistance." However, "DOD may not make arrests or directly participate in searches and seizures or intelligence collection activities related to enforcement of the statutes unless necessary for the immediate protection of human life and civilian law enforcement officials are not capable of taking action." This last provision will likely provide the necessary authority for the use of the military in a biological terrorist attack.

Seizure of Community and Private Assets

In a biological attack, the federal or state government could choose to assert authority over private entities to marshal resources and ensure public safety. This may include assuming control over scarce hospital facilities, ambulances, or land; private companies with access to antibiotics; and homes and automobiles of private individuals. State and federal governments are generally prohibited from taking private property without just compensation.[20] Historically, the ability to marshal such resources has been limited even in times of national crisis. Thus, when President Harry S. Truman sought to seize and operate steel mills in order to avert a strike during the Korean War, which was fought by the United States without a declaration of war, the Supreme Court ruled his actions unconstitutional absent specific congressional authority.[21] The Court supported the proposition that it was Congress, not the president, who could assert such authority over private property; stating that, "[t]he branch of government that has the power to pay compensation for a seizure is the only one able to authorize a seizure or make lawful one that the President has effected."[22]

In response to the limitations placed on executive authority over private property and privately produced goods, Congress passed the Defense Production Act of 1950.[23] This act affords the president an array of authorities to shape defense preparedness programs and take appropriate steps to maintain and enhance the defense industrial and technological base, in order to "reduce the time required for industrial mobilization in the event of an attack on the United States." The act contemplates that, once the president finds that such material is a scarce and critical ingredient to the national defense and that this need cannot otherwise be met, then the president is authorized to allocate materials, services, and facili-

20. U.S. Constitution, Fifth Amendment.

21. *Youngstown Sheet & Tube Co. v. Sawyer,* 343 U.S. 579 (1952). (Steel Seizure case).

22. Ibid., pp. 631–632. More recently, however, courts have been willing to recognize congressional approval even where there is no clear statutory authority. *Dames & Moore v. Regan,* 453 U.S. 654 (1981). (The president could, in executive orders, nullify private claims against the Iranian government in light of general broad congressional delegation of foreign policy power to the executive); *Haig v. Agee,* 453 U.S. 280 (1981). (Congress' silence is implicit approval of executive power to revoke passports on national security grounds).

23. 50 U.S.C. 2045, et. seq.

ties in such manner and to such extent "as he shall deem necessary or appropriate to promote the national defense."[24]

Thus, even under current law protecting private property, a properly constructed statute authorizing the taking of necessary materials to combat a biological terrorist attack could likely survive judicial scrutiny.[25] The 1950 Defense Production Act may be a starting point; the difficulty lies, however, in that this act was neither conceived of nor used to provide presidential authority during a domestic crisis. For example, FEMA's Federal Response Plan does not mention federal authority to marshal resources as in the Defense Production Act.

Explicitly legislating government authority to allocate resources is an essential tool in any effective consequence management plan. Such action could, of course, have disadvantages. U.S. society values the free market and private property; the authorized taking of private property has been limited to specific situations involving national security and foreign relations. A biological terrorist attack, however, likely qualifies for similar consideration. A statute that made clear the conditions under which the president was authorized to seize resources could prove extremely useful in consequence management.

Control of Transportation Terminals and Quarantine: Stay In or Go Out

Courts have long held that local officials may cordon off an area, establish a quarantine, or erect checkpoints for persons and vehicles entering or leaving an area. Both the need to prevent escape of suspected criminals[26] or carriers of contagion[27] and the individual's diminished right of privacy when either on foot or in a vehicle, support these rulings. In addition, U.S. officials are given significant leeway in control of national borders.

Because of the potential of quarantines to deprive individuals of their personal liberties, federal authority to quarantine apart from a congressionally-declared war is severely limited:

Special quarantine powers in time of war: To protect the military and naval forces and war workers of the United States, in time of war, against any communi-

---

24. 1950 Defense Production Act, 20 U.S.C. Sec. 220.

25. See *Dames & Moore,* supra.

26. *Laaman v. U.S.,* 973 F.2d 107 (1992). (Involving alleged terrorists who conspired to bomb military offices).

27. *Compagnie Francaise de Navigation a Vapeur v. Louisiana State Board of Health,* 186 U.S. 380 (1902).

cable disease specified in Executive orders . . . the surgeon general, on recommendation of the National Advisory Health Council, is authorized to provide by regulations for the apprehension and examination, in time of war, of any individual reasonably believed (1) to be infected with such disease in a communicable stage; and (2) to be a probable source of infection to members of the armed forces . . . Such regulations may provide that if upon examination any such individual is found to be so infected, he may be detained for such time and in such manner as may be reasonably necessary.[28]

This provision has never been utilized or interpreted to apply to any situation except for World War II, a congressionally-declared war. The detention of Japanese-Americans during World War II was approved by the Supreme Court because of the emergency situation and because Congress had passed a separate statute to authorize such detention. The Court found that this congressional authorization was an essential limitation on presidential authority.

The only other example of Congress authorizing the federal government to quarantine appears in public health laws. Regulations to control communicable diseases permit the apprehension, detention, or conditional release of individuals only for the purpose of preventing the introduction, transmission, or spread of communicable diseases specified in executive orders. These regulations, however, also apply only in limited circumstances when a person is known to be infected and is coming to a state from a foreign country or when a person is "reasonably believed to be infected with a communicable disease" and is about to move from one state to another state.[29]

The federal government is, therefore, limited in its ability to control the movement of citizens in wartime or when the movement affects interstate travel. Otherwise, pursuant to state law only, state and local officials are authorized to quarantine persons, buildings, and other designated areas in defined and limited ways. Governors and mayors, not presidents, may have that statutory authority.

To give the federal government broad authority to quarantine, present law would need to be modified and updated. The "special quarantine powers in time of war" would have to state explicitly that "war" includes a biological terrorist attack on U.S. soil. Even if the term "war" were flexible, new legislation would also have to account for the fact that there would be no time for surgeon general recommendations or advisory panels to convene and write regulations. The statute also contemplates that

---

28. 10 U.S.C. 238, et. seq.

29. 24 U.S.C. 24, et. seq.

those not carrying the disease, but who could later be infected, be released; effective consequence management, however, may require that those not yet infected remain detained.

Altering public health laws would also be difficult and expanding the federal law to include the ability to quarantine may not withstand judicial scrutiny. Consistent with limitations on congressional authority under the Tenth Amendment, public health laws only cover persons engaged in foreign or interstate travel. It may be that a president could quarantine a group of people under the reasonable belief that they all are infected with a disease and have the potential to move to another state. Whether that would justify the detention of a city employee who has a home in the suburbs is unclear.

Even if amending the law were possible, it may not be desirable as a policy matter. Expanding federal powers to include the right to quarantine has some advantages. The spread of the contagion could be confined to a limited geographic area and population. Decisive, albeit excessive, action by the federal government would ultimately save lives and resources. But the disadvantages are not only numerous, they are potentially disastrous. Current U.S. federal law limits the ability of the government to quarantine because it strikes at the core of a citizen's personal liberty and freedom of movement. Policymakers will need to consider the difficult task of predicting when and under which circumstances quarantine may be necessary. It is necessary first to delineate diseases that should be covered, ensure fair applications of the law, determine an acceptable time frame, and issue other protections. Only a carefully tailored statute applying to a biological terrorism outbreak would appropriately limit government authority and more effectively achieve the desired balance between civil liberties and public safety.

Required Notification of Appropriate Authorities in States and Localities

Many law enforcement rules, for example, those that do not permit the disclosure of grand jury testimony and historic communication divisions between state and federal actors as well as those between law enforcement and national security agencies, hinder timely and effective communication. Federal authorities are not required—indeed, in some cases, they are prohibited from doing so—to notify other federal, state, and local officials about potential terrorist attacks. In addition, a culture against information sharing, especially prevalent in U.S. intelligence agencies, is not easily overcome. Concerns regarding national security and the impact that notification could have on law enforcement capabilities tend to favor "close-hold" (few officials notified) situations, whereby the flow of information is tightly controlled.

The states have an essential interest in being well-informed as early as possible. Police powers, medical facilities, and other vital services all fall under the jurisdiction of the state. If state actors are not prepared, the effectiveness of consequence management is seriously undermined. There is, therefore, a serious dilemma between federal and state officials. This tension is mirrored in the rules established by FEMA on how to respond to a terrorist situation: "The federal government exercises primary authority to prevent, preempt, and terminate threats or acts of terrorism and to apprehend and prosecute the perpetrators; state and local governments provide assistance as required. . . . State and local governments exercise primary authority to respond to the consequences of terrorism; the federal government provides assistance as required."[30] However, crisis and consequence management are not sequential, but simultaneous.

The question, then, is: should state and local actors be notified of threats of a potential terrorist attack? One solution would be to permit narrow exceptions, in the case of biological terrorism threats, to congressional and federal law enforcement guidelines that often prohibit the sharing of criminal investigation information. Memorandums of understanding between federal and state law enforcement agencies that would provide for pre-release information flow may curtail unnecessary withholding of information.

This approach does have difficulties, however. For example, at what stage should notification be given? If notification occurs too early, it may compromise U.S. investigatory capabilities. It could also cause public distress, which in turn could harm the ability to control the situation. If notification occurs too late, it could undermine the consequence management capabilities and use up valuable time when state and local authorities could be preparing for an attack. Nonetheless, a specific triggering event, codified in law, would ensure that proper notification is given.[31]

Control of Access to Communication

The government may have an interest in curtailing wide dissemination of information about a threat or the cause of an outbreak. Such knowledge could create mass fear and hysteria, resulting in civil disorder. In the age

---

30. Federal Emergency Management Agency, *Federal Response Plan*, Terrorism Incident Annex, T1–1.

31. See Philip B. Heymann, "Law Enforcement and National Security: The Problem of Intelligence Collection to Prevent WMD Terrorism," positing a single organization

of the Internet and email, any control of the dissemination of information would be difficult but perhaps not impossible, especially in the early stages of the crisis. State and federal governments are generally prohibited from censoring materials in advance of publication. This is known as "the doctrine of prior restraint," which provides that such restraints are highly suspect, both substantively and procedurally, and are subject to a rebuttable presumption of unconstitutionality. An example of this was the invalidation of a restraint imposed on the publication of a classified study dealing with U.S. policy in the Vietnam War when the federal government failed to meet its burden of proof.[32] In the *Pentagon Papers* case, the Supreme Court implied, however, that the restraint was troubling because there was no federal statute authorizing it. Some of the justices felt that the presence of a statute may satisfy the heavy burden of justification necessary to authorize a prior restraint.

It is therefore essential to define the characteristics of the government's justification for using prior restraint.[33] A statute similar to the one that the Supreme Court seemed to endorse in the *Pentagon Papers* case would need to delineate when and where that restraint was justified. A statute confined to biological terrorism threats involving potential civil disorder may satisfy a court's exacting scrutiny regarding First Amendment guarantees.

Such a statute may be beneficial, in the short term, for controlling information. Whether it could be passed is another question, but not a legal question. The sanctity of the First Amendment is part of the popular belief that the free flow of ideas is beneficial to a democracy; the government is generally prohibited from placing any prior restraint on the publication of materials, during war or a normal domestic crisis, because of First Amendment protections of the right to free speech.

A less stringent alternative would be the adoption of a nonbinding resolution establishing an understanding between the press and the government that would facilitate government action in an emergency situation. This was attempted during the airline hostage situations of the 1980s, but the resolution was adopted by only one major news organization.[34] A similarly cooperative arrangement may be useful during a bio-

---

that would track collection, retention, analysis, and dissemination of grand terrorism threats. (Unpublished manuscript, on file with the author).

32. *New York Times Co. v. United States*, 403 U.S. 713 (1971).

33. *Alexander v. United States*, 509 U.S. 544 (1993).

34. See "Terrorism, the Press, and the Government," Congressional Research Service Report (1994).

logical terrorism crisis, but given its nonbinding nature and the advent of the Internet as a competitive form of communication, any such resolution would likely have limited benefits.

The desire to exercise some control of the media may be the result of the failure of the post–September 11 current domestic preparedness programs to develop and maintain effective public relations strategies. In other words, this desire may have less to do with the law and more to do with the failure of the United States to consider the policy implications of having a more open counterterrorism strategy.

More Liberal Interpretation of General Criminal Law Constitutional Standards; Detaining Individuals for Short Periods of Time; and Investigation of Groups before Required "Reasonable Suspicion" Is Met

This listing of necessary authorities is grouped together because they implicate similar constitutional norms. In a biological terrorism situation, are "emergency authorities" necessary or advantageous for law enforcement personnel or public health officials? This analysis does not implicate a typical criminal law investigation when there is a specific, suspected terrorist. In that case, the process for investigation is the same that it would be under normal—i.e., non-biological terrorism event—circumstances. A biological terrorism event, however, will likely require that the criminal law's focus on the suspect may have to be expanded. What concerns the legal norm, however, is those situations when the group of suspects cannot be easily narrowed, or the geographic locale is so broad that specificities of criminal law cannot easily be met. Biological terrorism is not akin to finding a bank robber on Main Street. The question is: what lawful authorities can be used against a broad group of persons whose relation to a suspect may be based merely on geography, ethnicity, or simply chance, but where—unless action is taken—there may be a demonstrable health or safety threat?[35] U.S. constitutional law requires specific and individual determinations of guilt and risk.[36]

The Fourth Amendment permits only "reasonable" searches. Determining reasonableness requires a detailed assessment of the nature and quality of the intrusion on an individual's privacy interests against the

---

35. For this section, I am indebted to Professor Barry Kellman of DePaul University Law School.

36. Lawrence O. Gostin, *Tuberculosis and the Power of the States: Toward the Development of Rational Standards for the Review of Compulsory Public Health Powers*, University of Chicago Law School Roundtable 219 (1995).

importance of the government interests in the specific action.[37] The existing law enforcement system has proved very successful in apprehending terrorists whose crimes, however heinous, were limited in time and impact (the Oklahoma City and the 1993 World Trade Center bombings). These crimes were not a part of sustained terrorist incidents. Though September 11, 2001, may be viewed as a continuation of a terrorist campaign, it is not the same experience, as in Israel, where several bombs will go off in sequence. A biological terrorism event, however, may be. The Fourth Amendment's rule that "no Warrants shall issue, but upon probable cause, supported by Oath or Affirmation, and particularly describing the place to be searched, and the persons or things to be seized" is an exceptionally complicated area of law. It applies to both state and federal law enforcement, though the contours of specific state laws may differ slightly. Generally, however, there are many circumstances in which arrests and searches may be made without a warrant.

These warrantless searches must satisfy the dual requirement of "reasonableness" and "probable cause":[38] "In dealing with probable cause . . . we deal with probabilities," . . . . [probable cause requires] "more than bare suspicion" and "less than evidence which would justify . . . conviction."[39] In order to justify warrantless searches or arrests, the government is also required to act under a "reasonableness" standard. Courts have generally defined the reasonableness standard in light of the circumstances surrounding the search. Exigent circumstances justifying a warrantless search or arrest may include those in which: (1) a crime of violence was involved; (2) the suspect was reasonably believe to be armed; (3) there was a clear showing of probable cause; (4) there was a strong reason to believe the suspect was within the premises; (5) it appeared likely that the suspect would escape if not swiftly apprehended; and (6) the entry was made peaceably.[40]

The Supreme Court has also recognized that special circumstances may call for greater discretion by law enforcement officials. This is

---

37. *O'Connor v. Ortega,* 480 U.S. 709, 719 (1987).

38. Arrests and searches that may be made without a warrant must not be "unreasonable" under the Fourth Amendment, and because the requirements in such cases "surely cannot be less stringent" than when a warrant is obtained, probable cause is (also) required in such circumstances. *Draper v. United States,* 358 U.S. 307, 311 (1959).

39. *Brinegar v. United States,* 338 U.S. 160 (1949).

40. *Welsh v. Wisconsin,* 466 U.S. 740 (1984).

known as the special needs doctrine, and this standard can justify a search absent a warrant. According to the special needs doctrine: "Where a Fourth Amendment intrusion serves special governmental needs, beyond the normal need for law enforcement, it is necessary to balance the individual's privacy expectations against the government's interests to determine whether it is impractical to require a warrant or some level of individualized suspicion in the particular context."[41] In such cases, the Court weighs (1) the privacy interest that the search disrupts (e.g., a home is different, legally, than a car); (2) the nature of the intrusion (invasive body searches are truly intrusive); and (3) the immediacy of the governmental interest and the effectiveness of the procedure.[42]

The Fourth Amendment may be, therefore, sufficiently elastic to permit careful and coordinated government action in times of crisis. Practitioners and policymakers should not view domestic preparedness challenges as situations where they need to overcome the Fourth Amendment. Where public health and security is at stake, the Constitution allows consideration of whether police searches directly promote a government interest that outweighs the individual's interest in avoiding the intrusion. Accordingly, the question ought to be about ensuring that the standards for government action provided in the law are effective and not merely abusive. More simply, policymakers must ask themselves: what is the government interest and how important is it? To satisfy the legal requirements, the government interest in a broad search must be significant, and the means of the search should have a close connection to the government's goals. Random searches of, for example, airport hand baggage are more acceptable than those that may stigmatize a specific person; indeed, broad searches are clearly less intrusive than any invasive search, such as a strip search. Searches based on group identity—religious, ethnic, or racial—are particularly subject to challenge. Searches cannot be a pretext for attempts to hide prosecutorial dragnets. Where health searches are necessary, evidence of other wrongdoing (such as keeping drugs in the house) should be ignored if not related to the terrorist attacks. Thus, in considering which authorities are necessary, it is essential to keep this realistic legal balancing in mind. By applying it to the desired authorities outlined above, the expectation that new authorities will be needed is less likely.

---

41. *National Treasury Employees Union v. Von Raab*, 489 U.S. 656 (1989).

42. *Vernonia School Dist. 47J v. Acton*, 115 S.Ct. 2386 (1995).

Mandatory Vaccinations and Other Medical Treatment

The courts traditionally have upheld compulsory medical procedures, including vaccination during disease outbreaks, if there is a reasonable expectation of some societal harm.[43] Local, state, and federal governments should face no obstacles to vaccinating those designated to be at risk. There may be different factors, however, for quarantining contagious individuals. Traditionally, courts have deferred to medical judgment (especially if the treatment was directly observed therapy). But, in the wake of the Acquired Immune Deficiency Syndrome (AIDS) epidemic and opposing medical assessments, courts are beginning to take a more critical view of medical necessity. Courts are now more likely to require a showing by the state of some necessity, even if the standard is low.[44] Indeed laws that would apply to the victims or potential victims of a biological terrorist attack should categorically distinguish between communicable and noncommunicable agents. Anthrax, for example, is not communicable; therefore, vaccination or quarantine may not be necessary in such a situation.

Public health authorities must consider how individuals are selected for testing or treatment and the justification for such action. This is a difficult enterprise—not merely for legal reasons. Because some biological agents have a two-to-four week incubation period, discovery may come too late to contain the outbreak. In addition, determining the source of some illnesses can be long and arduous, further hampering treatment. In the case of noncommunicable diseases, the necessity for invasive procedures may be questionable. Hence, requirements that public health officials have some rational articulation for limited and effective testing, which would be done because of a potential biological outbreak, are entirely appropriate.

Lowering the Threshold of "Reasonable Suspicion" and Sweep Searches

The Fourth Amendment requires that law enforcement conduct be "reasonable." Generally, the Fourth Amendment standard that "reasonable

---

43. Another action described in Table One is a desire to loosen confidentiality and licensing laws to permit broader access and interstate travel rights for health officials. Most laws governing confidentiality and the licensing of medical professionals are state laws and do not implicate any federal constitutional concerns. The ability of medical providers to go from state to state, therefore, would require merely a change in state laws to provide comity between states during a biological attack.

44. See *Hill v. Evans*, 1993 WL 595676 (M.D. AL)

suspicion" is required before an arrest or search is made is not a difficult standard to meet, especially if a suspect is identified by eyewitnesses. It is when a search is done more broadly that constitutional standards come into serious conflict. Sweep searches are highly suspect and often ruled invalid. It is important to note that no case has ever questioned the necessity of sweep searches overall—only the necessity in a particular instance. In those cases, state authorities had simply failed to show any law enforcement necessity for performing broad sweep searches.[45] In a recent Supreme Court case, for example, the Court ruled that an informant's statement alone would not satisfy probable cause, and the Court explicitly stated that this prohibition would not apply in an instance where the harm (such as a bomb) was so great as to justify a broad search.[46] The law requires what any democratic society would demand: that the emergency is grand and imminent.

Racial and Group Identification

Few law enforcement mechanisms have engendered as much controversy as the accusation that law enforcement uses racial and ethnic criteria to stop and detain suspects. One of the most recent examples is the "profiling" of Arab and Muslim U.S. residents and visitors by the Federal Bureau of Investigation (FBI) with assistance from state police. If detention before or after a biological attack is limited to only certain segments of the population, which standards are permissible?

The Fourteenth Amendment guarantees that, "No State shall make or enforce any law which shall deny to any person within its jurisdiction the equal protection of the laws." This rule applies to the states and to the federal government. When the government intentionally acts on the basis of race or national origin, courts will employ strict scrutiny: "[t]he clear and central purpose of the [Equal Protection clause] was to eliminate all official state sources of invidious racial discrimination . . ."[47] When race is used, the law is suspect and "subject to the most exacting scru-

---

45. Justified sweep searches may undermine legitimacy of the government in its counterterrorism efforts to the extent that the searches have critics on both the left and the right of the political spectrum.

46. *Florida v. J.L.*, 120 U.S. 1375, 1383 (2000). "The facts of this case do not require us to speculate about the circumstances under which the danger alleged in an anonymous tip might be so great as to justify a search even without a showing of reliability. We do not say, for example, that a report of a person carrying a bomb need bear the indicia of reliability we demand . . . "

47. *Loving v. Virginia*, 388 U.S. 1 (1967).

tiny."[48] The government has the burden of proving that the classification is necessary to a compelling interest: the government must show that the reason for the classification is essential and that there are no other alternatives to the classification. Application of this standard of review generally results in a holding that the law violates equal protection.[49]

Religious liberties and freedom of expression are similarly protected against state and federal deprivations. Direct and indirect burdens on religion are sufficient to invoke strict scrutiny review.[50] Yet, despite the fundamental right of citizens to hold and practice religious beliefs and be free to practice them without burden or classification by the state, the Court has held, in *Sherbert v. Verner*, that "[o]nly those interests of the highest order and those not otherwise served can overbalance legitimate claims to the free exercise of religion."[51] The Court has never found any interest to satisfy its "highest order" standard.

State and federal governments have reserved some authority to classify persons by race or religion, suggesting that in some cases they believe that it may be permissible for the government to act in a way that classifies persons based on their race or their religious beliefs (e.g., *Korematsu* refers to "extreme military danger"; *Sherbert* to "a(n) [governmental] interest of the highest order.") However overbroad, or likely to sweep in innocent members of society, the Court has consistently reserved "extreme military danger" as a legitimate basis for racial classifications. The government still must show that there is absolutely no other alternative. The classification must be narrowly tailored; it must be a perfect fit.[52]

Although state and federal governments may have the power to classify persons based on race or religion, exercising such options would likely have harmful consequences. It is difficult to imagine that law enforcement agencies have no better alternative than to so classify persons. Indeed, if a racial or religious classification is not overt but merely im-

---

48. *Palmore v. Sidoti*, 466 U.S. 429 (1984).

49. In *Korematsu v. United States*, however, the Court upheld the exclusion of Japanese-Americans from certain areas of the West Coast during World War II on the grounds of extreme military danger from sabotage.

50. *Wisonsin v. Yoder*, 406 U.S. 205 (1972).

51. *Sherbert v. Verner*, 372 U.S. 398 (1963). (Striking down state law that denied a Seventh Day Adventist unemployment benefits because she refused to work on Saturdays).

52. This essay does not address the use of racial classifications for "benign" or affirmative action purposes, because one must assume that in the context of a biological terrorism attack, such classifications would be for law enforcement purposes.

pacts a certain racial segment of society, then government action is given more deference. If, for example, police or federal agents target a restaurant and interview customers, all of whom are Japanese, there is no Fourteenth Amendment problem. In this case, impact alone is not determinative of racial animus. The government can justify the conduct of these law enforcement officers by arguing that there was reasonable suspicion that the restaurant customers may have had some evidence, and it is just a matter of coincidence that they were all Japanese.

Nonetheless, racial classifications are anathema to the understanding of permissible government conduct in a democracy. Such classifications are overinclusive and stigmatize an innocent population. Furthermore, they run counter to our notion of equal protection and fairness. Interestingly, no racial classification based on "extreme military danger" has been invoked since *Korematsu*, a case that has been roundly criticized for its racial bias and extreme deference to the executive and legislative branches.

Planning for a Biological Attack

Due to these loopholes and deficiencies in the law, some legal planning can be done to ensure proper and effective action. Congress and state legislatures can do much to delineate the implications of a biological terrorist attack and the authorities necessary in such an event. It could also require the Department of Justice to provide a handbook of legal authorities to prepare responders.[53]

Legislation addressing the legal authorities needed in a biological terrorist attack could provide important guidance to policymakers. First, it could set a definite triggering event—whether it be the use of a certain device, the potential for mass casualty, or a presidential order—that would automatically trigger certain law enforcement needs. A specific triggering event is essential, even though a number (for example, 10,000 casualties) may appear crude. Another standard, such as "very high casualties," is not only inexact but may leave too much room for interpretation. In this regard, the Model State Emergency Health Powers Act has gone far to delineate special powers necessary during a crisis, including the standards for declaration of an emergency, requiring access to facilities and property, and the safe disposal of corpses.

Second, the legislative process could provide for open debate and conversation about which kinds of government authorities the public

---

53. The National Commission on Terrorism recommended such a handbook in its June 2000 report "Countering the Changing Threat of International Terrorism."

would desire, even in a worst-case scenario. Only through such open debate could the public be heard. Counterterrorism legislation in the United States has been a perpetually growing enterprise. In other words, laws in place today are the baseline for determining what is acceptable when the next batch of legislation is proposed.[54] This is an important argument; yet, the alternative may be more risky. Without proper legal authority, the government would act too cautiously or too recklessly. Any effort to curb government power in times of crisis is therefore beneficial. A group of authorities, only to be used in a biological terrorist attack, would be made exceptional by their temporal specificity and triggering event.

Finally, legislation could allow for temporal specificity in the statute. Providing for a duration is essential to ensure that an emergency state not linger indefinitely. Providing for greater authority during periods of emergency and that it ceases when the threat no longer exists are both essential parts of any legislative scheme.

Conclusion

The U.S. legal system has achieved a fragile balance between national security, effective law enforcement, and personal liberties during times of war, peace, and national disasters. Terrorism does not fall easily into any of those categories; biological terrorism sometimes does not fit at all. It may be that the "rules of war" are too inflexible and permit more governmental powers than are desired in a democratic state. It may be that the "rules of personal liberty" are too soft and unduly tie the hands of government actors trying to avert a crisis with no historical precedent. It may be that the "rules for disasters" are too vague and assume a level of communication and preparation not possible in a biological terrorism situation.

More than offering a "new" set of rules though, this essay suggests where Congress and state legislatures can begin to make changes. There needs to be a clearer understanding of what the rules are. The law is not, and should not be, an impediment to protecting life. In the ongoing debate over terrorism, the argument that democratic norms will need to be sacrificed so that democracy can be preserved is often made or, at least, intuited. The premise of this argument is that the traditional balance between governmental powers and personal freedoms will not hold in the event of a catastrophic terrorism event. The balance will undoubtedly shift, but the assumption that the Constitution is an obstacle to adequate

---

54. Laura Donohue, "Facing the New Millenium: The Legacy of American Twentieth Century Counterterrorist Policy" (Unpublished manuscript, on file with the author).

domestic preparedness runs counter to the strength of our existing legal system and constitutional interpretation. With appropriate statutory revisions, a thorough search of authorities, and a clear triggering event providing for broader powers during a biological terrorist attack, legal preparation can be improved.

Ambulances to Nowhere: America's Critical Shortfall in Medical Preparedness for Catastrophic Terrorism

Joseph A. Barbera, Anthony G. Macintyre, and Craig A. DeAtley

The concern for large-scale terrorism resulting in mass casualties has grown steadily among the law enforcement and intelligence communities in the United States over the past decade.[1] Media coverage spotlighting this concern has raised the general public's awareness of the potential human consequences of an attack against unprotected civilians with weapons capable of widespread damage (known as weapons of mass destruction or WMD).[2] Although law enforcement and security capabilities are being enhanced to prevent acts of terrorism, not all of these events can be prevented, as the attacks on the Murrah Federal Building in Oklahoma City, Oklahoma (1995), the World Trade Centers in New York

---

1. Gilmore Commission, "Assessing the Threat: First Annual Report to Congress of the Advisory Panel to Assess Domestic Response Capabilities for Terrorism Involving Weapons of Mass Destruction" (Washington, D.C., December 15, 1999). Gilmore Commission, "Second Annual Report to Congress of the Advisory Panel to Assess Domestic Response Capabilities for Terrorism Involving Weapons of Mass Destruction" (Washington, D.C., December 15, 2000); Gilmore Commission, "Third Annual Report to Congress of the Advisory Panel to Assess Domestic Response Capabilities for Terrorism Involving Weapons of Mass Destruction" (Washington, D.C., December 15, 2001); National Intelligence Estimate (NIE) 1999, "The global infectious disease threat and its implications for the United States," NIE 99–17D, (Washington, D.C., January 2000). NBC News, "'Dateline' investigates terror support system supplying U.S. enemies with sophisticated weapons," (August 2, 2002), http://www.msnbc.com/news/788686.asp, accessed August 2, 2002.

2. Vernon Loeb, "Global threats against U.S. will rise, report predicts," *The Washington Post*, December 18, 2000, pp. A3–A4; J.P. Pinkerton, "We face war by terrorism, ready or not," *Long Island Newsday*, October 26, 2000, p. 45, accessed October 27, 2000 <ebird.dtic.mil/Oct2000/e20001027priorities.htm>.

City (1993 and 2001), the Pentagon in Arlington, Virginia (2001), and the anthrax dissemination (fall 2001) make clear. The general public expects adequate preparedness for consequence management by the emergency response community. A key component of consequence management is timely and appropriate medical care for victims of mass casualty incidents.

As concerns for WMD terrorism rise,[3] incorrect assumptions are being made about existing medical capabilities to treat mass casualties. In reality, hospital surge capacity and specialized medical capability across the United States has never been more restricted. While the public and the political communities assume that the health care systems are adequately preparing for terrorism incidents that would generate catastrophic casualty loads, the medical community is struggling just to maintain its everyday capacity. This essay outlines the current financial issues that restrict adequate hospital preparedness for mass casualty events and proposes model approaches for the United States to address this preparedness shortfall. Without prompt action, the nation faces the risk that victims of a mass casualty disaster might end up in "ambulances to nowhere."

Historical Perspective: Public-Trust Obligations of Hospitals

During the twentieth century, the delivery of acute medical care in the United States evolved beyond an ordinary business relationship to become a "trust" with patients.[4] The specialty of emergency medicine, which grew rapidly from its founding 30 years ago, has become a major component of this trust. Emergency medical services (EMS) have also evolved in the United States. EMS is expected to rapidly transport patients to the hospital, and once patients reach the hospital, it is expected that they will receive the best care possible. Thus, the "trust" expectation is extended to the hospital itself.[5] The Hippocratic Oath; the legal requirement to provide emergency medical care for everyone regardless of ability to pay;[6] the high esteem in which society holds physicians, nurses, and other medical personnel; the daily media headline reports of break-

---

3. Gilmore Commission, (Washington, D.C., December 15, 2000).

4. R. Flaste, R. Coles, P. Moffitt, *Medicine's Great Journey: One Hundred Years Of Healing* (Boston/Toronto/London: Little, Brown and Company, 1992), pp. 43–84.

5. J.R. Griffith, *The Well-managed Healthcare Organization*, 4th ed. (Chicago: Health Administration Press, 1999), p. 8.

6. Emergency Medical Treatment and Labor Act, 42 CFR 20.

throughs in health research; and the severity of judicial malpractice remedies for breach of medical standards are all evidence of the public's medical care expectations.[7]

The general public and public policy have traditionally extended expectations concerning available health care to include the disaster scenario. They have assumed that hospitals have an inherent obligation to the community for disaster preparedness. Justification for this assumption has included the following rationales:

- The concept of "medicine as a trust" has been extended from the individual patient to apply to the community as a whole;
- Financial support to hospitals by the community, including fundraising, municipal subsidies, and federal, state, and corporate grants, creates an expectation that hospitals will address the community's comprehensive health and medical needs, including disaster preparedness;[8]
- A reasonable cost for hospital preparedness for mass casualties was assumed to be a necessary cost of doing hospital business and was passed on through the fee-for-service system, through which Medicare and private insurance payments were handled until the 1990s. This hospital-generated, cost-based billing system allowed the costs of all medical functions, including emergency preparedness, to be recovered through payment for regular medical services.

This presumed obligation of hospitals toward community preparedness has become incorporated into public policy and is reflected in current laws and regulations. For example, Title III of the Superfund Amendment and Reauthorization Act of 1986 (SARA) established Local Emergency Planning Committees (LEPCs) to address risks generated by hazardous materials (HazMat) in every community in the United States.[9] The LEPC guidelines recommend that an individual local hospital be designated as a receiving facility for contaminated chemical casualties in at-risk communities. However, they do not specify how the development and maintenance of this expensive capability will be financed. Another example can be seen in the Health Care Financing Administration's

---

7. Ibid.

8. Griffith, *The Well-managed Healthcare Organization*, p. 6.

9. Superfund Amendment and Reauthorization Act of 1986 (also known as the Emergency Planning and Community Right to Know Act, EPCRA, 42 USC 11001); SARA Title III description accessed May 1, 2001, www.epo.cdc.gov/wonder/prevguid/p0000018/p0000018.asp#head004004000000000.

Medicare Certificate of Participation Agreement, which stipulates that, for any hospital providing full-time emergency services, "there must be adequate medical and nursing personnel qualified in emergency care to meet the written emergency procedures and needs anticipated by the facility."[10] Again, the cost of such surge capacity to meet anticipated needs is not addressed. A further example of unfunded requirements that hospitals face is incorporated into the preparedness standards of the Joint Commission on Accreditation of Healthcare Organizations (JCAHO).[11] While the regulations provide valuable incentives for hospitals to perform some preparedness activity, they do not provide funding mechanisms. Hospitals, therefore, rarely give these issues the attention necessary to meet requirements for a major emergency.

There appears to be very limited understanding of these mass-casualty medical care issues by the general public, the emergency response community, and policymakers. Instead, hospital operations are often perceived to function within a "black box": patients are admitted, difficult to understand but high quality medical care is somehow provided, and the best possible outcome is expected.[12] It is thus presumed that even if a large number of patients were brought simultaneously to a hospital, they would receive the same high-quality care as the individual patient does under regular hospital conditions. This confidence in today's health care system, however much appreciated by the medical community, is unfounded.

In a time when catastrophic terrorism is increasingly considered to be a significant risk, close examination of hospital preparedness capabilities reveals troubling issues. Historical expectations of casualty loads generated by traditional community disasters, such as transportation accidents, can best be described as "multiple casualties" rather than "mass casualties": expectations have been for numbers in the teens, not thousands, and planning has been performed accordingly. Mass terrorism casualty loads are, however, likely to be much greater.[13] In addition, tra-

---

10. 42 CFR 482.55(b) (2).

11. "Emergency Management Standards EC.1.4 effective January 1, 2002" in Joint Commission, *Comprehensive Accreditation Manual for Hospitals* (Oakbrook Terrace, Ill.: Joint Commission of Healthcare Organizations, January 1998).

12. J.A. Barbera, "The role of hospitals and the medical care system in chemical/biological terrorism," keynote panel presentation, Domestic Preparedness (Terrorism) National Stakeholders' Forum, Department of Justice, Washington, D.C., August 27, 1998.

13. H. Nozaki, N. Aikawa, Y. Shinozawa, et al., "Sarin gas poisoning in the Tokyo subway," *Lancet*, No. 345 (1995), pp. 980–981; *Top Officials (TOPOFF) 2000 Exercise Ob-*

ditional expectations of the type of casualty have focused on general trauma victims. Specialty casualties due to exposure to chemical, biological, or radiological weapons were rarely considered in the context of large numbers. For example, recent JCAHO regulations (1998) mandated only enough HazMat preparedness to manage just a single contaminated casualty.[14] Consideration must also be given to the special circumstances of chemical, biological, and radiation casualties. Among other dangers, contamination or infection from the victims may actually put health care providers at risk.[15] And finally, further complexity is added by the recognized danger that hospitals themselves might well be primary or secondary targets of terrorism.

Health care systems are only now beginning to adjust to each of these newly perceived threats and to recognize the vast shortfalls in preparedness. Hospitals are often unprepared for even a few chemically contaminated casualties.[16] They are "woefully unprepared" for biological or chemical terrorism.[17]

Current Medical Economic Realities: Counter-Incentives to Preparation

The assumptions used historically to justify the health care system's responsibility for disaster casualties have changed drastically over the

---

servation Report, Vol. 2: State of Colorado and Denver Metropolitan Area, prepared by the Office for State and Local Domestic Preparedness Support (OSLDPS), Office of Justice Programs (OJP), Department of Justice (DOJ), and the Readiness Division, Preparedness Training, and Exercises Directorate (PT&E), Federal Emergency Management Agency (FEMA) (Washington, D.C.), draft document circulated December 2000; T. Inglesby, "Lessons from TOPOFF," Presentation made at "The Second National Symposium on Medical and Public Health Response to Bioterrorism," Washington, D.C., November 28, 2000.

14.   Joint Commission, Comprehensive Accreditation Manual for Hospitals (Oakbrook Terrace, Ill.: Joint Commission of Healthcare Organizations, January 1998).

15.   R.J. Geller, K.L. Singleton, et al., "Nosocomial Poisoning Associated with Emergency Department Treatment of Organophosphate Toxicity, Georgia 2000," CDC, Morbidity and Mortality Weekly Report, Vol. 49, No. 51, January 5, 2001, pp. 1156–1158, accessed January 8, 2001, ov/mmwr/preview/mmwrhtml/mm4951a2.htm; D.A. Henderson, "The Looming Threat of Bioterrorism," Science, February 26, 1999, Vol. 283 pp. 1279–1282.

16.   D. Cone D and S. Davidson, "Hazardous materials preparedness in the emergency department," Prehospital Emergency Care, No. 1 (1997), pp. 85–90.

17.   S. Burling, "Study says emergency rooms unprepared for terrorism," Philadelphia Inquirer, October 25, 2000, accessed October 26, 2000, philly.com/content/inquirer/2000/10/25/city/ER25.htm.

past 10 years. The predominant reimbursement system for medical care has substantially transitioned from fee-for-service to an externally imposed, charge-based system. Managed care payments for services are now controlled by strict contract and often are not adequate to cover the total cost of providing even *regular* medical care (i.e., capital costs in addition to actual medical care costs). Federal regulations have changed the basis of Medicare and Medicaid payments from "costs incurred" to "charges allowed" and have strictly enforced limits on hospital billing for services. The 1997 Balanced Budget Amendment severely curtailed longstanding federal financial support for medical training programs, including those that had supported the trauma center capability in many jurisdictions.[18]

While hospital and physician charges have been constrained, no similar external controls have been applied to their business costs. New equipment acquisition, recently developed medications, capital construction, and facility maintenance have become increasingly expensive. Other adverse factors over the past decade have further increased the economic burden on the health care community, including:

- a decline in government support for public and private hospitals;[19]
- an increasing number of expensive, unfunded, or underfunded regulatory mandates;[20]
- a continued expectation that hospitals will maintain high levels of charity medical care;[21]
- a national shortage of nurses for acute care hospitals, resulting in the need for special compensation packages to attract personnel.[22]

---

18. The 1997 Balanced Budget Amendment, Public Law 105–33. C. Goldberg, "Teaching hospitals battle Medicare-money cuts," *New York Times*, May 6, 1999, accessed June 4, 2001, at <archives.nytimes.com>; Editorial, "Teaching hospitals in trouble," *New York Times*, May 31, 1999, accessed June 4, 2001, at <archives.nytimes.com>; J.K. Inglehart, "Support for academic medical centers: revisiting the 1997 Balanced Budget Act," *New England Journal of Medicine*, Vol. 341, No. 4, July 22, 1999, pp. 299–304.

19. Editorial, "Help the hospitals," *St. Petersburg Times*, March 24, 2001.

20. American Hospital Association, "Hospital preparedness for mass casualties: summary of an invitational forum," Washington, D.C., August 2000, available at www.aha.org.

21. B. Herbert, "In America: hospitals in crisis," *New York Times*, April 15, 1999, accessed June 4, 2001, at <archives.nytimes.com>.

22. R. Sorelle, "Ratios pit nurses against hospitals, doctors," *Emergency Medicine*

These conditions have created severe financial stress in the hospital industry. Few hospitals now have comfortable operating margins.[23] Many hospitals have been forced to close, downsize, consolidate, reconfigure, or, in the case of nonprofits, to "partner" with for-profit hospital corporations. These changes have led to the abolition or downsizing of specialty services crucial to disaster preparedness, including emergency departments and trauma centers.[24] Hospitals undergoing renovation or building new facilities are doing so only to meet daily operational needs, with no provision for extraordinary surge capacity or disaster casualty care. The military medical system has undergone similar transformations, including downsizing.

Current State of Hospital Preparedness for Mass or Specialty[25] Casualties

The health care system's financial crisis directly affects preparedness for mass casualty incidents in multiple ways. For example, most hospitals now use "just-in-time" inventory systems that provide for the minimum on-site storage of sterile supplies, vital equipment, and pharmaceuticals to meet immediate requirements.[26] This severely curtails what is available at any one moment to be used during a hospital response to a mass casualty event. Resupply and "backup" mechanisms are commonly shared by all local and regional medical institutions: a community's hospitals all count the *same* capability as their individual surge capacity.

News, Vol. 23, No. 3 (April 2001), pp. 1, 26, 29; M.C. Jaklevic and E. Lovern, "A nursing code blue," *Modern Healthcare*, Vol. 30, No. 51, December 11, 2000, pp. 42–44; W. Scott, "Nurse workforce: condition critical," *National Health Policy Forum Issue Brief* (Washington, D.C.: National Health Policy Forum, June 1, 2001), p. 763.

23. American Hospital Association, "Hospital preparedness for mass casualties: summary of an invitational forum," Washington, D.C., August 2000, available at <www.aha.org.>.

24. R. Sorelle, "Crisis Pushes California EDs to the Breaking Point: Fifty California emergency departments closed since 1990, leaving only 355, and 80% of those lost money in 1999, a total of $315 million statewide," *Emergency Medicine News*, Vol. 23, No. 30, April 2001, pp. 58–60.

25. "Mass casualties" refers to the number of patients exceeding the capacity to provide adequate care. "Specialty casualties" refers to patients requiring unusual types of medical care (decontamination, nerve agent antidotes, radiation illness treatment, and others), such that only a modest number of casualties may exceed the capabilities for adequate response.

26. P.I. Buerhaus and D.O. Staiger, "Trouble in the nurse labor market? Recent trends and future outlook," *Health Affairs*, Vol. 18, No. 1, January/February 1999, pp. 214–222.

Hospitals have also restructured their workforce, with a decline in the ratio of trained health care workers to patients, resulting in a marked increase in individual workload.[27] This is particularly evident in the dramatically higher patient-to-nurse staffing ratios that have developed over the past decade. The daily workload stress has caused a striking increase in personnel turnover, resulting in a decline in level of experience of hospital personnel.[28] This is further exacerbated by the heavy use of "agency" or temporary staff for the nursing workforce: these personnel are often unfamiliar with an individual hospital's emergency preparedness procedures. More worrisome is that these personnel often have commitments to multiple hospitals in any individual region; this could result in a serious shortfall of staffing when surge capacity is needed.

Hospitals are experiencing increasing difficulties in maintaining rosters of immediately available medical specialists.[29] Administrative hospital positions have also been reduced in number, with a resultant increase in the administrative burden on remaining personnel. Limited time and attention remains for emergency preparedness activities, and it can be overly taxing for individual institutions to participate in even low-key, pre-planned exercises.[30]

The net result of these factors is that hospitals are currently structured with a very limited surge capacity, even for normal fluctuations in patient volume.[31] Indeed, many regions of the country are regularly experiencing severe shortages of beds for normal acute care.[32] Hospital emergency departments are now frequently filled to capacity daily and must

---

27. Sorelle, "Crisis pushes California EDs to the breaking point."

28. Sorelle, "Ratios pit nurses against hospitals, doctors."

29. L.A. Johnson, T. B. Taylor, R. Lev, "The emergency department on-call back-up crisis: finding remedies for a serious public health problem," *Annals of Emergency Medicine*, Vol. 37, No. 5, May 2001, pp. 495–499.

30. DCHA Hospital Mutual Aid System, "November 15 [1999] Hospital Tornado Drill Outline (with Hospital Participation)" (Washington, D.C.: District of Columbia Hospital Association, November 11, 1999).

31. D. Ensor, "Experts: U.S. medicine unprepared for biological terrorism, com./U.S. May 10, 2001, accessed May 10, 2001, at com/2001/US/05/10/terror.attack/index. htm; J. Babula, "Crowded hospitals, paramedics caught in ER crisis: ambulance provider may start leaving patients unattended," *Las Vegas Review-Journal*, October 12, 2000, reprinted in *Emergency Physicians Monthly*, Vol. 7, No. 12 (December 2000) pp. 7, 13; A. Goldstein, "D.C. General refuses ambulances: nurses shortage behind decision to redirect trauma patients," *The Washington Post*, April 21, 2001, pp. B1, B4.

32. R.W. Derlet, J.R. Richards, "Overcrowding in the nation's emergency departments: complex causes and disturbing effects," *Annals of Emergency Medicine*, Vol. 35, No 1, January 20, 2000, pp. 63–68.

divert even critically ill emergency cases.[33] A telling sign of this crisis is a formal position statement released by the Arizona College of Emergency Physicians (AzCEP). In December 2000, they declared that AzCEP "hereby goes on record as stating that the emergency physician community has lost confidence in the emergency healthcare infrastructure in Arizona and that current resources supporting emergency care are inadequate to meet the needs of all patients at all times."[34]

Financial Challenges to Adequate Preparedness

Adequate preparedness for mass casualties requires an objective assessment of risks, analysis of needs, and development of systems. A component of risk assessment is a vulnerability analysis, which determines the impact of a hazardous event. An adequate health care response capability is specifically designed to meet the projected needs determined by this vulnerability analysis. In contrast, the concept of reasonable preparedness is defined as response capabilities established within the limits of available resources, including funding.

When analyzing the mass casualty needs of an incident involving deliberate release of chemical, biological, or radiation agents,[35] a clear disparity is evident between "reasonable" versus "adequate" health care response capabilities.[36] Among these vulnerabilities are the following:

- patients present a potential threat to health care workers and the facility itself unless appropriately managed;
- patient conditions require unusual and expensive capabilities for

33. A. Trafford, "America's ERs: in critical condition," *The Washington Post*, May 1, 2001, p. HE03, accessed May 1, 2001, at <washingtonpost.com/wp-dyn/health/A22680–2001Apr30.html>.

34. Arizona College of Emergency Physicians, "Position statement on the critical state of emergency care in Arizona," accessed April 30, 2001, at <www.azcep.org/er_crowding/position.pdf >.

35. A.G. Macintyre, G.W. Christopher, E. Eitzen, et al. "Weapons of mass destruction events with contaminated casualties: effective planning for health care facilities," *Journal of the American Medical Association*, 2000, Vol. 283, pp. 242–249; Biological Weapons Improved Response Program, "Improving local and state agency response to terrorist incidents involving biological weapons: interim planning guide," August 1, 2000, Final Draft, U.S. Army Soldier and Biological Chemical Command. Aberdeen Proving Ground, Md.; Radiation Emergency Assistance Center/Training Site; "Managing Radiation Emergencies: Guidance for Hospital Medical Care Management," accessed June 18, 2001 at http://www.orau.gov/reacts/emergency.htm.

36. Ibid.

adequate management, such as decontamination systems, isolation wards, ventilation requirements, and special medications;

- hospitals could themselves be primary or secondary targets, markedly increasing security requirements.

Adequate preparedness for terrorism is therefore expensive and time-consuming. Federal terrorism preparedness programs established and funded to improve the capabilities of first responders and the National Guard demonstrate this expense. Recent federal funding initiatives have provided millions of dollars to support WMD training and equipment for the public safety and first responder community.[37] In fiscal year 1999 alone, $43.8 million was provided to local emergency responders (primarily firefighters and police) for equipment purchases.[38] This financial support is regularly credited with aiding the development of local first responder capability.[39] Recently, the Department of Health and Human Services announced funds that would be provided to enhance local public health and hospital preparedness.[40] These monies, however, have neither reached individual institutions nor have they created any significant change in hospital system preparedness.[41]

Given current financial incentive structures, emergency preparedness might actually be imprudent financial practice for health care institutions. Developing "surge capacity" has little to do with normal hospital operations and provides no significant income. While the likelihood of a major terrorism incident somewhere in the United States is necessarily higher than it is in any one region or locality, only a low probability exists that any particular hospital's surge capacity would be utilized during the useful life of the equipment and training cycles. Even if an event requir-

---

37. U.S. Department of Justice (DOJ), Office for State and Local Domestic Preparedness Support (OSLDPS), Training Page, accessed April 30, 2001, <www.ojp.usdoj.gov/osldps/training.htm>.

38. U.S. DOJ, Office of Justice Programs (OJP), Funding Opportunities at OJP, accessed April 30, 2001, <www.ojp.usdoj.gov/fundopps.htm>.

39. J. Newton, "Bioterrorism drills: county specialized response team prepares for chemical attack," *The News Sun* (Lake County, Ill.), April 28, 2001, accessed May 1, 2001, at <www.copleynewspapers.com/NewsSun/>.

40. U.S. Department of Health and Human Resources, HHS News: "HHS announces $1.1 billion in funding to states for bioterrorism preparedness," hs.gov/news/press/2002pres/20020131b.htm accessed September 23, 2002.

41. M.L. Carius, "An emergency of unpreparedness," *Washington Times*, September 17, 2002, http://www.washingtontimes.com accessed 9/17/02. Furthermore, the allocation was a one year appropriation. It is unclear if there will be any *sustained* funding for what must be a continuously financed effort.

ing surge capacity occurs, chaotic circumstances and restrictive registration requirements may keep hospitals from assembling the documentation necessary to get full compensation for services rendered. These factors raise legitimate business and financial questions for hospital administrators and trustees in their decisions to participate in community emergency preparedness. A program to develop needed capabilities must address these financial realities.

Developing Hospital Surge Capacity in the Face of Economic Restrictions

Adequate preparedness requires sustained, directed funding sources with controls that promote true hospital preparedness for a defined surge capacity. Public policy must recognize that hospital preparedness for mass and/or specialty casualty scenarios is a public safety function, similar to fire suppression services, emergency medical services, and police services. It is economically unjust to expect the cost of this preparedness to be borne by a private sector business or by public medical facilities struggling to meet their current health care mandates. Adding more unfunded mandates to increase preparedness participation by the health care community is unlikely to improve capacity. Adequate hospital and health care preparedness for large and/or specialty casualty loads will be accomplished only when public policy recognizes this public safety premise and begins to address the legitimate responsibility for the costs of developing and maintaining preparedness capabilities. It is equally important that hospital preparedness guidelines accompany these funding streams, with a built-in accountability system to monitor reasonable and adequate preparedness efforts by hospitals.

To accomplish this, financial responsibility for the actual costs of preparedness should be assigned either to the public as a whole or to the activities and organizations associated with increased risk of mass or specialty casualties. Either approach would be an improvement over the current practice of arbitrarily expecting the costs to be assumed by the local health care community.

Among the sources of increased risk of mass or specialty casualties are industries that maintain or transport dangerous hazardous materials, such as manufacturers, rail companies, and power generating facilities. Another category of risk is represented by organizations that present an attractive target for terrorists by bringing together large numbers of individuals into one location. Examples include sporting and performing arts arenas, mass transit operations, parks with mass gatherings, and sites used for political demonstrations. A third category comprises organizations whose activities have historically generated a higher than average risk for mass casualties, including airlines, certain government agency installations, such as Internal Revenue Service offices, and other organizations, such as abortion clinics, that are historically targeted by terrorists.

It is operationally impossible to expect hospitals to fund the costs of adequately preparing for the risks generated by others. This key deficiency must be addressed by analytically establishing the cost of preparedness (development and maintenance) and then proportionately assigning responsibility for the costs.

Public policy precedent exists for funding similarly critical contingency systems that address risk generated by industry and for basing this funding upon an assignment of risk. The following alternatives suggest useful models for funding adequate surge capacity for mass or specialty casualties.

GENERAL TAX REVENUE MODEL

In a general tax revenue model, the risk is assigned to society in general. This approach assumes that the risk of mass casualties occurs across a large population and therefore, general tax revenues should be used to address the costs of preparedness. Most communities currently fund their other essential public safety initiatives (fire, police, emergency medical services, and emergency management) through general tax revenues, including the communities' capabilities for mass casualty incidents. The same level of emergency health care preparedness should be acknowledged as critical to the overall response system, on par with the other response disciplines. Public money would then be contractually obligated to health care resources, allowing development and maintenance of a well-defined patient surge capacity.

Public funding of these generally private reserve capabilities has a well-established precedent: the Civilian Reserve Air Fleet (CRAF) program provides federal funding to private sector airlines to maintain capacity for rapidly converting commercial passenger jets into patient evacuation aircraft for a major disaster or national security incident.[42] Over $700 million in federal funds was spent on this capability in 1999. A program modeled after CRAF could provide a reserve surge capacity for both public and private medical capabilities to respond to a mass casualty incident.

---

42. Civil Reserve Air Fleet Fact Sheet, accessed April 13, 2001, at <www.af.mil/news/factsheets/Civil_Reserve_Air_Fleet.html>.

HAZMAT ASSESSMENT OR SPECIALTY TAX MODEL

In a HazMat assessment model, risk would be assigned to appropriate segments of society that are tasked with the responsibility to fund public safety preparedness. Here, too, there is a precedent for requiring payment as compensation for generating community risk: many communities require a license fee for plant operators and transportation companies that deal with defined levels of hazardous materials. The license fee is considered a cost of doing business. In many locales, a portion of the license fee is used to fund the community hazardous materials response team.[43] Such fees, however, have rarely been used to assist the community's hospitals in preparing for the reception of chemically contaminated casualties from the licensed facilities.

Public policy could mandate that the HazMat license model be extended to include directed funding to aid hospitals in preparing to manage chemically contaminated mass casualties. The concept of licensing fees could be further extended beyond HazMat to encompass other activities and organizations that generate risk for mass casualties. Such fees could be included in entertainment licenses, mass gathering permits, and other special functions' regulation(s). Under this model, hospitals (like HazMat teams) would be required by government agencies to both commit to and meet a defined preparedness standard to be eligible for initial and continued funding. Thus, they would be "licensed," as well as funded, to perform the designated duties.

THE "WORST-CASE SCENARIO RESPONSE PLAN" OR "MSRC" MODEL

The "worst-case scenario response plan" model would assign risk to specific facilities that are tasked with the responsibility to develop adequate preparedness. The model for this approach is the Marine Spill Response Corporation (MSRC), which was created to meet the requirements of federal legislation passed after the Exxon Valdez oil spill in Alaska.[44] The MSRC is a quasi-public corporation developed to respond rapidly to major coastal HazMat spills.[45] The funding for the corporation is based on the requirement that all companies involved in the marine transporta-

---

43. Channel 4 Staff, "Anderson HazMat worried about preparedness: team has received anti-terrorism grant," February 11, 2001, accessed February 14, 2001, <www.thecarolinachannel.com/gs/news/andersonnewsroom/stories/andersonnewsroom-45570420010211–110254.html>.

44. Oil Pollution Act of 1990 (OPA-90), P.L. 101–380, enacted August 18, 1990; Marine Spill Response Corporation web site, accessed April 12, 2001, <www.msrc.org/>.

45. Marine Spill Response Corporation website, accessed April 12, 2001, <www.msrc.org/>.

tion of large quantities of hazardous materials must have a "worst discharge scenario" response plan in place. In order for a corporation to list MSRC as a spill response asset for its plan, the corporation must pay an annual fee that funds MSRC which, in turn, is expected to maintain a capacity to address these worst-case spill scenarios.

Similar legislation could require all organizations with a predetermined level of risk for mass or specialty casualties to develop a worst-case response plan. In order to list the hospital and community health care organizations as resources to care for victims of their worst-case scenario, organizations would be required to pay a fee to the government that would go toward improved hospital preparedness for such incidents. As in the HazMat assessment model described above, hospitals would be required by government agencies to commit to and meet a defined preparedness standard to be eligible for initial and continued funding.

RESPONDER "CERTIFICATION OF PREPAREDNESS REQUIREMENT" MODEL
In a Responder "Certification of Preparedness Requirement" model, risk would be assigned to specific facilities and their response resources. This model is similar to the MSRC model described above, with the financial obligations assigned to the organizations generating the mass/specialty casualty risk. The difference is that the organization that utilizes the health care resources as part of its response plan must obtain certification directly from the health care facility, specifying that the latter has adequate capacity to perform the functions expected of it during a worst-case scenario. The facilities that generate the risk would fund the development and maintenance of this certified health care capability.

Such a direct relationship may be the best way to maintain accountability by the health care system to the at-risk community for its response capability. The hospitals would be directly responsible to the payers, removing burdensome regulatory oversight. The role of government agencies would be limited to assuring that all parties maintain good faith practices in their planning, funding, and implementation of response capabilities.

Using these or other concepts, the public policy debate at the local, state, and national levels must establish a single or combination of remedies to resolve this critical health care funding issue.

Conclusions

The United States is currently developing public policy, law enforcement, and emergency response capacity to address the rising concern for mass terrorism. Glaringly absent from current practice is any clear, systems-oriented approach to funding preparedness for the health care community to manage the inevitable mass casualties. Current economic factors have adversely affected the capability of hospitals to fund preparedness. Only public policy recognition of this crucial public safety function can lead to adequate preparedness.

Funding methods must be identified and implemented through public policy declarations, legislation, and regulations. This effort could begin initially with legislation to require community funding of hospitals that prepare to receive a community's chemical casualties, perhaps by amending SARA Title III, since this is already in place and is currently an unfunded mandate for hospitals. This law could then be extended to include funding for health care facilities preparing to receive casualties from other unusual events. The models above, singly or in combination, could be used to develop sustained funding. It is equally important that, once a system of funding is established, hospitals are held accountable for establishing and maintaining the funded mass casualty capabilities.

The Exxon Valdez oil spill provides a sobering lesson. The United States did not develop adequate infrastructure for disastrous oil spills until after the Exxon Valdez incident. The United States cannot, however, afford to wait until it suffers an even greater mass casualty terrorism event than the September 11, 2001, attacks before addressing critical shortfalls in hospital surge capacity. Without conscious advance preparation, the nation may awaken to find that an extraordinary event has exceeded our capacity to save lives and health: our limited response capacity has created the unforgivable dilemma of "ambulances to nowhere."

Emergency Communications: The Quest for Interoperability in the United States and Europe

Viktor Mayer-Schönberger

Late on the morning of April 20, 1999, Eric Harris and Dylan Klebold, two sixteen-year-old students, entered Columbine High School and started a shooting spree that would leave 15 people dead, including Harris and Klebold, and dozens of others wounded.[1]

Within minutes of the first shootings, local police, paramedics, and firefighters arrived at the scene. Over the next several hours, they were joined by almost 1,000 law enforcement personnel and emergency responders. The task they faced was daunting. They did not know the number of attackers, their location, or the goal of the attack. Hundreds of

This research was supported by the Executive Session on Domestic Preparedness. This was to be a coauthored paper with my colleague Richard Falkenrath, now Special Assistant to the President and Senior Director for Policy and Plans with the Office of Homeland Security, who convinced me to look at interoperability. He deserves much of the credit for this paper. Deborah Housen-Couriel provided truly exceptional research assistance. Anatole Papadopoulos helped to track down hard-to-find sources in the final stages of the project. I am most grateful for many suggestions from Arnold Howitt and Robyn Pangi of the Executive Session on Domestic Preparedness as well as David Lazer, Thomas Oberlechner, Robert Heverly, and Gernot Brodnig for reading and extensively commenting on earlier drafts. I am especially grateful to Herbert Cordt for demonstrating that networks are not just technical artifacts and to Werner Senn, Herbert Nagy, and numerous interview partners in the Burgenland for generously taking time to answer my queries.

1. The description and analysis of the Columbine High School incident are based on the John F. Kennedy School of Government Cases "The Shootings at Columbine High School: Responding to a New Kind of Terrorism," Case No. C16–01–1612.0 and "The Shootings at Columbine High School: Responding to a New Kind of Terrorism Sequel," Case No. C16–01–1612.1.

screaming students were fleeing the school; many others were trapped in it, deadly frightened, and waiting to be freed. Scores of people were wounded and needed immediate medical attention. Seventy-six bombs and explosive devices set up by Harris and Klebold had to be identified and defused.

Yet as it turned out, the biggest challenge on that Tuesday afternoon was not battling the two attackers. They had already killed themselves by the time that the first law enforcement team entered the school. The biggest challenge was coordinating heavily armed and ready-to-fire police forces from half a dozen sheriffs' offices and 20 area police departments, 46 ambulances, and two helicopters from 12 fire and emergency medical services (EMS) agencies as well as personnel from a number of state and federal agencies. Coordination was difficult but not primarily because of turf wars or lack of crisis management. If anything, first responders, some of whom had taken part in Federal Emergency Management Agency (FEMA) training, were quite willing to work with each other.

The real challenge was simpler—and much more serious. Responders from the various agencies had no communications system that would permit them to communicate with each other. Agencies used their own radio systems, which were incompatible with those of others. With more and more agencies arriving on the scene, even the few pragmatic ways of communication that had been established, like sharing radios, deteriorated rapidly. Cellular phones offered no alternative, as hundreds of journalists rushed to their phones and overloaded the network. Within the first hour of the operation, the Jefferson County, Colorado, dispatch center lost access to the local command post because the radio links were jammed. Steve Davis, public information officer of the Jefferson County Sheriff's Office, later commented that "[r]adios and cell[ular] phones and everything else were absolutely useless, as they were so overwhelmed with the amount of traffic in the air."[2] The real miracle of Columbine High School is that nobody else was killed because of the complete communications breakdown, either through friendly fire or uncoordinated agency activity.

Yet the communications breakdown was to be expected. Analysis of the 1993 World Trade Center bombing, the 1995 Oklahoma City bombing, and the standoff between the Federal Bureau of Investigation (FBI) and Branch Davidians in Waco, Texas, in 1993, in which nearly 100 people died, all pointed to interagency communications as one of the weakest links in emergency management. In the immediate aftermath of the

---

2. "The Shootings at Columbine High School: Responding to a New Kind of Terrorism," p. 16.

Oklahoma City bombing, for example, the four radio channels available to the Oklahoma City police department instantly became congested.[3] Only one of a total of two channels accessible to the fire department was available for rescuers: the other channel had to be used to manage all other Oklahoma City fire coverage. Initial communication with the command post took place via cellular phones, until cellular phone networks, too, became overloaded. Similar miscommunication hampered emergency responses to the Amtrak train derailment in Arizona in 1995 and the Florida forest fires in 1998.[4] After each tragedy, the need for interoperability—for linking communications networks of the various agencies—was a significant issue. The lessons were visible for everyone in the field. Still nothing had fundamentally changed by 1999, the year of the Columbine tragedy.

Interoperability is "the ability of public safety personnel to communicate by radio with staff from other agencies, on demand and in real time."[5] Public safety agencies have used radio communications systems for many decades.[6] So far, however, most of these systems have been limited in reach and have enabled communication within a particular group or agency, but not across agencies. A group of firefighters, for example, can talk among themselves over their radios but not with paramedics or law enforcement officers and sometimes not even with fellow firefighters from a neighboring town or county. This severely curtails the utility of radio communications, especially in situations that demand large-scale immediate interagency communication and coordination.[7]

This is an essay about communications interoperability and its implementation in the United States and Europe. There are three required steps for interoperability: inventing the appropriate technology, setting common standards and frequencies, and providing adequate fund-

---

3. Public Safety Wireless Network (PSWN), Program Symposium Compilation Report, August 1997–December 1999, pp. 19–23.

4. Ibid.

5. PSWN, *Public Safety and Wireless Communications Interoperability—Critical Issues Facing Public Safety Communications*, p. 1.

6. The Detroit police department was the first to use mobile radio receivers in the 1920s; radio transmitters followed in the 1930s. See The First Two-Way Police Radio Systems, The Philip B. Petersen Collection (July 2, 1989) available online at http://www.infoage.org/p-29Police.html.

7. Interoperability concerns of communications networks in the public sector are not limited to public safety organizations. The military, too, has grappled with the problem. See Anthony W. Faughn, "Interoperability: Is It Achievable?," Program on Information Resources Policy (PIRP) Working Paper (Cambridge, Mass., September 2001).

ing.[8] This essay looks at each of these steps in both U.S. and European contexts and analyzes successes and failures, rendering a fuller picture of the challenges for interoperability and the best practices to meet them. Over the last few years (and surprisingly, given the complex political structures), the Europeans have pulled ahead of the United States in implementing interoperability, although with determination and the right set of strategies, U.S. policymakers can easily make up lost ground. Enhanced Federal Communications Commission (FCC) leadership in defining frequencies and standards and a clearly formulated and thoroughly executed comprehensive funding strategy, based either on public funds or innovative public-private partnerships, would go a long way toward enabling the establishment of communications interoperability.

But this essay is not simply about how to overcome obstacles on the path to interoperability. The case of interoperability, its elusiveness in the United States and its successes elsewhere, reveals a deeper, more troubling story—a story not so much of technical hurdles, as of structural and political hurdles, as more of perceived than actual constraints, unduly limiting the nation's ability to cope with an important public policy need. There are no abstract silver bullets to overcome the problem. Instead, policymakers have to look carefully at how well the policy strategy that they select is aligned with their means and the policy context. In the United States, interoperability has suffered from strategic misalignment and haphazard implementation. European interoperability policies have fared better, not because of a general advantage in the strategies chosen, but because of a better fit between means and ends. Interoperability provides an intriguing test case, highlighting the transcending importance of strategic alignment, agency innovation, and leadership.

The Path toward Interoperability and Its Three Obstacles

Over the course of the last decade, numerous public and private sector organizations have studied interoperability and the difficulties involved in achieving it.[9] Unfortunately, the three general obstacles that need to be

---

8. In addition to these three steps PSWN, "Public Safety and Wireless Communications Interoperability—Critical Issues Facing Public Safety Communications," mentions security as an additional obstacle to interoperability.

9. See for example PSWN, "Public Safety and Wireless Communications Interoperability;" National Institute of Justice, "State and Local Law Enforcement Wireless Communications and Interoperability—A Quantitative Analysis" (January 1998); European Radio Commission, Harmonisation of Frequencies for Police and Security Services in Europe, ERO Report No. 6 (1991).

overcome to establish interoperability—finding a suitable technology; defining a common frequency and standard; and securing the necessary funding—may reinforce each other, rendering the triad potentially even harder to tackle than they would be as individual barriers.

As an example, suppose five people speaking five different languages want to communicate with each other. First, they have to understand that each one of them is capable of learning a new, common language. In the interoperability context, this represents the technical hurdle. The next step is to define this new language, its grammar, and its vocabulary. This is the frequency and standards hurdle. Finally, they need to have the resources available to actually learn this new language. This represents the third hurdle, the need for appropriate funding. Obviously, overcoming one hurdle is necessary to overcome the next, but it does not make overcoming the next hurdle any easier, as each hurdle has its own unique difficulties. Worse, focusing energies on overcoming one hurdle may divert necessary resources from tackling the next, thus making it harder to overcome all three of them together.

FINDING A SUITABLE TECHNOLOGY

A truly interoperable public safety communications network will have to integrate the radio networks of law enforcement, firefighters, EMS, and other local, state, and federal public safety organizations. It will also have to accommodate the communications systems of neighboring public safety agencies, so that officers from one locality can talk with their colleagues in others. Hence, hundreds, even thousands, of users will have to be linked through a network extending beyond states and even nations.

Conventional analog radio equipment is ill-equipped to perform this integration task because it does not scale well—adding more users to the network quickly clogs communication channels. This is because participants using such equipment converse on a specific channel. The ability to speak and listen is shared among all the users. Multiple users cannot speak simultaneously. This limits the amount of information that can be exchanged. Adding channels eases the problem only temporarily, as extra channels require more bandwidth and, hence, a broader radio spectrum dedicated to public service communication. Radio spectrum, however, is not a boundless resource and must be shared with many other user groups. Moreover, even if bandwidth were endless and an unlimited number of extra channels available, managing who uses which channel with whom for what purpose poses a substantial coordination problem. In an emergency like the Columbine High School case, there is no time to sit down and coordinate rationally among the emergency responders how channels are to be used. Emergency planning and preparation may reduce the coordination problem, but it cannot prepare for all contingencies.

Interoperability requires a technology that scales, can accommodate many thousands of users efficiently, and can coordinate among them automatically to best utilize the scarce resource of available channels, while offering better voice quality and perhaps even additional services like data transmission. A simple walkie-talkie is hopelessly inadequate to fulfill these requirements. Yet almost all of the emergency responders in the United States today use equipment that differs little from traditional two-way radios.

DEFINING A COMMON FREQUENCY AND STANDARD

Once a suitable technology for interoperability has been identified, its success depends on its employment of a common frequency and standard. Without such commonality, even the best technology will be useless in terms of interoperability, and for an obvious reason: a common frequency allows all users to communicate over the same set of channels. Trying to communicate over different channels, when each party has access to only his or her own channel, is like attempting to watch channel 3 with a television set that receives only channels 5 and 6.

Understanding the need for a common frequency is intuitive, but meeting that need is hard. Various public service agencies, from law enforcement to firefighters to EMS, have traditionally used different (and limited) frequency bands for their radio communications.[10] For interoperability to work, a sufficiently broad spectrum needs to be reserved.

Even a common frequency, however, is not enough to establish interoperability. It requires not just a common frequency band but also a common standard—a common implementation of a selected technology. For example, many cellular phones in the United States use a common frequency band—the 1900 Megahertz (MHz) band. Still, users from one cellular phone operator cannot call through the network of another and could not even if both operators wanted to, because, although the networks use the same frequency band and the same basic technology platform (digital wireless), the concrete implementation of the technology differs among operators. Cellular phone operators use one of three com-

---

10. Twelve discrete portions of spectrum are currently allocated for public safety operations, including the 25–50 MHz, 72–76 MHz, 150–174 MHz, 220–222 MHz, 450–470 MHz, 470–512 MHz, 764–776 and 794–806 MHz, 806–821 and 851–866 MHz, 821–824 and 866–869 MHz bands for state and local agencies, as well as the 30–50 MHz, 138–150.8 MHz, 162–174 MHz and 406.1–420 MHz bands for federal agencies; see PSWN, Spectrum Issues and Analysis Report (1999).

peting standards,[11] so cellular phones are wedded to a particular operator's network, whether the users or even the operators like it or not.[12] They are not interoperable, even though they operate over a common frequency.

SECURING NECESSARY FUNDING

Even if the appropriate technology is identified and a common frequency and standard are selected, it is very unlikely that interoperability will happen overnight. For interoperability to be implemented, all existing radio communications infrastructure used by public service agencies must be replaced with new equipment. This involves more than just replacing the hundreds of thousands of radio sets currently in use. Every one of these agencies also operates a small radio network consisting of dispatcher stations, transmitters, and relay stations to link the individual radio sets with each other and with the command post, and this network infrastructure needs to be replaced as well. In addition to the new hardware (i.e., the radio sets and networks), hundreds of thousands of users may need to be trained to use the new equipment. Finally, this transition must take place in real time, while emergencies continue to happen that require first responders to be in active communication.

Such a large-scale shift to an interoperable infrastructure is a logistical challenge, in however staggered a fashion it may take place. Yet, the logistical challenge pales in comparison to the financial challenge. Studies have estimated that the total replacement value of radio equipment used by public service organizations in the United States exceeds $18 billion. More than 80 percent of the cost of replacement will have to be shouldered, not by federal or state, but by local agencies.[13] This amount does not include training costs. Moreover, every one of these tens of thousands of individual organizations will make its own procurement decision, based on its own preferences as well as available funds.

---

11. The current standards for digital cellular phones used in the United States are TDMA, CDMA, and GSM. In addition, some cellular phone operators still maintain analog networks.

12. Technical interoperability must not be confused with whether network operators actually permit interoperability. All cellular phone operators permit interoperability in the sense that any cellular phone user can call (and be called) by anyone on the global phone network, as long as they are within range of their cellular operator's network. Yet few cellular phone operators in the United States permit other operators' cellular phone users to temporarily use their networks. Experts call this flavor of interoperability "roaming." "Roaming" could be mandated through regulatory action, but only if operators used the same technology, standard, and frequency.

13. See PSWN, "LMR Replacement Cost Study Report" (June 1998), p. 5.

Interoperability may have a chance only if all three of these obstacles—technology, common frequency and standard, and funding—are overcome. Surmounting these obstacles is what some studies and reports have deemed the fundamental challenge for interoperability.[14]

Growing Hurdles: U.S. Policy toward Interoperability

Comprehensive communications interoperability among public safety agencies has been a long-standing goal of U.S. policymaking, reinforced by the tragedies of Oklahoma City and Columbine High School. Early on, experts identified the three hurdles that needed to be overcome, and significant effort was expended to surmount them. How successful was this strategy?

TECHNOLOGY: SUCCESS OF INNOVATION
Interoperability, as mentioned earlier, requires a technology that scales well and is capable of simultaneously accommodating many users, given the constraint of limited radio spectrum bandwidth. Technology's central task is to use the available bandwidth as efficiently as possible.

To increase the efficiency of bandwidth use, a communications network can take over the task of allocating channels for communications. Instead of human users flipping through channels and determining manually whether a given channel is "free" to be used, technology manages the assignment of these channels. Such assignment can be made based on a first-come, first-served system. When all available channels are in use, technology will—once a given conversation is over—automatically de-allocate the channel used for that conversation and assign it to the users next in line for a free channel. Unlike cellular phone conversations, most communication on public service networks tends to be short, permitting a high turnover rate and relatively short waiting times.

Such a system offers a substantial advantage over systems currently in use by eliminating the need to designate a particular channel for a particular use. There need no longer be a dedicated "dispatcher" channel, or a "group channel," for each team or group. Instead, network technology takes any request for a channel, finds a free one, allocates it, and establishes the connection. This is in essence what cellular phone networks do

---

14. See for example PSWN, "Public Safety and Wireless Communications Interoperability;" National Institute of Justice, "State and Local Law Enforcement Wireless Communications and Interoperability" (January 1998); European Radio Commission, "Harmonisation of Frequencies for Police and Security Services in Europe."

today. Only a limited number of channels are available, and the network automatically assigns them to users requesting to communicate.

Unlike cellular phone callers, however, users of a public service network typically cannot wait many seconds for the network to designate a channel for them. Instead, they require instant communication setup. In addition, networks allocating channels based on temporal priority—first come, first served—are not ideal for public service organizations. Channel allocation in such organizations should not be based on who asked first, but on whose communication need is most urgent. A police officer requesting a channel to communicate a routine status report should not get priority over his or her colleague's emergency call for mutual assistance just because his or her request was received first. A suitable network technology must assign channels based primarily on communication needs.

This implies a network capable of managing itself, understanding requests, allocating and de-allocating channels, and keeping on top of the traffic on the network. Public service organizations striving for interoperability require "intelligent" digital networks that are far more sophisticated than the radio networks currently in place. Such digital networks translate all communications into a unified digital code before routing them through the network. On the receiving end, bits are translated back into, for example, voice communication. The advantage of employing such a digital code is that the network can "manage" it easily. This is why interoperable public service networks are based on digital technology.

Digital networks receive communication requests from users along with information about the importance of the communication and queue the requests accordingly. Emergency communication requests get prioritized and may even prompt the network to de-allocate the lowest-priority communication under way—in effect kicking off users for an incoming emergency communication—a capability available neither in conventional analog radio networks nor in digital cellular phone networks. Digital technology also permits the compression of voice transmissions. Compressed transmissions in turn decrease the amount of data that needs to be transferred for the same communication, and less data requires smaller channels (less frequency bandwidth), for example, by compressing voice into a 6.25 kilohertz (kHz) instead of a 25 kHz channel. Hence, a given frequency band can fit more channels.

Managing channel allocation generally points toward a network technology with a strong center—a kind of superfast dispatcher in charge of assigning communication rights to users. Networks that employ this kind of technology are called "trunked" networks, implying that they have a strong trunk, or center, managing them. Yet efficient network management can also be based on a decentralized structure. Instead of being managed by a core, the network parts automatically coordinate the use and management of the network's resources among themselves. The Internet is such a network. The advantage of such a network is that it provides for ample redundancy. Even if a part of the network stops working, the rest will continue to operate. Trunked networks, on the other hand, will stop working if the managing center has been brought down. The advantage of decentralized networks, however, comes at a price. They require a much higher coordination overhead. Establishing a connection demands valuable time in decentralized networks: the more network links are involved, the greater the time required. This runs counter to one of the central requirements of emergency responder networks: instantaneous communication setup. On balance, most experts today advocate the use of digital trunked networks, rather than decentralized networks, to provide scalable interoperability for public service organizations.[15] They think that the chance of a trunked network failing because its center(s) has stopped working is small and thus a good trade-off (especially factoring in backup centers and similar resources), compared to unacceptably long communication setup times associated with decentralized networks.

COMMON FREQUENCY AND STANDARD: OUT OF SYNCH WITH THE PRESENT
The process of defining a common frequency and standard for interoperable digital radio networks got off to a good start. After an initial (and more general) congressional mandate in 1983,[16] the FCC issued a first "Report and Order" in 1987 envisioning intercommunication channels as part of a national plan for public safety agencies.[17] In 1993, as part of the Omnibus Budget Reconciliation Act, Congress asked the FCC to develop a framework to ensure that public safety communications needs are met through the year 2010. Interoperability was included in the request as a primary objective of this new framework.[18] The FCC was

---

15. The PSWN report "Comparison of Conventional and Trunked Systems" (May 1999), for example, concludes that "[t]ypically trunking allows a system to serve more users with the same amount of spectrum or less. Since spectrum has become a scare resource, this property of trunking will drive its use in the future." p. 46.

16. Federal Communications Commission Authorization Act 1983, P.L. No. 98–214, § 9(a), 97 Stat. 1467 (1983).

17. See Report and Order, 3 FCC Rcd 905; as well as the more daring Notice of Proposed Rule Making, 2 FCC Rcd 2869 (1987).

18. See 47 U.S.C. § 309(j)(10)(B)(iv), as added by P.L. No. 103–66 (1993); note that the

uniquely positioned to provide such a framework, as it not only maintains jurisdiction over the use of radio spectrum but may also condition spectrum use.

Unfortunately, the FCC approached the subject like any other spectrum allocation matter. Expending valuable time, it first studied the issue for two years and then set up an advisory committee (the Public Safety Wireless Advisory Committee, or PSWAC).[19] It soon became clear to the FCC that it faced numerous powerful stakeholders in its efforts to fulfill the congressional mandate.

The FCC's first task was to identify a portion of the radio spectrum that could be used nationwide by public safety organizations. This was difficult, as it required clearing the spectrum of existing users, most of whom had not only substantial investments in, but also valid legal claims to use, these frequency bands. Fortunately, the FCC was already negotiating with television stations their planned transition from analog to digital television (DTV). DTV transmits more information than analog television and, thus, requires a frequency band higher up in the radio spectrum than those currently in use for terrestrial transmissions of TV signals. In their shift toward a new portion of the radio spectrum that can accommodate DTV, TV network operators are vacating the radio spectrum that they have used for analog TV. A part of this spectrum, once vacated, may be rededicated for interoperable public safety radio networks.

After prolonged deliberation, in 1997, the FCC issued its order, allocating 24 MHz of vacated spectrum in the 700 MHz band to public safety services.[20] It also stated that it would initiate separate proceedings to set the conditions for use of this portion of the spectrum.[21] As part of these

---

congressional mandate was to provide a framework for public *safety* communications, which involves a narrower group than public *service* organizations. The FCC later redefined "interoperability" to encompass the wider definition of providing "an essential communications link within public safety and public service wireless communications systems which permits units from two or more different entities to interact with one another and to exchange information according to a prescribed method in order to achieve predictable results." "Development of Operational, Technical and Spectrum Requirements for Meeting Federal, State and Local Public Safety Agency Communications Requirements Through the Year 2010," WT Docket No. 96–86, First Report and Order and Third Notice of Proposed Rulemaking, 14 FCC Rcd 152, 189–90 ¶ 76 (1998).

19. Pursuant to the Federal Advisory Committee Act, 5 U.S.C. App. 2 (1988).

20. See "Reallocation of Television Channels 60–69, the 746–806 MHz Band," ET Docket No. 97–157, Report and Order, 12 FCC Rcd 22953 (1997).

21. Ibid.; see also "Advanced Television Systems and Their Impact Upon the Existing Television Broadcast Service," MM Docket No. 87–268, Sixth Further Notice of Proposed Rule Making, 11 FCC Rcd 10968–10980 (1996).

proceedings, the FCC issued its important First Report and Order and Third Notice of Proposed Rule Making, specifying use and service rules for this spectrum in the summer of 1998.[22] It appeared as though, five years after Congress mandated action, the FCC had finally embarked upon a specific plan to enable interoperability. It had identified a common frequency spectrum and initiated proceedings to define "service rules" for its use, providing the necessary groundwork for a common technical standard. But this apparently bright picture is darkened by some important caveats.

First, television broadcast stations have until December 31, 2006, to move from analog to digital broadcasting. Hence, only in 2007, 14 years after the initial congressional mandate was issued, will public safety organizations in the United States have spectrum available nationwide for interoperable communication. It almost seems as if the FCC misunderstood the congressional call to ensure that public safety communications needs were met *through* the year 2010 and instead aimed to meet them *by* the year 2010. Granted, the situation is not as bleak in reality as it looks on paper. In many areas of the United States, television broadcasters are not using channels 60–69—the portion of spectrum in question—and public safety organizations can utilize such unused spectrum right away. In many urban and suburban areas, however—exactly where public safety organizations have to communicate most frequently—these channels are still in use. Moreover, until September 2001, the FCC required television broadcasters wanting to move out of channels 60–69 to switch immediately to digital broadcasts. Given the minuscule number of digital receivers in use and the resulting smaller viewer base for such broadcasts, television stations had no incentive to vacate the spectrum earlier than by the end of 2006. Recently, the FCC has mitigated this situation by issuing an order permitting broadcasters to migrate to available spectrum for analog broadcasts and switch to digital broadcasts only in 2007—a positive move.[23] But another three important years were lost in the process.

Second, whereas the FCC has looked (too) far into the future when selecting a frequency band, its ventures into defining the communications standard have been fundamentally retrospective. Very early in the

---

22. "The Development of Operational, Technical and Spectrum Requirements for Meeting Federal, State and Local Public Safety Agency Communications Requirements Through the Year 2010," WT Docket No. 96–86, First Report and Order and Third Notice of Proposed Rulemaking, 14 FCC Rcd 152 (1998).

23. Action by the Commission September 7, 2001, by Order on Reconsideration of the Third Report and Order (FCC 01–258).

process of defining an appropriate technology, the commission understood the implications of large-scale interoperability within a limited portion of radio spectrum. As a result, it leaned toward trunked digital networks utilizing advanced compression of voice and data to accommodate as many interoperable channels as possible in the available 24 MHz. This was as prudent a move as it was obvious, given the advancements in technology and the requirements of interoperability.

At the same time, the FCC realized that interoperability depends not only on defining a framework but also on stakeholder buy-in. With tens of thousands of stakeholder organizations (some of which wield substantial power) on the local, state, and national levels, the FCC wanted to involve as many stakeholders as possible in the deliberations over rules and standards. This was not a novel situation for the FCC. In fact, the FCC's traditional deliberative process is designed to integrate stakeholder views. By also applying this process to the area of public safety communications, the FCC hoped to create a positive momentum furthering the acceptance of its envisioned framework.

Like the FCC, the stakeholders saw a need for interoperability, but for them, interoperability had to be balanced against a number of other needs and constraints. All public safety organizations, through their various national associations, expressed concern about the cost of a national interoperable network as envisioned by the FCC.[24] In addition, many of the local and state public safety organizations feared being marginalized by large, powerful federal agencies taking positions. The formation of the Public Safety Wireless Network (PSWN) program as a joint initiative of the Departments of Justice and the Treasury advocating interoperability did not help to alleviate their misgivings. Despite PSWN being targeted at helping state and local public safety agencies devise interoperability strategies, many of these agencies remained suspicious of federal involvement in what they perceived to be a largely local or regional issue. By the same token, federal agencies were convinced that a substantial technological step forward was necessary, especially in the wake of interoperability breakdowns like those that occurred during the response to the 1993 World Trade Center and 1995 Oklahoma City bombings. Realizing the resistance of local agencies only prompted them to push harder for an advanced solution.

---

24. For example, in its reply to the FCC, the Association of Public Safety Communications Officials International (APCO) stated that "[t]here are legitimate technical, operational, and feasibility reasons why some local governments must maintain conventional systems"; see Reply A96–86, available online at http://www.apcointl.org/gov/a96–86.doc.

The struggle was exacerbated by the fact that a number of public safety stakeholders, acutely aware of some of the technical shortcomings of their analog systems, had already engaged in years of deliberation over a potential new communications standard. The core of the standard that they had envisioned, however, was not just interoperability, but also limited backward compatibility, thus permitting older analog and new digital equipment to work together—to an extent. Moreover, they were wary of replacing existing networks with new hardware given their budgetary constraints. Their focus, therefore, was on small, evolutionary steps toward a more modern communications infrastructure. To that end, they had teamed up with the Telecommunications Industry Association (TIA) and the Electronic Industries Alliance (EIA). In addition, Motorola, a major vendor of radio communications equipment, became heavily involved in the process. The aim was to define a standard that would expand the capabilities of the communications networks and introduce some interoperability and also extend the life of analog networks. The resulting initiative, called Project 25, ultimately yielded a set of ANSI (American National Standards Institute)/TIA/EIA standards for communications networks. Its aim was to convince the FCC to require users of the 700 MHz band to use Project 25–compliant equipment.

The Project 25–based standard[25] differs in two fundamental ways from what the FCC had originally envisioned.[26] First, although it permits trunked networks, it does not *require* networks to be trunked, limiting the potential efficiency gains associated with trunking. It also features a less sophisticated compression technology than that envisioned by the FCC, using 12.5 kHz of spectrum for each voice channel and not just 6.25 kHz, as the FCC had originally hoped.[27] Hence, only half as many channels would be available in a given spectrum, and with no trunking requirement, these would not be managed to maximum efficiency. Second, the FCC had hoped for a vibrant market of hardware providers for the required radio network equipment. After all, more than $18 billion of investment was at stake in the United States alone. Yet by 2000, only one major vendor, Motorola, had released networking equipment capable of providing a Project 25–compliant trunked digital network,[28] and only a

---

25. I am referring here to a Project 25–based "standard," although it actually is a bundle of complementary standards. Yet, for reasons of brevity and readability, I will refer to it in the singular.

26. See "Project 25 Standards Explanation, February 2001," available online at http://www.motorola.com/publicsafety/docs/P25_white_paper.doc.

27. See First Report and Order, 14 FCC Rcd at 205 ¶ 113.

28. See http://www.motorola.com/publicsafety/70–10.shtml.

handful of smaller vendors offered equipment for less powerful, non-trunked networks. This ran counter to the FCC's idea of intense vendor competition prompted by open standards. How could public safety organizations ensure that they received value for their money when a single vendor effectively dominated the market?

For some, the FCC did not go far enough. But for many public safety organizations involved, it went dangerously far. They saw interoperability as one of the many challenges that they faced and estimated that the likelihood that they would have to confront a catastrophic event requiring comprehensive interoperability was slim. Their aim was to get the FCC to water down any strong interoperability requirements and thereby, to minimize any potential impact on their budgets.

Cognizant of how the stakeholders were lined up on the issue, the FCC tentatively opted for requiring public safety organizations using the 700 MHz band to use Project 25–compliant, trunked digital networks, proposing essentially a compromise between Project 25 and its own higher aspirations. Insisting that the networks be trunked, and suggesting what it termed a "migration path" toward a better compression technology using only 6.25 kHz of spectrum, the FCC had apparently hoped to maintain its ultimate goal by pushing it farther into the future.

Stakeholders' reaction to the FCC's tentative requirements was mostly negative. Many public safety organizations feared the financial consequences of such a mandate and pressured their national associations to lobby against it. Furthermore, they argued that oversight of interoperability should be performed at the state level, hoping to be more effective lobbyists there. When a group came forward advocating that the FCC adopt a much more sophisticated standard[29] called TETRA (Trans European Trunked Radio networks), which had already proven its operability in Europe, the Project 25 Steering Committee immediately sensed the danger of a strong competitor. Understanding that it had more to fear from TETRA than from reluctant public safety organizations, the committee decisively shifted its strategy. In tune with many public safety organizations, the committee started to downplay the need for comprehensive interoperability and began to argue that a limited number of interoperability channels, managed either through a trunked network infrastructure or even just manually, as in the old days of analog radio, would be sufficient for almost all emergency situations. At the same time, it began to emphasize potential disadvantages of trunked systems and to

---

29. Similar to the Project 25 "standard," the TETRA "standard" is a bundle of many complementary standards. For reasons of brevity, however, I will refer to it in the singular.

extol the virtues of a more gradual approach of including all stakeholders and providing backward capabilities. Finally, in a brilliant strategy of containment, Project 25 proponents set up an industry working group with some TETRA proponents to begin discussions about the possibility of an eventual second-generation common standard.[30]

Few insiders were shocked when the FCC, in its Fourth Report and Order and Fifth Notice of Proposed Rule Making, published in January 2001,[31] effectively rescinded its initial stance of comprehensive interoperability. A limited version of the Project 25 standard (termed "Phase I") was adopted, based on the less efficient 12.5 kHz channels. The original mandate for trunking was replaced by almost the opposite: a prohibition of trunking except in eight of the available 128 channels[32] originally allocated for narrow-band interoperability. And a possible migration path to a more spectrum-efficient compression technology was put on the back burner and relegated to "further study."

More than a decade has passed since the FCC ventured into developing a framework for interoperable communications among public safety organizations. Despite its understanding of the issues and its good intentions to involve the important stakeholders in the development process, so far the results have been dramatically misaligned with the needs of the present. Selecting a frequency band that would be fully available only at the beginning of 2007 for use by public safety organizations, the Commission looked far into the future, while at the same time selecting a technological standard wedded to a predigital, pre-information age. Therefore, despite all of the activities of an entire decade, substantial parts of the second hurdle remain in place.

FUNDING: CONCERNS

The difficulties of establishing a common frequency and standard pale when compared with finding funding for an advanced, interoperable public safety communications network. The situation is easy to describe

---

30. There is also a less cynical interpretation of the formation of this working group: a sincere desire to bridge the technological divide and create true global interoperability, especially after the events of September 11; see "Transatlantic Public Safety Partners meet in the wake of U.S. Terrorist Attacks," ETSI/TIA/Project Mesa press release (September 24, 2001); see also "New Transatlantic Partnership Addresses Mobile Broadband Specifications for Public Safety Applications" (October 20, 2001).

31. Fourth Report and Order and Fifth Notice of Proposed Rule Making, WT-Docket No. 96–86.

32. See the Third Memorandum Opinion and Order and Third Report and Order, 15 FCC Rcd at 19851–19860 ¶¶ 16–39.

and difficult to rectify. Most public safety agencies are acutely aware that their communications networks are outdated and need to be replaced, especially if the goal is comprehensive interoperability. Many plan to replace their equipment, but the overwhelming majority cannot find the funding to do so and do not expect to be able to in the near future. This dismal outlook is in line with studies estimating the total amount of investment needed, as well as the monies available now and in the foreseeable future through public (federal, state, and local) and private sources. Funding appears to be the final and most formidable hurdle on the road to interoperability.

There are almost 60,000 individual public safety organizations in the United States comprising more than 2.2 million personnel.[33] Thirty-seven percent of these organizations are (currently) planning to replace their aging radio systems with new equipment.[34] Forty percent of all fire and EMS agencies plan to switch to a trunked digital system,[35] and numbers for state and local law enforcement agencies' procurement plans are similar.[36] These agencies seem to have a good sense of the broad technological trends. Their individual procurement plans are well aligned with the general goal of increased interoperability. The problem is securing the necessary funding for the investments that they have planned. Agencies recognize the difficulty of the task of obtaining this funding. Sixty-nine percent of all law enforcement[37] and sixty-eight percent of fire and EMS agencies[38] recently stated that lack of funding was a severe obstacle on their path to interoperability.

Moreover, these are not just the subjective impressions of agencies that will have to make and fund the necessary upgrades. Independent studies have verified the need for tremendous amounts of funding to finance the necessary network upgrades for interoperability. One such study, undertaken by management consulting firm Booz-Allen & Hamilton on behalf of PSWN, estimated a total capital need of $18.3 billion to replace the existing communications infrastructure. Importantly, the costs to be borne by local agencies account for more than 80 percent of that amount ($15.4 billion), compared with $1.2 billion for federal and $1.7 bil-

33. PSWN, "A Priority Investment for America's Future Safety," p. 5.

34. Ibid., p. 4.

35. PSWN, "Analysis of Fire and EMS Communications Interoperability," p. 9.

36. National Institute of Justice, "State and Local Law Enforcement Wireless Communications and Interoperability" (January 1998), p. 1.

37. Ibid, p. 8.

38. PSWN, "Analysis of Fire and EMS Communications Interoperability."

lion for state agencies.[39] This implies that the organizations most burdened with finding sufficient funding are precisely the ones that have no direct access to larger federal or state budgets.

In addition, the amount of funding needed involves more than just the cost of replacing equipment. Provision also has to be made for planning, procurement, training, and maintenance costs over the entire life cycle of the new systems.[40] In fiscal year 2000, the White House sought, but Congress denied, a budget request for $80 million in "seed" money available to states to plan statewide public safety wireless communications systems and create demonstration projects.[41] Even if these public funds had been available (and the only federal funds for that purpose), it would have taken a staggering 225 years of funding at that level to replace the public safety radio networks nationwide.

Fortunately, there are other financial sources available on federal, state, and local levels to assist in funding communications network upgrades.[42] For instance, under the Community Oriented Policing Services–Making Officer Redeployment Effective Grants (COPS–MORE), up to $81 million in federal funding was available in 2001 to law enforcement agencies for the purchase of information technology equipment.[43] The Edward Byrne Memorial State and Local Law Enforcement Assistance program provides $63 million in discretionary federal funds.[44] Other federal funding sources include FEMA,[45] Local Law Enforcement Block (LLEBG),[46] National Telecommunications and Information Administra-

---

39. PSWN, "LMR Replacement Cost Study Report," p. 4

40. See Booz-Allen & Hamilton, "Report on Funding Strategy for Public Safety Radio Communications" (October 1998), p. ii.

41. This severe shortfall was in direct opposition to the recommendations made by the Interagency Working Group on Funding (IWGF) and was covered in the PSWN, "Report Card on Funding Mechanisms," p. ES-3 (last bullet point), 8 (section 3.2.1), 17 (recommendation 1). The original report by the IWGF in June 1998, pp. 23–26 recommended federal funding that would have totaled $162 million over four years, but was never appropriated.

42. See PSWN, "The Report Card on Funding Mechanisms for Public Safety Radio Communications" (August 2001) and Booz-Allen & Hamilton, "Report on Funding Mechanisms for Public Safety Radio Communications" (December 1997).

43. U.S. Department of Justice, COPS MORE Fact Sheet (Washington, D.C.) (May 2001).

44. PSWN, "Report Card," p. 20.

45. The total amount of FEMA grants in 2000 was $137 million, with $2.4 million the size of the average grant. Grant monies awarded by FEMA have to "improve and maintain state and local capabilities for addressing all hazards."

46. $523 million was provided in FY00 and FY01 for this grant program.

tion (NTIA),[47] and State and Community Highway Safety grants as well as the forfeiture funds of the Department of Justice[48] and of the Treasury.[49]

As good as this sounds, these funding sources have a number of disadvantages that are cumulatively quite discouraging. Most of the discretionary funds are heavily earmarked for very specific aspects or contexts (thus limiting their utility to fund interoperable communications systems), and many of the grant programs require matching funds from the agency applying for grants—from 25 to 50 percent of the total amount requested.[50] As local agencies have to reconcile buying into a new radio infrastructure with many other budgetary demands, matching even the 25 percent threshold may be difficult for them. Consequently, these federal grants may end up being accessible primarily to agencies that have already lined up significant seed funding of their own. Moreover, many of these funding sources are limited to specific parts of the system life cycle, like procurement, and do not cover other stages of the cycle, like planning or training.[51]

On the state level, the most promising funding source is an FCC-mandated surcharge levied on cellular phone operators for wireless 911 emergency services. In accordance with the FCC mandate, states have to use the income from the surcharge to improve 911 response capabilities. For example, for the state of Iowa, this surcharge generated quarterly revenues of more than $1 million in 2000 to enable the state to meet FCC emergency calling regulations.[52] Once states have complied with the initial FCC mandate to improve 911 capabilities, income from the surcharge may provide a more direct funding source for public safety communications. State budget appropriations, state grants, state targeted taxes, and state bond issues[53] may provide additional sources of funding. Similar local funding is possible as well, although its size is generally limited.

---

47. In FY00, a total of $15.5 million was awarded by the NTIA, with the average amount per recipient being slightly over $400,000.

48. Information on the Department of Justice Assets Forfeiture Fund is available online at http://www.usdoj.gov/jmd/afp/06fund/indextxt.html.

49. Information on the Department of the Treasury Forfeiture Fund is available online at http://www.ncjrs.org/htm/tff.htm.

50. PSWN, "Report Card," pp. 19–21.

51. This problem is detailed in PSWN, "Report Card," pp. 7–16.

52. Ibid, p. 23.

53. According to the PSWN, "Report Card," p. 27, the Commonwealth of Massachusetts successfully used a bond issue to construct a statewide 800 MHz radio communication system using trunking technology.

But none of these sources is targeted specifically at funding modern, interoperable radio communications networks. Being much more general in nature, they provide no incentives for agencies to choose an interoperable system specifically. Given the limited amounts of funding available, the requirements for matching funds, and the fact that agencies have legacy communications systems in place, there is a real danger that most funds obtained through these sources are going to be used to maintain and step up existing systems, not replace them. The funding mechanisms mirror and reinforce the crippling "small-steps" approach already permeating the frequency and standard-setting debates.

More unorthodox ideas, such as the sharing of systems among agencies and the promotion of partnerships with other public and even private sector actors, like utility companies, have been suggested and with some success implemented in individual cases.[54] Yet for most public safety agencies in the United States, moving to a new digital and interoperable communications network is still synonymous with planning, procuring, and maintaining a new infrastructure funded through a traditional mix of local, state, and federal sources. With limited funds available, such a strategy faces huge obstacles, pushing the ultimate goal of comprehensive interoperability far into the future.

As established above, three hurdles have to be overcome to achieve interoperability: technology, common frequency and standards, and funding. The appropriate technologies to enable interoperability are available. In addition, steps have been taken to designate a common frequency and set a common standard for the systems. With a common, nationwide frequency band not available before 2007, however, and the selection of an outdated standard, these steps hardly provide interoperability in the short to medium-term. Moreover, the limited funding available and the way that funding is targeted, make it very difficult for agencies to overcome the third hurdle. Unsurprisingly, agencies have looked elsewhere for pragmatic alternatives to mitigate the interoperability crisis.

PRAGMATIC ALTERNATIVES — AND THEIR PITFALLS
The focus of this essay thus far has been on achieving interoperability by creating a comprehensive digital network. In such a network, communication across agency lines happens seamlessly. Yet this is neither the only way that interoperability can be accomplished nor is interoperability a novel concern. Since the early days of radio communication, agencies

---

54. See, for example, the "Hamilton County Digital Communication Network," available online at http://www.mobilecomms-technology.com/projects.

have had a need to integrate operations. Over time, they have developed a variety of "low-tech" methods to work around communications incompatibilities, like posting representatives in dispatch centers to relay information and issuing mobile radios to other agencies.[55]

Such pragmatic solutions will work for many routine situations. But what catastrophes like the Columbine High School shootings and the Oklahoma City and World Trade Center bombings demonstrate is the need to have interoperability work not just in routine operations but also in extreme situations with hundreds of first responders from different agencies and locations. Simple low-tech methods cannot provide this level of interoperability.

There is another way, though, to provide "thicker" interoperability while utilizing the existing communications systems. Together with vendors, FEMA and other agencies have developed special equipment, so-called cross-band switches, to patch together two existing incompatible communications networks.[56] In simple terms, two radios are connected via these switches so that everything received by one radio is automatically retransmitted by the other and vice versa, creating the illusion of one interoperable network. FEMA has outfitted a number of trucks with this equipment, keeping them ready for deployment at its regional offices. Many other agencies, also facing interoperability challenges, have installed such equipment.[57]

This solution has a number of advantages. It is far superior to low-tech methods, as communication seems to flow freely between incompatible networks. Sophisticated Multi-Radio Vehicles (MRV) in use by FEMA can link a multitude of communication networks, if necessary to provide an almost seamless communication experience among different networks and across incompatible frequencies.[58] Unlike with "deep" interoperability, no new hardware is needed to implement this type of "shallow" interoperability, apart from the equipment linking the networks, which

---

55. See Mary J. Taylor, Robert C. Epper, and Thomas K. Tolman, "Wireless Communications and Interoperability Among State and Local Law Enforcement Agencies" Research Brief, National Institute of Justice (January 1998), p. 8.

56. For example, the ACU-1000 Intelligent Interconnect System by JPS Communications.

57. Roman W. Kaluta, "New Developments in Interjurisdictional Communication Technology" (January 2001), available online at http://www.iacptechnology.org/TechTalk/TechTalk0401.htm; see also "AGILE: Research, Development, Testing and Evaluation of Interoperability Technologies," available online at http://www.agileprogram.org/research.html.

58. See http://www.fema.gov/r-n-r/mers04.htm.

saves resources compared to the costs of a full conversion. Users can retain their radios, and agencies can still operate their conventional networks. Even new digital networks can thus be incorporated step-by-step and connected to existing analog networks. No common frequencies are needed, and no new standards must be set. The equipment is ready today, and deployment is comparatively simple and straightforward.[59]

Originally intended more as a stopgap measure, until the realization of a nationwide comprehensive interoperable network, this pragmatic solution has gained substantial momentum. At the same time, there are obvious downsides to network patching. Multi-radio equipment can link only those networks whose frequency and standards it supports. The greater the number of networks to be linked, the more complex and expensive the equipment necessary to link them. Linking may "create" one network, but it does not permit this network to be divided into subgroups. This, in turn, limits the ability of the network to accommodate a large number of users, making it difficult, if not impossible, to create interoperability on all levels of command. The technique uses existing radio networks with potentially poor reception and voice transmission quality. It is largely limited to voice; interconnecting data streams or other added services, like conference calling, faxing, or calling gateways, is difficult to implement, as is providing for encryption of communication. Moreover, interoperability is happening on a network level, not on the level of individual users. For example, when their network collapses, firefighters will be unable to use their radios with the police radio network. Also, emergencies may occur where there is no multi-radio equipment in place. Although FEMA has mobile units stationed around the country, it takes some time to get them on location and working. This will preclude interoperability in the hours immediately after an emergency, arguably the time interoperability is in highest demand. In sum, multi-radio equipment has severe limitations as a tool for interoperability. Fundamentally, it is little more than a patch until networks are deployed that provide comprehensive interoperability on the user level.

Yet there is an even deeper danger: cash-strapped public safety agencies may decide to substitute plans for advanced interoperable networks with multi-radio equipment, thinking that one is about as good as the other. There is already a trend toward doing this, and the potential consequences are dramatic. If this trend continues, tens of thousands of public safety agencies in the United States will exit the first decade of the new

---

59. The Capwin Initiative envisions a highly integrated version of such a cross-bound switch, which may overcome some but not all of the shortcomings of such a pragmatic approach; see <http://www.capwinproject.com.

millennium with the same equipment that proved insufficient for major emergencies 20 years earlier. Despite a head start in realizing the problem, the nation will have drawn out its interoperability crisis and will have long been overtaken by many other nations in terms of achieving interoperability.

Comprehensive interoperability is still an elusive concept in the United States. The hurdles that must be cleared to achieve it have been identified, but the strategies to overcome them have, at least so far, shown limited tangible results. One may argue that this is a general problem of interoperability, not one specific to the United States. But other nations have successfully mastered the challenge under even less fortunate circumstances. The following section analyzes how the Europeans have approached interoperability. Starting at about the same time as the United States did, yet handicapped by even more complicated political structures than those in the United States, the Europeans surprisingly have tackled the interoperability hurdles more forcefully and, so far, more successfully, than their colleagues in the United States.

European Interoperability: Succeeding against the Odds

Galtuer is an idyllic little village in the Austrian Alps, 5,250 feet high and at the end of a long valley on Tyrol's southwestern border; it is also a leading ski resort.[60] By the end of the 1990s, 3,000 beds in hotels and inns, run by its 700 inhabitants, accommodated thousands of tourists from around the globe.

The winter of 1998–99 produced one of the heaviest snowfalls in recent history. At the end of January 1999, it started to snow and hardly stopped for the next four weeks. By the second week of February, Galtuer was snowed in, the threat of avalanches making its only road downhill impassable. But most tourists in Galtuer hardly noticed. Their hosts, used to extreme winters, had stocked up on necessities.[61] To keep the tourists happy, the tourist office had even organized a tobogganing race at the town square on Tuesday, February 23.[62] A week earlier, the road had become usable again for a few days, and a new horde of skiers had come to the village.

---

60. The following description is based on press reports as well as interviews conducted in November 2001 by the author, including two interviews with Werner Senn.

61. "Schnee," *Der Standard*, February 11, 1999.

62. "Lawinenkatastrophe—Galtür: Die Lawine platzte mitten in ein Urlauberrennen," *Der Standard*, February 27, 1999.

Shortly after 4 P.M. on February 23, three gigantic avalanches slammed down the steep mountain slope, advancing right into town. The snow was heavy, "like concrete," eyewitnesses later commented; it buried 60 people. Within minutes hundreds of people began searching for those who were trapped under the snow. thirty-one people died that day in Galtuer, and scores more were injured.[63] Yet this was only the beginning. Snowfall made it impossible for rescuers to reach Galtuer by helicopter that day.[64] The road, still closed because of the snowfall, offered no alternative.

The avalanche had also cut the only power line. But Galtuer had diesel aggregates that provided sufficient electricity for all essential activities. And cellular phone relay stations, though quickly overloaded, seemed to work, even hours after the power was cut. On Wednesday morning, the weather was good enough for helicopters to rescue the wounded and to deliver food and fuel. Hope was growing in Galtuer. But by early afternoon, the weather had once again deteriorated. Shortly thereafter, another avalanche hit houses outside the village, burying another nine people.[65] Cellular phones stopped working, as the batteries in the relay stations, still without power, ran down. More than 12,000 tourists were trapped in Galtuer. The town's only remaining connection to the world was a one-channel analog radio link of the Austrian gendarmerie.

From his command post in Landeck, some 30 miles away, Werner Senn, assigned by the Ministry of the Interior to coordinate the Alpine gendarmes in the area, started organizing the rescue mission minutes after the first avalanches had hit Galtuer. Fortunately, the weather improved. Alpine gendarmes were flown into the village and the outlying hamlets to establish radio links. Over the next couple of days, the gendarmes' lone analog radio channel provided the communication infrastructure for a massive evacuation effort. With the help of 52 helicopters from Austria, Germany, France, and the United States, more than 12,500 tourists were flown out of Galtuer and the environs. To communicate with one another, they too, were equipped with the old radios of the Alpine gendarmerie. The true miracle of Galtuer, Senn recalls, was that in over 1,500 sorties flown through a tight, V-shaped valley with poor visi-

---

63. Nach Lawine 55 Menschen vermisst," *Der Standard*, February 24, 1999.

64. "'Es war einfach unmöglich': Warum Hubschrauber nicht fliegen konnten," *Die Presse*, February 25, 1999.

65. "Zweite Lawine krachte ins Tal: Suchhund rettete vierjähriges Kind," *Die Presse*, February 25, 1999.

bility and frequent snowfall, directed only by a single crackling analog radio link, more than 17,500 people were transported without a single accident.

For Europe, the drama of Galtuer was tantamount to that of Columbine High School in that it exemplified the interoperability crisis and restated the need for a communications solution. Through low-tech methods of deploying radios of the only working network to everyone involved, the rescuers of Galtuer could coordinate better, Senn maintains, than if each team of responders had used its own network. The forced interoperability had its advantages. It made everyone remain focused and informed. But the shortcomings of this setup were all too evident. Helicopter pilots shuttling tourists out of the steep valley could hardly make use of the radio. Despite everyone's trying to speak only when absolutely necessary, the channel quickly became overloaded. Rescuers wondered how long the old crackling network would last. Had that one available communications link broken down, Galtuer may have turned into a catastrophe. Not just for the hundreds of first responders involved in Galtuer did the need to have both an interoperable system and one with *more than one* channel become painfully obvious.

In Europe, the debate over interoperable radio communication networks emerged at about the same time as it did in the United States. But the process necessary to make interoperability a reality faced structural hurdles in Europe that were not present in the United States. Unlike the United States, the European Union (EU) is not a federal state. Individual member nations retain substantial decision-making power, making coordination among them more difficult. In addition, Europe's high-tech industry traditionally has lagged behind its U.S. counterparts. For decades, national regulatory bodies, not Europe-wide agencies, enacted frequency plans, splintering the radio spectrum geographically. The European Union was not in a position to help much either. Radio networks for public safety agencies were associated with law enforcement, a policy area originally excluded from EU decision-making. Some European nations had agreed on cross-border law enforcement cooperation, but these agreements were developed outside of the EU structures. Finally, the severe constraints imposed on EU members' national budgets since the mid-1990s by the so-called Maastricht criteria, shattered any hope for the spending flexibility needed to fund an interoperable radio network.

Still, Europe quickly overtook the United States in the march toward interoperability, partly through ingenuity and a can-do attitude and partly because of sheer luck. Today, it is well on its way toward an integrated continent-wide public safety radio communications network providing comprehensive interoperability on all levels.

TECHNOLOGY: PICKING A WINNER

Planning for a mobile digital trunked radio system (MDTRS) to be used by both the public and private sectors in Europe started in the late 1980s. MDTRS later evolved into a technology called TETRA.[66] TETRA is a trunked digital system permitting voice and data transmissions.[67] One of its strengths is its ability to scale, from a few dozen to hundreds of thousands of users across an entire continent.

TETRA technology offers comprehensive interoperability. Not only can TETRA-compatible *networks* easily be linked together: interoperability is implemented all the way to the level of individual radio *handsets*, enabling users from one TETRA network to use their handsets within the infrastructure of another TETRA network. Interoperability in TETRA is software-enhanced, permitting dispatchers to set up talk groups in advance, for example, among the commanders of various public safety agencies, as well as to create talk groups on the fly, generating communication links for task forces and emergency teams formed *ad hoc*.

Because of Europe's congested radio spectrum, spectrum efficiency plays a prominent role in TETRA. A sophisticated voice compression system, with voice channels taking up only 6.25 kHz of bandwidth, allows TETRA to bundle four such channels into a 25 kHz band—and not just two as with U.S. Project 25 technology.[68] As a Time Division Multiple Access (TDMA) trunked system, TETRA technology automatically manages channel allocation to maximize spectrum efficiency.[69]

Prioritization is an additional capacity that TETRA offers. All requests for communication are queued and allocated based on the level of priority, which is pre-selected for each radio handset. This permits commanding officers to get preferred access in times of congestion. Emergency priorities afford users with an immediate talk line, even if all channels are in use. And unlike conventional analog radio networks, TETRA incorporates a number of security features, from handset authentication[70]

---

66. See the discussion of the development of the Project 25 standard, *supra.*

67. For a description on how the TETRA standard was developed, see the following section, "Frequency and Standards: Working in Tandem."

68. See Tony Kent, "Understanding TETRA Voice Coding," available online at http://www.tetramou.com/Presentations/IIR/Codec.zip.

69. As noted above, one of the disadvantages of trunked systems is the coordination overhead required to set up a communication link. Because of optimization, TETRA is able to complete such a setup within 300 ms of the time the request is made by a user.

70. Such authentication enables the network to check whether a particular radio handset is "permitted" to take part in a specific (group) call, even if the handset is from outside the local network.

to optional two-way encryption.[71] Through multiple gateways, TETRA users are connected with other telecommunications networks and can place phone calls or make TCP/IP (Internet) requests.[72]

Second-generation TETRA technology, in use since the late 1990s, overcomes the primary Achilles heel of trunked radio systems: the need for a trunked infrastructure. In what is called "Direct Mode,"[73] TETRA users may talk with each other directly, even if they are out of reach of a network infrastructure (for example inside a building or in a steep valley). Basic communications services are available in direct mode, including communication prioritization for emergencies. Any second-generation TETRA handset can also act as a small relay station connecting direct mode users to the trunked network infrastructure, thus expanding network reach.

By 2000, more than a dozen large telecommunications corporations had commenced producing a wide variety of equipment—both network infrastructure and handsets—based on the TETRA technology, including Finnish cellular phone leader Nokia, British telecommunications provider Marconi, defense contractor Matra, Canadian telecommunications giant Nortel, and, perhaps most surprisingly, given its support for Project 25 in the United States, Motorola.[74] Despite initial U.S. technology leadership in this area, Europe leapt the first hurdle toward interoperability in stride.

FREQUENCY AND STANDARDS: WORKING IN TANDEM

Early discussions concerning a common, Europe-wide frequency for public safety communications did not start within the context of the European Union but within the Schengen group, a framework for enhanced cross-border coordination and cooperation of law enforcement agencies. In 1991, the Telecom working group of the Schengen framework con-

---

71. Gert Roelofson, "Introduction to TETRA Security," available online at http://www.tetramou.com/files/Tetra-sec.doc; Peter Wickson, "TETRA Security," available online at http://www.tetramou.com/Presentations/IIR/SecuritySIM.ppt.

72. Mehdi Nouri, "TETRA Standard Interfaces and Gateways," available online at http://www.tetramou.com/files/Mehdi%203.doc; Mehdi Nouri, "TETRA Standard Interfaces," available online at http://www.tetramou.com/Presentations/IIR/Interfaces.ppt.

73. For a description of "Direct Mode" see Ranko Pinter, "TETRA Direct Mode," available online at http://www.tetramou.com/files/TETRADMO.rtf.

74. See Pekka Blomberg, "TETRA: State-of-the-Art Global PMR Standard" (1999); see also the Tetra Memorandum of Understanding website at http://www.tetramou.com. Motorola markets its TETRA-compliant systems under the name of DIMETRA; see Motorola, "TETRA System Architecture," publication L0592 GBV 5 98–0.

tacted the European Radiocommunications Committee (ERC), which coordinates the use of radio spectrum in Europe, to "identify some harmonised spectrum for exclusive use by the police and security services across Europe."[75] ERC then negotiated with the North Atlantic Treaty Organization (NATO) to release initially six MHz, and later 10 MHz, of spectrum previously reserved for NATO use for such purposes.[76]

By 1993, the use of a harmonized spectrum had been broadened from law enforcement to all emergency services. The Schengen framework had been incorporated into the European Union's "third pillar,"[77] anchoring interoperability squarely within EU competency. At the same time, the European Telecommunications Standards Institute (ETSI)[78] initiated a fast-paced process for developing a TETRA standard for voice and data communications. Unlike the slow-moving inclusive process in the United States, ETSI proceeded swiftly. By 2000, more than 300 documents related to the TETRA standard had been published.[79]

Aware of ETSI's work, the Schengen group agreed upon a common communications specification and subsequently asked whether ETSI had a standard that met its specification.[80] ETSI replied that one of its standards, TETRA, did fulfill the specification. Although the European Union Police Co-ordination Council, which replaced the Schengen group when the Schengen framework was incorporated into the European Union, retained final decision power over the standard to be chosen for a Europe-wide interoperable communications system for public safety organizations, the choice for TETRA was a foregone conclusion.

In 1996, the ERC designated 10 MHz in the 380–400 MHz band for digital land mobile systems of emergency services.[81] A six MHz band was

---

75. ERC, "Harmonisation of Frequencies for Police and Security Services in Europe."

76. See also ERC, Harmonised Radio Frequency Channel Arrangements for Emergency Services Operating in the Band 380–400 MHz, Recommendation T/R 02–02 E (1993, revised 1997).

77. Treaty on European Union, articles 29–42, Official Journal C 340, 10.11.1997, pp. 145–172.

78. See http://portal.etsi.org/directives/home.asp.

79. These documents are available for download at http://www.etsi.org.

80. "ERC Decision of 7 March 1996 on the harmonised frequency band to be designated for the introduction of the Digital Land Mobile System for the Emergency Services" (ERC/DEC/(96)01).

81. Ibid. "1. To designate the bands 380–385 MHz and 390–395 MHz as frequency bands within which the requirements of the digital land mobile system be met[.]"

to be made available by 1998, with the remaining four MHz to follow shortly thereafter. Only systems compliant with ETSI standards were permitted to be used, in effect restricting the 10 MHz use to TETRA-compliant hardware.[82] Unlike FCC mandates, ERC decisions are not automatically binding. European member states need to decide to implement ERC plans. And they did: by 2001, 26 European nations had set aside the frequency bands designated in the ERC decision.[83]

Only four European nations refused to accept the common TETRA frequency and standard: France, Sweden, the Czech Republic, and Slovakia. Repeating telecommunications history, France, which decades earlier had selected an incompatible television standard called SECAM while the rest of Europe settled on PAL, developed and deployed its own secure but completely incompatible system called TETRAPOL.[84] Later, France obtained a waiver from the European Union to proceed with TETRAPOL and, consequently, did not implement the ERC decision.[85] With French support Czechoslovakia, too, opted for TETRAPOL.[86]

French exceptionalism, however, cannot obscure what is a success story under any view. Within a single decade and despite its complex, multilevel decision-making structures, Europe agreed upon and implemented a continent-wide common frequency and a common communications standard based on TETRA technology. Together frequency and standard form the regulatory basis for comprehensive interoperability of public safety organization communications systems in Europe.

FUNDING: UTILIZING TECHNOLOGY TO ATTRACT PRIVATE INVESTMENT

Europe's public safety organizations are similar to their U.S. counterparts with respect to their communications systems. Most of them still use old analog systems, but they are considering a switch to new digital systems.

---

82. Ibid. "2. [T]hat for the purpose of this decision a single harmonised digital land mobile standard for emergency services, adopted by ETSI, shall be used in the designated frequency bands[.]"

83. See http://www.ero.dk/documentation/docs/implement.asp?docid?1493.

84. TETRAPOL is not a standard recognized by ETSI or the ITU; in fact the ETSI General Assembly rejected the TETRAPOL standard in its meeting of April 22–23, 1999. TETRAPOL's main proponents are French law enforcement agencies, as well as French telecommunications and military hardware vendors.

85. See the TETRAPOL website at http://www.tetrapol.com.

86. Czechoslovakia later split into the Czech Republic and Slovakia. The fourth nation not signing on to the ERC decision, Sweden, did not want to dedicate the frequency band (designated by the ERC) exclusively to emergency services.

According to an EU estimate, most European public safety organizations will have moved to an interoperable digital system by 2010.[87] Unfortunately, as in the United States, finding sufficient funding for this replacement is going to be difficult. But unlike the United States and its budget deficits, European nations are still scrambling to balance their budgets in compliance with the Maastricht criteria of monetary union and the ensuing "stability pact." Only very limited public funding will be available, and, given reduced tax revenues due to the global recession, these dire financial circumstances may continue for some time. The need for substantial capital to rebuild Europe's public safety communications infrastructure could hardly have come at a more inopportune time.

Interestingly, however, European governments have not wavered in their commitment to interoperability. Instead, with the budget crisis as a backdrop, they looked at what the new communications networks could offer, not primarily in terms of monetary *needs*, but of monetary *savings*. For example, the Belgian government has instituted the ASTRID program, creating a nationwide TETRA-based digital radio infrastructure to be *shared* by all Belgian public service agencies.[88] This sharing arrangement saves agencies significant amounts of money, because it avoids the inefficiency of having multiple networks—one for each agency—covering the same or overlapping geographic areas.

Sharing communications infrastructure like transmitters and relay stations is nothing novel. In the United States, some agencies have been sharing infrastructure for years, and reports examining potential strategies for funding improvements in communications systems have advocated sharing arrangements as a way of reducing costs.[89] Simple sharing arrangements require that two or more agencies decide to share the cost of building infrastructure. But often procurement cycles and funding opportunities vary among communications agencies. Securing funding—hard already—is almost impossible to obtain at any specific moment in time. One could, of course, envision a sharing arrangement in which one agency, having received funding, builds the agreed-upon network and later lets another agency use it, perhaps for a fee. But why should one agency shoulder all the risk in building an infrastructure when it is uncertain that others will join?

---

87. See, e.g., ERC, "Harmonisation of Frequencies for Police and Security Services in Europe."

88. "ASTRID TETRA Network," available online at http://www.mobilecomms-technology.com/projects/astrid/index.html.

89. See PSWN, "Report on Funding Strategy," pp. 6–1 et seq.

This is a fundamental dilemma in funding network infrastructures. The early adopters of a new communications technology bear a higher risk than latecomers. Because it seems that acting early does not pay, everybody waits for others to make the first move. Political scientists call this a "collective-action problem."[90]

There are a number of ways that the collective-action problem can be overcome. An obvious one is for one agency to shoulder the financial burden when it needs an infrastructure anyway and the cost for permitting others to share is minimal. Or, an agency leader may just desire to be entrepreneurial, but these are exceptions. In most cases, public safety agencies have neither the funds nor the entrepreneurial spirit. A more promising solution is to have central coordination: the government steps in and finances the infrastructure buildup, shouldering the risk as a public good. This is precisely what the Belgian government did in the ASTRID program. This solution, too, is not novel. In the United States, numerous state governments have already financed shared communications infrastructure.

There is an important difference, however, between shared analog (or early digital) communications networks and a shared comprehensive system *a la* TETRA. Because of the limited number of channels available and the inefficiency of assigning them manually, many of the shared U.S. systems cannot accommodate *local*, only state public safety agencies. (Project Hoosier SAFE-T currently in its early stages will provide a fully integrated trunked digital network for the state of Indiana and is a most laudable exception.)[91] Moreover, these systems generally do not manage communications based on message priority, and access to communications channels is purely first come, first served. In an emergency, such networks may quickly produce a lot of noise (communications of limited importance), making it hard for users to filter out truly important information.

By contrast, TETRA and similar systems efficiently manage channels and, hence, scale well. They are designed to incorporate many different agencies and, with priority codes and the creation of talk groups on the fly, guarantee the level of flexibility needed when truly sharing a network among different user groups. Like the packet-switched Internet, TETRA and comparable advanced systems provide a high level of resource

---

90. See Mançur Olson, *The Logic of Collective Action* (1971).

91. "Hoosier SAFE-T Communications System—Indiana Statewide Digital Radio System," available online at http://www.mobilecomms-technology.com/projects/indiana/index.html; see also PSWN, *Case Based Tutorials on Shared System Development—Coordination and Partnerships* (December 2001).

efficiency, enabling the infrastructure to be used by many different user groups. In other words, the Belgian public safety agencies using the ASTRID network receive more benefits for less cost than in traditional resource-sharing setups. Building a truly shared digital network involves successfully leveraging a first important technological advantage, but there is more to be gained.

WALKY-TALKY IN THE BURGENLAND

The Burgenland, situated right next to the border with Hungary, is one of Austria's poorest states.[92] For 30 years, the state EMS agency had used the same analog radio system to communicate with its 70 EMS vehicles and seven base stations. By 1998, establishing radio communications had become difficult. Hungarian taxicab radio routinely interfered, and a national law constrained the organization from using more transmission power. The equipment was just too old.

Searching for a new radio system, Walter Adorjan, the EMS agency's radio officer, came across a group of entrepreneurs; soon they found common ground. In early 1999, Walky-Talky was incorporated. It had a simple mission: to build a statewide TETRA network infrastructure and to let public service agencies use it for a fee.

Having a private company construct and maintain the network infrastructure required for a shared communications system provides a number of advantages over public financing of a shared network. First, it requires no initial investment from the public sector. The network is built by a private sector actor that arguably has better financing expertise than a public sector organization and a keener desire to keep expenses in check. Agencies are charged a monthly flat fee per radio handset for using the network. This permits them to budget sensibly and to switch to the new network without having to pay up front for all, or even a portion, of the initial investment. Agencies have to purchase handsets[93] (although Walky-Talky has negotiated attractive agreements with Nokia, which operates a research center close by, for leasing handsets). The network provider calculates the monthly flat fee that it charges agencies based on the volume that it thinks it can attract and, thus, does not penalize early adopters. As with all network infrastructures, the setup offers strong incentives to the network provider to sign up more agencies to use the service. Although this does not solve the collective-action problem, it

---

92. The section is based on interviews by the author with Walky-Talky operators, users, and political decision-makers in September 2000, with follow-up interviews in November 2001.

93. Prices for radios range from $400 for a handset radio to $800 for a car radio.

shifts it to the network provider, who arguably has more expertise than agencies in how to overcome it. For example, as with other telecommunications markets, fee structures are possible that provide incentives for agencies to switch and the earlier the switch, the cheaper.

Walky-Talky took in Austria's incumbent telecommunications provider Telekom Austria and a private sector arm of the state government as equity partners.[94] In October 1999, Burgenland's EMS agency became Walky-Talky's first customer. In 2000, the network covered in excess of 90 percent of the entire state with capital investment of little more than $3.5 million. 25 fixed transmitter/relay stations and two portable transmitters were deployed, supporting 600 radios (and growing fast) and their users, from firefighters to law enforcement agencies.

Quickly Walky-Talky developed an understanding (and appreciation) for the different usage patterns of public safety agencies and for the way TETRA systems handled traffic. For example, EMS agencies have baseline traffic all day, as they tend to routine tasks and smaller accidents. Communication traffic swells in the case of a larger accident. In contrast, the traffic pattern for local firefighter units, consisting mostly of volunteers, is quite different: ordinarily there is almost no communication traffic, but once there is a fire, dozens and dozens of users have to be contacted at once. Whereas EMS agencies use a communications network continuously, firefighters essentially pay for its being provided in case of an emergency. This leaves a typical public safety network, over-provisioned to accommodate even heavy traffic in case of a large emergency, underutilized. Adding user groups with more continuous communication needs, like EMS or law enforcement agencies, may somewhat balance the load in times of no or only small emergencies. But the benefits of such a balance are lost once a large emergency requires all agencies —firefighters, police, and EMS—to use the radio network very actively.

What Walky-Talky needed, as a supplement to its public safety usage base, were public sector users that would want continuous, but not time-critical, communication. In times of emergencies, such users would find it acceptable to wait a few seconds (or even longer) for a free channel. Walky-Talky found such users not among public *safety* but among public *service* agencies with communication needs. Soon, highway gritting trucks were connected as well as park rangers and environmental protection officers. The TETRA network was used to transmit street temperature and other weather data along the interstate to central command and to control ice warning signals. With TETRA's built-in capability to

---

94. See Peter Martos, "5-Milliarden-Projekt Adonis wird vom Anbieter finanziert," *Die Presse*, October 31, 2001.

prioritize automatically depending on who wants to communicate, emergency agencies do not have to fear that weather data will constrain their communication needs during emergencies.

As we have seen, old analog public safety communications networks are inefficient from an economic perspective: their capacity is underutilized, except during emergencies. Sharing network infrastructures among public safety agencies, like the Belgian ASTRID network, will permit agencies to share the cost of building and maintaining the infrastructure. It will still be underutilized outside of emergencies, but at least every agency will not have to operate its own overprovisioned and underutilized network and, instead, will share it with other agencies. Walky-Talky takes this idea an important step further. Because of TETRA's communications prioritization capabilities, it can reach out to public *service* agencies with non-time-critical communication demands and, thus, truly balance network traffic loads. The enhanced network efficiency that results from such a balancing translates into higher revenues and, ultimately, lower costs for users. The success of Walky-Talky has prompted the Austrian government to abandon its initial plan, accelerated after the Galtuer tragedy, to construct a shared nationwide emergency communications network. Instead, it has asked the private sector to build it, based on TETRA.[95]

Would it then, one may ask, not make sense to extend the user base of such a TETRA network even further and have private corporations use the network as well? In theory, built-in communication prioritization should ensure that public safety organizations automatically get access to resources (channels) whenever they need to have it, and business users could provide an even better "load balancer" than public service organizations in nonemergency times. Walky-Talky, however, is reluctant to take on private users. It maintains that keeping its market limited to public sector users is prudent, not least of all for marketing reasons. It wants to be successful in convincing agencies to switch to an infrastructure that these agencies do not have immediate physical control over, and it feels that opening up the network to private sector use may make this task more difficult. Moreover (and more importantly), it points out that across Europe, the use of the 400 MHz band is reserved for the public sector.

Walky-Talky in the Burgenland sounds like a fairy tale, and, with only 600 radios, the size of the network is limited. A thousand miles northwest, however, the idea of a privately built and run TETRA network for public service agencies is rapidly turning into reality in a nation of

---

95. Ibid.

over 50 million people. The British government set out to use a funding mechanism similar to that employed by Walky-Talky for the creation and maintenance of a nationwide TETRA-based network infrastructure for the United Kingdom. The contract, worth £ 2.5 billion, was awarded to British Telecom (BT).[96] Understanding the economies of sharing a network and having selected a trustworthy private sector player to build the infrastructure, the government also decided to boost the new venture with an impressive "launch customer": all police forces in England, Wales, and Scotland. For the next 19 years, BT's TETRA-based Airwave network will provide the communications backbone not just for the police forces. Under the contract's terms, other public safety organizations may contract with BT and use the network. Lancashire's police were the first to use the system in March 2001.[97] By April 2001, Lancashire's fire service had signed on to Airwave and started using it the same year.[98] The rollout to all police forces is scheduled to be completed by 2005, with other public safety organizations added county by county.[99] Liberally defining public *safety* organizations more closely along the lines of public *service* agencies, the British government in 2000 released a long list of agencies permitted to use Airwave.[100] The list was later expanded to include even more public service agencies, like community health professionals and personnel of the environmental agency. In August 2001, the Ministry of Defense signed on to Airwave, extending coverage to additional user groups.[101] The Airwave network will replace aging noninteroperable technology for tens of thousands of users in a nation of over 50 million people, and the public will not have to pay a penny for the initial network buildup.[102]

---

96. "BT Wins Its Biggest Ever Government Contract to Set Up Police Digital Radio Service" (March 8, 2000).

97. "BT's Airwave Service Goes Live in Lancashire Today" (March 19, 2001).

98. "BT Signs First Airwave Contract With Fire Service" (April 25, 2001).

99. See http://www.airwaveservice.co.uk/Rolloutmap.cfm.

100. Department of Trade and Industry, "Users of Airwave Allowed Under the License," available online at http://www.airwaveservice.co.uk/attachments/allowedusers.doc.

101. "MoD Opens the Doors to BT's Airwave" (August 2, 2001).

102. Similar systems are under construction on the Isle of Man and in Malta. See "Isle of Man TETRA Radio System," available online at http://www.mobilecomms-technology.com/projects and "Malta Mobile Communications Network," available online at http://www.mobilecomms-technology.com/projects/malta/index.html; for a comprehensive assessment of the crucial factors to assess fee-for-service networks and how to best build them, see PSWN, *Fee-for-Service Report* (October 2001).

Enabling Collective Action

The need for public safety agencies to communicate through inter-operable radio networks is obvious. Of the three hurdles to developing this capacity identified earlier in this paper, the first—creating the appropriate technology—has turned out to be the least difficult to clear. Agreeing on common rules and creating a suitable funding mechanism, on the other hand, seem to be much more troubling issues (See Table 1).

Underlying these second and third hurdles is the same problem: how does one get a heterogeneous group of stakeholders to act, when the ones who take the first step are the ones who may have to pay the highest cost and, thus, reap the least benefits? Implementing interoperability requires one to overcome these two distinct collective-action problems.

When economist Mançur Olson analyzed collective action in his seminal study, he discovered that stakeholders would act if they could identify selective benefits and costs.[103] People, he maintained, are joining and working for interest groups and lobbying groups not primarily for the greater good of influencing public policy, but because these groups provide a very concrete, specific service for them. Consequently, public policies requiring collective action have to employ specific strategies to provide incentives for individual stakeholder action. Very generally speaking, two such strategies have been identified.[104] First, governments can take a "command-and-control" approach, mandating a certain behavior and prompting stakeholders to fall in line either by threatening them with fines or taxes or by inducing them to do so with subsidies. This "type-1" strategy has been the standard public policy approach for many decades. A second type of strategy that has gained some currency in recent decades focuses less on central decision-making and direct financial incentives. Instead, the "type-2" strategy turns to market forces and the private sector to provide an incentive framework. In the area of environmental policies, for example, polluters could be prompted to act either by direct regulatory mandates, enforced by fines or the loss of permits. Such strategies represent the "command-and-control" approach. But polluters could also be given "polluting rights" that could be traded

---

103. Olson, *The Logic of Collective Action* (1971).

104. Recently, a third strategy, called "management-based regulatory strategies," which has not been used either in the United States or in Europe in the TETRA context (and thus will be omitted in this essay) but holds tremendous promise, has been added to the toolset; see Cary Coglianese and David Lazer, "Management-Based Regulatory Strategies," KSG Regulatory Policy Program Working Paper No. RPP-2001–09 (July 2001).

Table 1. Strategies Used to Overcome Hurdles.

	Frequency/Standard Hurdle	Funding Hurdle
United States	Deliberative process	Offering some federal funding and some coordination
European Union	Swiftly setting up frequency and standard	Public-private partnerships

on markets. Polluters could invest in cleaner systems and gain financially from selling their polluting rights on the markets to others who continue to pollute but have to pay the price for it. Such an approach is more market-based and (as it lacks a commanding center) more network-centric. Neither strategy is inherently better in the abstract. The real trick is to select the appropriate strategy for a concrete collective-action problem, taking into account its specific context.

Very different strategies have been used by the United States and Europe to overcome the collective-action problems hampering the move to communication interoperability in the two areas.

ENABLING COLLECTIVE ACTION FOR A COMMON FREQUENCY AND STANDARD

In the quest for a common frequency and standard, at first sight, both the United States and Europe chose a traditional command-and-control approach. Yet the authorities in the United States hesitated to exercise their power. Instead, the FCC employed an inclusive, deliberative approach, involving as many stakeholders as possible and attempted to forge consensus and accommodate stakeholders even after the fact, as exemplified by its decision to modify its rules, once it encountered criticism from stakeholders. Its goal was a broad based buy-in: to convince the stakeholders that interoperability provided each of them with selective benefits by adding as many of their specific demands (like backward compatibility with legacy equipment) as possible to the overall interoperability policy. In contrast, the Europeans emphasized swiftness of process and the need for a "leap forward," a substantial break with the past. To be sure, stakeholders were involved, but the driving force was a desire to integrate and innovate, even if it meant a break with the past.

Institutionally, the FCC had a strong formal mandate and the unchallenged power to set the rules, yet it opted to facilitate the process more than to drive it. On the other hand, in Europe, players with comparatively weak formal powers—the intergovernmental pillar of the European Union, the ERC, and ETSI—pursued an ambitious course based on central coordination and leadership. This difference is intriguing. Facilitation to prompt buy-in and strong coordination through central leadership are common type-1 strategies to overcome collective-action problems. This fact should not surprise us. It is odd, though, that an institution with the power to push for central command-and-control chose facilitation, whereas its European counterparts, relatively weak on formal power, chose the opposite. One would think that neither of them selected a strategy aligned with its abilities. Yet one has succeeded—much more so than the other.

At first, it seems difficult to understand why the Europeans opted for a riskier approach with less power for national stakeholders, especially as the United States, usually more prone to risk taking, pursued the opposite path. Intuitively, one would have guessed things would have worked the other way around. But prior experiences, the path dependencies of the institutional structure that was involved in selecting a standard and frequency, may have played a decisive role. The FCC is attuned to deliberate processes, involving private and public sector stakeholders. Taking small, sensible evolutionary steps with long transition stages has played an important role in maintaining predictability and investment security for all involved in areas of FCC authority. It has been the blueprint for formulating regulations governing media and telecommunications—two sectors that have achieved sustained growth. Surely, the FCC must have thought that achieving public safety interoperability presents a similar challenge and will respond to a similar approach.

By the same token, the European institutions, too, remembered their successes.[105] In the late 1980s, they picked the fledging Groupe Special Mobile (GSM) standard for mobile telephony, creating a pan-European cellular phone market of tremendous proportions and establishing a global standard for mobile telephony more successful than any of its rivals. The GSM standard was chosen swiftly, without many years of deliberation. The EU selected it and declared it a winner—and it worked.[106] Enamored with this overwhelming success, the Europeans decided again to pick a winner, and they did. It seems that picking a winner and stick-

---

105. The result may have been different if they had also remembered picking losers, like the European digital television standard DMAC; see Xuidian Dai, Alan Cawson, et al., "The Rise and Fall of High Definition Television: The Impact of European Technology," *Journal of Common Market Studies*, Vol. 34, No. 2 (June 1996), pp. 149–166.

106. See Jacques Pelkmans, "The GSM-Standard: Explaining a Success Story," *Journal of European Public Policy* 432 (2001).

ing to it considerably shapes the playing field in favor of the selected. It is not enough to ensure success, but it certainly is of great assistance.

Understanding this path dependency helps to explain why the United States and the Europeans acted the ways that they did when facing essentially the same situation with respect to fostering interoperability of public safety communications systems. It does not explain, however, why one strategy was successful, and the other was not. We may have to look at and analyze the third hurdle to do that.

INTEROPERABILITY FUNDING: ENABLING COLLECTIVE ACTION WHERE IT
MATTERS

In the quest to establish appropriate sources of funding, the United States opted for public funding, with federal funds for the early stages. Unlike in selecting a common frequency and standard, the emphasis in funding was more on central leadership and coordination, less on process facilitation. In principle, this seemed an appropriate approach: federal and state budget surpluses enabled a command-and-control funding approach based on subsidies to be taken. Yet neither Congress nor many of the states decided to offer generous nationwide funding to upgrade public safety agencies' communications networks. Subsidies are a tried and proven strategy to overcome the funding hurdle, but the implementation of the subsidy programs was so haphazard that it largely failed. It was a missed opportunity. U.S. policymakers drastically underutilized the power of their purse (see Table 2).

On the other hand, the Europeans opted for a type-2 strategy to overcome the collective action hurdle: an untried market-based approach.[107] Did the Europeans suddenly turn themselves into public sector entrepreneurs? Unlikely. The European decision was almost completely driven by budgetary constraints. As there were no public funds available to finance the conversion to interoperable systems, alternatives had to be sought. The ingenuity, perhaps uncovered accidentally, was to leverage the power of the technology: (a) to share the infrastructure among the stakeholders and more importantly, (b) to create a private sector funding opportunity. Innovation occurred when there was no alternative option left. Surely, previous successes in taking risks had whetted their appetite to try a risk taking approach again.

---

107. It is important to note, however, that such private-public partnerships have very recently become more common in the United States. Four projects, in Florida, Illinois, and South Carolina as well as through the Federal Specialized Mobile Radio System (FEDSMR) were underway in 2001, with the first deployment expected in early 2002; see the insightful report PSWN, "Fee-for-Service Report."

Table 2. Types of Strategies Used to Overcome Collective-Action Hurdles.

	Frequency/Standard Hurdle	Funding Hurdle
United States	Type-1 strategy, but implementation underutilized available resources	Type-1 strategy, but implementation underutilized available resources
European Union	Type-1 strategy, successful in utilizing available resources	Type-2 strategy, successful in utilizing available resources

Clearly, path dependencies present may explain the actions taken, but not why one was a success and the other was not. A key to understanding the European successes lies in the successful alignment of means and ends, of strategies and context.

Transatlantic Lessons for Interoperability Policy

A number of important lessons can be learned from this analysis, both for U.S. public policy decision-makers, who—especially in the wake of the events of September 11, 2001—understand the importance of interoperability and want to correct previous missteps and accelerate the process of achieving it, and for those interested the broader picture of innovation and competitiveness in times of crisis.

PRAGMATIC STEPS TOWARD U.S. INTEROPERABILITY

There is no silver bullet for defining the most appropriate policy to provide interoperability of communications systems for public safety organizations. The best approach depends on the political contexts and the policymakers' strengths and weaknesses, as well as the type of "selective benefits" that will sway stakeholders to act. It would be shortsighted to attempt to transplant to the United States the solutions that worked for Europe. The Europeans were successful because the strategy they chose to overcome the two collective-action issues—commonality of frequency and standard and funding—were well aligned with their capacities and the overall political context in which they were operating. They played the cards that they were dealt very well.

Consequently, to achieve interoperability (perhaps sooner than originally planned), U.S. policymakers have to select a strategy based on the available means. For example, given the emphasis on domestic preparedness and homeland security, stakeholders today are clearly prepared to accept more central command and control. As a result, the FCC could now be more forceful than it has been in the past in freeing up frequency spectrum for interoperability before 2007 and in embracing technological standards more attuned to current technological possibilities.[108]

On the funding side, too, changed budget priorities as a result of the war against terrorism may make it feasible to establish more substantial federal and state-sponsored interoperability funds than before. Offering subsidies to tens of thousands of public safety agencies that make interoperability-related investments provides a very immediate "selective benefit" and will prompt them to act. Given the selected standard and the power lineup, this seems to be the most sensible strategy. Alternatively, one could of course also envision a market-driven funding strategy, akin to Britain's Airwave initiative or Walky-Talky. For such a type-2 strategy to succeed, however, the interoperability standard would probably have to be amended to ensure that calls could be prioritized (the prerequisite for sharing the infrastructure among public *service* agencies).

BROADER LESSONS FOR INNOVATION THROUGH PUBLIC POLICY

But there is more to the story. Perhaps one ought to look not so much at what differentiates the European strategy for establishing a common frequency and standard and obtaining the necessary funding from the ones in the United States than at what the two European strategies have in common. The Europeans overcame the standards hurdle and the funding hurdle by opting for less conventional, riskier solutions. Instead of deliberations, they swiftly identified and declared a "winner." This tactic can be dangerous, because they could have picked the "wrong" standard, a technologically inferior one, or one too advanced, requiring too much adaptation at too high a cost. But it seems that the sheer fact of picking a winner, announcing a strategy, and sticking to it created an environment conducive to success. Similarly, the funding hurdle seemed insurmountable. The Europeans succeeded in overcoming it by not attacking it through traditional means but by opting for an alternative, untried strategy. They took, perhaps out of necessity, the riskier route. In sum, the European strategies to overcome each of the two collective-action problems were similar. They were well aligned with and reinforced each other. The success of the strategy chosen for taking one hurdle bolstered the belief that that was the way to take the second as well.

Moreover, the Europeans aligned their overall strategy well with the first hurdle: technology. Unlike in the United States, where technology

---

108. The post–September 11, 2001, declaration of Project 25 and TETRA representatives that they will work toward a joint standard may be an early indication for some forward movement in these areas.

seemed to be either a given or something to be decided by consensus, the Europeans chose a technology that permitted them to overcome another obstacle, the funding hurdle. Traditionally one would see little connection between the choice of technology and the funding structures (apart from the amount of money needed to acquire the technology chosen). Only by leveraging the unique properties of digital trunked networks could the Europeans create an opportunity for the successful public-private partnerships that we have seen. The European perception that technology is neither an external constraint nor or an unrelated decision, but intricately linked to the social context of its use, reinforced the belief that interoperability requires a clear, comprehensive strategy. The United States, on the other hand, used two very different strategies to take the two hurdles. Hence, no similar strategic reinforcement could occur. Thus, a much broader (and perhaps simpler) lesson can then be drawn from the case of developing interoperability in public safety communications: when faced with interconnected collective-action problems, it may be most advantageous to devise a comprehensive strategy to tackle the entire issue and not just distinct parts.

Conclusions

This essay analyzed the activities in the United States and Europe over the last decade designed to solve the complex problem of interoperability of public safety organization communications systems. It identified three hurdles that have to be overcome to make such interoperability a reality: technology, common frequency and standard, and funding. It laid out the major debates for each of these hurdles on both sides of the Atlantic and their internal dynamic. So far, the Europeans are clearly ahead of the United States in the quest to implement such interoperability.

Policymakers concerned about interoperability may want to take a page from the European strategy and understand the importance of strategic alignment. The FCC could modify its stance and actively pursue an accelerated move toward a common frequency and standard. Federal, state, and even local governments could reassess their priorities and decide to fund a substantial part of the cost of transition from current systems to interoperable ones, under the assumption that interoperable communication networks are a "public good." Putting bruised egos aside, these may be the best options to put interoperability back on (the fast) track.

Policymakers who are more generally concerned with overcoming collective-action problems, as one frequently encounters in the network economies, may benefit from understanding the spectrum of solutions tried on the path to interoperability and their successes and failures. Examining the European strategy, the ingredients for its success become obvious: strong agency leadership, intentional risk taking, and public entrepreneurship were combined in a comprehensive overall strategy. It created a reinforcing belief in winning and the understanding that one may pick technology based on future requirements, not present needs. Leadership and risk taking entrepreneurship are not generally associated with Europe. But previous successes in both have made the Europeans more American. Strangely, the Americans—risk-averse, deliberative, and haphazard—seem to have become more European. These are core lessons to be drawn from a decade of interoperability policy. Instilling leadership, the willingness to take risks, and the ability to inject comprehensive strategies into the U.S. policy machinery may be the most promising long-term approach to public management and the most needed one.

But one must never forget: leadership, risk taking, and comprehensive strategic thinking are just the tools. The goal of interoperability is to have firefighters communicating seamlessly with their brethren from EMS, police officers, and the innumerable other first responders. When on September 11, 2001, the Pentagon stood ablaze, almost a decade after the first World Trade Center bombing and years after the Columbine High School shootings, responding fire companies from Maryland once again could not communicate with those from Washington, D.C., and Northern Virginia.[109] Runners had to be used instead—a shocking reminder of a crisis unsolved.

---

109. See Steve Twoney and Carol D. Leonnig, "Rush Is On to Boost Region's Response to Terror Attacks," *Washington Post*, September 30, 2001, p. A01.

Part IV
Lessons Learned from International Cases

Israel's Preparedness for High Consequence Terrorism

Ariel Merari

Since its creation in 1948, Israel has had to contend with the constant threat of terrorism. To meet this challenge, Israel has created and maintained an elaborate counterterrorism system. Much of the Israeli effort has focused on developing defensive measures designed to prevent attacks on the civilian population and minimize casualties. Israel has developed this strategy for two reasons. First, most Palestinian terrorist attacks as well as a smaller, yet significant, number of attacks by Lebanese groups have been random attacks against civilians. Second, all Israeli governments have been highly sensitive to civilian casualties.

In this essay, the term "high-consequence terrorism" refers to terrorist attacks that result in high numbers of casualties. To maximize casualties, terrorists may use large amounts of conventional explosives (e.g., car bombs); apply unique methods, such as crashing a hijacked airliner into a city neighborhood; or employ weapons of mass destruction (WMD), specifically chemical and biological agents. The focus of this essay is preparedness against WMD attacks.

The essay consists of four main sections. The first section is a review of Israel's experience with terrorism. It examines the form and scope of the problem and the countermeasures that Israel has adopted to deal with this persistent threat. The second section describes Israel's effort to prevent high-consequence conventional attacks. The third section examines Israel's preparedness for WMD attacks. This section describes the organization, responsibilities, and procedures related to the management of a WMD attack. The fourth section considers the debate in Israel concerning investment in preparations against a WMD attack. The essay ends with some observations on preparations.

An Overview of the Terrorist Threat and Israel's Responses

The Palestinian-Arab struggle against Israel has taken many forms: civil disobedience, riots, guerrilla warfare, several conventional wars fought by Arab states with minor Palestinian participation, and, of course, terrorism.[1]

PALESTINIAN TERRORISM

In the last quarter century, the terrorist campaign against Israel has been carried out mainly by organized Palestinian groups.[2] These groups have maintained offices and bases in Arab countries that have also been their main source of financial and logistical support.

The Palestinian organizations have been among the largest insurgent groups in the world, considerably larger than West European groups and similar in size and military capability to the Mujahedeen in Afghanistan and the Union for the Total Independence for Angola (UNITA). If other constituents of power that contribute to the overall strength of an organization, such as international political support and economic strength are factored in, the Palestinian organizations probably have been unparalleled worldwide.

From 1971 until the beginning of the second *intifada* (or popular uprisings) in September 2000, the annual number of Palestinian terrorist incidents has ranged from less than 200 to nearly 600.[3] About 80 percent

---

1. There are many definitions of terrorism that emphasize different aspects of this form of warfare. For an extensive survey and comparative analysis, see A. P. Schmid and A. J. Jongman, *Political Terrorism* (Amsterdam: North-Holland, 1988). In this paper, the main differences between terrorism and guerrilla warfare are the following: terrorists do not try to establish control of a territory (e.g., create "liberated zones"); guerrillas use relatively large units in operations—platoons, companies, or sometimes battalions or brigades—whereas terrorist operations involve very few people; and guerrillas use mainly regular armies' weapons and tactics, whereas terrorists employ specialized weapons and techniques (e.g., car bombs, improvised explosive charges, hijacking, and sophisticated bombs onboard aircraft).

2. Since 1982, Israel has also had to cope with Shi'ite groups. This strife, however, has been almost exclusively conducted in the form of guerrilla warfare on Lebanese territory.

3. From June 1967 until their expulsion from Jordan in September 1970, the Palestinian groups' main effort took the form of a guerrilla campaign against Israel, waged from neighboring Arab countries, particularly from Jordan. Their attacks included shelling across the border, mining roads, and ambushing. During that period there were 3,425 incidents along the Jordanian border, 346 incidents along the Syrian border, and 181 incidents along the Lebanese border. These figures exceeded by far the num-

of the attacks have been directed against civilians; the rest have targeted military installations and personnel. 45 percent of the attacks on civilian targets have consisted of explosive bombing; 28 percent, fire bombing; 14 percent, artillery shelling of towns and villages from across the border; and five percent, armed assaults. Two types of incidents have had particularly deep psychological and political impact: hostage incidents and suicide bombing attacks. The numbers of incidents and casualties have risen dramatically during the two years since the start of the second Palestinian *intifada*. In those two years, more than 600 Israelis have been killed in about 13,000 attacks, and the toll continues to rise weekly.[4] Yet, it remains true that a relatively low number of indiscriminate, spectacular terrorist attacks account for many of Israel's high casualty incidents. In 1974, for example, there were several such incidents, including the explosion in midair of a Trans World Airways (TWA) airliner (88 fatalities), the Kiryat Shmona attack[5] (18 fatalities), and the Ma'alot incident[6] (24 fatalities). In 1978, 35 of the 63 fatalities reported were passengers massacred on a bus hijacked along the coastal highway between Haifa and Tel Aviv. In the second *intifada,* as of September 2002, nearly half of the Israeli fatalities have been caused by about 80 suicide attacks, which have constituted less than one percent of the total number of terrorist incidents.

Palestinian terrorist operations can be divided into three categories: domestic attacks, operations launched against Israel from bases across the border, and international attacks.

---

ber of incidents inside Israel and the Territories. See Yehoshua Raviv, "Bitkhon Israel Ba'shana Ha'shlishit Le'milkhemet Sheshet Ha'yamim" [Israel's security in the third year after the Six Day War], *Ma'arachot,* January 1970, (Hebrew); and Hanan Alon, *Countering Palestinian Terrorism in Israel: Towards a Policy Analysis of Countermeasures* (Santa Monica, Calif.: RAND Corporation, 1980).

4. Testimony of BG Eli Amitai, the Head of the IDF Operations Division at the hearing of the Knesset's Committee of Foreign Affaris and Security, *Ha'aretz,* July 24, 2002, p. A5.

5. On April 11, 1974, a team of three members of the Popular Front for the Liberation of Palestine General Command penetrated the Israeli border town of Kiryat Shmona from Lebanon. Although they had apparently been instructed to take hostages, they instead entered an apartment building and killed all 18 residents that they found there, including nine children. The terrorists then barricaded themselves in one of the apartments and were eventually killed in an exchange of fire with Israeli forces.

6. On May 15, 1974, a team of three members of the Democratic Front for the Liberation of Palestine crossed the border into Israel from Lebanon and took more than 90 high school students hostage. A military rescue operation was launched when the terrorists, who had threatened to kill the hostages and commit suicide, refused to extend the deadline that they had set. During the rescue mission, one of the terrorists threw hand grenades at the hostages and sprayed them with automatic fire.

DOMESTIC TERRORISM

This first category includes attacks by local Palestinians within Israel and in the Administered Territories (hereafter referred to as the Territories). Domestic terrorism accounts for more than 90 percent of all terrorist incidents directed against Israel since 1970.[7] Most of these attacks have involved the placement of improvised explosive charges in public places. Until 1985, almost all domestic incidents in this category had been perpetrated by individuals or cells recruited, directed, and supplied by one of the Palestinian organizations—most often Fatah (the largest group of the Palestine Liberation Organization or PLO). From 1985 until the end of the first *intifada*, however, the proportion of "spontaneous" attacks—that is, incidents perpetrated by individuals affiliated with an organized group —grew steadily and constituted more than half of all domestic terrorist incidents. From the signing of the 1993 Oslo agreement between Israel and the PLO until the start of the second *intifada*, the majority of the attacks (including all spectacular, high-casualty incidents) have been perpetrated by organized groups, especially the fundamentalist Hamas and Palestinian Islamic Jihad (PIJ). In the second *intifada*, Fatah again has been responsible for most of the terrorist attacks, although Hamas has kept the lead in suicide attacks.

THE BORDER ARENA

Cross-border attacks in this category consist of two main forms: shelling across the border and incursions of terrorist teams into Israel. Cross-border shelling has been more common, but incursions have been considerably more disturbing. Practically all Palestinian terrorist organizations at one point or another have attempted to inject terrorist teams into Israel to carry out barricade-hostage incidents or engage in mass-killing operations. Almost all of these attacks were thwarted in process. Of those cross-border interdictions that have succeeded, some resulted in high casualties and caused a great shock in Israel, as was the case in the May 1974 attack in the town of Ma'alot in Northern Israel, in which 22 high school students were killed and more than 60 were wounded.

INTERNATIONAL TERRORISM

This last category includes attacks by Palestinian groups on Israeli, Jewish, Western, and Arab targets outside the borders of Israel and the Territories. The attacks started in 1968 and waxed and waned over the years

---

7. Estimates of domestic and border rates of terrorist attacks are based on Israeli Defense Forces press releases, IDF intelligence directorate reports, Israel police reports, and the database of the Political Violence Research Unit at Tel Aviv University.

for various reasons.[8] Their number ranged from 13 in 1975 to 85 in 1986. Since 1968, there have been 748 international Palestinian terrorist incidents, but only 206 of these were directed against Israeli targets. Since 1984, there have been only seven attacks against Israeli targets by Iranian-sponsored groups, especially Hizballah, outside Lebanon and Israel.[9]

ISRAELI COUNTERMEASURES

In many respects, the Israeli public and government have regarded terrorism as a war rather than as a problem of law and order that merely requires suitable police measures. Israel has perceived Palestinian terrorism as an existential problem, an extension of the comprehensive Arab struggle against the Jewish state. This perception, which has influenced all aspects of Israel's response to terrorism, was the result of the declared goal of the Palestinian groups to annihilate the state of Israel; the fact that the Palestinian struggle was taking place within the broader political-strategic context of the Arab confrontation with Israel; and the assistance that Arab states provided to the Palestinian groups.

As surprising as it may seem, Israel has never formally devised a comprehensive doctrine or strategy for dealing with Palestinian political violence. In agglomeration, however, the measures that Israel has taken to fight terrorism amount to a *de facto* strategy. For better or for worse, Israel has developed countermeasures to respond to problems as they have arisen, rather than conducting an assessment of the overall threat and then planning a comprehensive set of responses.[10] The result has been an extremely practical and efficient policy of combating terrorism. However, this policy has at least three major drawbacks.

First, it reflects an apparent lack of strategic planning: Israel has always preferred to leave the conceptual initiative to its adversaries. As a result, Israel was surprised and unprepared when Palestinian organizations started a campaign of international terrorism in 1968 and again in

---

8. See John W. Amos, *Palestinian Resistance: Organization of a Nationalist Movement* (New York: Pergamon Press, 1980); Ariel Merari and Shlomi Elad, *The International Dimension of Palestinian Terrorism* (Boulder, Colo.: Westview Press, 1986); and Yezid Sayegh, *Armed Struggle and the Search for State: The Palestinian National Movement, 1949–1993* (Oxford: Clarendon Press, 1997).

9. Data for the period 1968–1983 are based mainly on IDF press releases. The data after 1983 are derived from the database of Tel Aviv University's Political Violence Research Unit.

10. According to Alon, "the countermeasures taken by Israel were introduced gradually, in response to innovations taken by the Palestinian terrorists; countermeasures were introduced as crash programs, without a detailed analysis." Alon, *Countering Palestinian Terrorism in Israel*, p. viii.

1971, when the PLO shifted its main arena of operations from Jordan to Lebanon. In addition, Israel was caught off guard politically, strategically, and logistically when the first *intifada* erupted in December 1987. Israel has demonstrated a similar lack of foresight in the tactical domain. For example, only after an Israeli aircraft was hijacked in July 1968 (Israel's first such incident) were sky marshals put on board El Al airliners and measures taken to better screen passengers. Only after an El Al airliner was attacked on the tarmac, just six months later, did Israel invest in security measures for airplanes and passengers on the ground.

Second, Israel's lack of comprehensive strategic planning can be linked to its overall investment in the struggle against Palestinian terrorism and the allocation of resources to deal with this struggle. With regard to the relative proportion of funds for combating terrorism in the national budget, Hanan Alon has noted that Israeli countermeasures "were designed mainly to minimize the number of casualties inflicted by terrorism. Yet there seems to be a gross inequality between the amount of resources invested by Israel to counter terrorism and those allocations to counter other sources of casualties."[11]

Third and most important, Israel has not engaged in a strategic overview of its *ad hoc* counterterrorism policymaking procedures. In some cases, these policies have become institutionalized—despite their failure.[12] The most notable example is the policy of retaliation, which is discussed below.

Defensive Measures

Israel's greatest investment in combating terrorism has been, by far, in the development of defensive measures in all three categories of terrorist operations. All together, these measures have resulted in the thwarting of a high proportion of planned terrorist attacks and have undoubtedly been the single most effective category for coping with the terrorist threat.

TARGET HARDENING

Efforts to harden potential targets have focused on two types of terrorist operations: cross-border raids and attacks on Israeli installations abroad. This emphasis has been the result of the terrorist preference for launching spectacular raids in both types of operations and, again, has been reactive

---

11. Ibid, p. viii.

12. Ibid., pp. viii–ix.

rather than proactive. In practically all cases, Israeli investment in antiter-rorist measures came only after a terrorist attack.

Along its borders, Israel has built, at great cost, a complex counter-terrorist system comprising electronic fences, minefields, detection de-vices, and patrols. Israel has also invested in fortifying its diplomatic mis-sions abroad in response to the rise in international Palestinian terrorism. The main investment to counter international terrorism, however, has been in civil aviation security. Measures designed to prevent terrorist at-tacks on passengers and aircraft from takeoff to landing have been insti-tuted piecemeal in response to a series of terrorist attacks in the late 1960s and early 1970s.

Target hardening within Israel has centered mainly on border vil-lages. Here, too, decisions have been made on the basis of actual experi-ence rather than on foresight. Border villages have been fortified only after they became an evident target for terrorist attacks. Public places, such as theaters, museums, supermarkets, government buildings, and schools (including kindergartens), have guards posted at their entrances to check visitors' bags.

PUBLIC PARTICIPATION

Public participation has been one of the cornerstones of Israeli defensive measures against terrorism in the domestic arena. In July 1974, in the wake of a series of hostage incidents earlier that year, the government es-tablished a civil guard. Designed as a civilian volunteer force, subordi-nate to the national police, the guard established units in all urban locales. In 1982, the civil guard had 84,000 volunteers and 1,200 com-manders and paid staff.[13] The guard's ranks dwindled in the 1980s and 1990s, when spectacular terrorist attacks inside the country were rare but has grown again during the second *intifada*, which started in September 2000. Over the years, the civil guard has been used increasingly as an auxiliary police force, undertaking ordinary police duties. By an official Israel Police account of 2002, the guard included about 50,000 volunteers, of whom 75 percent were adult males, 10 percent were adult females, and 15 percent were teenagers. The volunteers also include Arab citizens of Israel. The volunteers are committed to serve at least four hours each month, and most of them carry out patrol duties in their neighbor-hoods.[14] In addition to its law enforcement functions, the guard has prob-

---

13. *Yediot Aharonot,* January 15, 1982, p. 15.

14. See <www.police.gov.il>.

ably acted as a substitute for vigilantism by furnishing the public with a controlled, legal outlet for responding to domestic threats.

Much of the success Israel has experienced in thwarting terrorist bombings can be attributed to public awareness. The majority of explosive devices placed in public sites, such as bus stations, supermarkets, and shopping centers, have been discovered by civilians who were able to alert the police before the bombs went off. Public alertness has been encouraged by police advertisements on television and in other media, but the main reason for this high-level awareness has undoubtedly been the Israeli public's identification with the struggle against terrorism.

Two generalizations can be made concerning Israel's massive defensive effort. First, it has been reactive; new defensive measures or the expansion of existing ones always followed in the wake of some terrorist success. Second, the primary and almost only criterion for instituting new defensive measures is their level of effectiveness in preventing casualties. Cost has not been a limitation, and no resources have been spared in an effort to deny any terrorist success.

PREEMPTIVE STRIKES

Preemptive strikes are intended to thwart terrorist operations by eliminating the personnel and the physical infrastructure involved in the preparation of a terrorist attack. In the Israeli-Palestinian struggle, in which the terrorist infrastructure has been located by and large in Arab states and, during the second *intifada*, in the area controlled by the Palestinian Authority, outside Israeli-controlled territory, preemptive operations have ordinarily taken the form of military strikes rather than police actions. These strikes have included commando raids or air force bombings of headquarters and bases used by Palestinian organizations for preparing attacks on Israel. The success of this policy depends on the availability, in real time, of extremely accurate intelligence. Although Israel has engaged in preemptive strikes, there are no comprehensive statistical data on the scope of these strikes and no easy way to assess their effectiveness. The value of thwarting a terrorist attack is self-evident. In addition, preemptive strikes are morally and legally justified when carried out against terrorists on enemy territory. Problems arise, however, when clandestine antiterrorist operations are carried out on neutral or friendly countries' territory.

LEGAL MEASURES

With some modifications, Israel's antiterrorist measures are legally based on the 1945 British Defense Regulations (State of Emergency). The British mandatory government designed these measures to address Palestine's worsening internal strife. The regulations placed certain types of offenses under the jurisdiction of military courts and allowed for the imposition of severe punishment for terrorism-related offenses. For example, carrying a firing weapon or an explosive device may be punishable by death (Article 58);[15] unauthorized production or possession of weapons or explosives is punishable by life imprisonment (Article 59); unauthorized wearing of a police or military uniform is also punishable by life imprisonment (Article 60). The regulations empower authorities to censor mail, press, and books that contain material which, if disseminated, could jeopardize state security, public security, or public order (Articles 86–91). In addition, the measures allow authorities to restrict a person's movement or area of residence (Articles 108–110); to confiscate and destroy by military commander's order any house that was used for terrorist activity (Article 119); to confiscate the property of a person engaged in such activity (Article 120); and to impose, again by a military commander's order, a curfew on any area (Article 124).

The British mandate's regulations proscribed "unlawful associations," defined as groups that advocate, incite, or encourage the bringing down of the government by violence or that carry out acts of terrorism against the government or its employees (Article 84). In 1948, Israel's Provisional State Council enacted the Directive for Prevention of Terrorism, which defined a terrorist organization as "a group of people which uses acts of violence that may cause the death or injury of a person, or threats to carry out such acts."[16] Membership in a terrorist organization is punishable by five years imprisonment, and a leadership role is punishable by 20 years.[17] Article 8 of the directive authorized the government to declare certain groups as terrorist organizations until otherwise proven. In 1986, in accordance with this article, the Israeli government declared 21 Palestinian insurgent groups, including the PLO, to be "terrorist organizations." In 2002, the Supreme Court upheld the new law allowing for the forceable relocation of the relatives of Palestinians involved in violent

---

15. It should be noted, however, that no terrorist has ever been executed in Israel. In one case, a terrorist (Mahmud Hijazi) was sentenced to death, but his sentence was commuted to life imprisonment. Prosecutors in Israel do not seek capital punishment, even in trials of terrorists accused of multiple murders of civilians. The policy has apparently been adopted by the government on the recommendation of security agencies, despite public sentiment.

16. Directive for Prevention of Terrorism, 1948 (No. 33), Article 1.

17. Ibid., Articles 3 and 2, respectively.

acts.[18] Another recently adopted law legalizes the indefinite detention of "illegal combatants" who are suspected of "taking part in hostile activity against Israel, directly or indirectly."[19]

Preparedness for Conventional Mass-Casualty Attacks

Scenarios of terrorist attacks resulting in high casualties have included such esoteric methods as the use of a liquefied natural gas (LNG) cloud (liquefied gas is kept at –259 degrees Fahrenheit). It is transported in tankers and kept at special terminals. If released into the air, it forms a highly combustible cloud that can be set off by any spark. To date, however, all terrorist attacks that have produced high fatalities (say, more than 100) have involved explosives or explosions. With the exception of fuel-laden airliners or bombs placed on board airliners, large amounts of explosives are generally necessary to kill many people. This has usually been achieved by using car bombs.[20] In Israel, most of the terrorist attacks that cause numerous casualties are suicide bombing attacks. In the period spanning January 1993 to June 2002, 149 suicide attackers struck in Israel. Although the spate of suicide attacks that emerged during the first *intifada* declined from 1998 to 2000, the second *intifada* (September 2000 to 2003, and continuing) has been marked by an increase in the frequency and lethality of suicide attacks. On the eve of Passover 2002, for example, an attack on the Park Hotel in Netanya killed 29 Israelis.[21]

Even before the intentional crashing of commercial airliners into the World Trade Center and Pentagon in the United States, Israeli intelligence (since the 1970s) had issued warnings that some Palestinian groups had contemplated taking such actions. In a couple of cases, members of the Abu Nidal Organization (ANO) carried out attacks designed to culminate in the crashing of a hijacked airliner into Tel Aviv but were prevented from carrying through with their plot. In the first instance, members of ANO who staged the attack on El Al ticket counters at Rome Airport on December 27, 1985, said under interrogation that this had

---

18. Harvey Morris, "Israel's Supreme Court Endorses Punitive Expulsions," *Financial Times*, September 4, 2002, p. 7.

19. Human Rights Watch News, "Opportunistic Law Condemned," <www.hrw.org>

20. In some cases, terrorists were able to smuggle large quantities of explosives into buildings (e.g., the bombing of the King David Hotel in Jerusalem by the Irgun in 1946).

21. Nachman Tal, "Suicide Attacks: Israel and Islamic Terrorism," *Strategic Assessment*, Vol. 5, No. 1, (June 2002).

been their ultimate objective.[22] The same organization commandeered a Pan Am airliner in Karachi Airport on September 5, 1986, with the same purpose. The damage estimate of an airliner crashing into the middle of a city does not differ from that caused by a large bomb, so no special preparations had to be made for damage control in such an eventuality. However, Israel has been ready to go to great lengths to prevent attacks of this kind. In 1973, a Libyan airliner that entered Sinai Peninsula airspace by mistake was shot down by Israeli combat airplanes when its pilots ignored orders to land. Nearly all of the passengers and crew perished.

As a routine matter, Israel has made an effort to prevent the smuggling of explosives. Systematic and thorough searches are conducted at all border crossing points between Israel and the Territories. At times, the practice has had negative consequences, including extremely long lines of trucks hauling goods from the Gaza Strip, damage to the Palestinian economy, and perturbation among the Palestinian population. Despite these repercussions, the searches have continued and should probably be credited with the fact that, unlike in Lebanon, no sizeable car bomb has ever been detonated in Israel.[23]

Searches of Palestinian cars at random roadblocks inside Israel are also conducted. These are generally rare, except when tensions are running high—for example, when intelligence information indicates that an attack is imminent. Searches of bags at entrances to public places, such as theaters, sports stadiums and arenas, museums, and universities have been routine for more than 25 years.

Presumably, the inability of terrorist groups to smuggle car bombs through the border has been a major factor in their decision to use suicide "human bombs" as their preferred mode of spectacular terrorist attacks inside Israel. The amount of explosives used in these attacks is limited to what a person can carry in a handbag or wrap around his or her body, which is usually less than 10 kilograms. In the worst attacks of this kind, (e.g., on a bus in Jerusalem on February 25, 1996; at the Dolphinarium Disco in Tel Aviv on June 1, 2001; at the Park Hotel in Netanya on Passover Eve on March 27, 2002) the number of casualties was between 20 and 30 fatalities and more than 100 wounded, compared with hundreds of fatalities in large car bomb attacks.

Following a series of suicide bombings in March 1996, the United

22. Yaakov Perry, *Strike First* (Tel Aviv, Israel: Keshet, 1999), p. 285.

23. Most car bombs in Lebanon have contained between 70 and 150 kg of explosives. Some, however, have contained considerably more (e.g., the truck bomb that destroyed the U.S. Marine barracks in October 1983).

States gave Israel $100 million in emergency aid—half in 1996 and the other half in 1997—mainly to purchase counterterrorism equipment. By the end of 1999, Israel had spent only $61 million of this sum. Thirty million dollars were earmarked for detection equipment at border crossing points, including 16 explosives detection systems, eight of which are located at the Karni border crossing—the main point of entry for merchandise coming in from the Gaza Strip. The remaining eight detection systems are designated for use at the permanent border crossings from the West Bank into Israel, which have not yet been determined. On July 31, 1996, the government decided to improve border control by introducing a "smart system" for documenting persons entering the country. This project was supposed to include a computerized system that would connect all entry points into the country and all security organizations involved in border control. A supplementary project was begun to equip police patrol vehicles with computers that are connected to a central data bank and contain information on suspects. The United States has financed both projects, which are being directed by the planning division of the police. To date, however, neither project has been completed. A third project, involving screening large containers at seaports, has also not been fully implemented yet.[24]

Preparedness for Attacks Using Weapons of Mass Destruction

Attacks by weapons of mass destruction (WMD) have several characteristics that make them more difficult to manage than conventional terrorist attacks. These include the following:

1. WMD attacks can potentially cause significantly higher numbers of casualties and can affect a large area;
2. WMD attacks require detection and identification equipment and trained personnel;
3. The units at the scene of an event must use protective clothing and gas masks;
4. The symptoms of exposure are less clear than the effects of a conventional injury, resulting in a large number of unaffected people seeking treatment;
5. WMD attacks have a much greater psychological impact on the public.

---

24. Alex Fishman, "Terrorist Attacks Can Wait," *Yediot Aharonot*, February 18, 2000.

With the exception of an unsuccessful attempt to pour parathion, an extremely toxic insecticide, into Israel's water system in 1965, no other attempts have been made to use WMD weapons in Israel. Israel's defense against WMD attacks has developed within the context of its wars with its unfriendly neighbors, not in the context of terrorism. To manage a terrorist WMD attack, Israel would rely on its existing wartime civil defense system. It has not developed a separate system for managing WMD events caused by terrorists, as opposed to states. The logic behind this decision is that the worst terrorist attack would presumably still be less severe than a barrage of Iraqi or Syrian missiles carrying chemical or biological warheads.

ORGANIZATION AND RESPONSIBILITIES

In terrorist incidents lasting days or weeks, such as hijackings and kidnappings, political-strategic decision-making has been done at the cabinet level. This was true, for example, during the hijacking of an El Al airliner to Entebbe, Uganda, in 1976.[25] Similarly, policy decisions in the Persian Gulf crises—the 1991 war and the regional tension during February 1998—were made at the top level. In the February 1998 crisis, for example, the top level decision making was conducted among a small group, including Prime Minister Benjamin Netanyahu, Minister of Defense Yitzhak Mordechai, and Chief of Staff, Lieutenant General Amnon Shahak. The prime minister also consulted with cabinet members Ariel Sharon and Rafael Eitan whose advice he valued because of their military experience, although their formal responsibilities were not relevant to the preparedness issue. The cabinet and the government were kept informed of events. The actual management of the situation was handled by the minister of defense with a team that included the chief of staff and his deputy, the director of military intelligence, the director general of the ministry of defense, and his special assistant, Major General (res.) David Ivri. The team met frequently and dealt with issues of intelligence, public information, civil defense, coordination with the United States, and preparation of proposals for military responses in case Israel was attacked.[26]

Incidents of short duration, such as major bombings and even hostage crises that last less than several hours, have been managed at the operational level with minimal or no intervention at the political level. Although the minister of defense was on-site during several barricade-

---

25. Itzhak Rabin, *Pinkas Sherut* (Tel Aviv, Israel: Sifriat Ma'ariv, 1979), pp. 526–527.

26. Benziman, *Ha'aretz*, February 27, 1998.

hostage incidents, the decisions were usually made by the supreme military echelon at the scene, ordinarily the chief of staff and the regional commanding general. Major bombing incidents have been managed by the police. On-site decisions have usually been made by the district commander.

OPERATIONAL RESPONSIBILITY FOR THE MANAGEMENT OF TERRORIST INCIDENTS

A 1974 government decision charged the police with responsibility for handling terrorist incidents within Israel's borders. It also made the Israeli Defense Forces (IDF) responsible for managing incidents up to five kilometers from the borders, in the Negev Desert, which encompasses the southern half of the country (with the exception of cities and towns there), and in the Territories. The minister of defense, however, may declare a "limited state of emergency," thereby transferring comprehensive responsibility for managing an incident to the military. The declaration of a state of emergency allows military authorities to take actions to ensure public security and the uninterrupted supply of vital services. It allows the military to force people to stay in bomb shelters, to obtain means of defense as determined by the military, and to shut down schools and other public services and workplaces. The state of emergency cannot restrict the written or electronic media. By law, the declaration must be made public through radio, television, and newspapers as early as possible. It can remain in effect for a maximum of five days. After that, it must be endorsed by the Knesset, the Israeli parliament.

To date, all hostage incidents have been managed by the military, including those that have taken place within the designated area of police authority. This departure from the formal regulation has been done without a declaration of a state of emergency and is the result of several factors, including the military's superior capabilities for handling these situations and the higher esteem in which key government figures—namely the minister of defense and the prime minister—hold the Israeli military.

In conventional terrorist incidents, the police are capable, in principle, of assuming comprehensive responsibility. This is not the case, however, in unconventional incidents, such as terrorist WMD events. At present the police are unable and unequipped to manage an unconventional incident. For instance, they are neither trained nor equipped to detect and identify chemical substances. The Army's Home Front Command (HFC) is the only organization that can manage an unconventional incident and would be in charge in a case of this kind. Judging from experience, however, the management of a WMD incident would not belong solely to the HFC, which would have to rely heavily on other IDF resources. The chief of staff and general headquarters would probably be directly involved in managing the event. In peacetime, the IDF can afford to allocate these resources, but this may not be true in wartime.

Major General Meir Dagan, the former head of the Combating Terrorism Headquarters in the office of the prime minister (1997–1999), maintained that the police should assume full responsibility for managing terrorist WMD incidents, and that it could do so if given the means.[27] Other recommendations have implied major organizational changes. After the 1991 Gulf War, a committee headed by Major General (res.) Herzl Shafir concluded that in a time of general war, the military command would be too busy at the front to attend to civil defense. The committee therefore recommended the establishment of a national guard that would incorporate the HFC as well as fire brigades and other rescue services. Another commission, headed by Lieutenent Gen. (res.) Moshe Levi, reexamined civil defense in a workshop initiated by the minister of defense in 1998 for reviewing Israel's security conception. Like the Shafir report, the 1998 review recommended that, as a first step, HFC be transferred from the ministry of defense and be placed within the ministry of internal security (whose main responsibilities include the police and prisons).[28] One commentator suggested enacting a "home defense law" that would give local municipalities the authority and responsibility for managing all kinds of emergencies.[29] As of 2003, HFC is still part of the IDF.

ORGANIZATION AND RESPONSIBILITIES OF THE HOME FRONT COMMAND
The Home Front Command has a comprehensive responsibility to be prepared for and manage states of emergency within Israel's borders (excluding the Territories, where regional commands are in charge). Although HFC is part of the IDF, most of its budget comes directly from the treasury, not from the ministry of defense.[30] HFC has a national command and three regional commands—north, center, and south—that report to the national command.

In performing its duties, HFC relies by and large on Israel's extensive system of readiness for war rather than on its own standing force. This gives HFC access to Israel's manpower and equipment reserves. Like other components in the Israeli army, HFC is made up mostly of reserve

---

27. Personal interview, January 14, 2000.

28. Amnon Barzilai, *Ha'aretz*, November 25, 1998.

29. Avirama Golan, *Ha'aretz*, April 25, 1996.

30. Interview with Major General Uzi Dayan, Deputy Chief of Staff of IDF, January 14, 2000; and *Ma'ariv*, February 2, 1998.

soldiers who can be called up immediately in a state of emergency. The same rule applies to certain kinds of equipment. For example, in Israel, all heavy mechanical equipment (e.g., tractors, bulldozers, cranes, et al.) is registered with the military and may be requisitioned for service in an emergency. In addition, bus companies must maintain a predetermined number of buses to evacuate victims of a mass-casualty attack and to transport forces to the site of the incident. For research and development, HFC relies on the special means branch of the ministry of defense, which is responsible for developing the means to deal with unconventional warfare for both the IDF and the civilian population.[31]

HFC is responsible for establishing operating procedures, planning and supervising exercises, and monitoring the preparedness of organizations that respond to high-consequence attacks, including the medical system, municipalities, transportation, and electricity. The procedures set forth by HFC are very specific. With regard to medical treatment, for example, HFC issues binding directives for treating individuals exposed to any number of chemical substances.

HFC preparedness has three main organizational goals:

1. To create a common terminology among all of the agencies that would be called upon in the event of high-consequence attack. This step is essential for ensuring rapid, mistake-free mutual understanding of people coming from different organizations. This objective is achieved primarily through HFC's development of standard operating procedures that are issued to all organizations responding to an incident, and through the use of joint exercises;
2. To establish a smoothly functioning central command post that controls resources during an emergency;
3. To establish a clear delineation of responsibility at every stage of crisis management.

For the detection, identification, and decontamination of chemical warfare substances, HFC maintains a unit at constant readiness. Similar but smaller units are located in the less-populated northern and southern districts. In addition, civilian teams trained and equipped to detect and identify harmful chemical substances, including chemical warfare substances, are housed within the ministry of environmental protection and can be called up if needed. Like other first-response forces, these units are equipped with gas masks and protective clothing.

The Home Front Command is in charge of communicating with the

---

31. Amnon Barzilai, *Ha'aretz*, February 18, 1999.

public in the event of an attack and maintains a unit for this purpose. The unit is assisted by HFC's regular duty and reserve psychologists. All media outlets, including television and radio stations and newspapers, are required by law to provide the military with immediate access to their broadcasting and publication outlets in an emergency. Presumably, however, a mass-casualty incident, particularly a WMD event, would have such enormous national and international significance that it would quickly overwhelm HFC's resources. Under these circumstances, HFC's communication with the public would probably be limited to issuing instructions for behavior in the affected area.

OPERATIONAL PROCEDURES

A terrorist incident in an urban area is usually reported first to the police, who immediately distribute a report of the attack to other agencies on a predetermined distribution list, including IDF's headquarters operations branch and HFC. Following a preliminary assessment of the nature of the incident and its apparent scope, IDF's operations branch may decide to activate HFC and allocate other units and resources as necessary. Once activated, HFC sends first response units to the site. Concurrently, it sets up two types of command posts:

- Inner-perimeter command post at the site of the incident that controls rescue activities, including fire fighting, detection and identification of chemical substances, searching for victims, searching for explosives and deactivation of explosive devices, preliminary triage, decontamination, and evacuation to hospitals;
- Outer-perimeter command post that has general command of the incident. It controls all contacts with other organizations, including the political echelon, military and police headquarters, municipal authorities, medical services, and public communications outlets. This command center ensures the sealing of the affected area, allocation of forces to the incident, distribution of casualties to hospitals, etc.

The outer-perimeter command post includes key people from HFC headquarters (logistics, intelligence, spokespeople, legal advisers, et al.), as well as representatives from all other agencies and organizations that have a role in managing the incident, including:

- Medical services, with representatives from the ministry of health and the ambulance service;
- Firefighters;
- An evacuation unit;

- Police, in charge of sealing off the area of the incident and securing routes for the transportation of forces, casualties, and evacuees;
- The municipal civil engineering department with information on buildings plans, telephone lines, electricity, water pipelines, gas stations, et al.; and
- The municipal welfare department, which allocates temporary housing to evacuees and provides other basic necessities such as mattresses, blankets, and food.

Every representative maintains constant contact with and direct computer access to his or her parent organization and the organization's data and systems.

The command-and-control structure described above is implemented in incidents involving a chemical warfare substance and/or a very large amount of explosives. Biological attacks are distinct in several crucial respects and require different, generally simpler, organization and procedures. In such incidents, there is no need for an inner-perimeter command post, and some of the elements of the outer-perimeter command post are unnecessary. The time frame for detecting a biological incident, identifying its parameters, and managing it is considerably longer.

THE MEDICAL SYSTEM

Like other components of the preparedness system, the medical complex relies on procedures designed to deal with the greater threat of unconventional attacks by regular armies and does not maintain special readiness for WMD terrorist attacks. Although the capability of states, such as Syria, to spread chemical or biological warfare substances is immensely greater than that of any terrorist group, the number of casualties in an unconventional attack by an enemy state would not necessarily be greater than the number of casualties in a terrorist incident.

A WMD attack by a state would probably be preceded by a warning period. People would presumably keep their gas defense kits (GDKs) within reach, shelters would be prepared, and an attack would find most of the population well protected. Even in the case of a surprise attack, the approaching missiles would be detected by radar, and sirens would be sounded. In this case, part of the population would have a few minutes to find shelter, although, presumably, would not be able to reach their GDKs.

A terrorist WMD attack, on the other hand, would occur without warning, leaving people no time to protect themselves. The number of casualties per fixed quantity of chemical or biological substance (i.e., the effectiveness ratio) would therefore be considerably higher than in the case of a state-sponsored WMD attack. This difference is even more pronounced with regard to unannounced biological terrorist attacks. In wartime, an enemy missile carrying biological warfare material would likely be immediately identified as such, leaving enough time for preventive treatment. An unannounced terrorist biological attack, on the other hand, could cause many casualties before the source is identified, and the exposed population gets proper treatment.

Israel's capacity for hospitalizing victims of a massive terrorist chemical attack, as estimated by senior officials in the medical system, is barely sufficient, with Shiba Hospital (the largest in Israel) taking up to 600. Israel's medical system can handle several thousand casualties. The hospital would need four hours to reach maximum capacity. (In the Tokyo sarin attack, approximately 5,000 persons applied for medical treatment, although supposedly only about 200 were actually affected by the gas).[32]

Israel's health ministry maintains a rotation list of hospitals for an event involving mass casualties. In a declared state of emergency, HFC has authority over hospitals and other medical facilities. In consultation with the ministry of health and the IDF's medical corps, it would also determine the distribution of casualties to hospitals.

In the event of an attack, the hospital next on the rotation list receives notification. It is also notified if a chemical agent is suspected, even before detection and identification have been performed. The hospital then sets in motion its emergency procedures.

The initial sorting out and decontamination of casualties is performed on site by an HFC medical team. A senior HFC medical officer supervises the evacuation of those needing further treatment. The evacuation is carried out by civilian and military ambulances and, if necessary, by buses called up for emergency service. The police make sure that evacuation routes to the hospitals have been cleared. Upon reaching the hospital's entrance, the casualties are assessed by the medical staff. Chemical attack victims requiring hospitalization are taken to the vicinity of the emergency room where showers have been set up for decontamination.[33] Treatment by type of substance is given according to binding orders of HFC. Long-range treatment and follow-up is provided by the civilian community medical services (sick funds).

For Israel's medical system, preparedness for a biological attack

32. John Parachini, presentation, Belfer Center for Science and International Affairs, John F. Kennedy School of Government, Harvard University, February 25, 2000.

33. Interview with Mordechai Shani, director-general of Shiba Hospital, January 11, 2000; and interview with Shaul Mukhtar, head of Shiba Hospital's Emergency System, January 12, 2000.

means awareness of symptoms and readiness for treatment. The ministry of public health monitors the incidence of contagious diseases throughout the country, particularly those diseases that could be used in biological warfare. By law, hospitals must immediately report the occurrence of such diseases.

In the event of a biological incident, HFC can call upon teams of soldiers to canvass the affected area. Going door to door, the teams give residents the appropriate medicines and printed follow-up instructions.

Maintaining a sufficient stock of medicines for full WMD warfare preparedness constitutes an economic burden. At times when there is no palpable danger, the natural tendency is to allocate resources to other needs. In the 1990–1991 Gulf War, for example, Israel would have had enough antibiotics to treat victims of an anthrax attack. In the 1998 tension in the Persian Gulf, however, it was reported that the stock was outdated. Only after the report was published did HFC receive 183 million shekels (about 52 million U.S. dollars at the time) to buy masks and other equipment and another 57 million for medicines.[34]

A RECENT TEST OF A LIMITED STATE OF EMERGENCY
The organizational limitations of Israeli preparedness were tested in early February 2000. At the height of tensions along the Israeli-Lebanese border, the threat of Hizballah rocket attacks prompted the minister of defense to declare a state of emergency in northern border towns. On February 8, the towns' inhabitants were ordered into bomb shelters. Although the state of emergency lasted only 48 hours, it was long enough for management problems to surface, even though no rockets were ever launched. Citizens and municipal officials complained about the inefficient distribution of food and mattresses to the people in the shelters. Doctors (except for emergency medical teams) were also required to stay in shelters and were unable to attend to patients.

In a meeting of HFC commanders and municipal officials, it was decided that, in future states of emergency, the command posts in the main towns should be manned by representatives of the prime minister's office, northern command, HFC, ministry of labor and public works, and the ministry of industry and commerce. Food distribution will be coordinated by the municipalities with the participation of the military.[35]

---

34. Yoav Limor, *Ma'ariv*, February 2, 1998. With regard to the anthrax inoculation, see also Zeev Schiff, *Ha'aretz*, February 1, 1998.

35. *Yediot Aharonot*, February 11, 2000.

The Debate on Investing in Homeland Preparedness against Unconventional Weapons

Awareness of the threat of missile attacks on Israeli cities has stimulated public debate on the need to invest in the defense of the civilian population. The debate has intensified when danger has seemed more imminent, most recently during the 1998 tension in the Persian Gulf and in the wake of U.S. punitive actions against Iraq.

For many years, Israel has emphasized an offensive rather than a defensive policy. Since the 1967 war, Israeli military planners have assumed that the air force would be able to guarantee a "clean sky" over Israel. This position became untenable, however, once enemy states acquired missiles capable of reaching Israeli population centers. The development of chemical and biological warfare capability by Syria, Iraq, and Iran has made the WMD threat more ominous. The existence of missiles equipped with chemical warheads in the arsenals of enemy states has spurred a debate in Israel on whether to continue investing in defense measures to protect the civilian population.[36] Opponents of investing in civilian defense argue that the number of casualties in attacks on civilian population centers has been very small. Iraqi Scud attacks resulted in only one fatality in the Gulf War, and hundreds of Katyusha rockets fired on Israeli towns along the Lebanese border in the last two decades have caused very few casualties. According to the opponents, the best way to cope with this threat is through deterrence, that is, to threaten to respond to an attack with an overwhelming counterattack. This is the position of David Klein, who conducted a study of the home front defense expenditure for Tel Aviv University's Jaffee Center for Strategic Studies. He also argues that a passive defense should have only a secondary role: limiting the damage once an attack has occurred.[37] In Klein's view, because even a huge additional investment in homeland defense will decrease the number of casualties by only a very small margin, expenditures on homeland defense should be reduced.[38]

---

36. The term "passive defense" as used here refers to measures that are designed to protect the population after an attack has occurred, as opposed to measures to prevent the missiles or bombs from reaching their target.

37. David Klein, "Home Front Defense: Examination of the National Investment," *Strategic Assessment*, Vol. 2, No. 2 (September 1999), pp. 1–7 Tel Aviv University, Jaffee Center for Strategic Studies.

38. David Klein, *Home-Front Defense: An Examination of the National Cost*. Tel Aviv University, Jaffee Center for Strategic Studies, Memorandum No. 58, April 2001, pp. 44–45 (Hebrew).

Some proponents of investment in homeland defense have under-scored public sensitivity to attacks, citing, for example, damage that can be done to the economy when people feel that an attack is imminent.[39] During the Gulf War, many people left the Tel Aviv area for safer places. Although only 38 Scud missiles reached Israel and just one person was killed, the government reacted by recommending that people stay at home, unless they were employed in vital services. Kindergartens, schools, and even universities shut down for a week and then reopened only partially. On September 4, 1996, after a U.S. punitive cruise missile attack against Iraq, Israelis again began exhibiting heightened anxiety, manifested, for example, in long lines at GDK distribution centers. Pre-sumably, an unconventional weapons attack would result in all but com-plete paralysis of the economy for the duration of the threat. In all likeli-hood, a very large number of inhabitants in areas either under attack or likely to be attacked would be able to reach safer places, and those that remained could stay home, near a shelter. Against the backdrop of this assessment, investment in home front defense is necessary for a psycho-logical reason: to give people a sense of security, so that they will con-tinue to function in an emergency.

Yair Evron, former Head of the Security Studies Program at Tel Aviv University, has offered another reason for investment in homeland de-fense.[40] In his view, a chemical or biological attack on Israeli civilians re-sulting in mass casualties could put public pressure on the Israeli govern-ment to retaliate with nuclear weapons. Strategically, this would be disastrous and could hasten the acquisition of nuclear weapons by enemy states as well as dangerously alter the Middle Eastern military balance, at the very least. To prevent such an eventuality, Israel's home front must have the defensive means necessary to minimize losses in an unconventional attack and, thus, remove the temptation of nuclear re-taliation.

Israel began preparing for unconventional attacks in the early 1980s, at a time when enemy capability for attacking civilian population centers with missiles carrying chemical warheads became possible. People began buying kits for defense against gas attacks. A typical kit included a gas mask and an atropine syringe. Purchases were funded by the National Social Security. In 1986, however, Israel decided that the stock was sufficient, and procurement was halted. Preparations were resumed in

---

39. LTC Avi Bitzur, "The Home Front in the Israeli National Security Conception," *Ma'arachot*, No. 354 (1997), pp. 25–28.

40. Yair Evron, "Leave Nuclear Weapons Aside," *Ha'aretz*, February 23, 1998.

1990, following Iraq's invasion of Kuwait. At that time, against the back-drop of an acute threat of Iraqi missile attacks on Israel, the government began distributing GDKs to the population. People were instructed to prepare a sealed room in their homes to prevent the penetration of gas from the outside. The recommended method of sealing was simple: cover windows with nylon sheets taped to the wall and block spaces under doors with a wet rag. The IDF medical corps has determined that GDKs also offer good defense against biological weapons (e.g., anthrax). The HFC found that a sealed room provided a defense against chemical and biological weapons that is 10 times more effective than staying outside in the open air, and that the combined defense of a sealed room and a gas mask is 1,000 times more effective than staying outside with no mask.[41]

The Debate on Distributing GDKs to the Population

A strong argument in favor of distributing GDKs to the general population before the outbreak of hostilities in the Persian Gulf was, of course, that this was the only way to ensure prompt access to them in case of a chemical attack. Reluctance to distribute the GDKs stemmed from the notion that GDKs are better maintained in government storage than in citizens' hands and, therefore, should be distributed to the public only when the danger is clearly imminent. Thus, the argument against the distribution of GDKs was essentially related to costs and reflected a downgraded estimate of the likelihood of a chemical attack. In more recent periods of tension, when the threat of an Iraqi attack seemed much less concrete than it had been in the Gulf War, questions concerning the political-strategic repercussions of distributing GDKs to the public were again raised. An argument in favor of distribution was that it may, in fact, reduce the likelihood of unconventional weapons attacks, because it signals to the potential users that such attacks would not be effective. Some, however, were concerned that enemies may interpret the distribution in a different way. One commentator suggested that distributing GDKs was not only a waste, but politically unwise, because it signaled to potential WMD users that Israel is extremely sensitive to this form of warfare.[42]

The Home Front Command was established as a response to some of the lessons of the Gulf War. The government initially decided to allocate to HFC about 1 billion shekels annually for civil defense equipment. This would allow for the periodical renewal of gas kits held by the population,

---

41. Yoav Limor, *Ma'ariv*, February 2, 1998.

42. Uzi Benziman, *Ha'aretz*, February 27, 1998.

so as to maintain constant readiness. In 1996, however, the government decided to suspend this program. In the wake of this decision, Yossi Sarid, member of the Knesset's Foreign Relations and Defense Committee, appealed to the Supreme Court in a move to force the government to continue maintaining these gas kits. The government agreed to continue the program, but the funds to keep it going were not allocated; as a result, the program suffered. The gap between existing equipment and what was needed gradually increased, so that by early 1998 the stocks were in short supply. Hundreds of thousands of Israeli citizens and permanent residents, in addition to about 200,000 foreign workers, lacked gas kits.[43] At the time, Major General Gabi Ofir, commander of HFC, said that only two-thirds of the population had satisfactory defenses against missile attacks. Problems with facilities and equipment were detected in hospitals, schools, and residences, and billions of shekels would be needed to correct the situation. One-third of the schools did not have sufficient shelters.[44] The ministry of defense estimated that the 220 million shekels would be needed annually to properly maintain the entire population's GDKs.[45]

Public opinion weighed heavily in the political leadership's decision to refurbish the GDKs held by the population. Then Minister of Defense Yitzhak Mordechai, responding to criticism, bluntly stated in February 1998: "I would like to see the wise guy who would be able to explain to the public why we had not distributed kits, had there been 200 fatalities here."[46] According to a media account of the decision-making process, the IDF's chief medical officer pressed to provide the public with all available means of civil defense.[47] His main concern, however, was psychological as well as physical. He argued that a chemical or biological attack would result in immense public panic, which could be reduced by early distribution of a means of defense. The decision to refurbish the GDKs held by the public was the result of presumed public pressure and the IDF's determination that it could not complete distribution to the en-

---

43. Yoav Limor, *Ma'ariv*, February 2, 1998.

44. *Ha'aretz*, February 20, 1998, quoting Col. Yuri Sufrin, head of HFC's Defense Department; *Ma'ariv*, February 1998, quoting Major General Gabi Ofir, HFC's commanding officer.

45. *Ha'aretz*, February 27, 1998.

46. Quoted in Amos Harel, *Ha'aretz*, February 27, 1998.

47. Uzi Benziman, *Ha'aretz*, February 27, 1998.

tire population within 36 hours of a war. Defense against biological attacks were also considered.

Yehoshua Matza, former minister of public health, and the ministry's professional staff objected to early distribution of antibiotics in the event of an anthrax attack. They argued that, unlike the effects of a gas attack, the effects of an attack with a biological agent like anthrax are not immediate and antibiotics would be effective as long as the first dose is taken within a day of exposure to the infectious agent. In their judgment, it would be possible for the health services to distribute antibiotics to the affected population within this critical time frame, a view supported by the IDF's Center for System Analysis. The Home Front Command, however, refusing to take any risks, recommended the inclusion of two doses of antibiotics in each GDK. The government adopted the HFC's cautious position, choosing to include antibiotic pills for adults and the liquid form for children. The minister of the treasury suggested that payment for the antibiotics would be levied from the public, but the government adopted the public health minister's position that the antibiotics should be distributed free of charge. The decision had not yet been implemented, however, when the tension in the Gulf subsided.

Conclusion

Given its unique experience in managing significant terrorist events and its nationwide readiness for a state-sponsored chemical or biological attack, Israel is probably better prepared than any other country for an unconventional terrorist attack. From the point of view of civil defense, it may be argued that the Scud missile attacks during the 1991 Gulf War were a strategic gift to Israel. They provided Israel with an opportunity to test its defense system and exposed problems involved in this kind of warfare at a cost of well below the damage that can be expected in a full-scale missile war.

In addition, Israel is probably the only country in which every citizen, including infants, is supposed to have a chemical defense kit at home. In theory, this should make the country better prepared to deal with a terrorist WMD attack. In reality, having GDKs at home are of little value, however, in the event of a chemical terrorist attack because of the element of surprise. In time of war or even during a period of high tension that precedes war, people keep their GDKs within reach at all times. Furthermore, even with the short ranges of Israel's strategic arena, missiles launched from enemy territory can be detected in time to allow sirens to be sounded a few minutes before the missiles reach population centers. A chemical terrorist attack, on the other hand, will surely find the population unprepared and without their GDKs. A terrorist biological attack also poses greater difficulties than a biological attack by an enemy state's missiles. Whereas biological warfare material carried by an enemy missile is likely to be detected and identified soon after landing, leaving enough time for preventive treatment, a terrorist biological attack would probably be identified as such only after the symptoms relating to the attack have been diagnosed.

A surprise chemical attack is likely to induce large-scale anxiety in the affected area. People will not only be undefended at the time of attack but also frightened and disoriented. Developing an authoritative mechanism for issuing immediate instructions is, therefore, of utmost importance. The speed at which this mechanism can operate will be a major factor in the management of the incident.

A critical problem stemming from any chemical or biological attack is the potentially large number of "worried well," who are likely to flood the evacuation and medical systems and hinder their ability to handle genuine casualties. Immediate initial diagnosis at the site of incident and along hospital routes is necessary to reduce this problem. Sufficient medical manpower should be trained and organized for this purpose.

Finally, unlike other kinds of terrorist events (e.g., hostage incidents), it is practically impossible to exercise the management of terrorist WMD attacks under near-realistic conditions, because in a WMD exercise the critical factor of public response cannot be simulated. Models of public behavior in panic-generating situations should be developed on the basis of data collected on non-malicious disasters and epidemics and incorporated into the crisis management plans as estimates.

Consequence Management in the 1995 Sarin Attacks on the Japanese Subway System

Robyn L. Pangi

In the early to mid–1990s, the group known as Aum Shinrikyo amassed and used against innocent civilians, an arsenal of chemical and biological weapons. A large body of literature details the evolution of Aum Shinrikyo, its shocking attacks on both a housing complex in Matsumoto and five subway lines in Tokyo using a chemical weapon, and Japanese society's reaction to the attacks. Not much analysis, however, has been done on the lessons learned about consequence management from these first significant terrorist attacks with weapons of mass destruction (WMD) to occur in modern times.[1] Recent events in the United States, including the dispersal of anthrax spores through the mail and scores of

The author thanks Arnold Howitt for the thorough substantive and stylistic comments that he provided on this essay; Naofumi Miyasaka, Tetsu Okumura, Yoshihide Kuroki, Nozomu Asukai, Masaaki Iwaki, Makato Tsuruki, and all of the participants of the Japan Society Roundtable, "Terrorism: Prevention and Preparedness, New Approaches to U.S.-Japan Security Cooperation" October 30–31, 2000, Tokyo, Japan, for their candid reflections on counterterrorism policies; Shun'ichi Furukawa and Mark Tice for their thoughtful review of this essay; and Teresa Lawson for providing outstanding editing skills.

1. For the purposes of this essay, weapons of mass destruction include biological, chemical, nuclear, and radiological weapons. Attacks resulting in mass casualties have also occurred through other means, most notably the use of fuel-laden commercial aircraft to attack the World Trade Center towers and the Pentagon in September 2001. However, this essay focuses on the ways in which consequence management after a biological, chemical, nuclear, or radiological attack differs from consequence management after an attack with a conventional weapon like a high-yield explosive. The Aum Shinrikyo attacks represent the first significant WMD attacks in modern times.

hoaxes alleging use of anthrax, have brought the issue of terrorism using weapons of mass destruction closer to home. The handling of the Aum Shinrikyo attacks offers the opportunity for policymakers, emergency response personnel, and other relevant professionals to learn about WMD consequence management.

An attack with a chemical weapon (as in Tokyo) or with a biological weapon (as in the United States) is different from a conventional attack, because the potentially catastrophic effects of the attack can be substantially reduced with prompt intervention. In a large explosion, such as the aircraft bombings of the World Trade Center in New York City and the Pentagon in Washington, D.C., in September 2001, the actual impact of the explosion cannot be mitigated. The only hope is to save lives by rescuing people from the rubble and keeping potential victims away from the unstable structures. However, in a chemical or biological weapon attack, proper decontamination and rapid prophylaxis can often save lives and prevent the spread of disease or chemical exposure to the larger population.[2]

The Aum Shinrikyo case study is a good learning tool for policymakers and emergency response professionals seeking to form a coherent domestic preparedness strategy.[3] A review of the scenario, starting in 1994 and early 1995 with the sarin attacks, reveals potential opportunities to preempt such an attack or to mitigate its effects.[4] This essay begins with a brief introduction to Aum Shinrikyo. It then reviews the sarin attacks in the town of Matsumoto in 1994 and in Tokyo in 1995. Following the case studies, the essay details the municipal and national governments' rescue and recovery operations. It then summarizes many of the policies that Japan has implemented since 1995 to strengthen response plans and preparedness. Finally, the essay analyzes several lessons that emerged from the experience and examines implications for the United States.

---

2. This is even more evident after a biological weapons attack, when rapid agent identification and appropriate medical treatment can significantly reduce the spread of the disease and the number of casualties.

3. After the sarin attack on the Tokyo subway in 1995, the United States revised its assessment of the threat of terrorism to include the new threat of terrorism with a weapon of mass destruction. Since then, U.S. government spending on counterterrorism programs has risen exponentially. The various initiatives, known collectively as the domestic preparedness program, represent a major effort to improve the nation's ability to respond to an act of catastrophic terrorism.

4. Sarin is isopropyl methylphosphonoflouridate.

Case Studies

BACKGROUND

Aum Shinrikyo, or Aum Supreme Truth,[5] based its teachings on the belief of impending Armageddon. Led by Shoko Asahara, a partially blind man whose given name was Chizuo Matsumoto, cult members believed that only devout followers of Asahara ("the guru") would be saved at the end of the world. The cult was well financed and diverse: by 1995, it had a worldwide membership of 40,000 people and assets estimated at one billion dollars.[6] Cult members represented many different segments of society, but a characteristic that set Aum apart from other groups was that many members had a relatively high level of education and wealth. In fact, Aum recruited at universities, focusing particularly on physics, engineering, and computer departments.[7]

Most Japanese initially dismissed the cult as an oddity. Peculiar rituals, such as drinking Asahara's blood to achieve enlightenment or wearing headgear referred to as the Perfect Salvation Initiative, clearly set followers apart from mainstream society.[8] Aum was subjected to further ridicule in the 1990 elections, when 25 Aum members, including Asahara, ran for parliament seats and suffered an overwhelming defeat, earning fewer votes than the number of cult members who were eligible voters.[9]

The elections brought Aum and the cult leadership into the public eye. Thereafter, Asahara and his followers turned down a more antisocial path.[10] A series of events led to a greater isolation of cult members and

---

5. The cult lost its status as a religious organization under Japanese law in 1995. However, it retained a following and officially regrouped in 2000 under the name "Aleph."

6. The members were located around the world: 30,000 in Russia, 10,000 in Japan, and the remainder in the United States, Germany, and elsewhere. David A. Kaplan, "Aum Shinrikyo," in Jonathan B. Tucker, ed., *Toxic Terror* (Cambridge, Mass.: MIT Press, 2000), pp. 207–226.

7. David E. Kaplan and Andrew Marshall, *The Cult at the End of the World: The Incredible Story of Aum* (London: Hutchinson Press, 1996).

8. The Perfect Salvation Initiative headgear delivered a shock of six volts to adults and three volts to children. Each treatment cost members $7,000 per month.

9. During the campaign, the cult members wore white suits and giant paper mache masks that looked like Asahara.

10. "The humiliations resulting from this public rejection intensified Aum's own gradual estrangement from the world: one is tempted to speculate that this rejection, when in Aum's eyes Japanese society spurned the chance to be saved . . . might well have pushed Aum's leadership into feeling that society was damned and should be

radicalization of cult ideals. Part of this trend included increasingly aggressive and ultimately violent responses to internal and external critics. Members were threatened and punished for transgression against Asahara's teachings, outsiders who interfered with cult activities were abducted, and cult members experimented with biological and chemical weapons. Eventually some of those dangerous agents were put to use.

Prior to the 1995 attacks, Aum was able to escape police scrutiny largely because of institutional barriers against religious persecution in Japan. In 1951, the Japanese government passed the Religious Corporation Law, which strengthened constitutionally-guaranteed religious freedoms by relieving any organization that could be identified as "religious" of tax obligations and providing these groups with unusually strong protection from government intrusion.[11] "The Japanese police, like the governmental bureaucracy, exercised extreme caution in handling complaints made against official religious groups. Partly as a reaction to the harsh suppression of religious freedom by Japan's prewar military government, the postwar constitution and police policy nationwide called for scrupulously avoiding even the appearance of religious persecution."[12] Aum Shinrikyo exploited the laws guaranteeing religious freedom and, under the protective umbrella of these laws, was left virtually untouched by the authorities.[13]

Aum also benefited from a second type of restraint practiced by the post–World War II government: loosely organized and relatively weak intelligence gathering. To some extent, this resulted from limitations in the Japanese Constitution. For instance, there were legal bans on police use of preventive surveillance techniques. In addition to legal restrictions, the rivalries among prefectural police forces hindered information sharing.

---

abandoned. It also meant, once its hopes of influencing society through legal, democratic means, such as political campaigns, were wrecked, that if Asahara's contention that spiritual action was no longer enough to fulfil its mission were correct, it had to look elsewhere for the means by which to influence control of Japanese society." Ian Reader, *Poisonous Cocktail* (Denmark: Nordic Institute of Asian Studies Special Report, 1996), p. 45.

11.   An emphasis on religious freedom is pervasive in postwar Japan. The Japanese Constitution, which was drafted and imposed by the United States during its military occupation of Japan following World War II, emphasizes the individual's right to freedom from government intrusion.

12.   D.W. Brackett, *Holy Terror: Armageddon in Tokyo* (New York: Weatherhill, Inc., 1996), p. 13.

13.   "Aum seemed to enjoy a curious immunity from public complaints. The police investigated each charge made against the sect promptly, yet it never went any farther and there were never any arrests." Brackett, *Holy Terror,* p. 49.

Shielded by this combination of civil liberties and limited governmental powers, Aum Shinrikyo was able to accumulate extensive stockpiles of cash and dangerous chemical and biological materials without raising police suspicion, and Aum was able to execute not one, but two lethal attacks on civilian populations.[14]

CULTURAL CONTEXT

Prior to the sarin attack in 1995, many Japanese took comfort in their perceived isolation from the high crime rates and corruption of other highly developed countries.[15] Japan is a strikingly homogenous and relatively peaceful society.[16] "Peace (*heiwa*) and fundamental human rights (*jinken*) are twin cultural concepts that have been enshrined in national and international security policy."[17] The Japanese Constitution "denounces any type of war," and the Self Defense Force "technically are not interpreted as a military force."[18]

Until recently, terrorism was a phenomenon rarely discussed by government officials or Japanese citizens. This reticence is partially cultural: Naofumi Miyasaka, professor at the National Defense Academy, points out that, "the Manichaean belief of peace and war hinders one from con-

---

14. "[A] contributing factor to Aum's behavior was the degree of impunity that the cult enjoyed. Despite an extraordinary six-year crime spree, the sect met with surprisingly little resistance from Japanese officials, who were hampered by jurisdictional problems, a reluctance to probe religious organizations, and a lack of investigative initiative. Only after the Tokyo subway attack did authorities move quickly against the cult." Ian Reader, *Religious Violence in Contemporary Japan: The Case of Aum Shinrikyo* (United Kingdom: Curzon Press, Nordic Institute of Asian Studies Monograph Series No. 82, 2000), p. 223.

15. Japan is widely considered to be a safe society. Anthony Head explores this perception and concludes that, although Japan is safer than the United States, it is not the non-violent utopia that it is often depicted to be. For example, Japan is not "gun-free"; there are many illegal handguns, and Japan has more handgun deaths each year than the United Kingdom. Moreover, there is significant underreporting of crime in Japan, especially of rape and domestic violence, much of which results from the stigma of being a victim. Anthony Head, "Japan and the Safe Society," *Japan Quarterly*, April–June 1995.

16. Ethnic Japanese are 99.4 percent of Japanese citizens; 0.6 percent are classified as "other" and are mostly of Korean heritage. "Ethnicity and Race by Country" at <www.infoplease.com/ipa/A0855617.html>.

17. Naofumi Miyasaka, "Terrorism and Antiterrorism in Japan: Aum Shinrikyo and After," prepared for the Japan Society Roundtable on Terrorism: Prevention and Preparedness, October 2000, p. 3, on file with the author.

18. Shun'ichi Furukawa, "An Institutional Framework for Japanese Crisis Management," *Journal of Contingencies and Crisis Management*, Vol. 8, No. 1 (March 2000), pp. 3–15 at p. 4.

sidering an in-between [such as terrorism]."[19] This ethos of peace and human rights gives rise to three national ideas on terrorism: first, terrorism is believed to have root causes such as poverty or prejudice or to be a response to an oppressive government.[20] Second, Japan's antiterrorism policy is extremely risk-averse: sparing lives is paramount to the Japanese when dealing with a terrorist situation.[21] Third, terrorism remains a taboo subject that is rarely discussed; incidents such as the hijacking of 1999 ANA Flight 61 or the 1994 and 1995 sarin gas attacks are seen as unique cases and are not widely labeled "terrorist" acts.[22]

Partly as a result of this sympathetic attitude shared by the Japanese people and government, and partly owing to the overwhelming nationwide support for a free society, "terrorism is not seen as a threat to the nation's core values: democracy, prosperity, and national unity. Rather, counterterrorism is seen as a grave danger to peace and fundamental human rights."[23] Only recently has public opinion widely favored harsh punishment for convicted terrorists. Thus, prior to 1995, counterterrorism policies, where they existed at all, consisted of loosely organized measures that did not give government officials much power. By and large, the only terrorism situations with which the government was prepared to deal were hostage crises.

THE MATSUMOTO ATTACK

On June 27, 1994, a group of Aum cult members drove a converted refrigerator truck to Matsumoto, a village of approximately 300,000 residents

---

19.   Miyasaka, "Terrorism and Antiterrorism in Japan," p. 4.

20.   Ibid., p. 5.

21.   Ibid., p. 6. "Risk-averse policy is intuitively viewed as the best choice." One component of a risk-averse policy is a fear of casualties—either hostages or terrorists. The operational norm for police is not to kill terrorists. A second component is to remain neutral regarding international terrorism. Japan does not specify enemies in international society and applies the label of "terrorist" only to domestic organizations. Japan does not have a legal or officially agreed definition of terrorism, and it judges terrorist acts only under criminal or civil law.

22.   Ibid., pp. 6–7. "The perception of terrorists is so limited that the media did not label, for example, the maniac who hijacked ANA 061 and killed the pilot in July 1999, or the high school math teacher who bombed a neighboring school in February and March 1999, as terrorists. Furthermore, there is no consensus among people in general whether Aum is a terrorist organization or not." Additionally, the spate of attacks in Japan in the 1970s and 1980s, including aircraft hijackings and hostage takings, were widely perceived not as terrorist attacks, but rather as actions taken by marginalized individuals and groups to draw attention to social inequalities.

23.   Ibid., p. 6.

located 322 kilometers northwest of Tokyo. The target was a dormitory inhabited by three judges who were about to decide a civil case over land rights to which Aum was a party.[24] In an effort to stop the verdict from being issued, Aum intended to incapacitate the judges.[25] The Aum members released sarin into the evening air. Poor dispersal technique and contrary wind patterns prevented the attack from being a complete success. However, the devastation was great: seven people were killed and 500 hospitalized as the result of the attack. Moreover, the judges were injured, resulting in the delay of the decision.[26]

At first the local police in Matsumoto appeared incapable of understanding what had happened: a chemical weapons attack in a relatively small and quiet Japanese town . . . seemed beyond the bounds of comprehension. The police appeared incapable of even conceptualizing the event as a deliberate act of terrorism or mass murder, and their first step was to blame a local man. . . . According to the police, [main suspect] Kono [Yoshiyuki] had accidentally created the poisonous gases while mixing fertilizers in his garden.[27]

The media were more persistent than the investigators. They emphasized the improbability of making sarin by accident and raised the possibility of a link between Aum Shinrikyo and the Matsumoto attack.[28] This link was substantiated in 1994, when soil taken from outside of an Aum compound revealed traces of sarin. Yet the police still refused to adopt a more aggressive stance and actively investigate Aum Shinrikyo. As a result, no arrests were made in connection with this attack until *after* the 1995 subway attack.

The sarin attack on Matsumoto had surprisingly little impact on the community, the nation, or the world. "The sarin attack on Matsumoto was a precedent-shattering episode in the history of modern terrorism, but no one, either inside Japan or out, seemed to attach much significance to the fact that a highly deadly World War Two–era nerve gas, an agent all but unknown in Asia, had been unleashed with deadly results in a re-

---

24. Aum believed that the judges were likely to rule against them.

25. The Matsumoto attack may have been a trial run for the subway attack. A secondary effect was "to punish the judges and citizens of Matsumoto for having opposed Aum." Reader, *Religious Violence in Contemporary Japan*, p. 209.

26. Kyle Olson, "Aum Shinrikyo: Once and Future Threat?" *Emerging Infectious Diseases*, Vol. 5 No. 4, July–August 1999 at <www.cdc.gov/ncidod/EID/vol5no4/olson.htm>.

27. Reader, *Religious Violence*, p. 221. Kono remained a suspect until Aum members confessed to the crime in the summer of 1995.

28. Ibid., p. 211.

mote mountain town in central Japan."[29] Matsumoto, it turns out, served as a practice session for the cult's future exploits in WMD terrorism.

THE TOKYO SUBWAY ATTACK

Between 7:30 and 7:45 A.M. on March 20, 1995, five cult members boarded an inbound subway on one of three different subway lines—Hibiya, Chiyoda, and Maronouchi—at different stations, bound in a total of five different directions.[30] Beginning at 7:48 A.M., each cult member pierced one or more bags of sarin and then fled the subway. Shortly before 8 A.M., the five trains converged on the Kasumigaseki station of the Tokyo subway system.[31] Kasumegaseki is home to most of Tokyo's government offices and is considered to be the power center of the city. The attack left 12 dead, hundreds injured, and thousands terrorized.

Fortunately, the enormous potential for catastrophic damage was not actually achieved. The more than 30 train lines of the public and private transit system in Tokyo sprawl through 400 miles of underground tunnels and above-ground tracks. Over nine million passengers ride the subway daily. A rush-hour attack could thus have caused chaos and massive numbers of casualties and fatalities.[32] However, the sarin used in the subway attack—like that used in the Matsumoto attack—was only 30 percent pure, thus sparing most of the subway ridership the disaster of a successful attack. In its pure form, as little as one drop of sarin on the skin is colorless, odorless, and lethal. Impure sarin is less lethal, and when diluted (as in this case), it takes on an odor, which alerted subway passengers and emergency responders to the presence of a foreign chemical.[33]

The rudimentary method of delivery also prevented greater devastation. Aum's scientists were unable to master the construction of an aero-

---

29. Brackett, *Holy Terror*, p. 53.

30. The five cult members had left their hideout at around 6:00 A.M. in the morning in separate vehicles, each with its own driver. Four had two plastic bags filled with sarin (one member had three bags), and each also had an umbrella with a sharpened tip. On the way to their respective subway entry points, each purchased a newspaper or bag with which to conceal the sarin.

31. All of the trains involved in the attack converge at one point: Kasumigaseki. There is speculation that this attack was intended to cripple the National Police Agency: the station serves the NPA, and the attack was timed to coincide with the 8:30 A.M. shift change.

32. Reader, *Religious Violence*, p. 23.

33. Early calls to emergency assistance switchboards complained of "strange smells" and "powerful odors" in the subway system. Brackett, *Holy Terror*, p. 1.

sol delivery vehicle. The sarin was instead poured into plastic bags that were then wrapped in paper, placed on the ground, and punctured with sharpened umbrellas. Most of the sarin was not released into the air in respirable droplets, which would have effectively entered the lungs, landed on the skin of passengers, and caused mass casualties. By merely puncturing the bags, only those in immediate proximity to the release or to severely poisoned individuals suffered severe physical injuries or death.

Even with impure sarin and primative delivery techniques, thousands of passengers were affected. Subway stations were forced to evacuate passengers *en masse*, many choking, vomiting, and blinded by the chemicals. They fled up the stairways and collapsed in the streets, while fire, police, and emergency medical responders, most unprotected, ran down the stairs to assist the victims. The scene was immediately broadcast over television and radio. Images of confusion and chaos dominated the nine o'clock news and provided Tokyo and the world with its first glimpse of an act of terrorism with a weapon of mass destruction.

Consequence Management

The historical and cultural reluctance among Japanese officials to prepare for or even discuss terrorism was reflected in underdeveloped consequence management capabilities, which hindered the response effort in both sarin attacks.[34] Consequence management comprises those essential services that mitigate or ameliorate the effects of a disaster—in this case, catastrophic terrorism. Management of the consequences of natural or unintentional man-made disasters includes fire fighting, rescue and recovery operations, medical treatment, emergency transportation, law enforcement, psychological assistance by medical professionals, securing of buildings and infrastructure, and the provision of clean water and food. After a WMD terrorism attack, additional capabilities are required, including specialized mass-casualty medical operations, including triage, prophylaxis, and decontamination; possible quarantine or evacuation; environmental analysis; dissemination of public information; and specialized psychological assistance.

CONSEQUENCE MANAGEMENT IN JAPAN: BASIC PRINCIPLES
In any large-scale disaster, response personnel from multiple agencies and various levels of government must work together. This includes public, private, and volunteer agencies from the local, regional, and national

---

34. This assertion is supported by the general consensus expressed by participants at a conference sponsored by the Japan Society in Tokyo (2000).

levels.[35] The first trained personnel to arrive on the scene are almost always from local or state emergency services, with state and national resources following. After the sarin attack, for example, the response involved fire, police, emergency medical services, and medical professionals from the municipal, prefectural, and national governments.

METROPOLITAN RESPONSE

The Japanese system is set up so that "in disaster management, most functions are to be borne by local governments."[36] This includes planning and implementing disaster response.[37] In the subway sarin attack, the Tokyo metropolitan government had these responsibilities. The metropolitan police have primary jurisdiction over law enforcement, investigation, maintenance of law and order, and prevention of further attacks. Under the Tokyo regional disaster plan, the Tokyo Metropolitan Fire Department (TMFD) is responsible for providing first aid to victims, selecting the hospital(s) to which victims will be transported, and providing transportation to hospitals. To fulfill its mission of providing non-hospital emergency medical care, the TMFD has 182 emergency medical teams and 1,650 emergency medical technicians ready to serve the Tokyo metropolitan area.[38] Each emergency medical team is staffed by one emergency lifesaving technician (ELST) who provides basic medical treatment and may provide advanced treatment only with the express permission of a medical doctor. There is no system that provides for doctors to ride along with ELSTs, but the Tokyo Metropolitan Ambulance Control Center (TMACC) has a staff physician on call 24 hours a day who may permit ELSTs to perform advanced medical procedures.

The disaster response plan in place in 1995 recognized that local resources could be overwhelmed in a large-scale disaster. Thus, several provisions for extra assistance were in place. The plan called for staff

---

35. As with most disasters, the earliest first responders were victims and bystanders, who were not trained to deal with the aftermath of a disaster, especially a chemical weapons attack.

36. Furukawa, "An Institutional Framework," p. 5. In Japan, "the fundamental law of disaster management" assigns responsibility for managing disasters to the emergency management offices in the wards in metropolitan areas like Tokyo and in other cities, towns, and villages.

37. Tetsu Okumura, Kouichiro Suzuki, Atsuhiro Fukuda, Akitsugu Kohama, Nobukatsu Takasu, Shinichi Ishimatsu, and Shigeaki Hinohara, "The Tokyo Subway Sarin Attack: Disaster Management, Part 1: National and International Response," *Academic Emergency Medicine*, Vol. 5, No. 6 (1998), pp. 613–617, at p. 625.

38. Ibid., p. 614.

from surrounding hospitals to be dispatched to the disaster scene to assist local ELSTs. Similarly, mutual aid agreements, in which other localities and prefectures lend assistance to the disaster-stricken site, were in place prior to the sarin attack.[39] Prefectures, which comprise (but do not have legal authority over) several municipalities, provide assistance and support when a disaster overwhelms municipal resources. As one of 12 designated "large cities" in Japan, Tokyo functions almost like a prefecture in terms of resource allocation, yet the "wards" that make up the city have less autonomy than municipalities. Moreover, because it is the capital of Japan, Tokyo is home to national government agencies as well as city agencies. Thus, Tokyo is more able to coordinate resources and personnel across agencies and levels of government than most prefectures of other large cities.[40]

NATIONAL CRISIS MANAGEMENT AGENCIES

In Japan, the governor of the affected prefecture is in charge during an emergency. Local government must request assistance from the appropriate national agency in order to secure assistance from that agency.[41] For instance, a request to the Japanese Self Defense Force (part of the Defense Agency) must originate from the local government. Moreover, because the legal head of the SDF is the prime minister, the subsidiary of the Defense Agency cannot act without the prime minister's consent. The SDF possesses a wide knowledge of chemical warfare agents and possesses some decontamination abilities. It also has the ability to rapidly assemble communications systems and medical triage units. There are two bureaucratic hurdles to overcome, however, before the SDF can enter the disaster area or carry out rescue operations: receipt of a request and approval.[42]

If the disaster is of such magnitude that it requires national emergency measures and is labeled a "major disaster," the national government establishes a Headquarters for Major Disaster Countermeasures. The National Police Agency plays largely a support role but does have the authority to coordinate and command local law enforcement and to

39. Ibid.

40. Furukawa, "An Institutional Framework," p. 4.

41. However, a governor may not have the best information, as was the case following the great Hanshin Kobe earthquake of 1995. In other cases, the governor may be reluctant to request help for a variety of political reasons. Interview with Shun'ichi Furukawa, Institute of Policy and Planning Sciences, University of Tskuba, November 1, 2000.

42. Okumura et al., "The Tokyo Subway Sarin Attack," p. 614.

assign police from other prefectures to assist police in the affected municipality.[43]

Major Consequence Management Issues

There are several lessons to be learned from Tokyo's experience regarding actions that can be taken to mitigate the consequences of a WMD terrorist attack. Emergency response has immediate, near-term, and long-term phases. Actions may overlap from one stage to the next, but specific actions may be necessary at particular stages. This section of the essay examines the consequence management actions that were taken after the subway sarin attack and outlines the changes made to Japanese consequence management plans in the years following the attack.

PROBLEM RECOGNITION

Problem recognition, or the ability to gather information, construct a pattern with that information, and disseminate both up the chain of command, is an immediate to near-term response activity. Gathering information is the responsibility of first responders—those best positioned to arrive on the scene to begin rescuing victims upon receiving report of a crisis. In the subway attack scenario, transit workers were the first responders because of their proximity to the attack sites.

There was a significant delay in recognizing the nature of the problem during both sarin attacks, as is illustrated by the chronology of the subway attacks. Sarin was released in the subway cars shortly before 8 A.M. Immediately after the release, sick passengers staggered from the five affected trains at several stations. By 8:10 A.M., the transit workers operating the Hibiya line recognized that something was amiss. Their announcements to passengers on the trains and in the stations progressed from "sick passenger" to "explosion occurred at Tsukiji," then "Tsukiji next stop," and finally, "evacuate, evacuate, evacuate."[44] Despite these alarming announcements and the influx of emergency response personnel into the station, the Hibiya line train departed Tsukiji and headed for Kasumigaseki, only seven minutes late. Not for several more minutes did subway officials direct passengers to leave the station and halt service.[45]

---

43. Interview with Yoshihide Kuroki, Chief Superintendent, Special Advisor for Counterterrorism, National Police Agency, October 31, 2000.

44. Kaplan and Marshall, *The Cult at the End of the World*, pp. 248–249.

45. Ibid.

Meanwhile, on the Chiyoda line, passengers pointed out two packages leaking an unknown fluid onto the floor of a train car. Station employees responded by mopping up the mess with newspaper and their bare hands and sending the train on its way. Two of these employees later died from sarin exposure. When the full impact of the situation was realized, station employees posted handmade signs outside of the stations announcing that they were closed "owing to a terrorist attack."[46]

The Marunouchi line continued to run until 9:27 A.M., long after the others closed down, leaving a trail of sarin up and down the entire line.[47] This potentially contaminated several additional stations and could have exposed countless passengers and transit employees to sarin.

It is not surprising that transit workers were unable to identify the nature and scope of the situation. They were not trained to identify or respond to chemical or biological weapons, and they did not have a centralized system to monitor disturbances at the various stations. Thus, in most stations, the employees thought they had isolated incidents of sick passengers or chemical spills.

Police and emergency medical technicians are better equipped to identify and respond to a crisis. However, even though the metropolitan police began receiving calls shortly after the attack, it was not until 8:44 A.M. that the National Police Agency (NPA) became convinced that a major problem was at hand and a serious response effort was required.[48] Before 9 A.M., the NPA suspected that a chemical agent was the cause of illness. The NPA called upon the Self Defense Force to send two chemical warfare experts to assist emergency operations units. Yet, even though police at all levels of government believed that there was a major problem, trains continued to run until 9:27 A.M., almost an hour and a half after the metropolitan police began receiving calls and over 30 minutes after the NPA determined that a major incident had occurred.

Neither the identity of the agent nor the effectiveness of the dispersal methods were known to most victims or emergency response personnel until several hours after the attack. Police and military authorities did not identify the agent as sarin for nearly two hours after the attack.[49] They did not share that information with other emergency response agencies

---

46. Ibid.

47. Ibid., p. 250.

48. It is unclear whether there was a lack of reporting or a lack of recognition.

49. Although accounts vary, most assert that police identified the agent prior to 11 A.M. All agree that the diagnostic tool was chromatograph–mass spectrometer analysis.

for another hour; according to many sources, hospitals were never officially informed of this assessment.[50]

In Tokyo, the delay in halting service and evacuating passengers had several root causes. First, this type of attack was virtually unprecedented. Thus, it presented a completely novel situation for most government employees at all levels.[51] No response plans or training existed to prepare response personnel for a WMD attack.

Second, the coordinated, multi-site nature of the attack was initially unknown to train operators and other first responders. Each station thought that it had an isolated sick passenger situation. When passengers pointed to the leaking bags that contained the sarin, station employees cleaned them up, assuming they were unrelated incidents. Not for one full hour after the attack were enough calls aggregated at the police emergency switchboard to allow authorities to connect the incidents and formulate an assessment of the situation.

Third, no contingency plans detailing how to respond to a WMD attack existed outside of the military. Thus, even if the inexperienced response personnel had identified the nature of the incident, they would not have had a plan to guide them as to how to proceed.

Finally, bureaucratic barriers hindered the immediate recognition and response. *Tatewari,* a term that translates roughly as "compartmentalized bureaucracy," describes the stovepiped agencies that comprise the Japanese government. The agencies do not usually work together, but rather work separate from—or even in competition with—one another.[52] Even when each agency does its job, the lack of cross-agency communication and cooperation hinder effective response and recovery operations.

---

50. Physicians at St. Luke's Hospital asserted that, "the police did not inform us directly." According to several reports, a physician who treated victims of the Matsumoto attack contacted St. Luke's hospital after seeing news coverage of the subway situation and suggested the possibility that the causative agent was sarin. The physician, from Shinshu University Medical Department, personally phoned all Tokyo regional hospitals and faxed them information on sarin. See Okumura et al., "The Tokyo Subway Sarin Attack," p. 621. See also Haruki Murakami, *Underground* (New York: Vintage Books, 2000), pp. 217–219.

51. At the time of the Tokyo attack, the Matsumoto attack was still officially labeled an accident. A link between Aum Shinrikyo and the use of sarin in Matsumoto had been established with soil samples from an Aum compound in November 1994, but police did not investigate this connection after the subway attack. The newspaper *Yomiuri Shimbun* had run a story in January 1995 outlining the link and pushing for an investigation. However, the gardener, Kono Yoshiyuki, remained a suspect until Aum confessed to the crime in the summer of 1995. See Reader, *Religious Violence,* p. 221.

52. Interview with Nozomu Asukai, Department of Psychiatry, Tokyo Institute of Psychiatry, November 1, 2000.

This was particularly acute following the Kobe Hanshin earthquake of 1995 and was also evident in the aftermath of the sarin attack, when the highly independent nature of government agencies contributed to the delay of agent identification.[53] In both of these disasters, agencies did not communicate with one another; thus, information and expertise were not readily shared.

SUBSEQUENT REVISION TO IMPROVE PROBLEM RECOGNITION: WMD
TRAINING FOR FIRST RESPONDERS

The first responders in the subway attack were transit workers, police officers, emergency medical technicians, firefighters, and physicians. Many of them did not have the requisite training to recognize—and function in—a contaminated environment. One lesson that was acted upon by Japanese officials after the attacks was that response personnel need WMD-specific training.

After the sarin attack, the SDF began providing information to the police and the media on dangerous chemical agents. According to a senior military official, "since the Tokyo sarin attack, nerve agents have become a recognized measure of terrorism. Therefore, information on nerve agents has become open, and a manual for emergency medical services personnel has been published."[54] In addition to education in agent identification, on-the-ground training for police and fire personnel is now being provided by the SDF.[55] The Tokyo Metropolitan Fire Department is working with Tokyo University on emergency planning. Volunteers are being trained to respond to chemical and biological weapons. For example, during the sarin attack, it was quickly discovered that volunteer and professional responders should not rush in to assist without first donning personal protection because of the risk of secondary contamination.[56] This contradicted the working assumption that rescue workers should enter the disaster as soon as possible, in their standard professional attire, to rescue victims.

Training is being reinforced with simulations. A large-scale disaster drill in Tokyo in September 2000 provided multiple agencies at all levels of government with the opportunity to apply their new skills in a simu-

53.   See also Furukawa, "An Institutional Framework."

54.   Okumura et al., "The Tokyo Subway Sarin Attack," p. 626.

55.   Interview with Colonel Masaaki Iwaki, Chief, Operations Research Office, Japan Defense Agency, October 31, 2000.

56.   Interview with Makato Tsuruki, Professor, University of Tokyo, and President of the Antiterrorism Section of the Police Policy Studies Association, October 31, 2000.

lated catastrophe. This type of large-scale simulation is relatively new to response agencies in Japan.

Despite the progress in training and exercising, however, agencies remain divided in their training and duties. Although one SDF official notes that the SDF has a better working relationship with the police and with other countries now than it did prior to the sarin attack, collaboration has not become a regular part of the relationship between the agencies.[57]

Incident Management

Incident management is an immediate priority in any disaster situation. In Tokyo, within five minutes of determining that the situation merited a serious response, which had occurred at 8:44 A.M., the NPA requested the assistance of two SDF chemical warfare experts. The NPA and SDF immediately established a joint police/army investigative unit. A second emergency unit was established to coordinate the police, fire, rescue, and medical responders. There were, nevertheless, significant planning, logistical and operational difficulties that contributed to the delay in the reaction by transit workers and public safety officials.[58]

Two main issues led to the lack of strong incident management. First, the delay in problem recognition meant that operations began without a properly established incident management system (IMS):

IMS is a generic term for the design of ad hoc emergency management teams that coordinate the efforts of more than one agency under a unified command. It is a functionally based organizational template that facilitates information flow, decision-making, and operational coordination . . . [that] is designed to manage complex or multisite emergency events.[59]

Because the multi-site nature of the incident was initially overlooked, there was no effort to coordinate the provision of resources to each contaminated area. The first emergency call came into the Tokyo Metropolitan Fire Department at 8:09 A.M. For the next hour, calls came in from

---

57. Interview with Iwaki, October 31, 2000.

58. In a WMD attack, time is crucial. For example, prophylaxis for victims of a biological attack must often be initiated in the first hours or days after exposure in order to be effective.

59. Hank Christen, Paul Maniscalco, Alan Vickery, and Frances Winslow, "An Overview of Incident Management Systems," *Perspectives on Preparedness*, No. 4, Executive Session on Domestic Preparedness, John F. Kennedy School of Government, Harvard University (September 2001), at <www.esdp.org>.

15 different subway stations. However, the TMFD failed to rapidly establish a link among these events. Approximately one hour after the attack, the TMFD set up emergency response operations headquarters at the affected stations. However, the rapid onset of symptoms meant that the establishment of response centers came after the most severely affected patients had been triaged.[60]

Another example of the problems caused by a lack of coordinated command-and-control was poor unit assignment. Upon receiving the first call for assistance, the fire department sent all of their personnel to the Tsukiji station—the first station to call in the emergency—leaving minimal resources for other emergency calls. When calls began pouring in from the other affected stations, there were no firefighters left to respond.[61]

A second barrier to efficient incident management was the lack of established interagency relationships.[62] Physicians who worked at St. Luke's International Hospital (SLIH) at the time of the subway attack say that, "during this disaster, the concerned organizations acted independently and there was too little communication among them."[63] The police, fire department, and Hygienic Department of the Tokyo Metropolitan Government functioned simultaneously but without any central coordination.[64]

This problem was particularly acute between agencies at different levels of government. For months following the Matsumoto attack, for example, the Self Defense Force had been unwilling to cooperate with the police.[65] The police agency had primary responsibility for crisis management and authority to call in the SDF when support was required. However, "at the early stage of this disaster, the full abilities of the Japanese Self Defense Forces were not used. Complicated formalities delayed the implementation of these forces."[66] This was especially unfortunate, given

---

60. Okumura, et al., "The Tokyo Subway Sarin Attack," p. 615.

61. Interview with Asukai, November 1, 2000.

62. "The Aum affair teaches us that . . . coordination among concerned governmental agencies are absolute necessities in preventing and responding to future terrorism." Miyasaka, "Terrorism and Antiterrorism in Japan," p. 8.

63. Okumura et al., "The Tokyo Subway Sarin Attack," p. 616.

64. The Hygienic Department of the Tokyo metropolitan government is directly responsible for metropolitan disaster planning. See Okumura et al., "The Tokyo Subway Sarin Attack," p. 626.

65. Interview with Tsuruki, October 31, 2000.

66. Okumura et al., "The Tokyo Subway Sarin Attack," p. 626.

that SDF personnel had far more chemical and biological weapons training than the police did, as well as decontamination capability.

The sharp bureaucratic divisions, coupled with an organizational culture that did not emphasize cooperation, also stymied the subway attack investigation. The lack of cooperation between the NPA and SDF eventually grew so problematic that some specialists quit the SDF, so that the police could hire them as trained personnel to investigate the scene.[67]

SUBSEQUENT REVISIONS TO INCIDENT MANAGEMENT: CREATING PLANS

Perhaps the most important change has been in the way that officials think about terrorism and, more specifically, terrorism as a subset of consequence management for all natural and man-made disasters. The government views the threat of terrorism through a broader lens and no longer focuses solely on left-wing activities and hostage taking in its response plans. Moreover, terrorism with a weapon of mass destruction has moved to the front of the stage to join hijackings on the list of "serious incidents" under the Crisis Classifications for Preparing Response Plans.[68] Japan's government held its first bioterrorism conference in 1999, and in the same year, the SDF secured its first budget for anti- bioterrorism preparedness.[69]

At the time of the subway attack, "there [were] no concrete articles in the Japanese legal system providing for a single, coordinated headquarters for disaster management."[70] The national government has worked since 1995 to enhance not only its response capabilities, but also its overarching response plan. A formal response plan has been agreed upon, as detailed below in a graphic supplied by the Cabinet Office for National Security and Crisis Management.

SUBSEQUENT REVISIONS TO IMPROVE INCIDENT MANAGEMENT: BRIDGING INTERAGENCY DIVIDES

In an effort to remedy the lack of an agreed incident management structure and the lack of interagency cooperation, revisions were made at the national level. The management issues are summarized in Figure 1. Ele-

---

67. Interview with Tsuruki, October 31, 2000.

68. The two other categories are natural disasters and serious accidents. See Cabinet Office for National Security Affairs and Crisis Management handout on file with the author.

69. Mike Green, Conference Report, "New Approaches to U.S.-Japan Security Cooperation," proceedings from Japan Society Conference, October 30–31, 2000 (Tokyo, Japan), p. 11, on file with the author.

70. Okumura et al., "The Tokyo Subway Sarin Attack," p. 626.

Figure 1. Formal Response Plan.

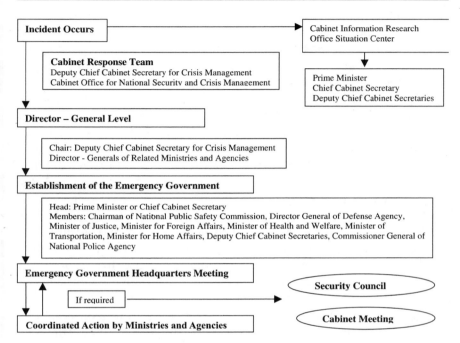

ments of interagency cooperation that have been targeted for improvement include:

- Clarifying information liaisons and establishing a chain of communication up to the prime minister;
- Providing equipment for information transmission between ministries, agencies, and the prime minister;
- Defining procedures for convening emergency meetings of officials at the prime minister's residence; and
- Establishing the position of Deputy Chief Cabinet Secretary for Crisis Management.[71]

The fourth revision enumerated above—the post of Deputy Chief Cabinet Secretary—was created in April 1998 to "make primary decisions on initial government response to emergencies and perform overall coordination among measures taken by related ministries and agencies . . .

---

71. Furukawa, "An Institutional Framework," p. 6.

and to prepare various government response plans to different types of emergencies and coordinate those of related ministries and agencies."[72] A second entity, the Office for Crisis Management in the Cabinet Secretariat, was established to support the Deputy Chief Cabinet Secretary. The primary function of the two entities is to assist with preparation and co-ordination among national agencies. This effort to facilitate interagency cooperation represents a relatively new operating procedure for post-war Japan, and is greatly needed if agencies are going to break the long-standing tradition of working independently of one another.

More recently, the Council Against NBC Terrorism was created to tackle various issues related to counterterrorism. The council, a meeting of Japanese government officials chaired by the Deputy Chief Cabinet Secretary for Crisis Management, began meeting in August 2000 and has since met twice (August 2000 and April 2001). Other participants include Directors-General of ministries and agencies, such as Police, Defense, Fire and Disaster Management, Foreign Affairs, Science and Technology, Health, Economy, Trade and Industry, and the Coast Guard. At the 2001 meeting, various agencies described the measures that they took in response to the sarin attack and discussed plans to improve response in the future. Indeed, these meetings are designed to facilitate discussion among the national-level agencies involved in terrorism response, as well as to create a strong national response plan. Thus, several new efforts at bridging interagency divides, at least at the national level, are underway.

The new national response plan will not solve all of the incident management problems that emerged during the response to the subway attack. Deeply entrenched political norms, some of which are embodied in the response plan, remain a hindrance to effective response.

First, the Japanese political system is *designed* to be cautious. After World War II, "coordination and integration functions of the administration were carefully constructed to ensure checks-and-balance systems in the inter-rivalry compartmentalization of bureaucratic organizations."[73] The combination of relatively weak authority and massive bureaucracy fosters slow and deliberate decision-making, which can be problematic in a crisis situation.

Second, the new response plan shown above assumes a "top-down" structure in which national-level agencies coordinate the immediate

---

72. Kazuharu Hirano, Cabinet Councilor, Cabinet Office for National Security and Crisis Management, notes presented on October 30, 2000, at the Japan Society Conference.

73. Furukawa, "An Institutional Framework," p. 5.

disaster response. However, local and regional governments are almost inevitably the first responders in a terrorist attack or a natural disaster. This is true primarily because of proximity to the disaster site, but also because local and regional response agencies are often better equipped to handle disasters, because they routinely respond to natural disasters, and because they possess the primary legal authority to respond. Thus, national agencies should not presume that circumstances or knowledge will permit them to dictate the terms of the response from the top.

Third, the response plan is designed for national agencies. According to the Cabinet Office for National Security and Crisis Management, comparable response plans for terrorism do not widely exist at the prefecture or local level.[74] Local response plans tend to be generalized to apply to all disasters, although specific contingency plans for earthquakes typically exist. The national cabinet office is encouraging prefectures to emulate the national model establishing specific contingency plans for terrorism as one potential type of disaster.[75] Because local and regional personnel will arrive at the scene before national agency personnel, response plans must be developed at the local and regional levels, not just at the national level. Moreover, national response plans should be based on, or at least designed to work in concert with, local plans.

Communication

The need for strong communication spans the temporal spectrum but is particularly important immediately following the attack, when a proactive communications strategy can aid rescue and recovery efforts. A good intergovernmental communication strategy facilitates allocation of resources, implementation of response plans, and establishment of a chain of control. Communication between the government and the public can minimize panic, facilitate smooth evacuation or quarantine, and provide instructions and information to victims and others.

In the immediate aftermath of the subway attack, communication across agencies was hindered by a variety of technical and cultural barriers. On the technical front, for example, the Tokyo Metropolitan Ambulance Control Center (TMACC) could not effectively manage the dispatch of emergency medical technicians, in part because "information regard-

---

74. Correspondence from government official (who requested anonymity) from the Cabinet Office for National Security and Crisis Management, September 7, 2001, on file with the author.

75. Ibid.

ing this disaster exceeded their ability to manage communications," which led to a system overload.[76] As a result of communications overload, emergency medical technicians lost radio contact with the TMACC and were thus unable to secure permission to perform advanced medical treatment, such as intubations. This directly affected patient care: all but one victim had to wait for hospital admission to receive intubation and adequate ventilation.[77]

Another result of communication system overload was that ELSTs could not acquire hospital availability information and were thus forced to find out which hospitals had beds available via public telephone, or simply to take patients to the nearest or largest hospital.[78] This method made tracking the number, location, and medical status of patients all but impossible.

Difficulties were neither confined to the medical arena nor were they all technical: communication infrastructure and information sharing were inadequate across disciplines and levels of government. Channels of communication among local emergency response workers, transit workers, and medical personnel were poor. Although police had information confirming that sarin was the source of the problem by 11:00 A.M., the hospitals and the TMFD were never officially notified that sarin was the agent used in the attack. Some personnel found out by watching the news, some learned it from patients who were watching the news, and others were assisted by tips from physicians who had responded to the Matsumoto attack and recognized the symptoms described by television and radio.[79]

An extended form of cross-agency communication involves working with similarly situated agencies in other countries that have reason to be concerned about the disaster. Communication with the international community about either sarin attack was all but absent. Anxious nations, including those with Aum chapters based within their borders, were not

---

76. Okumura et al., "The Tokyo Subway Sarin Attack," p. 614.

77. Ibid.

78. Ibid., p. 615.

79. It was not until three hours after the incident that the Tokyo Metropolitan Police communicated the positive identification of sarin to the public at a press conference. Once the medical staff receiving patients were convinced sarin was involved, they were able to tailor patient treatment accordingly. Nozomu Asukai, "Health Effects Following the Sarin Attack in the Tokyo Subway System," unpublished manuscript on file with the author. See also Okumura et al., p. 615; Amy Smithson and Leslie-Anne Levy, "Ataxia: The Chemical and Biological Terrorism Threat and U.S. Response," Stimson Center Report No. 35 (October 2000), p. 97.

promptly briefed by Japanese officials; most learned of the attack and subsequent investigation via television and radio. Aum had members in Russia and the United States, and some members had visited Australia, where they performed experiments that left livestock dead. The United States, in particular, was worried about a possible attack due to Aum's strident anti-Western teachings. The silence persisted through the near- and long-term periods following the attack. Federal Bureau of Investigation (FBI) officials and other members of the U.S. government were frustrated by the lack of cooperation and information sharing by the Japanese government. One U.S. official complained that he "found out more from the morning paper than from our briefings from the Japanese."[80]

Equally important is communication with the public—victims and concerned citizens alike. A public affairs campaign can provide the public with information about evacuation, transportation, and treatment. This did not occur in the subway sarin attack: the government did not rapidly identify the nature of the situation or the appropriate response, and no public affairs strategy had been prepared for a mass casualty terrorist attack. The first confusing messages were transmitted to the public by the transit department. False announcements on trains added to the confusion among victims and responders. Further messages were transmitted via the media. The images portrayed on the 9 A.M. news, which may have exacerbated the nervous frustration of victims and concerned parties, were of confusion and chaos: victims were shown becoming ill, staggering around the city, and searching for answers.

Communication between the government and the Japanese people was no clearer in the early or near-term period after the attack than it had been during and immediately following the attack. According to one account, "in contrast to the cult's loud declarations of innocence, Japanese authorities seemed intent on keeping the public in the dark."[81] The silence practiced by most government agencies began immediately after the attack and continued for days. This perpetuated the general fear within the population and among victims, who knew only that the perpetrators were at large and thus could launch a follow-up attack. As a result of the government's silence, "Aum was winning the propaganda war hands down."[82] Cult members even attracted throngs of teenaged groupies who clipped pictures of the charismatic young Aum spokesman and other accused members.

---

80. Kaplan and Marshall, *The Cult at the End of the World*, p. 265.

81. Ibid., p. 259.

82. Ibid., p. 273.

The media, already heavily focused on the sarin attack, became obsessed with Aum Shinrikyo. However, the emphasis was on the nature of Aum and its members, the disintegration of Japanese society and standards, and the loss of safety in society, rather than on the phenomenon of terrorism or weapons of mass destruction. The continuing fixation with Aum certainly influenced society's long-term impression of the attack. The constant media coverage and the revelation of new discoveries over several months "heightened the sense of unease [among Japanese] and called into question, [for] many people, the competence of the public authorities."[83]

SUBSEQUENT REVISIONS TO IMPROVE COMMUNICATION: INFRASTRUCTURE AND STRATEGIES

Underdeveloped communications systems and strategies resulted in difficulties at all three stages of response: immediate, near-term, and long-term. Since 1995, the government has undertaken several initiatives designed to repair communications deficiencies. Most of these improvements have focused on infrastructure and the interagency relationships that need to be in place in order for that infrastructure to be useful in information sharing. There has not been a strong focus on building a public affairs strategy that would enable the government to communicate effectively with the public.

One example of a technical advancement involves "a communication system for disasters, including video and satellite communication systems, [which] has been developed in central and local governments."[84] In tandem with this effort, outdated systems were repaired. In addition, a new disaster reporting system was instituted whereby authorized taxi drivers report details on disasters to a taxi control center via their standard radios.[85] Until the communication infrastructure is widely improved, however, a robust reporting system will exist only in plans and will be ineffective in practice because telecommunications lines will be overwhelmed and will become disabled, as they were after the sarin attack.

Improving communication is not limited to repairing and expanding physical infrastructure. Some of the biggest problems experienced after the sarin attack resulted from organizational and cultural, rather than technical, deficiencies. Repairing these deficiencies is difficult, however,

---

83. Reader, *Poisonous Cocktail,* p. 108.

84. Furukawa, "An Institutional Framework," p. 6.

85. Okumura et al., "The Tokyo Subway Sarin Attack," p. 617.

because many officials prefer to wait until they can provide full and accurate information before offering any information at all. Communication problems stemmed from two sources: the rigid divides between public safety agencies that discouraged information sharing among agencies and professional reluctance to divulge information that may be incomplete or uncertain. In the first case, many of the organizations and individuals involved in the recovery operation in Tokyo had not often worked together previously and therefore lacked established relationships. For instance, police, fire, medical, and transportation personnel had not necessarily established a trust that could facilitate information sharing. In the second case, communication between agencies, with the public, and with the international community was limited where information was unconfirmed or incomplete. The lesson learned in Tokyo, and in many other disasters around the world, is that officials must share the information that they do know in a timely manner. If the media do not have an authorized spokesperson to turn to, they will fill that void with information, correct or otherwise, from whatever sources will step up to the camera.

Personal Protection and Decontamination

Protecting personnel who enter contaminated environments and decontaminating the site are immediate and near-term concerns. In the subway attack, primary contamination claimed the lives of 10 passengers and two transit workers. Secondary contamination—response workers sickened indirectly by exposure to victims who had been in direct contact with the chemical—incapacitated, but did not kill, many response personnel in Tokyo. Natural decomposition of sarin's strength and the fact that the sarin used was only 30 percent pure were mitigating factors that reduced the casualty count. If Aum had used pure sarin, advanced delivery technology, or a biological agent, the lack of rapid decontamination of the subway and the victims could have been fatal to far more people.

The first responders in this incident were, because of their proximity to the attack site, subway workers. Ignorant about the source of the illnesses, many well-meaning transit workers handled sick passengers or touched the sarin while cleaning up the spillage. Two workers died after they had removed the newspaper that had concealed the agent and absorbed some of it.

The second wave of the response included firefighters, police, and emergency medical technicians. At 8:20 A.M., the first call came into the Tokyo emergency switchboard with a complaint of a foul odor in the Kamiyacho station on the Hibiya line. At 8:33 A.M., the fire department emergency squad received a call that six passengers had collapsed at the Nakano Sakaue Station on the Marunouchi line. Emergency workers without appropriate gear took care of severely poisoned victims. Many were overcome by sarin exposure.[86] Emergency medical service personnel at the scene were contaminated by sick victims: of 1,364 ELSTs, 135 suffered acute symptoms and required medical treatment.[87] Others were contaminated while transporting victims to the hospital. After witnessing the effects of secondary contamination, police ordered response personnel to wear masks. At 9 A.M., police finally began blocking access to subways that transit officials had not yet closed.[88]

Almost simultaneous with the influx of traditional emergency response personnel into the subways and surrounding areas was the involvement of hospital workers. Because no information that the incident was caused by poison gas was available in the first few hours of the attack, patient decontamination was not initially attempted, and 23 percent of the 472 house staff that were exposed to contaminated patients showed signs of sarin poisoning.[89] Table 1 depicts staff symptoms.[90]

After St. Luke's Hospital staff learned that the victims were suffering from exposure to a nerve agent, they decontaminated patients "by having them change clothes and shower." This was a time-intensive ordeal, because "it took time to determine the cause of the victims' illness . . . and [there was] not enough space for changing clothes and showering."[91] The hospitals lacked adequate decontamination facilities and training and, therefore had to rely on this rudimentary method of decontaminating patients.

In 1995, the only agency that possessed the ability to decontaminate an area exposed to a chemical or biological agent was a specialized task force of the Self Defense Force.[92] Between 4:50 P.M. and 9:20 P.M.[93]—over

---

86. See Asukai, "Health Effects Following the Sarin Attack," p. 3.

87. Okumura et al., "The Tokyo Subway Sarin Attack," p. 615.

88. Smithson, *Ataxia*, p. 93.

89. None were seriously affected. See Sadayoshi Ohbu, Akira Yamashina, Nobukatsu Takasu, Tatsuo Yamaguchi, Tetsuo Murai, Kanzoh Nakano, Yukio Matsui, Ryuzo Mikami, Kenji Sakurai, and Shigeaki Hinohara,"Sarin Poisoning on Tokyo Subway," (Tokyo, Japan) at <www.sma.org/smj/97june3.htm>.

90. Okumura et al., "The Tokyo Subway Sarin Attack," p. 620.

91. Ibid.

92. According to a high-ranking official in the National Police Agency, the police had no decontamination capabilities.

93. Smithson, *Ataxia*, p. 94.

Table 1. Secondary Exposure Symptoms in 472 Hospital Workers at St. Luke's Hospital.*

Symptom	Number	Percent
Eye symptoms	66	14
Headache	52	11
Throat pain	39	8.3
Dyspnea	25	5.3
Nausea	14	3
Dizziness	12	2.5
Nose pain	9	1.9

* Okumura et al., "The Tokyo Subway Sarin Attack," p. 620.

eight hours after the attack—the task force decontaminated the subway cars with a bleach and water mixture.[94] The subway was back in service later on the day of the attack. The SDF did not assist hospitals that were attempting to decontaminate patients.

SUBSEQUENT REVISIONS TO PROTECTION AND DECONTAMINATION: EQUIPMENT AND INFRASTRUCTURE

Since 1995, the Japanese national government has invested in protective gear and decontamination equipment. One concrete example is the introduction into police training and response of protective gear, decontamination kits, and detectors purchased with a one-time expenditure of one billion yen. Forty-seven local police forces benefited from this investment.[95] Another is that a special U.S. Marine Corps unit for chemical and biological weapons management was deployed to Japan to assist with training.

Despite these investments, decontamination capabilities remain underdeveloped.[96] According to an official in the Cabinet for Crisis Management, the NPA decontamination capability is intended for use on police

94. This process was shown on the evening news. Interview with senior Cabinet Officer for National Security and Crisis Management.

95. Correspondence from Yoshihide Kuroki, Special Advisor for Counterterrorism, National Police Agency, November 1, 2000.

96. Correspondence from Tetsu Okumura, Department of Acute Medicine, Kawasaki Medical School, September 19, 2001.

officers, not civilians or buildings. The SDF has a more extensive capacity to decontaminate roads, buildings, and members of the public. However, as in both sarin attacks, the bureaucratic barriers to rapid response by the SDF may render this resource ineffective. The Fire Disaster Management Agency has some decontamination equipment that is available for both personnel and the public. Although at least three national agencies and several local police departments possess at least some decontamination equipment, an official notes that the national plan has not yet "determined the specific role or responsibility of [each] agency at the scene."[97] Therefore, what decontamination capability exists may not be rapidly or effectively deployed.

Finally, hospitals' decontamination capability requires further attention. The Japanese government distributed decontamination equipment and personal protection equipment to hospitals beginning in 2000. By 2002, nearly 80 hospitals were to have some decontamination capability. However, the budget allows for only four personal protection suits for each hospital, and additional units must be purchased at the expense of the hospital.[98] Because of budget constraints and competing priorities, hospitals may choose not to expand on the government-initiated capacity to operate in a contaminated environment or to create decontamination facilities.

Medical Surge Capacity

Medical surge capacity is the ability of the health care system to handle an influx of patients that exceeds the normal patient load. Surge capacity includes physicians, nurses, hospital staff, medication, physical space, beds, equipment, and communication infrastructure.

One component of medical surge capacity is the system's ability to assess and attend to patients' vital needs at the disaster site: to allocate immediate care capabilities by determining which patients need urgent care, which can safely wait, and which are beyond help. A complementary component is the ability of the medical community to "flex," so that it can accommodate the needs of a high volume of patients. Approximately one hour after the subway attack, the TMFD set up emergency response operations headquarters at the affected stations. The TMFD requested assistance from the regional medical association, and 47 doctors,

---

97. Correspondence from government official, Cabinet Office for National Security and Crisis Management, September 7, 2001.

98. Correspondence from Tetsu Okumura, September 19, 2001.

23 nurses, and three clerks responded. In addition, St. Luke's hospital, the nearest medical facility, sent eight doctors and three nurses. However, the rapid onset of symptoms meant that the establishment of response centers came after the most severe patients had been attended to,[99] and, by the time supplemental personnel arrived, the patients in most serious need of attention had been transported to the hospital. The hospitals, ironically, had been depleted of key personnel because they had sent them out into the field. In essence, the system "flexed" at the wrong time and, therefore, in the wrong direction.

A second aspect of surge capacity is the ability to transport patients to functioning medical facilities. By the end of the day on March 20, 1995, 1,364 emergency medical technicians and 131 ambulances had responded to patients at 15 subway stations.[100] The emergency medical system and medical transportation were overtaxed: 688 patients of the sarin attack were transported by ambulances during the course of the day.[101] Hospitals outside the center of the disaster area offered to help the overcrowded hospitals, such as St. Luke's, but they could not be fully used due to lack of available transportation.

In several local hospitals, capacity was also put to the test. Approximately 5,500 people went to 280 medical facilities on the day of and the days following the attack. In all, 1,046 patients were admitted to 98 hospitals.[102] The best data comes from St. Luke's International Hospital, which saw the most patients from the attack. At 8:40 A.M., patients began flooding into St. Luke's; within an hour, the hospital had received 150 patients. In total, St. Luke's saw 641 patients that day and over 1,400 patients the following week.[103] Like other hospitals in the metropolitan area and beyond, St. Luke's was overwhelmed. Exhausted physicians who had sarin victims added to their existing caseloads treated patients in hallways. At 9:20 A.M., St. Luke's Hospital administrators declared an emergency, canceling routine operations and outpatient services. All hospital facilities, including chapels and halls, were used to treat sarin victims.[104]

Hospital communication systems were also overwhelmed. St. Luke's reported that jammed systems made it impossible to communicate

---

99. Okumura et al., "The Tokyo Subway Sarin Attack," p. 615.

100. Ibid., p. 614.

101. Smithson, *Ataxia*, p. 95.

102. Asukai, "Health Effects Following the Sarin Attack," p. 2.

103. Okumura, et al., "The Tokyo Subway Sarin Attack," p. 619.

104. Ibid., p. 621.

from one department to the next. As a result, "hospital staff resorted to shouting down the halls or personally hunting down a particular colleague."[105]

Part of what overwhelmed the medical system was a category of affected people called the "worried well." The worried well included exposed and unexposed individuals that sought, but did not really require, medical care. Some may have been exposed to the attack but not physically affected. Others may have heard about the attack and were concerned for their welfare, even though they had not been exposed to the chemical. Still others exhibited psychosomatic symptoms that led them to believe they were in danger. Some people associated preexisting conditions with symptoms described by sarin victims, such as eye pain or nausea.

Of the more than 5,000 patients whose hospital visits were directly related to the attack, less than 20 patients were admitted and treated in intensive care units.[106] At St. Luke's, only five patients were deemed to be in critical condition, while 43 men and 63 women were admitted in "moderate" condition—a small proportion of the 641 victims seen by medical practitioners on the day of disaster. People who did not exhibit symptoms of exposure—easily over one half of the patients seen at St. Luke's alone—represented the worried well that clogged the system and postponed treatment of affected individuals.[107] Because the source of the attack and the symptoms of patients were unknown, physicians were unable to distinguish exposed patients in need of medical intervention from the thousands of worried well that flooded hospitals all around Tokyo.

SUBSEQUENT REVISIONS TO MEDICAL CAPACITY: EXPANDED SURGE CAPACITY

There is a concern on behalf of hospital administrators and staff that, if hospitals must tend to large numbers of casualties following a disaster, quality of care will suffer because the facilities are unprepared to handle the unexpected influx of patients who flood the system as a result of the disaster.[108] Yet this issue of building adequate medical surge capac-

---

105. Smithson, *Ataxia*, p. 96.

106. Asukai, "Health Effects Following the Sarin Attack," p. 3.

107. Headache and malaise were the most common persistent, generalized symptoms noted after discharge from the hospital.

108. Correspondence from Tetsu Okumura, December 1, 2001.

ity—the resources to handle excess casualties—is difficult to solve. According to Tetsu Okumura, M.D., "because of tight medical economics, almost all hospitals in Japan do not have sufficient surge capacity."[109] This is unlikely to change, particularly given the fact that, "directors of Japanese hospitals think that expenses against disasters and terrorism are unprofitable."[110]

In part as an attempt to remedy the lack of adequate medical capacity, the Tokyo National Disaster Center was founded in July 1995. This hospital represents the first disaster-oriented hospital in Japan. In non-disaster times, the hospital serves as an educational facility. In times of crisis, the hospital provides hundreds of extra beds.

Although this facility is a thoughtful step forward in creating medical surge capacity, this approach ignores the fact that surge capacity requires more than hospital beds. Medical capacity in general must be strengthened: transportation, communication, pharmaceutical supplies and delivery channels, and medical professionals, all factor into this equation. Thus, Japan has yet to solve the question of how to provide adequate medical surge capacity.

SUBSEQUENT REVISIONS TO MEDICAL CAPACITY: HOSPITAL PLANS
In Tokyo, at the time of the sarin attack, most hospitals did not have extra capacity or specific plans to deal with mass-casualty disasters. Even where emergency response plans were in place, resources were inadequate to handle the demand. A physician at St. Luke's observed that, "to aid the house staff in achieving and maintaining a proper level of disaster preparedness, SLIH conducts routine disaster drills. The nerve gas attack was so unprecedented in nature and site, however, that management guidelines were inadequate; we had no means of handling such an extraordinarily large number of simultaneously affected patients."[111]

After the attacks, hospitals began developing plans to manage mass casualties. The planning is still in a formative stage and varies from one facility to the next.[112] The Kawasaki Medical School Hospital, a teaching facility, developed a manual for managing WMD disasters. Dissemination of these standards to other Japanese hospitals will advance preparedness.

---

109.   Correspondence from Tetsu Okumura, September 19, 2001.

110.   Ibid.

111.   Ohbu et al., "Sarin Poisoning on Tokyo Subway."

112.   Correspondence from Tetsu Okumura, December 1, 2001.

Law Enforcement

Much of the near-term and long-term response to the sarin attack is in the area of law enforcement. Two different aspects of law enforcement were present: investigation, detention of suspects, and trial; and the passage of legislation intended to facilitate trial and punishment of the perpetrators of the crime and to prevent future crimes.

In the days after the attack, more than 2,000 police officers mobilized for a nationwide investigation into the sarin attack and Aum Shinrikyo members and facilities. On March 22, 1995, only two days after the subway attack, authorities raided the Aum commune at Kamikuishiki. Preparing for the worst, police wore gas masks and carried canaries into the residence. That same day, police raided the 25 offices, compounds, and complexes throughout Japan belonging to the cult. However, even though police raided Aum centers equipped with full protective gear, they refused to publicly acknowledge any link between the sarin attack and the cult.[113]

It was not until days later that the government revealed that Aum had a cache of weapons and weapons-grade chemicals. By the end of the first week in April, the police had gathered enough evidence to begin arresting members of Aum Shinrikyo. More than 150 cult members had been arrested by late April, but none of the arrests were based on a connection with the sarin attack. By mid-1996, over 400 cult members had been arrested on charges ranging from kidnapping to drug production to participation in the sarin attack.[114]

On October 30, 1995, the Tokyo District Court ordered the dissolution of the cult's status as a religious organization. Aum appealed but lost the case, and on December 19, 1995, its religious status was officially revoked. Legally, this did not prevent Aum members from practicing their faith or running affiliated business ventures. Rather, the cult lost the legal protections guaranteed to religious groups, including its tax-exempt status.[115]

SUBSEQUENT REVISIONS IN LAW ENFORCEMENT: A NARROW LEGAL FRAMEWORK

The sarin attack spurred the passage of several pieces of legislation. Some, such as the legislation increasing undercover police powers, had

---

113. Kaplan and Marshall, *The Cult at the End of the World,* p. 255.

114. Mark Mullins, "The Political and Legal Response to Aum-related Violence in Japan: A Review Article," *The Japan Christian Review* (Tokyo), Vol. 63 (1997).

115. Ibid.

broad impact on law enforcement.[116] Most, however, were narrowly tailored to apply to Aum Shinrikyo and the sarin attack.

Less than one month after the subway attack, the Japanese parliament passed the "Law Related to the Prevention of Bodily Harm Caused by Sarin and Similar Substances." The law prohibits the manufacture, possession, and use of sarin and similar substances.[117] The laws guaranteeing religious freedom were also modified after the sarin attack. On December 8, 1995, the Diet passed revisions to the "Religious Corporations Law" that granted authorities "greater leeway in monitoring potentially dangerous religious organizations."[118] The government also began reevaluating laws restricting police actions, antiterrorism policies, and consequence management plans. In June 1996, the "Police Law" was revised "to enable prefectural police to extend their authority out of their border by their own judgment and responsibility in dealing with transprefectural organized crimes."[119] Finally, "The Group Regulation Act of 1999" was passed to regulate groups that have committed indiscriminate mass murder. The law does not refer directly to Aum Shinrikyo, but it did allow police to put Aum under surveillance for a maximum of three years.

Although several pieces of legislation were passed in direct response to the sarin attack, the government chose moderate language and limited the measures that restricted civil liberties. Some government officials suggested invoking "The Anti-Subversive Activities Law of 1952" with regard to Aum Shinrikyo. The law would have prohibited Aum from recruiting and fund-raising, training followers, and publishing materials promoting its beliefs. In addition, the law would have permitted ongoing surveillance of the group by the police. To invoke the law, the National Police Agency first had to exhaust all other legal remedies and then prove that the violence committed by the group "was politically motivated and that there is a strong possibility that future acts of violence will be committed."[120] In this case, however, officials decided not to apply the law because both other remedies were available, and they determined that Aum did not pose a credible future threat. Moreover, although there was significant political and public support for the measures that were invoked, the majority of the population did not support invoking the

116. Abigail Haworth, "The Naked City," *Tokyo Journal*, July 1995, pp. 32–37, p. 37.

117. Brackett, *Holy Terror*, p. 155.

118. Mullins, "The Political and Legal Response," p. 63.

119. See <ww.npa.go.jp/keibi2/it8.htm>.

120. Mullins, "The Political and Legal Response."

Anti-Subversive Activities Law, which many saw as compromising freedom of speech and other civil liberties.

One expert noted that the laws that were passed "can be located between the Anti-Subversive Activities Law, which the government failed to apply to Aum in 1997, and 'doing nothing'."[121] The narrow focus of the measures passed after the Aum attack means that they may not be useful should another chemical attack, or even a biological attack, take place in Japan. Although it may be difficult to secure the focus of lawmakers in the absence of an emergency situation, laws pertaining to the possession, transfer, and use of biological and chemical agents should be on the books before another disaster occurs.

Compensation for Damages

The government has not taken significant steps to correct all of the shortcomings revealed in the aftermath of the sarin attacks. One shortfall has to do with financial compensation. Victims are still responsible for much of the cost of their long-term recovery.

Compensation for damages is both a near-term and a long-term concern. The families of 18 individuals who were killed or severely injured by the Matsumoto and Tokyo attacks received a total of U.S. $424,000, which averages out to just over $23,000 each.[122] Many other injured Japanese were able to submit worker's compensation claims for damages resulting from the attack. In Japan, an injury received while in transit to or from a place of employment qualifies as a work-related injury. As of September 1995, more than 4,000 individuals had filed worker's compensation claims relating to the sarin attack.[123] Of those claims, almost all were recognized as "involved in the accident resulting from commutation and over 300 as having been involved in the accident in the course of duty."[124] The Labor Ministry has incurred $2.6 million in expenses associated with these victims.[125] However, many of the victims' claims remain unpaid.

Aum Shinrikyo, not the national or local government, is actually

---

121. Miyasaka, "Terrorism and Antiterrorism in Japan" p. 7.

122. These figures are in 1998 dollars. Mari Yamaguchi, "For Victims of the Subway Nerve Gas Attack, the Nightmare Goes On," Associated Press, March 18, 1998.

123. In addition to the worker's compensation claims, the restitution was made to the families of those killed in the attack in the amount of $23,000 USD each.

124. The government estimates that these claims will total over 3 million yen. "Victims of Sarin Incident on Tokyo's Subway System Recognized as Eligible for Workmen's Compensation," Public Policy, Vol. 34, No. 12 (December 1, 1995).

125. Yamaguchi, "The Nightmare Goes On."

responsible for paying most of the compensation. Under Japan's worker's compensation laws, the state can claim damages for insurance benefits it pays to a third party in a case where the damage is caused by another entity.[126] In this case, the government has refused to pay for medical or other damages suffered by the victims because Aum, the culpable third party, is considered liable for these expenses. The Health and Welfare Ministry, relying on this legal distinction, has neither offered any payment for comprehensive follow-up care or other support nor has it offered to provide these services.[127] Unfortunately, the cult's assets at the time of dissolution were approximately one billion yen, not even close to the five billion yen in claims filed by victims.[128] Furthermore, Aum declared bankruptcy on December 14, 1995.[129] In the end, an estimated 80 percent of the claims against Aum will go unpaid.[130] Not until 1999 did Aum formally acknowledge that two of its members were involved in the attack and offer to pay some compensation to victims.[131]

SUBSEQUENT REVISIONS TO COMPENSATORY SERVICES: GOVERNMENT FORFEITURE
In early 1998, state and some local governments announced that they would forfeit their claims against Aum, which total 520 million yen. This move is an effort to allow more individual victims to recover greater shares of the cult's assets.[132] This government action, although thoughtful and appropriate, does not address the systemic shortcomings of the remediation system. In many instances, victims had to pay their own medical bills and were not reimbursed by the worker's compensation system. This led to some degree of financial suffering for all involved.

Psychological Recovery

Most individuals affected by the attack—both directly and indirectly—have successfully managed the trauma associated with the event. "The first anniversary of the world's largest ultraterrorist attack came and

---

126. Ibid.

127. Ibid.

128. Tetsushi Kajimoto, "Aum Three Years Later: Victims Struggle for Redress" *Japan Times*, March 18, 1998.

129. Mullins, "The Political and Legal Response."

130. Kajimoto, "Aum Three Years Later."

131. Miyasaka, "Terrorism and Antiterrorism in Japan," p. 2.

132. Ibid.

went with only modest observance and emotion. Prime Minister Ryutaro Hashimoto visited the station, transit officials and families held a brief ceremony, families laid small tributes, such as flowers."[133] Subsequent anniversaries have received incrementally less attention. Most of the victims of the sarin attack have recovered physically from the sarin exposure. However, psychological effects linger for many victims and their families.

One survey of victims of the sarin attack questioned 35 inpatients in a metropolitan hospital six months after the event. The results showed that 26 percent of the patients were at high risk for post-traumatic stress disorder (PTSD). The overall conclusion drawn from the study was that 20–25 percent of at least moderately poisoned victims suffered from PTSD or subthreshold PTSD symptoms.[134] The same hospital surveyed 20 patients who visited for a checkup two years after the event: 10 percent were identified as suffering from PTSD; 10 percent were identified as recovered from PTSD. Although a few victims have suffered permanent long-term debilitating physical effects, the more common issue has been the psychological trauma associated with the attack.

SUBSEQUENT REVISIONS TO IMPROVE MENTAL HEALTH CARE: AWARENESS AND TRAINING

After the sarin attack, there was no concerted effort to address the unique psychological challenges of WMD terrorism. Those patients who were admitted to hospitals that had psychological services were offered assistance. Patients at smaller hospitals had to seek out private treatment on their own. All care was the financial responsibility of the patient.

No official government response has occurred in the ensuing years. Five years after the attack, a group of mental health specialists offered psychiatric intervention for victims. Considering the delay in service, a surprisingly high number—84 victims—attended the clinic on the first day of operation.[135] Psychiatrists involved in the effort acknowledge that early intervention would have been much more useful in facilitating rapid and more complete recovery for victims.

In light of this understanding, Japan is making an effort to train physicians and other emergency responders to recognize and treat symptoms of post-traumatic stress disorder. Until 2000, the Ministry of Health provided a daylong lecture on PTSD. Beginning in 2001, the training will last

---

133. Brackett, *Holy Terror*, p. 181.

134. Asukai, "Health Effects Following the Sarin Attack," p. 5.

135. "Sarin Victims Say More Must be Done," *Asahi Shimbun*, March 20, 2000.

for three days. Thus far, more than 2,000 people have been trained to deal with PTSD among victims.

Lessons and Implications for the United States

The islands of Japan face myriad natural disasters—including typhoons, earthquakes, and volcanoes—on a regular basis. As a response to one such disaster—the Hanshin Kobe earthquake of January 1995—Japan had already begun revising its disaster management plans before the Tokyo sarin attack occurred.[136]

After Aum Shinrikyo attacked civilians with sarin on two separate occasions, thereby introducing terrorism with a chemical agent into an urban setting as a new disaster threat, the Japanese government and civil organizations became much more concerned with incorporating anti-terrorism efforts and WMD response planning into general disaster plans.[137]

Japan has now made concrete improvements to many consequence management capabilities. This section analyzes some of the lessons of the attack and provides suggestions for further enhancements to consequence management plans that can also be implemented in the United States.

Many of the lessons learned in Japan offer insights for the United States: relationships between various governmental and medical components need to be built; telecommunications infrastructure strengthened; medical surge capacity enhanced; laws passed to enable appropriate surveillance and prosecution methods; and psychological care capabilities improved. The United States has confronted several of these challenges, some with greater vigor and success than others. By and large, the U.S. approach has been to enhance the "all-hazards" approach to disaster management, rather than to "specialize," when preparing to handle the aftermath of a WMD terrorist attack.

There are, however, considerations that distinguish a WMD terrorist attack from a natural or other man-made disaster. These considerations have been evident in the response to the anthrax attacks on members of Congress and journalists in the United States in the fall of 2001, which taxed the public health and medical systems, revealed shortfalls in the ability of government officials to communicate effectively with one an-

---

136. Furukawa, "An Institutional Framework," p. 3. Over 6,000 people lost their lives in the Hanshin Kobe earthquake.

137. Interview with Tsuruki, October 31, 2000.

other and the public, and created a sense of fear across the country. Some of the considerations that are unique to WMD terrorism represent relatively new issues for the public safety community, while others reinforce the importance of problems that are already acknowledged, yet remain unsolved.

One issue that is specific to a hazardous materials or public health emergency is that primary and secondary contamination may cripple response efforts.[138] Decontamination is an issue not only for the disaster scene, but also for emergency transportation, hospital workers, and others. Numerous agencies and facilities must be able to recognize contamination, provide decontamination, and function in a "dirty" environment. In Tokyo, for instance, even though the SDF was the only organization with decontamination expertise, the SDF role was largely limited by protocol to the decontamination units that cleaned the trains after the recovery operations were over.

Second, a mass-casualty attack will require medical surge capacity, including sufficient medical personnel to attend to increased casualty loads. At the time of the Tokyo subway attack, mutual aid agreements—intended to improve response—had an unexpected adverse effect on patient care. 55 doctors and 26 nurses were dispatched from area hospitals to affected stations. However, by the time the doctors and nurses arrived at the scene, severe cases had been transported to the hospital. Doctors and nurses in the field treated non-critical patients, a job that could have been done by the ELSTs. Meanwhile, the hospitals were suffering a shortage of staff. For example, 11 personnel had been dispatched from St. Luke's, the hospital that saw the most patients that day. The lesson from Tokyo is that, in a disaster that consumes resources from throughout the region, localized mutual aid agreements may simply pull resources from one area that needs them to another that needs them as much, or less than, the home location. Governments must think creatively about contingency plans to provide and allocate medical surge capacity after an attack.[139]

Third, well-established working relationships and a willingness to prioritize cooperation over interagency or intergovernment competition is essential to planning for and responding to a WMD attack. As evidenced by the various initiatives described above, the Japanese govern-

---

138. This is especially true for biological agents that cause contagious diseases.

139. For more on the lack of surge capacity and the consequences for the United States, see Joesph Barbera, Anthony G. Macintyre, and Craig A. DeAtley, "Ambulances to Nowhere: America's Critical Shortfall in Medical Preparedness for Catastrophic Terrorism," in this volume.

ment is trying to build relationships that bridge interagency divides. As with many post-sarin attack initiatives, however, these efforts focus on the national government. Although the response plan encourages cooperation between the ministries and between local agencies, there is no avenue or mechanism to implement this suggestion.[140] This is an important aspect of preparedness, but it is too narrow a focus. Local and prefectural governments must be included in planning, training, and even routine meetings. The same is true in the United States. Federal law enforcement and other federal agencies must work closely with state and local law enforcement, public health, fire, EMS, and recovery services. Although agencies such as the Federal Bureau of Investigation and the Federal Emergency Management Agency play lead federal roles, state and local agencies will be "on the ground" at the beginning and conclusion of any disaster. Communication between levels of government will facilitate the building of relationships and alert the national government to the needs of local response agencies. Additionally, in both Japan and the United States, relationships must be established between military personnel and civilian first responders *before* a disaster occurs. These two groups need to plan and practice interacting with one another through drills. This is the best way to ensure that, in a mass casualty attack, the military has a clear role commensurate with the constitution and the society's expectations.

Fourth, legal preparation is a vital but often overlooked aspect of domestic preparedness. Japan was forced to pass a variety of laws after the sarin attack that were retroactively applied to Aum Shinrikyo. The legal system in the United States would not permit retroactive application of the law. Therefore, it is even more essential that laws be in place before an attack occurs. This enables the nation to determine, with appropriate rational debate, the limitations of investigative and other law enforcement powers. Additionally, robust legal preparedness affords law enforcement the necessary powers to investigate and prosecute those who possess or attempt to use dangerous, but not yet illegal, chemical, biological, or nuclear components or weapons.[141]

Fifth, although evidence shows that people behave rationally in the face of disaster, including the sarin attacks, there is a heightened risk of immediate panic, short-term trauma, and long-term post-traumatic stress disorder following a WMD attack. Therefore, it is important to tailor psy-

---

140. Correspondence from government official, Cabinet Office for National Security and Crisis Management, September 7, 2001.

141. For more information on the status of the law and recommendations for legal preparedness, see Juliette Kayyem, "U.S. Preparations for Biological Terrorism: Legal Limitations and the Need for Planning," in this volume.

chological intervention to the demands of the occasion. The United States has successfully set up hotlines and trauma centers following terrorist attacks. Contingency plans for WMD terrorism should be put in place, so that counselors are prepared to deal with the particular traumas associated with intentional use of weapons of mass destruction.

As the attack on the Tokyo subway system showed, most of the emergency response efforts, especially in the immediate aftermath of an attack, will be carried out by local transit police, fire, and medical personnel. Assistance from the federal level is necessary, but the federal government cannot and will not be the dominant player in the first minutes or hours after an attack. Therefore, it is essential that emergency responders in state and local governments be prepared to deal with an unannounced attack with a weapon of mass destruction. At the same time, national-level coordination is vital to ensure that both training and equipment are provided to localities in accordance with their needs, and exercises are carried out that involve personnel from multiple agencies and levels of government.

In addition, responders from all relevant agencies and all levels of government must practice skills in simulations that involve all aspects of response. Only in this way can these agencies, which may not be accustomed to working together, converge on the scene of a disaster and effectively carry out rescue and recovery operations.

Civil Liberties, Terrorism, and Liberal Democracy: Lessons from the United Kingdom

Laura K. Donohue

In 1922, the Unionist government in Northern Ireland sought to quell rising violence through the temporary use of emergency powers. Fifty years later, the 1922–1943 Civil Authorities (Special Powers) Acts remained ensconced in the Northern Ireland constitution. Upon the assumption of direct rule, Britain incorporated these measures into the 1973 Northern Ireland (Emergency Provisions) Act. Although intended to operate for a short period, the emergency provisions remain in place. Similarly, Westminster Parliament's temporary adoption of legislation to counter the Irish Republican Army (IRA)'s 1939 mainland campaign led to the entrenchment of emergency law in the United Kingdom. Allowed to expire in 1953 and repealed in 1973, the 1939 Prevention of Violence (Temporary Provisions) Act was reintroduced in 1974 as the Prevention of Terrorism (Temporary Provisions) Act. The statute remained in effect until replaced by the Terrorism Act of 2000.

These "temporary" measures posed a significant challenge to civil liberties, contributed to the disaffection of the minority community in Northern Ireland, led to the suspension of the Northern Parliament, and provided a basis for successive cases brought against the United Kingdom (UK) in the European Court of Human Rights. Yet the Northern Ireland and British governments maintained and even expanded many of these emergency powers. Why was this so? Was it because successive governments in Northern Ireland were faced with emergency situations

Previous versions of this essay appeared as an article in the Stanford Journal of Legal Studies and as the final chapter in Laura Donohue, Counterterrorist Law and Emergency Powers in the United Kingdom 1922–2000, (Dublin, Ireland: Irish Academic Press), 2000.

that required extraordinary measures, or were the reasons more complex? Is there something about emergency law that, once introduced, leads to its entrenchment? Is there something about terrorism that demands these types of statutes? What lessons can be drawn for other liberal, democratic states facing a terrorist challenge? Are any of the elements that contributed to the UK's introduction and use of emergency law similarly at work in other states?

This essay examines these questions and proposes that a confluence of primary factors and secondary circumstances—many of which are common to liberal, democratic states—perpetuated the emergency measures beyond their intended life. The first of five primary factors, the seeming efficaciousness of the measures, provided a clear reason for their retention. Put simply, they appeared to work. Second, the sheer persistence of the Northern Ireland conflict, built on deep divisions in the province and a long history of paramilitarism, suggested that the issue that the legislation sought to address was not going to just disappear. Third, Britain's previous use of emergency law in Ireland and, fourth, the continued perception in Westminster of Northern Ireland as a place that allowed—indeed demanded—the use of such measures also contributed to the statutes' retention. Finally, the symbolic importance of the legislation provided further justification for their continuation. Repeal of the measures would have meant either that violence was no longer an issue (the long-standing nature of the Northern Ireland conflict would suggest otherwise) or that some measure of violence was somehow acceptable. Neither of these claims was made.

Several secondary conditions contributed to the retention of emergency law by helping to create an environment in which such measures could be used. First, within Britain, the counterterrorism provisions greatly overlapped with ordinary criminal law. Most of the activities banned, particularly after 1972, were already illegal. What made them a part of counterterrorism legislation was the intent of those engaged in such behavior, extensions of the penalties associated with such actions, and alterations to the court system for those suspected of acting with terrorist intent. Second, the international context within which the British state operated, while it mitigated the more extreme aspects of emergency law, also supported the establishment and operation of the statutes. Various international treaties protected the right of contracting states to introduce emergency legislation, and confusion existed in the international arena, particularly in international law, over how to handle terrorist violence. Third, the use of the liberal discourse further defended the use of emergency law. In Northern Ireland from 1922 to 1972, this took the form of appeal to reason of state—that the state could take any and all such measures deemed necessary to protect itself. In Westminster 1972 to 2000, a hierarchy of rights emerged, wherein "lesser" rights could be suspended to protect the most important: the right to life and property.

Many, if not all of the primary factors and secondary conditions that contributed to the retention of emergency law in the United Kingdom are also at work in other liberal, democratic states faced with a terrorist challenge. The essay highlights these elements, concluding with additional lessons, such as the importance of the social and political context into which domestic statutes are introduced, parallel obligations held by states, the use of liberal discourse to undermine itself, and the significance of precedent in counterterrorism, that come from observing Northern Ireland and the United Kingdom.

The Northern Ireland Conflict: A Brief History

Passage of the 1921 Articles of Agreement for a Treaty between the Irish Free State and Britain resulted in a violent civil war between those who accepted the 26 county unit and those wanting to press for full Irish independence. Immediately following partition, which was formalized in the 1921 treaty, the Unionist government introduced a series of emergency measures aimed at consolidating control of the province. The 1922 Civil Authorities (Special Powers) Act (SPA) was by far the most wide-sweeping of these measures and became instrumental in maintaining Unionist control of Northern Ireland.[1] Amended in 1943, the act empowered the Northern Ireland Parliament to impose curfew; proscribe organizations; censor printed, audio, and visual materials; ban meetings, processions, and gatherings; restrict the movement of individuals to within specified areas; and detain and intern suspects without bringing charges. The statute authorized extensive powers of entry, search, and seizure; altered the court system; and, most importantly, empowered the Civil Authority (the executive in Northern Ireland): "to take all such steps and issue all such orders as may be necessary for preserving the peace and maintaining order." The Unionist government introduced more than 100 regulations under this last clause, levying the vast majority against the minority population.[2] The 1922 SPA became one of the central grievances voiced during the civil rights marches of the late 1960s and ultimately led

---

1. 1922 SPA, Civil Authorities (Special Powers) Act (Northern Ireland), 1933, 23 & 24 Geo. V, c. 12, and Civil Authorities (Special Powers) Act (Northern Ireland), 1943, 7 & 8 Geo. VI, c. 2. [Hereafter 1922–1943 SPAs].

2. See L. Donohue, "The 1922–43 Special Powers Acts: Regulating Northern Ireland," *Historical Journal*, Cambridge University Press, Vol. 1, 1999.

to the downfall of the Northern Ireland Parliament. Unionists, however, had intended this statute to be temporary. The Executive initially defended enactment of the legislation by claiming its use as a distinctly provisional measure necessary to secure law and order. Section 12 of the Act limited the duration of the statute to one year, unless otherwise determined by the Northern Ireland Parliament. Within a few years, however, the government's rationale for maintaining the legislation shifted: what had been an interim means to establish peace became a necessity for maintaining the North's constitutional position. In April 1928, the Unionist government called for the permanent entrenchment of the SPAs. In 1933, Parliament made the 1922 SPA indefinite, and in 1943, it introduced a second act that made minor amendments to the 1922 statute. For purposes of this essay, these statutes are referred to the 1922–1943 SPAs.

The late 1960s and early 1970s witnessed spiraling violence in Northern Ireland. In 1972, Britain prorogued the Northern Ireland Parliament. Direct rule did not, however, eliminate the emergency legislation. Although the British government claimed to replace the 1922–1943 SPAs with the 1973 Northern Ireland (Emergency Provisions) Act (EPA), the latter statute simply renamed the vast majority of the Special Powers regulations. The 1973 EPA retained the government's extensive powers of detention, proscription, entry, search and seizure, restrictions on the use of vehicles, the blocking of roads, the closing of licensed premises, and the collection of information on security forces. In addition, the statute eliminated juries from the court system and established certain crimes as "scheduled" offenses, regardless of the perpetrator's motivation. It also retained the general powers allocated to the Civil Authority in Northern Ireland, authorizing that the Secretary of State for Northern Ireland "may by regulations make provisions additional to the foregoing provisions of this Act for promoting the preservation of the peace and the maintenance of order." Initially, the 1973 EPA also was intended as a temporary measure. In 1974, the Secretary of State for Northern Ireland claimed, "The [1973 EPA] makes emergency provisions and is by its nature temporary, to cover the period of an emergency."[3] For 26 years, however, this legislation remained in force. In 1975, the British government amended the 1973 Act and three years later consolidated the two statutes into the 1978 EPA. Further replacements in 1987, 1991, and 1996 did little to change the content of the earlier acts except to expand certain powers and allow a small number of others to lapse.[4] As with the justification for the 1922–1943

3. Merlyn Rees, *HC Debs,* July 9, 1974, Vol. 876, col. 1273.

4. Northern Ireland (Emergency Provisions Amendment) Act, 1975, Eliz. II, c. 62;

SPAs, the rationale behind the retention of the 1973–1996 EPAs changed subtly: they became seen as a critical part of the ongoing fight against terrorism.

Not only did emergency legislation become a permanent feature of the Northern Ireland legal system, but, for more than 60 years, Westminster has retained emergency provisions aimed at countering Northern Irish violence in the UK. In January 1939, the IRA initiated a mainland bombing campaign. The British government responded by passing the 1939 Prevention of Violence (Temporary Provisions) Act (PVA),[5] which introduced powers of expulsion, prohibition, arrest, and detention. It too was intended as an interim statute: "We have tried to make it clear . . . that the Bill . . . is a temporary measure to meet a passing emergency. We have expressly restricted the duration of the Bill to a period of two years."[6] Although the IRA's mainland bombing campaign ceased within a year of the statute's introduction, it was only in 1953 that Westminster allowed the 1939 Act to expire, and it was not until 1973 that the government repealed it.

In 1974, the IRA bombing of two pubs in Birmingham left 21 people dead and 160 injured. The British government responded by reintroducing powers contained in the 1939 act, with the addition of proscription—a provision employed under the 1922–43 SPAs and the 1973 EPA. Again, this legislation was intended to be in place for a limited period: during his introduction of the 1974 Prevention of Terrorism Bill, British Home Secretary Roy Jenkins asserted, "I do not think that anyone would wish these exceptional powers to remain in force a moment longer than is necessary."[7] The government built mechanisms into the statute to prevent it from remaining on the books simply as a result of inertia. The 1974 Prevention of Terrorism (Temporary Provisions) Act (PTA), however, belied its title: not only did it reintroduce measures in place from 1939 to 1973, but it remained in force over a quarter of a century later.[8] In 1991, Jenkins wrote, "I think that the Terrorism Act helped to both steady opinion and to provide some additional protection. I do not regret having introduced

---

Northern Ireland (Emergency Provisions) Act, 1978, Eliz. II, c. 5; Northern Ireland (Emergency Provisions) Act, 1987, Eliz. II, c. 30; Northern Ireland (Emergency Provisions) Act, 1991, Eliz. II, c. 24; Northern Ireland (Emergency Provisions) Act, 1996, Eliz. II, c. 22.

5. Prevention of Violence (Temporary Provisions) Act, 1939, 2 & 3 Geo. VI, c. 50. [Hereafter 1939 PVA]

6. Sir S. Hoare, Home Secretary, *HC Debs*, July 24, 1939, Vol. 350, col. 1054.

7. Roy Jenkins, *HC Debs*, November 28, 1974, Vol. 882, col. 642.

8. See footnote 9.

it. But I would have been horrified to have been told at the time that it would still be law nearly two decades later. . . . [I]t should teach one to be careful about justifying something on the ground that it is only for a short time."[9]

Primary Factors Contributing to the Retention of Emergency Law

A combination of primary factors and secondary conditions contributed to the retention of emergency measures in the United Kingdom. This section focuses on the first. The seeming efficaciousness of the provisions, the long history of the Northern Ireland conflict, Britain's previous use of emergency law in Ireland, perceptions in Westminster that such measures were both necessary and acceptable outside of the UK, and the symbolic importance of counterterrorism measures provided a direct impetus for the introduction and continued operation of the extraordinary provisions.

One of the most obvious reasons for maintaining the emergency laws was their seeming effectiveness. Declining levels of violence in Northern Ireland and the UK immediately followed the introduction of the 1922 SPA, 1973 EPA, 1939 PVA, and 1974 PTA. In Northern Ireland, a high of 80 murders and 58 attempted murders in April 1922 plummeted to one murder and 11 attempted murders by September of that year. These figures continued to fall throughout the balance of 1922 and into 1923.[10] Similarly, immediately following the introduction of the 1973 EPA, the number of deaths and injuries in the province decreased: from a high of 467 deaths in 1972 to 250 in 1973 and 216 in 1974. Injuries also dropped: from 4,876 in 1972 to 2,651 in 1973 and 2,398 in 1974.[11] As already noted, within a year of the introduction of the 1939 PVA, the IRA's mainland campaign had ceased. When violence rose again in the 1970s in the UK, immediately following the introduction of the 1974 PTA, a similar drop in the number of deaths related to political violence occurred.

It is uncertain to what degree special powers were responsible for these decreases. For instance, following the establishment of direct rule in 1972, the increased effectiveness of the security forces, improved intelligence, growing rejection by the communities in Northern Ireland of the use of violence for political ends, the 1974 IRA cease-fire, the drying up of

---

9. R. Jenkins, *A Life at the Centre* (1991), p. 397.

10. Letter from the Imperial Secretary to the Under Secretary of State, Home Affairs, June 21, 1923, PRO HA 267/362.

11. *Northern Ireland Annual Abstract of Statistics* and Irish Information Partnership.

IRA funding from the United States, greater selectivity of terrorists in choosing targets, greater cross-border cooperation with the Irish Republic, and increased media attention, all may have played significant roles in helping to reduce the violence. However, statistics on the operation of the 1973 EPA and the 1974 PTA suggest that wide use was made of provisions relating to the collection of information during the first few years of the statutes' operation: under the 1973 EPA, 4,141 people were arrested in 1975, 8,321 in 1976, and 5,878 in 1977.[12] *Pari passu,* under the 1974 PTA, the British armed forces detained 1,067 people in 1975, 1,066 in 1976, and 853 in 1977.[13] This brought the number of people held for questioning over the three-year period under powers provided by emergency legislation to more than 21,000. From its introduction in 1974 until its renewal in 1996, some 27,000 people were arrested under the PTA alone. Although the security forces subsequently charged fewer than 15 percent of those arrested with a crime,[14] the information gathered during questioning most likely had a significant impact on the level of violence. Certainly under the 1922–43 SPAs, which were considerably more far-reaching than their post-1972 counterparts, Northern Ireland suffered significantly fewer deaths and injuries due to political violence. Members of Parliament (MPs) from Northern Ireland highlighted this fact in Westminster.[15] The effectiveness of the 1922–43 SPAs became the basis for the shift in the justification of the measures: they came to be defended as a means of maintaining the status quo rather than as a means to establish law and order. This same alteration marked British defense of emergency measures: their efficaciousness became a reason for their retention. Considering the wide-ranging nature of the powers exercised under the legislation, the acts' seeming effectiveness does not come as a great surprise: it appears at least arguable that if more leeway is afforded the security forces and less stringent measures required in the court system, more information can be gleaned and more convictions obtained.

---

12.   *Statistics on the Operation of the Northern Ireland (Emergency Provisions) Act 1991 for 1993.* Northern Ireland Office Statistics and Research Bulletin 1/94. Table 7a, 9.

13.   *Statistics on the Prevention of Terrorism (Temporary Provisions) Acts 1974 and 1976—First Quarter 1980.* Home Office Statistical Bulletin. April 29, 1980. Issue 7/80. Tables 1, 5.

14.   Mr. Canavan, *HC Debs,* March 14, 1996, Vol. 273, col. 1162.

15.   See Ian Paisley, *HC Debs,* December 8, 1977, Vol. 940, col. 1736. For an examination of the 1922–1943 SPAs as breeding subsequent violence, see Gerry Fitt, *HC Debs,* March 18, 1981, Vol. 1, col. 382 and *Disturbances in Northern Ireland: Report of the Commission appointed by the governor of Northern Ireland.* September 1969. Session 1969/70 Cmnd 532, para 229(a).

In addition, there also existed a tendency within the security forces to support the extension of such measures as part of their arsenal in the fight against terrorism. Once the powers had been gained, those wielding them were unwilling to see them diminished. Parliamentarians realized this during the 1981 renewal of the PTA.[16] As time passed and the security forces became familiar with the operation of a particular statute, significant alterations may be considered inconvenient.

Was emergency law maintained simply because an emergency continuously existed? The numbers would suggest otherwise. Northern Ireland was distinguished, in part, from 1922 to 1968 precisely by the lack of immediate violence. Was there something beyond the absence of violence—something about the nature of the Northern Ireland conflict, the contrary demands of the two dominant ethnic groups, and the intractable nature of the violence—that created a situation within which emergency legislation tended to permanence? Despite the lack of overt violence signifying division, Northern Ireland politics from 1922 were built around deep ethnic divisions and divergent political aspirations. Housing distribution, employment patterns, education, interpersonal relationships, and social activities all cut along ethnic lines.[17] Divergent constitutional aspirations underscored the Catholic-Protestant divide. Appeals to past events further served to legitimate grievances, signaling the persistence of the Northern Ireland conflict. For Republicans, the twelfth-century Norman invasions, sixteenth-century Surrender and Re-grant treaties and Nine Years' War, and seventeenth and eighteenth century plantations and penal laws provided grounds for their struggle against the Loyalists. The sixteenth century risings by the Irish Catholics, the 1689 Siege of Derry, the 1690 Battle of the Boyne, and agrarian risings throughout the eighteenth century supplied the basis for Loyalist claims. Repeated reference to past events served to justify not only the Republican view of the British government as an outside, conquering power, but also physical force organizations as a "legitimate" tool to rid the country of British presence. From Theobold Wolfe Tone and the 1791 Society of United

---

16. E.g., "It is my impression that once a government have these powers in their control they are very reluctant to give them up." (Gerry Fitt, *HC Debs,* March 18, 1981, Vol. 1, col. 382).

17. For more detailed discussion of the entrenched divisions in Northern Ireland, see D. Boulton, *The UVF 1966–1973: an Anatomy of Loyalist Rebellion* (1973); F. Boal and J. N. Douglas, *Integration and Division: Geographical Perspectives on the Northern Ireland Problem* (1982); F. Boal and A. Robinson, "Close Together and Far Apart: Religious and Class Divisions in Northern Ireland," *Community Forum,* No. 3 (1972); F. Burton, *The Politics of Legitimacy* (1978); and J. Darby, *Northern Ireland: Background to the Conflict* (1986).

Irishmen to the Young Ireland movement, Fenian Brotherhood, Irish Republican Brotherhood and the Defenders, Republican violence was directed against the state and its institutions. In turn, the Loyalist counter-revolutionary tradition sought to uphold the authority of the state. The Planters' home guards in the 1780s, the Rifle clubs, and Young Ulster at the end of the nineteenth century professed devotion to the British Crown. These physical force organizations both emphasized and further entrenched divisions between the communities. By the time of partition and throughout Unionist rule of the North from 1922 to 1972, two very different histories had been constructed, further reinforcing divisions within the province.

Following partition in 1922, violence erupted in both Northern Ireland and the Irish Free State, leading Unionists to feel under siege. Even after Unionists restored civil order in the province, sporadic outbreaks of Republican violence occurred, reminding the new leadership that the divisions between the communities had the potential to assume deadly proportions. Moreover, just over the border a distinctively Irish, Catholic state was being formed: in the 1932 Free State general election, Eamon de Valera and Fianna Fáil gained control of the Southern Parliament. The Northern Executive expanded its emergency powers: between 1922 and 1949 alone, the Unionist government issued statutory instruments adjusting more than 50 regulations.

As Britain assumed direct rule, the conflicting aims of Nationalists, Republicans, Unionists, and Loyalists continued to influence the existence of emergency law. Just as a threat had existed during the operation of the Northern Parliament, violent opposition faced Britain. Even though Westminster did not share the Unionists' urgency in terms of the impact on the survival of the British—versus Northern Irish—state, Britain too became caught in the deep provincial divisions. The long history of Republicanism and Loyalism and their respective ideologies made it difficult for Westminster to respond to the conflict through ordinary legislation. The sense that whatever statutes the British government might introduce would be rejected by paramilitaries safe in their own communities permeated parliamentary consideration of the measures. Measures implemented by the British government, such as the Diplock courts (which provided for a single judge with no jury to try individuals accused of terrorist acts), the withdrawal of special category status, the supergrass trials, and the media ban were directed toward isolating "terrorists." Attempts to bridge the ideological divide, though, met with little success. Emergency legislation became hailed as necessary in the distinctively Northern Irish context.

Following World War II, the Unionist government slightly relaxed provisions introduced under the 1922–1943 SPAs by suspending a handful of regulations. This was the first and only time that the Northern government actually withdrew any of the emergency powers. They were swiftly reintroduced.[18] What was significant, though, was the temporary repeal of the regulations. One explanation for this lay in the impact of World War II: having demonstrated their loyalty to the Crown in contrast to the South's neutrality, Northern Unionists could look upon their links with Britain with increased confidence. Winston Churchill's leadership and implacable support for Unionists secured their position in the United Kingdom. Moreover, the passage of the 1949 Government of Ireland Act reaffirmed that Northern Ireland would remain part of the United Kingdom until a majority in the Northern Parliament decreed otherwise.[19] Unionists had established such a clear hold on the political machinery that the possibility of losing a majority in Parliament seemed increasingly unlikely. Unionists' newly found confidence, together with the relative calm in Northern Ireland and the lack of an immediate threat from the IRA, thus contributed to the repeal of the emergency provisions. Although divisions in Northern Irish society remained, the degree of security felt by the Unionists, in juxtaposition to the constitutional threat wielded by nationalism and Republicanism, had increased. The advent of the 1956–1962 IRA campaign, however, led to the swift re-enactment of emergency measures.

The entrenched ideologies of the two dominant ethnic groups, and in particular the two extremes, lent its own dynamic to the maintenance of emergency law from 1922 to 1972. Because the central issue rested on the constitutional status of the North, minority aspirations threatened the foundation of the state. Any Nationalist or Republican attempt to gain power or to garner support for a united Ireland was perceived as an attack on the Northern Ireland constitution. As defenders of the state, Unionists immediately exercised their authority to secure the Northern government: they hailed emergency legislation as critical to gaining control of the province. To have lost control, particularly at the time of partition, would have meant not just civil disorder, but a change in the structure of government. Because of the political aspirations of both Nationalism and Republicanism—a united Ireland and the absence of ties to the UK—the threat to the constitutional position of the North remained long after the violence had subsided. The history of force in Irish affairs

---

18. S.R.O. 147/1949 and S.R.O. 187/1951 repealed a number of regulations under the 1922–43 SPAs. See also S.R.O. 176/1955 and S.R.O. 199/1956.

19. Government of Ireland Act, 1949, 12 & 13 Geo. VI, c. 41.

and the episodic use of violence as advocated by Republicanism was enough to remind Unionists of the threat in their midst. Emergency measures had to be maintained.

Prior Emergency Measures

Not only did a long history of division and a physical force tradition accompany governmental consideration of emergency law, but there was a long history of Britain enacting emergency measures in Ireland. This precedent played a role in influencing, on the state side at least, the acceptability of employing emergency legislation to address Northern Irish affairs. Between 1800 and 1921, the government introduced more than 100 Coercion Acts in Ireland to minimize violence and to establish law and order.[20] For instance, in 1803 the government followed "An Act for the Suppression of the Rebellion which still unhappily exists within this Kingdom, and for the Protection of the Persons and Properties of His Majesty's faithful subjects within the same"[21] with "An Act for the Suppression of Rebellion in Ireland, and for the Protection of the Persons and Property of His Majesty's Faithful Subjects there."[22] These were succeeded in 1833 by "An Act for the More Effectual Suppression of Local Disturbances and Dangerous Associations in Ireland"[23] and "The Protection of Life and Property in Certain Parts of Ireland Act."[24] Responding to the land war agitation, the British government enacted the Protection of Person and Property (Ireland) Act in 1881.[25] In the following year, it passed the Prevention of Crime (Ireland) Act.[26] The preamble of the latter statute explained the purpose of emergency measures in the Irish context:

---

20. M. Farrell, "The Apparatus of Repression," Field Day Pamphlet (1986), p. 1. For other accounts of emergency legislation in Ireland and the United Kingdom prior to 1921, see C. Campbell, *Emergency Law in Ireland 1918–1925* (1994); Osborough, "Law in Ireland 1916–26," (1972) 23 N.I.L.Q., 48–82; and E. Mulloy, "Emergency Legislation: Dynasties of Coercion," Field Day Pamphlet (1986).

21. "An Act for the Suppression of the Rebellion which still unhappily exists within this Kingdom, and for the Protection of the Persons and Properties of His Majesty's faithful subjects within the same," 1799, 39 Geo. III, c. 11.

22. See footnote 1.

23. "An Act for the more effectual Suppression of Local Disturbances and Dangerous Associations in Ireland," 1833, 3 Will. IV, c. 4.

24. "The Protection of Life and Property in Certain Parts of Ireland Act," 1871, 34 & 35 Vict., c. 25.

25. Protection of Person and Property Act, 1881, 44 & 45 Vict., c. 4.

26. Prevention of Crime (Ireland) Act, 1882, 45 & 46 Vict., c. 25.

"Whereas by reason of the action of secret societies and combinations for illegal purposes in Ireland the operation of the ordinary law has become insufficient for the repression and prevention of crime, and it is expedient to make further provision for that purpose, [this statute is now] enacted." Similar to the 1973 EPA, this legislation allowed for the suspension of trial by jury in cases of treason, murder, attempted murder, manslaughter, aggravated crimes of violence against the person, arson, and attacks against the dwelling-home. The statute was the first to make an offense of intimidation. Like the 1922–1943 SPAs, the Prevention of Crime Act included powers against rioting, unlawful associations, curfew, freedom of movement, and newspapers advocating offenses against the Act, and it empowered security forces to search for illegal documents and arms. It withdrew privilege against self-incrimination from witnesses, enabling magistrates to summon witnesses and compel them to answer questions under oath.

In 1887, the government passed the Criminal Law and Procedure (Ireland) Act,[27] which drew on previous coercion measures, granted powers of inquisition to magistrates, and empowered the Attorney General to conduct interrogation in private. "Whereas it is expedient to amend the law relating to the place of trial of offenses committed in Ireland, for securing more fair and impartial trials, and for relieving jurors from danger to their lives or property, and business," trials could be transferred to different counties where a "more fair and impartial trial" could be held with or without a special jury. Thus, interestingly, the same concerns addressed by Lord Diplock in 1972 were at issue in the nineteenth century. The 1887 act also allowed the Lord Lieutenant and Privy Council to proscribe organizations. The nineteenth century witnessed a series of Peace Preservation (Ireland) Acts,[28] adjustments to the judicial procedure, and tightening of explosives and firearms measures. In sum, the historical use of special powers to address unrest punctuating rule of Ireland created a sort of internal legitimacy that supported the continued use of similar measures immediately following partition and through direct rule.

The perception in Westminster of Ireland as a "place apart" helped to

---

27. Criminal Law and Procedure (Ireland) Act, 1887, 50 & 51 Vict., c. 25. This statute was not repealed until the 1973 Northern Ireland (Emergency Provisions) Act.

28. See, for example, the Peace Preservation (Ireland) Act, 1870, 33 & 34 Vict., c. 9; the Peace Preservation (Ireland) Acts Continuance Act, 1873, 36 & 37 Vict., c. 24; the Peace Preservation (Ireland) Act, 1875, 38 & 39 Vict., c. 14; the Peace Preservation (Ireland) Act, 1881, 44 & 45 Vict., c. 5; and the Peace Preservation (Ireland) Continuance Act, 1886, 49 & 50 Vict., c. 24.

legitimize further Britain's application of similar measures from 1972 to 2000. The view that Northern Ireland bears a unique history within which special powers are acceptable, or even necessary, played a role in annual consideration of emergency legislation. In 1972, one Member of Parliament commented: "I have great sympathy with those who have protested in this debate that the [Northern Ireland] order provides for internment in another and more sophisticated form. But internment has been one of the facts of Irish history and one of the means for securing the State in Ireland, north or south."[29] Another MP asserted: "We have never been able to maintain a Northern Ireland state, since its very inception, without some kind of repressive law."[30] Parliamentarians viewed Northern Ireland as different from the rest of the United Kingdom. In 1979, the Secretary of State for Northern Ireland, Humphrey Atkins, contended, "Northern Ireland, for reasons that cannot be undone, is not like any other part of the United Kingdom. New structures of government must be based on a recognition of that fact."[31] Atkins later added, "I hope that it will be clear to the House that the Government are [sic], and will continue to be, sensitive to the special problems of Northern Ireland."[32] Responding to protestations that the powers in the 1975 EPA would not be accepted in Britain, the Minister of State for Northern Ireland replied, "Of course, but the same situation does not apply in England."[33] During deliberations over the elimination of juries in the 1973 EPA, A.W. Stallard asserted, "The . . . impression I got . . . was that . . . this step would never be taken [in England] but that it was good enough for Northern Ireland."[34] More than two decades later, MPs were still voicing similar sentiments: Kevin McNamara stated, "no one in Britain will undergo the [EPA] procedures that apply in Northern Ireland."[35] Commenting later on the government's decision in 1974 to introduce the Prevention of Terrorism (Temporary Provisions) Bill, Roy Jenkins wrote: "I always believed in keeping as much as possible of the contagion of Northern Irish terrorism out of Great Britain. I thought we had responsibilities in North-

---

29. *HC Debs*, December 11, 1972, Vol. 848, col. 80.

30. J. Maynard, *HC Debs*, July 2, 1979, Vol. 969, col. 987.

31. Humphrey Atkins, *HC Debs*, July 2, 1979, Vol. 969, col. 928.

32. *HC Debs*, July 2, 1979, Vol. 969, col. 930.

33. J. D. Concannon, *HC Debs*, December 6, 1978, Vol. 959, col. 1580.

34. A.W. Stallard, *HC Debs*, Standing Committee B, 1972–1973, Vol. 2, col. 52.

35. Kevin McNamara, *HC Debs*, February 19, 1996, Vol. 272, col. 61.

ern Ireland, both to uphold security and to assuage the conflict, but I did not think they extended to absorbing any more than we had to of the results of many generations of mutual intolerance."[36] Tom Litterick commented: "I view with trepidation the prospect of discussing the internal affairs of a foreign country. Ulster is a foreign country. I have been there and it is, in every sense, unmistakably a foreign country."[37] Thus, in the view of many British legislators, Northern Ireland was alien territory with its own ingrained history. "We should remember that we cannot allow ourselves to be swayed too much by our sometimes frantic considerations of present events because, as the House should know, present events are very similar in Ireland to what has gone on before. There is nothing exceptional about them."[38]

The brevity and perfunctoriness of the procedure for renewing emergency legislation further reflected the perception such measures were somehow acceptable in the Northern Ireland context. In the House of Commons, debates tended to be held late at night, rarely lasting more than 90 minutes. Even shorter and less detailed debates marked consideration of the measures in the House of Lords.[39] Not only did the British government allocate limited time for the consideration of emergency legislation, but after the introduction of the 1973 EPA, it appended the renewal of other statutes to the debates surrounding the emergency measures. Within a few years, Parliament began considering the renewal of the 1974 Northern Ireland (Young Persons) Act[40] and the 1974 Northern Ireland Act concurrent with retention of the 1973–1975 EPAs.[41] This allowed for even less direct discussion of the emergency measures under review. In addition, attendance at the annual renewals steadily eroded in the years following the introduction of emergency law, which further reflected the general view in Westminster of the acceptability of applying emergency law to Northern Ireland.

---

36. Jenkins, *supra*, p. 377.

37. Tom Litterick, *HC Debs*, December 8, 1977, Vol. 940, col. 1710.

38. Tom Litterick, *HC Debs*, June 30, 1978, Vol. 952, col. 1784.

39. *Review of the Operation of the Prevention of Terrorism (Temporary Provisions) Act 1976.* By the Rt. Hon. Earl Jellicoe, DSO, MC. February 1983. Session 1982/83 Cmnd 8803, para.14. [Hereafter Jellicoe Report]

40. Northern Ireland (Young Persons) Act, 1974, Eliz. II, c. 33.

41. See for instance *HC Debs*, June 26, 1975, Vol. 894, col. 814; *HC Debs*, June 30, 1977, Vol. 934, cols. 633; and *HC Debs*, December 8, 1977, Vol. 940, col. 1678.

Import of Emergency Legislation

As political violence increased in both Northern Ireland and the UK after 1972, broad support within Britain for more stringent measures grew. The 1974 Birmingham bombings provided the main impetus for the enactment of the 1974 Prevention of Terrorism Act.[42] As repeatedly cited by MPs in Westminster, the need to be *seen* as responding to this event—and indeed to the slew of terrorist incidents in Britain immediately preceding Birmingham—was as important as the specific aspects of the statute itself. In urging fellow members to pass the 1974 Prevention of Terrorism Bill, Lord Hailsham stated, "Apart from [the Bill's] practical value . . . its moral impact is hardly less important and would, I fear, be considerably blunted if we did not accede to the Government's request to enable the Bill to receive the Royal Assent so as to place it on the Statute Book tomorrow. . . . I would suggest to pass it without amendment."[43] He later added, "If one yields to terrorism of this kind other terrorists in Britain will draw the obvious moral that the gun and the bomb pay off because the British do not have the courage to resist them."[44] Statements in both Houses of Parliament frequently supported the use of emergency measures to demonstrate Britain's rejection of terrorism. No real indication was given in any of the statutes as to which circumstances would have to change, or to what extent, to justify their repeal. This made it less than clear as to when the legislation could be rescinded without altering the initial connotation entailed in its enactment. Because of this, any repeal or repudiation of the measures assumed new import. In the absence of a cessation in terrorist activity, repeal might have indicated a level of acceptance, either of some degree of violence or of the use of violence for political ends.

Proscription, which outlawed membership of specific organizations, provides a poignant example of the need felt by politicians to appear to be acting in accordance with the aim of protecting the life and property of their constituents. The central purpose underlying the introduction of proscription in the UK was to reduce the affront caused to the public by seeing overt support for Republican organizations.[45] For instance, the

---

42. *HC Debs*, November 28, 1974, Vol. 882, cols. 634–944; and *HC Debs*, November 25, 1974, Vol. 882, cols. 29–45.

43. *HL Debs*, November 28, 1974, Vol. 354, col. 1509.

44. *HL Debs*, November 28, 1974, Vol. 354, col. 1517.

45. Roy Jenkins, *HC Debs*, November 28, 1974, Vol. 882, col. 636.

government-commissioned Jellicoe Report, issued in 1983, noted that proscription bore both a practical and presentational value: "At the least practical level it enshrines in legislation public aversion to organizations which use, and espouse, violence as a means to a political end."[46] If public displays supporting proscribed organizations could be prohibited, public outrage and disorder might likewise be avoided. Lord Shackleton juxtaposed considerations of civil liberties with the moral disapprobation assigned Republican paramilitary activity. Although there seemed to be agreement that freedoms should not be lightly infringed, the great offense caused by seeing support for the IRA outweighed other considerations.

Unwillingness to rescind emergency measures once enacted was linked to the moral import assumed in their enactment. Withdrawing them would have been akin to surrendering to terrorism: "I welcome the legislation because it is a signal to the men of violence that the Government will not weaken in their fight."[47] Although Viscount Colville, who conducted the 1986 review of the PTA, noted the limited use made of proscription within the bounds of the legal system, he recoiled from recommending its repeal. He was concerned that it would be perceived as "a recognition . . . that the leading merchants of Irish terrorism were no longer disapproved."[48] Thus, the statutes were transformed from "emergency provisions" into "antiterrorist legislation."[49] This verbiage demonstrated a rejection of terrorism, which became inextricably linked to the renewal of emergency measures. In the annual debates on the Prevention of Terrorism Act, the Labour Party went out of its way to indicate that in opposing the legislation, it was by no means going soft on terrorism.[50] Likewise, anyone who called for an inquiry into the operation of the

---

46. *Jellicoe Report*, Rt. Hon. Earl Jellicoe, DSO, MC. February 1983. Session 1982/83 Cmnd 8803, para. 207.

47. Ian Paisley, *HC Debs*, February 19, 1996, Vol. 272, col. 104.

48. *Review of the Operation in 1986 of the Prevention of Terrorism (Temporary Provisions) Act 1984*. By the Viscount Colville of Culross QC. Session 1986/87, para. 13.1.6. [Hereafter Colville 1987].

49. Compare *HC Debs*, April 17, 1973, Vol. 855, cols. 275–392 and *HC Debs*, April 18, 1973, Vol. 855, cols. 627–628 to *HC Debs*, January 9, 1996, Vol. 269, cols. 31–115 and *HC Debs*, February 19, 1996, Vol. 272, cols. 41–108.

50. "I hope that our debate today will be conducted on the understanding that, whatever our disagreements, we all occupy . . . common ground. Certainly I do not propose . . . to accuse the Home Secretary of being negligent in the cause of civil liberties, and I suspect that neither he nor his Minister will want to accuse us of being irresponsible in the face of terrorism." (Roy Hattersley, *HC Debs*, March 7, 1983, Vol. 38, col. 569). See also *HC Debs*, January 9, 1996, Vol. 269, col. 94.

emergency measures risked being seen as retiring from the fight on terrorism. Concerning suggestions in 1981 that the government institute a review of the emergency measures, the opposition stated: "My right hon. and hon. Friends supported the motion calling for an inquiry, but there should be no misunderstanding about our reasons. We do not believe that there should be any lowering of our guards against terrorist activity and the continuing threat of it. Our vote did not signify any complacency or moral weakness, faced as we are by deadly, clandestine groups in our midst."[51] Labour's later decision in 1996 not to oppose the renewal of the Prevention of Terrorism Act primarily rested on the party's decision that it could not be seen as tolerant of terrorism.

Given the import of the enactment of emergency measures, their repeal might have been interpreted as meaning either that rejection of paramilitary violence had altered or that the threat was no longer relevant.[52] From 1973 to 1996, however, no sustained breaks in paramilitary activity in either Northern Ireland or Britain occurred. Even after the 1994 cease-fires, punishment beatings, movements of arms, and racketeering continued, suggesting that paramilitary activity was not so much ended as funneled into other channels. Either violence still existed within society, in which case the moral import of the enactment of emergency measures proved a stumbling block to removing them, or a cessation in violence had occurred. In the latter case, the onus was on those opposing emergency legislation to demonstrate that the threat no longer remained. This transferred the burden of responsibility from those seeking to extend antiterrorist law to those seeking to repeal it. This transfer guaranteed the survival of emergency measures beyond their temporary intent. The British government ultimately made the repeal of the Prevention of Terrorism Act dependent on a solution to the Northern Irish political situation. "Until [the conflict] is resolved and until there is an end to the threat, we must be able to look for the protection that the [PTA] provides."[53] MPs repeatedly cited this as a reason for voting for renewal of emergency legislation. For instance, during consideration of the 1996 EPA, one MP stated, "I [support the Bill] for one clear and simple reason—the conditions that originally made the emergency powers necessary have still not gone away. . . . [I]n Northern Ireland, there is still no

---

51. Neville Sandelson, *HC Debs*, March 18, 1981, Vol. 1, col. 379.

52. Fear that paramilitary interpretation of the withdrawal of emergency legislation would be to see it as a concession or as an "invitation" to intensify the armed struggle further discouraged the relaxation of the statutes. B. Dickson, "Northern Ireland's Emergency Legislation—the Wrong Medicine?," (1992) Public Law, 597.

53. Mr. Gardner, *HC Debs*, March 18, 1981, Vol. 1, col. 351.

universal renouncement of violence for political ends."[54] The 1994–1996 cease-fires did not diminish this threat: "The PTA will remain necessary even if the temporary cease-fire is reinstated."[55] Similarly, "Even if the cease-fire were continuing, we would have to keep in place some emergency measures for quite some time."[56] And again, from a Northern Ireland Unionist politician, "It is important that we do not lose the protection that the Prevention of Terrorism Act and the Northern Ireland (Emergency Provisions) Act provide with regard to terrorist acts. It is not wise to leave the United Kingdom without some permanent protection."[57] Why? Because "there is always a need to be cautious when dealing with terrorism. . . . [I]t is, to a great extent, unpredictable. There is always a danger of resurgence."[58]

Not only did the danger exist, but no politician would want to be seen as responsible for violence, should it occur after the statute had been repealed. In 1984, the Prevention of Terrorism Act was extended to include international terrorism, making the statute's repeal even more remote. Between 1984, and 1996, more than 21 percent of those detained under either the 1984 or the 1989 PTA and subsequently charged with an offense were involved in international terrorism. In 1995, the figure rose to 50 percent. This led one MP to comment that it was vital for Britain to "continue to have on the statute book legislation which will enable a democratic society to respond to the ever-present threat of international terrorism, regardless of the situation in Northern Ireland."[59] During his introduction in the renewal debates in 1996, the Home Secretary agreed that "there is always likely to be terrorism of an international kind. . . . [T]he manifestations of it are increasing; and . . . the need for the [PTA] in order to counter them therefore remains."[60] Basing the withdrawal of a temporary statute on the cessation of international terrorism undermined the act's claim to transient status and placed repeal even further beyond reach. As long as violence continued, in relation either to Northern Ireland or to international disputes, the use of emergency legislation as a

---

54. David Wilshire, *HC Debs*, January 9, 1996, Vol. 269, col. 54.

55. David Wilshire, *HC Debs*, March 14, 1996, Vol. 273, col. 1147.

56. A.J. Beith, *HC Debs*, March 14, 1996, Vol. 273, col. 1149.

57. David Trimble, *HC Debs*, March 8, 1995, Vol. 256, cols. 379–380.

58. Piers Merchant, *HC Debs*, January 9, 1996, Vol. 269, col. 90. As long as this threat remained, "[i]t would be criminally irresponsible to foreswear the use of the power of internment." (David Trimble, *HC Debs*, February 19, 1996, Vol. 272, col. 96)

59. Andrew Hunter, *HC Debs*, March 14, 1996, Vol. 273, col. 1143.

60. Michael Howard, *HC Debs*, March 14, 1996, Vol. 273, col. 1129.

way to condemn terrorism added to the propensity of such legislation to remain in force.

The primary factors outlined above—the seeming efficaciousness of the measures themselves, the long history of conflict in Ireland—north and south, perceptions in Westminster of Northern Ireland as a place where such measures were somehow acceptable, and the moral import associated with the introduction of counterterrorism legislation—played a direct role in the introduction and retention of emergency law. At least three secondary factors—the overlap between criminal law and counterterrorism measures, the formal impeccability of the legislation, and the context within which the two states operated—created an environment within which such measures could be maintained.

Overlap between Criminal Law and Counterterrorism Measures

With regard to the first of these secondary elements, the sense of the emergency legislation introduced in the Northern Irish context, particularly by Westminster after 1972, was that while some civil rights otherwise protected were violated, many of the acts prohibited by the statutes already were forbidden under criminal law. What made these offenses "terrorism" was the motivation and organization of entities using them for political or ideological ends. In this respect, emergency legislation was employed to reject the use of violence for political means by: highlighting the aims of individuals engaging in such behavior; increasing penalties associated with otherwise ordinary criminal activity; and altering the manner in which the state addressed transgressions of the law.

Scheduled offenses under the 1973 EPA included violations of common law, such as murder, manslaughter, arson, and riot, and infringements of already existing criminal statutes.[61] The government's determination to defeat terrorism (defined in the 1973 EPA as "the use of violence for political ends [including] any use of violence for the purpose of putting the public or any section of the public in fear")[62] caused these acts to be incorporated into emergency legislation. Under the 1973 EPA, sum-

---

61. This included statutes such as the Malicious Damage Act, 1861, 24 & 25 Vict., c. 97; the Prison Act (Northern Ireland), 1953, 2 Eliz. II, c. 18; the Firearms Act (Northern Ireland), 1969, Eliz. II, c. 12; the Theft Act (Northern Ireland), 1969, Eliz. II, c. 16; and the Protection of the Person and Property Act (Northern Ireland), 1969, Eliz. II, c. 29.

62. 1973 EPA, Part IV, section 28.

mary conviction or conviction on indictment, while applied to offenses in ordinary law, carried tougher penalties than could otherwise be levied. From 1973 through 1996, the government altered provisions of the EPAs relating to scheduled offenses on only one occasion: the 1985 Northern Ireland (Emergency Provisions) Act 1978 (Amendment) Order that granted the attorney general greater discretion to certify out cases relating to kidnapping and false imprisonment and offenses carrying less than a five-year penalty, allowing accusations related to these offenses to be tried in ordinary criminal courts. The government subsequently incorporated this order into the 1987 EPA. Although this alteration allowed the attorney general to certify out specific cases, after the formation of the 1973 EPA, the British government did not remove any scheduled offenses from the statute.

Not only were offenses already cited in other statutes appended to emergency legislation, but some of the measures introduced under the 1922–1943 SPAs, 1973–1996 EPAs, and 1974–1996 PTAs gradually influenced ordinary law. For instance, Regulation 4 of the 1922 SPA empowered the civil authority to ban meetings, assemblies, and processions. At its repeal in 1951, the Public Order Act was introduced and became the primary instrument used to prohibit marches and processions.[63] The Unionist government used this statute, amended in 1963 and again in 1970, in the same way that it had previously operated Regulation 4.[64] Regulation 24C of the 1922–43 SPAs prohibited the display of the Tricolour. Responding to widespread support from the Unionist population, in 1954 the Northern Executive incorporated the measure into the Flags and Emblems (Display) Act (Northern Ireland).[65] Because Britain had recognized the Republic of Ireland in the interim, the new statute did not follow Regulation 24C in banning the Tricolour outright. Instead, it forbade interference with the flying of the Union Jack and empowered the security forces to ban any flags or emblems likely to lead to a breach of the peace. More recently the Criminal Evidence (Northern Ireland) Order 1988 limited an individual's right to silence.[66] According to one account,

---

63. Public Order Act (Northern Ireland), 1951, 14 & 15 Geo. VI, c. 19.

64. Public Order Act (Northern Ireland), 1963, Eliz. II, c. 52 and Public Order Act (Northern Ireland), 1970, Eliz. II, c. 4.

65. Flags and Emblems (Display) Act (Northern Ireland), 1953, 2 & 3 Eliz. II, c. 10.

66. For background on the introduction of the order, see J. Jackson, "Recent Developments in Criminal Evidence," (1989) 40 Northern Ireland Legal Quarterly, pp. 105–130, and J. Jackson, "Curtailing the Right to Silence: Lessons from Northern Ireland," (1991) Crim LR, p. 404. For criticism of the statutory instrument, see SACHR, *Fourteenth Report of the Standing Advisory Commission on Human Rights*, HC 394 (988/89).

"the Order was prompted primarily by the need to encourage those who were suspected of terrorist activity to answer questions when there was not enough evidence to convict them."[67] It reflected the widespread belief among the security forces that maintaining silence was evidence of training in "anti- interrogation techniques."[68] The government aimed this provision at individuals suspected of involvement in terrorist activity or paramilitary financial affairs.[69] However, because it was enacted by means of the Order in Council procedure, it applied to all criminal suspects in Northern Ireland. The impact of the emergency measures also can be seen in the powers incorporated into the 1984 Police and Criminal Evidence Act.[70] Reflecting steps by Westminster to counter Republican violence in the UK, "the widely increased police powers within the police and Criminal Evidence Bill suggest that the emergency nature of the [PTA] will to an even greater extent be subsumed within everyday police practice." As a result, "what was abnormal in 1982 becomes normal in 1983; likewise emergency measures become standard and unexceptional."[71] In Northern Ireland, the norms shifted so as to incorporate what had hitherto been emergency measures into ordinary law.

In brief, the incorporation of already existing statutes into emergency measures mirrored the gradual impact of the emergency measures on ordinary legislation. Because many of the crimes cited in the 1973 and subsequent EPAs fell under ordinary criminal legislation, their inclusion did not represent a significant point of departure. What was unusual was the measures' focus on the political intent behind the actions themselves, the alteration in penalties associated with engaging in such activities with terrorist intent, and the court system in which cases relating to breaches of the measures were conducted.[72] These elements recognized the unique

---

67.   J. Jackson, "Curtailing the Right of Silence: Lessons from Northern Ireland," (1991) Crim. L.R., 404–415, quote from p. 413.

68.   Home Office Circular, para. 41, cited in C. Walker, *The Prevention of Terrorism in British Law,* second ed., (Manchester: Manchester University Press, 1992), fn. 30, p. 74.

69.   Tom King, *HC Debs,* November 8, 1988, Vol. 140, cols. 183–187.

70.   Police and Criminal Evidence Act, 1984, Eliz. II, c. 60.

71.   J. Sim and P. Thomas, "The Prevention of Terrorism Act: Normalising the Politics of Repression," (1983) 10 Journal of Law and Society, p. 75. See also M. O'Boyle, "Emergency Situations and the Protection of Human Rights," (1977) 28 N.I.L.Q., pp. 160–187.

72.   For further discussion of the assimilation of emergency legislation into normal law, see D. Walsh, "Arrest and Interrogation: Northern Ireland 1981," (1982) 9 B.J.L.S., pp. 53–57; and D. Bonner, "Combating Terrorism in the 1990s: The Role of the Prevention of Terrorism (Temporary Provisions) Act 1989," (1992) Public Law, pp. 473–474.

nature of the challenge being mounted against the state and indicated rejection of the use of violence for political ends, tying into the import borne by the introduction and operation of the emergency provisions.

International Influence: Treaties and Laws

As the U.S. civil rights marches in the late 1960s played a role on the world stage, agitation from the international community influenced the shape of British counterterrorist measures. Prior to this time, emergency provisions were largely considered an internal UK concern. Internal demands, internal reviews, and increasing international attention worked together to, on the one hand, mitigate some of the more extreme aspects of the measures and, on the other, validate the existence of exceptional provisions. There are a handful of examples of the first. For instance, the security forces drew the interrogation techniques introduced in the early 1970s from British operations in Palestine, Malaya, Kenya, Cyprus, and elsewhere. When they appeared in the Northern Ireland context (i.e., within the United Kingdom), they drew international condemnation, which forced Britain to abandon their use. Although extended detention and its disparate application to the minority community in the North continued well into the next decade, challenges made in the European Court of Human Rights contributed to the abandonment of internment and made Britain's subsequent derogation for seven-day detention subject to question.

Exclusion also underwent dilution during the tenure of direct rule. In response to Unionist agitation, Britain included the principle of reciprocity in the 1974 Prevention of Terrorism (Supplemental Temporary Provisions) (Northern Ireland) Order. The government later incorporated this instrument, with some alterations, into the 1976 PTA.[73] Two years later, in response to Lord Shackleton's recommendation that a survey of exclusion orders be conducted to determine if any of them should be revoked, Westminster announced that it would implement a standard review of exclusion orders to be instituted three years after the making of the initial order. In 1982, Lord Jellicoe proposed that exclusion orders be retained with some modifications.[74] The government accepted his findings and al-

---

73. The time limit for making representations against an exclusion order after being served with notice increased from 48 hours to 96 hours, and, in the event that the individual had not already been removed from the UK with his or her consent, the right to a meeting with an advisor was made absolute, rather than being dependent on whether the secretary of state determined the request to be "frivolous."

74. See Jellicoe Report, para. 188.

tered the appropriate provisions in the 1984 Prevention of Terrorism (Temporary Provisions) Act. The statute limited exclusion to a period of three years, after which time the secretary of state could renew the order. It exempted any British citizen resident in the UK three or more years prior to consideration of exclusion.[75] Westminster's introduction of the 1996 Draft Prevention of Terrorism (Temporary Provisions) Regulations further modified the provisions in accordance with the European Covenant on Human Rights. These changes gradually reduced the more severe effects of exclusion, making the presence of the measure, while still exceptional, more palatable than previously.

Other alterations, such as the extension of the requirement of reasonable suspicion for the exercise of various powers and the extension to detainees of certain rights they otherwise would hold under the Police and Criminal Evidence Act, demonstrated the "normalization" of emergency law. This very dilution contributed to the entrenchment of the legislation.[76] Parliamentary scrutiny of the measures highlights this process of normalization, as well as the growing acceptance of emergency legislation throughout the 1980s and into the 1990s. Following the 1976 general review of the PTA, the terms of reference for independent reports consistently accepted "the continuing need for legislation against terrorism."[77] Analysis was based on the operation of the statute and not on whether the legislation was necessary or appropriate. By the early 1970s, the government had established a framework within which minor adjustments could be made.

TREATIES PROTECTING THE ABILITY OF CONTRACTING STATES TO INTRODUCE EMERGENCY LEGISLATION

Not only did the British state operate within certain limitations imposed by its governmental structure, but the international community likewise legitimized and, indeed, encouraged Britain's alteration of emergency law. Various treaties to which the United Kingdom was a signatory protected the ability of contracting states to introduce emergency measures in times of need. For instance, Article 4 of the International Covenant on

---

75. Similarly, an individual resident in Northern Ireland three or more years could not be excluded from the province. Clause 7 made an absolute right of appeal for individuals to meet with an advisor to make representations protesting the issuance of exclusion orders. The length of time within which such meetings were arranged was extended from 96 hours to seven days after the initial order was made.

76. While many of the measures were diluted, others, such as those relating to financial support of proscribed organizations, grew more strict.

77. See, for instance, Shackleton Report.

Civil and Political Rights allowed for deviation from obligations under the treaty in times of public emergency.[78] Upon ratification of the covenant in 1976, the British government entered such a derogation in respect to Northern Ireland. Britain withdrew the derogation in 1984, only to reinstate it in 1988.[79] Similar to Article 4 of the International Covenant, Article 15 of the European Convention on Human Rights and Fundamental Freedoms allowed that "in time of war or other public emergency threatening the life of the nation any High Contracting Party may take measures derogating from its obligations under this Convention to the extent strictly required by the exigencies of the situation, provided that such measures are not inconsistent with its other obligations under international law."[80] During the introduction of emergency measures, MPs appealed to the derogations provided by these agreements: "We know that every human rights convention admits of some circumstances in which ordinary principles may be set aside."[81]

In its exercise of emergency powers after 1972, the UK government chose to avail itself of the right to derogate from the standards when it was brought before the European Court for violations of the Covenant.[82] In *Brogan and Others v. UK,* four people, detained between four and seven days under the PTA on suspicion of involvement in Northern Irish terrorism, submitted complaints to the European Commission on Human Rights that the United Kingdom's actions had violated the convention.[83] Article 5, paragraph 3 of the document demanded that anyone arrested "be brought promptly before a judge or other officer authorized by law to exercise judicial power and . . . be entitled to trial within a reasonable

---

78. See *International Covenant on Civil and Political Rights 1966,* in I. Brownlie, *Basic Documents on Human Rights,* third ed., (Oxford: Clarendon Press, 1992), p. 127. Although some articles were exempted from derogations, such as those relating to the right to life, the right not to be subjected to torture or to cruel, inhuman or degrading treatment or punishment, and the right not to be enslaved or held in servitude, a general derogation could be established.

79. For the text of this subsequent derogation see <www.law.qub.ac.uk>.

80. *European Convention on Human Rights and Its Five Protocols,* in Brownlie, *supra,* p. 331. Britain withdrew its derogation under Article 15 in 1984 as part of its criminalization of terrorist violence. See Jackson, *supra,* p. 235.

81. *HC Debs,* July 5, 1973, Vol. 859, col. 812. See also EPA debates, *HC Debs,* April 17, 1973, Vol. 855, col. 298.

82. For discussion of multiple cases under consideration by the European court of Human Rights see Jackson, *supra,* pp. 507–535.

83. Publ Eur Ct HR, Ser A, No. 145-B.

time or to release pending trial."[84] In November 1988, the European Court ruled that even the shortest period for which one of the four individuals had been held, four days and six hours, violated the convention. Because no provisions existed in the UK to allow the government to compensate the individuals, the country was also found in violation of Article 5, paragraph 5, which stipulated that anyone who had been the victim of arrest or detention should have an enforceable right to compensation. The British government insisted that seven-day detention was required and examined two possible courses of action.[85] Either a judicial element could be inserted into the procedure to extend the seven-day detention, or the United Kingdom could derogate under Article 15.[86] In December 1988, Britain announced that it would pursue the second route, and a year later, it reaffirmed the derogation, stating that it would be maintained as long as deemed necessary.[87] Although *Brannigan & McBride v. UK* subsequently challenged the validity of this derogation, once again contesting the length of detention, the court found in the United Kingdom's favor.[88] According to the preconditions for derogation, that there existed a "war or other public emergency threatening the life of the nation," that the derogation was "strictly required by the exigencies of the situation," and that measures were not inconsistent with the state's other international obligations, the court determined that the derogation was valid.[89] Simultaneously, the court noted its concern about the long-

---

84. *European Convention on Human Rights and Its Five Protocols,* in Brownlie, *supra,* p. 329.

85. Douglas Hurd, *HC Debs,* December 6, 1988, Vol. 143, cols. 210–211.

86. The derogation was an option in *Brogan and Others v. UK;* it had not been possible in the first case to come before the court: *Ireland v. UK* (1978) 2 E.H.R.R. 25, since the breach established in that case was non-derogable under Article 3.

87. Written Answer by Mr. Waddington, *HC Debs,* November 14, 1989, Vol. 160, cols. 209–210, reprinted in S. Marks, "Civil Liberties at the Margin: the UK Derogation and the European Court of Human Rights," (1995) 15 O.J.L.S., 71.

88. Publ Eur Ct HR, Ser A, No 258-B. For other applications challenging the validity of the derogation, see Application No.s 14672/89, 14705/89, 14780/89, 14880/89, 18317–18320/91, 18414/91, 18627–18628/91, 19431/92, 19504/92, and 20440/92. Reprinted in Marks, *supra,* fn 18, p. 71.

89. "The Jurisprudence of the Commission and Court of Human Rights has established the following characteristics of an emergency where Article 15 of the Convention is invoked: (i) the emergency must be actual or imminent, (ii) its effects must involve the whole nation; (iii) the continuance of the organized life of the community must be threatened; and (iv) the crisis or danger must be exceptional in that the normal measures or restrictions, permitted by the convention for the maintenance of pub-

term, apparently unexceptional character of the "emergency" in Northern Ireland.[90]

These international agreements became a yardstick by which Britain could measure its incursions into civil rights.[91] In 1972, Lord Diplock sought to adjust existing criminal procedures in a manner consistent with Article 6 of the European Convention. In his 1975 review of the 1973 EPA, Lord Gardiner wrote, "The British Government has acted legitimately, and consistently with the terms of the European Convention for the Protection of Human Rights and Fundamental Freedoms, in restricting certain fundamental liberties in Northern Ireland."[92] These findings followed on concerns voiced in the House of Commons that emergency measures introduced by Westminster and, particularly with respect to the Diplock Court system, would lower the United Kingdom's standing in the international community.[93] Reviewers frequently examined powers under the 1973–1996 EPAs and 1974–1996 PTAs against findings by the

---

lic safety, health, and order, are plainly inadequate." K. Boyle, "Human Rights and Political Resolution in Northern Ireland," Yale Journal of World Public Order, Vol. 9, (1982), p. 159. For further discussion of the margin of appreciation granted in emergency circumstances, see C. Feingold, "The Doctrine of Margin of Appreciation and the European Convention on Human Rights," Notre Dame Lawyer, Vol. 53 (1977), pp. 90–106 and the European Court of Human Rights' decision in *Lawless v. Ireland* (1961) 1 E.H.R.R. 15. For analysis of *Lawless,* see A. Robertson, *Human Rights in Europe* (1st ed., 1977), pp. 51–53, 111–114, 212–221.

90. Only four states of emergency were declared in Northern Ireland between 1972 and 1980 under the Emergency Powers Act (Northern Ireland),1926, 16 & 17 Geo. V, c. 5 and the Emergency Powers (Amendment) Act (Northern Ireland), 1964, 12 & 13 Eliz. II, c. 34: (i) issued: February 10, 1972, withdrawn: November 16, 1973; (ii) issued: November 16, 1973, withdrawn: May 19, 1974; (iii) issued: May 19, 1974, withdrawn: September 19, 1974; (iv) issued: January 11, 1979, withdrawn: January 14, 1979, <www.law.qub.ac.uk>.

91. Following *Ireland v. UK* and *Brogan and Others v. UK, Fox, Campbell and Hartley* was the third finding by the European Court of Human Rights that Britain's counterterrorism legislation violated the European Covenant. This case focused on requirements of "suspicion" versus "reasonable suspicion" and the use of arrest to gather information. For analysis of this case see W. Finnie, "Anti-terrorist Legislation and the European Convention on Human Rights," (1991) 54 M.L.R., pp. 288–293.

92. *Report of a Committee to Consider, in the Context of Civil Liberties and Human Rights, Measures to Deal with Terrorism in Northern Ireland.* Chairman: Lord Gardiner. January 1975. Session 1974/75 Cmnd 5847, chapter 7, no. 4.

93. "When we sit in and observe trials in [other] countries, our position and the respect in which British law is held in those countries will be severely diminished and hampered." *HC Debs,* April 17, 1973, Vol. 855, col. 315).

European Court.[94] Colville's 1987 review cited the damaging effects of exclusion on the British government's civil rights reputation in the eyes of the international community. The existence of this provision prevented the United Kingdom from ratifying Protocol Four of the European Convention on Human Rights, which declared the right to move freely and to choose where to live within one's own country. Not only did the international community allow for derogation, but, as its influence led to a watering-down of emergency measures, an "acceptable level" of the suspension of human rights was obtained.

The international arena also influenced Britain's counterterrorist legislation through the European Convention for the Suppression of Terrorism. The United Kingdom ratified the Convention on July 24, 1978, and installed it as domestic law on June 30, 1978.[95] Although the first article technically eliminated the possibility for a requested state to invoke the political nature of an offense in order to oppose an extradition request,[96] Article 13 allowed contracting states to make exceptions with regard to the application of Article 1.[97] Seven of the 18 initial signatories, including Denmark, France, Germany, Italy, Norway, Portugal, and Sweden, chose to avail themselves of this option. At the same time, Britain was implementing its policy of Ulsterization (transferring primary security responsibility to provincial forces) and criminalization (criminalizing individuals convicted of paramilitary activity by removing political status from the prisons). Both the international support for the criminalization of terrorist acts (such as that signified by the European Convention on the Suppression of Terrorism) and the concurrent tightening of counterterrorism measures within other member states, created a context within which the adoption of emergency law reflected an accepted international norm.

CONTRADICTIONS IN INTERNATIONAL LAW REGARDING COUNTERTERRORISM PROVISIONS

The international community has said very little about the issue of counterterrorism law. This stems in part from the failure of the interna-

---

94. See, for example, *HC Debs*, February 19, 1996, Vol. 272, cols. 42–44, pp. 81–84, 89–90 and *HC Debs*, March 14, 1996, Vol. 273, col. 1160.

95. Suppression of Terrorism Act, 1978, Eliz. II, c. 26.

96. Explanatory Report, para. 31.

97. "Any state may, at the time of signature or when depositing its instrument or ratification . . . declare that it reserves the right to refuse extradition in respect of any offense mentioned in Article 1 which it considers to be a political offense, an offense connected with a political offense or an offense inspired by political motives." (Article 13)

tional community to agree on a common definition of "terrorism."[98] Failure to operate under a common definition of terrorism limits the international community's ability to direct the scope and direction of counterterrorist statutes. The lack of clarity in determining what constitutes a terrorist act also reflects jurisprudential disagreement over whether terrorism constitutes its own formal branch of international law, or whether it is simply a manifestation of acts conducted within the auspices of other areas, for example, the law of the seas and air and space law.

Some aspects of the principles that underlie the structure of the United Nations (UN) and the international community impacted the international community's lack of guidance on domestic counterterrorism law, which has (to some extent) served to perpetuate emergency measures in the United Kingdom and would have similar impact on other liberal, democratic states considering counterterrorism law.

The principle of equal rights and the self-determination of a "people" are at the heart of the UN Charter.[99] This document also presupposes a vision of state sovereignty, territorial integrity, and political independence. As the scope of "self-determination" has expanded—particularly since 1945—these principles have come into frequent conflict. Ethnic groups live across modern geographic demarcations, but the context of nationality must operate through traditional mechanisms of sovereign state administration. Thus, while most states in the world agree to the principle of self-determination, international law views the exercise of the right to self-determination as subject to participation in democratic processes.[100] Yet the majority/minority mechanisms present in liberal, democratic states often preclude the possibility of minority self-determination. Additionally, it is less than clear exactly which rights entitlements are involved in self-determination. How can international law determine which "peoples" can exercise this entitlement? This issue links directly to the Northern Ireland situation, where Republican organizations claim the

---

98. In 1937 the world community agreed in principle as to what constitutes international terrorism. Since then, however, states have failed to accept a common definition. For further discussion of this point see, for example, Yonah Alexander, *International Terrorism: National, Regional, and Global Perspectives*, ed., (New York: Praeger Publishers, 1976).

99. For further discussion of definition of a "peoples" and the conflict between self-determination and state sovereignty, see E. Chadwick, *Self-Determination, Terrorism and the International Humanitarian Law of Armed Conflict*. (The Netherlands: Martinus Nijhoff Publishers, 1996).

100. Chadwick, *Self-Determination*, p. 3.

right of self-determination applies to the whole of Ireland and not just to the people living in the area currently referred to as Northern Ireland.

In addition, the application of the principle of self-determination, if backed at an international level, contradicts the principles of state sovereignty and the territorial integrity of the existing state. The principle of nonintervention encourages states to handle domestic disputes independently of any international customary law. Yet self-determination suggests that nationalist movements are themselves legitimate actors in the international arena and, thus, subject to protection under international norms. The 1977 Protocol to the Geneva Conventions of August 1949 addresses the Protection of Victims of International Armed Conflicts, and the International Humanitarian Law of Armed Conflict extends to attempts to establish self-determination. The crucial difference in the 1977 extension of international humanitarian law is that state actions, in particular those dealing with domestic armed conflicts, are no longer beyond the scope of international inquiry. Further, acts of terrorism perpetuated by or on behalf of people struggling for their right to self-determination constitute a separable and different phenomenon than those which could be prosecuted under international humanitarian law. However, the UN regulates states only in their use of force. International humanitarian law generally applies between states party to the same treaties or other parties that accept the same treaties. For example, it relates to domestic liberation conflicts through states' acceptance of the 1949 Geneva Conventions. Reflective of the aim of states to deny the challenge to state political legitimacy posed by nationalist terrorist movements, ruling governments have stopped short of advocating the application of international humanitarian law to sub-antistate terrorist organizations. Governments prefer to deal with terrorism as criminal activity and prosecute it within a sovereign, domestic framework of penal law.

In the case of the United Kingdom, the government made every effort to address the violence through domestic statutes. It repeatedly denied the Republic of Ireland or the international arena any role in what it claimed were the "internal workings" of the state. It was only in the early 1980s, with the initiation of the Anglo-Irish process, and, more formally, in 1985, with the signing of the Anglo-Irish Agreement, that the British government recognized any role that a state external to the United Kingdom may have *vis-à-vis* Northern Ireland. By handling the violence as an internal UK matter, the state sought to deny legitimacy to terrorist organizations. This refusal of states to elevate these organizations to equal status in the international arena prevents international humanitarian norms relating to conduct in war from being applied to measures adopted by either the terrorist organizations or by the states themselves.

If the states were to involve international humanitarian law in wars of self-determination, it would imply that the manner in which the state ensures its own survival no longer lies within its domestic jurisdiction. This of course violates the principle of state sovereignty. So while most states are prepared cautiously to allow that the right to self-determination is a principle of the UN system and international customary law, they are not prepared to accept the practical impact of such a concession: the legitimization of antistate terrorist organizations, the possible fragmentation of state territory, constitutional alteration, the application of international humanitarian law, the erosion of state sovereignty, and limitations on the state's right to self-defense.

The Establishment of a "Hierarchy of Rights"

The international legal system contributed to the retention of emergency measures through the rights discourse inherent in liberal, democratic thought. The propensity of Britain to appeal to this discourse served to further entrench emergency law in the United Kingdom. To understand this apparent contradiction, it is helpful to compare the Northern Ireland Parliament's justification of emergency law to that enacted by Westminster.

In Northern Ireland, justification for the 1922 SPA rested in part on the claim that for those who did not challenge the state, such measures in no way infringed upon their freedom: "One great feature about this Act which we now propose to continue is that while it places great powers in the hands of the government in regard to dealing with disorder and the disorderly elements in our midst, it does not tend in any way to infringe on the liberty of any law-abiding subject."[101] This assertion not only reflected the security Unionists felt in that the measure would not be applied to those individuals supporting the constitutional position of the Northern state, but it also ignored the impact of legislation that violated, in any measure, the rights of any citizens in the state.

MPs in Westminster recognized that both the 1973 EPA and the 1974 PTA violated the rights of citizens. The MPs justified the measures, however, in terms of the duty that the government bore to protect its citizens: "If the Government are not to forfeit their right to be called a Government, if the rule of law is to be anything other than a hollow mockery, if the Government are to be entitled to the regard and obedience of their citizens, it is their solemn duty to consider how these murders can be

---

101. Second reading in the Senate, 1928, PRONI HA/32/1/619.

ended."[102] This implied that the citizens bore a right to be protected by the government, a right that, in turn, placed a correlative duty on the government to create and enforce measures protecting its citizens. This right was clearly a derivative of the most basic right of all: the right to life, which imposed a duty on citizens to abstain from causing death. The state's obligation to enforce the duty corresponded to a separate right of the citizens to protection from the government, creating a duty for officials to pursue and effectuate individuals' rights.[103] Not only did international covenants to which the United Kingdom was a signatory recognize the right to life and the duty of others to abstain from taking that life, but the articles delineating derogations implied the entitlement of the citizen to expect protection from the government. Furthermore, the international arena widely recognized the right to life as the most fundamental right within a state, along with the ability of the state to suspend other rights to protect that entitlement.

With this rationale driving Parliament and reflected in its international agreements, a hierarchy of rights emerged in Westminster in which the government was called on to protect the most basic of individual entitlements. Those of lesser importance had to be sacrificed to protect the more basic rights of the citizenry: "Where there is a terrorist situation in any country, the rights of the individual in the community have to be surrendered to a degree in order that his real rights may be defended and eventually maintained. We must keep that principle before us. We have to surrender certain rights in Northern Ireland for the greater welfare of the whole community, so that the rights of the individual may be defended."[104] William Whitelaw, secretary of state for Northern Ireland, emphasized, "[the PTA] infringe[s] our shared concept of civil liberties. But that is the price which the House has always accepted must be paid for protecting the most fundamental liberty of all—the liberty not to be killed or maimed when going about one's lawful business."[105] The basic right to life and protection from physical harm was placed even above the right to self-determination: "More important to most people than the right of

---

102. John McQuade, *HC Debs*, July 2, 1979, Vol. 969, col. 948.

103. The concurrence of these two rights was a matter of practicality and not logic, as one did not necessarily entail the other. The right of the citizen to be protected against other citizens could be simply a nominal right; however, in any operative legal system, the officials will be under a moral duty and perhaps also a legal duty to take all reasonable steps to avert and rectify violations of basic rights.

104. Ian Paisley, *HC Debs*, December 8, 1977, Vol. 940, col. 1737.

105. William Whitelaw, *HC Debs*, March 18, 1981, Vol. 1, col. 341.

self-determination is the right to stay alive—which is why we must accept the necessity, however regretfully, of these emergency powers."[106]

In protecting this most basic entitlement—the right to life—the Northern Ireland Parliament and Westminster violated what they considered to be the lesser rights or freedoms of the citizens. To act in this manner, however, was to risk further alienating the population. In the case of Northern Ireland, where the aim of Republican paramilitarism was to draw an ever sharper distinction between the state and the citizens, this was a route of maximum possible risk. For instance, government ministers recognized that internment had done more harm than good. The secretary of state for Northern Ireland, Merlyn Rees, said, "I feel that the key is internment. Whoever one talks to in the minority group in Ulster, one can be in no doubt that since internment the political situation has changed radically. Internment has hardened attitudes."[107]

Not only was this a risky approach for Westminster to adopt, but the hierarchical claim made in Parliament mistook the psychological effect of terrorism for the physical impact of the violence. The legislation did not, in fact, establish that the right to life and property were the two most important rights, and, thus, all lesser rights could be suspended. Rather it established that the most important right that a citizen bore was the right not to be afraid. The actual impact that terrorism had on life and property in the United Kingdom was much less than the impact of other acts. For example, each year more people are killed in driving accidents in Northern Ireland than have been killed by terrorist violence in 30 years of the Troubles. Yet the government did not suspend all civil rights with counter-accident legislation to protect the life and property of citizens. The main function of counterterrorism law was to respond to the fear engendered by terrorism. Secondly, it attempted to control the risk associated with the loss of property or life, or both.[108] Terrorism, by its very nature, however, is not a controllable event. By introducing emergency law, some sense of control over a situation in which one would otherwise be afraid is gained. This is a very different claim than that put forth in Parliament:

---

106. John Biggs-Davison, *HC Debs,* December 8, 1977, Vol. 940, col. 1748.

107. Merlyn Rees, *HC Debs,* November 25, 1971, Vol. 826, col. 1661, re-quoted in *HC Debs,* December 11, 1975, Vol. 902, col. 762. See also *HC Debs,* April 17, 1973, Vol. 855, col. 354.

108. When an individual gets into a car, s/he perceives some sort of control over whether s/he will get into an accident and/or be hurt. S/he can wear a seat belt, drive more carefully, come to a full halt at four-way stops, and so on. There is some sense that the risk associated with this behavior can be controlled.

rather than life and property as the first concerns, the right not to be afraid played a central role in the adoption and maintenance of emergency legislation. It is the fear of losing life and property and not the actual loss thereof, which provided the underlying justification for Westminster's introduction—and retention—of emergency law.

CONCLUDING REMARKS: LESSONS FOR LIBERAL, DEMOCRATIC STATES

There is very little either new or temporary about emergency measures enacted to combat political violence in the United Kingdom. The 1922–1943 SPAs and the 1973–1996 EPAs derive from a common history and, to an extent, incorporate similar measures to try to address political violence in Northern Ireland. The 1939 PVA and 1974–1996 PTAs also share a significant degree of overlap in the provisions contained in the statutes and in their entrenchment in British policy toward the North. This essay suggests that a number of factors contributed to the longevity of such measures. Ultimately, the use of special powers depended upon the Northern Ireland and UK governments' ability to justify their use. In Northern Ireland, this took the form of appeal to the concept of reason of state to prevent the North from being incorporated into a united Ireland. In contrast, Westminster claimed to be protecting the lives and property of individuals within the state. In both cases, emergency measures initially intended as a temporary solution became constitutionally entrenched: their presence became inextricably linked to the politics of Northern Ireland. The Terrorism Act 2000 finally permanently codified measures repeatedly hailed as temporary.

To a great extent, the elements that contributed to the entrenchment of emergency law in the United Kingdom can be seen at work in other liberal, democratic regimes. Many of the same elements that contributed to the Northern Ireland Executive and, later, the British government's retention of emergency powers would likewise play a role in the retention and evolution of counterterrorism measures in liberal, democratic regimes. The extension of state powers may well be effective in its application; the more efficacious such measures are perceived to be, the greater the pressure will be on governments to retain them to prevent future loss of life or property. Similarly, the import assumed in the adoption of "counterterrorism" or "antiterrorism" measures will be shared by any liberal state faced with such challenge. Terrorism strikes at the very core of an open society, playing on the vulnerabilities inherent in the freedoms and rights of its citizens. The wholesale rejection of terrorist techniques as a means to draw attention to the aims of those inflicting the damage will be a central element in the introduction of countermeasures. Once these countermeasures become law, as in Britain, the onus will be transferred from those needing to prove that an emergency exists to those seeking to repeal the measures to demonstrate that they are no longer necessary. The very nature of terrorism, though, makes it difficult to gauge at what point the threat posed by an individual, a terrorist organization, or an entire movement no longer poses a danger to either the citizens or the state. And what happens if, as in the United Kingdom, counterterrorism measures aimed at one particular conflict are used to address other violence within the state? The possible repeal of such measures would become even more remote.

Not only may primary factors play a role in the retention of such measures, but the secondary factors creating conditions favorable to the retention of counterterrorism law exist in other geopolitical regions. The crossover with criminal statutes may similarly be an issue, as will, if enacted properly, the formal consistency of the measures themselves. The context and international arena in which Britain finds itself are extremely similar to that in which other states operate—most directly those in Europe and adjunctly others, such as the United States, Australia, New Zealand, Canada, and elsewhere. Treaties to which other liberal states are party and confusion in the international arena over how to handle terrorist violence will influence other states facing a terrorism challenge. The general support within the international arena for the enactment of some sort of counterterrorism legislation, and the simultaneous lack of real direction on which form it should take, would lead other states to retain their own measures, just as Britain retained its domestic legislation. It is unlikely that the international arena will be able to provide more detailed guidance until such time as fundamental principles—such as self-determination, state sovereignty, territorial integrity, and a state's right to self-defense—can be reconciled. Possible application of international humanitarian law and the construction of a common definition or understanding of terrorism would likewise need to be broached. Regardless, liberal states' adherence to the discourse of rights and the tendency of British Parliamentarians, in particular, to view counterterrorism legislation as reinforcing a hierarchy of rights, wherein the right to life and property assume dominance, are likely to be reflected in other liberal regimes. The right not to be afraid deserves particular attention here in the possible introduction and operation of emergency legislation in other states, because it is this entitlement that justifies the suspension of "lesser" rights and the retention of emergency law.

Aside from the tendency of counterterrorism measures to become permanently embedded in state law, what other lessons can be drawn from Northern Ireland and Britain's experience in the introduction and operation of counterterrorism law? Perhaps less obvious than the connection between foreign policy and international terrorism is the link between domestic policy and domestic terrorism. Britain's experiences highlight the importance of the social and cultural context into which domestic statutes are introduced. Whereas in Northern Ireland the disparate application of such measures played into centuries-old ethnic, social, and political divisions, the danger of the disparate use of wide powers in a state's social and political context cannot be taken lightly. In Northern Ireland, the use of these powers contributed substantially to the proroguement of the Northern Parliament and the ongoing grievances of the minority community throughout the Troubles. Attempts in the present round of talks to address parity of esteem and meet the demands of the vast majority of political parties to repeal special powers directly relate to the operation of such measures throughout the twentieth century. In addition to the liberal, democratic state's obligation to protect the life and property of the citizens—liberal values that became trump cards in the British context—the parallel obligations that governments bear toward their populations must not be lost.

In the United Kingdom, the emergency measures shared a common initial perception: they represented extraordinary moves designed to meet the needs of a passing emergency. Over time, however, they became standard and unexceptional—a baseline from which further extraordinary powers could be introduced. The repeal of the measures that may reverse this steady progression, however, became extremely unlikely in light of the primary and secondary factors that were addressed earlier in this essay. Britain's experiences highlight the importance of not borrowing blindly from other countries, but rather of carefully evaluating the measures to be introduced, how they will be implemented, and the full impact that they are likely to have on those who constitute the state itself.

Throughout the twentieth century, terrorist violence in the United Kingdom fluctuated. At times when the level sharply increased, the Northern Ireland and British governments were placed under severe pressure to enact counterterrorism measures. Although such provisions were to some extent effective, there were some significant costs, as discussed in the introduction of this essay, with regard to civil liberties. These costs included increased friction in the North between the minority and majority communities, the proroguement of the Parliament, and unwelcome international attention to the domestic affairs of the United Kingdom. When violence linked to terrorist attacks decreased, the government did not repeal emergency measures. Factors playing a role in maintaining emergency laws, both in the face of immediate violence and its aftermath, are not singular to the United Kingdom. In adopting counterterrorism law, countries need to be cognizant of both the possible domestic impact of counterterrorism measures and elements forcing temporary measures into permanent entrenchment in domestic law.

About the Authors

Ashton B. Carter. *Co-Director, with William J. Perry, of the Preventive Defense Project and Professor of Science and International Affairs, John F. Kennedy School of Government, Harvard University.* From 1993 to 1996 Carter served as Assistant Secretary of Defense for International Security Policy; he was responsible for national security policy concerning the states of the former Soviet Union (including their nuclear weapons and other weapons of mass destruction), arms control, countering proliferation worldwide, and oversight of the U.S. nuclear arsenal and missile defense programs; he also chaired the North Atlantic Treaty Organization (NATO)'s High Level Group. He was twice awarded the Department of Defense Distinguished Service medal, the highest award given by the Pentagon. Carter continues to serve DOD as an adviser to the Secretary of Defense and as a member of its Defense Policy Board, Defense Science Board, and Threat Reduction Advisory Committee. From 1998 to 2000, he served in an official capacity as Senior Advisor to the North Korea Policy Review. Before his government service, he was director of the Kennedy School's Center for Science and International Affairs and chairman of the editorial board of *International Security.* He received bachelor's degrees in physics and in medieval history from Yale University and a doctorate in theoretical physics from Oxford University, where he was a Rhodes Scholar. In addition to authoring numerous scientific publications and government studies, he is the author or editor of a number of books, including *Preventive Defense: A New Security Strategy for America* (with William J. Perry). His current research focuses on the Preventive Defense Project, which designs and promotes security policies aimed at preventing the emergence of major new threats to the United States. He is a Senior Partner of Global Technology Partners, LLC, a member of the Advisory Board of MIT Lincoln Laboratories, the Draper Laboratory Corporation, and the Board of Directors of Mitretek Systems, Inc. He is a consultant to Goldman Sachs and the MITRE

Corporation on international affairs and technology matters, a member of the Council on Foreign Relations, the Aspen Strategy Group, and the National Committee on U.S.-China Relations, and a fellow of the American Academy of Arts and Sciences.

Arnold M. Howitt. *Director, Executive Session on Domestic Preparedness, and Executive Director, Taubman Center for State and Local Government, John F. Kennedy School of Government, Harvard University.* Howitt specializes in state and local public management and intergovernmental relations. The Executive Session on Domestic Preparedness, which began in 1999, is a Kennedy School research program on terrorism, sponsored by the U.S. Department of Justice, which works closely with local, state, and federal officials in emergency management, health, and law enforcement professions. In related activity, Howitt serves on the Governor's Bioterrorism Coordinating Council in Massachusetts and was a member of an Institute of Medicine/National Academies of Science panel on Evaluation of the Metropolitan Medical Response System. He has served as a faculty member at the National Governors Association Policy Academy on Homeland Security and Bioterrorism. Howitt has been a faculty member and administrator at Harvard since 1976. In other research, he directs a multiyear study of transportation and air quality policymaking in the federal government and fifteen states. He received his B.A. degree from Columbia University and an M.A. and Ph.D. in political science from Harvard University. Among other writings, Howitt is the author of *Managing Federalism,* a study of the federal grant-in-aid system, and coauthor and coeditor of *Perspectives on Management Capacity Building.*

Robyn L. Pangi. *Research Associate, Executive Session on Domestic Preparedness, John F. Kennedy School of Government, Harvard University.* Pangi is a 2000 graduate of the Master in Public Policy Program at the John F. Kennedy School of Government. In addition to her contributions to this volume, she is coeditor of the forthcoming *First to Arrive: State and Local Responses to Terrorism* (MIT Press). She is author of "Preparing for Terrorism: What Governors and Mayors Can Do," and coauthor of "Preparing for the Worst: Mitigating the Consequences of Chemical and Biological Terrorism." She received her bachelor's degree from Columbia University.

Philip B. Heymann. *James Barr Ames Professor of Law, Harvard Law School; Director of Center for Criminal Justice; and Faculty Chair of the Project on Justice in Times of Transition.* From his first job as clerk to U.S. Supreme Court Justice John Harlan to his post as deputy U.S. attorney general (1993–1994), Heymann has spent much of his career in government. A former Fulbright Scholar with degrees from Yale University, Harvard Law School, and the Sorbonne, he has been assistant U.S. attorney general in charge of the criminal division (1978–1981) and assistant to the solicitor general in the Justice

Department, acting administrator of the State Department's Bureau of Security and Consular Affairs, deputy assistant secretary of state for the Bureau of International Organizations, and executive assistant to the undersecretary of state. In addition, he was an associate prosecutor and consultant to the Watergate Special Prosecution Force.

Jonathan P. Caulkins. *Professor of Operations Research and Public Policy at Carnegie Mellon University's Heinz School of Public Policy and Management.* A faculty member at Carnegie Mellon's Heinz School since 1990, Caulkins regularly teaches courses in management science, decision analysis, criminal justice policy, and drug policy. He also conducts a Ph.D. seminar and occasionally advises project courses. He has taught at the RAND Graduate School and the Technical University of Vienna. Caulkins's research focuses on modeling and analyzing problems pertaining to drugs, crime, and violence and how policies affect those problems. Caulkins was chosen as the 1999 winner of the prestigious David R. Kershaw Award and its $10,000 honorarium by the Association for Public Policy Analysis and Management (APPAM). He is the first operations researcher/management scientist to win the Kershaw Award, which recognizes individuals under the age of forty who have made distinguished contributions to the field of public policy analysis. In addition, Caulkins won the Heinz School's Martcia Wade Award for Teaching Excellence in 1999 and has been named a National Young Investigator by the National Science Foundation. In 1987, he received bachelor's degrees in systems science and engineering, computer science, and engineering and policy, and a master's degree in systems science and mathematics from Washington University in St. Louis, Missouri. During the summers of 1984–1987, he did internships at IBM and Eastman Kodak and was a research collaborator at Brookhaven National Laboratory. After completing his studies at Washington University, he went on to the Massachusetts Institute of Technology, where he earned a master's degree in electrical engineering and computer science in 1989 and a doctorate in operations research in 1990.

Mark A. R. Kleiman. *Professor of Policy Studies and Director of the Drug Policy Analysis Program at the School of Public Policy and Social Research, UCLA.* Kleiman teaches methods of policy analysis, political philosophy, and drug abuse and crime control policy. He is also the Chairman of BOTEC Analysis Corporation, a Cambridge, Massachusetts, firm that conducts policy analysis and contract research on illicit drugs, crime, and health care. Previously, he held teaching positions at the John F. Kennedy School of Government and the University of Rochester. Kleiman's primary research interests are drug abuse and crime control, with special attention to illicit markets and the design of deterrent regimes. His past positions include: Director of Policy and Management Analysis for the Criminal Division of the U.S. Department of Justice, Deputy Director for Management of the Office of Management and Budget for the City of Boston, Special Assistant to Edwin H. Land at Polaroid Corporation, and Legislative Assistant to congressman Les Aspin. He directed a study of the Drug Enforcement Administration for the Clinton transition team. Currently, he chairs the drug policy committee of the Federation of American Scientists and edits its *Drug Policy Analysis Bulletin*. Kleiman received his bachelor's degrees in economics, philosophy, and political science at Haverford College and his Ph.D. in public policy at the John F. Kennedy School of Government in Cambridge, Massachusetts.

Peter Reuter. *Professor of Public Policy at the University of Maryland, College Park.* Reuter teaches in the School of Public Affairs and the Department of Criminology. In July 1999, he became editor of the *Journal of Policy Analysis and Management*. From 1981 to 1993, he was a Senior Economist in the Washington office of the RAND Corporation. He founded and directed RAND's Drug Policy Research Center from 1989 to 1993; the Center is a multi- disciplinary research program that was begun with funding from a number of foundations. His early research focused on the organization of illegal markets and resulted in the publication of *Disorganized Crime: The Economics of the Visible Hand* (MIT Press, 1983), which won the Leslie Wilkins award as most outstanding book of the year in criminology and criminal justice. Since 1985, most of his research has dealt with alternative approaches to controlling drug problems, both in the United States and in Western Europe. He and Robert MacCoun recently published *Drug War Heresies: Learning from Other Places, Times, and Vices* (Cambridge University Press). Recent papers have appeared in *Addiction, Journal of Quantitative Criminology, American Journal of Public Health, Journal of Policy Analysis and Management,* and *Science.* Reuter was a member of the National Research Council (NRC) Committee on Law and Justice from 1997 to 2002. He currently serves on a NRC Panel on Firearms Research. He also is a member of the Office of National Drug Control Policy's Committee on Data, Research and Evaluation. The Attorney General has appointed him as one of five nongovernmental members of the Interagency Task Force on Methamphetamine. Reuter has testified frequently before Congress and has addressed senior policy audiences in many countries, including Australia, Chile, Colombia, and the United Kingdom. He has served as a consultant to numerous government agencies and to foreign organizations including the United Nations Drug Control Program and the British Department of Health. Reuter received his Ph.D. in economics from Yale.

Gregory D. Koblentz. *Doctoral Candidate, Department of Political Science, MIT.* Koblentz is currently a Pre-Doctoral Fellow in National Security at the John M. Olin Institute for Strategic Studies at Harvard University. His research focuses on the international security implications of biological warfare and strategies for reducing the threat posed by biological weapons and biological terrorism. He was previously a Research Specialist with the Executive Session on Domestic Preparedness and is a recent graduate of the Master in Public Policy program at the Kennedy School of Government. Prior to attending the Kennedy School, he worked on the Nuclear Non-Proliferation Project at the Carnegie Endowment for International Peace. He is the coauthor of *Tracking Nuclear Proliferation* (1998) and has published articles in *Jane's Intelligence Review* and *The Nonproliferation Review*. He graduated from Brown University with a B.A. in political science.

Jim Walsh. *Executive Director of the Managing the Atom Project at the Belfer Center for Science and International Affairs at Harvard University's John F. Kennedy School of Government.* Walsh's research and writings focus on international security and, in particular, topics involving weapons of mass destruction, terrorism, and the Middle East. Earlier this year, Walsh testified before the U.S. Senate Governmental Affairs Committee on the issue of nuclear terrorism. Walsh's comments and analyses have appeared in the New York Times, the Washington Post, the Los Angeles Times, the Times of London, the Christian Science Monitor, and other domestic and foreign publications. He also served as historical consultant for a documentary, "Fortress Australia," commissioned by the Australia Film Board and televised by the Australia Broadcast Corporation. Closer to home, Walsh is the on-air consultant for the NBC-TV affiliate in Boston (WHDH) and appears regularly on CNN. Walsh's writings have appeared in several scholarly journals including *Political Science Quarterly*, *The Nonproliferation Review*, *International Studies Review*, and *Contemporary Security Policy*. He serves as editor for the book series, *Terrorism: Documents of International & Local Control [Oceana]*, and is currently working on a book about Iran. Before coming to Harvard University, Walsh was a visiting scholar at the Center for Global Security Research at Lawrence Livermore National Laboratory, one of the country's three nuclear weapons labs. Previously, he was named a Jennings Randolph Peace Scholar by the United States Institute for Peace and won the Hubert Humphrey Fellowship from the U.S. Arms Control and Disarmament Agency. Walsh received his Ph.D. from the Massachusetts Institute of Technology.

Jason Pate. *Deputy Director, Chemical and Biological Weapons Nonproliferation Program and Manager of the WMD Terrorism Project, Center for Nonproliferation Studies, Monterey Institute of International Studies.* A certified emergency medical technician (EMT), Pate's primary interest is first responder/law enforcement response to and emergency planning for terrorist incidents. His research focuses on understanding motivations and patterns of behavior associated with terrorism involving weapons of mass destruction, the militia and Christian Identity phenomenon in the United States, and the causes of violence. Pate is coauthor of "The Minnesota Patriots Council," in Jonathan B. Tucker, ed., *Toxic Terror* (MIT Press, 2000), a case study of a militia group that acquired a biological toxin for possible use against local law enforcement officials. He has been interviewed extensively by regional, national, and international television and print media on issues including terrorism, response planning for terrorist incidents, the September 11, 2001, terrorist attacks, the anthrax letters, and chemical and biological weapons issues. Pate is the author or coauthor of several other publications on WMD terrorism and WMD proliferation and has taught graduate-level courses on WMD terrorism at Monterey Institute of International Studies (MIIS). In addition to his work at the Center for Nonproliferation Studies (CNS), Pate has participated in biological terrorism tabletop response exercises, chemical terrorism functional response exercises, and the Nunn-Lugar-Domenici domestic preparedness training programs for the San Francisco Bay Area. Prior to his affiliation with CNS, Pate was a Research Assistant for the Science and Technology Committee at the North Atlantic Assembly, NATO's interparliamentary body in Brussels, where he worked on chemical and biological terrorism, military technology proliferation, and non-lethal weapon systems. Pate holds an A.B. in international relations and national security studies from Stanford University and a Master of public management in international security and economic policy from the School of Public Affairs at the University of Maryland.

Gavin Cameron. *Lecturer in Politics and Military History, School of English, Sociology, Politics, and Contemporary History, University of Salford, England.* Cameron's research focuses on terrorism, nonproliferation of nuclear, biological, and chemical weapons, and comparative governmental responses to non-traditional threats. He was formerly a Senior Research Associate at the Center for Nonproliferation Studies at the Monterey Institute of International Studies in California. During 2000–2001, he held a Visiting Fellowship at the Belfer Center for Science and International Affairs, Harvard University. Cameron is a member of the editorial board of the journal *Studies in Conflict and Terrorism*. His book, *Nuclear Terrorism: A Threat Assessment for the 21st Century* (Palgrave), was published in 1999. Cameron has contributed articles that have appeared in such scholarly journals as: *Studies in Conflict and Terrorism, The Nonproliferation Review, Terrorism and Political Violence, The Journal of Conflict Studies,* and *Low Intensity Conflict and Law Enforcement.* He received his doctorate in international relations from the University of St. Andrews in Scotland.

Michael A. Vatis. *Director of the Institute for Security Technology Studies (ISTS) at Dartmouth College and Chairman of the Institute for Information Infrastructure Protection (I3P).* ISTS is a principal national center for counterterrorism and cyber security research, development, and analysis. The I3P is a consortium of major research organizations whose mission is to develop a national research and development agenda for cyber security, foster collaboration among researchers, and facilitate and fund research in areas of national priority. Vatis joined ISTS in March 2001 and led the establishment of the I3P in 2001–2002. Vatis is also an attorney with the international law firm of Fried, Frank, Harris, Shriver, and Jacobson, specializing in e-commerce, security, and Internet law issues. Prior to joining ISTS, Vatis founded and served as the first Director of the National Infrastructure Protection Center (NIPC) in Washington, D.C., an interagency center located at the FBI. The NIPC, now an important building block of the new Department of Homeland Security, was the principal federal agency responsible for detecting, warning of, and responding to cyber attacks, including computer crime, cyber terrorism, and cyber espionage. Vatis has also served in the U.S. Departments of Justice and Defense. As Associate Deputy Attorney General and Deputy Director of the Executive Office for National Security, he coordinated the Justice Department's national security activities and advised the Attorney General and Deputy Attorney General on issues such as counterterrorism, counter-intelligence, foreign affairs, national defense, infrastructure protection, high-tech crime, and encryption. At the DOD, he served as a Special Counsel in the Office of General Counsel, advising the Secretary of Defense, the Deputy Secretary of Defense, and the General Counsel on sensitive legal and policy issues; he received the Secretary of Defense Award for Excellence. Vatis also practiced law with the firm of Mayer, Brown & Platt in Washington, D.C., specializing in Supreme Court and appellate litigation. Before that, he served as a law clerk for U.S. Supreme Court Justice Thurgood Marshall and for then-Judge Ruth Bader Ginsburg when she served on the U.S. Court of Appeals for the District of Columbia Circuit. Vatis earned his law degree from Harvard Law School in 1988, where he served as Supervising Editor of *Harvard Law Review*. He received his undergraduate degree from Princeton University in 1985, where he studied at the Woodrow Wilson School of Public and International Affairs.

Juliette N. Kayyem. *Executive Director of Executive Session on Domestic Preparedness, John F. Kennedy School of Government, Harvard University.* The Executive Session on Domestic Preparedness is a terrorism and homeland security research project at Harvard University. From 1999 to 2001, Kayyem served as former House Minority Leader Richard Gephardt's appointment to the National Commission on Terrorism. Before that, she was a legal advisor to the Attorney General and Counsel to the Assistant Attorney General for Civil Rights at the U.S. Department of Justice. In related areas, she serves as a member of the bipartisan Constitution Project's program on Liberty and Security, the Council on Foreign Relations, the American Bar Association's committee on National Security Law, and the Advisory Committee of the Migration Policy Institute. She has also served as adjunct faculty at Boston University School of Law and has taught at the Institute of Politics at the Kennedy School of Government. She has testified before Congress and serves as an advisor to a number of governmental and private institutions. She writes frequently in the field of counterterrorism law, domestic preparedness, and the legal implications of U.S. national security strategy. Her work has appeared in the *New York Times*, the *Los Angeles Times*, the *Christian Science Monitor*, and the *Washington Post* as well as academic journals such as the *Boston Review*, *National Defense*, and *Studies in Conflict and Terrorism*. She is coeditor of *First to Arrive: The State and Local Response to Terrorism* (MIT Press, 2003). Kayyem also serves as an analyst for NBC News and National Public Radio WBUR's On Point. She is a 1991 graduate of Harvard College and a 1995 graduate of Harvard Law School.

Joseph A. Barbera, *Co-Director of the George Washington University Institute for Crisis, Disaster, and Risk Management; Associate Professor of Engineering Management; and Clinical Associate Professor of Emergency Medicine at The George Washington University.* Dr. Barbera was the lead medical consultant for the Federal Emergency Management Agency in the development of the National Urban Search & Rescue (US&R) Response System and participates as a medical officer for the Office of Foreign Disaster Assistance International Search & Rescue Program and the FEMA US&R Incident Support Team. He has participated in scene responses to hurricanes, mine disasters, earthquakes (Baguio City, Philippines; Northridge, California; Tou-Liu, Taiwan), mass terrorism (the Oklahoma City Bombing and the September 11, 2001, Pentagon and World Trade Center attacks), and biological terrorism. He has helped plan and execute medical contingency capabilities for high security events (presidential inaugurations, State of the Union addresses, the NATO fiftieth anniversary summit) and participated in numerous mass casualty exercises, including the development and execution of the TOPOFF Bioterrorism exercise in Denver, Colorado, in May 2000. Barbera was medical director for the emergency preparedness committee at Bronx Municipal Hospital Center for four years and chair of the emergency preparedness committee at The George Washington University Hospital for another four years. He coordinated the implementation of a mass patient decontamination and treatment facility at the old George Washington University Hospital, one of the first in the United States. At the request of the U.S. Public Health Service, Barbera led the development of a national hospital preparedness model for chemical terrorism. As founder and chair of the District of Columbia Hospital Association (DCHA) Emergency Preparedness Committee, Barbera led the implementation of a comprehensive Hospital Mutual Aid System (HMAS) for Washington, D.C. The HMAS structure and communications system became the medical information distribution and healthcare interaction system for the National Capital Region (NCR) during the September 11, 2001, terrorist attacks and the October/November 2001 anthrax bioterrorism. Barbera established (and moderated) a daily conference call among all the hospitals, public health authorities, and major medical practitioner groups in the NCR. Dr. Barbera teaches Masters and Doctoral level academic courses at The George Washington University. He has also completed multiple research projects focusing on health and medical issues in emergency response, the most recent being a Sloan Foundation–supported project that defined a single system for managing bioterrorism or any other mass casualty incident.

Anthony G. Macintyre. *Associate Professor of Emergency Medicine, Department of Emergency Medicine, George Washington University Medical Center.* Macintyre is a Board Certified Emergency Physician and Associate Professor with the Department of Emergency Medicine at The George Washington University. His academic career has focused on medical emergency preparedness at various levels. In particular, he has assisted in developing a mass decontamination capability for The George Washington University Hospital (key concepts recently published in JAMA) and has served as a medical advisor and coordinator for the federally sponsored bioterrorism exercise, TOPOFF 2000, held in Denver, Colorado. Macintyre has served as the medical director for Fairfax County's Urban Search and Rescue team since 1995. His work with the team has involved deployments to the bombing of the Alfred P. Murrah building in Oklahoma City (1995), the bombing of the U.S. Embassy in Nairobi (1998), the 2001 Pentagon incident, and to several international earthquakes.

Craig A. DeAtley. *Deputy Director, Institute for Public Health Emergency Readiness, Washington Hospital Center, and Associate Professor, Emergency Medicine, George Washington University School of Medicine and Health Sciences.* DeAtley is currently the Deputy Director of the Institute for Public Health Emergency Readiness at the Washington Hospital Center, the District of Columbia's largest hospital, and an Associate Professor of Emergency Medicine at George Washington University, where he worked fulltime for twenty-eight years before leaving to help start the Institute. He also works as a Physician Assistant at Fairfax Hospital, a Level-One Trauma Center in Northern Virginia. In addition to being a Physician Assistant, he has been a volunteer paramedic with the Fairfax County Fire and Rescue Department since 1972 and a member of their Urban Search and Rescue Team since 1991. He currently serves as the Medical Team Coordinator. He also serves as the Assistant Medical Director of both the U.S. Customs Service and the Fairfax County Police Department. Those positions involve his working with the special operations personnel (SWAT, Civil Disturbance, Marine Patrol, and Helicopter operations) in those agencies. He has particular interest in hazardous material/WMD planning and response and was a founding member of NMRS-DC-1, the nation's first U.S. Public Health Service trained and equipped civilian NBC incident response team. For the past five years, he has been working as a consultant with Research Planning, Inc., on projects related to DOD's/DOJ's WMD Domestic Preparedness Program and the CDC's Public Health Department self-assessment program. Those projects have led to his working with police, fire, EMS, hospitals, and public health personnel to develop and exercise their Hazmat/chem-bio response plans. He also worked for the HHS Office of Emergency Preparedness in developing and facilitating a new Public Health Emergency Practicum Program for medical, emergency management, public health, and public safety personnel in Utah.

Viktor Mayer-Schönberger. *Associate Professor of Public Policy, John F. Kennedy School of Government, Harvard University.* Mayer-Schönberger's work focuses on business, legal, and policy issues of information and telecommunication infrastructures. He is also an expert on the European Union, especially its regulatory framework, and business-government relations. In 1986, he founded Ikarus Software, a company focusing on data security, and developed "Virus Utilities," which became the best-selling Austrian software product. He was voted Top-5 Software Entrepreneur in Austria in 1991 and Person-of-the-Year for the State of Salzburg in 2000. He holds a number of law degrees, including one from Harvard, and an MSC in economics from the London School of Economics. Mayer-Schönberger advises businesses, governments, and international organizations on technology policy issues.

Ariel Merari. *Director, Political Violence Research Unit at Tel Aviv University.* Merari is the Director of the Political Violence Research Unit at Tel Aviv University, Israel. He received a B.A. degree in psychology (1964) and in economics (1965) from the Hebrew University in Jerusalem, and a Ph.D. in psychology from the University of California, Berkeley, in 1969. He has been a faculty member of the Department of Psychology, Tel Aviv University, since 1969 and chaired the department (1982–1985). During the period of 1978– 1989, he was also a Senior Fellow at the Jaffee Center for Strategic Studies at Tel Aviv University, where he founded and directed the Project on Terrorism and Low Intensity Warfare. He has been a Visiting Professor at the University of California, Berkeley, and at Harvard University. From 1998 to 2000, he was a Senior Research Fellow with the International Security Program at Harvard's Belfer Center for Science and International Affairs, John F. Kennedy School of Government. Merari has studied political terrorism and other forms of political violence for more than twenty-five years. He has authored, coauthored, or edited several books and many articles, monographs, and chapters on these subjects. He established the Israeli Defense Forces' Hostage Negotiations and Crisis Management Unit and commanded it for more than twenty years. He has served as a consultant to various branches of several governments. He presently chairs the Advisory Commission on Combating Terrorism at Israel's National Security Council.

Laura K. Donohue. *Visiting Fellow at the Center for International Security and Cooperation and Acting Assistant Professor in the Political Science Department, Stanford University.* In April 2001, the Carnegie Corporation named Donohue to its Scholars Program, awarding her two years' funding for her project: Security and Freedom in the Face of Terrorism. Her research focuses on liberal, democratic states' legal, political, military, and economic responses to political violence. This work builds on research she completed while a post-doctoral fellow at the Kennedy School of Government, Harvard University, on U.S. counterterrorist measures from 1960 to 2000. At Harvard, she also served as a fellow on the Executive Session for Domestic Preparedness, which examined the U.S. emergency response abilities for mass-casualty attack. Her book, *Counter-terrorist Law and Emergency Powers in the United Kingdom 1922–2000*, drew from her Ph.D., which she received from Cambridge University in 1998, and her M.A. in war and peace studies, which she obtained with Distinction from the University of Ulster, Northern Ireland. Some articles she has written include "Fear Itself: Counterterrorism, Individual Rights, and U.S. Foreign Relations Post 9–11," "Bias, National Security, and Military Tribunals," "Capital Punishment and Political Challenge," "Toward a Counter-terrorist Taxonomy," "The 1922–43 Special Powers Acts: Regulating Northern Ireland," "In Time of Need: Terrorism and the Liberal Constitution," and "Temporary Permanence: the Constitutionalisation of Emergency Powers in Northern Ireland."

Index

BCSIA Studies in International Security

Published by The MIT Press

Sean M. Lynn-Jones and Steven E. Miller, series editors
Karen Motley, executive editor
Belfer Center for Science and International Affairs (BCSIA)
John F. Kennedy School of Government, Harvard University

Allison, Graham T., Owen R. Coté, Jr., Richard A. Falkenrath, and Steven E. Miller, *Avoiding Nuclear Anarchy: Containing the Threat of Loose Russian Nuclear Weapons and Fissile Material* (1996)

Allison, Graham T., and Kalypso Nicolaïdis, eds., *The Greek Paradox: Promise vs. Performance* (1996)

Arbatov, Alexei, Abram Chayes, Antonia Handler Chayes, and Lara Olson, eds., *Managing Conflict in the Former Soviet Union: Russian and American Perspectives* (1997)

Bennett, Andrew, *Condemned to Repetition? The Rise, Fall, and Reprise of Soviet-Russian Military Interventionism, 1973–1996* (1999)

Blackwill, Robert D., and Michael Stürmer, eds., *Allies Divided: Transatlantic Policies for the Greater Middle East* (1997)

Blackwill, Robert D., and Paul Dibb, eds., *America's Asian Alliances* (2000)

Brom, Shlomo, and Yiftah Shapir, eds., *The Middle East Military Balance 1999–2000* (1999)

Brom, Shlomo, and Yiftah Shapir, eds., *The Middle East Military Balance 2001–2002* (2002)

Brown, Michael E., ed., *The International Dimensions of Internal Conflict* (1996)

Brown, Michael E., and Šumit Ganguly, eds., *Fighting Words: Language Policy and Ethnic Relations in Asia* (2003)

Brown, Michael E., and Šumit Ganguly, eds., *Government Policies and Ethnic Relations in Asia and the Pacific* (1997)

Carter, Ashton B., and John P. White, eds., *Keeping the Edge: Managing Defense for the Future* (2001)

de Nevers, Renée, *Comrades No More: The Seeds of Political Change in Eastern Europe* (2003)

Elman, Colin, and Miriam Fendius Elman, eds., *Progress in International Relations Theory: Appraising the Field* (2003)

Elman, Colin, and Miriam Fendius Elman, eds., *Bridges and Boundaries: Historians, Political Scientists, and the Study of International Relations* (2001)

Elman, Miriam Fendius, ed., *Paths to Peace: Is Democracy the Answer?* (1997)

Falkenrath, Richard A., *Shaping Europe's Military Order: The Origins and Consequences of the CFE Treaty* (1994)

Falkenrath, Richard A., Robert D. Newman, and Bradley A. Thayer, *America's Achilles' Heel: Nuclear, Biological, and Chemical Terrorism and Covert Attack* (1998)

Feaver, Peter D., and Richard H. Kohn, eds., *Soldiers and Civilians: The Civil-Military Gap and American National Security* (2001)

Feldman, Shai, *Nuclear Weapons and Arms Control in the Middle East* (1996)

Feldman, Shai, and Yiftah Shapir, eds., *The Middle East Military Balance 2000–2001* (2001)

Forsberg, Randall, ed., *The Arms Production Dilemma: Contraction and Restraint in the World Combat Aircraft Industry* (1994)

Hagerty, Devin T., *The Consequences of Nuclear Proliferation: Lessons from South Asia* (1998)

Heymann, Philip B., *Terrorism and America: A Commonsense Strategy for a Democratic Society* (1998)

Heymann, Philip B., *Terrorism, Freedom, and Security Winning without War* (2003)

Howitt, Arnold M., and Robyn L. Pangi, eds., *Countering Terrorism: Dimensions of Preparedness* (2003)

Kayyem, Juliette N., and Robyn L. Pangi, eds., *First to Arrive: State and Local Responses to Terrorism* (2003)

Kokoshin, Andrei A., *Soviet Strategic Thought, 1917–91* (1998)

Lederberg, Joshua, ed., *Biological Weapons: Limiting the Threat* (1999)

Shaffer, Brenda, *Borders and Brethren: Iran and the Challenge of Azerbaijani Identity* (2002)

Shields, John M., and William C. Potter, eds., *Dismantling the Cold War: U.S. and NIS Perspectives on the Nunn-Lugar Cooperative Threat Reduction Program* (1997)

Tucker, Jonathan B., ed., *Toxic Terror: Assessing Terrorist Use of Chemical and Biological Weapons* (2000)

Utgoff, Victor A., ed., *The Coming Crisis: Nuclear Proliferation, U.S. Interests, and World Order* (2000)

Williams, Cindy, ed., *Holding the Line: U.S. Defense Alternatives for the Early 21st Century* (2001)

The Robert and Renée Belfer Center for Science and International Affairs

Graham T. Allison, Director
John F. Kennedy School of Government
Harvard University
79 JFK Street, Cambridge, MA 02138
(617) 495-1400
http://www.ksg.harvard.edu/bcsia   bcsia_ksg@harvard.edu

The Belfer Center for Science and International Affairs (BCSIA) is the hub of research, teaching and training in international security affairs, environmental and resource issues, science and technology policy, human rights and conflict studies at Harvard's John F. Kennedy School of Government. The Center's mission is to provide leadership in advancing policy-relevant knowledge about the most important challenges of international security and other critical issues where science, technology, and international affairs intersect.

BCSIA's leadership begins with the recognition of science and technology as driving forces transforming international affairs. The Center integrates insights of social scientists, natural scientists, technologists, and practitioners with experience in government, diplomacy, the military, and business to address these challenges. The Center pursues its mission in four complementary research programs:

- The **International Security Program** (ISP) addresses the most pressing threats to U.S. national interests and international security.

- The **Environment and Natural Resources Program** (ENRP) is the locus of Harvard's interdisciplinary research on resource and environmental problems and policy responses.

- The **Science, Technology and Public Policy** (STPP) program analyzes ways in which science and technology policy influence international security, resources, environment, and development, and such cross-cutting issues as technological innovation and information infrastructure.

- The **WPF Program on Intrastate Conflict, Conflict Prevention and Conflict Resolution** analyzes the causes of ethnic, religious, and other conflicts, and seeks to identify practical ways to prevent and limit such conflicts.

The heart of the Center is its resident research community of more than 140 scholars: Harvard faculty, analysts, practitioners, and each year a new, interdisciplinary group of research fellows. BCSIA sponsors frequent seminars, workshops and conferences, maintains a substantial specialized library, and publishes books, monographs, and discussion papers.

The Center's International Security Program, directed by Steven E. Miller, publishes the BCSIA Studies in International Security, and sponsors and edits the quarterly journal *International Security*.

The Center is supported by an endowment established with funds from Robert and Renée Belfer, the Ford Foundation and Harvard University, by foundation grants, by individual gifts, and by occasional government contracts.